Painter IX for Photographers

Dedicated to

My wife Doreen

Painter IX for Photographers

Creating painterly images step by step

Martin Addison

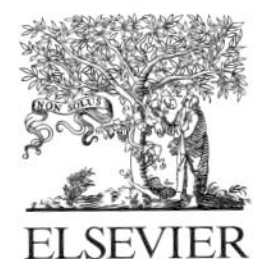

AMSTERDAM • BOSTON • HEIDELBERG • LONDON • NEW YORK • OXFORD
PARIS • SAN DIEGO • SAN FRANCISCO • SINGAPORE • SYDNEY • TOKYO
Focal Press is an imprint of Elsevier

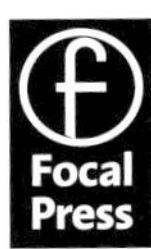

Focal Press
An imprint of Elsevier
Linacre House, Jordan Hill, Oxford OX2 8DP
30 Corporate Drive, Burlington MA 01803

First published 2005

British Library Cataloguing in Publication Data
A catalogue record for this book is available from the British Library

Library of Congress Cataloguing in Publication Data
A catalogue record for this book is available from the Library of Congress

ISBN 0 240 51982 5

For information on all Focal Press publications visit our website at:
www.focalpress.com

Typeset by Charon Tec Pvt. Ltd, Chennai, India
website: http://www.charontec.com
Printed and bound in Italy

Contents

Foreword

As a painter and photographer, I have used and enjoyed Corel Painter software since Fractal Design Painter first was introduced – and I barely had been introduced to a computer. Struggling to learn both was a steep hill to climb, and Painter software books and teachers were few and far between. Students today are so much more fortunate, and Martin Addison's book is a great contribution to bring that steep learning curve down to a manageable slope.

It's rare that a computer book can hold your attention, but even though I have my own style, I found that I was eager to try everything that Mr. Addison suggested, and I looked forward to the next chapter until I finished the book. I am convinced that the tools and techniques described will have an influence on the artistic interpretation of all those who read it and actually utilize the tutorials included.

The author has done a real service to those both new to Painter, and those who have used it for some time. He is clear and concise in his explanation of the tools and techniques, and photographers who feel they are not artists will find methods that will enable them to create artistic paintings from their photographs. The visual explanation of each major brush category and their internal variations clearly demystify the confusion that even a seasoned Painter user might have, and the likelihood of users to expand their repertoire is greatly increased.

There is a concentration and explanation of cloning throughout the chapters that make the techniques easy to replicate and invites readers to a whole new world of imaginative style.

Martin Addison's readers will enjoy delving deep into the mysteries of Painter brushes, papers and textures, especially those in Painter IX, as they expand their photographic and artistic horizons. The book will become a well-used reference for digital artists and photographers alike.

Helen Yancy
PPA Certified, Professional Photographers of America
Master Photog., Master Artist, MEI, Cr Hon.M.Photog.
Fellow and Associate, ASP
Fellow, BIPP
Past President, Professional Photographers of America

Preface

Photography is about documenting the reality around us, the photographer deciding how to interpret that reality through the choice of lenses, viewpoint and composition. Sometimes however, this reality is not enough; it doesn't reflect the feelings that we originally experienced. This is not surprising, of course, as the conditions have changed, the sensory pleasure has been lost, the smells, sounds and atmosphere are all gone, and all we now have is a one-dimensional piece of film, print or electronic image.

So we often want to take our picture further to better reflect what we felt at the time and to communicate this to the viewer, who has no recall of the original experience. Usually, the first step is to use a general photo-editing program such as the excellent Adobe Photoshop. Here we can subtly or perhaps dramatically change the appearance of the picture using the many tools available. Another route is to take a more artistic approach, and this is where the Painter program comes in. This fabulous program is quite unique and gives us the opportunity to take our pictures into another dimension altogether, revealing the hauntingly beautiful, mysterious and alluring world of the imagination.

The purpose of this book is to give you a sound knowledge of the tools which Painter provides and of the techniques needed to use them. There is a wide range of skills to be learned, and this book guides you through them in a simple, logical and exciting way. Of course, this is only the starting point; good technique does not ensure that you make a good picture, but it is essential to master this first. Once that is done, your own imagination and ways of expression will lead you to make the great pictures that you are visualizing.

As the title suggests, this book is aimed solely at photographers. There are other books which teach you how to use Painter from a painter's point of view, but this is the only one to focus solely on the photographic aspect. This approach has the great advantage that everything in the book is relevant and useful to photographers.

Painter IX for Photographers progresses step by step from very simple techniques to more advanced technical expertise. Throughout the book, the many illustrations are intended to provide ideas and inspiration combined with clear instructions to make the very best of your own image.

The book begins with a simple guide to the Painter program; this is for the total beginner and takes a brief look at the main tools and palettes. If you have used Painter before, you could skip this section and go straight on to the first cloning chapter. Cloning is the process through which we transform photographs from their original state to a new and exciting existence. Even at this early stage of the book, you will be able to make beautifully soft images and we are still only on the first chapter!

Paper textures are an essential part of using Painter; they provide depth and texture to the picture, and the program has hundreds to choose from. The second chapter gives more information on using textures and explains how they are chosen and adapted.

Step-by-step examples are the basis for much of the book and, following the informative chapter on textures, we return to more exercises to follow, from which you will learn about the use of colored backgrounds; these give a very different ambience to those made in the earlier chapters. All the image files for the step-by-step examples are provided on the accompanying CD; use these first and then try out the technique on your own photographs.

Brushes are at the heart of everything we do in Painter, and understanding which brush to use and how it works is crucial to working creatively. The two chapters on brushes illustrate every one of the main brush categories and explain how they differ. Examples of finished pictures are provided as a source for ideas and inspiration. The following chapter shows how the standard brushes can be customized using the Brush Creator.

More step-by-step examples show how you can clone from more than one original photograph; this offers considerable creative opportunities to merge and blend images together. The use of layers extends this further, providing the ability to build pictures in many different ways; the step-by-step example combines cloning and the use of layers to powerful effect.

The chapter on watercolor, oil and pastel includes complex step-by-step examples – building the image by gradually bringing in detail, with the finished result looking more like a traditional painting. We also take a further look at paper textures, showing how to apply them after the picture is completed. Three more step-by-step clones complete this part of the book, including the fascinating 'Mosaics' section, where you can make your own Roman mosaic!

The final few chapters explain how Painter can be used to enhance photographs in other ways. Toning and hand tinting is a fascinating subject, and Painter excels in providing all you need to make delicate tinted alternatives, which are so popular as a way of making pictures that little bit different. There are also lots of special effects available, everything from simulating burnt paper to making kaleidoscopic images. This section is great fun and packed full of colorful examples. At the end of the book is a reference section illustrating every one of the hundreds of papers available in Painter which you can use for painting and cloning; this makes choosing a texture so much easier.

If you have used Painter before and are following my step-by-step instructions, it may be advisable to return the brushes to their default settings before you begin, or they may not react as predicted. To do this, click on the small triangle on the Brush Selector that is at the top right of the screen and select Restore All Default Variants.

This book has been written on a PC and all the screen shots reflect that platform. Painter operates virtually identically on both PC and Macintosh computers. Keyboard shortcuts are of course different; the Ctrl key on Windows becomes the Cmd key on the Macintosh, and likewise the Alt becomes Opt.

Whether you are new to digital imaging or are already familiar with Painter and other graphics programs, I am confident that this book will help you to expand your creative abilities and make many brilliant new pictures from your photographs.

Acknowledgements

I would like to thank the following people for their help in the making of this book.

Kay Montclare for her encouragement to start this book and for her help in editing and commenting on the first draft.

Clive Haynes, Malcolm Haynes, Sara Bunn, David Eaves and Kay Montclare for kindly providing gallery pictures for the accompanying CD.

Albert Tinsley for loaning me the original photograph of the lion, from which the picture in Chapter 6 was created.

Donna for allowing me to use my photographs of her in several chapters of the book.

Ian at Threkeld Mining Museum in Cumbria for permission to use his portrait in Chapter 2.

Permajet Ltd of Warwick, UK (www.permajet.com), for providing me a range of their excellent inkjet papers and ink systems.

Adi Sethna for his unfailing support, advice and friendship.

Ric Champagne, product manager for Corel Painter, for his help and advice.

Marie and Georgia of Focal Press for their encouragement and assistance at all stages of the book.

Helen Yancy for writing the excellent Foreword.

Most of all, to my wife Doreen, without whom none of this would have been possible.

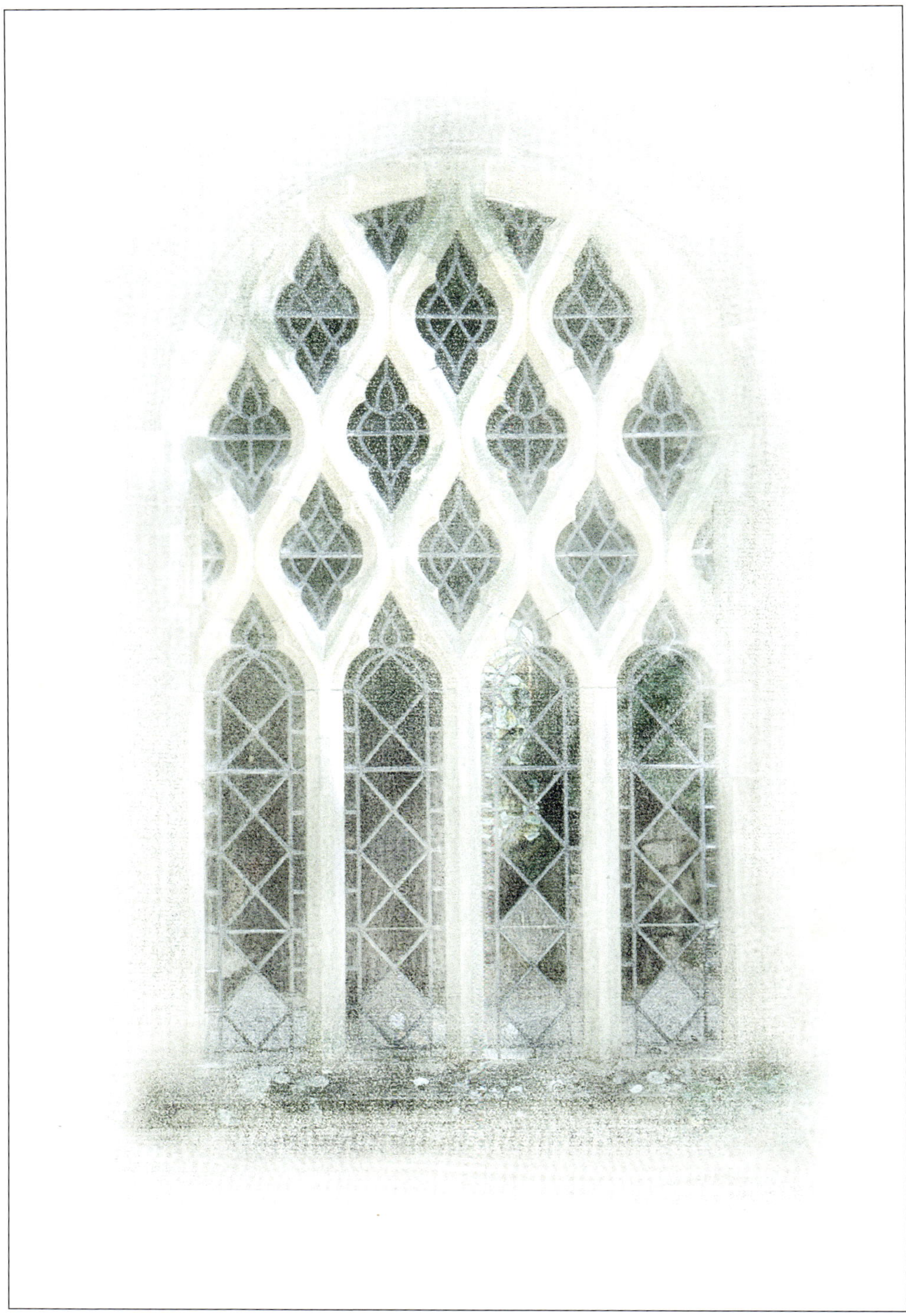

Figure 1.1 Window, St Conan's Kirk

Chapter 1
Getting started in Painter

The first part of this chapter is intended for complete beginners to Painter and contains a series of simple exercises to guide the user in identifying the key areas of the workspace prior to starting Chapter 2. If you have used a previous version of Painter or are experienced in other digital imaging programs such as Photoshop, you may wish to skim or skip this section.

The second part of the chapter contains information to help in customizing the program to your own requirements and covers the use of graphic tablets, setting Preferences and some basic tips on using Color Management in Painter.

Both sections can be used as a quick reference guide to the key elements as you work through the step-by-step examples in later chapters.

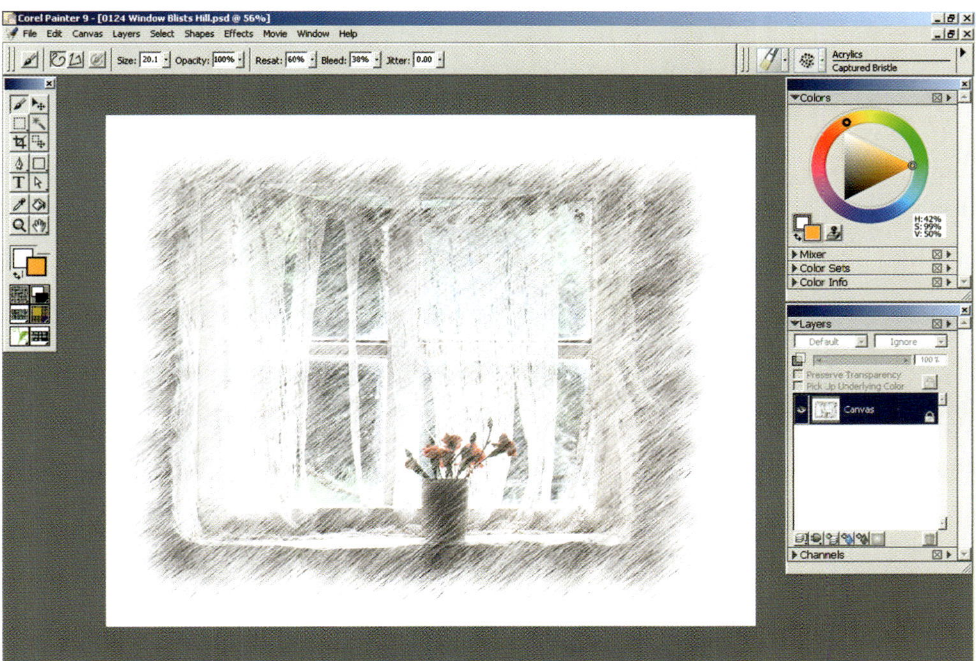

Figure 1.2 The Painter IX workspace

The Painter IX workspace

The default view

Figure 1.3 shows the default view of Painter IX, showing the File bar at the top of the screen, the Properties bar just beneath, leading to the Brush Selector on the right. The Tools are on the left and a selection of palettes on the right.

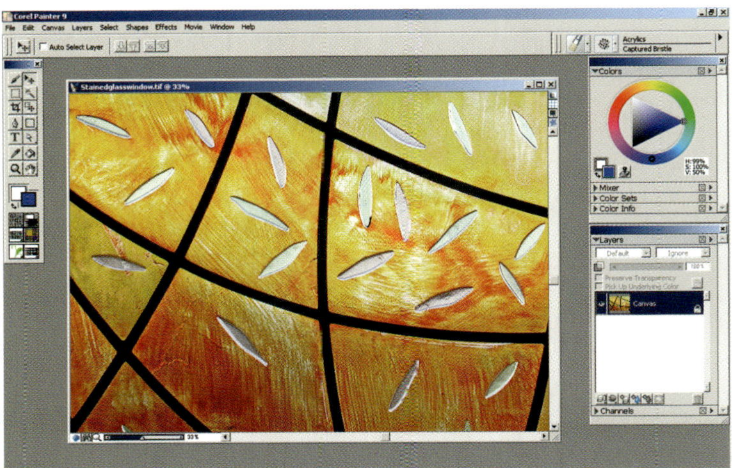

Figure 1.3 The default view of Painter IX

Importing a picture into Painter

Painter is able to use several different types of pictures. If you are bringing in pictures from a digital camera, the most common file types are JPEG or TIFF format. If you are importing a picture that has been saved in Adobe Photoshop, the file type is likely to be PSD. Painter will happily use all these file types and several others. Painter does have its own file type called RIFF; however, when using photographs it's not necessary to use this in the majority of cases.

It is generally desirable not to use very large image files as they will slow the program down, and some of the complex brushes in particular can be very slow.

If the image is to be printed then a resolution between 150 and 300 dpi is preferable, which means a file size of between 10 and 20 mb. For web use a much smaller file size can be used, in most cases around 1 mb.

Figure 1.3 shows the first picture on the CD, which is opened from the File bar by going to *File>Open>CD>Step-by-step files>'01 Stained Glass Window'*. If you prefer you may use your own photograph.

The Brush Selector

The Brush Selector is where the type of brush is chosen; brushes are at the heart of everything in Painter and are dealt with in greater depth in Chapters 5 and 6.

On the right of the Properties bar is the Brush Selector. Click the brush icon on the left and the drop-down menu will reveal the extensive range of brush categories that are available. Drag down the right bottom corner of the menu to see the full list of brush categories. Select the Oils category.

Click on the right-hand icon to reveal another drop-down menu that shows the list of variants for the Oils brush category. Once again, you will need to drag down the list to reveal all the variants. This is a very large category and will give some idea of the huge number of brushes available. Click on the Bristle Oils 30 brush as illustrated in Figure 1.4.

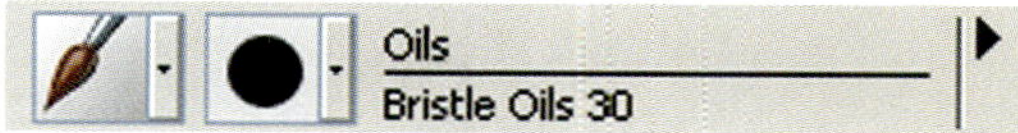

Figure 1.4 The Brush Selector

Picking a color from the Colors palette

To choose a color with which to paint go to the Colors palette, which should be visible on the right of the screen. If this is not the case, go to *Window>Color Palettes>Show Colors* and it will appear.

Figure 1.5 shows the Colors palette. Click in the outer colored circle to choose the hue or color. The inner section defines the brightness of the color; the pure color is on the right, the darker colors bottom left and lighter at the top. Click within the triangle to choose the tone. The orange square shown bottom left in Figure 1.5 is the Main color and confirms which color has been chosen. The Colors palette is explained in more detail in Chapter 12.

Draw some lines on the picture to get a feel for the brush. If you are using a graphic tablet you will see that the brush responds differently depending on the angle used; this is common to many of the brushes. I recommend that you use a graphic tablet, as it is essential for getting the most out of the program. At the end of this chapter there are some tips on setting up your graphics tablet for Painter.

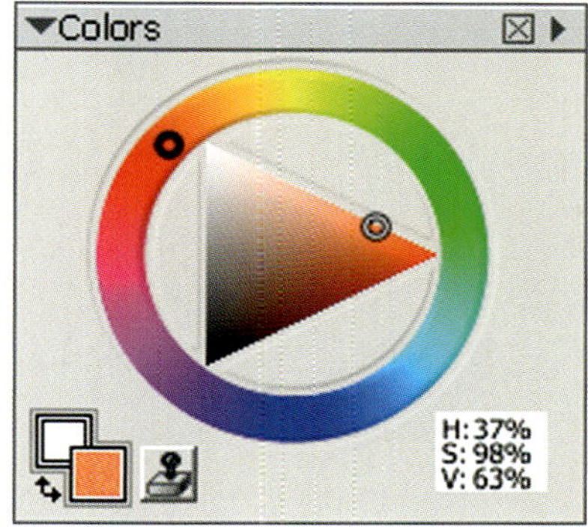

Figure 1.5 The Colors palette

Now try a brush from the Chalk brush category; click on Square Chalk 30, which is very different to the Oil brush. Try some of the other brush categories yourself, but for the moment avoid the Watercolor and Liquid Ink categories as they need a special layer to work on and will be explained in more detail in Chapter 9.

The Properties bar

Figure 1.6 shows the Properties bar – this is a context-sensitive bar and changes to whatever tool is currently active. In the example shown it is relevant to the Brush and is where the brush size is usually changed. Alongside this is the Opacity setting, which affects the density of color being put onto the paper. The other settings will be dealt with in more detail later.

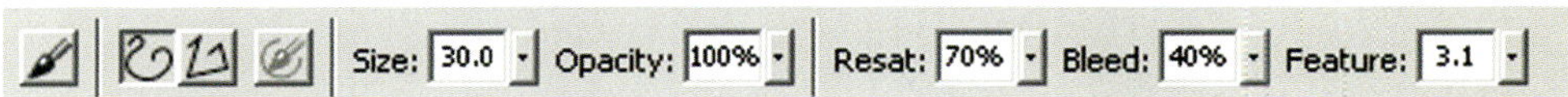

Figure 1.6 The Properties bar

Correcting mistakes

Your image will now be covered with paint strokes, so this is a good point to show how to correct mistakes and if necessary return a picture back to its original state.

The very valuable Undo command is found in the Edit menu and as we have been using a brush, the line will read Undo Brush Stroke. Click on this and the last brush stroke will be undone; click on it again and the previous brush stroke will also be undone. As you can see, the command works backwards and continues to remove the last action taken until you reach the maximum numbers of Undo, which is 32 steps. This number can be changed in the Preferences menu, which is covered later on in this chapter.

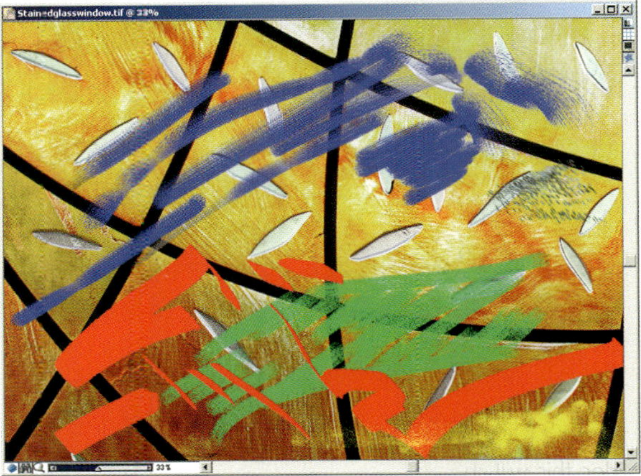

Figure 1.7 Correcting mistakes

Rather than go to the menu every time you want to use the Undo, it is much quicker to use the keyboard shortcut, which is *Ctrl/Cmd + Z*. If you are a Photoshop user you will need to be aware that the Undo command in Painter works differently and is not a toggle action.

To ReDo an action, go to *Edit>ReDo* or use the shortcut *Ctrl/Cmd + Y*.

If you want to get back to the original, go to *File>Revert*. Confirm you want to do this by clicking Revert in the pop-up dialog box and the picture will return to its original state. This will work provided the original picture is still in the same place from which it was loaded, either on your computer or on the CD.

Moving around the picture

One of the great advantages with all graphic programs is the ability to enlarge the picture to work at a more detailed level. The quickest way of doing this is to use the keyboard shortcuts, but I will give the Toolbox method as well.

Click on the Magnifier in the Toolbox and click in the picture; this will enlarge the picture by 25% each time you click. To reduce the magnification, hold down the Opt/Alt key and click in the picture again.

When the Magnifier tool is active there are three buttons on the Properties bar that give preset views.

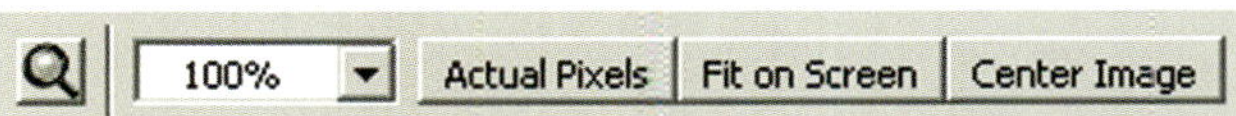

Figure 1.8

Actual Pixels show the image at 100% enlargement, which is very useful for checking detail. Fit on Screen will show the whole picture on the screen as large as possible without being hidden by anything else. Center Image will return the image to the center when it has been magnified.

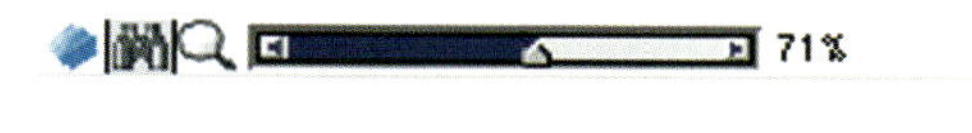

Figure 1.9

Another way to change the magnification is to use the slider at the base of the document window (Figure 1.9). The percentage number shown on the right of the bar is the current magnification of the picture. Type in an amount and press enter to go to a specific magnification.

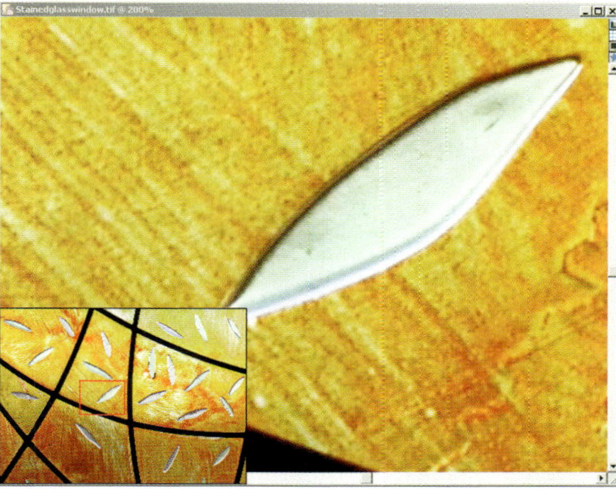

Figure 1.10 Using the Navigator

Increase the magnification significantly then click on the binoculars icon shown in Figure 1.9 to the left of the slider; this will show you which part of the image is being magnified.

Click and drag inside the rectangle to move the point of magnification. The window is shown in Figure 1.10 with the enlarged area in the red rectangle.

Click the Grabber in the Toolbox and the cursor will change to a hand click and drag in the window to move the image. Double-click on the Grabber icon in the Toolbox and the picture will change from a magnified view to the full picture being visible on screen.

Rotating the canvas

The Grabber is one of several tools that have alternative options in the Toolbox. Click and hold the Grabber and select the second icon with a circular arrow. This is the Rotate Page tool and allows the picture to be rotated to make it easier to paint with certain brushes. Don't get this confused with the Rotate Canvas command in the Canvas menu – this tool simply turns the picture around in the same way a traditional artist might move a canvas around to get a better angle. Activate the tool by clicking on the icon, then click and drag in the document window and see the image rotate. To return to the original position, click once on the canvas or double-click on the Rotate Page icon in the Toolbox. Figure 1.11 shows the canvas after being rotated.

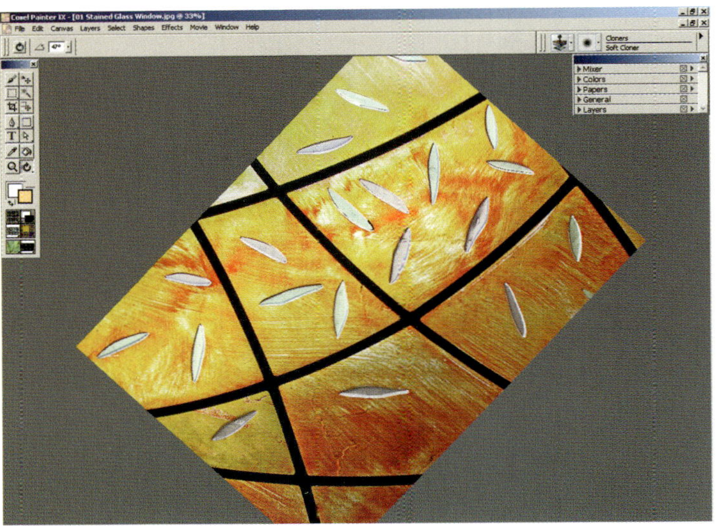

Figure 1.11 Rotating the canvas

Keyboard shortcuts for the screen

- *Ctrl/Cmd* + '+' will magnify the image.
- *Ctrl/Cmd* + '–' will reduce the magnification.
- *Ctrl/Cmd* + 0 will make the image fit on the screen.
- Pressing the Spacebar while painting will activate the Grabber and enable the image to be moved.

Normal view

The Normal view is shown in Figure 1.12 and the picture is contained within its document window. The Full Screen option frees the image from the confines of the document box and fills the entire screen, including behind the palettes and Toolbox. This is a good way to work, as it allows more freedom to move the image around on screen and removes much of the clutter.

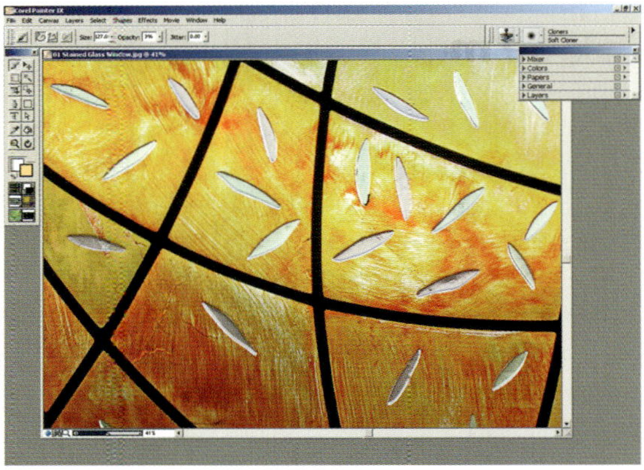

Figure 1.12 Normal view

Full Screen view

Figure 1.13 shows the Full Screen view; to use this mode either go to the Window menu and click on Screen Mode Toggle, or use the keyboard shortcut *Ctrl/Cmd* + *M*. This is a toggle action, so pressing the keys again should revert to the Normal view; however, this often does not work, so you may need to click the minimize button on the top of the document window.

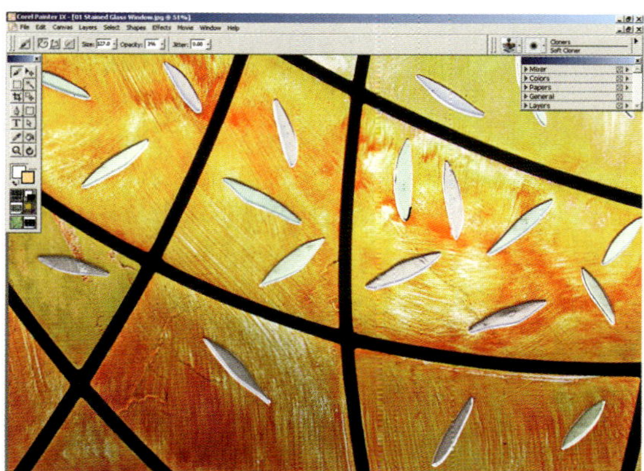

Figure 1.13 Full Screen view

Using and organizing palettes

There are over 30 palettes in Painter IX, and even though they will collapse and stack very neatly, they do take up room on the screen that could be used for the image. Many of them are not usually needed when using photographs, so fortunately they are easy to organize and unwanted ones can be removed.

To remove a palette from the screen, click on the cross in a square on the palette header. To show palettes not visible on the screen, go to the Window menu and click on the name of the palette you want; some of the palettes are arranged in groups for convenience.

To expand or close a palette, click either on the triangle on the left, or on the name of the palette itself. To move and link palettes together, click on the blank area to the right of the palette name and drag the palette over another palette and they will dock together.

Figure 1.14 shows the palettes that I keep on the screen and use regularly; they are usually kept collapsed as shown and opened when required.

Figure 1.14 Useful palettes to keep on screen

Palette menu

One further note regarding palettes: on the right side of the palette name is a small triangle (circled in Figure 1.15) that indicates the palette contains a palette menu. This is a further selection of options relevant to that particular palette; click and hold on the triangle to see the drop-down menu. The various palettes will be looked at in more detail as you work through the step-by-step examples in the book.

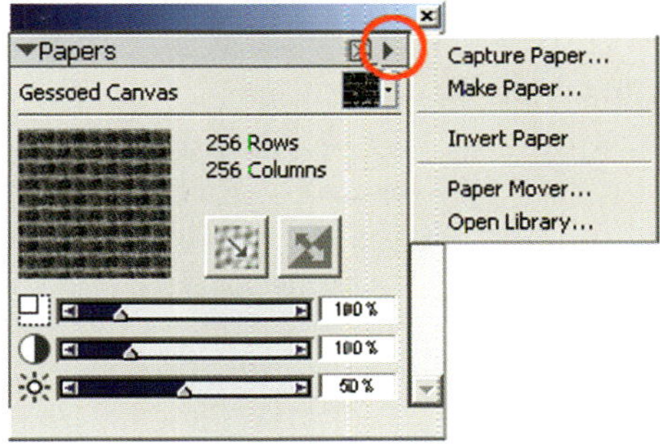

Figure 1.15 The palette menu extended

Basic cloning techniques

Cloning is the name of the process used in Painter to take imagery from an original photograph and reproduce it in an artistic style, using the brushes and textures supplied in the Painter program.

Painter IX has considerably simplified the initial steps for setting up a clone copy. Open a new picture or use one from the CD. Go to the File menu and click on Quick Clone; this will achieve several steps which in earlier versions had to be done separately. A copy of the original picture is created, all the imagery is removed ready to clone, a brush from the Cloners category is selected and the Tracing Paper option activated. Figure 1.16 shows the screen after the Quick Clone command has been used; the picture is now ready to start cloning. Chapter 2 includes three step-by-step examples to lead you through the cloning process.

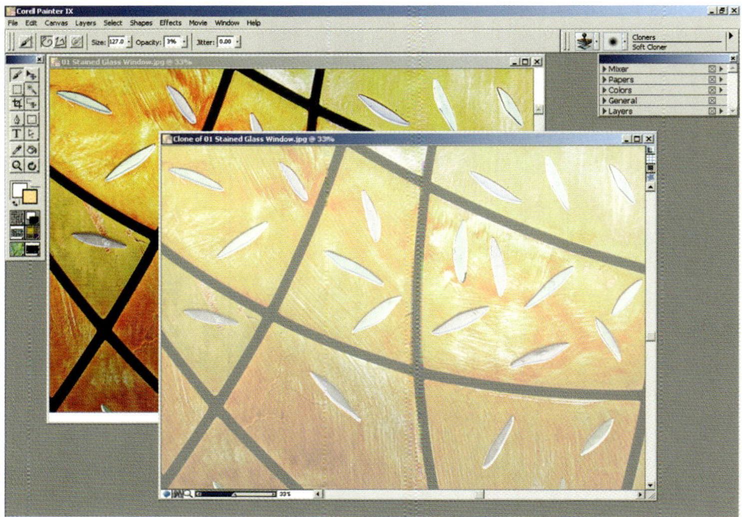

Figure 1.16 Screen showing the Tracing Paper option

Tracing Paper

Tracing Paper is a semi-transparent overlay of the original picture that assists in the early steps of making a clone copy. The overlay can be clearly seen in Figure 1.16 and when the Tracing Paper option is turned off the clone copy will be empty. It is created automatically when the default Quick Clone procedure is used and can be turned on and off at any time. To turn the Tracing Paper on and off, click the top icon on the right of the document window, just above the grid icon. If you cannot find this, look at Figure 2.4 in Chapter 2. The keyboard shortcut is *Ctrl/Cmd + T* and this is a toggle action.

You may wish to try painting a clone copy now with one of the Cloners brushes or wait until the next chapter, where the cloning techniques will be explained fully.

The Brush Creator

The Brush Creator is covered in some detail in Chapter 6, but gets a quick mention here as it is used in a few step-by-step examples in earlier chapters.

This palette, which is accessed by the *Ctrl/Cmd + B* shortcut or from *Window>Show Brush Creator*, houses the controls for customizing brushes. Clicking on a category from the list on the left opens the relevant sub-palette and reveals the sliders and options available. On the right is the Scratch Pad, where brushes can be tried out prior to use.

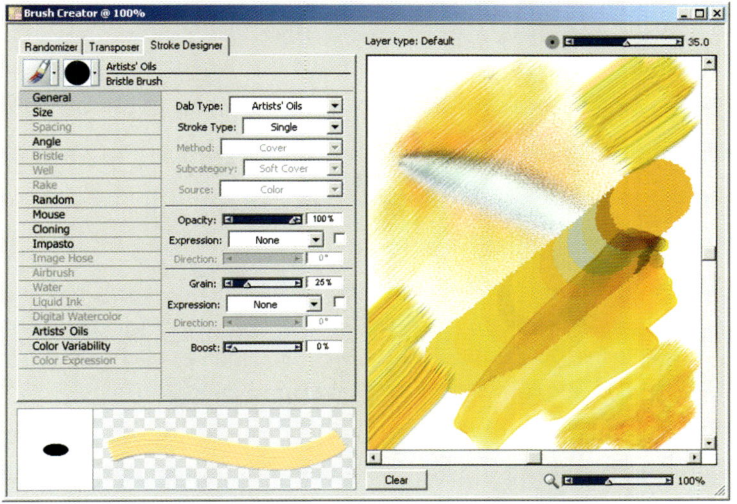

Figure 1.17 The Brush Creator

In Painter IX, all the sub-palettes are also available as separate palettes that can be brought on the screen individually, which is very useful as many of the palettes are rarely used. The palette I recommend you keep on screen is the General palette and this is available from *Window>Brush Controls>General*. If you are using Painter 8 this is not available separately, but can be used from the Brush Creator.

Using a graphic tablet

A graphic tablet with a pressure-sensitive stylus is a must to obtain the Painter brushes' full potential; Wacom are the leading brand of tablets and have a large range from small to very large sizes. I personally find the A5 (6 × 8 inch) size ideal – it is large enough to have ample room for brush strokes yet not take up too much space on the desktop.

How you set up the button configuration for your pressure-sensitive pen is a matter of personal preference; once the software has been installed on your computer, the controls can be accessed via the Control Panel for Windows or in Applications on Mac OS X.

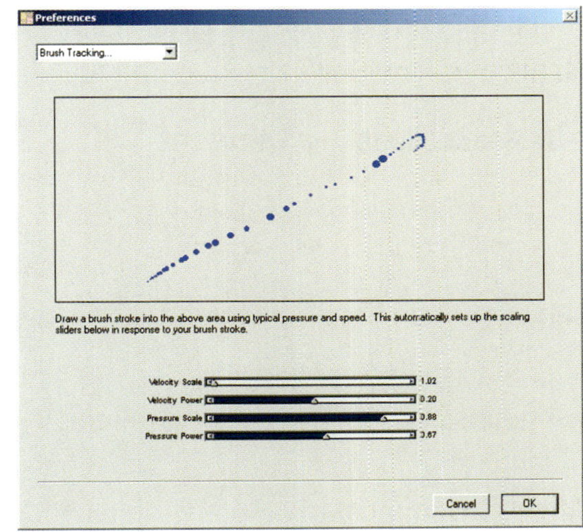

Figure 1.18 Brush Tracking

All the brush and opacity settings used throughout the book are for use with a graphic tablet. If you are using a mouse you will need to reduce the specified opacities quite considerably.

Brush Tracking is a control within Painter to adjust the sensitivity of the pen to suit your own hand. In the Edit menu, go to Preferences and select Brush Tracking in the dialog box.

Make a few sample strokes in the Scratch Pad as in Figure 1.18 and Painter will automatically adjust the pen sensitivity to your own hand pressure.

Saving images

There are three options for saving images available from the File menu:

- Save will save the image, overwriting the original file.
- Save As will save a copy under a different name if required.
- Iterative Save is a new option in Painter IX and is very useful when you need to keep interim versions of the image showing different stages of completion. Each time the image is saved, Painter adds an incremental number to the file, 001 then 002 and so on. This is a very useful option for returning to an earlier stage; usually these interim saves are deleted when the image is completed.

Painter will save images in several file formats, but generally it should be saved in the same file type in which it was originally opened. In the case of photographs this will usually be PSD if it has come via Photoshop or TIFF if from a digital camera.

Images that started as JPEG files should be saved as a PSD, TIFF or RIFF (see below) while being worked on in Painter, as continually saving in JPEG format will degrade the image quality.

The native file format for Painter is RIFF, which would be chosen were the program being used for original painting rather than working from photographs. When certain brushes such as Watercolor are used, the brush strokes can be edited at a later date if saved in RIFF format. Mosaics are another case where it is useful for RIFF to be used. There are some circumstances where we need to save photographic clones in RIFF format and these will be mentioned later in the book.

Setting up preferences

Preferences – General

Apart from the Brush Tracking already mentioned, there are a number of other important and useful settings to be found in the *Edit>Preferences* menu.

Figure 1.19 shows the controls under the General heading and the top left controls the appearance of the cursor.

The Cursor type is usually best set to Brush and a shape can be selected from the menu alongside.

Enable Brush Ghosting means that the size of the brush can be seen on screen before painting; it changes to the cursor during actual painting.

Brush size increment controls the amount of increase or decrease in brush size when the square brackets keyboard shortcut is used.

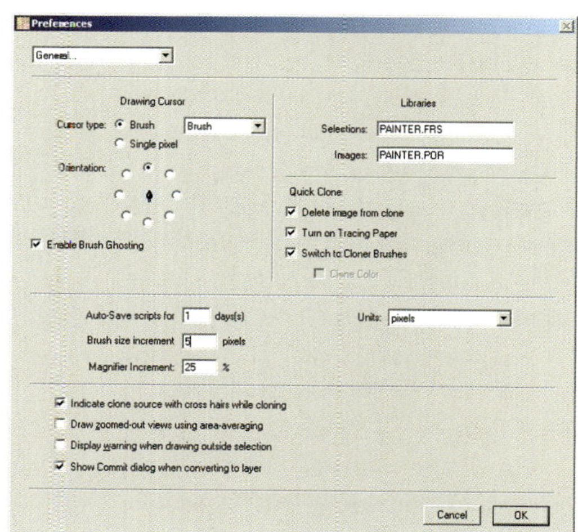

Figure 1.19 Preferences, General section

The Quick Clone options control the steps that are carried out when Quick Clone is used. I suggest that you leave them all ticked at first.

All other options can be left on the default settings.

Preferences – Undo

In this dialog box the number of steps of 'Undo' Painter will remember is specified. The decision on the number to set will be based largely on the amount of RAM that is installed on the computer. The higher the number, the more flexible the Undo is, but the downside is that this uses more memory as Painter keeps track of the Undo steps. The maximum number is 32.

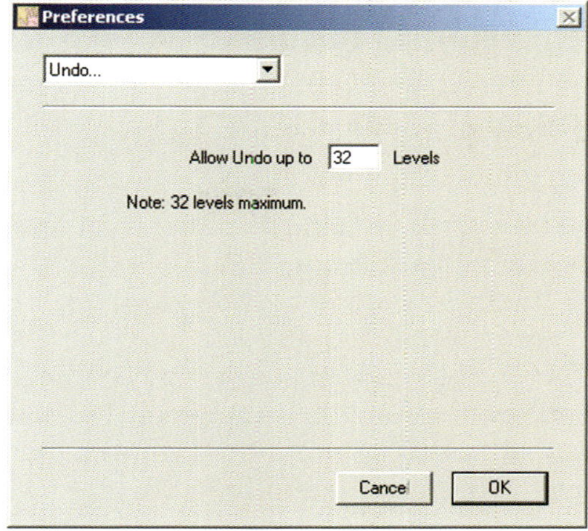

Figure 1.20 The Undo dialog box

Preferences – Customize Keys

For those people like myself who use keyboard shortcuts a lot, the Customize Keys option is superb. It allows shortcuts to be made for all the main functions in Painter and you can also change the default ones if you wish. It is particularly useful if you use another program, like Photoshop for instance, as you can use the same shortcuts in both programs.

The option existed in earlier versions of Painter, but in Painter IX the dialog box has had an overhaul and is much more user friendly.

To bring up the dialog box, go to *Edit>Preferences>Customize Keys.* Figure 1.21 shows the dialog box at this stage. It is all very easy to follow, but to show an example, here is how to make a shortcut for the Revert option, which has the function key F12 in Photoshop.

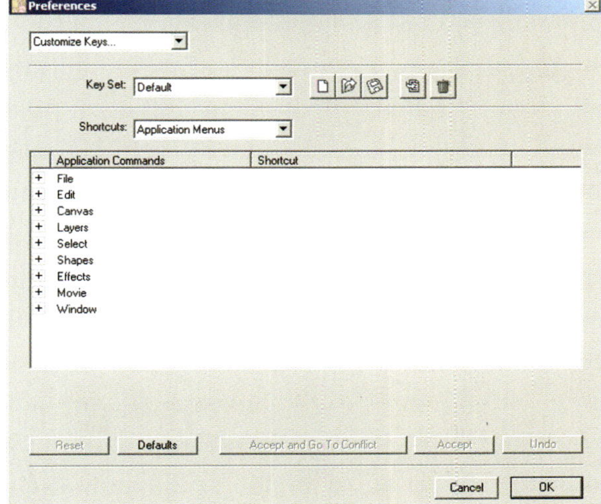

Figure 1.21 The Customize Keys dialog box

Open the dialog box and click on the plus sign to the left of the word File; this will bring up the list of commands in the File menu. Highlight Revert and as you will see there is no shortcut allocated to it. Press the F12 key to set this as the shortcut, make any more shortcuts in the same way then press OK to accept all the changes you have made. It is that simple.

Apart from commands in the menu bar, keyboard shortcuts can be set for the palette menus and tools; to access the other areas change the option in the Shortcuts dialog box.

The changes you have made will be saved for immediate and ongoing use, but if you have to reload the program they may be lost; you can therefore save your own set by pressing the save icon.

Color management

Color management plays an important part in getting the printed image as close as possible to the image we see on the computer screen. The whole subject of color management is very complex and is the subject of several books, so the following notes are a brief summary and include some practical tips on what settings to choose.

The Color Management controls are available from the Canvas menu and the dialog box is shown in Figure 1.22 with its default settings.

If you are using Painter in conjunction with Adobe Photoshop, I recommend that you import the picture in Photoshop PSD format, work on it in Painter and, after saving the picture, return to Photoshop and print from there. Photoshop has much better facilities for setting and previewing print options. If you follow this procedure you can leave all the Color Management settings in Painter on default and use your existing settings in Photoshop. This is the method I use and find it very satisfactory.

If you are using Painter IX as a standalone program, the following notes will help you with the settings required.

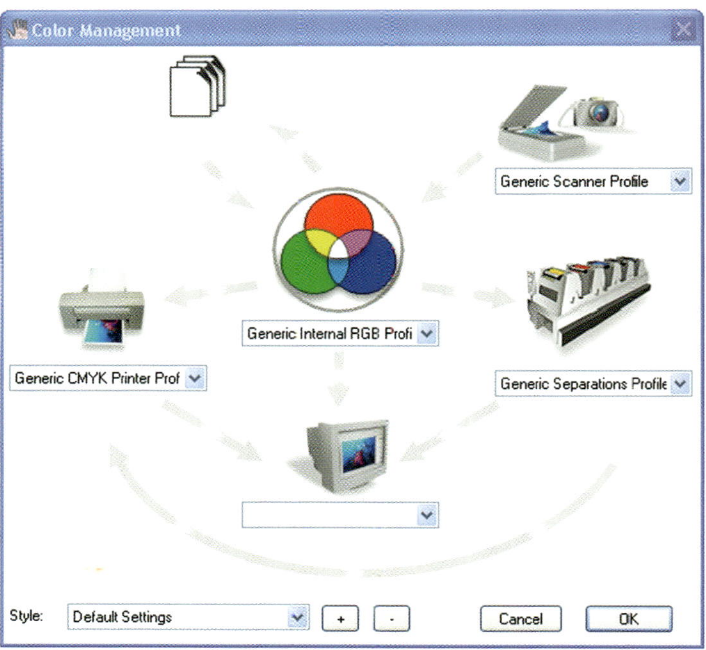

Figure 1.22 The Color Management dialog box

Color profiles

Each device, whether it is a printer, monitor or scanner, has a different way of using colors and to get them all working together means that they must communicate their own method to the other parts of the system. This is achieved by creating a color profile for each device which contains all the necessary information. The profiles are called ICC profiles and are controlled through the Kodak Color Management System.

Color profiles can be provided in various ways; the most accurate result will be by employing a specialist to calibrate your system. They will use expensive specialist equipment to analyze each device and will create a custom set of profiles for you to use.

The next best is to purchase calibration equipment yourself; there are several devices available at various price levels. These will be specific to your own devices and will therefore be reasonably accurate, depending on the system used.

The cheapest option is to use generic profiles provided by the equipment manufacturers; these are usually available from the suppliers' websites at no cost. They will based on the manufactured device, but not specific to your particular equipment. They may or may not be accurate, but are worth trying if you cannot get the profiles written any other way.

Using profiles in Painter IX

Go to *Canvas>Color Management* and the dialog box will appear as seen in Figure 1.22 – you must have an open document in Painter to access this. There are a series of grayed out arrows going in various directions; click on any one and the arrow color will turn to orange, which indicates that Color Management is now active for that particular link.

Selecting profiles

Click on the drop-down menu below the computer monitor icon and a list of profiles will appear. If you have created a monitor profile, click on the name to select it. If you have a monitor profile and it does not appear in this list, click on 'get profile from disc' and navigate to where your profile has been saved.

Use the same process to allocate profiles for your printer and scanner. Bear in mind that you will need to change the printer profile when you print on a different paper.

Click the drop-down menu below the RGB color icon in the center, and select a color space from the list (Figure 1.23). If you are already using a color space for other programs, select that one; otherwise, use the Generic Internal RGB profile.

Click on the pages icon top left to reveal the Advanced Import/Export Settings (Figure 1.24).

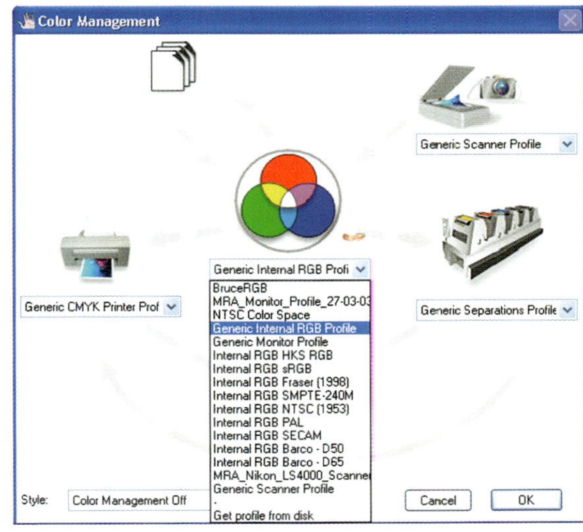

Figure 1.23 Selecting the profile

Color space profiles can be embedded as part of the image file when using programs such as Photoshop and Painter, and this dialog box determines how Painter will handle these profiles when importing or exporting.

At the top are buttons to choose CMYK or RGB and the series of options beneath will control whether profiles will be used.

In the Import section it is generally better to select the 'Convert using embedded ICC profile' option, as this will keep whatever profile the image already contains. The other choices are to change the profile or to ignore the profile.

In the Export section the first option will export the picture with the color profile and this is the option most used. The other options will specify which profile is to be embedded and, again, to ignore the ICC profile.

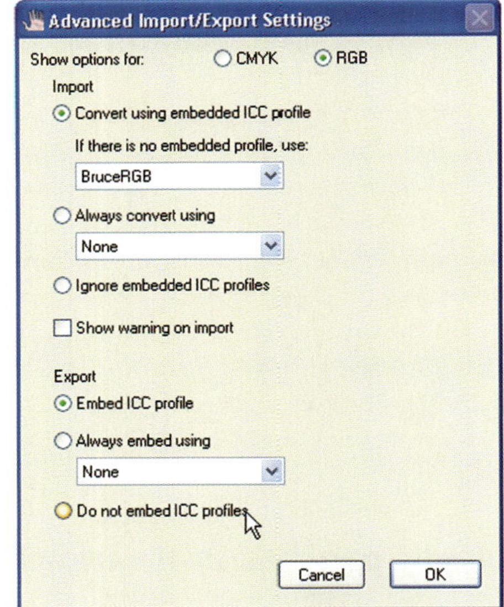

Figure 1.24 Advanced Import/Export Settings

Click the grayed out arrows to activate the profiles you are using; this can be seen in Figure 1.25. When you have set all the various options and are happy that they are right for you, the settings can be saved. Click the '+' button at the bottom of the dialog box and enter a name in the Save box. In the Style box, click to reveal the drop-down menu and select the name for the setting you have just saved; this will make them active.

This quick overview should help you set up the key options for Color Management; it is difficult to be more specific as the requirements are different due to the many ways in which Painter is used. For a more detailed description of color management issues, go to *Help>Welcome* ... and click on the bottom tab of the new Welcome screen which opens when Painter is started.

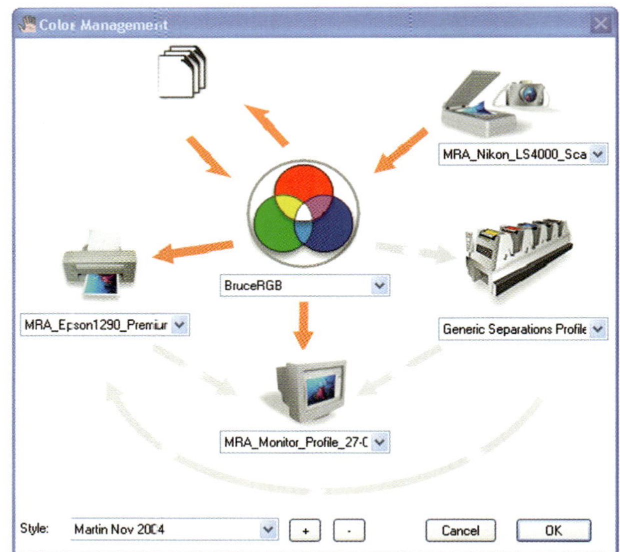

Figure 1.25 Showing the Color Management arrows active

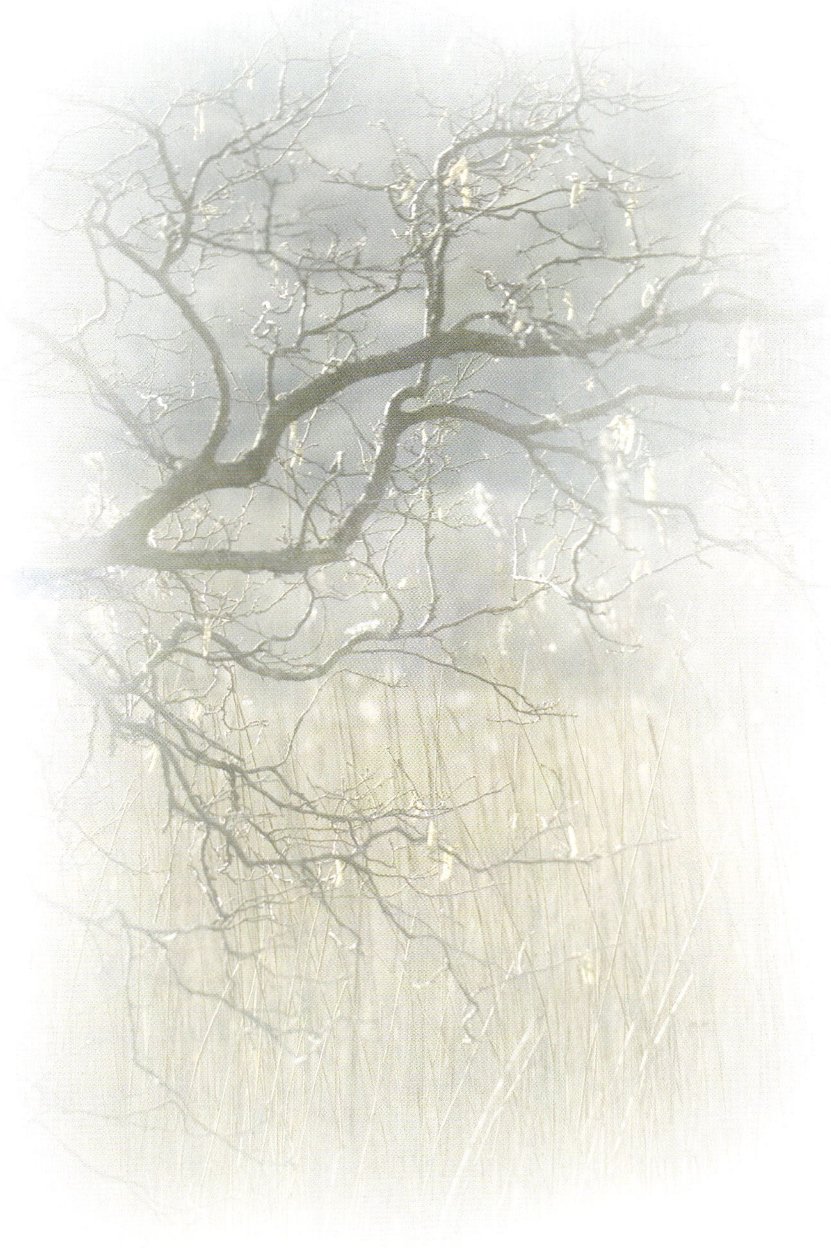

Figure 1.26 Catkins

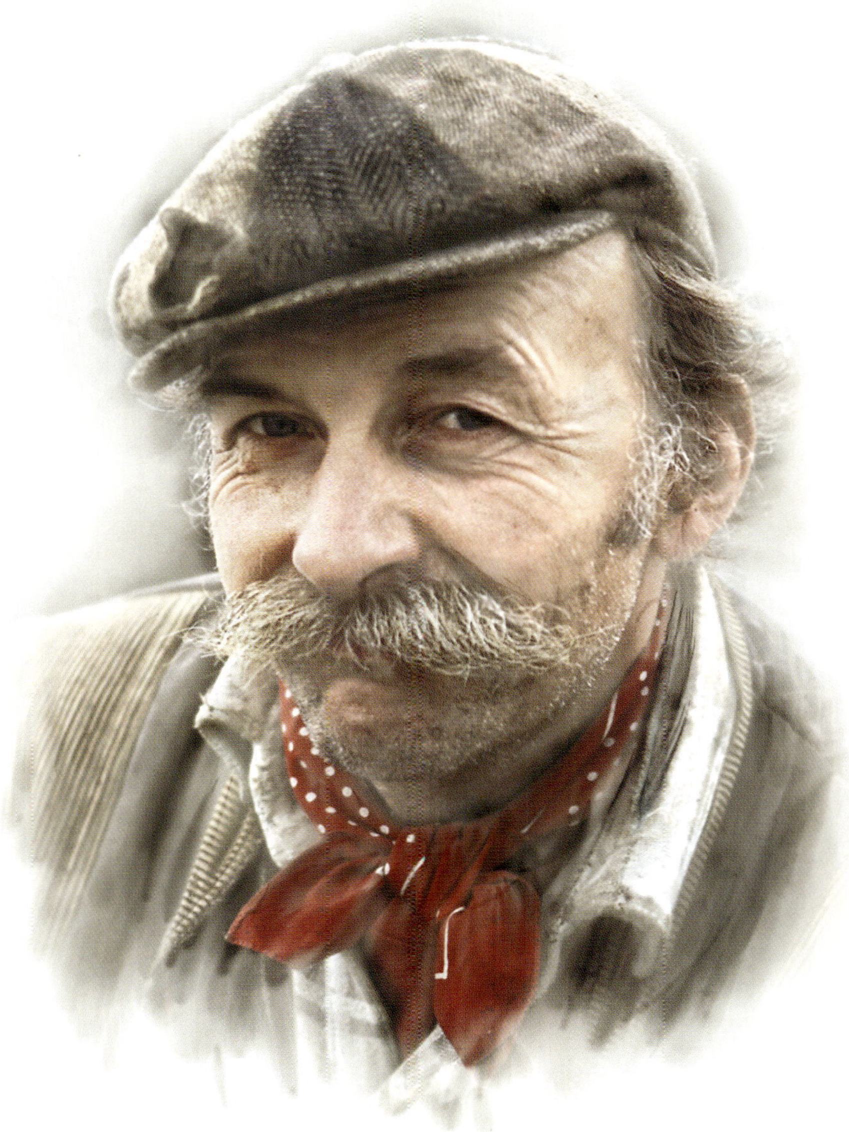

Figure 2.1 The workman

Chapter 2
First steps in cloning

The major part of this book deals with cloning techniques of all kinds, so it is worth explaining just what cloning means in this context. The term has a different meaning in other graphic programs such as Photoshop, where cloning tools are chiefly used for retouching images. It can mean this in Painter too, as there are tools which do just that; however, when I discuss cloning photographs I am referring to the process which takes the imagery from an original photograph and reinterprets it in an artistic manner through the use of Painter brushes and paper surfaces.

In this chapter you will learn, through step-by-step examples, the basic clone types in Painter. They are very easy to create and by the end of the chapter you will understand how to make artistic clones from photographs. The remainder of the book builds on these basic techniques and will gradually introduce more complex ideas and other ways to adapt photographs.

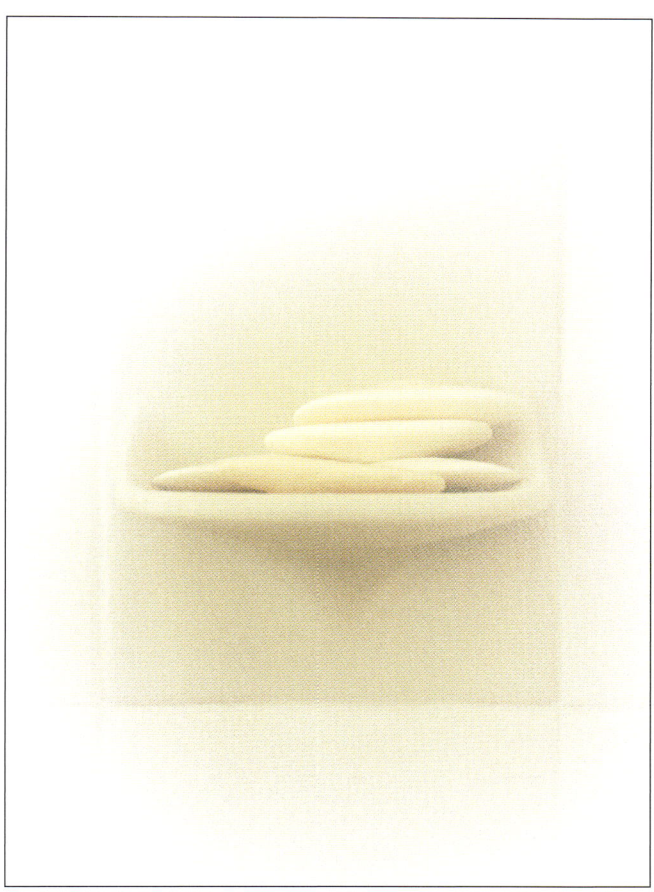

Figure 2.2 Soap

A simple soft clone

The first step-by-step example in this chapter is what is called a 'soft clone' – this is a clone that does not use any paper texture but has a very smooth finish. It is a simple clone that can result in a beautiful delicate picture and is a good one to start with. Try it with the picture that is on the CD; it has been tested with this image so it will be easier to follow. Throughout the book, the precise settings will be given for each brush and it is most important that you follow these carefully to achieve the desired result.

Dandelions and grasses

Step 1 *File>Open>CD>Step-by-step files>'02 Dandelions and Grasses'.*

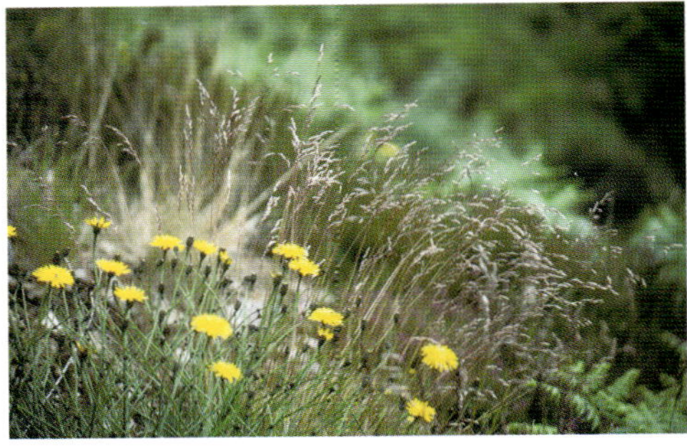

Figure 2.3 Original photograph

Step 2 *File>Quick Clone*; this will complete several steps at once. A copy of the original picture is made, the copy is cleared of imagery and the Tracing Paper overlay will be applied. The brush category will also be set to Cloners. The Quick Clone steps are included as the default settings when Painter is first loaded, but they can be altered in the *Edit>Preferences>General section* if required.

The Quick Clone command is new to Painter IX, so if you are using an older version of Painter you will need to take the following steps. Open the photograph from the CD. *File>Clone, Select>Select All, Edit>Cut, Canvas>Tracing Paper.*

Step 3 Click on the document bar at the top of the clone and drag it to see the original underneath. Figure 2.4 shows the screen at this point. The tracing paper overlay is hiding what is now an empty canvas; click the Tracing Paper icon (shown in Figure 2.5) in the top right corner of the clone document window to check that this is indeed empty, then click again to reapply the tracing paper.

Remember that the original image must stay on the screen at all times, as the brush strokes you are about to make will be coming from that linked photograph.

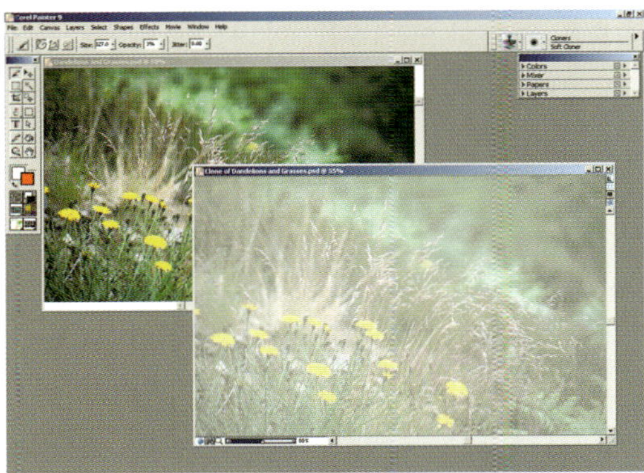

Figure 2.4 Original with clone copy in front

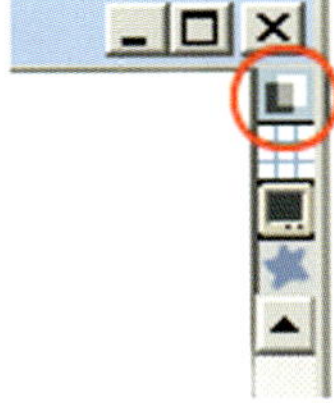

Figure 2.5 Tracing Paper icon

Step 4 The Brush Selector is on the right of the Properties bar and is seen in Figure 2.6. The brush category should now be Cloners and if it is not, click the brush icon on the left and select Cloners in the drop-down menu.

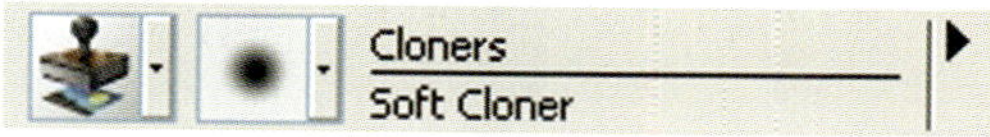

Figure 2.6 The Brush Selector

To select a Brush Variant, click the icon to the right and a long list of Variants in the Cloners category will drop down. All these brush variants have been set up to work as Cloners with no adjustments needed, which means they are ready for use immediately. Select the Soft Cloner; this variant will give a very smooth and gentle effect.

Step 5 Check the Properties bar at the top and change the settings to those in Figure 2.7. Enter 127.0 in the Size box; this can be done either by clicking on the arrow to the right of the figures and using the slider, or by typing the amount in and pressing Enter. This is a very large brush size, which will work well with the low opacity set in the next step.

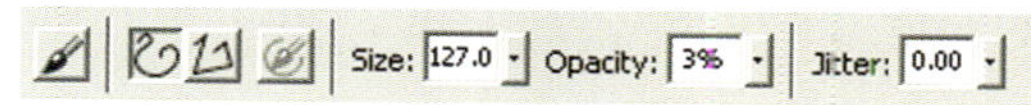

Figure 2.7 The Properties bar

Step 6 Change the opacity to 3%; small adjustments of the slider can be made by clicking on the arrows at either end. Very low opacities are common when cloning from photographs, but each type of brush will need a slightly different setting. Before starting to paint, make sure you can see the original picture underneath as well as the copy. As you paint into the copy you will see the crosshairs cursor move in the original photograph; this is showing where the clone source is coming from. Make a few light strokes in the clone copy, start in the lower left corner and sweep out the strokes in the direction the grasses are growing. You will probably not see any difference immediately because the Tracing Paper hides the very light strokes you are making. Turn off the Tracing Paper to see what you have painted so far. The Tracing Paper is usually only needed for the first few strokes and then it is better to remove it, as it disguises the result. Switch it back on every now and then if you need to check progress.

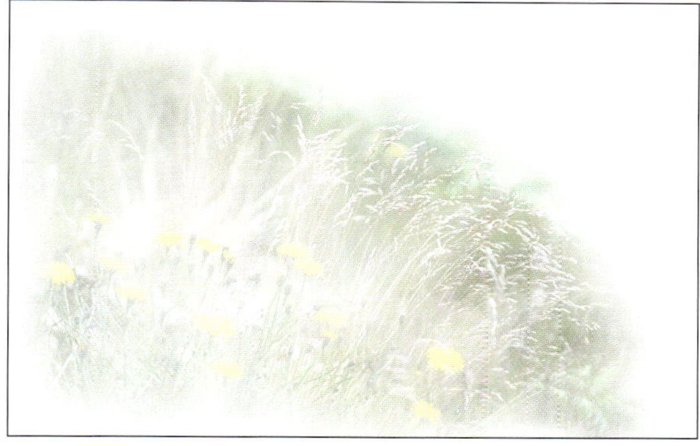

Figure 2.8 The first stages

Step 7 Continue to paint the image into the clone copy; the low opacity brush will allow you to do this very gradually. The effect to aim at is a very soft, delicate and dreamlike quality. Check Figure 2.8 to see where you should be at this point. Follow the lines of the grasses with your brush strokes and leave the edges white.

Step 8 Reduce the brush size to around 31.4 and paint over the yellow flowers a few times to emphasize the color. If you need to enlarge any part of the picture to see more clearly use the slider at the base of the document window. Press the Spacebar and click and drag in the picture to move the enlarged section around the screen.

If you need to undo any step use the keyboard shortcut *Ctrl/Cmd + Z* or go to the File menu and click Undo. The Undo function will continue to undo the previous action until it reaches the limit set in the Preferences section. Setting the preference value is covered in Chapter 1.

Step 9 A very light smooth finish is required to create the soft ethereal effect, but even by painting with great care there are often areas which are rather darker than is ideal. This is very easy to correct by painting white over the top of the area that you have cloned. Go to the Brush Selector and choose the Acrylics brush category and select the Dry Brush 30 as the variant. Change the brush size to around 79.0 and make the opacity 7%; leave the other settings unchanged.

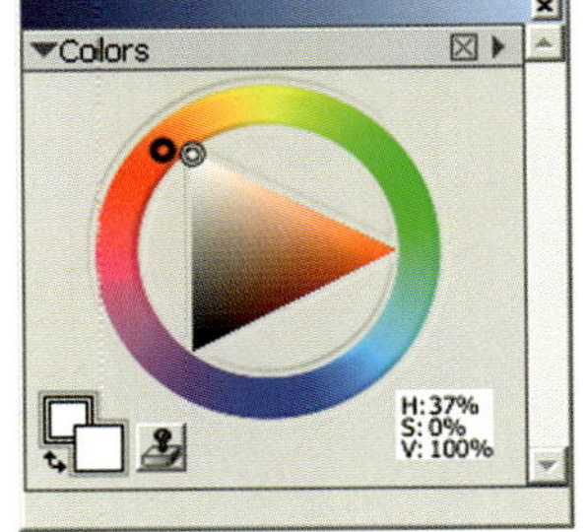

Figure 2.9 The Colors palette

Step 10 Now that the brush is selected you must ensure that you will be painting with white as the color. If the Colors palette is not on screen, go to the Window menu and in the Color palettes section click on Show Colors. Click on the arrow to the left of the palette name to open the palette if it is not already open. On the inner colored triangle, move the circular indicator to the white corner. Check the two overlapping squares in the bottom left of the palette; the one on top is the Main color and indicates the color that will be used for painting, and this should be White, as in Figure 2.9.

Step 11 Lightly paint over the dark areas in your picture until the finish is very smooth and even. If you overdo this stage, simply change back to the Soft Cloner brush and clone some imagery back from the original picture. The whole process is very flexible and can be repeated as often as is necessary.

Step 12 This finishes the first cloned photograph; now it is time to find some photographs of your own on which to try the technique. Choose a picture that will benefit from the very soft treatment – an important part of making successful images is matching the right picture with the right technique. You may wish to save your picture for future reference.

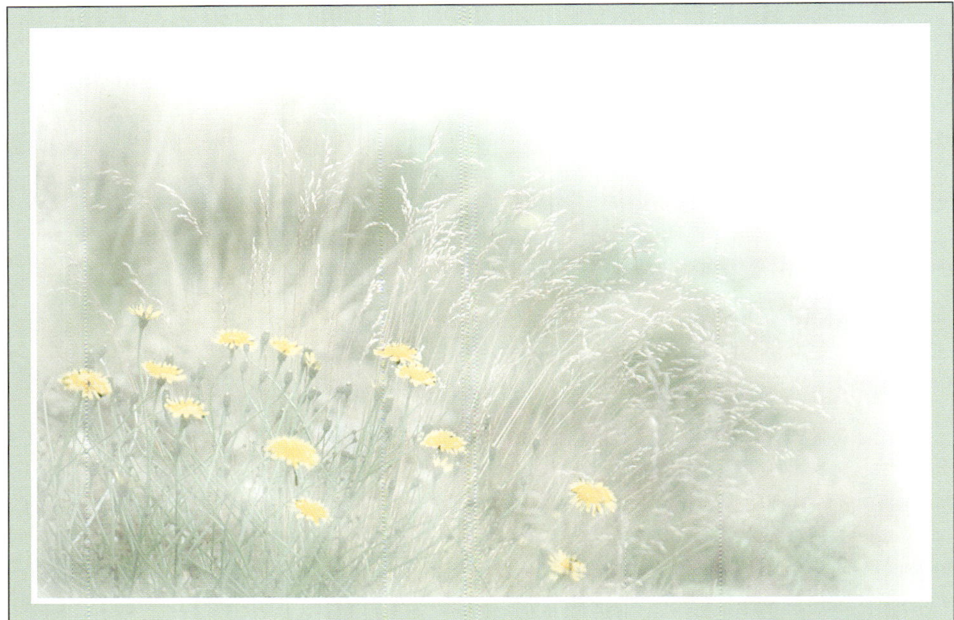

Figure 2.10 Dandelions and grasses

A bristle brush clone

The second step-by-step example uses a brush that has bristles and, as you will quickly see, the technique needed to make a good picture is rather different to the soft clone. More care is needed when placing the individual brushstrokes to ensure that the textural detail is retained.

Flower petal

Step 1 *File>Open>CD>Step-by-step files>'02 Flower Petal'.*

Step 2 *File>Quick Clone.*

Step 3 Select the Brush icon in the Toolbox.

Step 4 From the Brush Selector bar, choose the Cloners category and select Bristle Brush Cloner as the Brush Variant. Using the controls on the Properties bar, change the brush size to 32.2 and the opacity to 65%.

Step 5 Using the Tracing Paper as a guide, paint in all the areas except the center stamens, dragging the brush outwards from the center. Make the brush strokes fairly loose.

Step 6 Paint in the center of the flower; this time dab with the brush rather than making long strokes. Figure 2.12 shows the picture at this point seen with the Tracing Paper turned off.

Step 7 Turn the Tracing Paper off and paint over the picture again until all the white areas are filled; paint the center with brush dabs as before.

Step 8 To put the finishing touches to the picture, change the brush size to 9.6 and the opacity to 100%. This will give contrast to the areas painted and enhance the texture. Follow the darker lines in the petals, and paint with short brush strokes – don't be too exact as this is not intended to be an exact copy of the original photograph. Figure 2.13 shows the final version.

This particular cloning brush partially smears the cloned image, and later in the book other brushes that have this same characteristic in a more pronounced manner will be explored.

Another similar brush in the Cloners category is the Smeary Bristle Cloner which, as its name suggests, smears the image rather more than the brush used in this example.

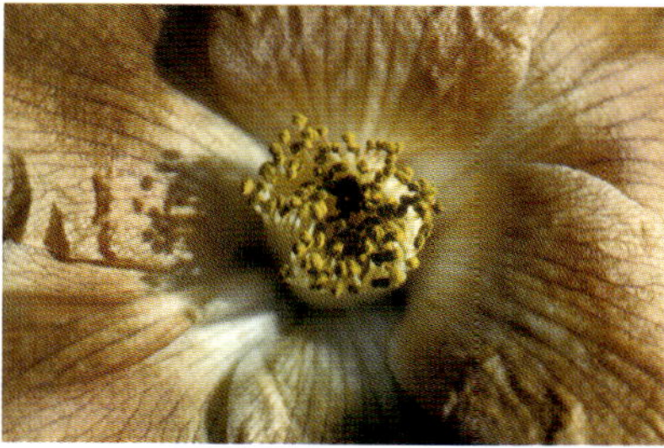

Figure 2.11 Original photograph

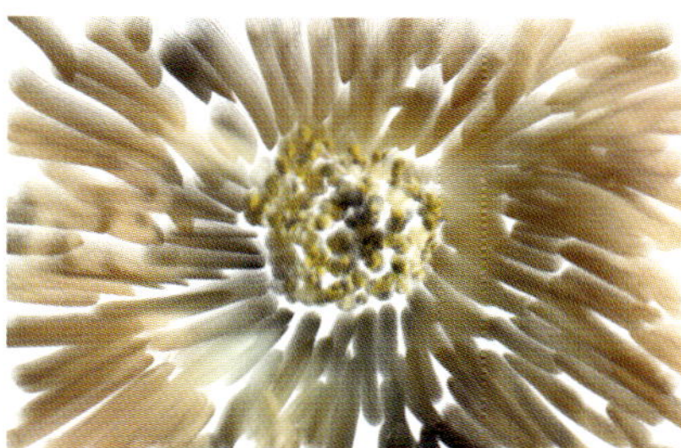

Figure 2.12 The initial brush strokes

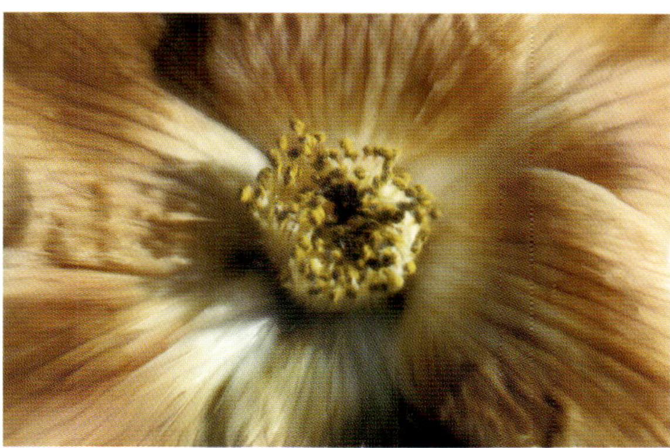

Figure 2.13 Flower petal

A simple textured clone

Before a painter using a 'traditional', i.e. non-digital, method starts to paint, two important decisions have to be made. Firstly, which medium to use (which might be oil, watercolor, pencil pastel and so on) and then the surface on which to paint (perhaps paper, board, sandpaper, etc.).

What Painter does is to replicate as closely as possible the result of the chosen combination. A soft camel hair brush on a smooth board will give a clear-edged smooth color, whereas when using a piece of hard chalk on a heavily textured paper the chalk will skim the surface, leaving the paper indentations with no paint – in other words, a very rough effect. These choices will have a major influence on the finished look of the artwork.

It is very similar when a photograph is cloned using the brushes and surfaces available in Painter; the huge range of brushes and papers covers virtually every type available to the traditional artist and many that are not.

There are something like 600 different papers in Painter, some of which have to be loaded separately from the program CD, so the combination of 900 brushes combined with 600 papers is pretty mind-boggling!

Figure 2.14 shows a small selection of the hundreds of textured papers available.

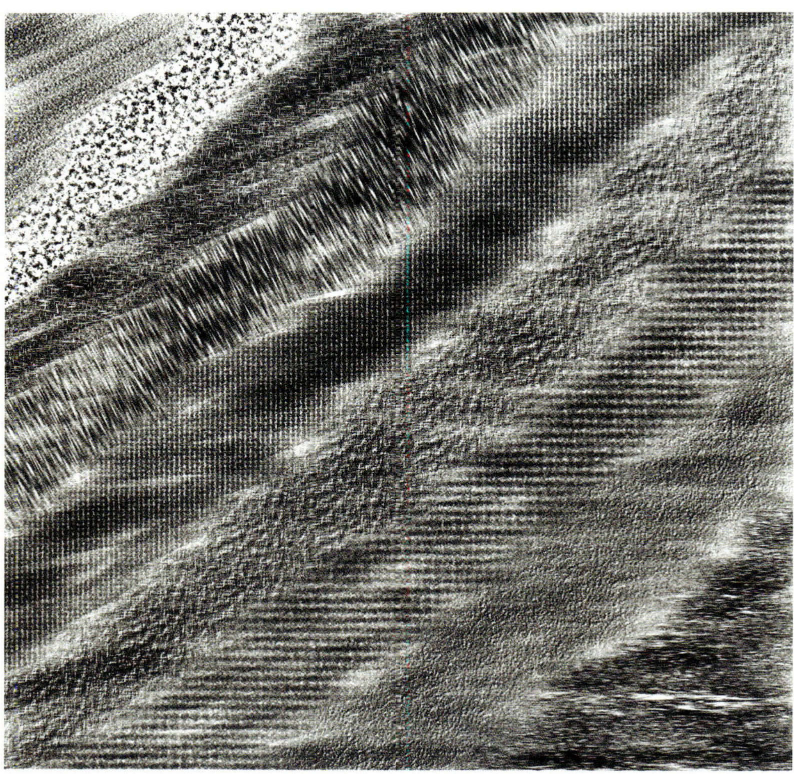

Figure 2.14 Some of the default set of paper textures in Painter IX

St Conan's Kirk

This next step-by-step example will look at how to use paper textures when making clones. You will learn how to change the appearance of a photograph to give the impression of painting on a coarse textured paper. The range of paper textures and how to use them is explored in more detail in the next chapter.

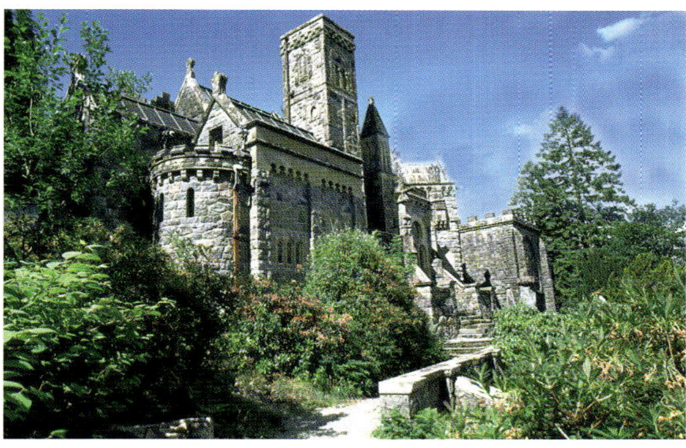

Figure 2.15 Original photograph

The photograph of St Conan's Kirk in Scotland had some simple repair work done in Photoshop prior to opening in Painter. The contrast was increased slightly and the blue sky was extended down to cover some eye-catching white clouds. It is not necessary to get this very precise, as the cloning process will cover up any minor imperfections.

Step 1 *File>Open>CD>Step-by-step files>'02 St Conans Kirk'.*

Step 2 *File>Quick Clone.*

Step 3 Select the Brush icon in the Toolbox.

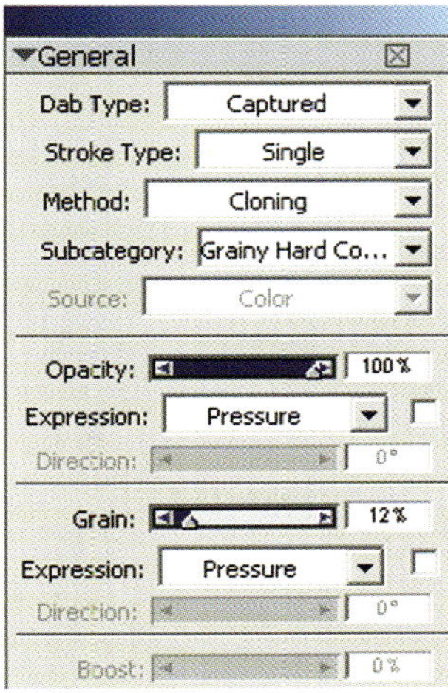

Figure 2.16 The General palette

Step 4 From the Brush Selector bar, choose the Chalk category and select Square Chalk 35 as the Brush Variant. This brush is not in the Cloners brush category and therefore you will have to change it from the default setting, which is painting color, to cloning mode, so that the brush picks up detail from the original image. This applies to all brush categories except Cloning. If the General palette is not on screen, go to *Window>Brush Controls>Show General.* You will get all the Brush Control palettes on screen, so click on the General palette heading and drag it out from the rest; you can then remove the other palettes which will not be needed from the screen by clicking on the 'x' at the top right of the palette stack.

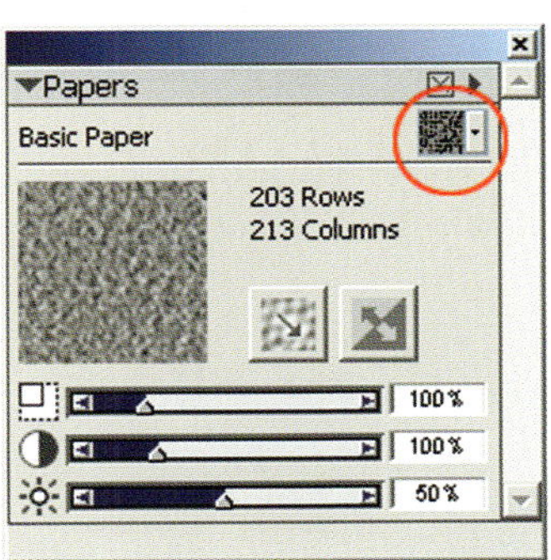

Figure 2.17 The Papers palette

Step 5 There are two controls to be adjusted to change this brush to work as a cloner. In the Method box, change the setting to Cloning; this will make the brush use the original picture as the source for color. Then, in the Subcategory box, select Grainy Hard Cover Cloning; this will tell the brush to use the paper texture when painting.

Step 6 Change the brush size to 35.0 and the opacity to 5%. If you are using a mouse rather than a pressure-sensitive pen, I suggest you use 1% or 2% opacity – this will enable you to build up the textures more slowly.

Step 7 You now need to choose a paper texture and if the papers palette is not on the screen, go to *Window>Library Palettes>Show Papers*. Open the Papers palette and click on the small paper icon highlighted in Figure 2.17. This will reveal a drop-down menu showing the Painter IX default set of papers, as shown in Figure 2.18. Select the Italian Watercolor Paper.

Step 8 Paint the main lines of the building with the Tracing Paper turned on. These initial marks should be very light and you will need to turn the Tracing Paper on and off many times to see what you have painted. Once you have all the main building areas indicated on the picture, you can turn off the Tracing Paper. See Figure 2.19 for an indication of the clone picture at this point.

Step 9 Gradually build up the picture, working from the building outwards keeping the textures light. Your brush strokes should be following the direction of the building; never simply stroke the brush across the picture, always think about which way the brush strokes will look best. Once the whole picture has been lightly covered, start to go over the buildings again, using the same opacity, and this will slowly make the details more distinct. You can slightly increase the opacity if necessary, but it is generally better to allow the brush strokes to build the picture – that way, you have more control.

Basic Paper
Small Dots
Artists Rough Paper
Sandy Pastel Paper
Rough Charcoal Paper
Retro Fabric
Hard Laid Paper
Gessoed Canvas
Fine Dots
New Streaks
Wood Grain
Artists Canvas
Charcoal Paper
Simulated Woodgrain
Thick Handmade Paper
Coarse Cotton Canvas
Fine Hard Grain
Worn Pavement
Italian Watercolor Paper
Linen Canvas
Pebble Board
Hot Press
French Watercolor Paper

Figure 2.18 The default Painter papers

Step 10 Use the magnifier slider below the image to work at a bigger magnification, and then reduce the brush size to about 10.0 and paint over the building outlines, making them more prominent. Increase the opacity to 10% and emphasize the shadow areas in the buildings. Figure 2.20 shows the picture at this stage.

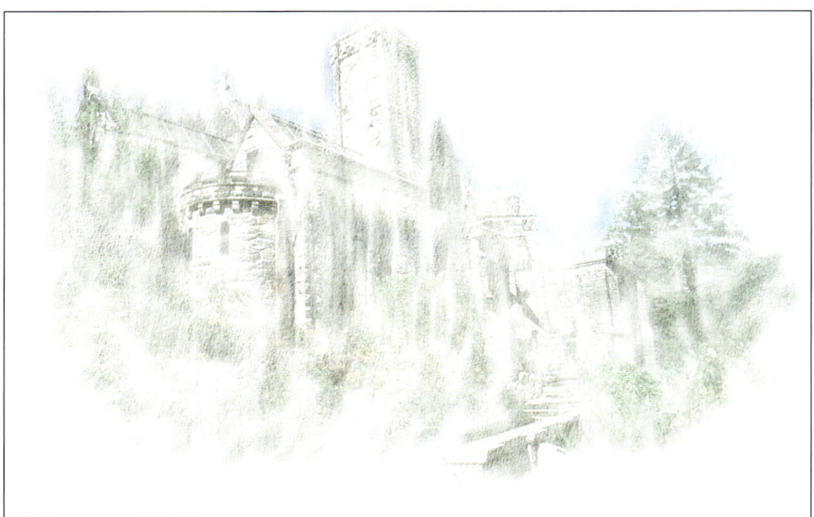

Figure 2.19 Keeping the textures light

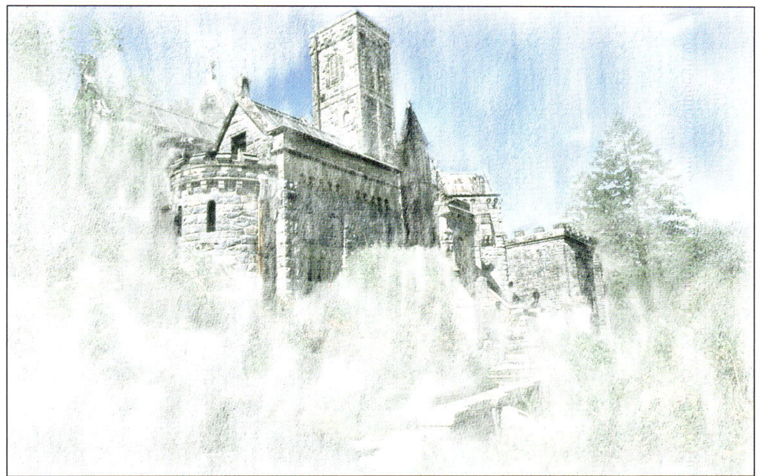

Figure 2.20 Increasing the density of the picture

Step 11 Experiment with different brush sizes and opacities to see how they affect the picture. Try brush size 72 with 5% opacity and sweep over the main areas; this will bring more detail in and smooth out some of the irregularities caused by the brush strokes. One of the most difficult decisions is to know when to stop, as it is easy to overwork a picture and bring back too much of the original image. Figure 2.21 shows the final picture.

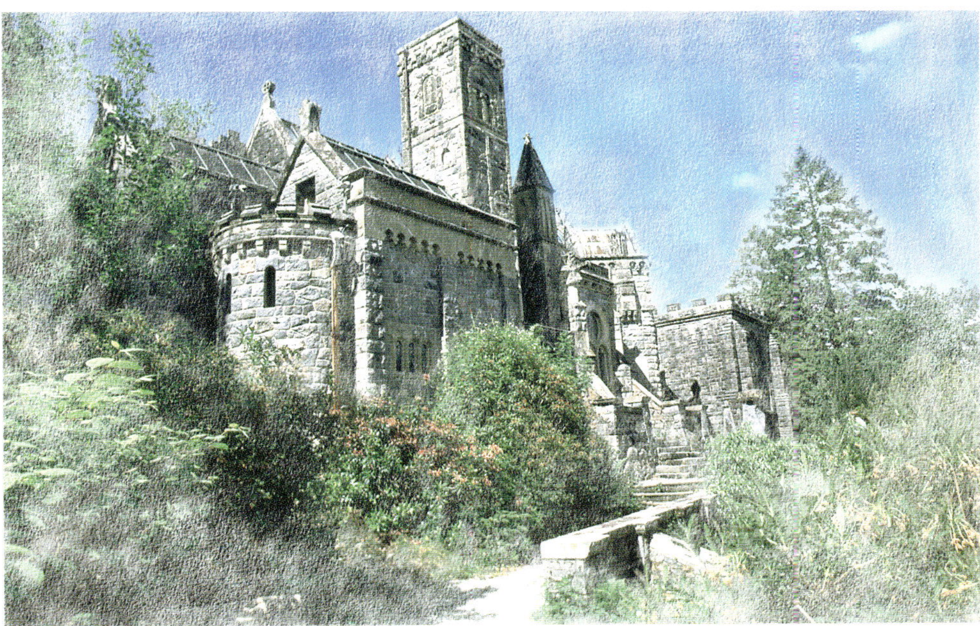

Figure 2.21 St Conan's Kirk

In the next chapter we will look at paper textures in more detail, learning how to choose different papers and to alter them to suit the style of the picture.

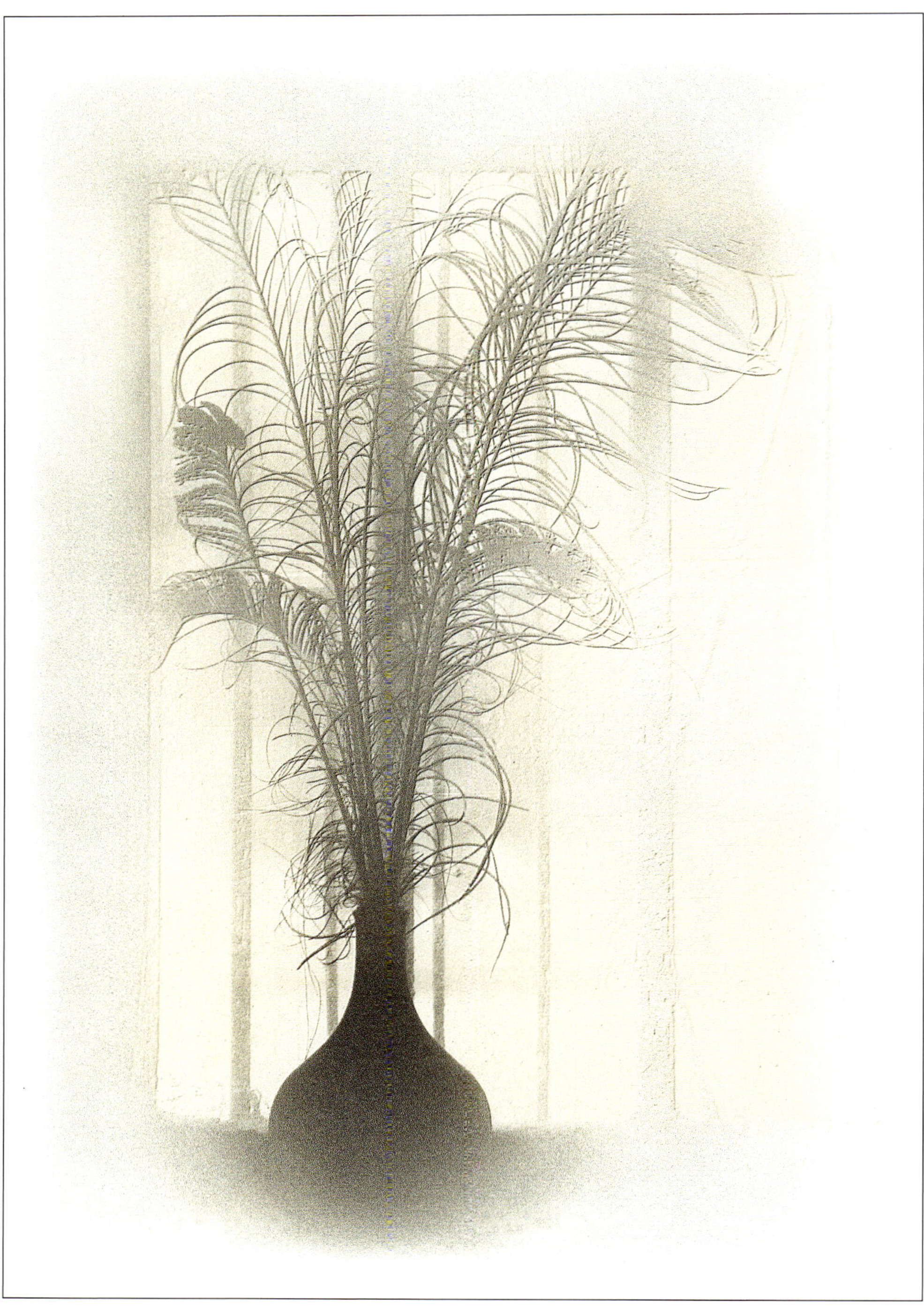

Figure 3.1 Window silhouettes

Chapter 3
Exploring paper textures

The huge range of paper textures is one of the main reasons that Painter is so attractive to photographers, and choosing the right texture can transform a picture quite dramatically.

In this chapter you will explore the library of paper textures that come as the default set, altering the size of the texture and also the contrast and brightness, all of which will change the appearance of the finished picture.

In addition to the default paper library there are many more papers available to load into the Painter program. You can also make your own paper; this is explained later in the chapter.

The picture on the preceding page used several different paper textures to achieve the desired result.

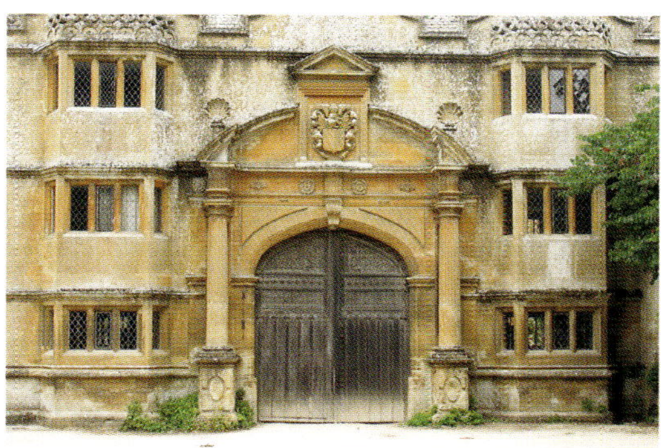

Figure 3.2 Original photograph

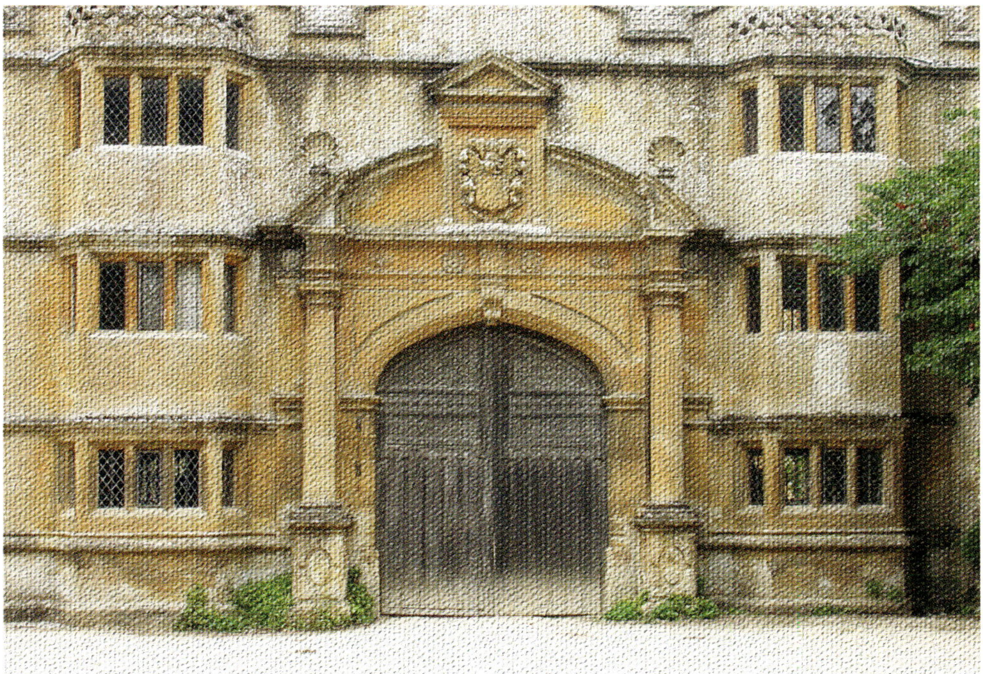

Figure 3.3 Manor house

Making a paper texture test print

To illustrate how different textures will change the appearance of your picture, this step-by-step example explains how to make a test print from one of the images on the disc using sample papers from the default range which are loaded with the Painter IX program.

Step 1 *File>Open>CD>Step-by-step files>'03 Manor House'.*

Step 2 *File>Quick Clone.*

Step 3 Select the Brush icon in the Toolbox.

Step 4 Select Chalk/Square Chalk 35 from the Brush Selector.

Step 5 Open the General palette; if it is not on screen, go to *Window>Brush Controls>Show General.* Change the Method to Cloning and the Subcategory to Grainy Hard Cover Cloning. Move the opacity slider to 32% and the grain to 9%.

Step 6 Change the brush size to about 99.6.

Step 7 Open the Papers palette and select Italian Watercolor Paper.

Step 8 Turn off the Tracing Paper and paint a few brush strokes down the left side of the paper. If you want to keep the test panels separate as in Figure 3.5, make a tall narrow selection with the Rectangular Selection tool and paint inside the selection area. When you have completed the first panel, go back to the Selection tool and click and drag inside the selection to move to the right.

Step 9 Change the paper to Artists Canvas and make more strokes next to the original one. Note how different the texture looks. Try some more papers and you see how the texture changes.

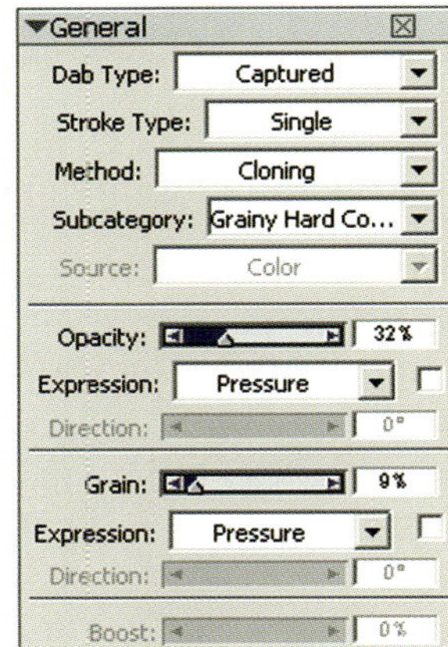

Figure 3.4 The General palette

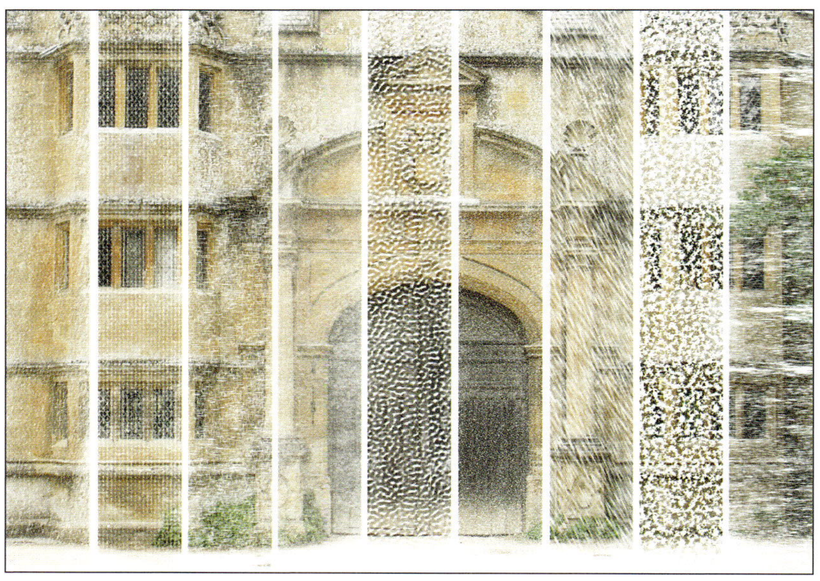

Figure 3.5 A selection of paper textures from the default Papers palette

Changing the paper scale

The Paper Scale slider controls the size of the texture on the paper. This is particularly useful when different file sizes are used. Generally, the larger the file size, the larger the Paper Scale needs to be to show a significant effect. The size to suit the particular picture is, of course, an artistic decision.

Step 1 Use the same photograph as in the last example.

Step 2 *File>Quick Clone* and hide the Tracing Paper.

Step 3 Select Chalk/Square Chalk 35 from the Brush Selector.

Step 4 In the General palette, change the Method to Cloning and the Subcategory to Grainy Hard Cover Cloning. Move the opacity slider to 32% and the grain to 9%.

Step 5 Change the brush size to about 99.6.

Step 6 Select Simulated Woodgrain from the Papers palette.

Step 7 The top slider of the three in the Papers palette controls the scale of the paper grain. Move the slider to the far left (25%) and draw a few brush strokes on the left-hand side of the picture. You will notice that the texture is finer than the picture you did earlier.

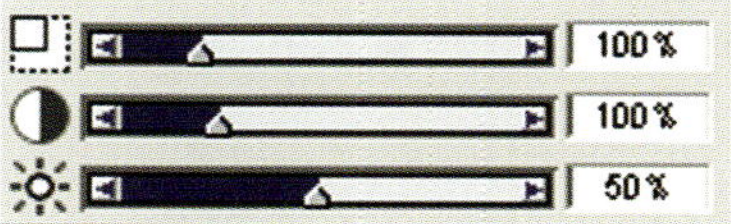

Figure 3.6 The sliders in the Papers palette

Step 8 Move the slider to 50% and make more brush strokes next to the original one.

Step 9 Continue to make more brush strokes with the slider at 100%, 200%, 300% anc 400%.

You will see from your own example, and from Figure 3.7, that the paper texture becomes much larger and coarser as you increase the scale.

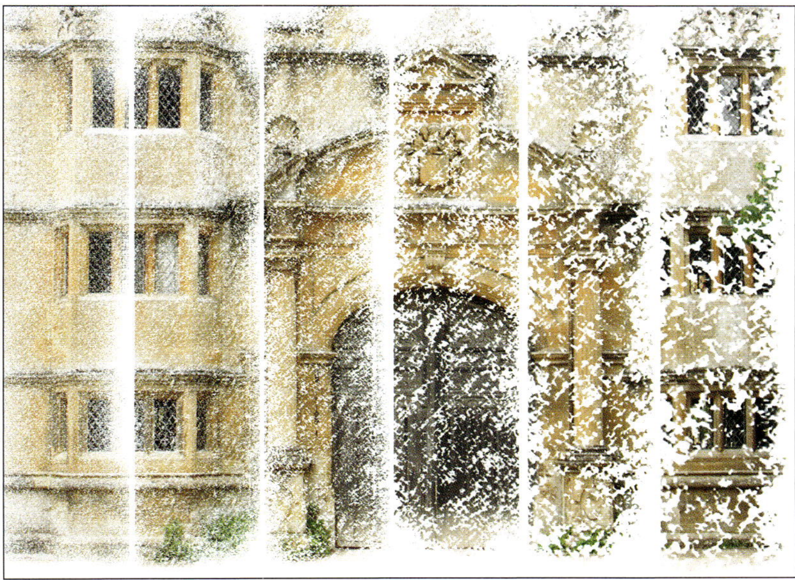

Figure 3.7 The Paper Scale slider at 25%, 50%, 100%, 200%, 300% and 400%

Changing the paper contrast

Beneath the scale slider is the Paper Contrast control, which increases or decreases the amount of contrast present in the texture. The higher the setting, the more pronounced the texture appears relative to the picture.

Step 1 Use the same photograph as in the last example.

Step 2 *File>Quick Clone* and remove the Tracing Paper.

Step 3 Select Chalk/Square Chalk 35 from the Brush Selector.

Step 4 In the General palette, change the Method to Cloning and the Subcategory to Grainy Hard Cover Cloning. Move the opacity slider to 32% and the grain to 9%. Brush size 99.6.

Step 5 Select Thick Handmade Paper from the Papers palette.

Step 6 Move the Paper Contrast slider to the far left (0%) and make some brushstrokes down the left side of the picture. You will notice that the texture is very smooth.

Continue with more test stokes, using 50%, 100%, 200% and 400%. The later ones will have a very hard contrasty appearance and the grain texture is emphasized. At the highest settings the texture is very strong. Different sizes and different paper textures can be mixed within one picture if that is appropriate.

In the Papers palette, the small square icon highlighted in Figure 3.8 will invert the paper texture and make the paint go into the hollows of the paper. This will have the effect of removing the texture, which is useful if you want to bring back more of the original picture.

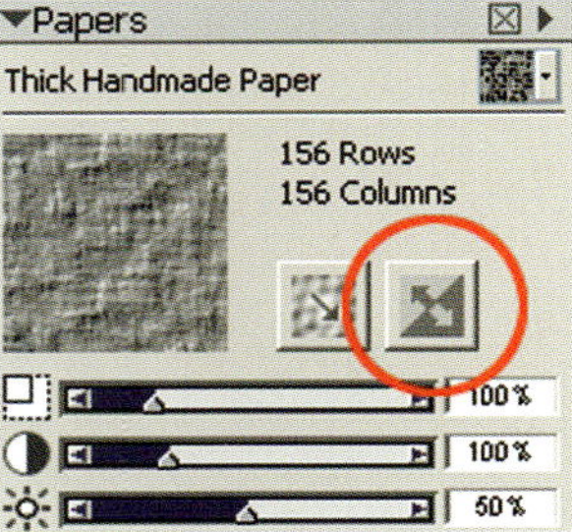

Figure 3.8 Inverting the paper grain

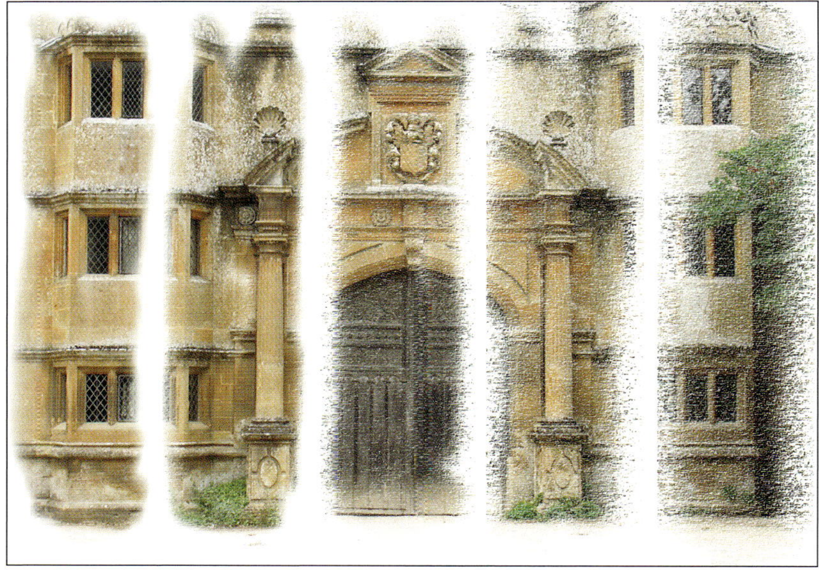

Figure 3.9 The Paper Contrast slider at 0%, 50%, 100%, 200% and 400%

Changing the paper brightness

The last of the three sliders in the Papers palette controls the brightness of the paper texture. The brightness is effectively the depth of the paper grain; the shallower the grain, the less texture is visible. In common with the other two controls, as the brightness level is raised the texture becomes more pronounced. At very low levels the texture is hardly visible, while at 100% the picture is only just discernible and the texture itself dominates the picture.

Step 1 Use the same photograph as in the previous examples.

Step 2 *File>Quick Clone* and remove the Tracing Paper.

Step 3 Select Chalk/Square Chalk 35 from the Brush Selector.

Step 4 In the General palette, change the Method to Cloning and the Subcategory to Grainy Hard Cover Cloning. Make the opacity 100% and the grain 13%. Brush size 206.0.

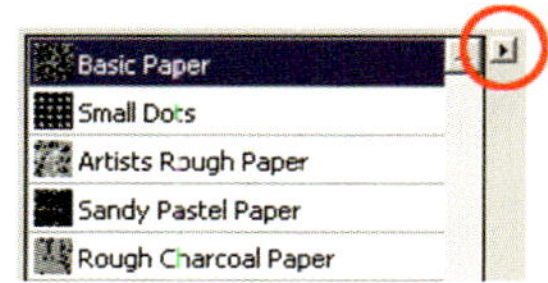

Figure 3.10

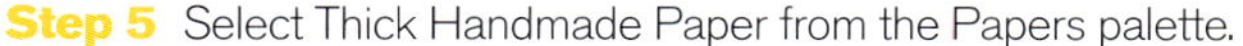

Step 5 Select Thick Handmade Paper from the Papers palette.

Step 6 Move the Brightness slider to the far left (0%) and make some brushstrokes down the left side of the picture. Continue with more test stokes, using 25%, 50%, 75% and 100%. By combining the effects of the three sliders, the original paper texture can be changed from a very smooth finish to an extremely rough worn texture in different parts of the picture.

Figure 3.11 shows an alternative way of viewing the papers in the Papers palette. Click the paper icon to show the drop-down list of papers, then click on the next tiny arrow in that menu (highlighted in Figure 3.10) and select Thumbnails.

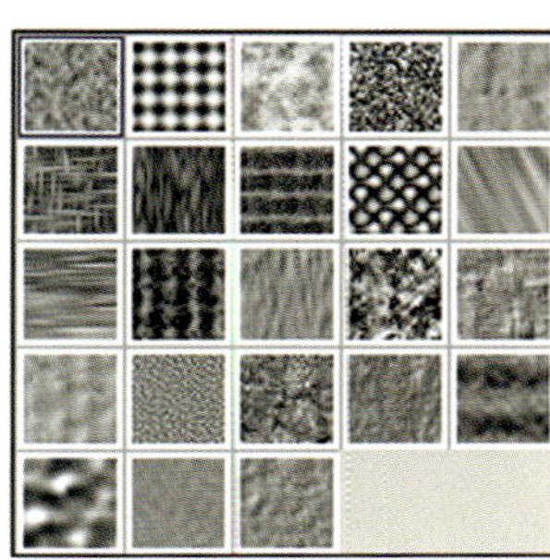

Figure 3.11 The thumbnail view of the papers

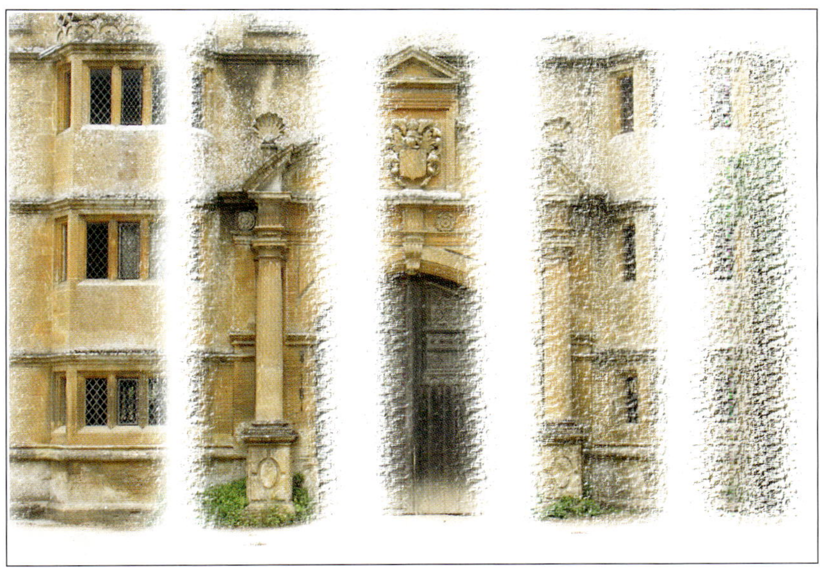

Figure 3.12 The Paper Brightness slider at 0%, 25%, 50%, 75% and 100%

Using extra paper libraries

Painter IX contains many extra paper texture libraries which are not automatically loaded with the program; in earlier versions of Painter these were contained on a second CD.

You will need to copy the folder containing these files and place them within the Painter program on your computer; they can be found in the Extras folder on the Painter CD.

Once you have done this follow the instructions below.

Step 1 On the far right of the Papers palette, click the small, right-facing triangle to reveal the drop-down palette menu.

Step 2 Click on Open Library and a warning message will appear asking whether you want to Append or Load the new library – click on Load. The Choose Papers dialog box will appear as in Figure 3.13; go to the Corel Painter program files and open the Paper Textures folder.

Step 3 Highlight the Library you want to load and click Open. The selected library will appear in the Papers palette, replacing the existing default library.

Step 4 Try out the papers in that library and make a note of any that look interesting. Repeat the process with some of the other libraries.

Step 5 To return to the original paper library, click on Load Library again and in the Choose Papers dialog box, go up one level out of the Paper Textures folder and you will see a solitary file named Painter.pap amongst the folders. Select this file and click it open to reinstate the default paper set.

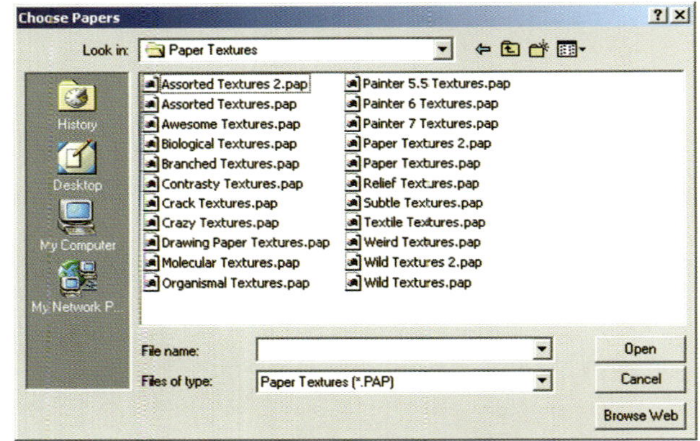

Figure 3.13 Loading additional paper libraries

Painter does not offer an easy way to view all these papers as each paper library has to be loaded into the program before it can be viewed. A printed copy of all the paper textures available is included in Chapter 14. The thumbnails should prove very useful to help you decide which paper to choose and therefore which library you will need to load.

Creating your own paper texture

In addition to the many paper textures supplied with Painter, paper textures can also be made from a pattern or a photograph of your own.

Step 1 Use the same photograph of the manor house for this exercise.

Step 2 Click on the Rectangular Selection tool in the Toolbox.

Step 3 Make a selection of the wall just under the top left window in the image, as shown in Figure 3.14. The selection can be rectangular or square.

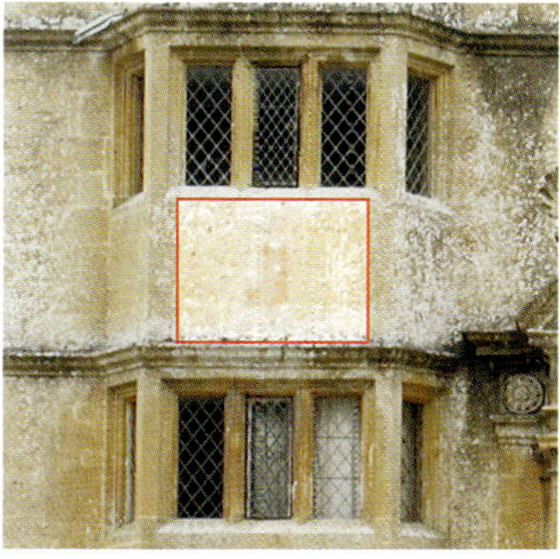

Figure 3.14 Making a selection from the photograph

Step 4 Select Capture Paper in the Papers palette menu and in the dialog box that appears, type in a name for the paper and click OK. Go to *Select>None* to remove the selection.

Step 5 Your new paper texture will appear at the bottom of the Papers palette; click the name to make it ready for use.

Step 6 *File>Quick Clone.*

Step 7 Select the Square Chalk 35 brush from the Brush Selector; it should still be set up for cloning from the last example. If not, change the Method and Subcategory in the General palette as previously.

Step 8 On the Properties bar, set the brush size to 60.0, opacity to 26% and grain to 10%.

Step 9 In the Papers palette, move the size slider to 400%, the contrast slider to 29% and the brightness slider to 14%.

Step 10 Clone the right half of the picture using these settings, then change the size slider to 25% and clone the other half.

Using these two very different size settings will illustrate how the captured pattern reacts when used on a picture; this can be seen in Figure 3.15. The 25% setting reduces the selected area to a small tile that is repeated across the entire picture, resulting in a strong pattern; contrast this with the 400% setting, which creates a very rough texture where the pattern effect is much larger and broken up. These tiling effects can be reduced significantly if the tile has a very even texture. These are extreme settings and usually a more moderate size is used, but they clearly illustrate the effect of the slider settings.

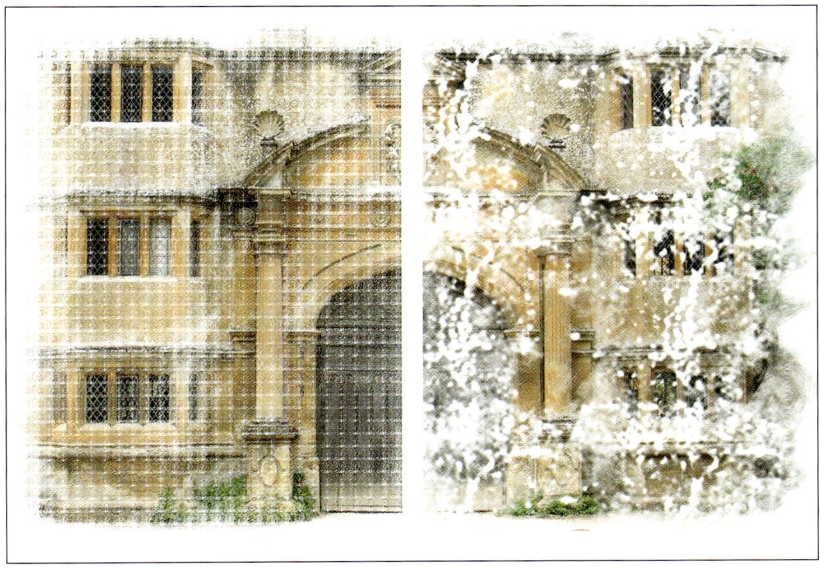

Figure 3.15 Two examples using a captured brush at different Paper Scales

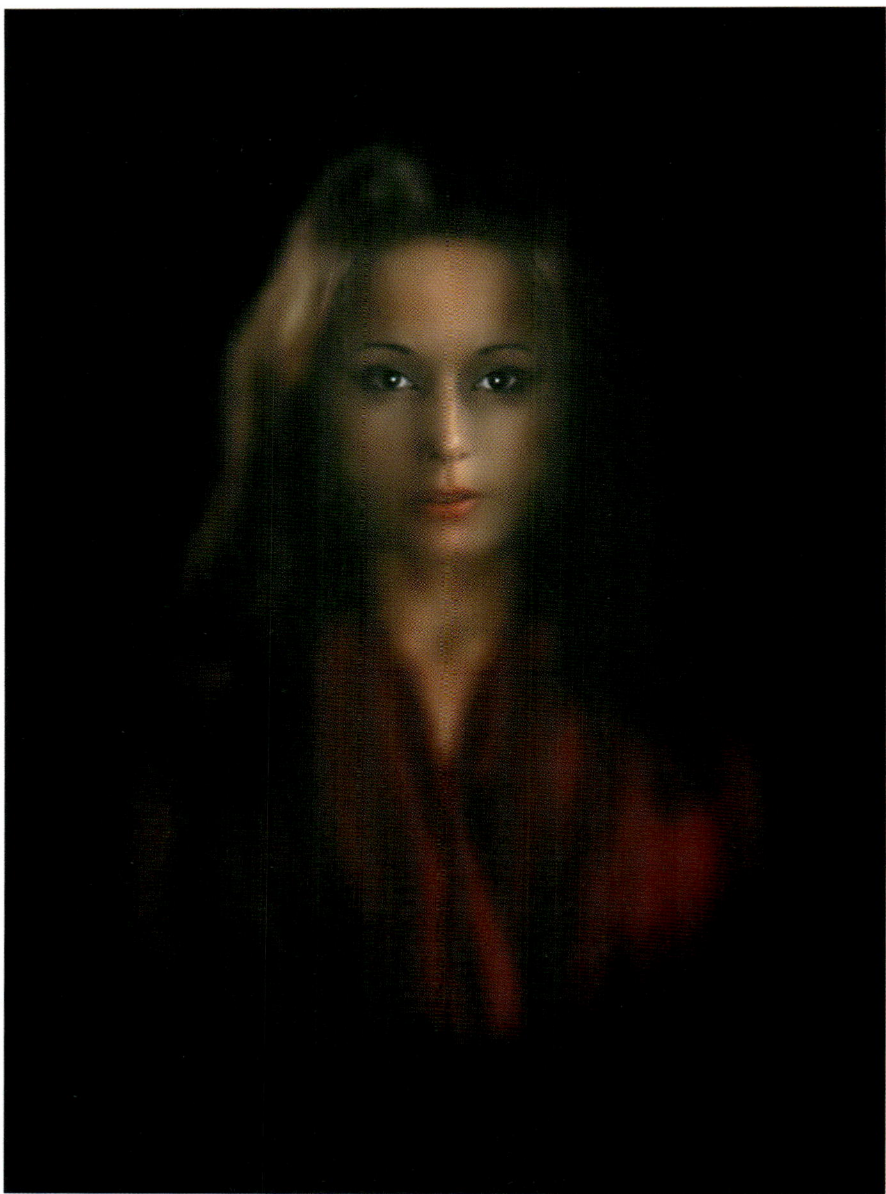

Figure 4.1 Mysterious portrait

Chapter 4
Dark and colored clones

The pictures made so far have all had a white background and this has given them a light, airy feeling. In this next chapter the step-by-step examples have dark or colored backgrounds and the technique for making these clone images is different in the earlier stages.

By using this technique you can make very moody pictures, as Figure 4.1 on the opposite page shows. When this image was created I had in mind the feeling one might encounter on finding a very old oil painting in a deserted house. It is thickly covered in dust, and as you brush away the dirt to see the painting those startling eyes seem to jump out of the canvas. Who is she? Why do those eyes seem so riveting?

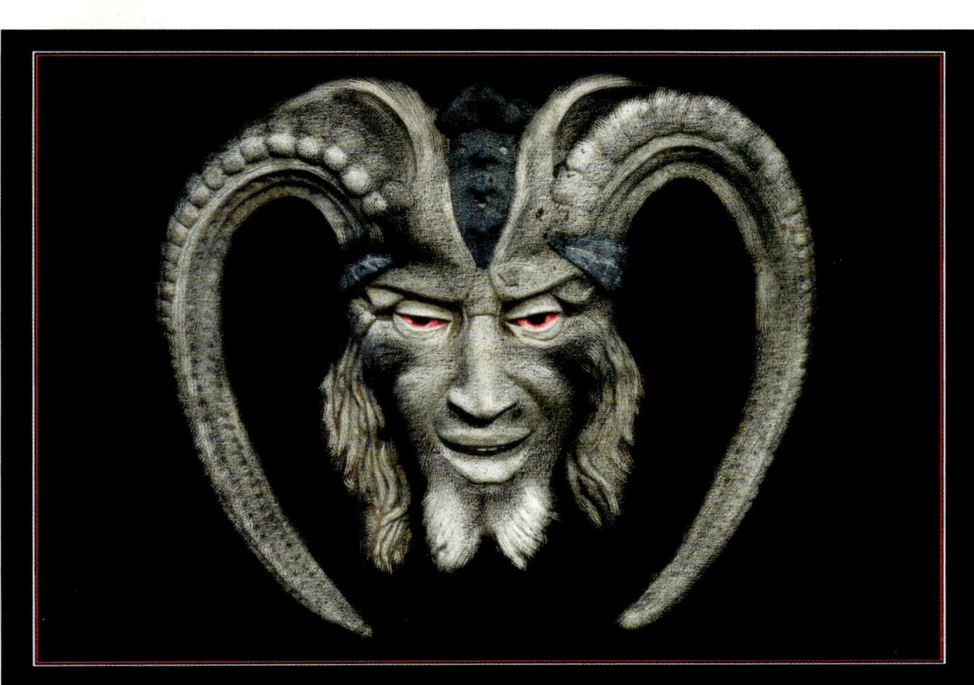

Figure 4.2 Dark statue

Dark statue

This first example starts with a black background and into this will be cloned this rather devilish statue.

Step 1 *File>Open>CD>Step-by-step files>'04 Dark Statue'.*

Step 2 *File>Clone.* Unlike the Quick Clone option that we have used in the earlier chapters, this will make a clone copy, but not clear the picture or reset the brushes.

Step 3 Go to the Colors palette and in the inner triangle click the black corner; the front square that shows the main color should now be black. If the colors are grayed out the brush may still be in cloning mode; if so, click on the rubber stamp icon to take it back to normal.

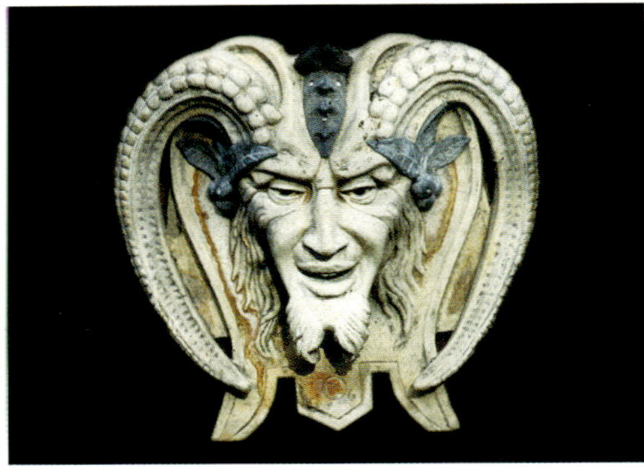

Figure 4.3 Original photograph

Step 4 *Effects>Fill.* Select Current Color at 100%. The clone copy should now be filled with black, obliterating the original picture.

Step 5 Select the Brush from the Toolbox.

Step 6 Select the *Chalk>Square Chalk* variant from the Brush Selector.

Step 7 Open the General palette and change to these settings: Dab Type Static Bristle, Method Cloning, Subcategory Grainy Hard Cover Cloning, opacity 55%, grain 12%. Make the brush size 54.0 on the Properties bar.

Step 8 This picture uses a paper texture from the Painter 8 library, so open the Papers palette menu, click on open and answer Load in the next dialog box. When the open dialog box appears, go to the Painter program files and load the library called Painter 8 Textures. Select Pacific Laid as the paper to use.

Step 9 Turn on the Tracing Paper and lightly trace the outlines of the face and surrounding area with the clone brush. Turn the Tracing Paper on and off as you work to review the result. Start from the center and gradually build up the lightness in the picture. Once the outlines are established, turn off the tracing paper and continue to build up the detail. At this stage the picture, with the Tracing Paper turned off, should look something like Figure 4.4.

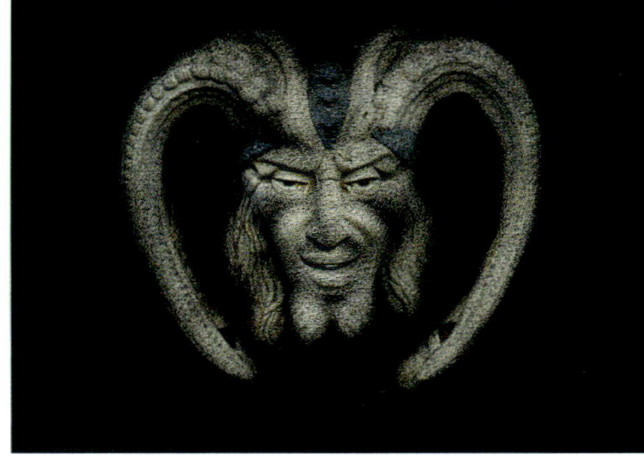

Figure 4.4

Step 10 Return to the General palette and change the Subcategory to Grainy Soft Cover Cloning, reduce the brush size to 20.0 and the opacity to 30%. Paint selected areas rather than all over to enhance the textural feel of the picture. Brush over the eyes, face and parts of the surrounding area to lighten and bring out more detail. Check the screenshot in Figure 4.5 to see the direction and intensity of the brush strokes. Note how the brush strokes follow the lines of the picture, picking out certain lines, but leaving others; this gives the picture more depth.

It is useful to enlarge the picture on the screen at this point, either by moving the slider at the base of the picture or by using the keyboard shortcuts *Ctrl/Cmd* ++ to enlarge the picture and *Ctrl/Cmd* +– to make the picture smaller.

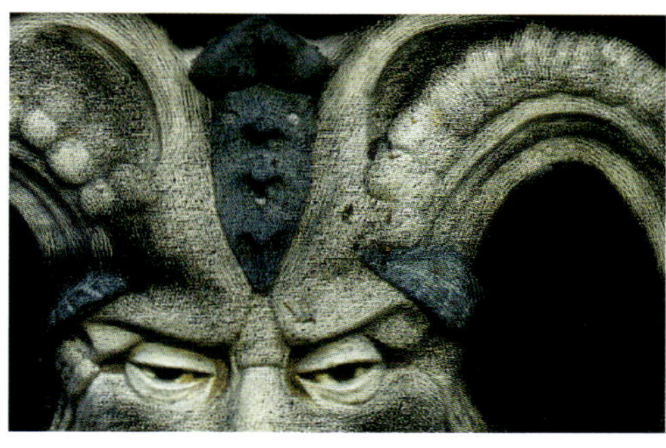

Figure 4.5 Building the contrast

Step 11 To bring out more of the texture, reduce the brush size to 10%, increase the opacity to 60% and paint over some of the main features again. At this brush size and opacity the separate brush strokes show up more clearly and this helps the painterly effect.

To complete the devilish appearance you may wish to add a spot of red in the eyes, as I have done in Figure 4.7. The use of layers is explained in detail in Chapter 8, so for now follow these simple instructions. Bring the Layers palette on screen with *Window>Show Layers*.

Step 12 *Layers>New Layer* will create a new empty layer above the existing Canvas. Change the layer composite method from Default to Color by clicking on the word Default at the top of the Layers palette and selecting Color from the drop-down menu.

The Color composite method is very useful for coloring areas as it does not block out the detail beneath.

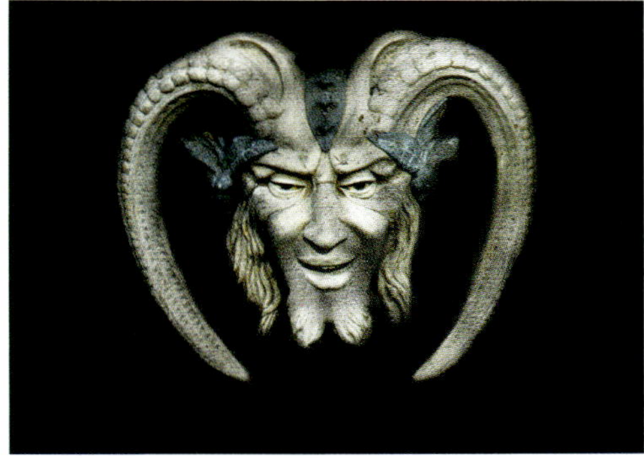

Figure 4.6

Step 13 Change the brush to *Airbrushes>Broad Wheel Airbrush 20*, brush size 1.5 and opacity 10%. In the Colors palette, select red in the outer ring and click the red corner in the inner triangle.

Step 14 Enlarge the picture so that the eyes almost fill the screen and paint with red into the white of the eyes. If the red looks too strong, move the opacity slider in the Layers palette to the left to reduce the effect. This adjustment is possible as the red is on a different layer to the rest of the picture.

That completes your picture. If you want to go back over any other parts of the image you will need to return to the Canvas layer; do this by clicking on the Canvas layer in the Layers palette to make it active. Figure 4.2 on the first page of this chapter shows the final picture.

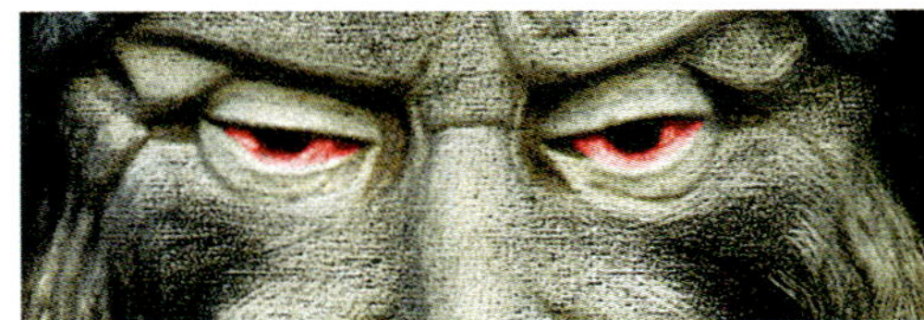

Figure 4.7 Making the eyes red

Setting the paper color

In the same way that a traditional artist can choose to work on a colored paper, Painter allows us to set a paper color at the outset and even change it later if required. In the last example the background color was changed by filling the clone copy with black; however, this was not changing the paper color and had we used an eraser to remove parts of the image it would have revealed white, as that is the default color.

In the next step-by-step example the paper color is changed to an orange and the eraser will be used later on. Which method you decide to use is a matter of choice, but generally setting the paper color in advance is usually the more flexible option.

To set the paper color choose the color you want to use first in the Colors palette, go to the Canvas menu and click on Set Paper Color. You will not see any change until you use an eraser, but if you create a quick clone then the paper will appear as the color you have set.

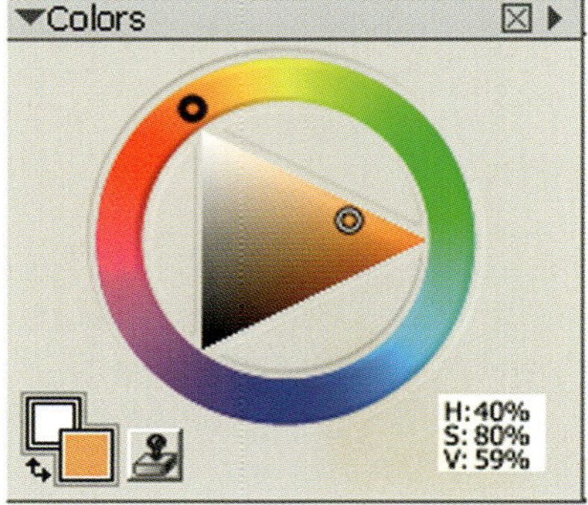

Figure 4.8 The Colors palette

Pencil sketch

Step 1 *File>Open>CD>Step-by-step files>'04 Carving'.*

Step 2 Choose an orange color in the Colors palette then go to the Canvas menu and click on Set Paper Color. You will not see any change until the next step.

Step 3 *File>Quick Clone.* Turn off the Tracing Paper and you will see that the cloned copy now has a colored background.

Step 4 *Select the Chalk>Square Chalk.* This is a very useful brush when you want to emphasize a grainy paper texture. Bring up the General palette and make the following settings: Dab Type Static Bristle Method Cloning, Subcategory Grainy Hard Cover Cloning, opacity 75%, grain 12%. Select brush size 52.2.

Step 5 In the Papers palette, load the Wild Textures paper library using the same method as the previous example. Select Drawer Surface to use on this picture.

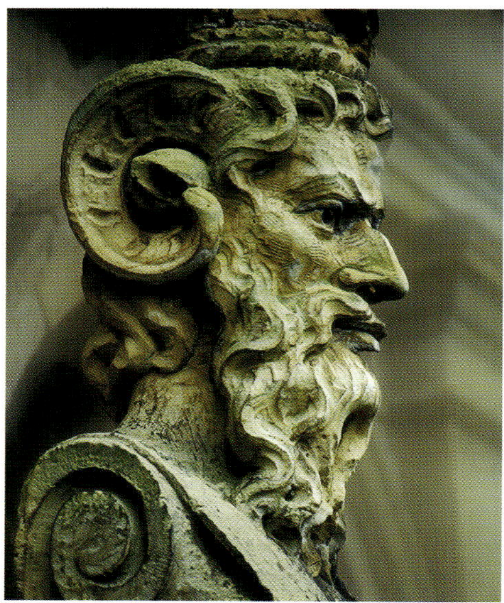

Figure 4.9 Original photograph

Step 6 Turn the Tracing Paper option back on and sketch lightly all over the carving; don't worry about going over the edges, that adds to the effect and can be adjusted afterwards. Use the brush in a diagonal direction as this emphasizes the pencil quality. Your picture (with the Tracing Paper turned off) should look like Figure 4.10.

Step 7 Continue to build up the detail but keep the picture fairly light. Enlarge the picture to see more detail and paint in the edges of the face to strengthen the shapes.

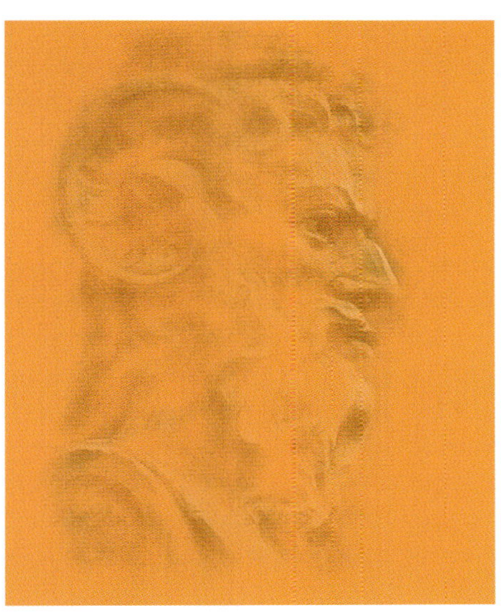

Figure 4.10 Step 6

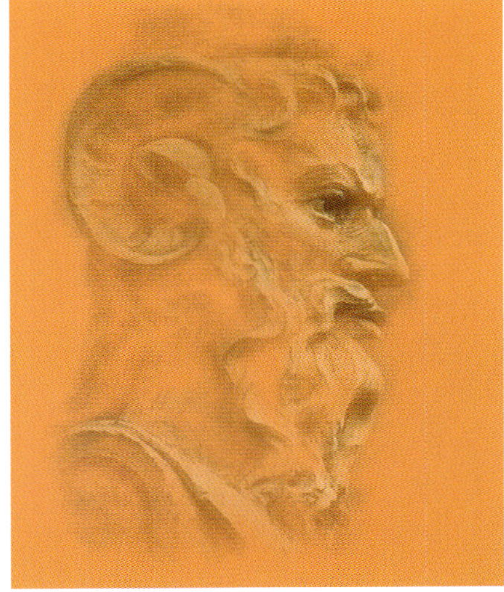

Figure 4.11 Step 7

Step 8 In the Papers palette, change the Contrast slider to 215% and the Brightness slider to 16%, and paint over the picture again to bring in more detail. (The Contrast slider is the middle slider of the three and the Brightness the one beneath.) This will give more texture and detail to the picture.

Step 9 Now reduce the opacity to 25% and paint over all the picture including the background; this will give a light, airy texture to the background and help to bring the whole picture together. Figure 4.12 shows an enlarged detail at this stage.

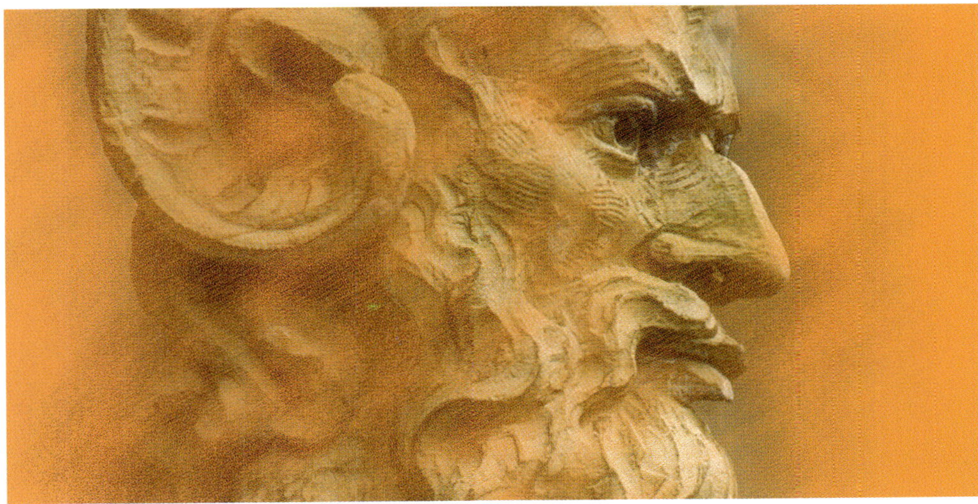

Figure 4.12 Detail at step 9

Sometimes a computer-controlled brush makes a stroke that is too regular and the Random palette allows a degree of randomness to be introduced into the painting. This randomness can affect the brush stroke, the color and the paper texture, and in this example it will be used to break up the regularity of the paper grain.

Step 10 *Window>Brush Controls>Show Random*. Tick the Random Brush Stroke Grain option. Brush over the figure to deepen the density and detail. Remember to change the Random option back to normal when you have finished.

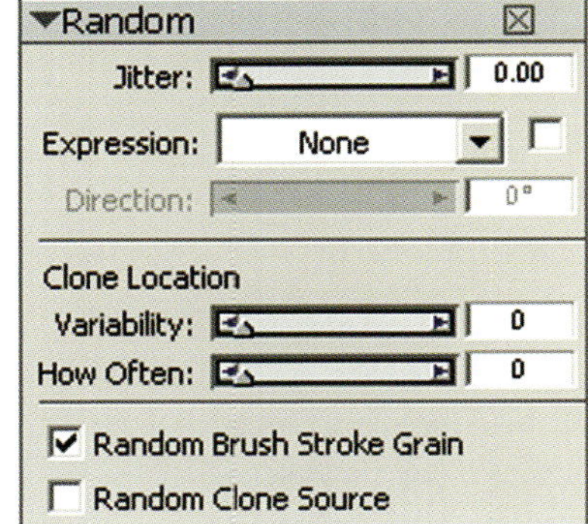

Figure 4.13 The Random palette

When the picture is looking good you may have some areas where the black is too heavy. These can be lightened or removed altogether, although it is better not to tidy it up too much. Because the paper color was changed to orange when the picture was started you can use an eraser and erase back to the paper color.

Step 11 Go to the General palette and change the Method to Eraser and the Subcategory to Soft Paper Color. Use brush size 52.0 and opacity 10%, and gently brush over any areas that are too dark. If you overdo this, simply return the brush to cloning method and paint over the picture again.

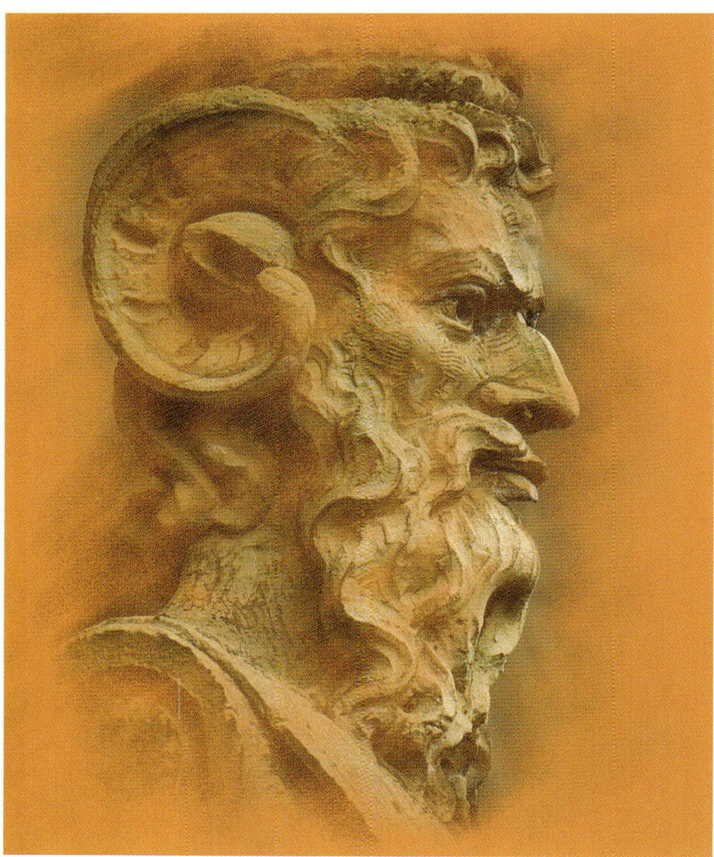

Figure 4.14 Carving

Moody portrait

This example starts with a studio portrait and transforms it to a dark and moody low light picture. The process is simple and easy to follow.

Step 1 *File>Open>CD>Step-by-step files>'04 Studio Portrait'.*

Step 2 *File>Clone.* Do not clear the picture.

Step 3 Using the Eyedropper, click on a point behind her head to sample the color, which is a dark red. *Edit>Fill* with the current color.

Step 4 Select *Cloners>Soft Cloner* brush, size 72.1 and opacity 2%. Lightly brush in the face; with this opacity the face will just be visible.

Step 5 Reduce the opacity to 1% and brush in the rest of the body.

Step 6 Increase the opacity to around 5% and go over the face again to make this brighter. Figure 4.16 shows the picture at this stage.

To finish off the picture I added a surface texture called Artists Canvas; this is covered in detail in Chapter 10.

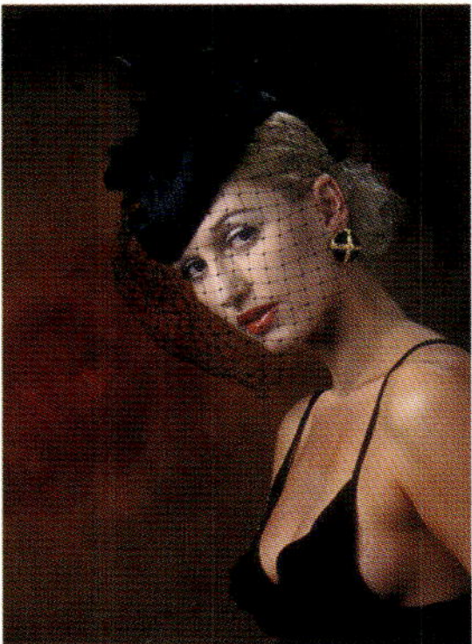

Figure 4.15 Original photograph

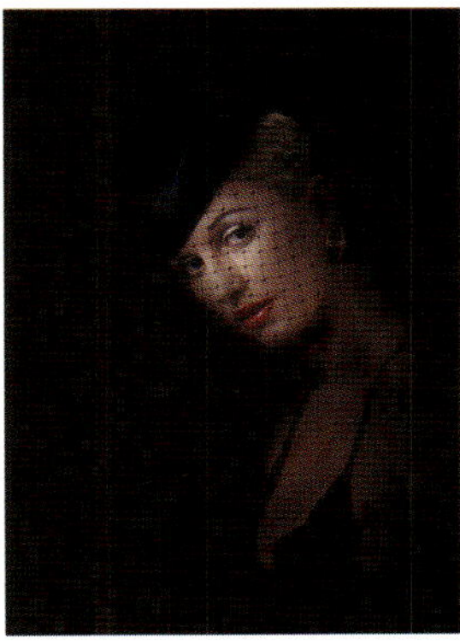

Figure 4.16 Cloned copy

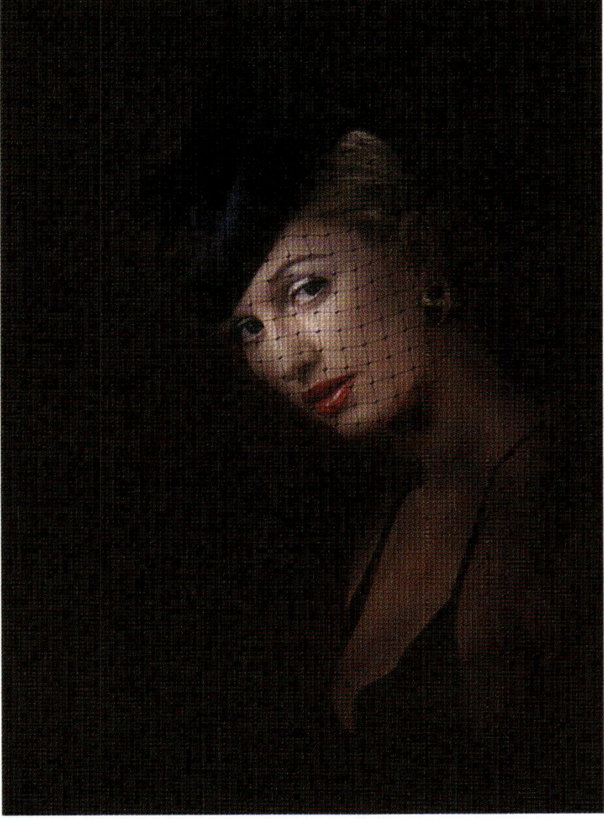

Figure 4.17 Low light portrait

Pastel-colored backgrounds

As a contrast to the earlier strong colored pictures in this chapter, this example uses a pastel-colored background The original photograph was taken on a sunny day, but the cool background and technique suggests the title.

Step 1 *File>Open>CD>Step-by-step files>'04 Horses in the Snow'.*

Step 2 Choose a light lilac color in the Colors palette then go to the Canvas menu and click on Set Paper Color.

Step 3 *File>Quick Clone.* Turn off the Tracing Paper and you will see that the cloned copy now has a lilac-colored background.

Step 4 Select the *Acrylic>Wet Soft Acrylic 30 brush*, size 30.0. This brush gives a very attractive brushy texture that will suit the subject.

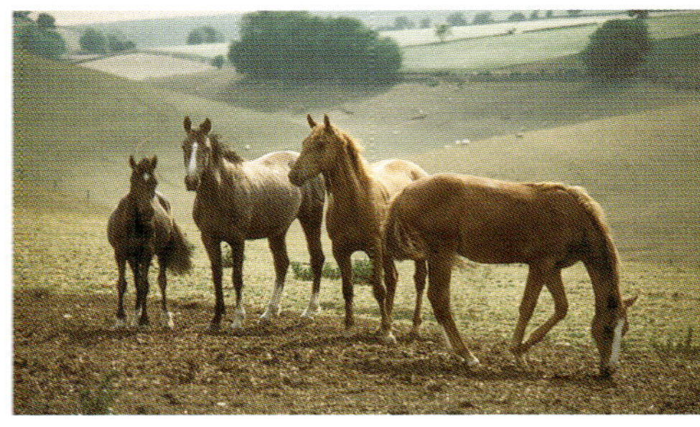

Figure 4.18 Original photograph

Step 5 In the General palette, change the Method to Cloning, change the opacity to 100% and leave the other settings on default (the Subcategory stays on Soft Cover Cloning).

Step 6 Turn the Tracing Paper on and paint lightly over the horses but not the background. Remove the Tracing Paper and you will have a soft impression of the horses similar to that in Figure 4.19.

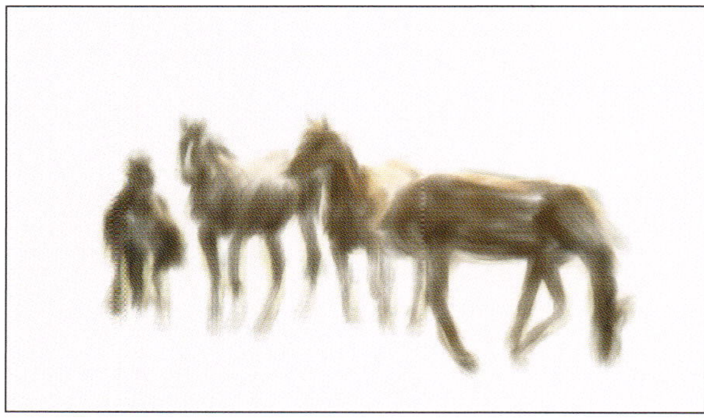

Figure 4.19

Step 7 Reduce the brush size to 15.0 and paint over the horses until the density increases; keep turning the Tracing Paper on and off. Reduce the brush size to 6.5 to bring in more fine detail, particularly in the hair. Make your brush strokes follow the direction of the hair; it will take quite a while for the picture to build up, so do not be impatient!

Step 8 The horses need something to stand on, so paint in some ground beneath their hooves using a brush size of 50.0 and 30% opacity. Increase the brush size to 50.0 and reduce the

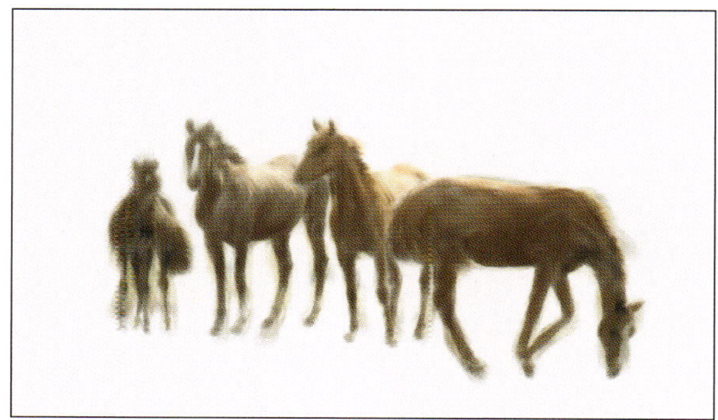

Figure 4.20

opacity to 20%. Lightly paint in some brush strokes just to hint at a background.

Step 9 Change the brush method to Eraser and the Subcategory to Soft Paper Color. Use brush size 38.0 and opacity 6%, and lightly paint over parts of the horses to add highlights to the coats. Clean up any edges around the horses where you have cloned too much, particularly around the legs; use brush size of 9.5 and opacity 12%.

Figure 4.22 shows the final picture and Figure 4.21 has an enlarged section to show the detail of the brush strokes.

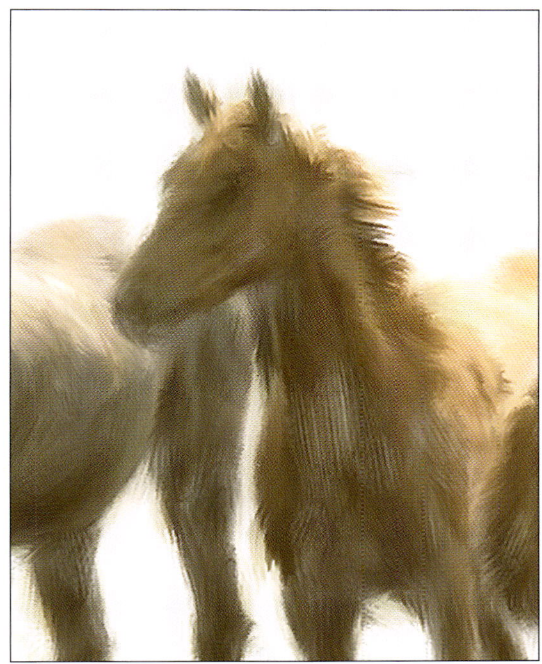

Figure 4.21 Detail of brush strokes in the final picture

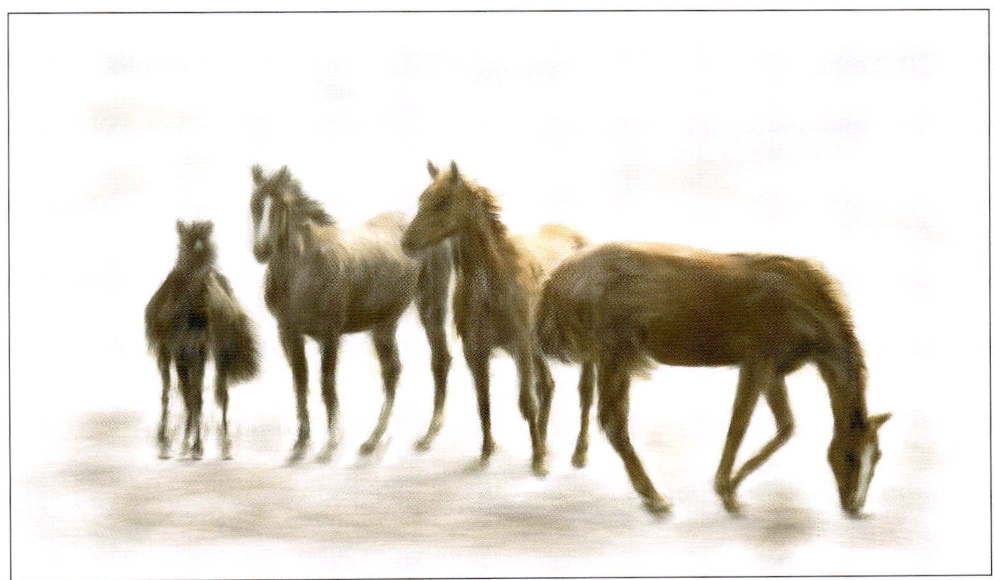

Figure 4.22 Horses in the snow

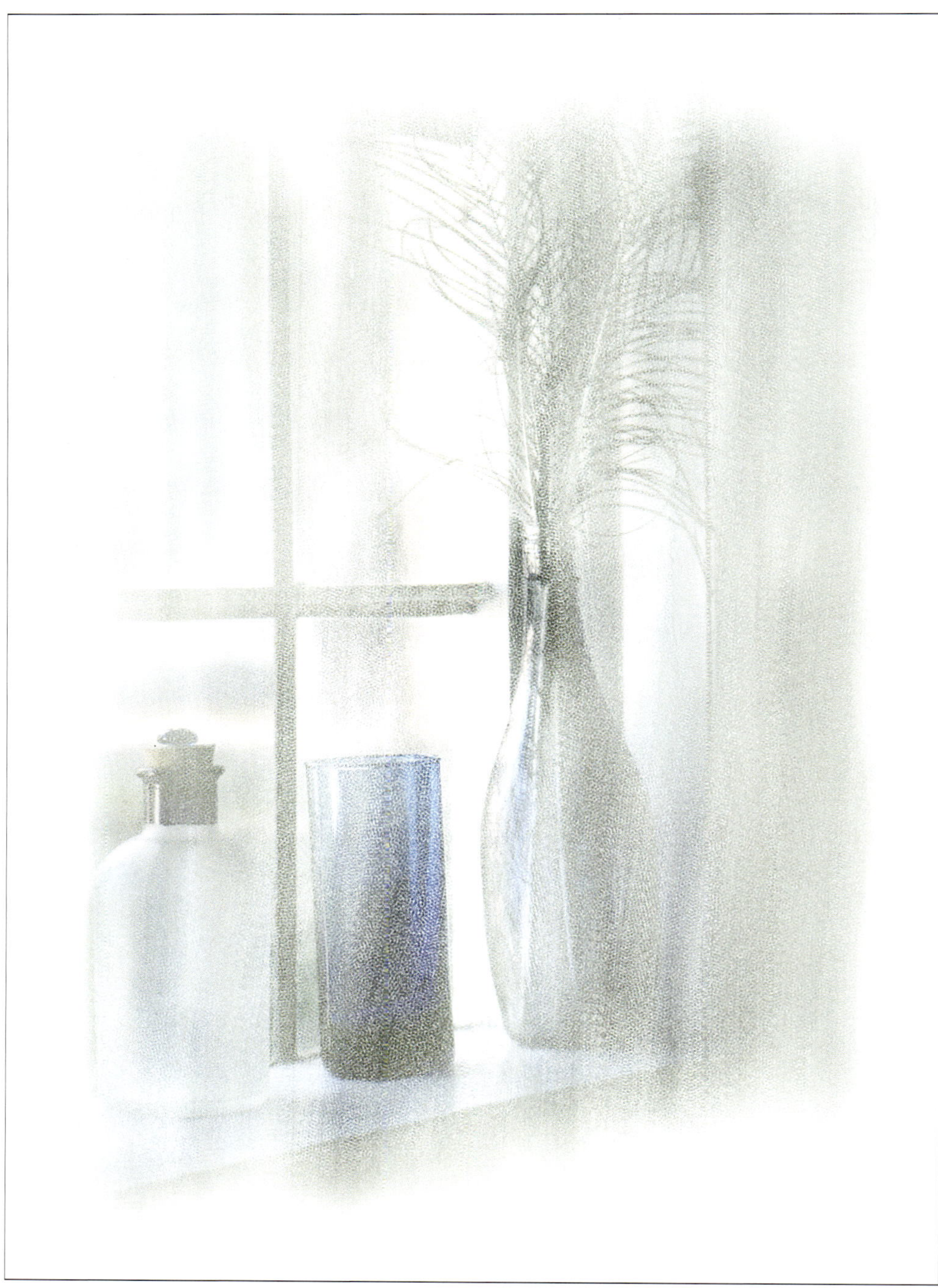

Figure 5.1 Shades of blue

Chapter 5
Choosing brushes

Brushes are at the heart of everything in the Painter program and it is the sheer volume of choice that confuses many first-time users. In this first chapter covering the subject of brushes, every brush category in Painter IX has two pages devoted to it. The first page has a short introduction to the category and a series of examples of some of the brush variants available.

There are two examples for each variant, the first showing how the brush stroke looks when cloned from a photograph and then another showing a close-up detail of the same picture to illustrate the brush strokes more closely.

The examples shown on the following pages should prove helpful when deciding which brush to use for a particular image. If you look, for instance, at the first two categories, which are Acrylics and Airbrushes, you can immediately see that the Acrylics have a strong brushy texture, while the Airbrushes are quite different and show no brush marks. On the other hand, Chalks show grain texture extremely well. All the examples have been used at the default setting with just the cloning option changed.

On the second page of each brush type is a clone picture using one or more of the brush variants in the particular category to illustrate just one of the many ways in which the brushes can be used.

The picture of the bottles in a window on the previous page illustrates how using the correct brush with an appropriate paper texture can considerably enhance the finish of the picture.

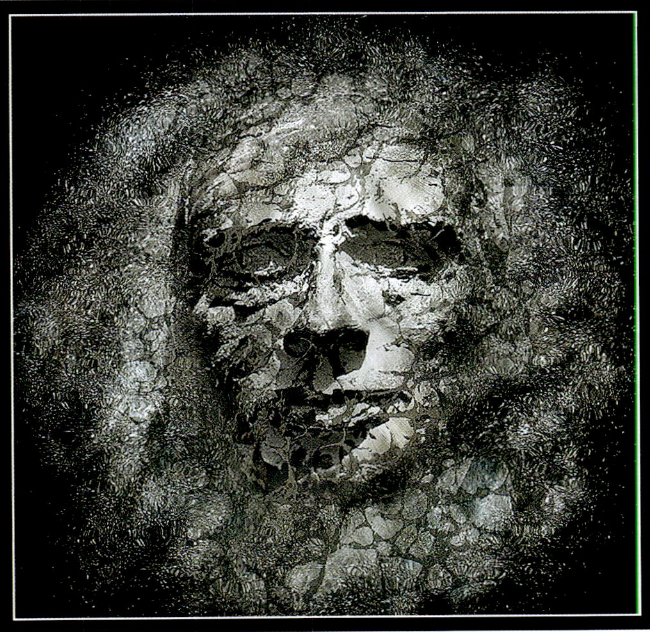

Figure 5.2 The unseeing

Acrylic brushes

The Acrylic range of brushes is ideal for making pictures that need to show the brush strokes clearly; the range is large and distinctive.

The Thick Acrylic variants use Impasto to give a stronger impression of depth to the brush strokes. Impasto is explained in more detail in the next chapter, but essentially it means that the brush strokes have a three-dimensional appearance.

The Wet variants blur the cloned image; this applies particularly to the larger brush sizes, but even with smaller brushes it is difficult to retain much detail.

The Dry Brush variant is a very useful brush for cloning, as it paints quickly and gives an attractive brush texture.

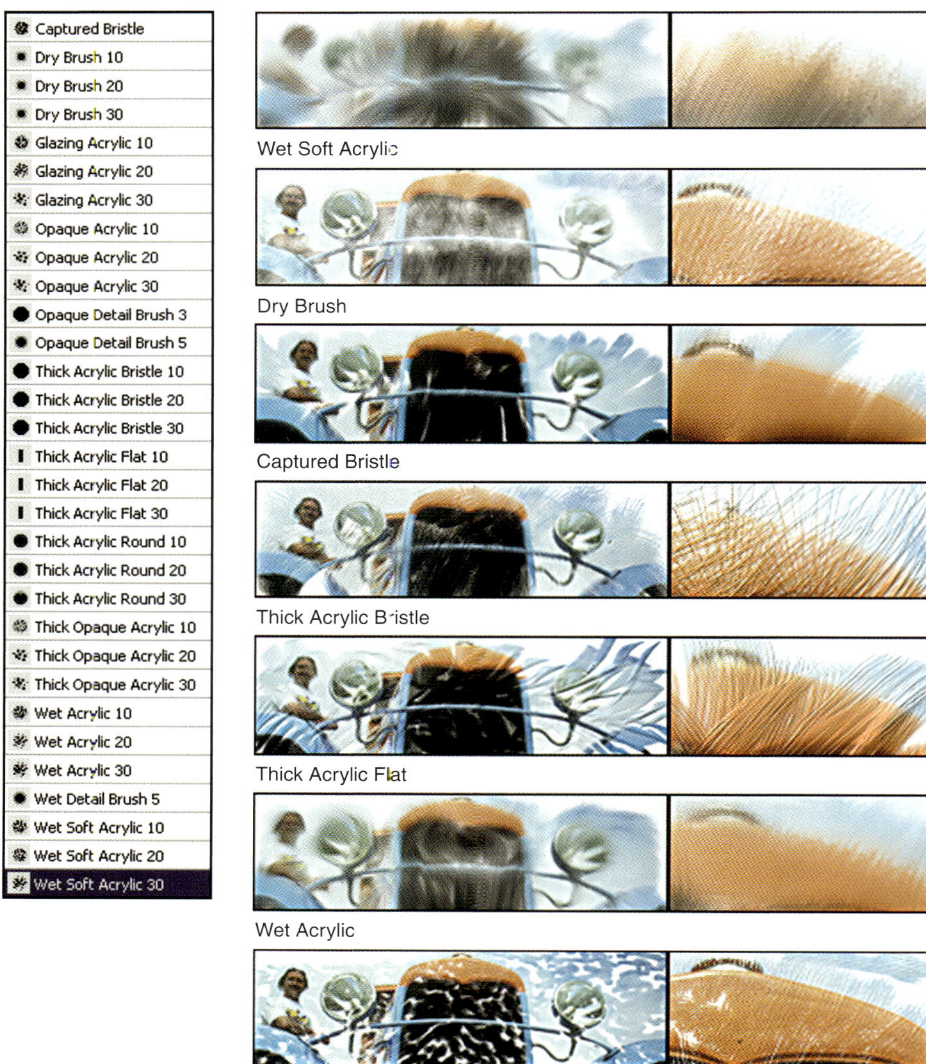

Wet Soft Acrylic

Dry Brush

Captured Bristle

Thick Acrylic Bristle

Thick Acrylic Flat

Wet Acrylic

Thick Opaque Acrylic

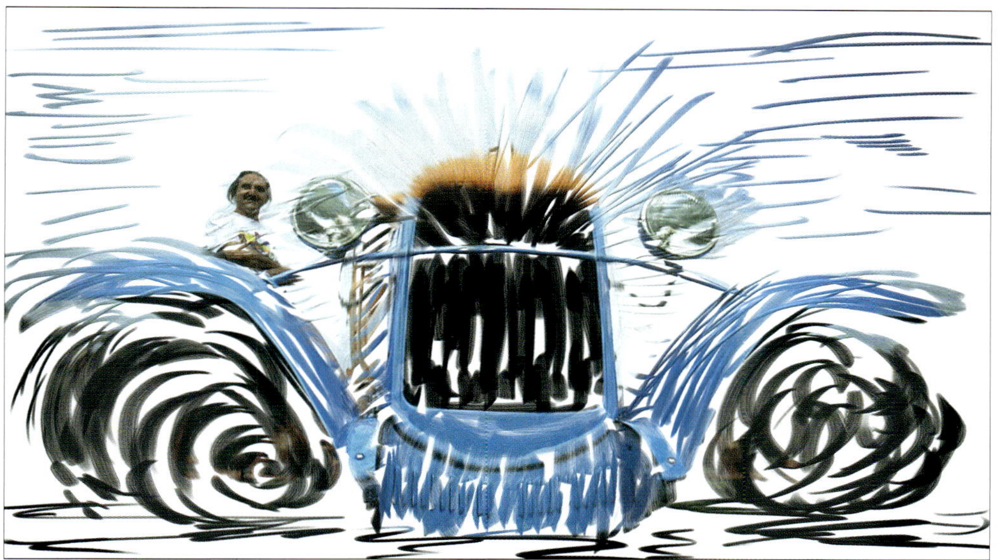

Figure 5.3 The proud owner

The Thick Acrylic Flat 30 brush was used to make this clone picture and the flat brush gives strong directional strokes that stand out well.

The picture has a strong illustrative feeling rather than being purely photographic and emphasizes the exuberant impression of this car.

A pressure-sensitive stylus is essential for this type of picture in order to be able to get the elongated strokes; when the pen is held at an angle, the shape of the strokes changes.

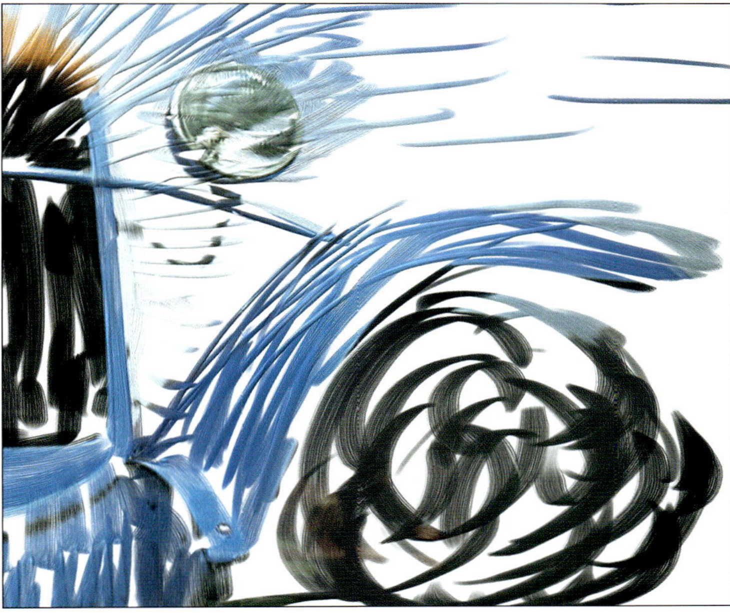

Figure 5.4 Detail of the Acrylic brush strokes

Airbrushes

Many of the brushes in this category spray in the direction in which the tablet stylus is angled. These spray-type airbrushes include Broad Wheel, Coarse Spray, Fine Spray, Fine Wheel and Finer Spray, most of which give a fairly smooth finish.

Some of the smeary airbrushes, Digital, Detail, Fine Detail and Fine Tip Soft, all move the underlying imagery and do not have the typical airbrush spray.

Variable Splatter, Tiny Splatter and Pepper Spray throw out a very coarse spray that looks very blotchy on a small file size.

The Soft Airbrush is one of the few to use paper textures.

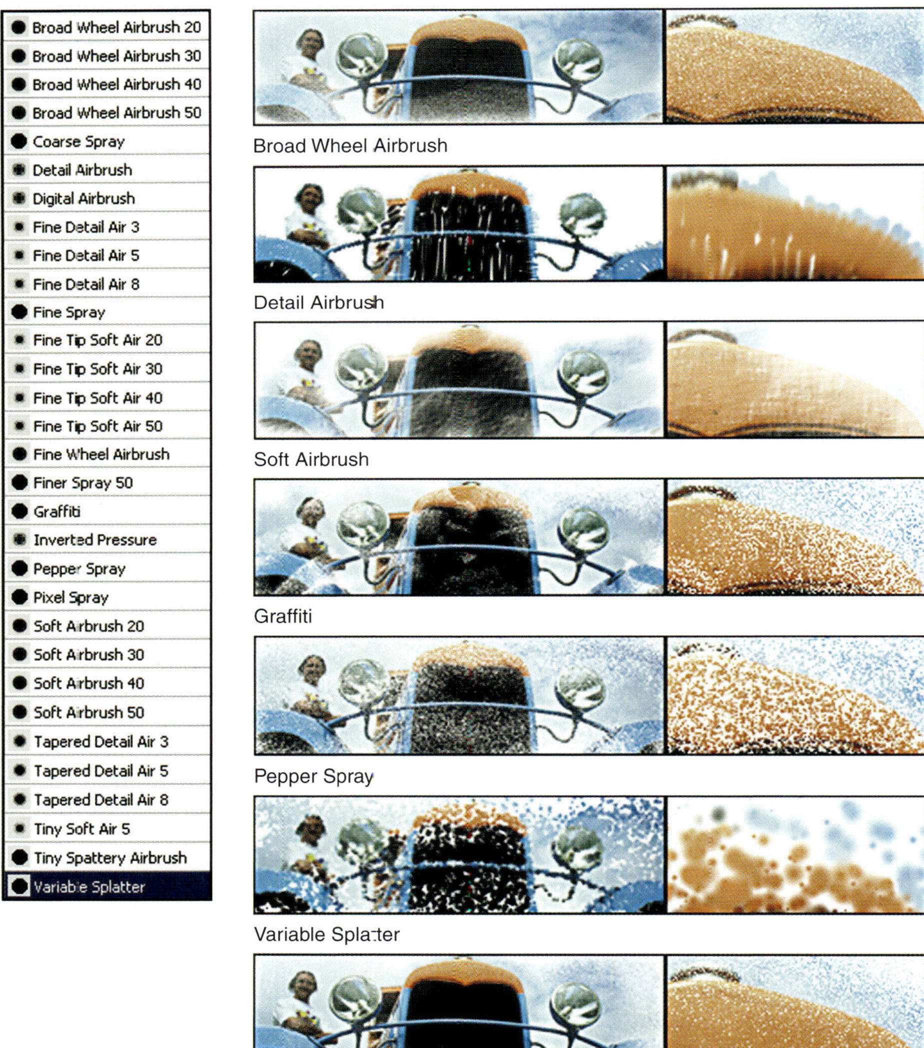

Broad Wheel Airbrush

Detail Airbrush

Soft Airbrush

Graffiti

Pepper Spray

Variable Splatter

Pixel Spray

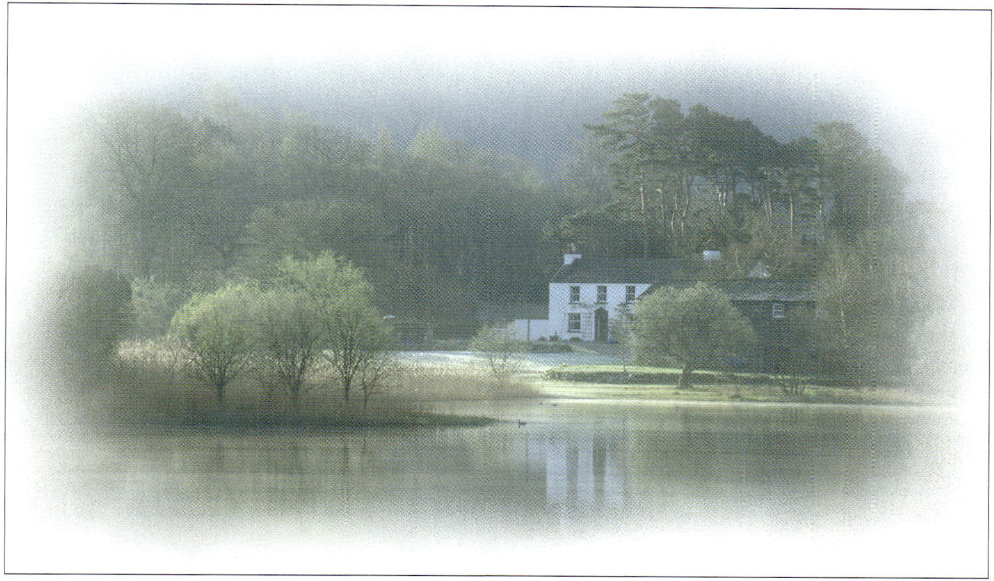

Figure 5.5 Across the lake

This photograph was taken early one morning looking across part of Derwentwater in the English Lake District. The atmosphere was placid and the only things moving were the ducks on the water.

The Broad Wheel Airbrush was used to paint over most of the picture; this is a very useful brush for covering large areas very lightly and gives the spray effect seen on the edges of the picture above. The density in the image was gradually increased, mainly in the central areas.

The Soft Airbrush was used to finish the picture and brought in more clarity to the central area. This brush has a much smoother texture and does not have the spray texture of the Broad Wheel Airbrush.

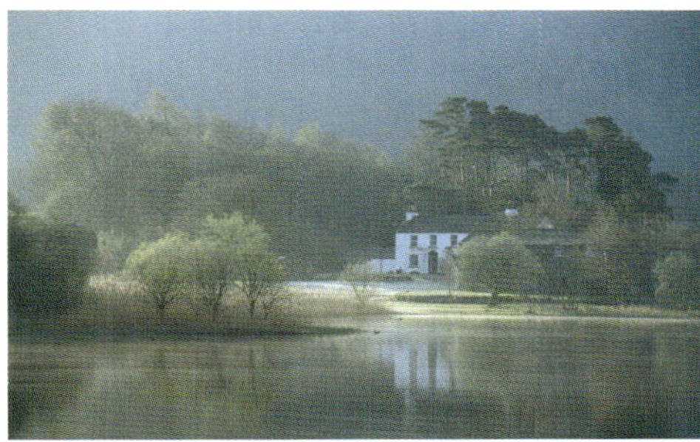

Figure 5.6 Original photograph

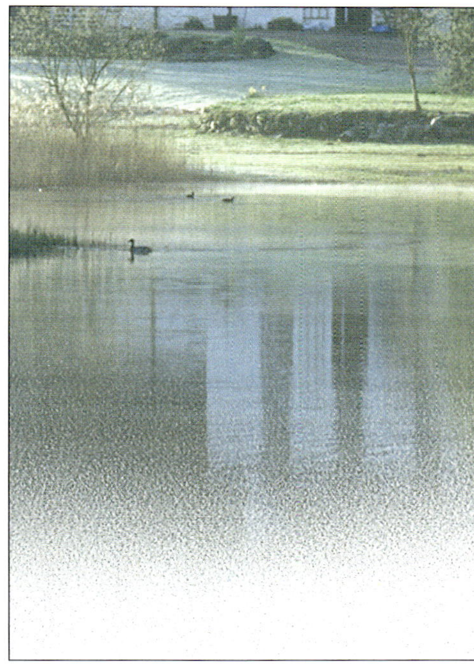

Figure 5.7 Detail showing textures

Artists' Oils

Artists' Oils are new in Painter IX and are an exciting new development for painters. The brushes replicate the use of real brushes more closely than ever before; the paint can be taken directly from the Mixer palette and a blend of colors picked up on the brush. The brush only takes up a specific amount of paint so the brush stops painting when it runs out of paint. The brush also interacts with any paint already on the canvas, just as it would on a real oil painting.

When the brushes are used on photographs they do not work as cloners in the same way as other brushes. They will pick up colors from the source image and continue to paint with those colors, disregarding what has changed, so painting a full clone copy is not possible. In the example on the next page, the brush has been used as a cloner and the brush strokes have been kept very short, thereby retaining the shapes but getting a very painterly result.

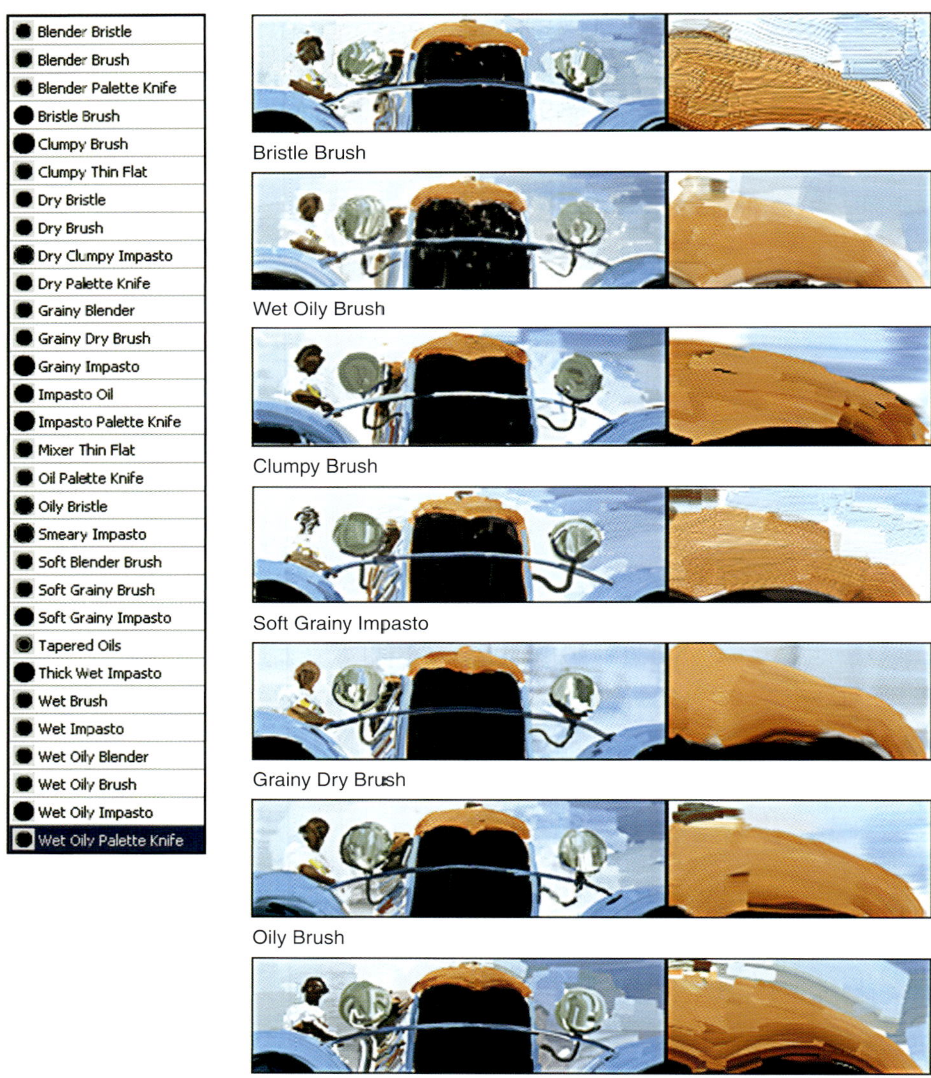

Bristle Brush

Wet Oily Brush

Clumpy Brush

Soft Grainy Impasto

Grainy Dry Brush

Oily Brush

Dry Brush

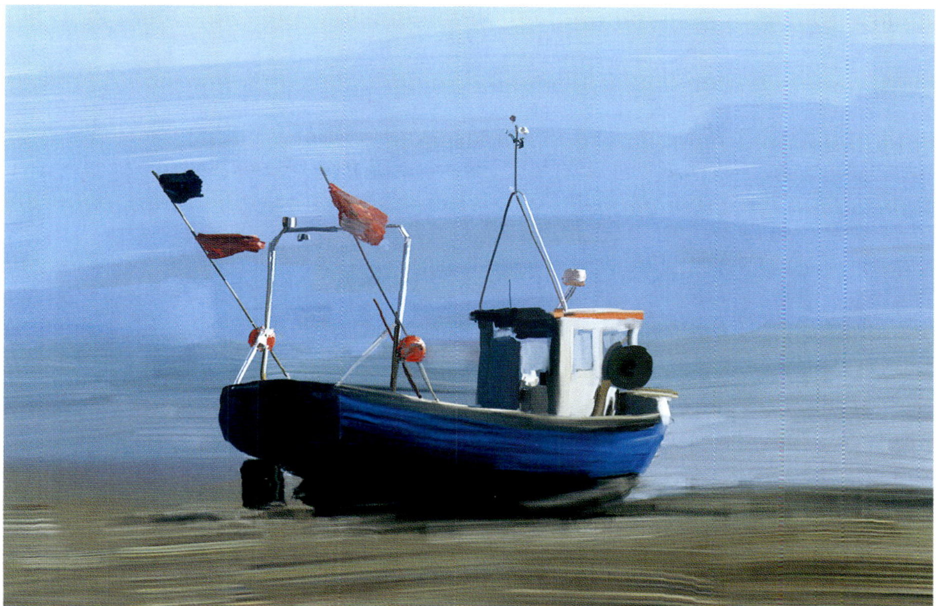

Figure 5.8 Colorful boat

The technique used to create this picture of a colorful boat on the seashore was to make a clone copy and clear the image. A new layer was made and the Artists' Oils Dry Bristle brush was used at a large size to paint over the background to establish the sky, sea and shoreline.

A new layer was made on the top of the layers stack and the Artists' Oils wet brush, size 20.0 and opacity 100%, was used to paint in the boat. The brush was reduced to size 3.2 to paint the rigging and flags and to go over some of the detail of the boat.

Another new layer was created to give more emphasis to the line between sea and sky.

The various elements were blended together using the Artists' Oils Grainy Blender at various sizes and opacities; this softened the transition between the background and the more detailed boat.

The technique of using multiple layers is dealt with in detail in Chapter 8.

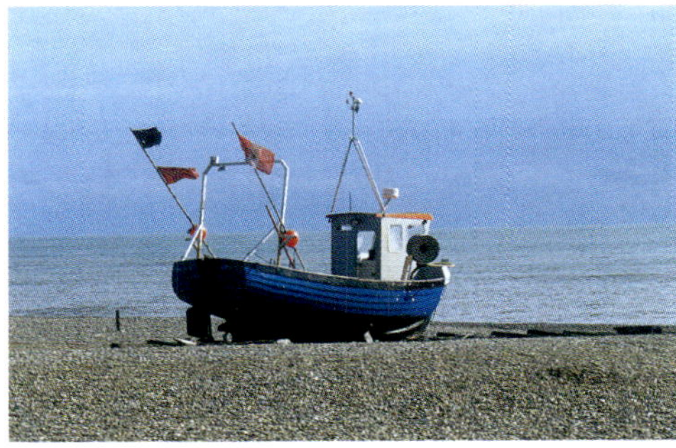

Figure 5.9 Original photograph

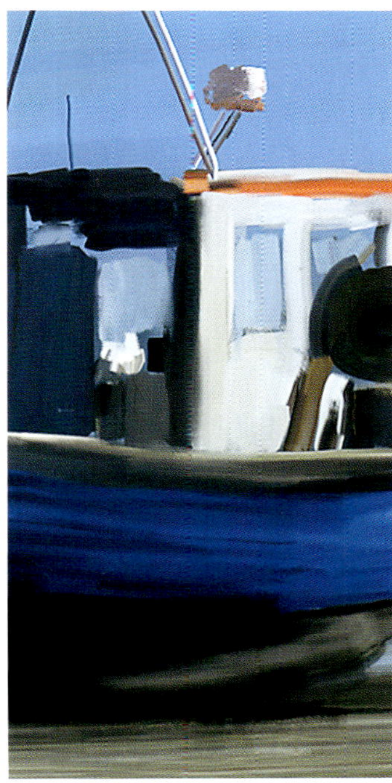

Figure 5.10 Detail

Artists

It is perhaps surprising that this set of what one might call curiosity brushes all work perfectly well as cloners. All of the brushes except Tubism are able to use the Cloning Method while Tubism has to use Clone Color.

The final example, titled Auto Van Gogh (on Auto), has been created in a different manner. The brush was set to Auto Van Gogh and the Cloning Method chosen. A clone copy was made and cleared, then I went to *Effects>Esoterica>Auto Van Gogh* and immediately the 'Van Gogh' effect was applied. There are no controls, it just does the one clone. Try it and see.

- Auto Van Gogh
- Impressionist
- Sargent Brush
- Seurat
- Tubism
- Van Gogh

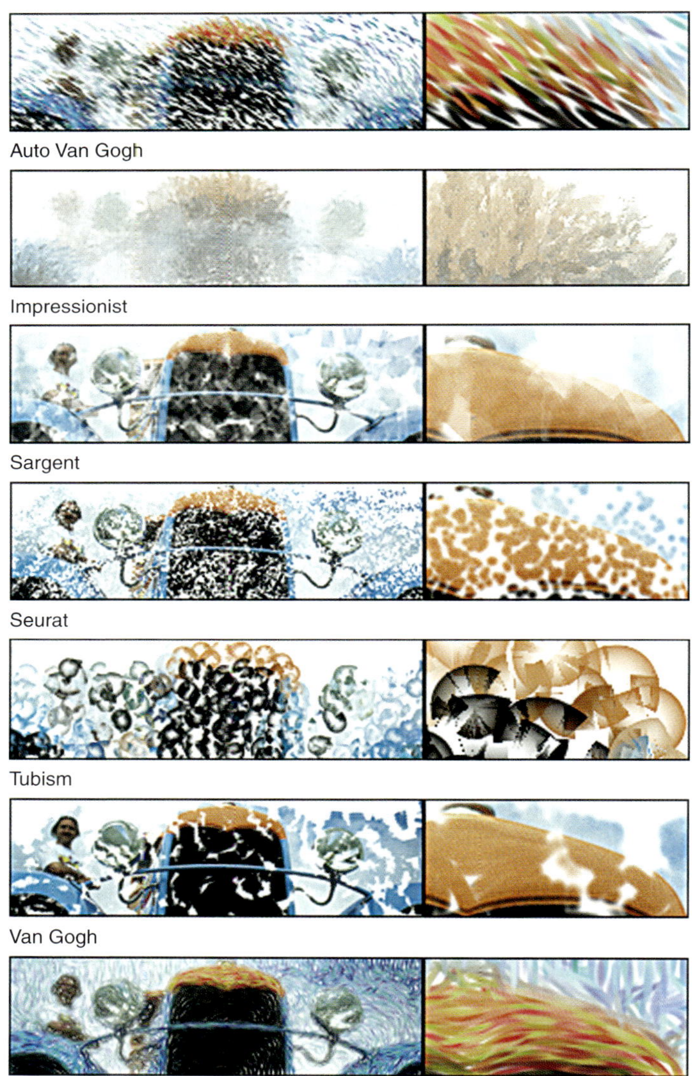

Auto Van Gogh

Impressionist

Sargent

Seurat

Tubism

Van Gogh

Auto Van Gogh (on Auto)

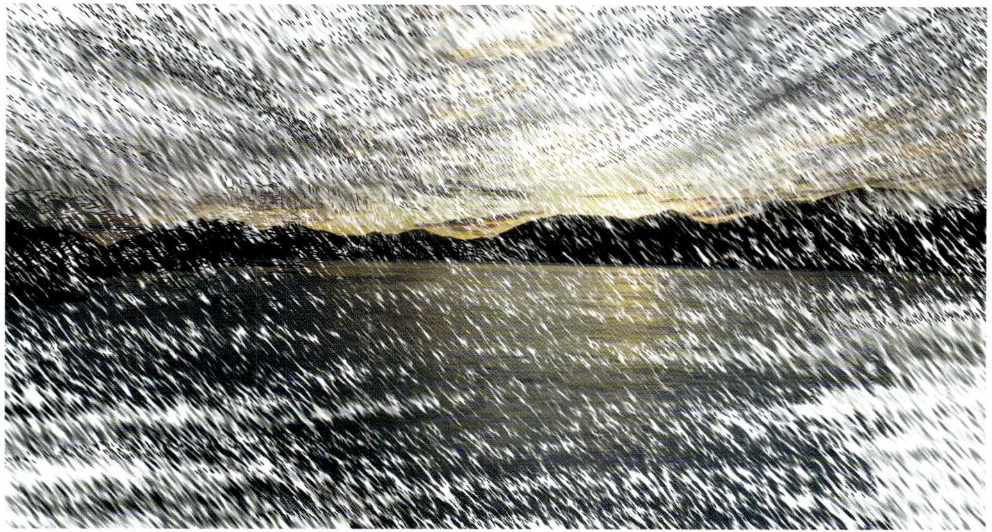

Figure 5.11 Sunset over the mountains

The Auto Van Gogh brush was used to paint this view of a sunset over the sea and distant mountains.

The main contours were painted first using the default brush size of 12.9. This gave a hard scratched appearance and you can see the smaller lines in the detailed view in Figure 5.13. The brush size was increased to 34 and the picture painted once again, and at this size the color started to come back in.

Finally, the opacity of the brush was reduced to around 12% and worked over all the picture, softening some of the roughness.

The original picture is shown in Figure 5.12.

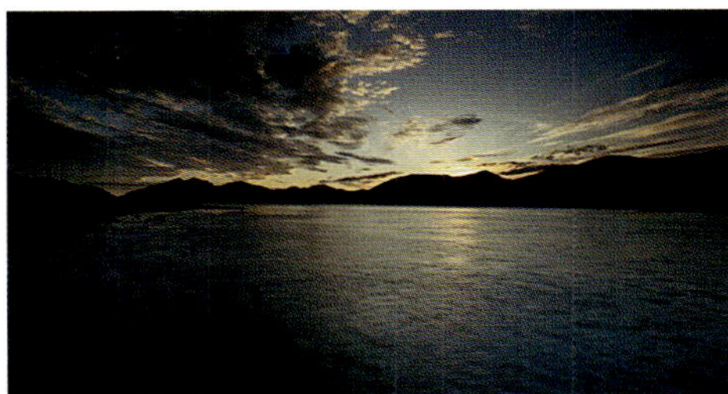

Figure 5.12 Original photograph

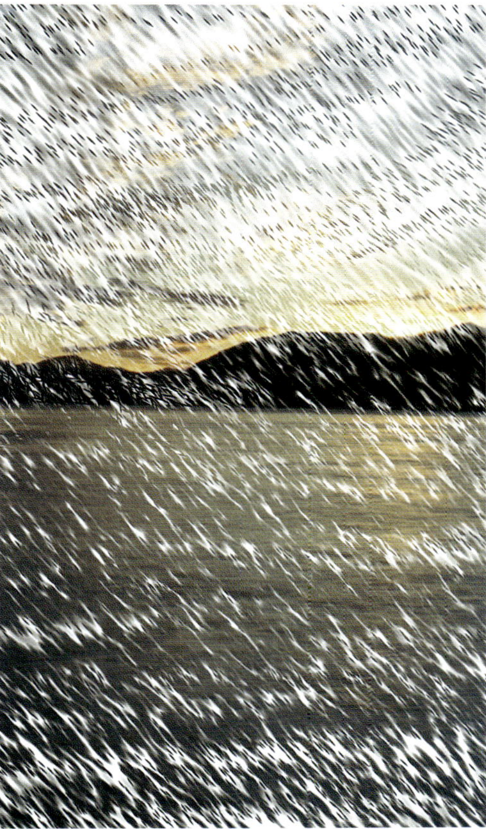

Figure 5.13 Detail of the finished picture

Blenders

Blenders are not brushes for cloning but they do have some very interesting and useful features. They can be used directly on photographs imported into Painter and can be used upon finished clones to add a further dimension.

Several of the variants, such as Diffuse Blur and Round Blender Brush, smear the image and give it a furry look. Others, like the Detail Blender, smooth the image but retain the overall shape and color.

The Soft Blenders smooth and blur the picture and can be used for creating a background prior to adding detail with another brush.

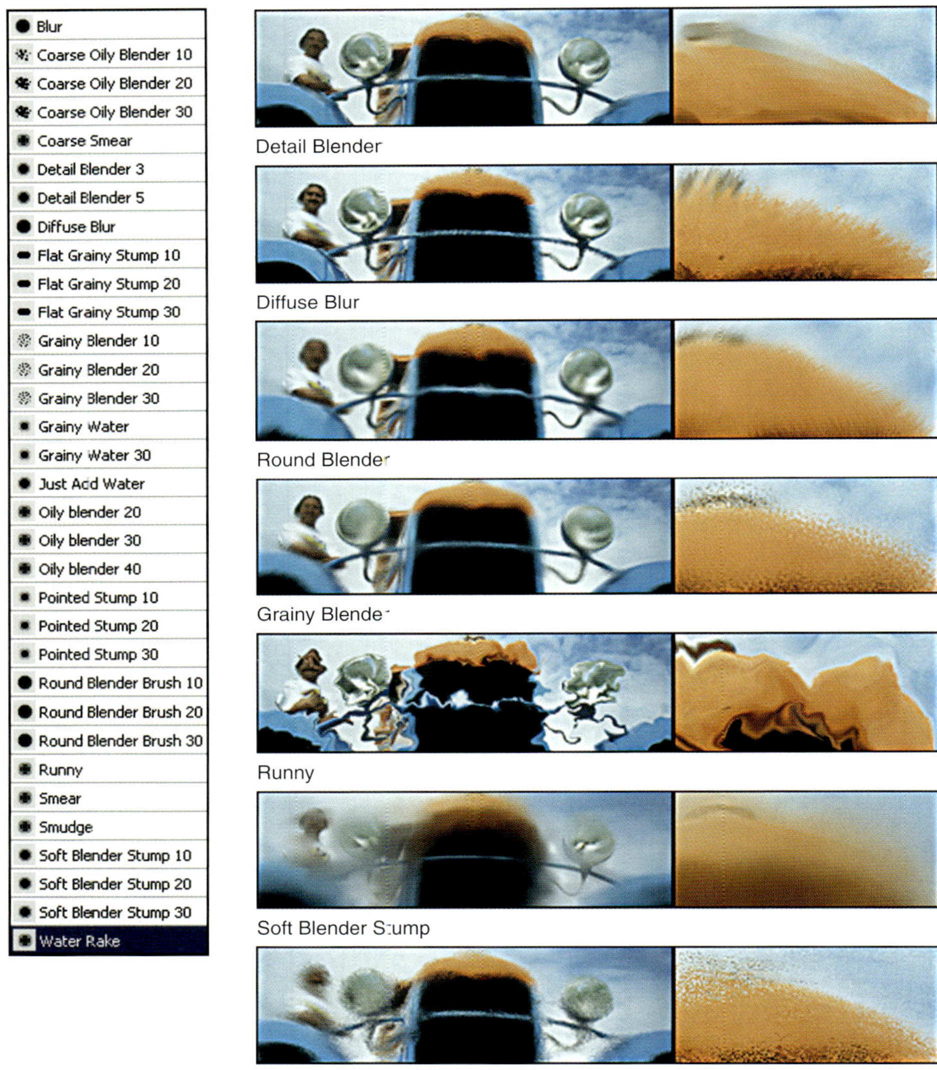

Detail Blender

Diffuse Blur

Round Blender

Grainy Blender

Runny

Soft Blender Stump

Coarse Smear

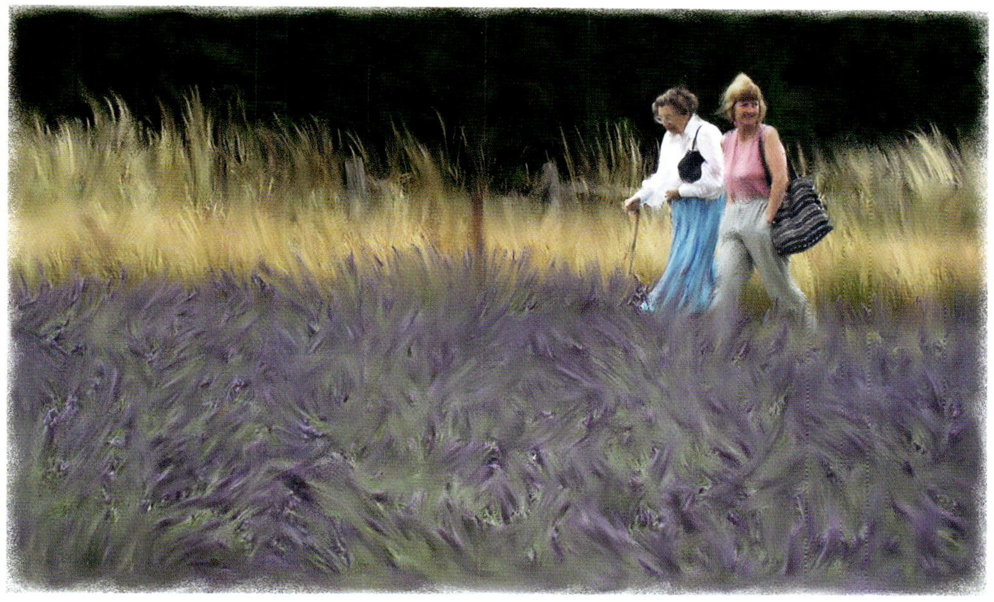

Figure 5.14 The lavender walkers

The Coarse Smear Blender was used to make this picture. I painted all over the photograph, making flowing lines in the lavender and streaking the grasses out against the dark background; look at the detail in Figure 5.16 to see the brush strokes.

The Coarse Smear Blender was used once again on the clothes but changed to the Detail Blender 3 to work on the faces and fine detail.

The picture was taken at the Lavender Farm in the Cotswolds, England.

The blender range of brushes creates lovely textures and is well worth experimenting with.

It is usually better to make a clone copy and work on that, which gives you the opportunity to bring back detail from the original image.

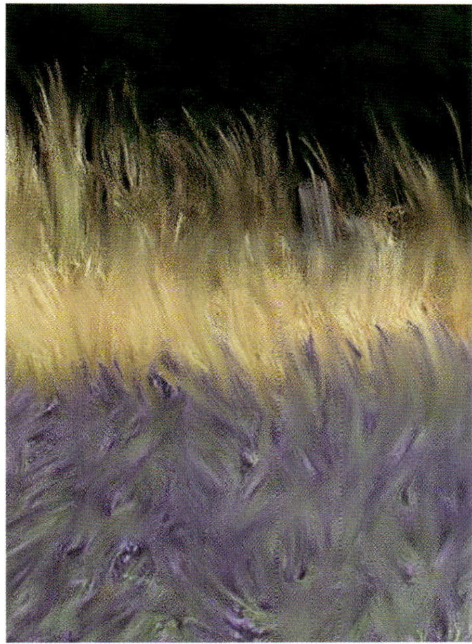

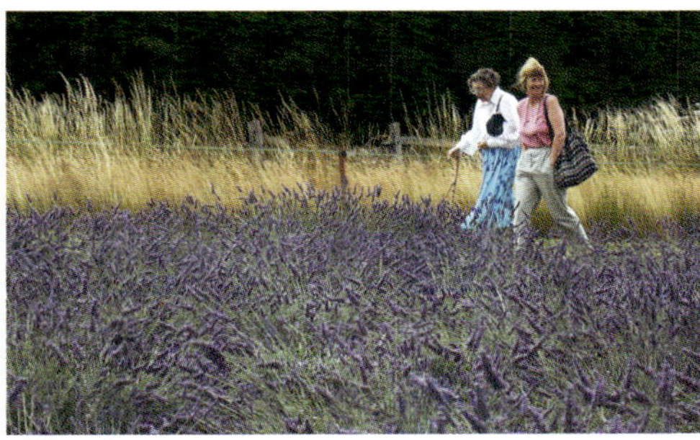

Figure 5.15 Original photograph

Figure 5.16 Detail of brush strokes

Calligraphy

The major characteristic of the Calligraphy brushes is the sharp angle of the brush stroke, one edge narrow and the other broad.

All of these brushes use the Cloning Method and are therefore very good for using with paper textures.

In the examples below, the first three brushes have been used at their default settings and have the opacity and grain at high levels.

The other examples have had both the opacity and grain reduced to around 20%, and this gives them quite a different appearance. The strokes are very similar, however; it is the texture that is different.

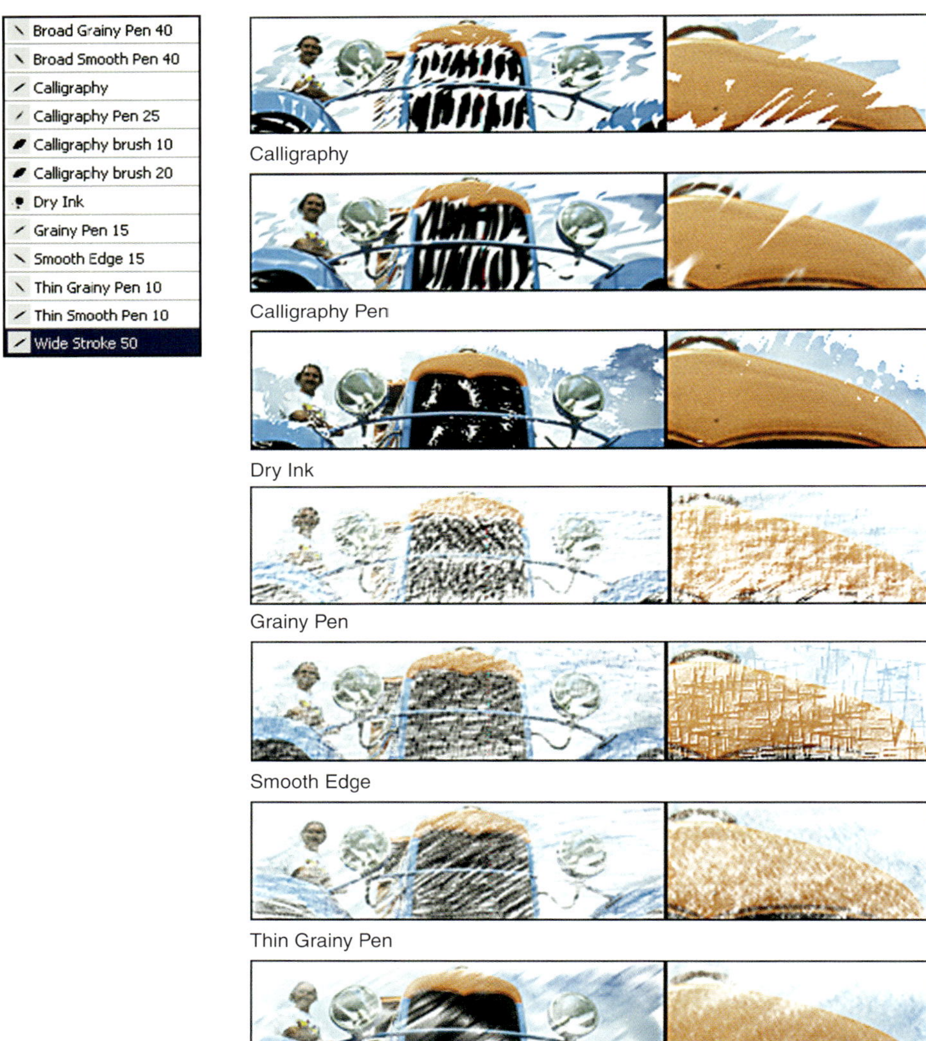

Calligraphy

Calligraphy Pen

Dry Ink

Grainy Pen

Smooth Edge

Thin Grainy Pen

Wide Stroke

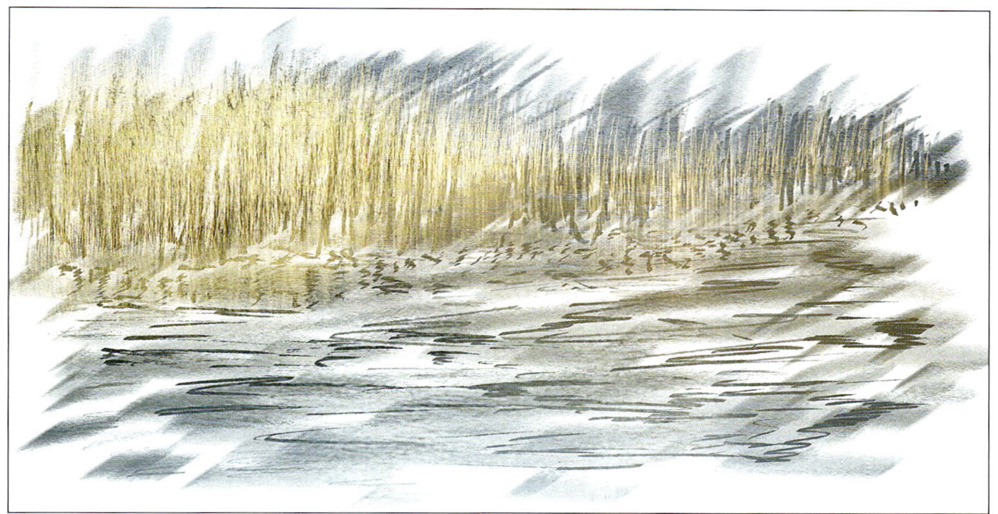

Figure 5.17 Lakeside reeds

The Calligraphy Thin Smooth Pen 10 was used to make this picture. The brush grain setting was reduced to around 21% in order to emphasize the grain. The opacity varied between 5% and 100% and the brush size between 8.0 and 45.0.

The small brush was used at a high opacity to sketch in the lines of the reeds and add some lines in the water. You can still see the dark lines in the water where they were put at the start of the picture, with more added at various opacities at the end. Washes of color were painted with the larger brush sizes at a low opacity.

The brush was used in a very definite calligraphic style to make full use of the thin and wide strokes that are characteristic of these brushes.

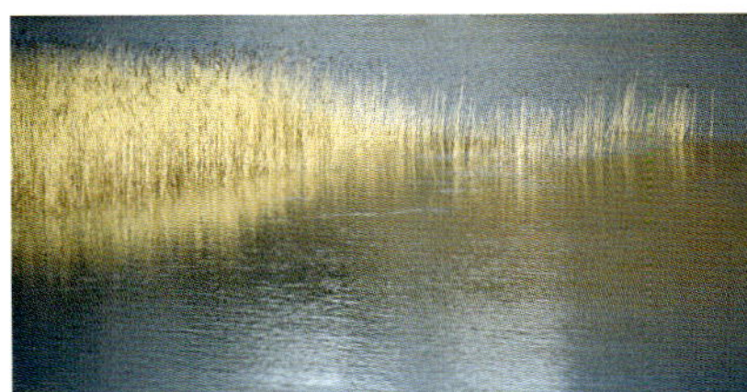

Figure 5.18 Original photograph

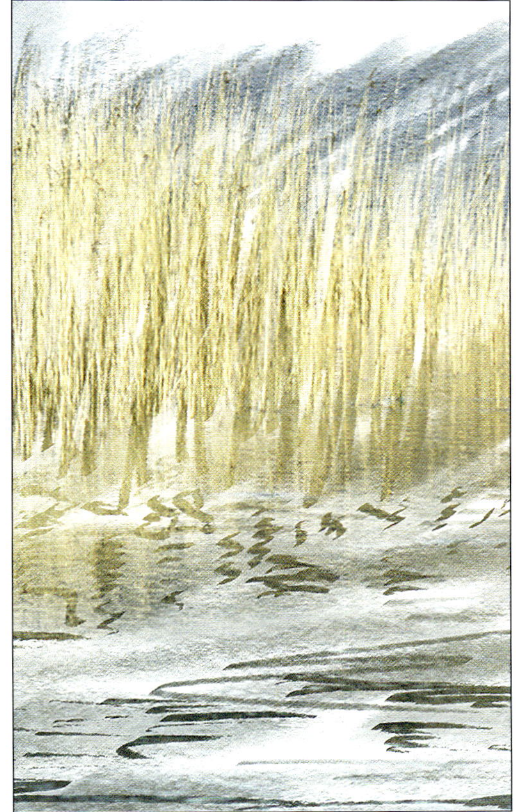

Figure 5.19 Detail of brush strokes

Chalk

The Chalk brushes are particularly good for using with paper textures; many of them use very rough captured dabs, which scrape over the paper surface and emphasize the grain. Some of the dabs are square and the icons in the list of brushes on this page give an indication of the shape.

In most of the examples below, the grain and the opacity settings have been reduced to emphasize the paper grain. The papers chosen vary and it is the differing papers that have changed the appearance of the texture.

The Tapered Artist Chalk is particularly smooth, yet it also brings out the texture. The Sharp and Square Chalks give the roughest finish.

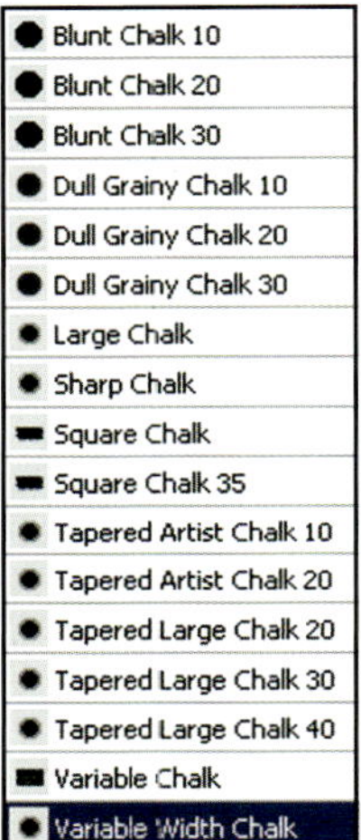

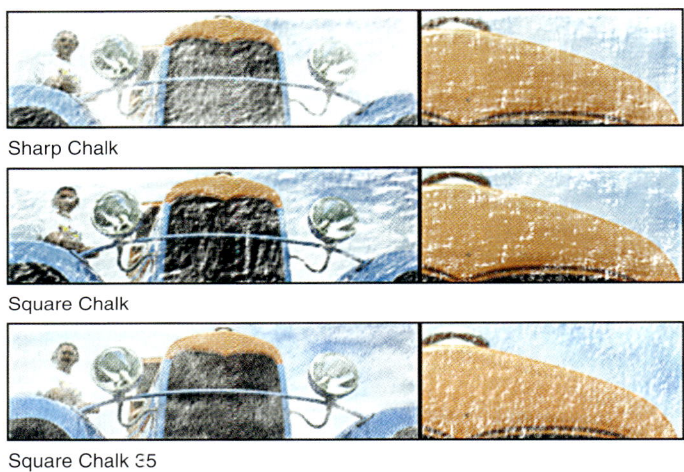

Sharp Chalk

Square Chalk

Square Chalk 35

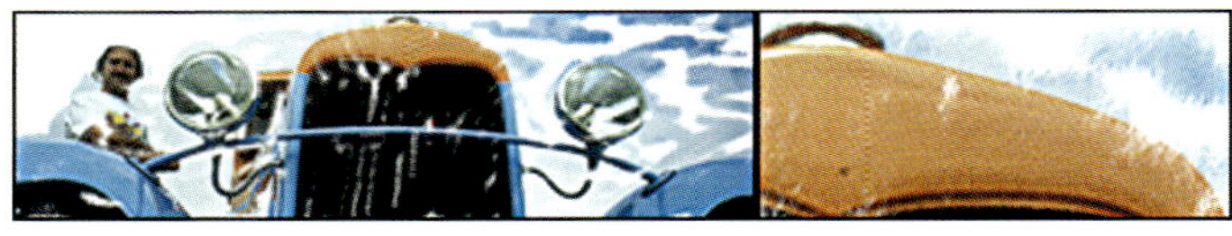

Tapered Artist Chalk

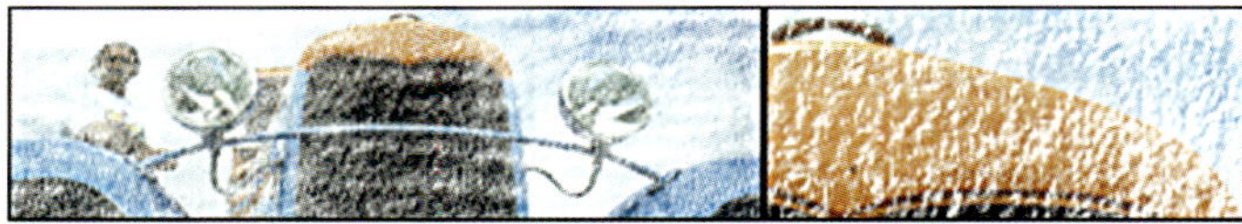

Tapered Large Chalk

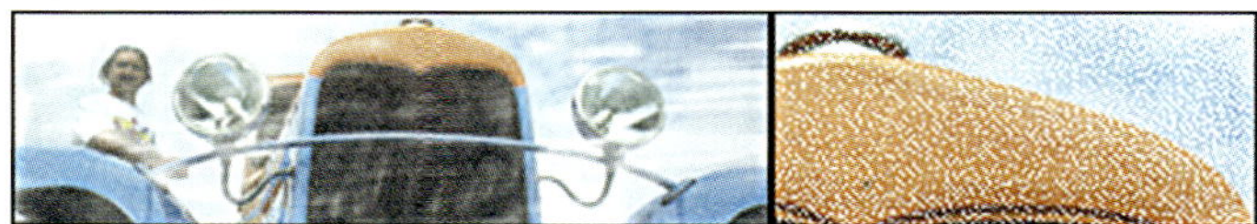

Variable Chalk

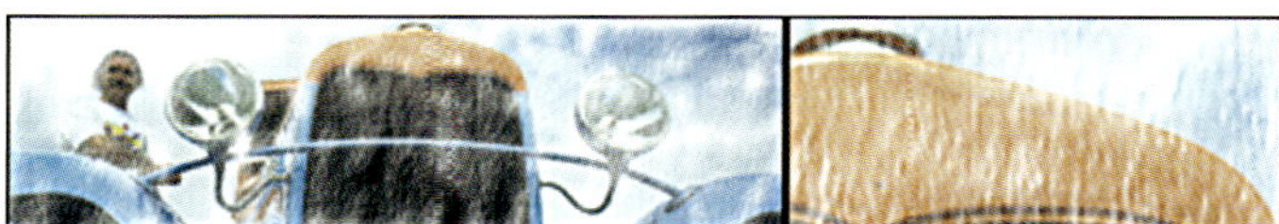

Variable Width Chalk

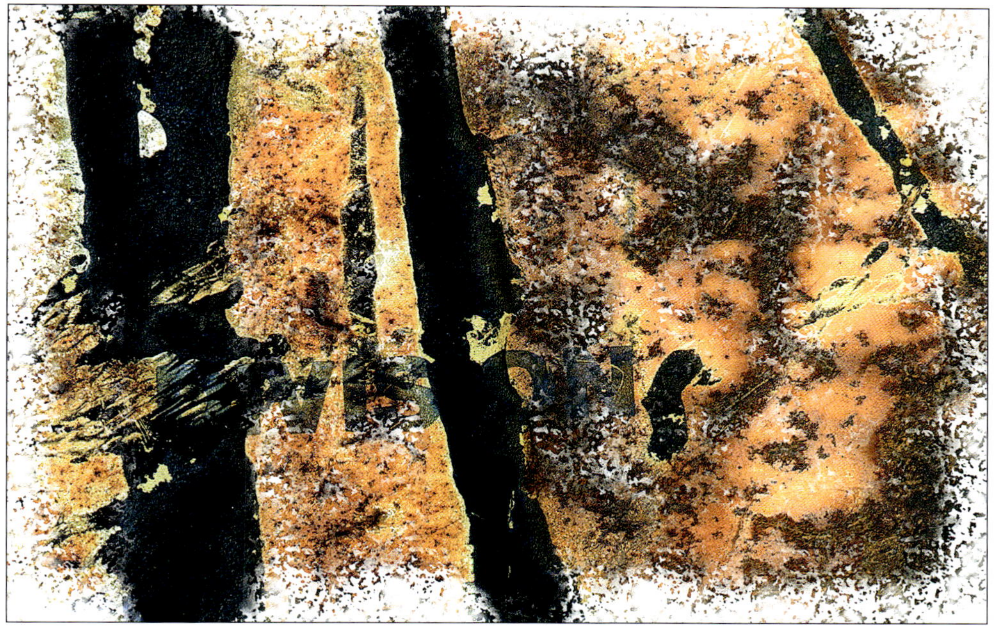

Figure 5.20 Rust

The original picture of rust on the side of an old vehicle was very striking already and the clone has given it even more impact.

The Tapered Large Chalk variant was used to paint a very rough texture that reacted well to the strong colors and shapes.

Harsh Texturing paper from the Relief set of paper textures was the paper used; this additional brush library can be found within the Painter program.

The brush size was initially 250.0, then using more opacity and less grain the colors and textures were gradually built up.

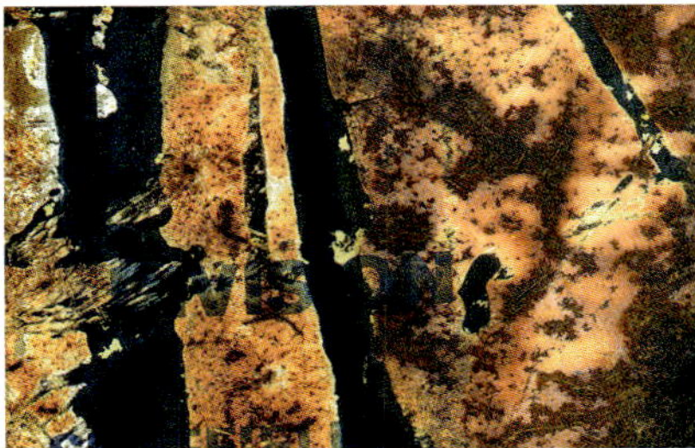

Figure 5.21 Original photograph

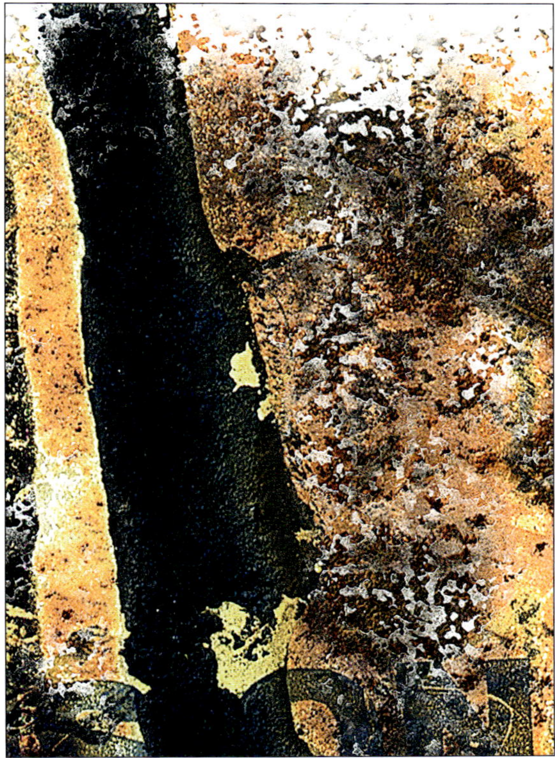

Figure 5.22 Rust detail

Charcoal

Like the Chalk variants, the Charcoal brushes are very hard and rough. They are excellent for interacting with grain textures; in most cases you will need to reduce both the grain and opacity settings.

The Sharp Charcoal Pencil seems to work almost like an airbrush in the way it lays down clumps of clone image.

A variant that is quite different is the Soft Vine Charcoal, which shifts around the cloned image and blurs it out of register with the original.

The Soft Charcoal Pencil also does this but to a much lesser extent.

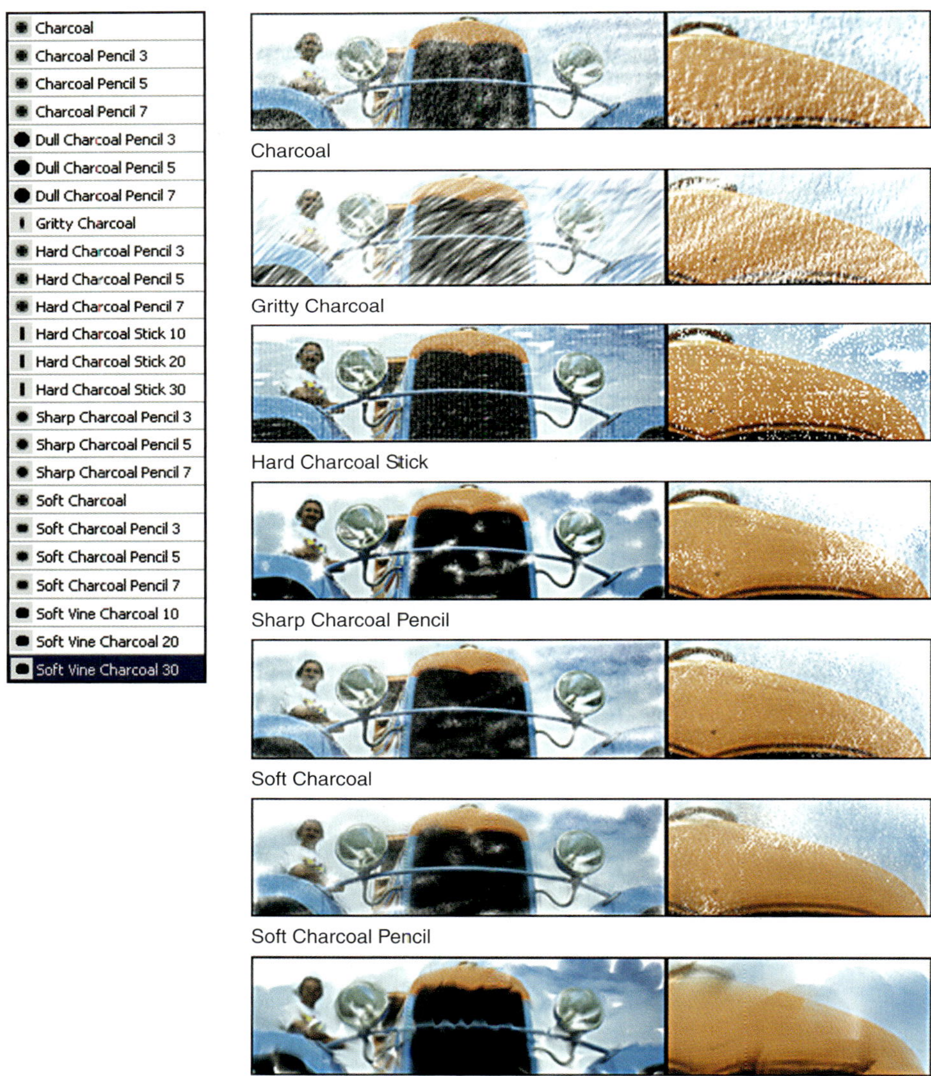

Charcoal

Gritty Charcoal

Hard Charcoal Stick

Sharp Charcoal Pencil

Soft Charcoal

Soft Charcoal Pencil

Soft Vine Charcoal

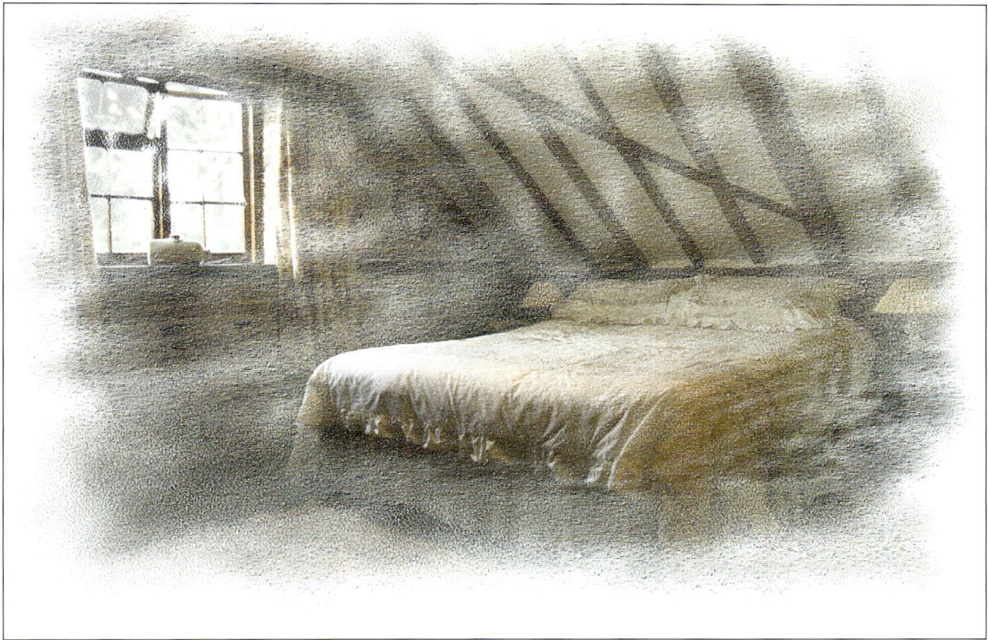

Figure 5.23 The bedroom in the loft

The Sharp Charcoal Pencil was used to create this picture. A large brush size was used for the early stages and then various smaller sizes to bring in more detail.

The Method was Cloning/Hard Grainy Cloning and Pacific Laid was the paper, which produced the distinctive horizontal streaks.

To complete the clone the paper was changed to Basic Paper, which helped to even out the texture.

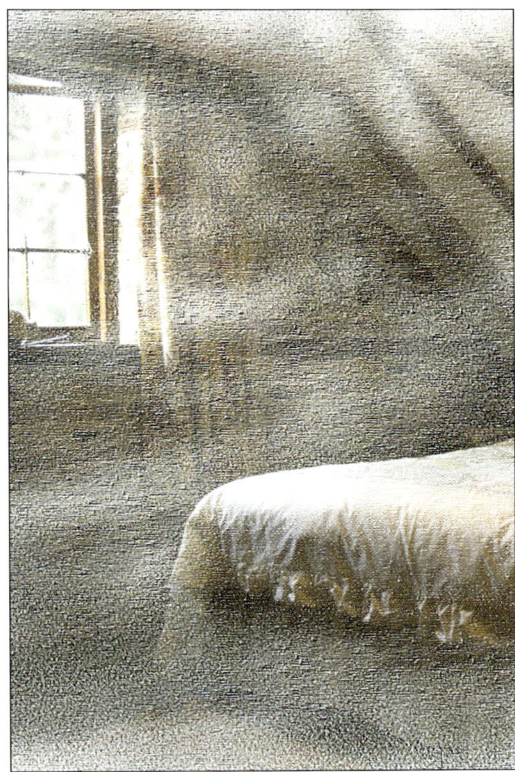

Figure 5.25 Detail of texture

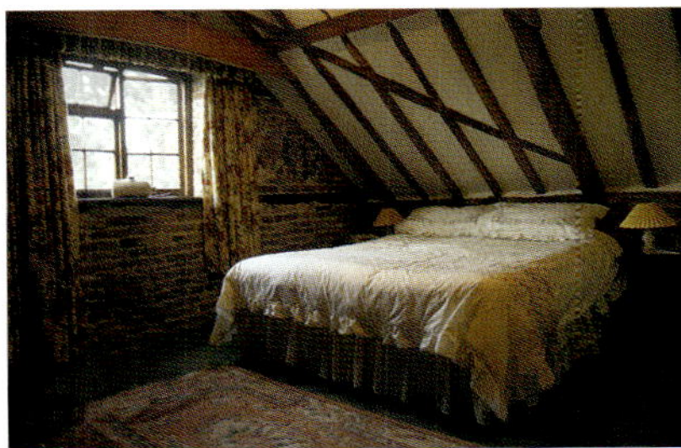

Figure 5.24 Original photograph

Cloners

This set of brushes has been chosen specifically for cloning and brings together brushes from several other brush categories. All the brushes have been set up ready for cloning with no adjustments needed.

There is no sense of strong identity with this set as they have been presented together for convenience. Some, like the Splattery and Texture Spray Cloners, are very rough while the Camel Cloners are smooth and smear the original picture.

The Water Color and Oil Cloners use the Clone Color option and will smear the cloned image.

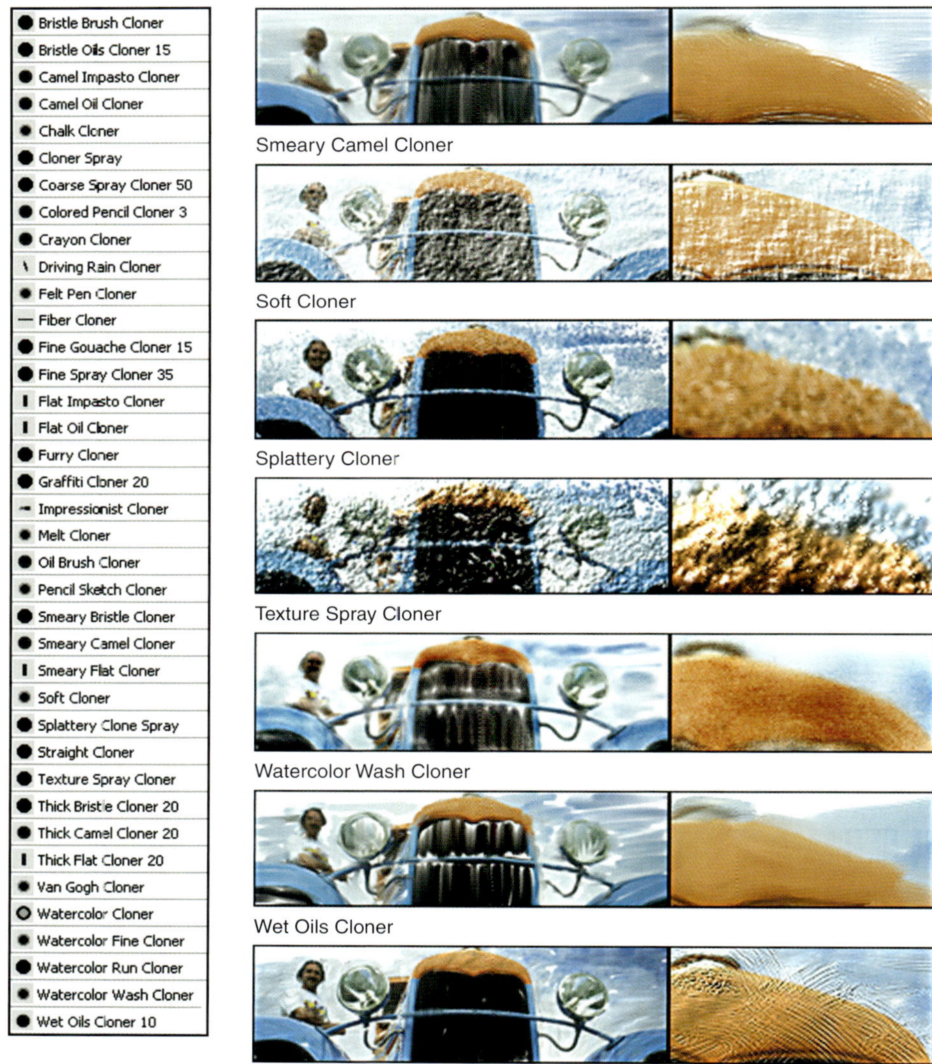

Smeary Camel Cloner

Soft Cloner

Splattery Cloner

Texture Spray Cloner

Watercolor Wash Cloner

Wet Oils Cloner

Thick Camel Cloner

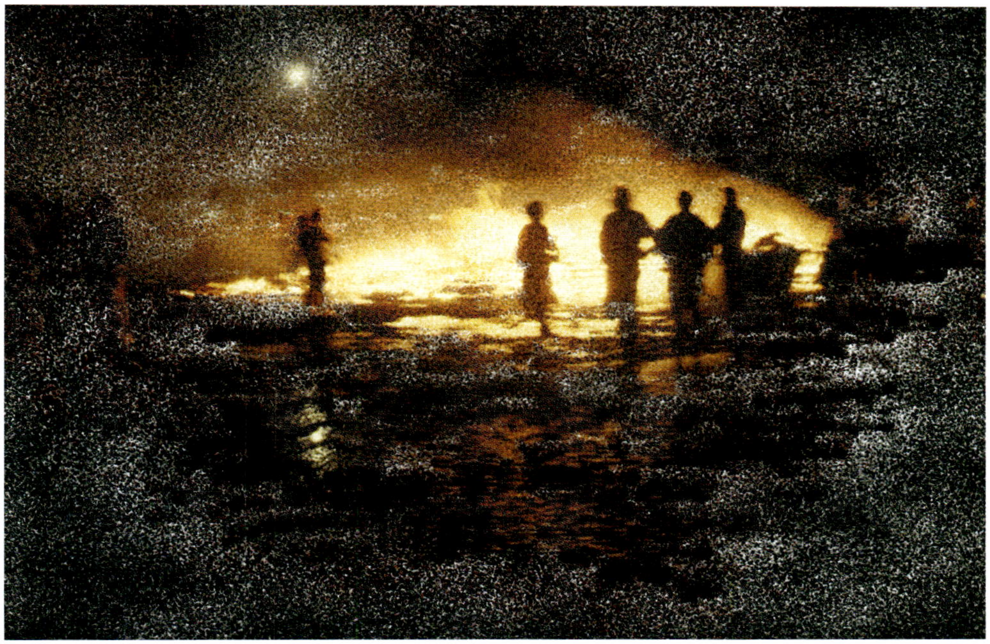

Figure 5.26 Bonfire night

This photograph was taken at a large bonfire night event. The fire had subsided to a small but still intensely hot mound and I liked the ghostly silhouettes of the figures as they stood in front of the glow.

The clone was made using the Splattery Clone Spray, which suited the inky blackness with the many pinpoints of light.

The brush was used at the default settings with various sizes and opacities; it uses an airbrush setting to spray on the picture.

This section of brushes has been considerably expanded in Painter IX and includes a wide variety of brush types suitable for cloning.

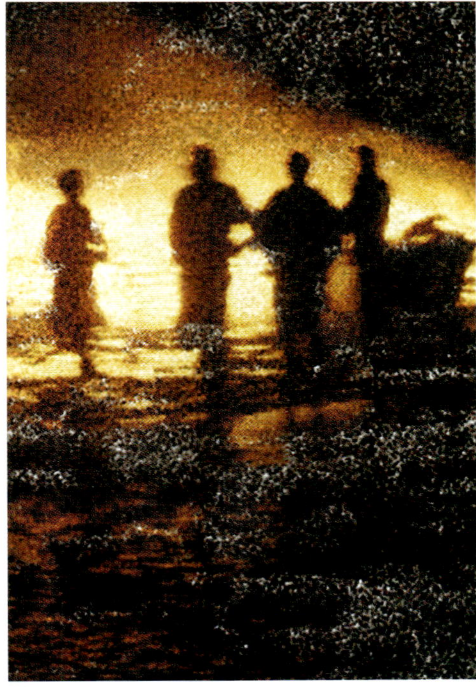

Figure 5.28 Detail

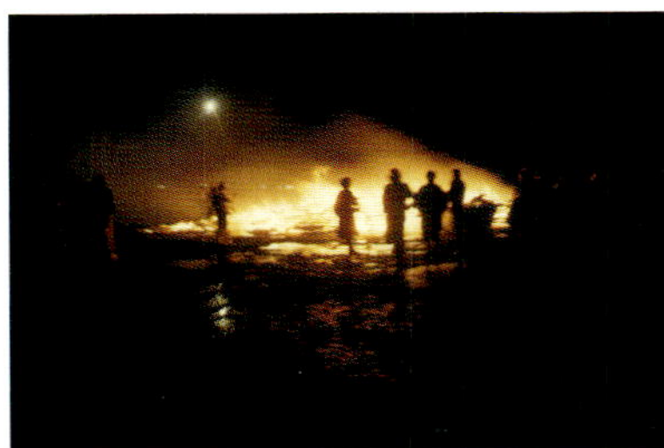

Figure 5.27 Original photograph

Colored Pencils

This group of brushes is not very easy to use for cloning.

The first three examples can be used in the Cloning Method but they have a rather unique style. When you make a brush stroke, the brush picks up the color first clicked on, continues painting with that color and ignores the source image. Some variants gradually fade out while others continue with the same color.

The rest of the examples cannot be used for cloning at all, or at least, none that I have found. They can, however, be used to work directly upon a picture so perhaps it might be best to think of them as a sort of blender.

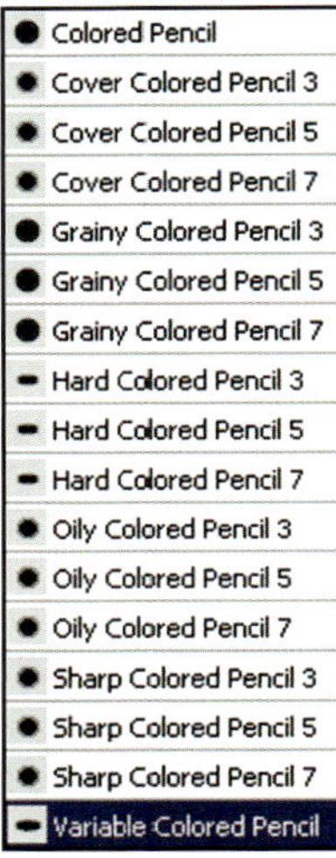

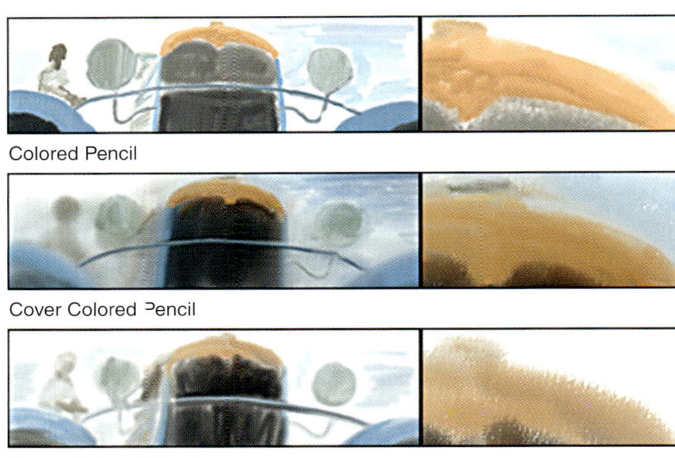

Colored Pencil

Cover Colored Pencil

Grainy Colored Pencil

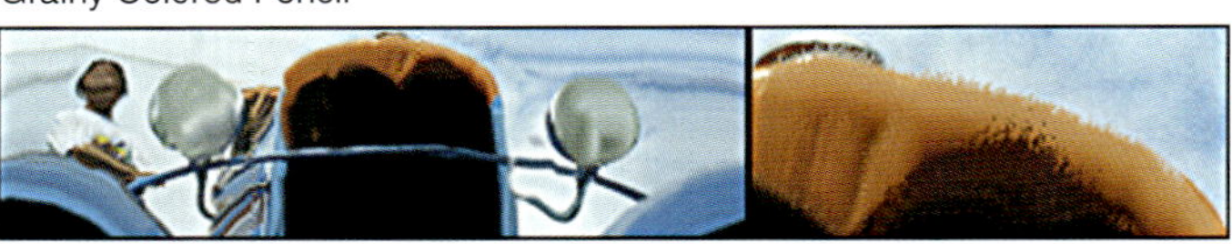

Hard Colored Pencil

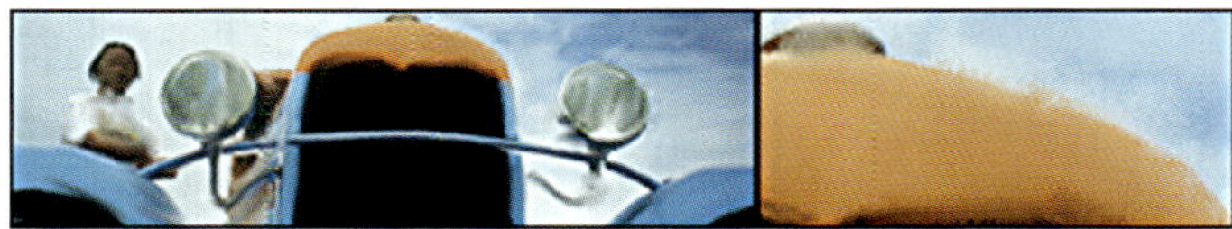

Oily Colored Pencil

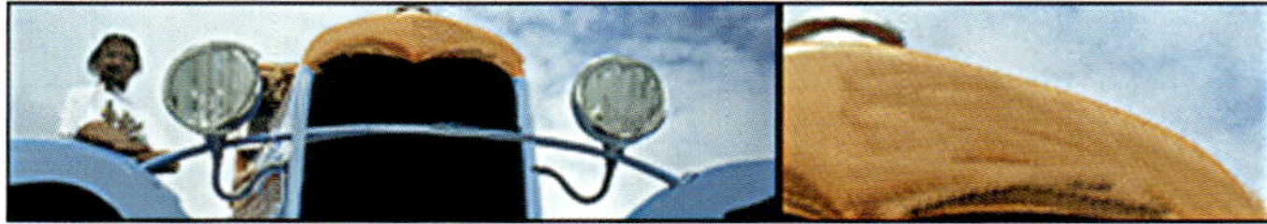

Sharp Colored Pencil

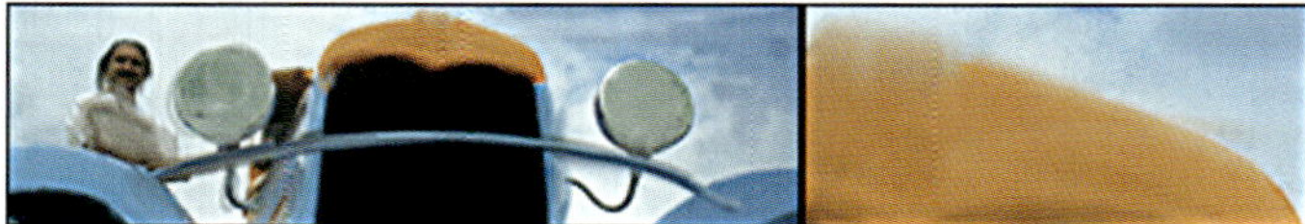

Variable Colored Pencil

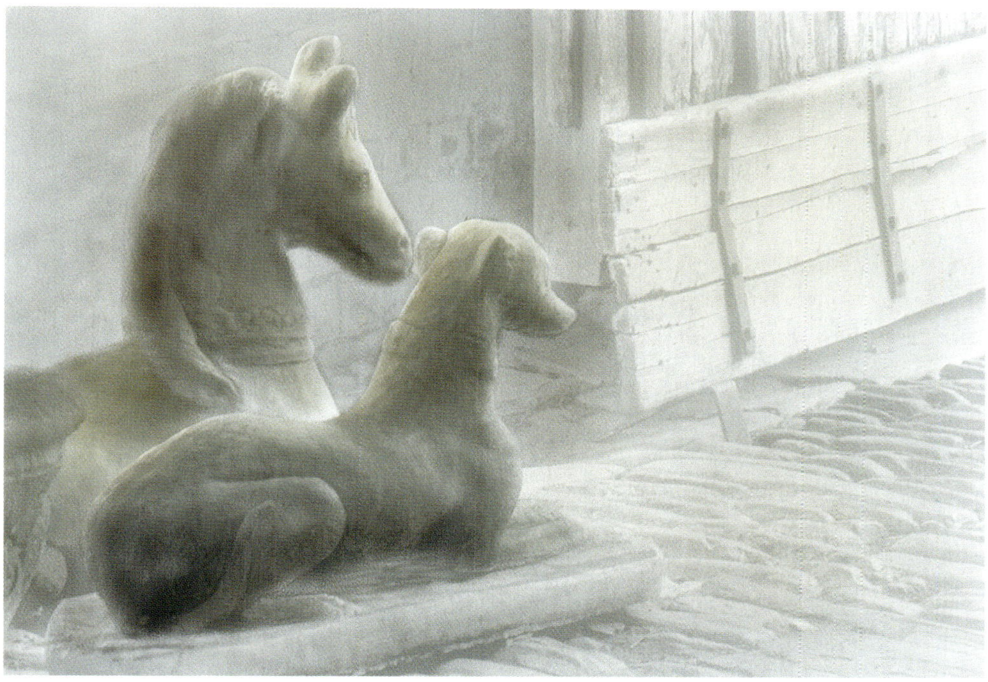

Figure 5.29 Stone horse and dog

This picture was created using the Grainy Colored Pencils variant. The outlines of the statues were traced with a narrow brush at a low opacity, then a larger brush size filled in the shapes. A medium brush integrated the two brush sizes.

To finish the picture the original image was selected and copied, then pasted into the clone document on top of the clone layer.

The layer composite method of the top layer was changed to Luminosity and the opacity to 32%. More detail on using layers can be found in Chapter 8.

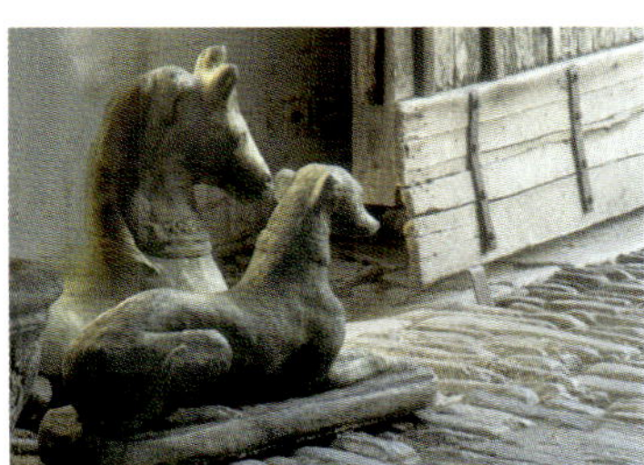

Figure 5.30 Original photograph

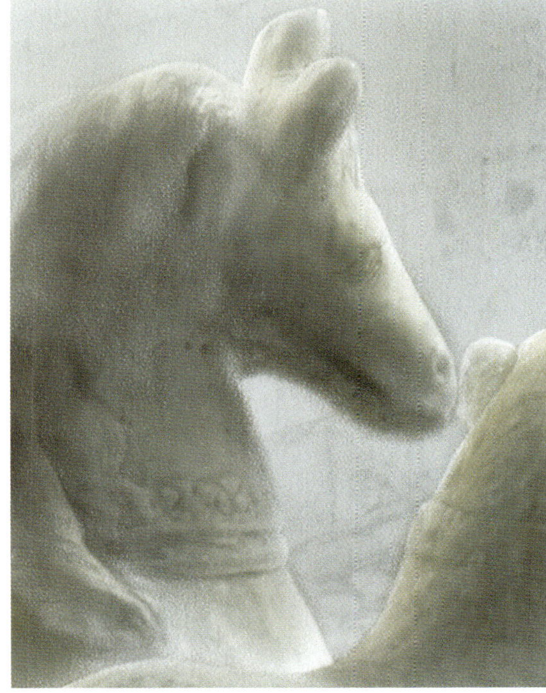

Figure 5.31 Detail

Conte

As you will notice from the list of variants on the left, this is a very small section. When you remove the different sizes there are only three different variants of the Conte Brushes.

Like the Chalk and Charcoal categories, these brushes are excellent at picking up a paper texture as they have a very rough finish. They can all use the Cloning Method.

In the examples below, the brushes have been shown using both the Cloning Method and the Clone Color option.

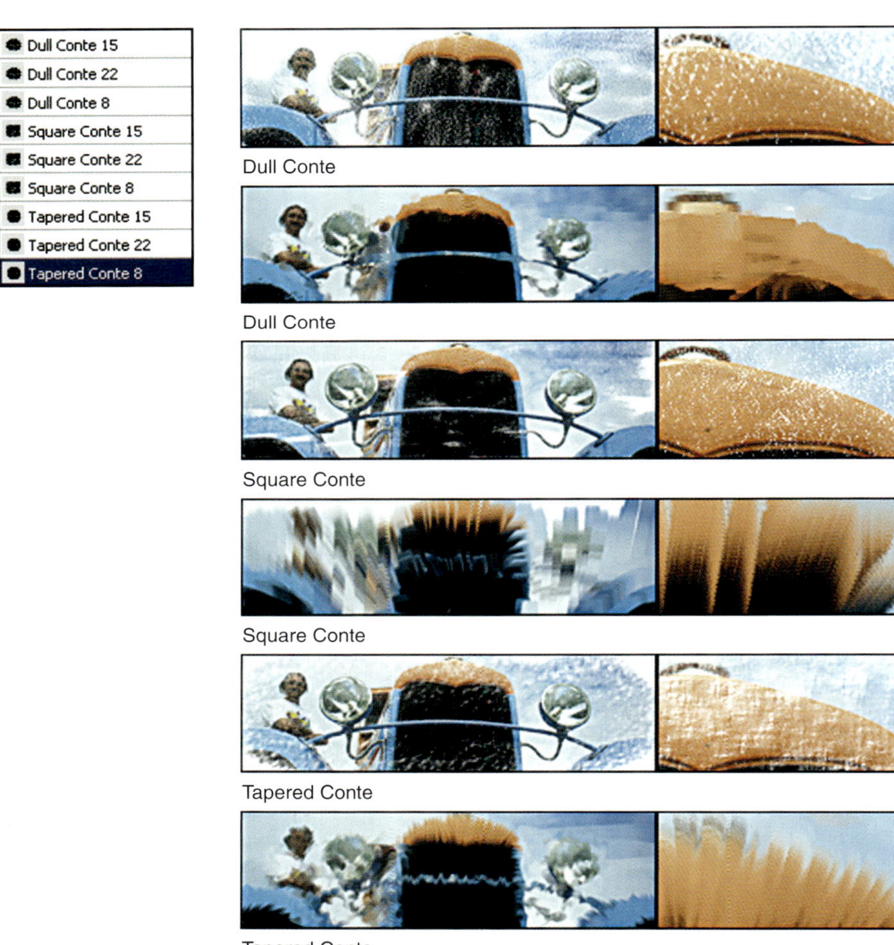

Dull Conte

Dull Conte

Square Conte

Square Conte

Tapered Conte

Tapered Conte

Tapered Conte

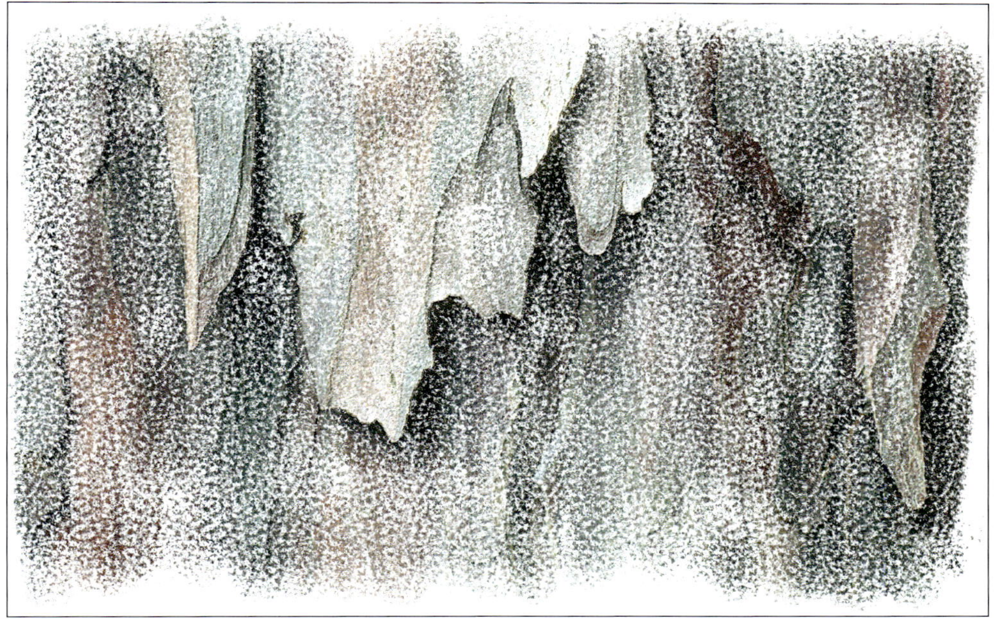

Figure 5.32 Bark patterns

This tree had a wonderful bark pattern and I was particularly attracted to the lovely range of colors.

The Tapered Conte brush was used to make the picture above, brush size 21.5 and opacity 75%. In the General palette, the Method was changed to Cloning and the Subcategory to Grainy Hard Cover Cloning.

After lightly cloning most of the picture, the opacity was then increased to 100% to emphasize the main lines of the pattern.

The paper used was the Artists Rough Paper.

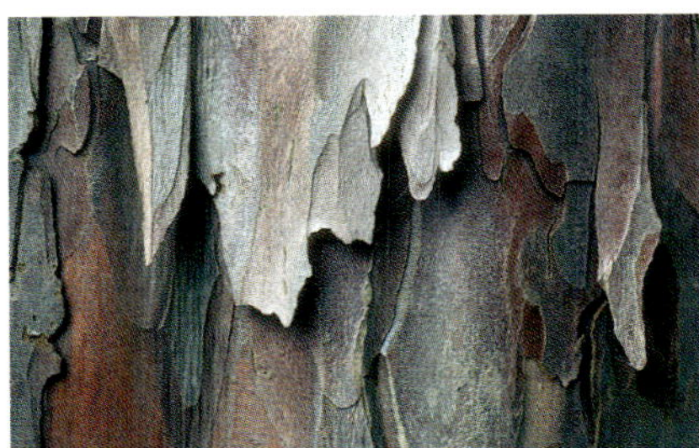

Figure 5.33 Original photograph

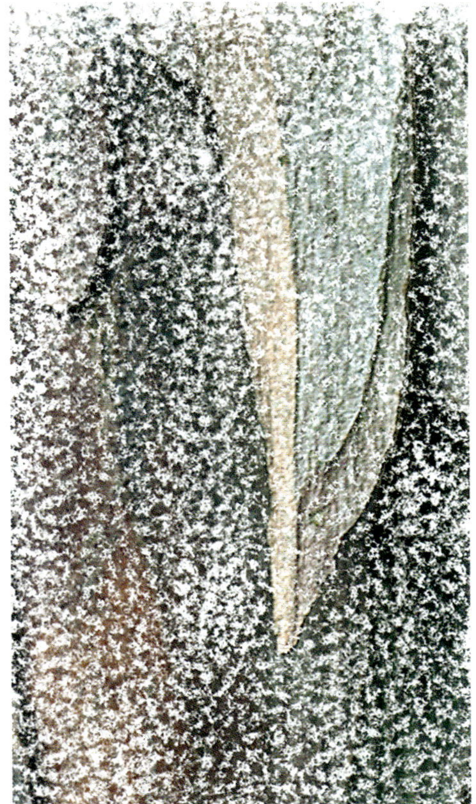

Figure 5.34 Detail

Crayons

Like the Chalk and Conte brushes, the Crayon group takes up the paper texture very well, as you can see from the examples below.

The two odd ones are the Grainy Hard Crayon and the Waxy Crayon, both of which smear the cloned image.

The second example of the Dull Crayon brush uses a paper called Crystalline Formation from the Molecular library, which is one of the extra paper libraries that can be loaded when required.

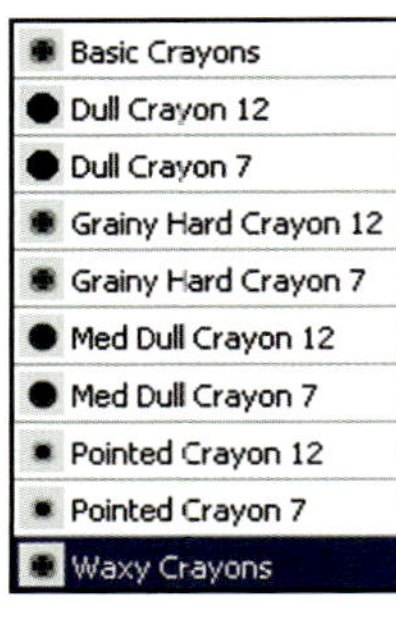

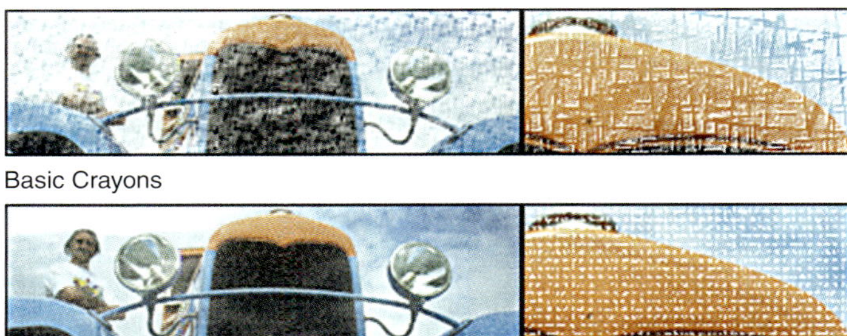

Basic Crayons

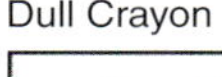

Dull Crayon

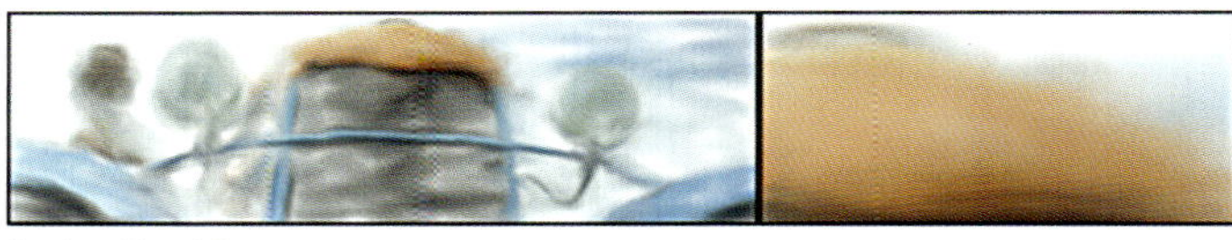

Grainy Hard Crayon

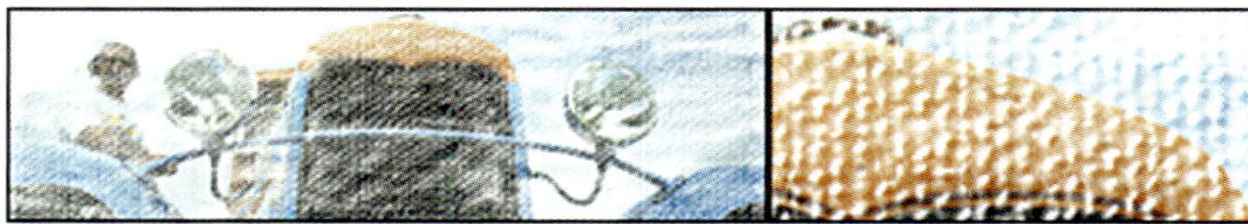

Medium Dull Crayon

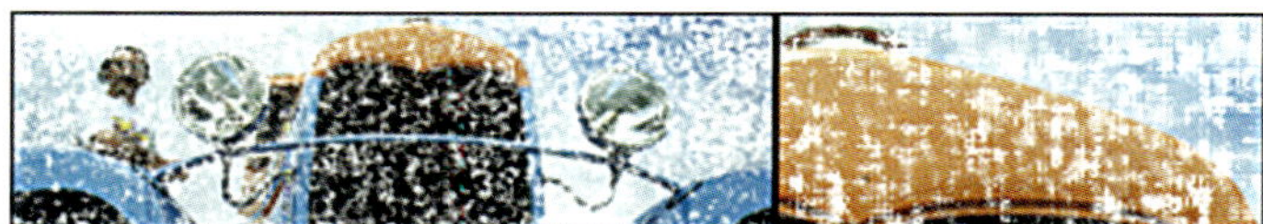

Pointed Crayon

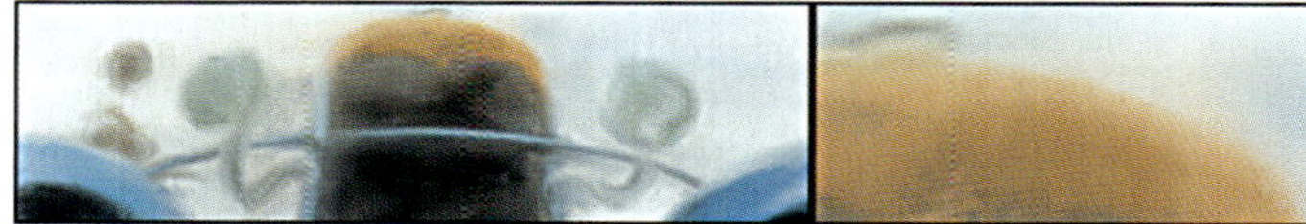

Waxy Crayons

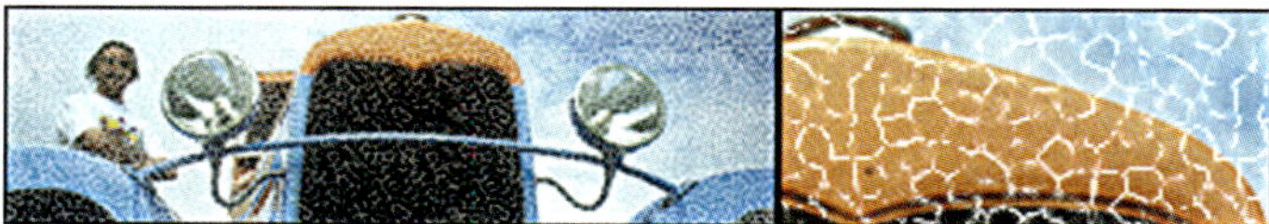

Dull Crayon

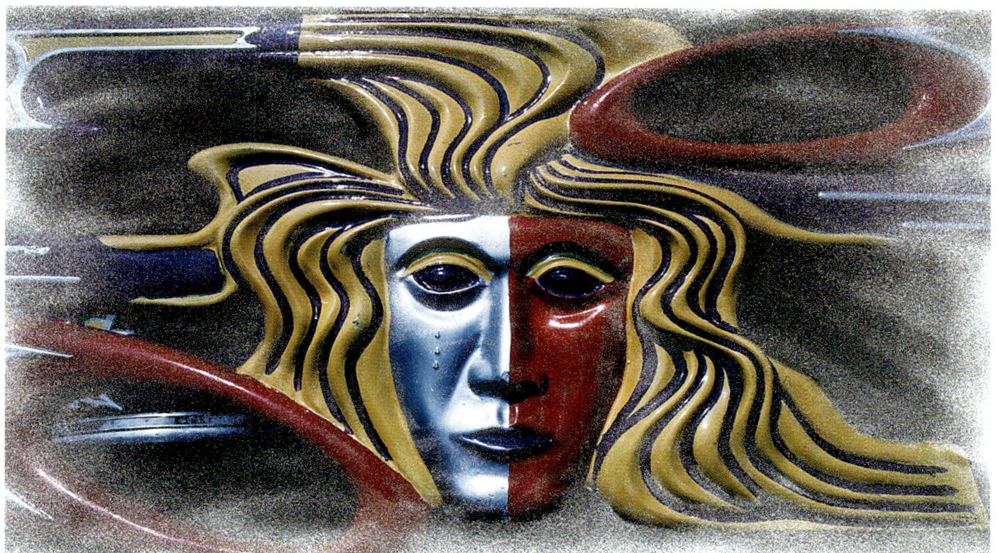

Figure 5.35 Fairground decoration

The picture above was initially painted with the Painted Crayon, brush size 108.0, opacity 28%, grain 14%. This gave a light texture over all the photograph.

The Dull Crayon was then used to bring in more detail. Brush size 78.2, opacity 9% and grain 20%.

The settings for the Dull Crayon were changed to brush size 12.0 and opacity 30%, which brought in more detail.

Most of these brushes show the paper texture very well when used in the Grainy Hard Cover Cloning method, as these were here.

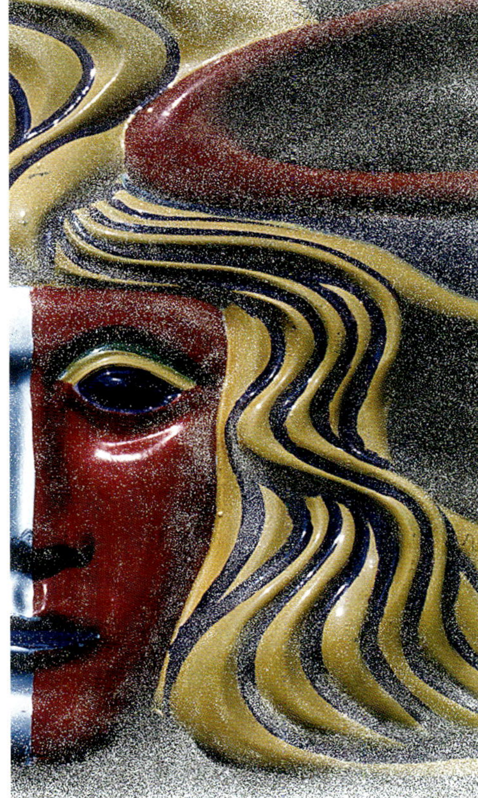

Figure 5.37 Detail

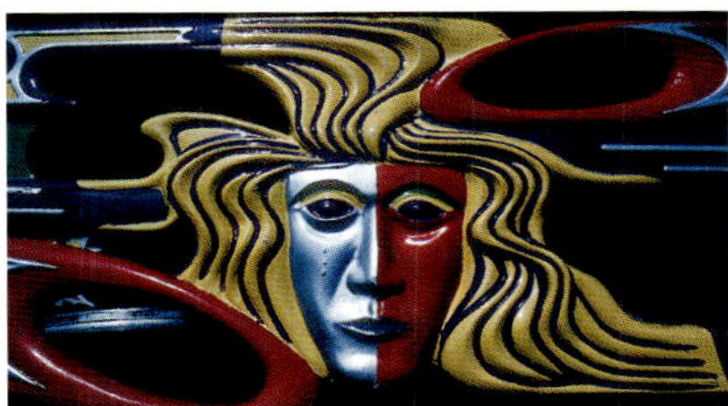

Figure 5.36 Original photograph

Digital Watercolor

Digital Watercolor was first introduced in Painter 8 and offers an alternative to the existing Watercolor brushes. The chief difference is that the brushes can be applied to a normal layer, unlike Watercolor, which must have its own dedicated layer. This makes it more versatile as it is now possible to use both Digital Watercolor and other brush categories on the same layer.

As can be seen below, the brushes vary considerably from smooth strokes to very diffused ones. With the exception of the Flat Water Blender, all the examples below use the Clone Color option, which retains the impression of watercolor.

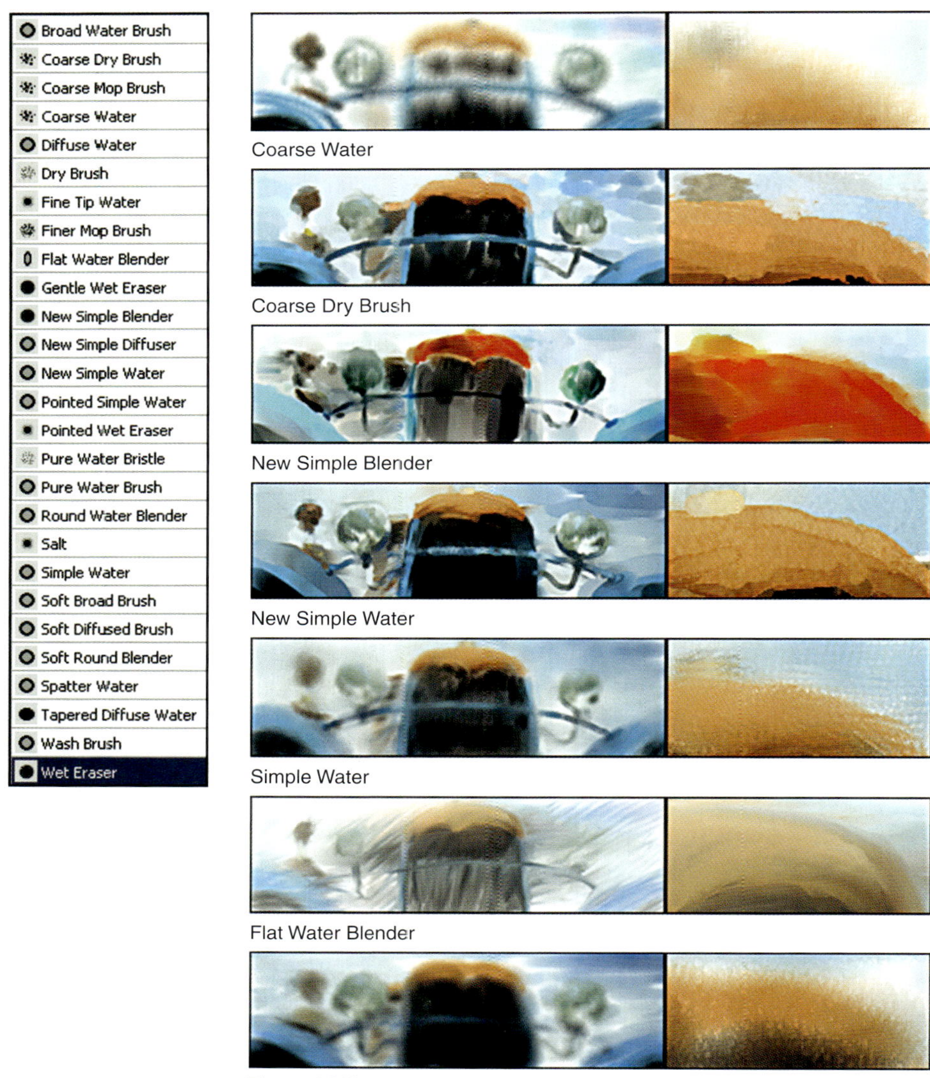

Coarse Water

Coarse Dry Brush

New Simple Blender

New Simple Water

Simple Water

Flat Water Blender

Tapered Diffuse Water

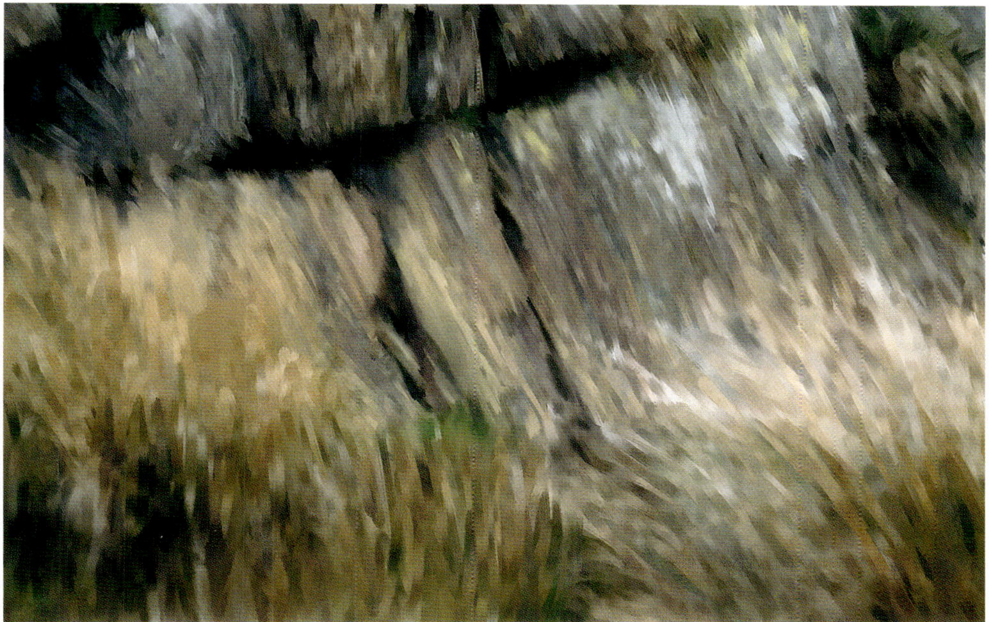

Figure 5.38 Rock and grasses

The brush used for this picture was the Digital Watercolor Dry Brush.

When used in a medium or large brush size, the result will be very diffused with no detail, which is useful as a base color wash.

The brush size was 23.6, opacity 20% and grain 100%. The Clone Color option was ticked in the Colors palette.

To bring in some detail the brush size was reduced to 5.4 and the whole picture painted over at an enlarged size. It was useful to rotate the canvas so that the brush strokes followed the lines of the grasses and rock strata. Rotating the canvas is explained in Chapter 1.

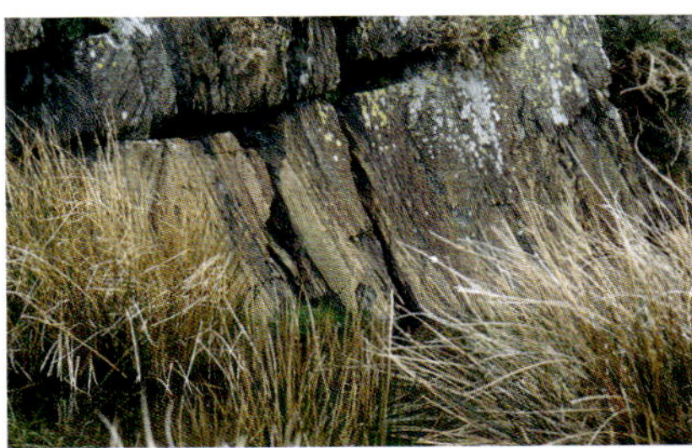

Figure 5.39 Original photograph

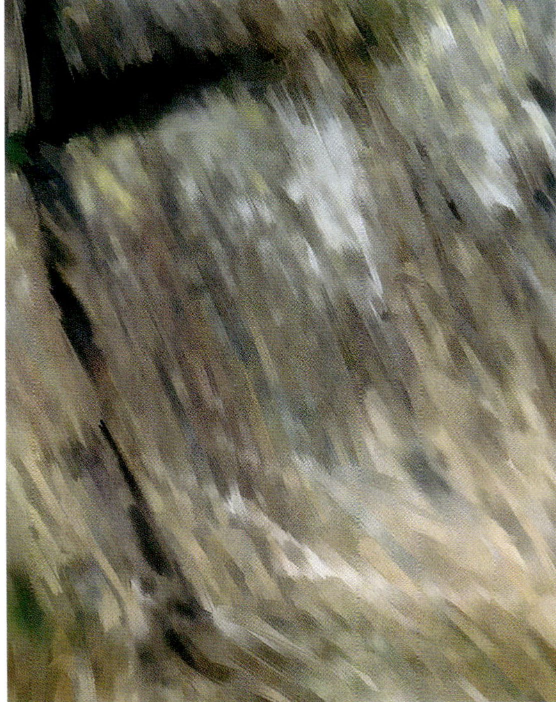

Figure 5.40 Detail

Distortion

This brush category is not suitable for cloning but is great fun to play around with, as the brushes move around and distort the original picture.

The brushes create spikes, swirls, circles and distortions of every type.

The Hurricane brush seems to send the image to another planet!

Although generally these brushes are not made for cloning, it is possible to use a few in this way. Marbling Rake and Water Bubbles can both be used as cloners.

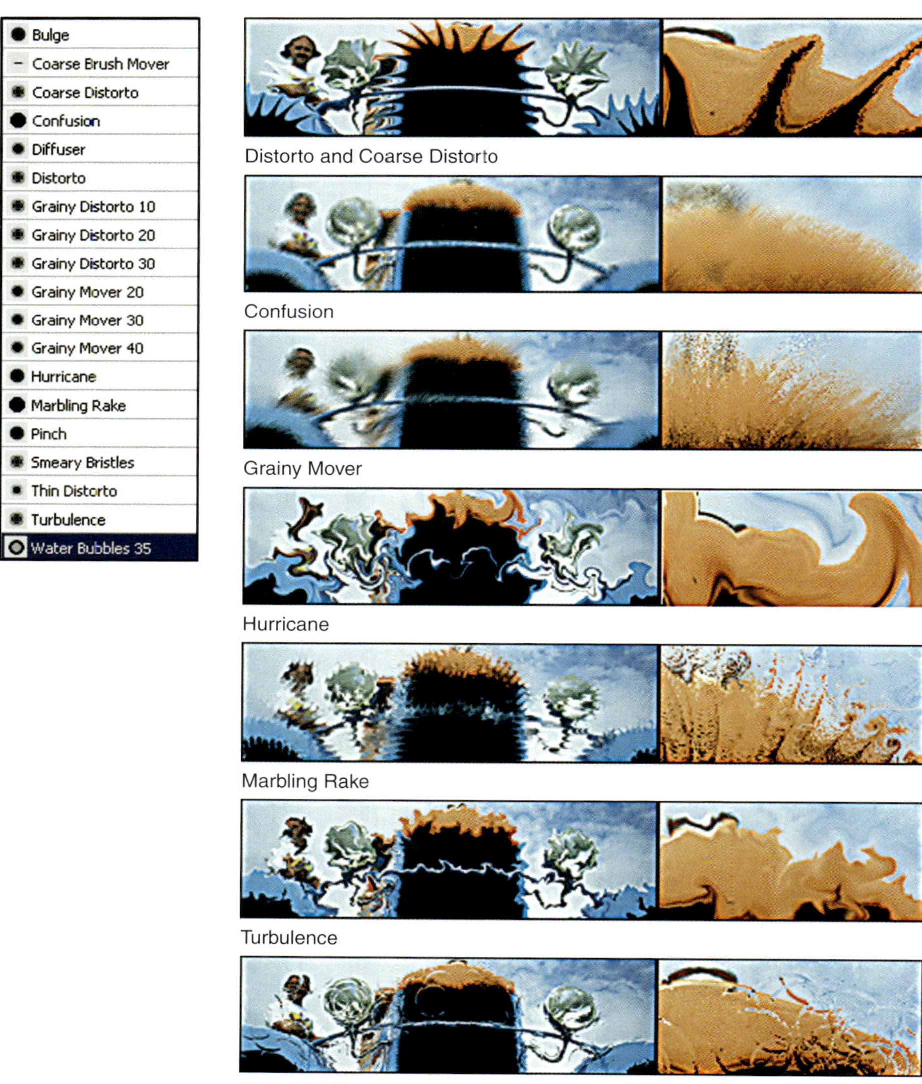

Distorto and Coarse Distorto

Confusion

Grainy Mover

Hurricane

Marbling Rake

Turbulence

Water Bubbles

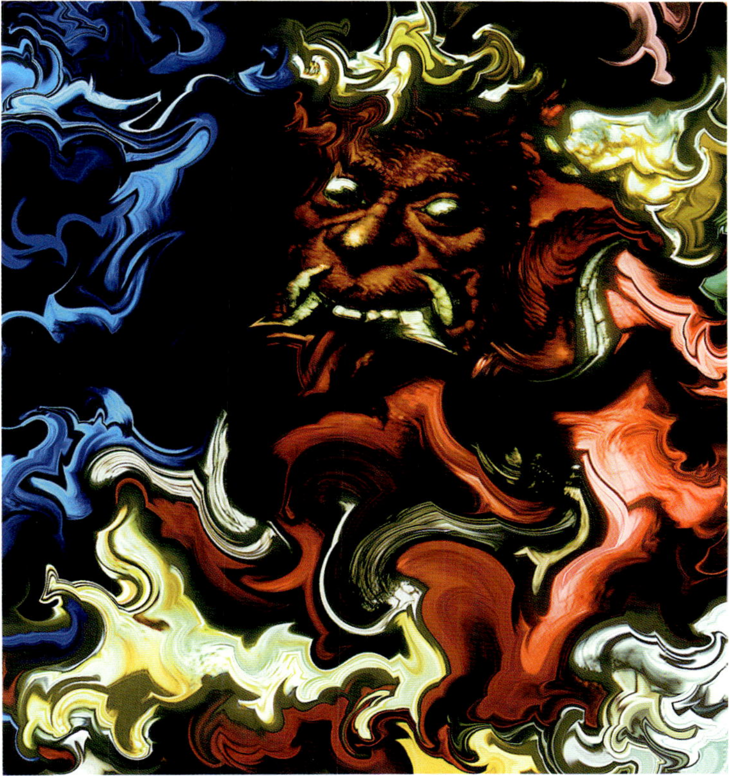

Figure 5.41 The fiery furnace

The original photograph was of a stained glass church window and from the Distortion set of brushes the Hurricane brush was used to make these wild distortions.

I rather felt that it suited the idea of being thrown in the maelstrom, with the Devil waiting there for you!

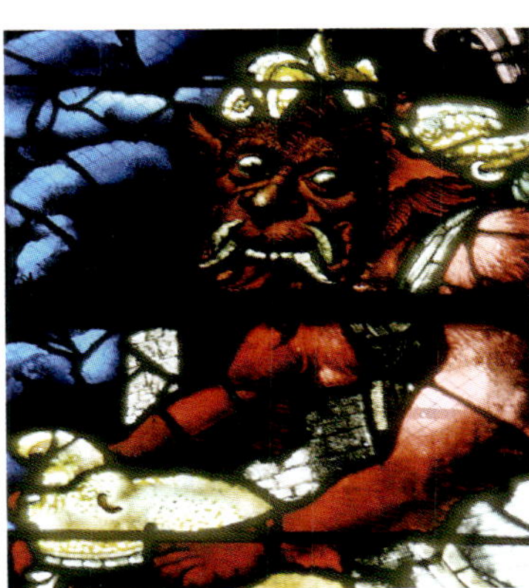

Figure 5.42 Original photograph

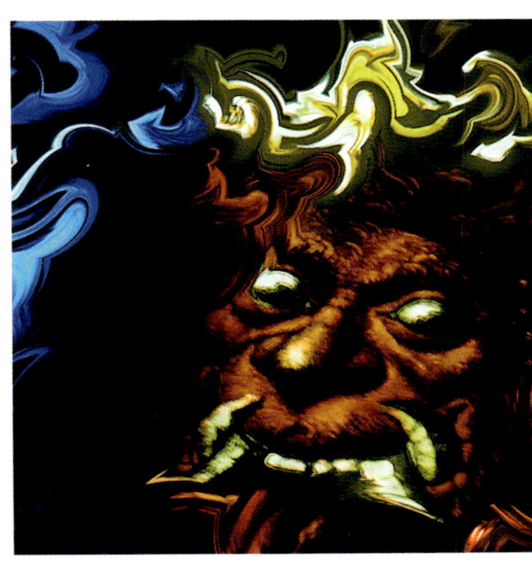

Figure 5.43 The Devil in close-up

Erasers

When it is necessary to erase parts of a picture, it is often better to change the Method to Erasers in order to retain the same brush stroke characteristics. There are times, however, when it is more convenient to use the Erasers in this category, as you can then swap very easily between the cloning brush and the eraser.

There are several brushes that have uses other than as erasers. The darkener can be used to enhance modelling by darkening shadows.

The Gentle Bleach will do the opposite and brighten areas. When used with large brush sizes and a low opacity, many erasers will lighten or darken whole areas.

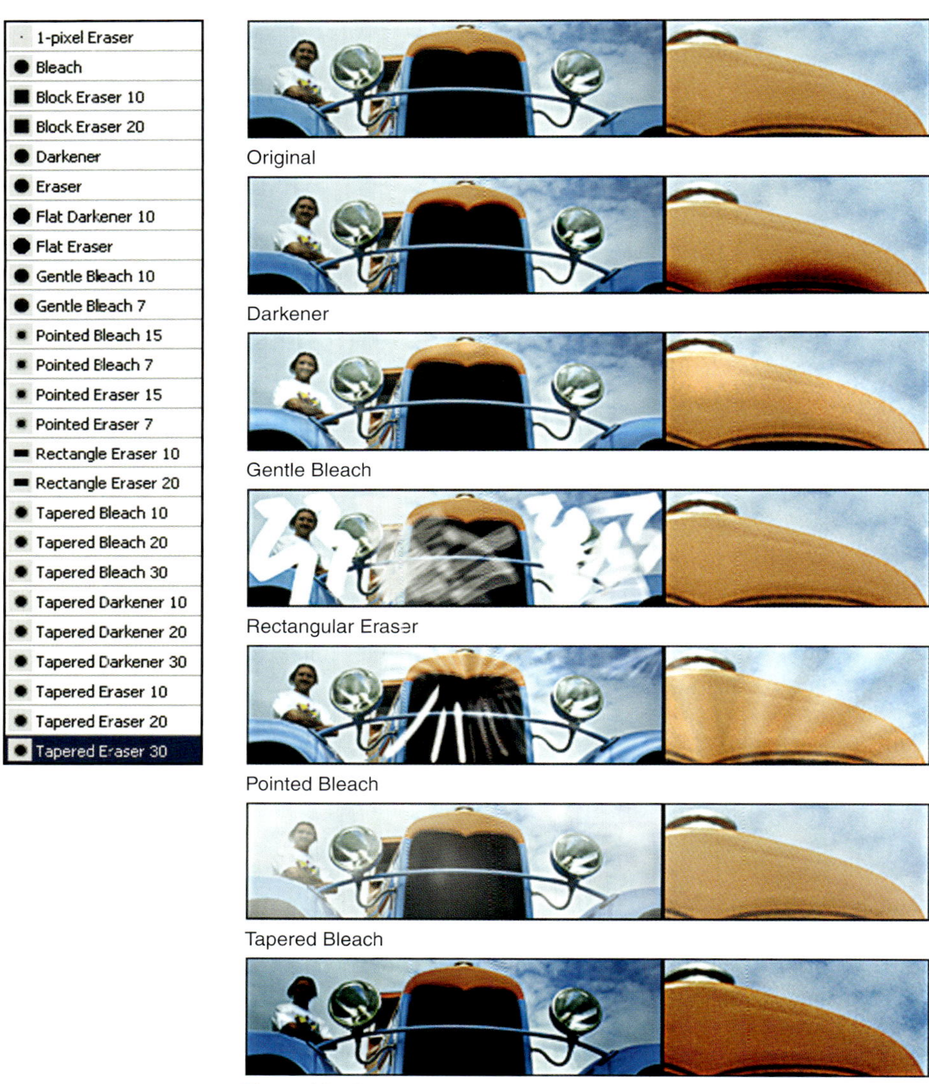

Original

Darkener

Gentle Bleach

Rectangular Eraser

Pointed Bleach

Tapered Bleach

Tapered Darkener

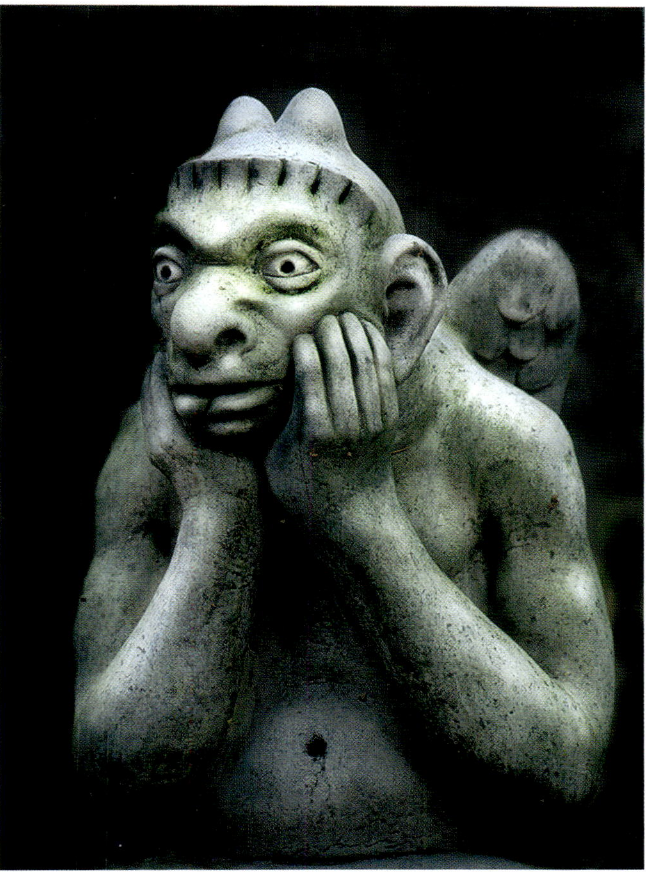

Figure 5.44 Thoughtful

The photograph of this rather grotesque statue was taken on a very dull overcast day and the resulting picture was lacking in contrast.

Two of the Eraser brushes were used to improve the contrast and brightness.

The Darkener was used to paint in the background to remove the bright areas, then the Gentle Bleach to paint over the eyes and areas where the light would be expected to fall.

Various brush sizes and opacities were used and alternated until the picture was complete.

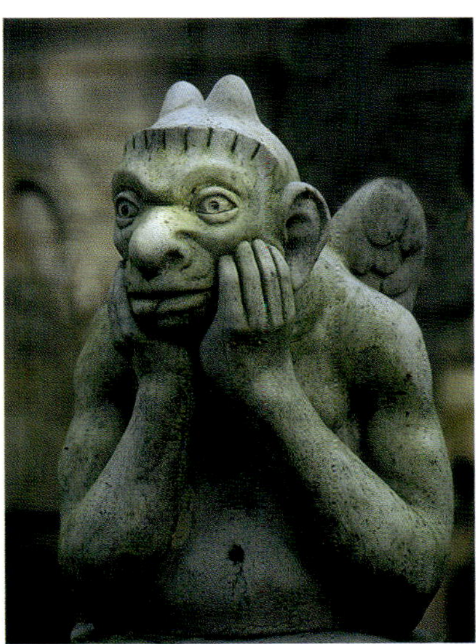

Figure 5.45 Original photograph

F/X

The name F/X immediately tells us that this group of brushes is intended for special effects. Some of the brushes, such as Graphic Paintbrush, Furry Brush and Piano Keys, will also work well as cloners; they will all produce some very unusual pictures.

Other brushes work directly upon the picture. In the examples below Glow, for instance, lights up the headlights of the car, while Fire seems to set light to it.

Shattered imposes a broken structure over the original as though it is being seen through broken glass. The Furry Brush and Hair Spray both use the airbrush effect and shoot out the paint in the direction that the stylus is angled.

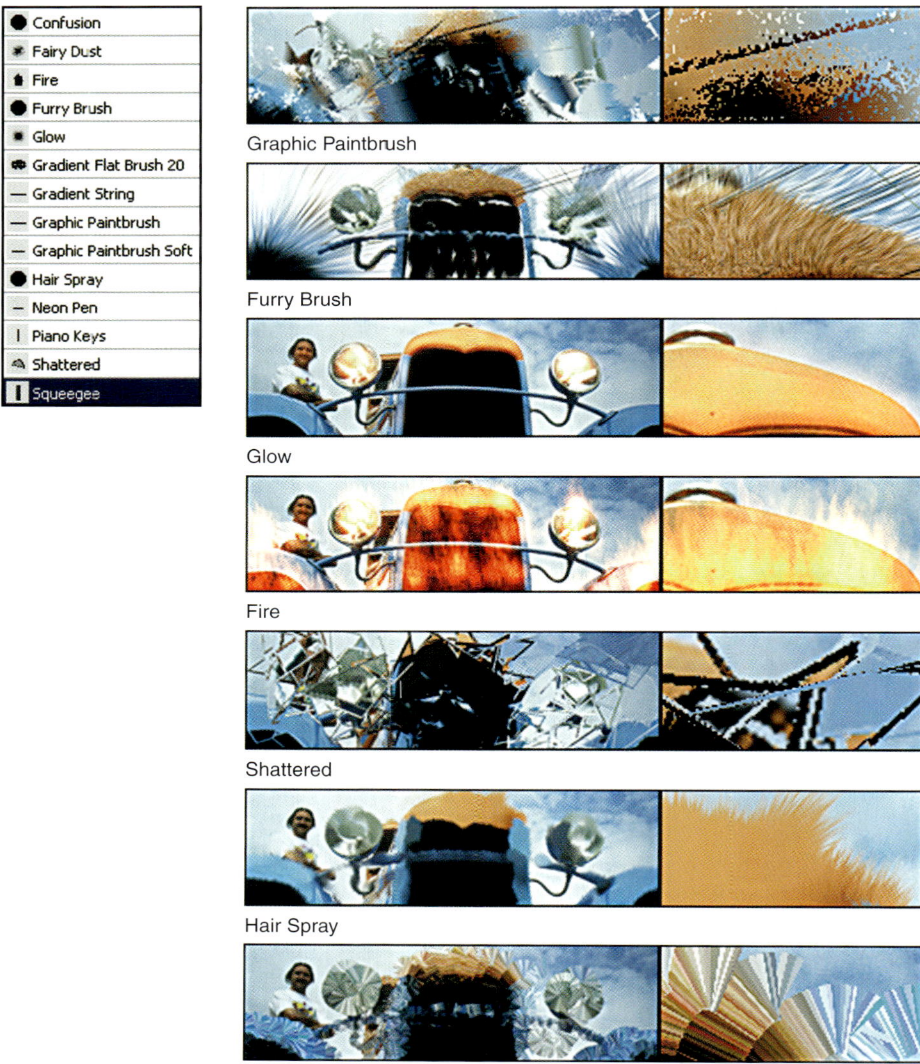

Graphic Paintbrush

Furry Brush

Glow

Fire

Shattered

Hair Spray

Piano Keys

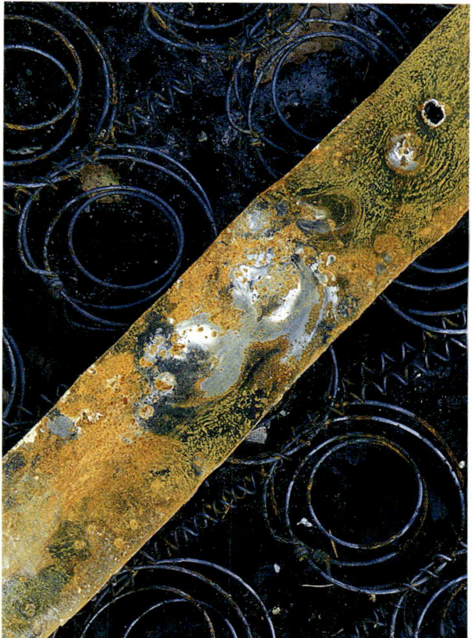

Figure 5.46 Original photograph

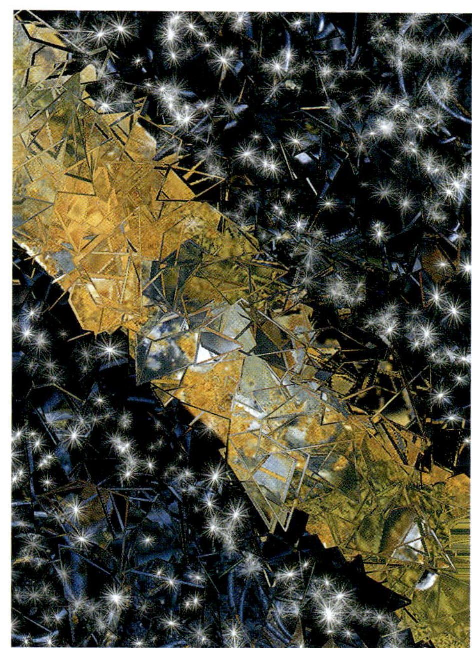

Figure 5.47 Shattered and Fairy Dust

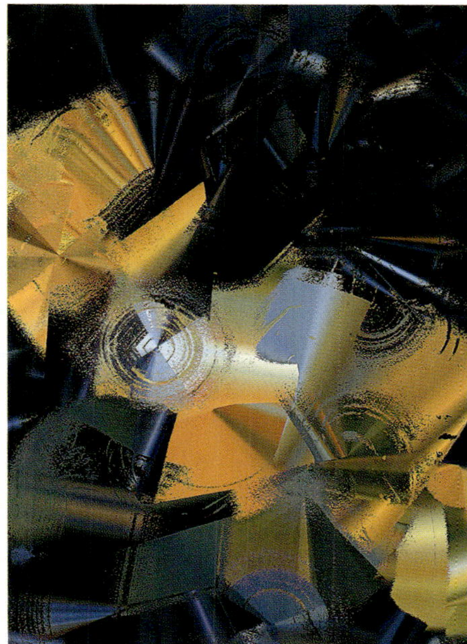

Figure 5.48 Graphic Paintbrush Soft

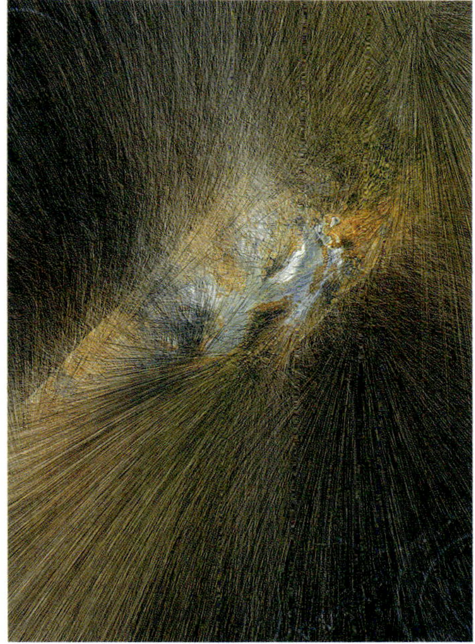

Figure 5.49 Furry Brush

The examples above show how brushes in this category may be used to create unusual abstract pictures. Figure 5.47 used the Shattered brush initially then the Fairy Dust brush added the stars over the top of the picture.

The Furry Brush is illustrated in more detail in Chapter 11.

Felt Pens

Felt Pens are graphic tools and are best used for pictures that need a strong energetic style. One of the distinguishing characteristics of Felt Pens is that when you repeat brush strokes the density increases and the color builds quite quickly to black. Most of the Felt Pens in this category work on this same principle.

The Design Marker is very rough and increases the contrast and color quite strongly.

In the last two examples the Method has been changed to Grainy Hard Cover Cloning and paper textures used to change the style. Using this method the pens no longer build to black.

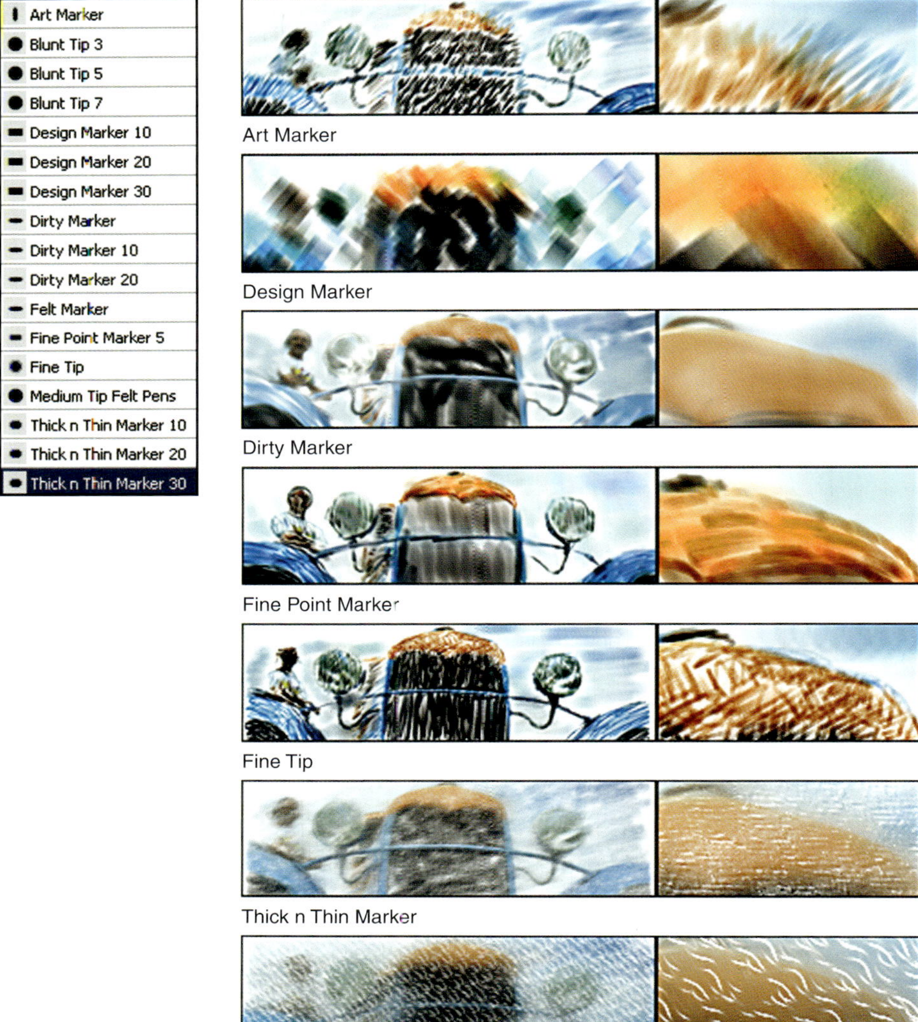

Art Marker

Design Marker

Dirty Marker

Fine Point Marker

Fine Tip

Thick n Thin Marker

Blunt Tip

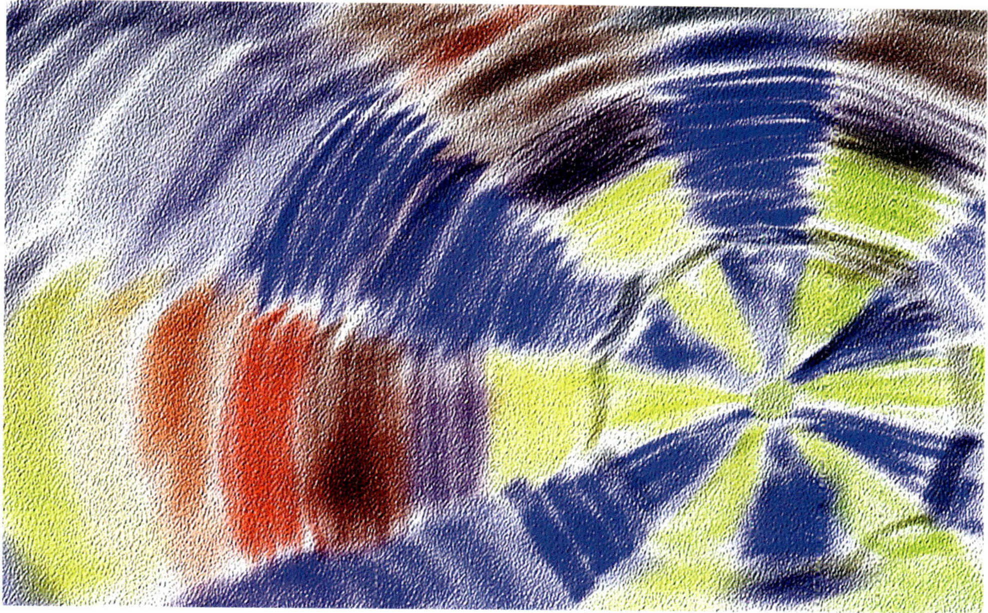

Figure 5.50 Balloon canopy

The Art Marker was used for this picture, which gave a rough unfinished look but with quite a lot of impact. The brush was on the default settings but with the Clone Color option selected. Brush sizes were between 8.0 and 24.0 and opacity 10%.

The original photograph of the balloon canopy was shot from inside the balloon while it was being inflated. Once the first stage of the clone copy was finished, as shown in Figure 5.52, a surface texture was added based on the paper pattern, which was Basic Paper.

Another layer of texture was applied, this time based on the image luminance.

The textures added to the overall appearance of the finished picture and helped to harmonize together the brush strokes.

The procedure for adding surface textures is covered in Chapter 10.

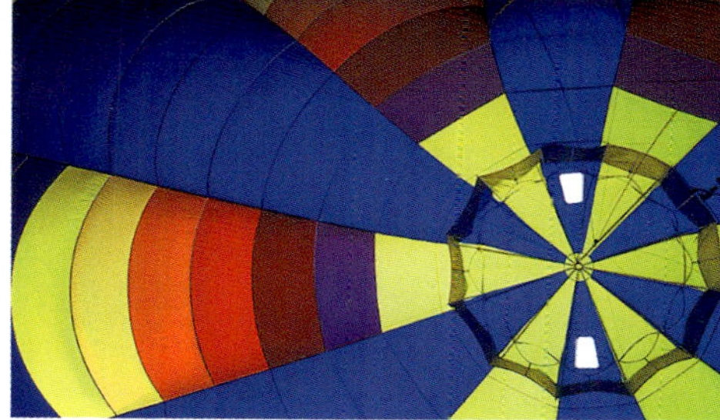

Figure 5.51 Original photograph

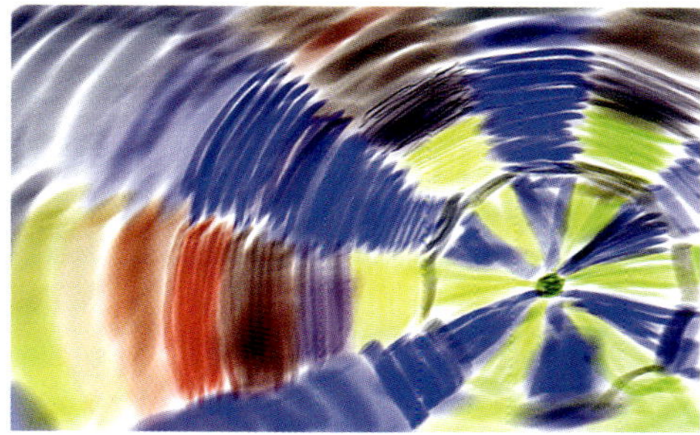

Figure 5.52 Before the texture was applied

Gouache

All the Gouache brushes have a very pronounced brush stroke and several have three-dimensional depth.

The first few examples below use an airbrush style and spray paint in the direction that the stylus is angled.

Most of the brushes use the Clone Color option, but the Opaque Smooth brush can also change the Method to Cloning and it is shown below in that mode using the Smooth Handmade Paper.

The Wet Gouache Round brush smears the picture in a style reminiscent of watercolor.

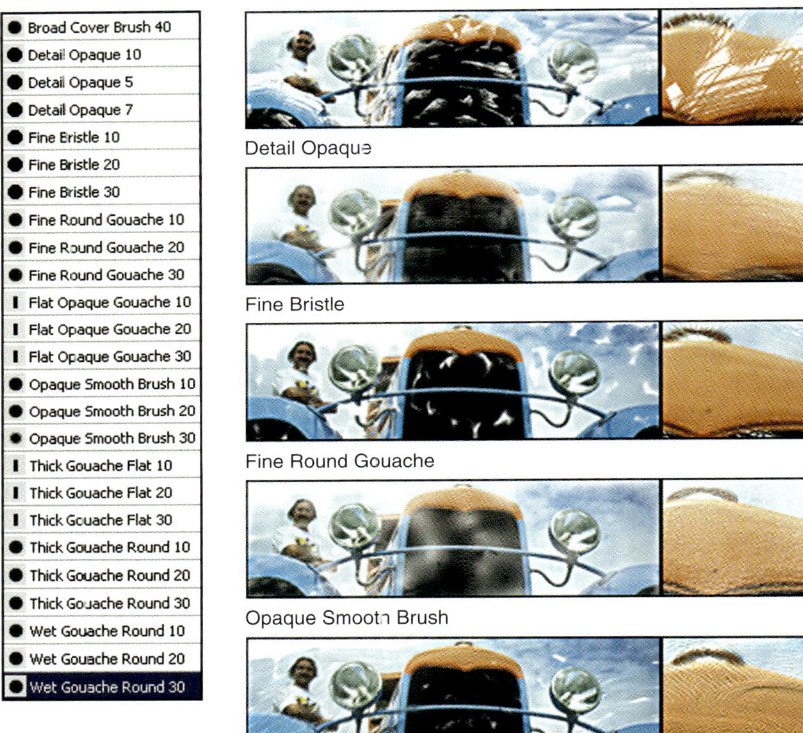

Detail Opaque

Fine Bristle

Fine Round Gouache

Opaque Smooth Brush

Thick Gouache Flat

Thick Gouache Round

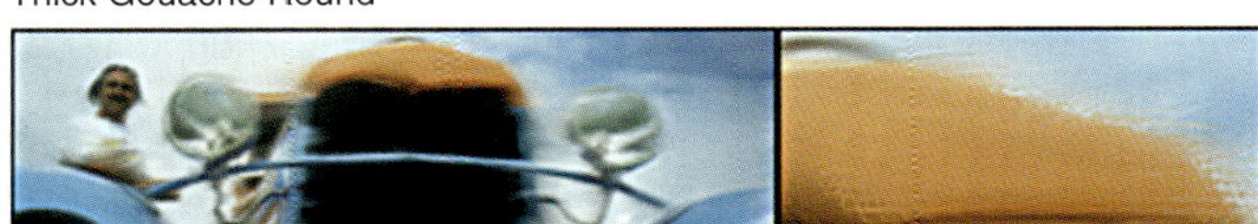

Wet Gouache Round

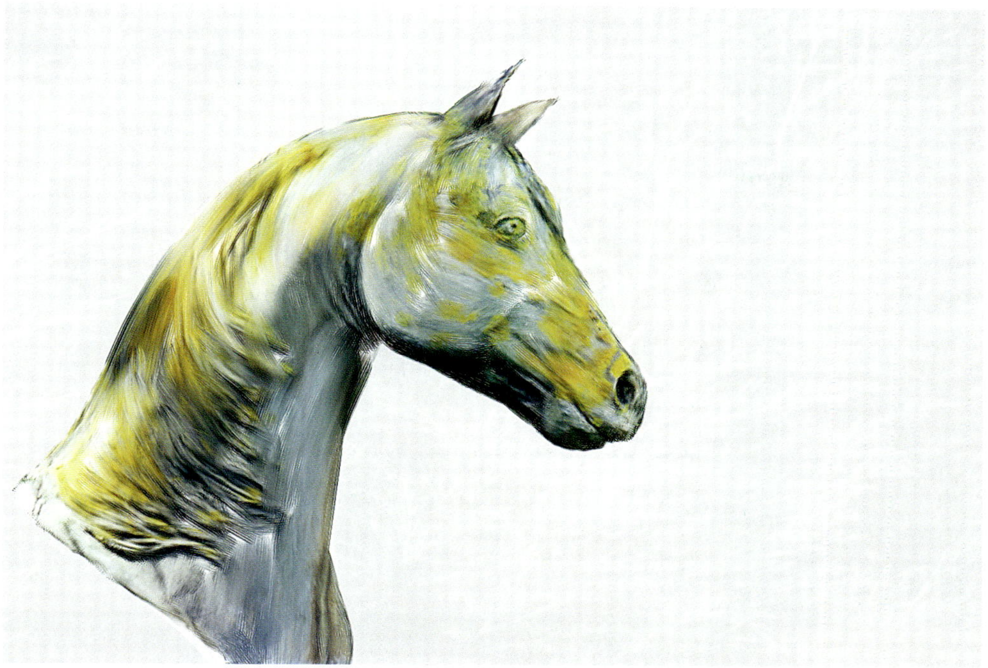

Figure 5.53 Horse statue

The Wet Gouache Round brush was used for this statue of a horse's head. The brush size was 30.0 initially then 10.0 for the more detailed areas, with the opacity at 100% for most of the time.

Only the statue was cloned and not the background, as the color was too strong and distracting.

When the head was finished, the original image was copied and pasted into the cloned copy on the top of the layer stack.

The canvas was then copied and moved to the top of the layer stack and the Layer Composite method was changed to Gell, which removed the white around the head.

Finally, the opacity of the layer underneath was reduced to just 11% to provide this very light background with just a hint of the original trees.

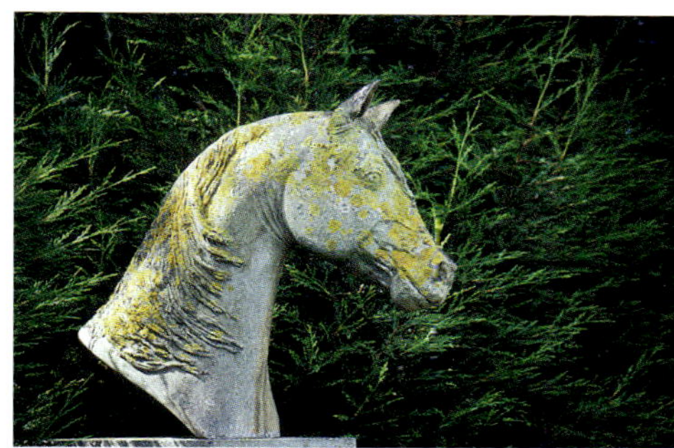

Figure 5.54 Original photograph

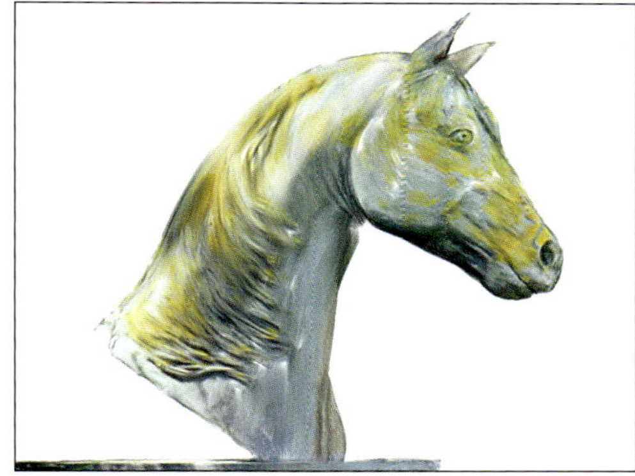

Figure 5.55 Before the background was added

Image Hoze

The Image Hoze is quite unlike any other brush category as it cannot make clones or paint pictures and does not resemble any traditional artist's tool.

What it does is to spray out images which have previously been stored in the Image Hoze nozzle. There are many nozzles in Painter to choose from and some samples from the libraries that come with the program are shown below.

What is also very interesting is the ability to make Image Hoze nozzles from your own images. It is certainly a tool to explore and have fun with.

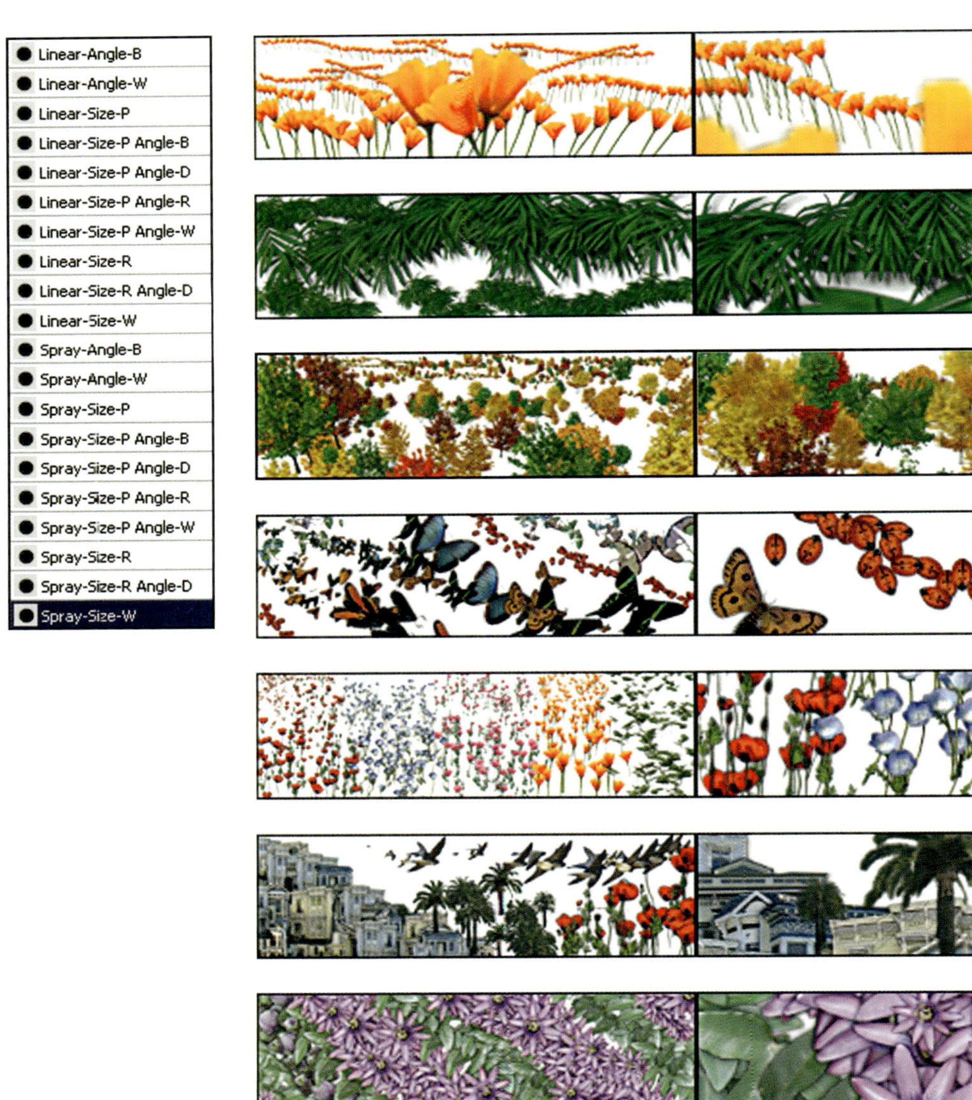

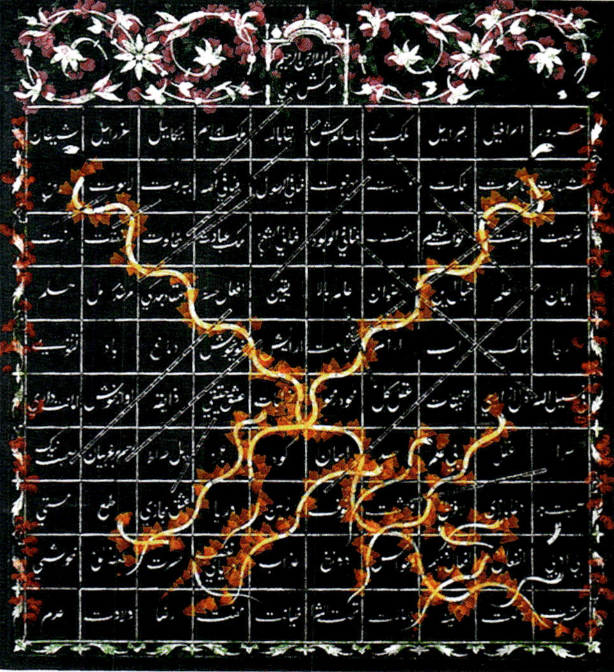

Figure 5.56 Snakes and ladders

Several Image Hoze nozzles have been applied over a photograph of a very old snakes and ladders board game.

The brush variants listed for this category refer to the manner in which the images are put on the paper, in lines or sprays and in what order.

To access the images to be sprayed, click on the bottom right icon in the Toolbox and select the nozzle required. Image Hoze pictures can be used to make abstract patterns, as the pictures below illustrate.

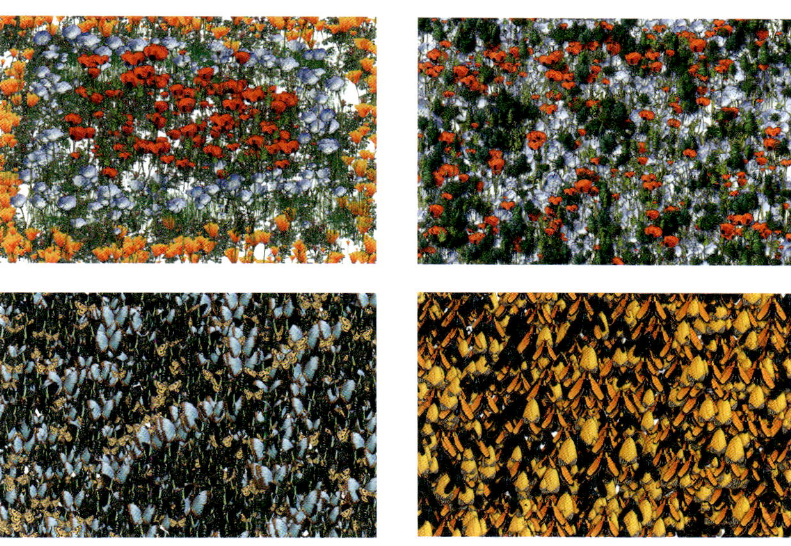

Impasto

Impasto is both the name given to this group of brushes and also the name of the style used for many of the other brushes, particularly in the Acrylics and Oils categories.

The Impasto effect is based upon the traditional technique of painting with a very thick paint to create the impression of depth.

Painter recreates the look of Impasto by using lighting effects to create a three-dimensional impression, which is applied as the brush stroke is made.

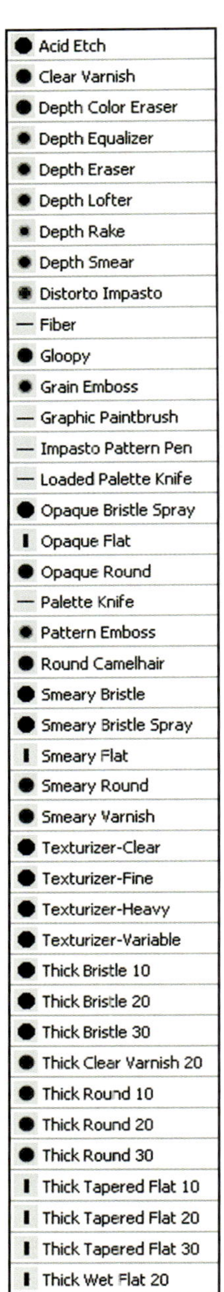

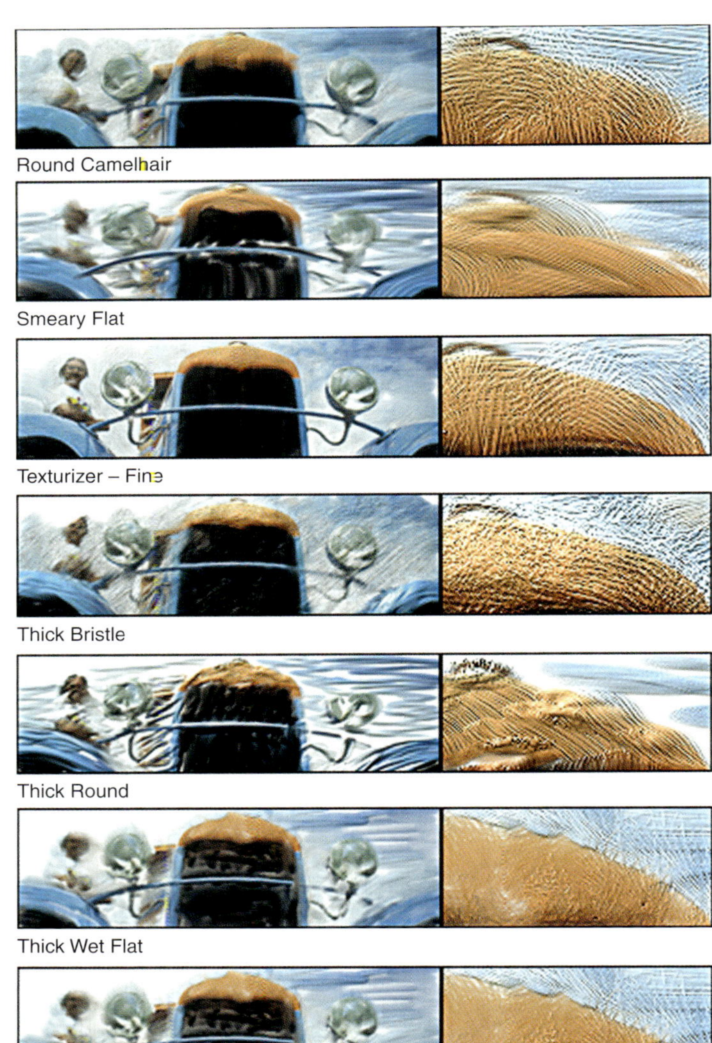

Round Camelhair

Smeary Flat

Texturizer – Fine

Thick Bristle

Thick Round

Thick Wet Flat

Wet Bristle

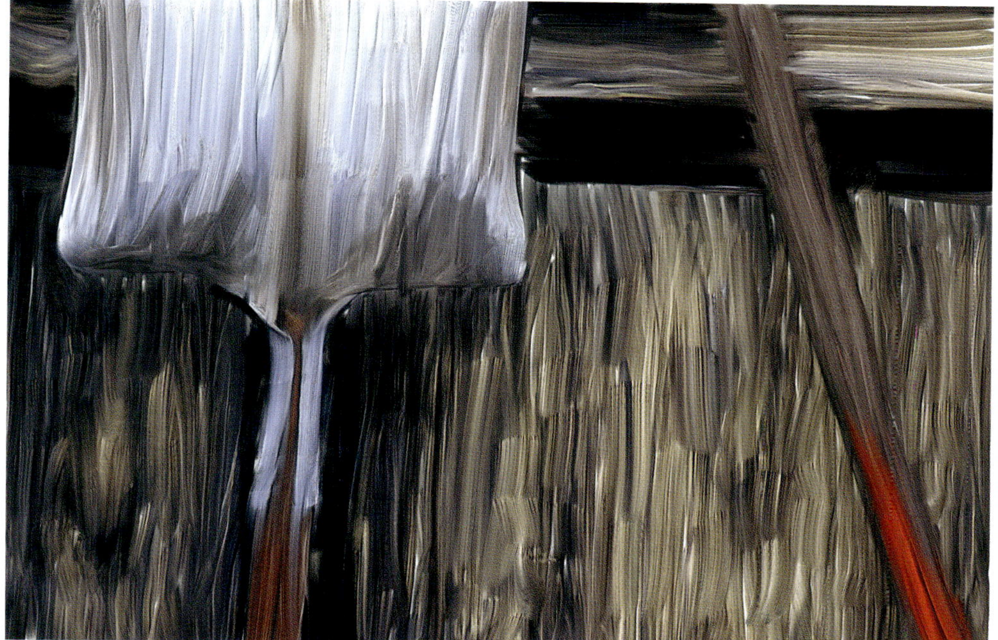

Figure 5.57 Shovel

This old shovel and another tool were hanging on the side of an old boat and I liked the contrast between the metal and the wood.

The Smeary Flat brush was chosen for the clone picture to emphasize the textures of the wood and metal. The brush sizes were between 20.0 and 50.0 and opacity 63%. The Clone Color option was ticked in the Colors palette.

One useful technique is the ability to turn the canvas around to make it easier to paint in a particular direction. In this case I wanted to paint downwards to go with the wood grain, but that way the flat brush was being used on its short edge while I wanted to use the wide edge.

With a traditional canvas you can just turn it around, so you will not be surprised that Painter also allows you to do this. Click and hold the hand symbol in the Toolbox until the circular symbol appears. Click into the picture and drag until the canvas is in the position where it is most convenient to use and continue painting.

To revert to the normal upright position, simply double-click in the picture.

You may also notice that the brush strokes appear different. That is to be expected, as you are now painting using the side of the brush and the brush strokes reflect that.

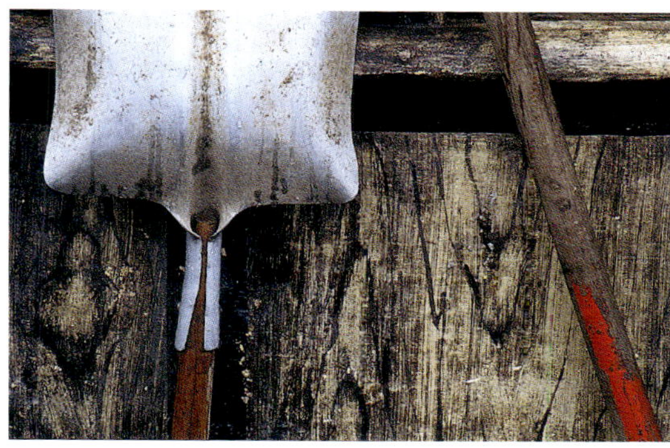

Figure 5.58 Original photograph

Liquid Ink

Liquid Ink is a large group of brushes which replicate the use of ink-based artist's materials. The ink flows very fast, covers the paper quickly and has a graphic appearance.

All Liquid Ink brushes use a special layer and a new Liquid Ink layer is created automatically when you use one of the brushes.

The Liquid Ink section in the Brush Creator has many controls for adjusting the brushes, in particular the amount of ink. If this slider is very high the inks spills over the paper in pools.

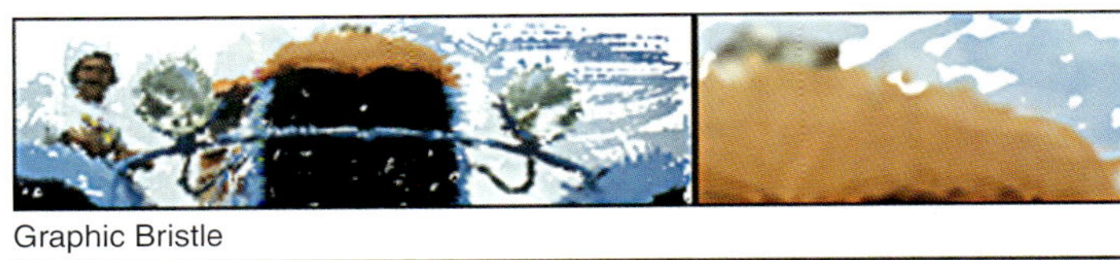
Graphic Bristle

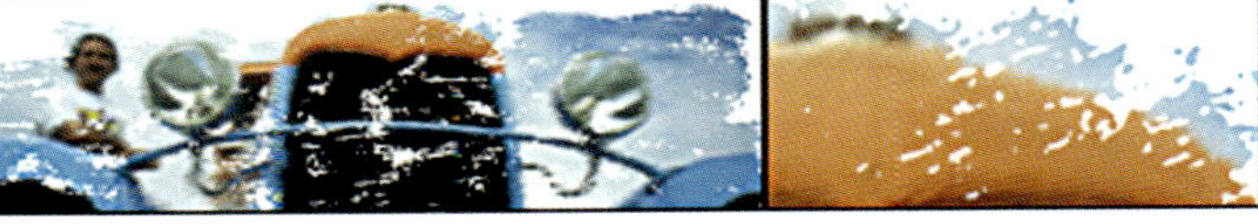
Graphic Camel

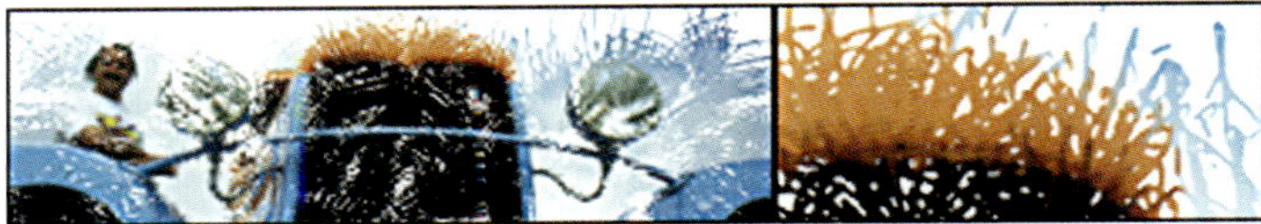
Sparse Bristle

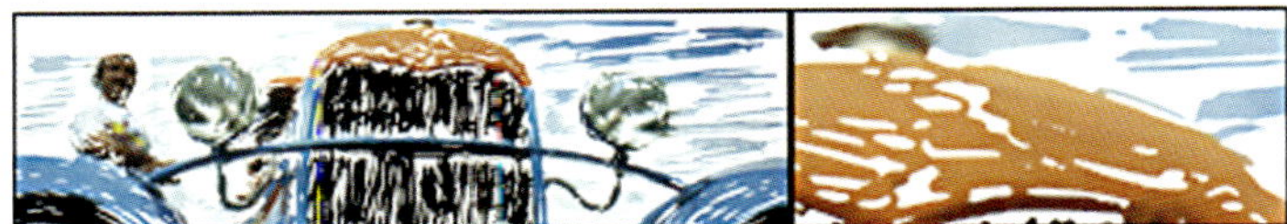
Sparse Camel

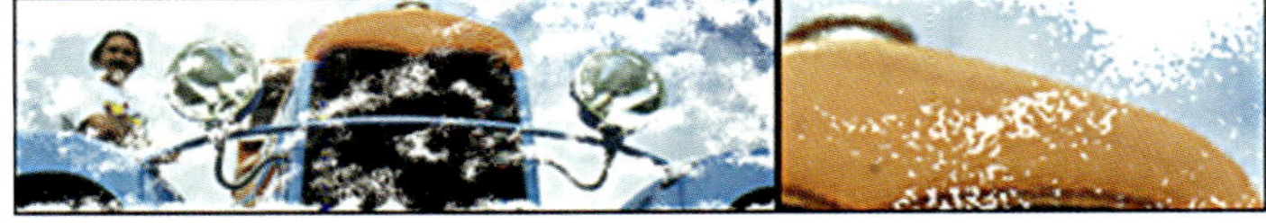
Velocity Airbrush

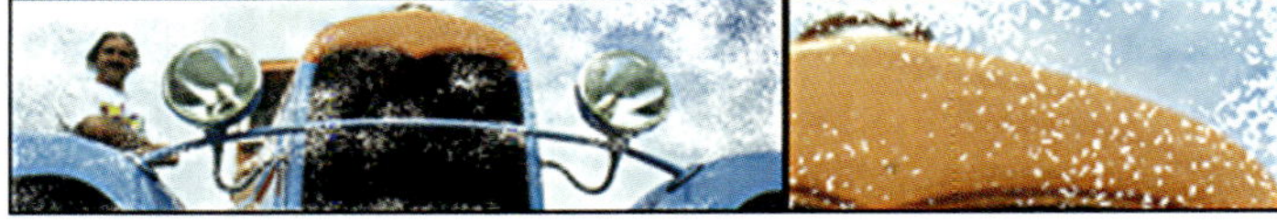
Velocity Sketcher

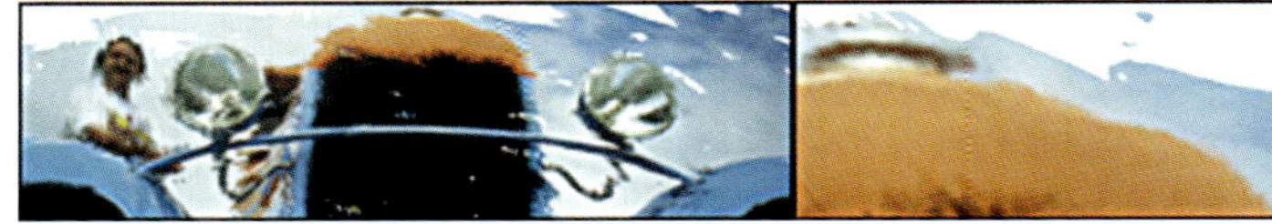
Sparse Flat

- Airbrush
- Airbrush Resist
- Calligraphic Flat
- Calligraphic Flat 15
- Clumpy Ink 4
- Coarse Airbrush
- Coarse Airbrush Resist
- Coarse Bristle
- Coarse Bristle Resist
- Coarse Camel
- Coarse Camel Resist
- Coarse Flat
- Coarse Flat Resist
- Depth Bristle
- Depth Camel
- Depth Flat
- Drops of Ink 4
- Dry Bristle
- Dry Camel
- Dry Flat
- Eraser
- Fine Point
- Fine Point Eraser
- Graphic Bristle
- Graphic Bristle Resist
- Graphic Camel
- Graphic Camel Resist
- Graphic Flat
- Graphic Flat Resist
- Pointed Flat
- Serrated Knife
- Smooth Bristle
- Smooth Bristle Resist
- Smooth Camel
- Smooth Camel Resist
- Smooth Flat
- Smooth Flat Resist
- Smooth Knife
- Smooth Rake
- Smooth Round Nib
- Smooth Thick Bristle 12
- Smooth Thick Flat 12
- Smooth Thick Round 12
- Soften Color
- Soften Edges
- Soften Edges and Color
- Sparse Bristle
- Sparse Bristle Resist
- Sparse Camel
- Sparse Camel Resist
- Sparse Flat
- Sparse Flat Resist
- Tapered Bristle 15
- Tapered Thick Bristle
- Thick Bristle
- Velocity Airbrush
- Velocity Sketcher

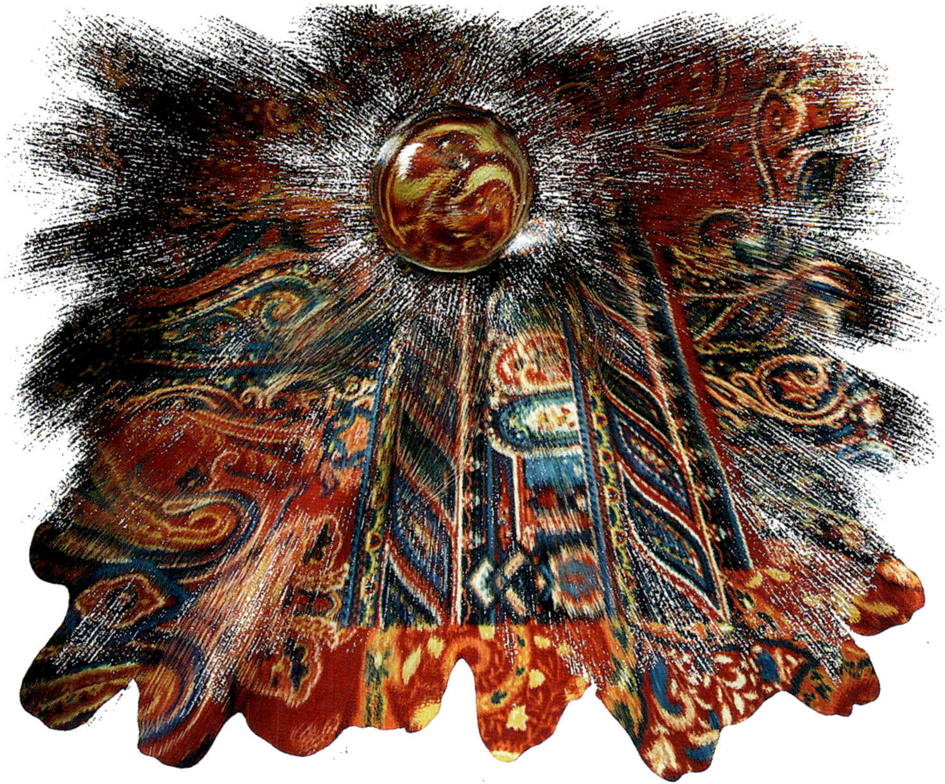

Figure 5.59 Paperweight on colored cloth

This paperweight on a strongly patterned cloth was painted with the Graphic Camel Liquid Ink brush, brush size 66.0, opacity 5%. This brush gives a different result depending on whether the brush strokes are fast or slow.

The brush size was reduced when painting the paperweight in order to give it more clarity.

In order to break areas up where the picture had become too dense, white streaks were painted using the Sparse Bristle brush, brush size 84.0, opacity 1%, volume 6%.

Finally, the Soften Edges and the Soften Edges and Color brushes were used on the bottom edges of the picture to create the impression of pooled ink.

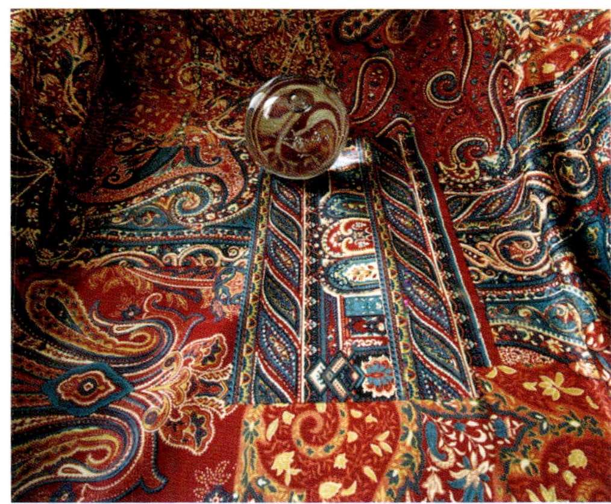

Figure 5.60 Original photograph

Oil Pastels

The brushes in the Oil Pastel category all use a very loose chunky style of applying paint, but when the brush size is reduced to a small size the detail can be brought back into the picture.

Oil Pastel brushes will show paper texture if the opacity and grain sliders are reduced considerably. Compare the two examples of the Chunky Oil Pastel shown below, the default setting at the top and the reduced grain setting at the bottom.

Some brushes will use the Cloning Method and the Oil Pastel is shown in its default version below and also at the bottom of the examples using the Cloning Method. This does not show the grain at all but smears the original image.

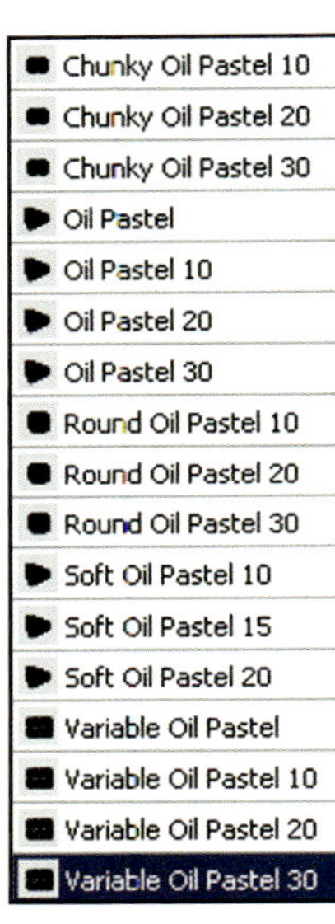

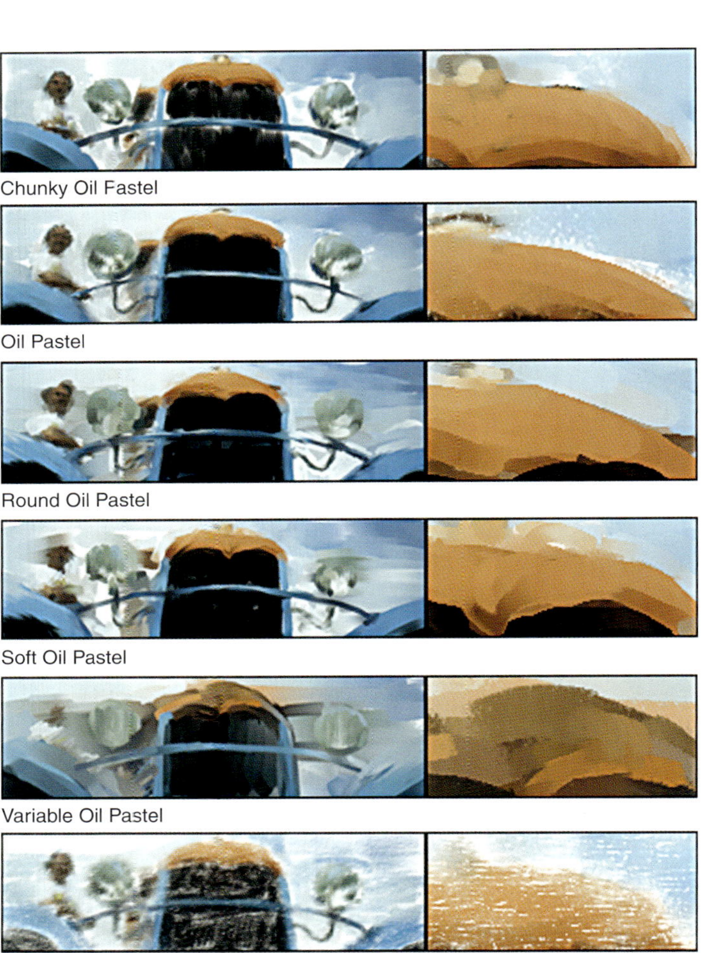

Chunky Oil Fastel

Oil Pastel

Round Oil Pastel

Soft Oil Pastel

Variable Oil Pastel

Chunky Oil Pastel with grain

Oil Pastel – Cloning Method

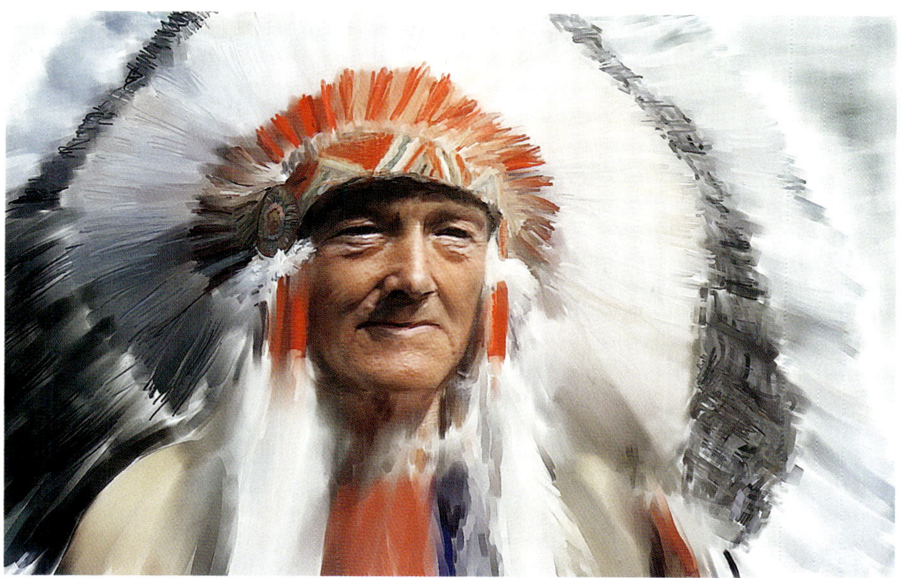

Figure 5.61 The chief

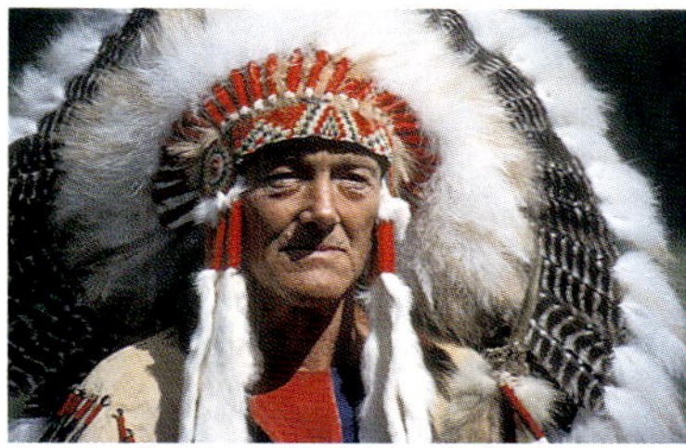

Figure 5.62 Original photograph

A Variable Oil Pastel was used to make a clone of this photograph of a man with a splendid feather head-dress.

The first step was to roughly block out the main shapes with brush size 30.0 and opacity 100%.

The same brush and one slightly larger but with reduced opacity was used to paint all over the picture, softening and merging the brush strokes together.

In stage 3, a smaller brush brought out more detail and the opacity was increased to enhance the color and contrast.

Finally, the original image was pasted back into the clone and using a layer mask some of the face was brought back to add more realism and detail.

The use of layer masks is explained in Chapter 8, which deals with all aspects of the Layers palette.

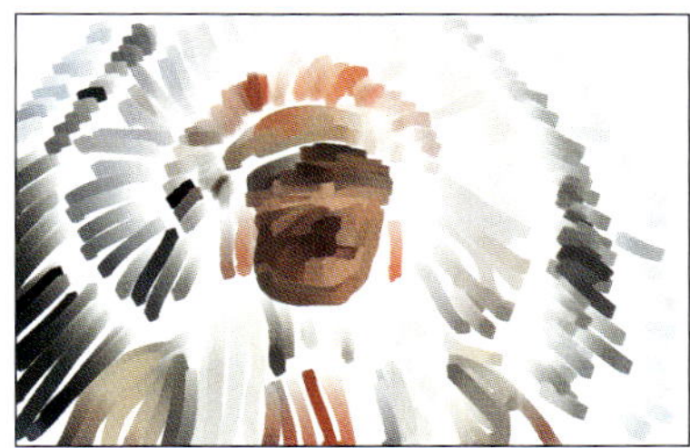

Figure 5.63 Stage 1

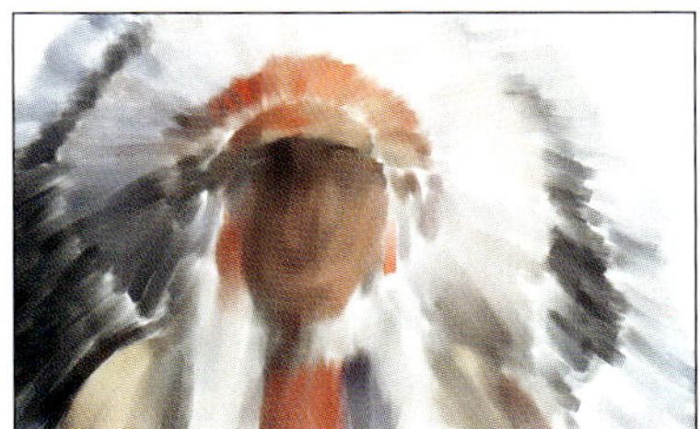

Figure 5.64 Stage 2

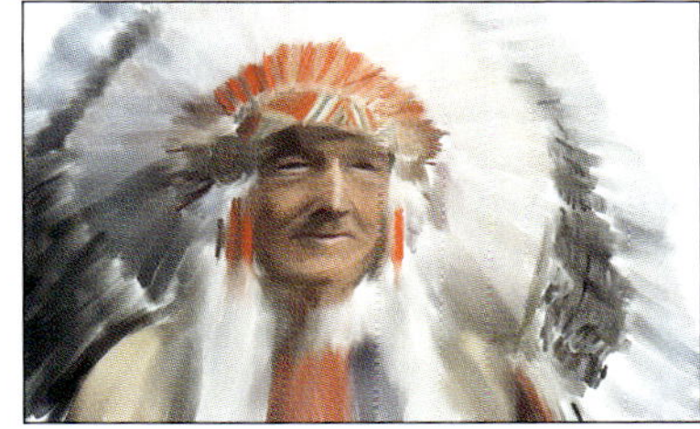

Figure 5.65 Stage 3

Oils

- Bristle Oils 20
- Bristle Oils 30
- Detail Oils Brush 10
- Detail Oils Brush 15
- Detail Oils Brush 5
- Fine Camel 10
- Fine Camel 20
- Fine Camel 30
- Fine Feathering Oils 20
- Fine Feathering Oils 30
- Fine Soft glazing 20
- Fine Soft glazing 30
- Flat Oils 10
- Flat Oils 20
- Flat Oils 30
- Flat Oils 40
- Glazing Flat 20
- Glazing Flat 30
- Glazing Round 10
- Glazing Round 20
- Glazing Round 30
- Meduim Bristle Oils 15
- Meduim Bristle Oils 25
- Opaque Bristle Spray
- Opaque Flat
- Opaque Round
- Round Camelhair
- Smeary Bristle Spray
- Smeary Flat
- Smeary Round
- Tapered Flat Oils 15
- Tapered Round Oils 15
- Thick Oil Bristle 10
- Thick Oil Bristle 20
- Thick Oil Bristle 30
- Thick Oil Flat 10
- Thick Oil Flat 20
- Thick Oil Flat 30
- Thick Wet Camel 10
- Thick Wet Camel 20
- Thick Wet Camel 30
- Thick Wet Oils 10
- Thick Wet Oils 20
- Thick Wet Oils 30
- Variable Flat
- Variable Round

None of these Oil brushes use the paper texture but nearly all have a lovely brush texture. The majority of them use the Clone Color option with just a few able to switch to the Cloning Method.

These brushes are really useful for creating a painterly look; they can be used initially as large brushes to create a textured background and then, by reducing the brush size, more detail can be brought into the clone picture.

The Glazing Round brush has a fine gentle texture which is unusual in this category.

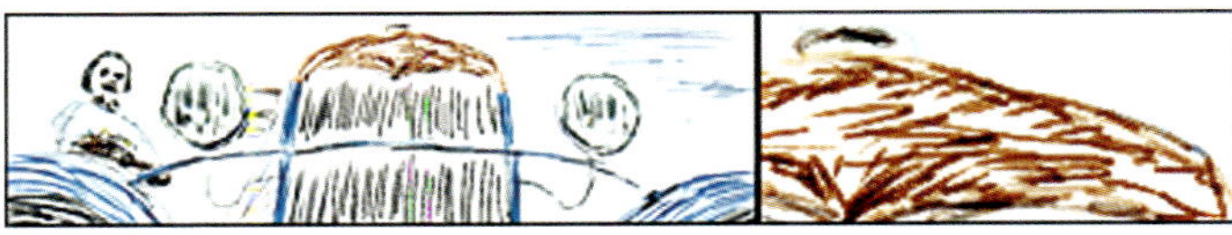

Detail Oils Brush

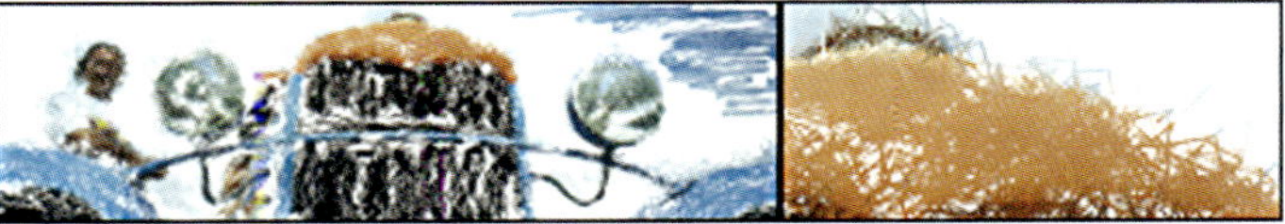

Flat Oils

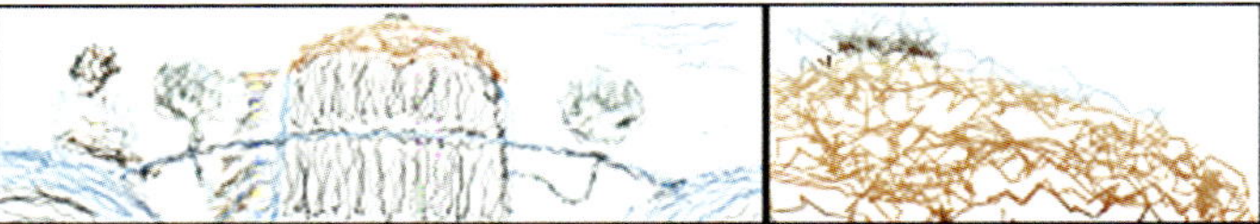

Medium Bristle Oils

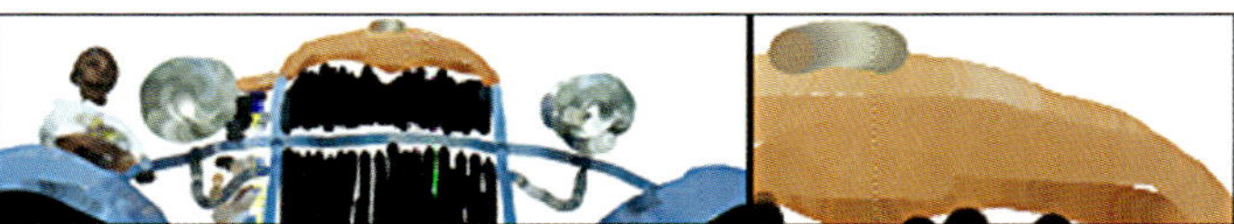

Glazing Round

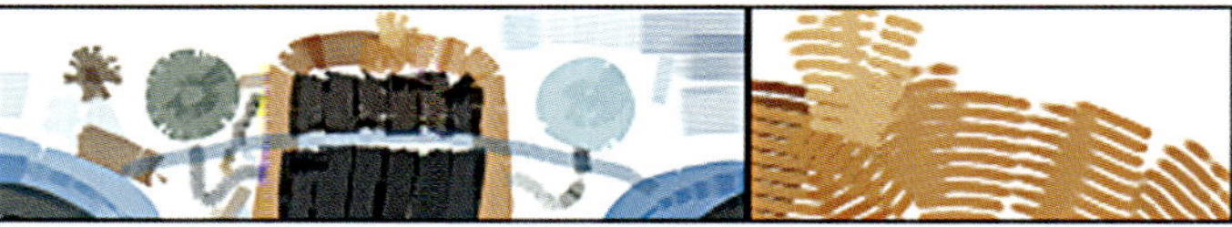

Thick Oil Bristle

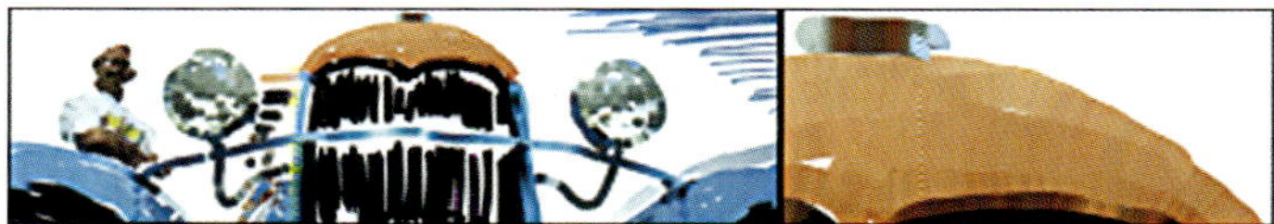

Thick Wet Camel

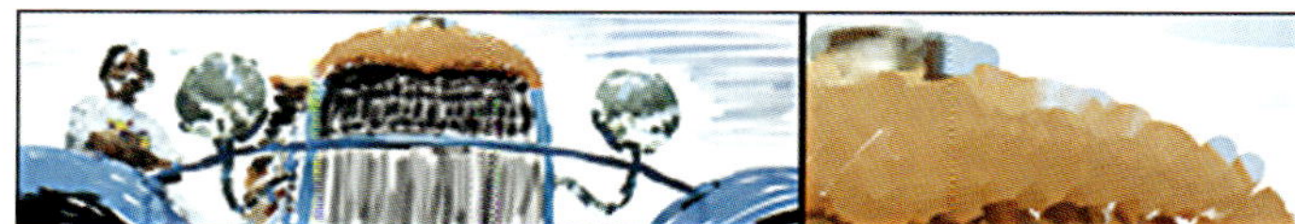

Thick Wet Oils

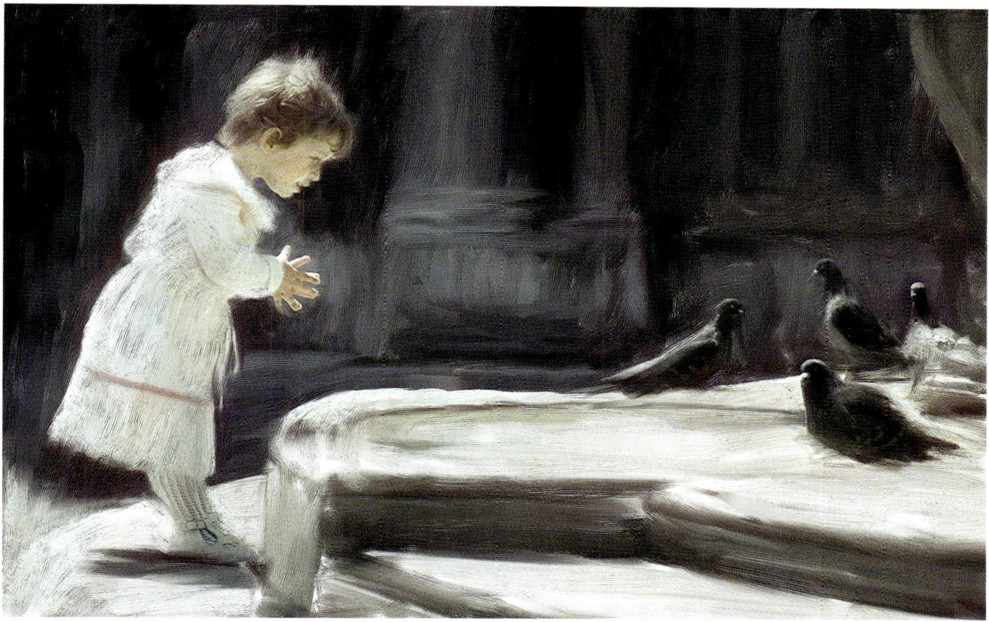

Figure 5.66 Hello there!

This charming scene of a child watching the pigeons bathing in the fountain was photographed in Venice and I loved the delight that showed in her face and in the way her hands were clasped together.

The Thick Wet Oils brush was used to block in the main areas, then the Thick Wet Camel to bring in more detail and texture.

It was quite difficult to get good detail into the face and hands of the child, so when the clone was finished the original was pasted back into the clone copy.

A layer mask (see Chapter 8 on how to apply and use layer masks) hid most of the original picture, and just the face and hands were revealed. This gave the clarity and definition that the picture needed.

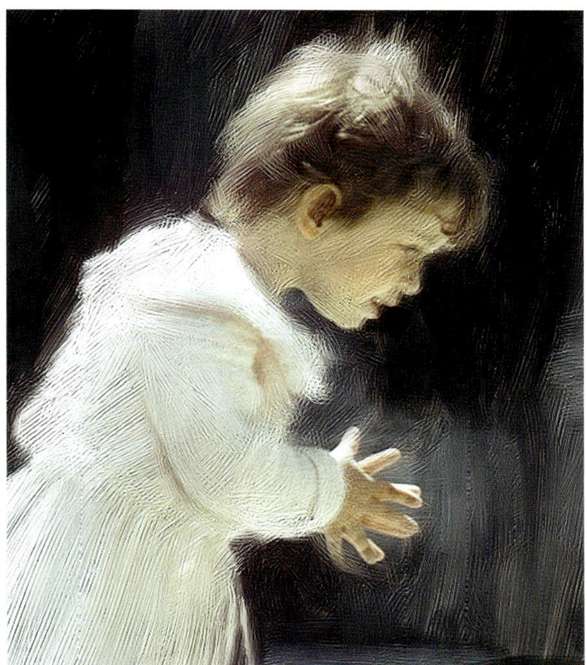

Figure 5.67 Detail of finished picture

Palette Knives

The Palette Knife brushes are not the easiest to use as clone brushes as they jump around and are quite difficult to control. The Loaded Palette Knife shown below is a good example. The Tiny Palette Knifes are easier to handle, probably because they are so much smaller.

Another way of using these brushes is to work directly on the original and not use the Cloning option. The brushes then push the picture around like the Blenders and this can be very successful with the right picture. The examples below for the Subtle Palette Knife and Tiny Subtle Knife have both been used directly upon the image.

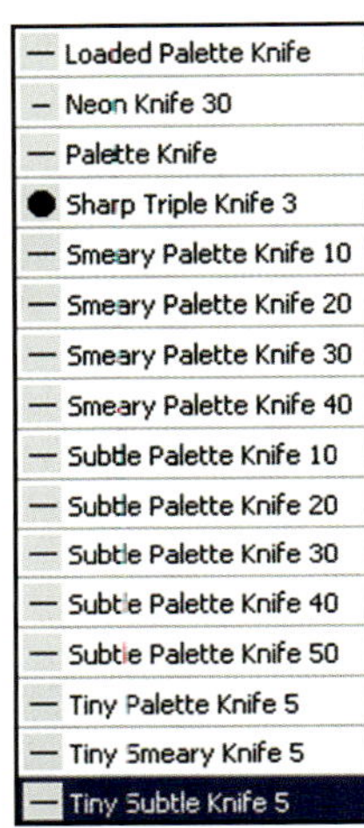

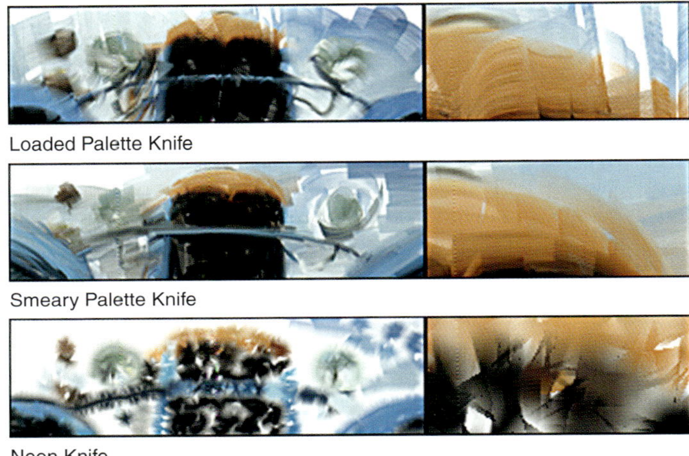

Loaded Palette Knife

Smeary Palette Knife

Neon Knife

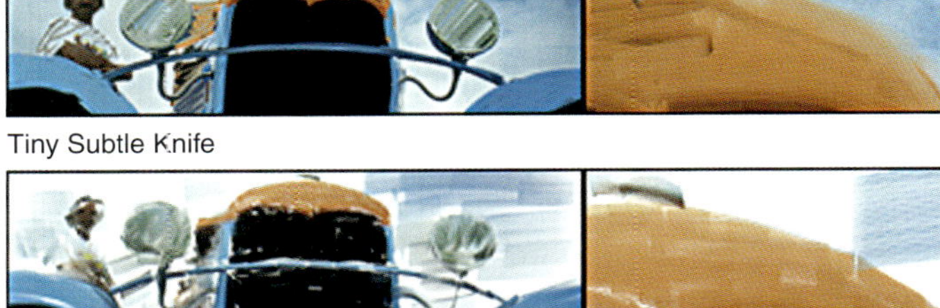

Tiny Subtle Knife

Tiny Smeary Knife

Subtle Palette Knife

Tiny Palette Knife

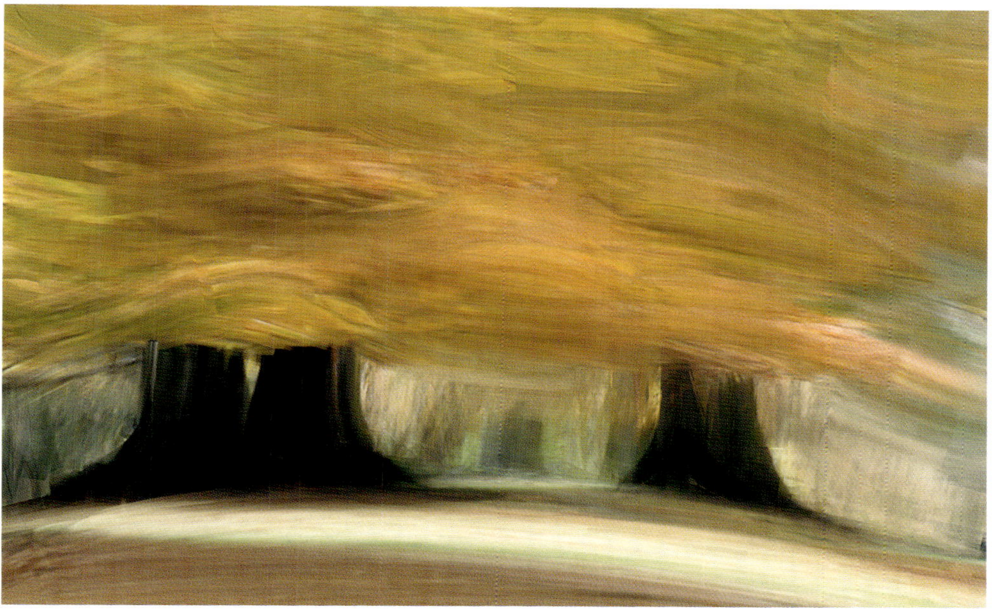

Figure 5.68 Autumn gales

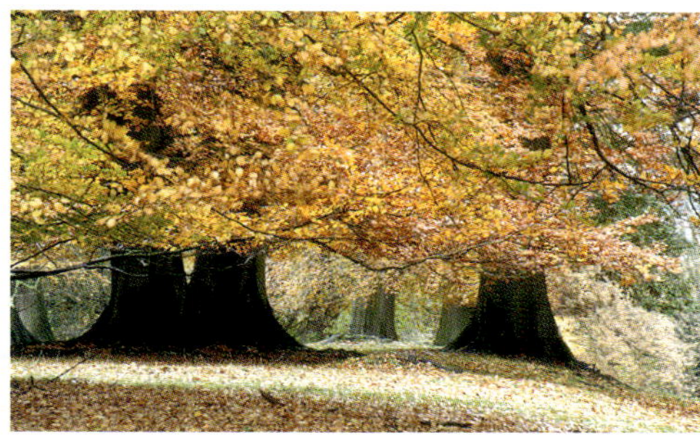

Figure 5.69 Original photograph

The Subtle Palette Knife was used on these trees in their autumn colors; the brush was used on a clone copy but with the image not cleared. The brush smeared the photograph as it recreated the picture, treating the imagery as though it was wet paint.

The brush size was mainly 40.0 and opacity 77.0%. It was necessary to rotate the photograph in order to have the knife painting in the desired direction.

These brushes work in a similar manner to the Blender brushes and Figure 5.70 shows an alternative version using the Grainy Blender brush. This is actually a much easier brush to use; the brush size was 66.60 and opacity 80%.

It's fun doing this sort of picture. The brush is fast to use, and you can easily make several versions and decide later which is the better one.

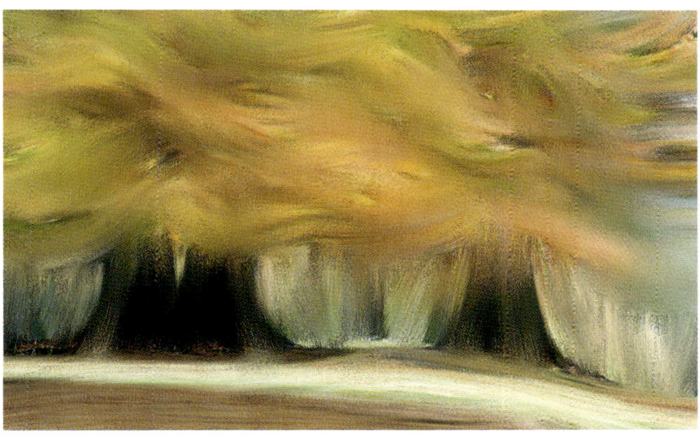

Figure 5.70 Another version made with a Blender brush

Pastels

The Pastel brush category has a rather loose smeary finish when used at a large brush size, but more detail can be brought back when the brush size is reduced.

Most variants can be used in Cloning Method, but to get the distinctive pastel finish it is generally more useful to use the Clone Color option.

The Blunt Hard and the Square Hard Pastels use the paper textures very successfully without any brush modification.

The various Soft Pastels all smear the picture, some very substantially.

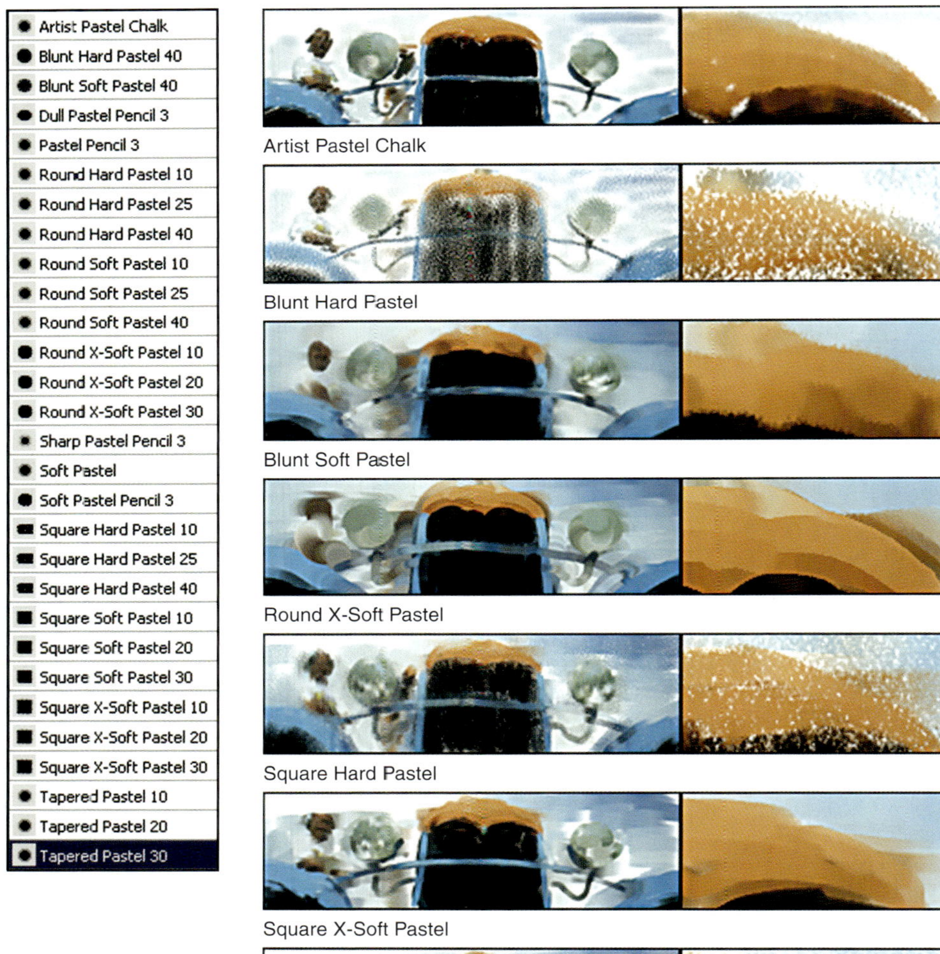

Artist Pastel Chalk

Blunt Hard Pastel

Blunt Soft Pastel

Round X-Soft Pastel

Square Hard Pastel

Square X-Soft Pastel

Tapered Pastel

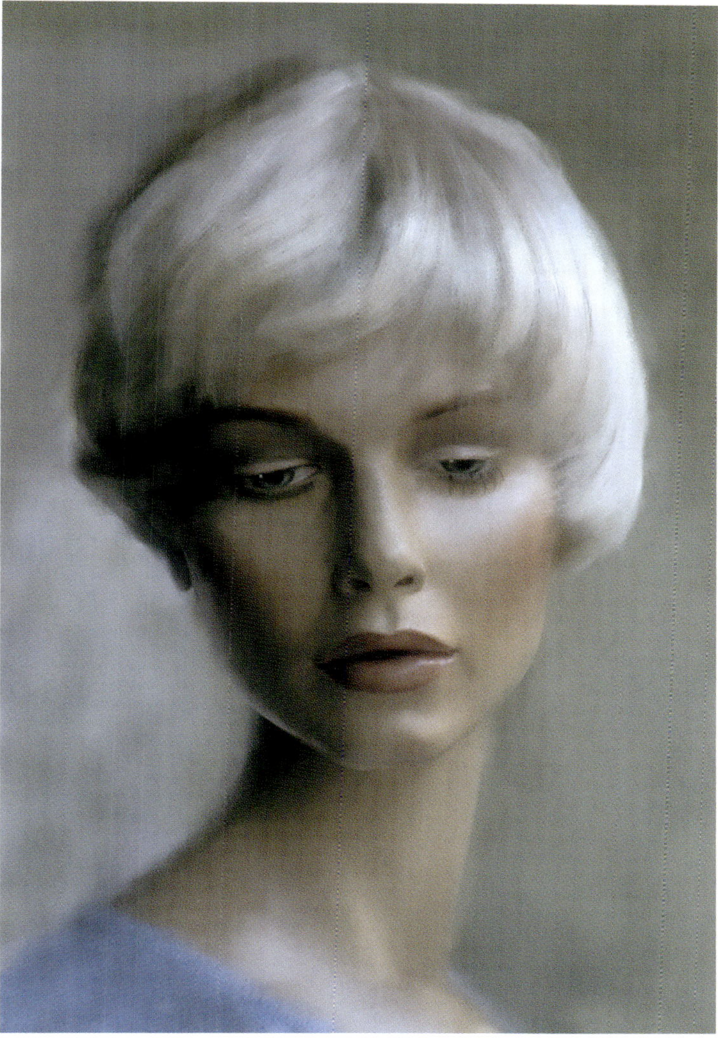

Figure 5.71 Window model

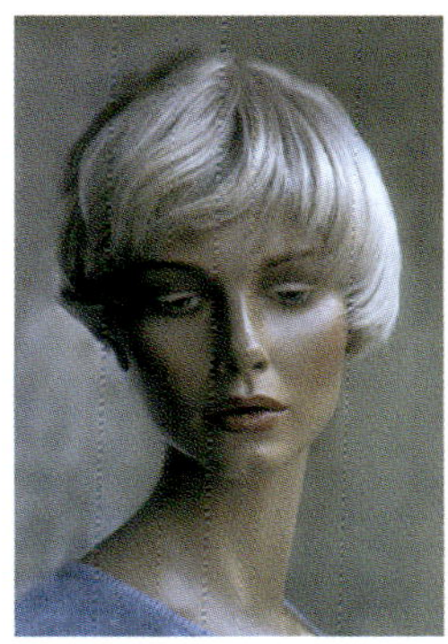

Figure 5.72 Original

A clone copy was made of the photograph of the window model and the image was not cleared. The hair, neck and shoulders were painted over with the Round Hard Pastel, brush size 40.0, opacity 100% and grain 12%.

The paper chosen was Sandy Pastel Paper, which added a fine texture to the picture and gave it the distinctive look of pastel.

The face was painted with the same pastel and a reduced opacity of 65%, which gave it a lighter and more detailed texture.

Smaller sizes and varying opacities were necessary to complete the details of the face.

Pattern Pens

Well, what are we to make of this brush category? It is very different and definitely not designed for accurate cloning.

The name of the brush category says it all: Pattern Pens are designed to make patterns out of images. Some of the brush variants can use the Cloning Method, but the result is much the same, an unusual sampling and mixing of the original picture.

The pens vary slightly. The Pattern Marker mutes the colors and gives a pastel finish, while the Pattern Pen is strident and full of bold colors. The Soft Edge and Transparent Pens both have softer and slightly veiled looks.

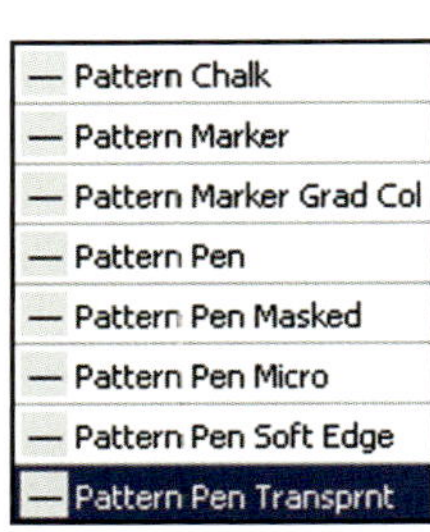

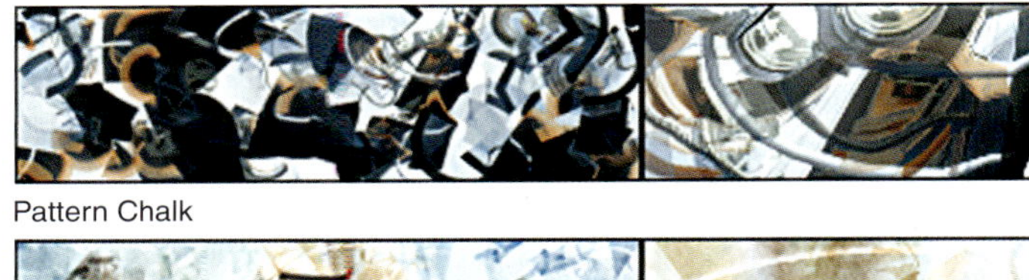

Pattern Chalk

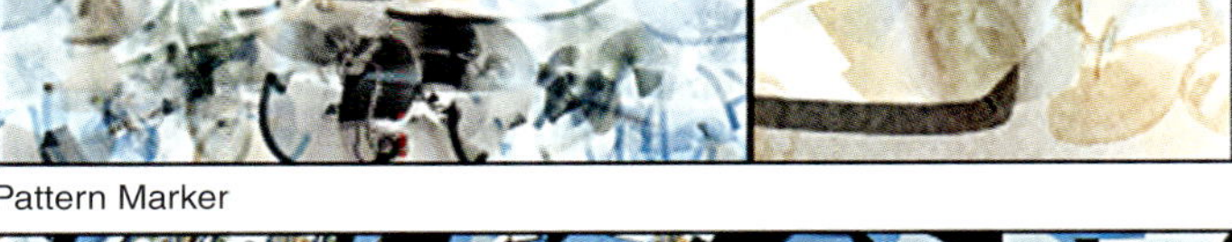

Pattern Marker

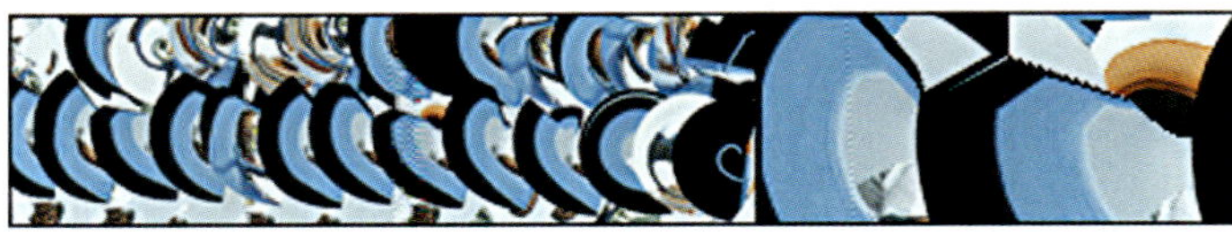

Pattern Marker Grad Color

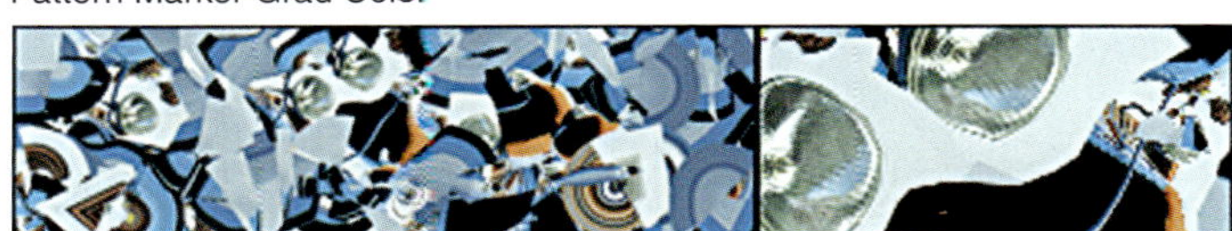

Pattern Pen

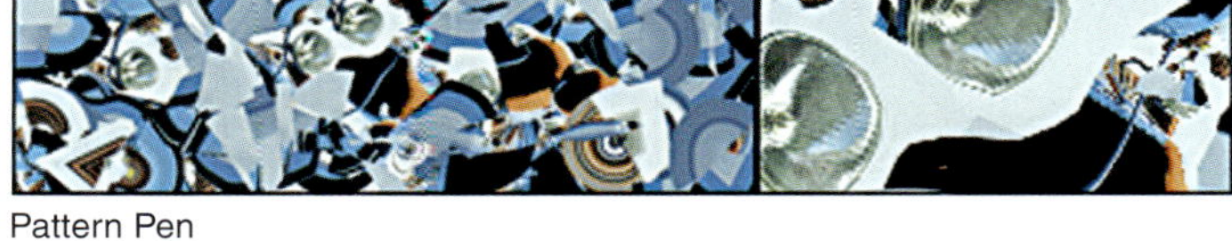

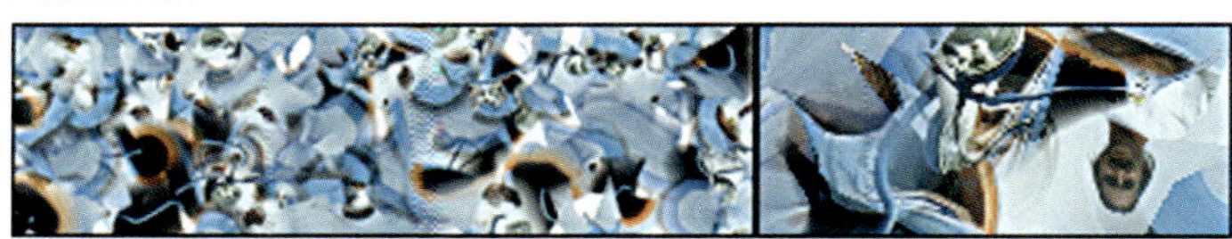

Pattern Pen Masked

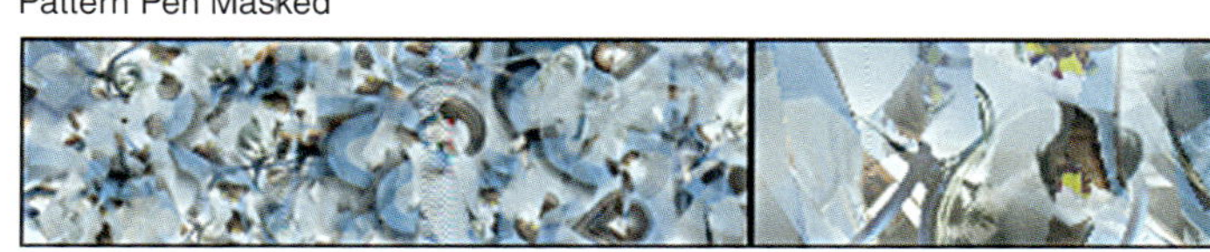

Pattern Pen Soft Edge

Pattern Pen Transparent

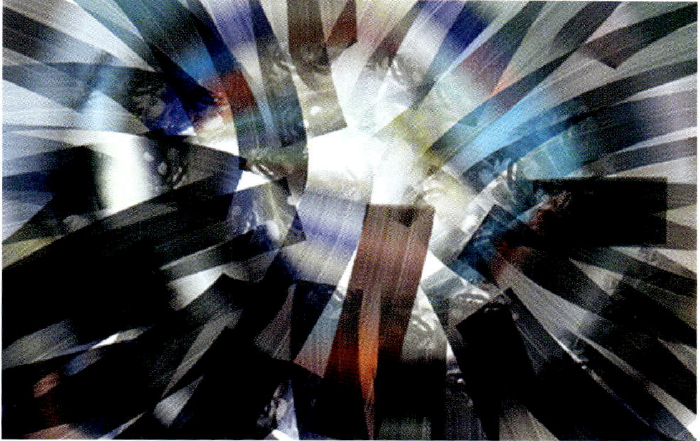

Figure 5.73 Interleaved

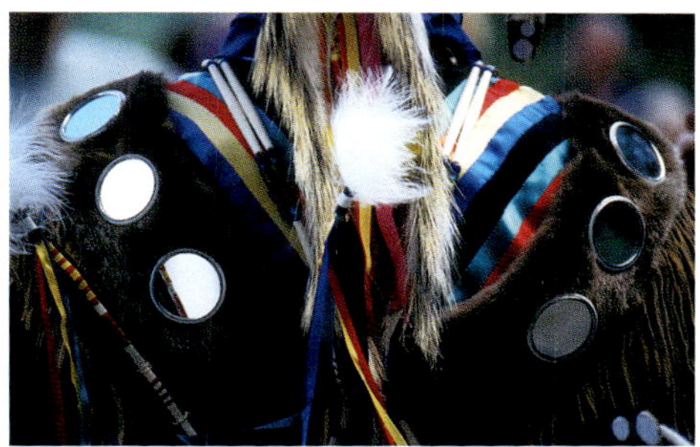

Figure 5.74 Original photograph

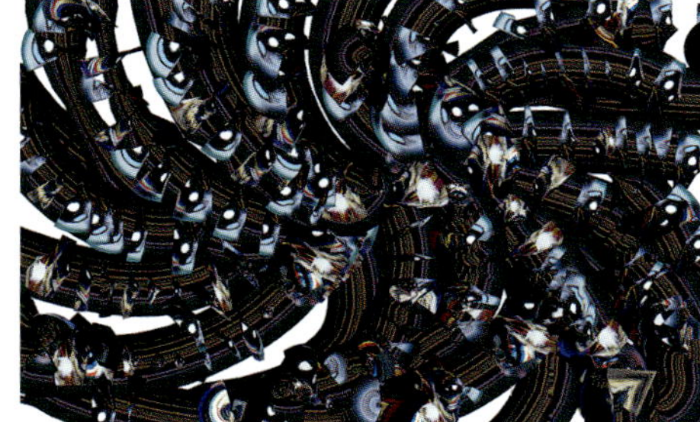

Figure 5.75 Swirl

Various brushes from the Pattern Pen category were used to make the abstract patterns on this page. Figure 5.74 shows the original photograph.

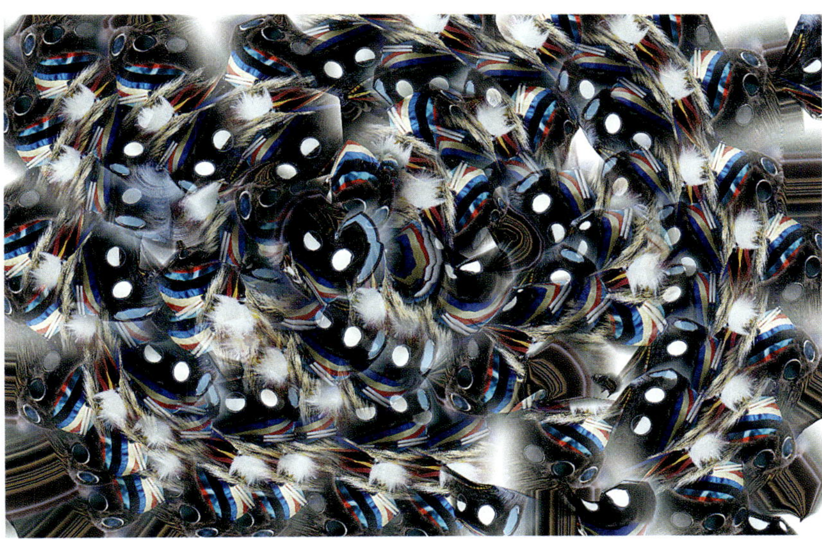

Figure 5.76 Eyes

Pencils

The Pencil brush category, not surprisingly, consists of thin brushes suitable for sketching. Here I have used them all as cloners, but they may be more successful to use as simple pencils.

Several of the variants use the Buildup Method, so they will get darker as the brush continues to paint. If you want to avoid this you could use the Grainy Cover Pencil, as this works differently.

Both the Greasy Pencil and the Oily Variable Pencil smear the image so are less accurate in making clones. All the Pencils interact well with the paper grain.

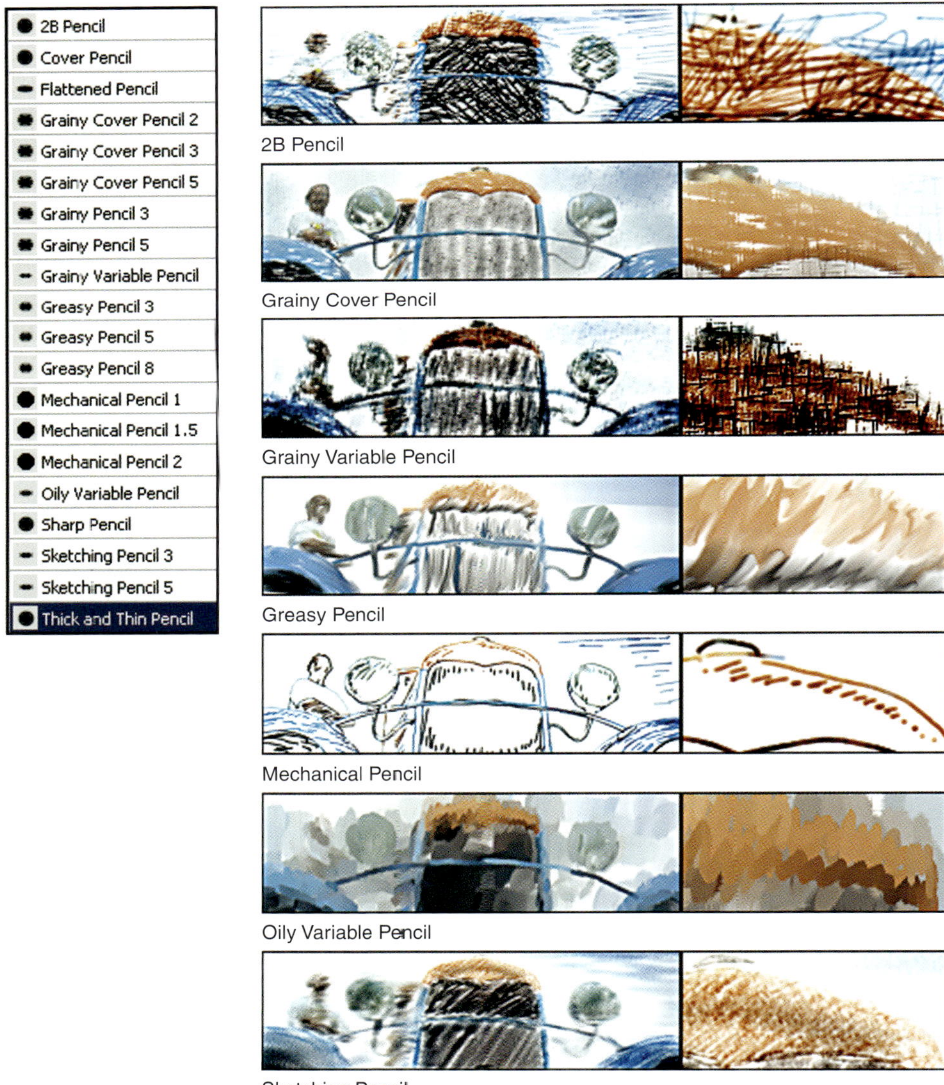

2B Pencil

Grainy Cover Pencil

Grainy Variable Pencil

Greasy Pencil

Mechanical Pencil

Oily Variable Pencil

Sketching Pencil

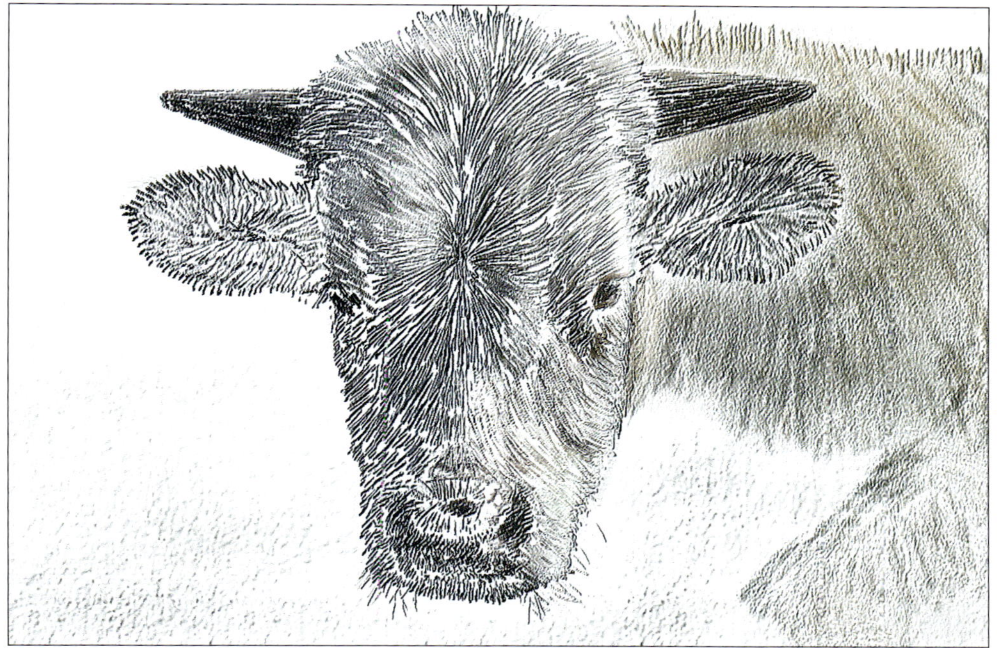

Figure 5.77 Bullock

This picture was painted with the Grainy Cover Pencil variant, the brush size was around 3.0–5.0 for most of the picture, with the opacity at 100%.

The picture was intended to look like a pencil sketch and this brush gave a hard finish to the brush strokes. The Clone Color option was used with the other settings on default.

When the head was finished a larger brush size, around 10.0, with a lower opacity of 10% was used for the body of the bullock.

Light texture was added to the bottom of the picture to give the impression of ground for the animal to lie on; this was cloned using Rough Charcoal as the paper grain.

Finally, Surface Texture was added based on the image luminance and in addition another texture using 3D brush strokes, which gave the picture more body.

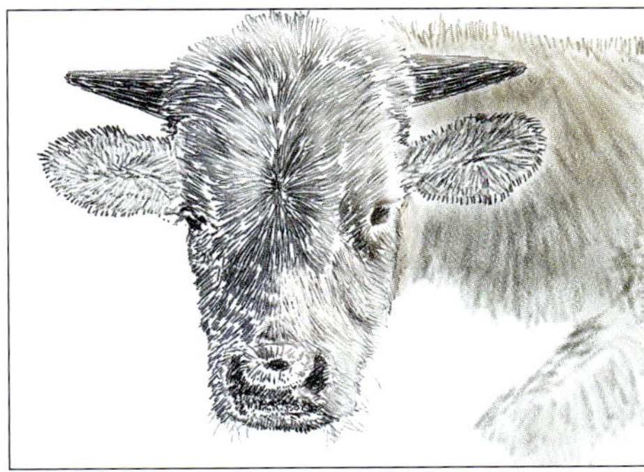

Figure 5.78

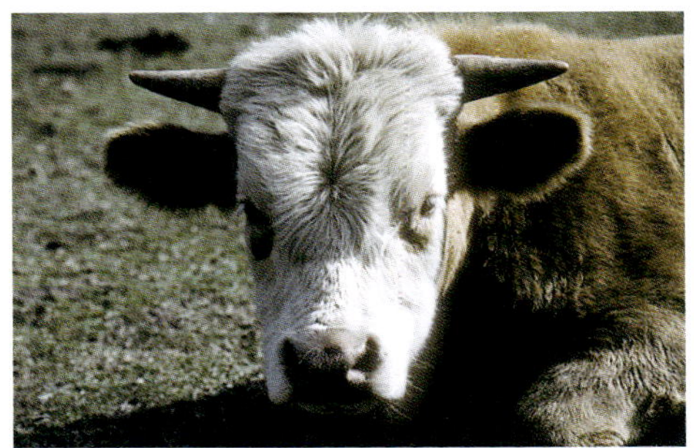

Figure 5.79 Original photograph

Pens

As you may expect, the Pens brush category includes a fair selection of thin brushes, which give a ball pen style of painting. There are, however, some rather unusual and interesting variants – the barbed wire pen, for example, which spreads random lines around the brush stroke.

The Nervous Pen is great fun; it might also be described as a drunken pen, as the brush stroke is so irregular. The Scratchboard Rake is also quite different, painting everything with multiple separate brush strokes.

Variants like the Smooth Ink Pen and the Round Tip Pen both give strong colorful strokes and smear the original clone information around to some extent.

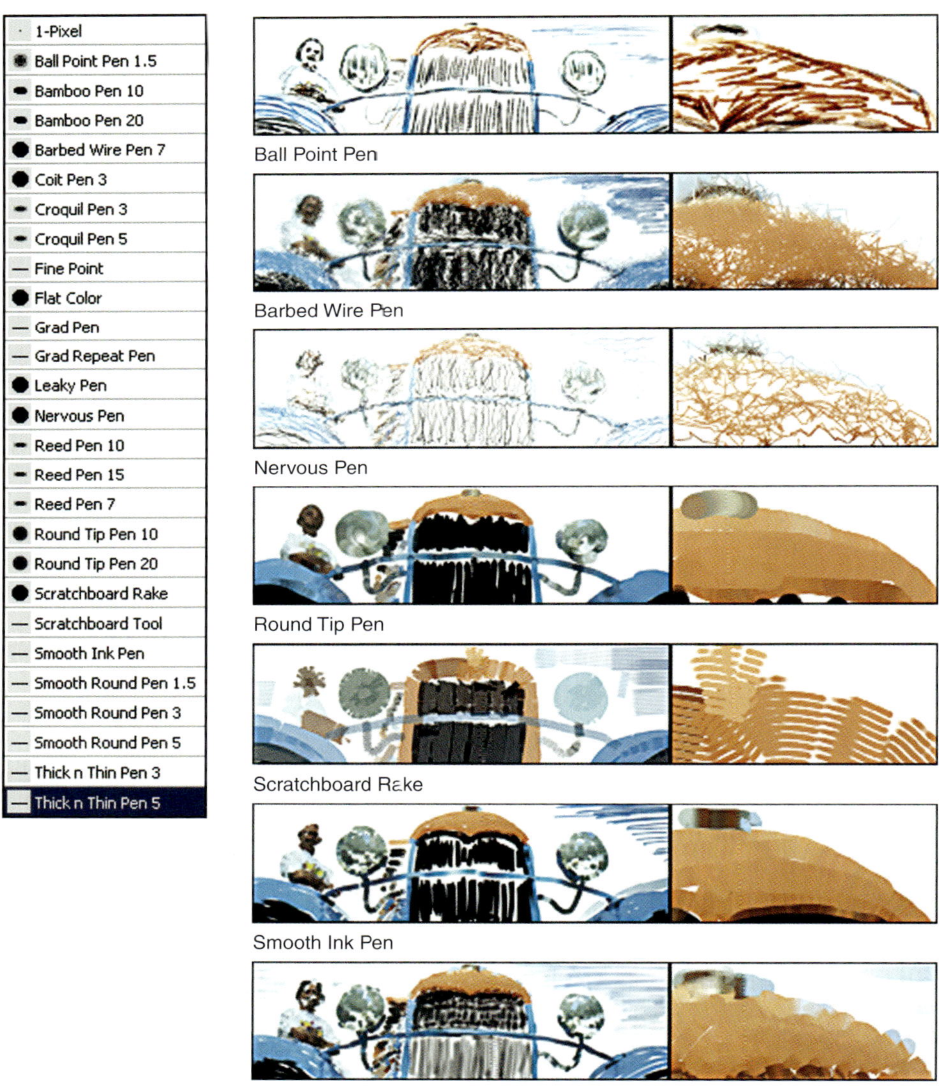

Ball Point Pen

Barbed Wire Pen

Nervous Pen

Round Tip Pen

Scratchboard Rake

Smooth Ink Pen

Thick n Thin Pen

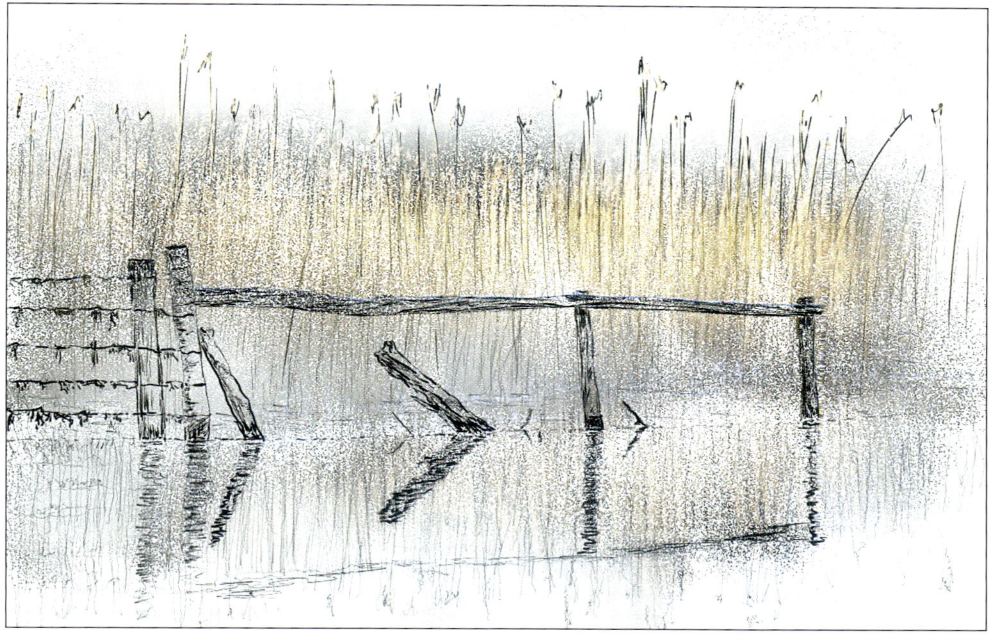

Figure 5.80 Lakeside reeds

This clone was painted with the Smooth Ink Pen. The outlines of the posts were sketched first using the Tracing Paper as a guide; the brush size was 5.0 and the opacity 100%.

The reeds at the top were painted using brush sizes of between 1.0 and 3.0, and 50% and 100% opacities.

The reflections of the reeds were made with the Nervous Pen. This was ideal as the nervous movement of the pen was perfect for indicating the subtle movement of the reflections in the water. The picture showing this stage can be seen in Figure 5.81.

To complete the picture shown in Figure 5.80, an empty layer was placed on the top of the layer stack and, using the Coarse Spray Airbrush, color was cloned back in. Some of the color was later partially removed with an eraser to keep the picture very light and delicate.

The original slide is shown in Figure 5.82.

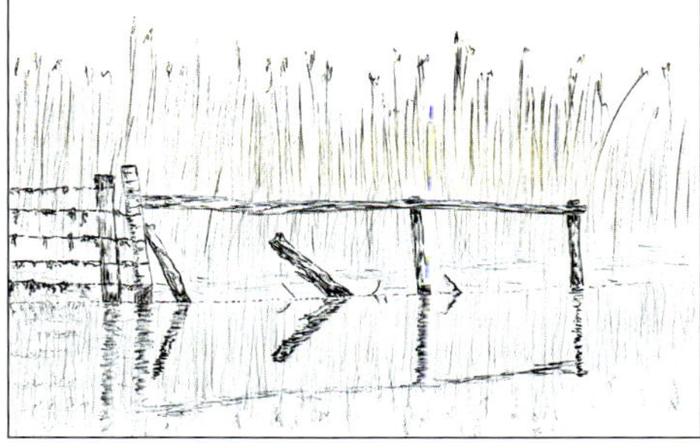

Figure 5.81 Stage 1

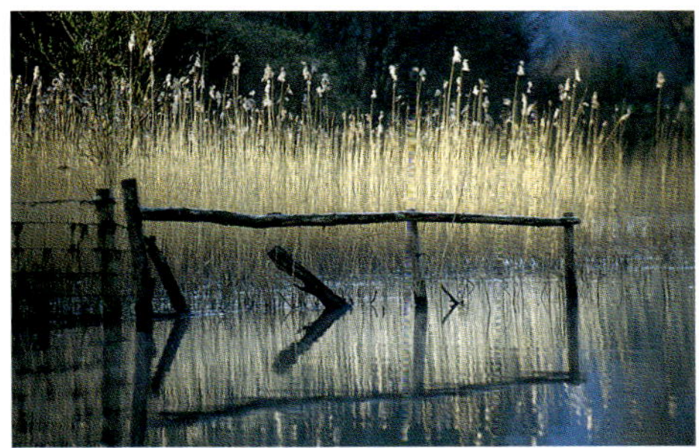

Figure 5.82 Original photograph

Photo

The Photo category of brushes is intended to give easy access to tools which photographers typically use to fine-tune their photographs. They include Sharpen, Blur, Dodge and Saturation, and are applied directly on the photograph with brushes rather than by making selections.

The Add Grain Brush is interesting as texture is copied from the Papers palette and painted directly on the photograph.

The diffusers are very similar to those in the Diffusers brush category.

In the examples below, I have been rather heavy handed to enable the result to be seen in a small picture. Normally, the effect would be done with more subtlety.

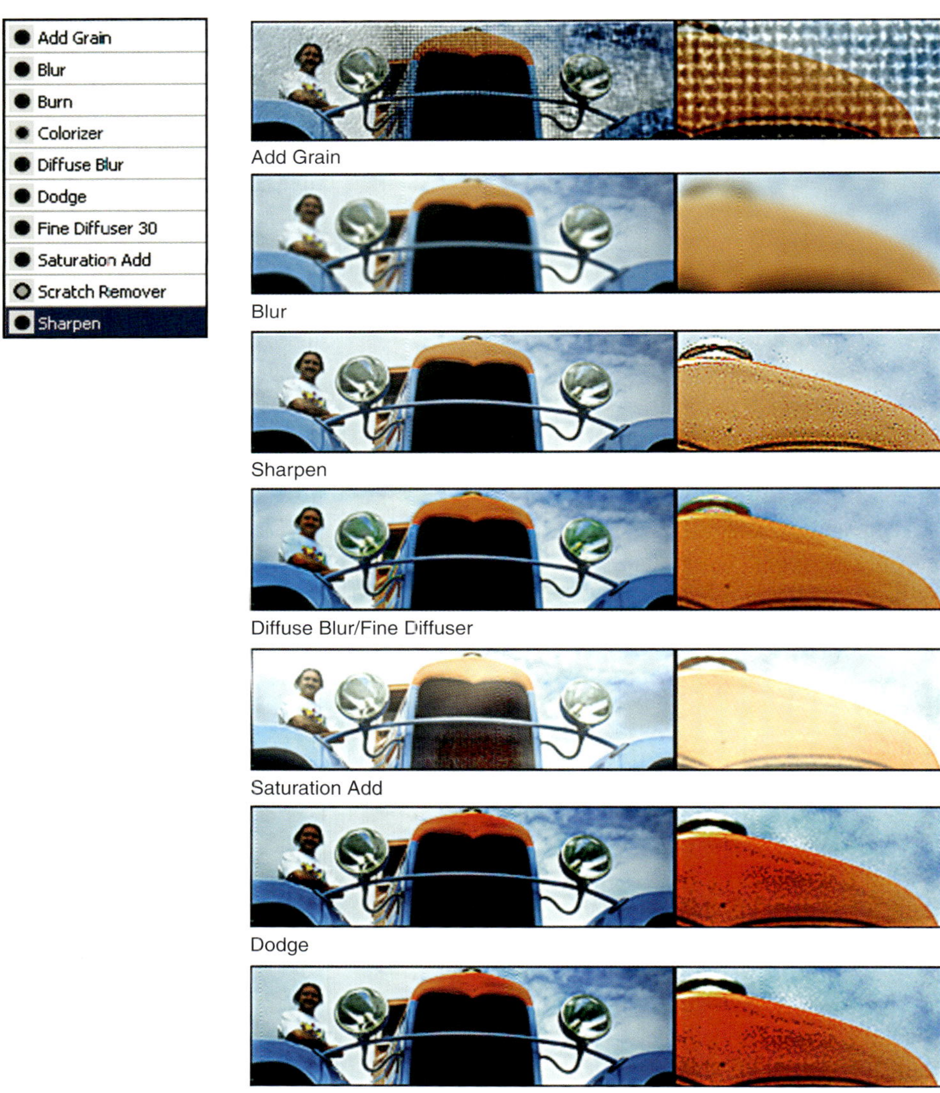

Add Grain

Blur

Sharpen

Diffuse Blur/Fine Diffuser

Saturation Add

Dodge

Burn

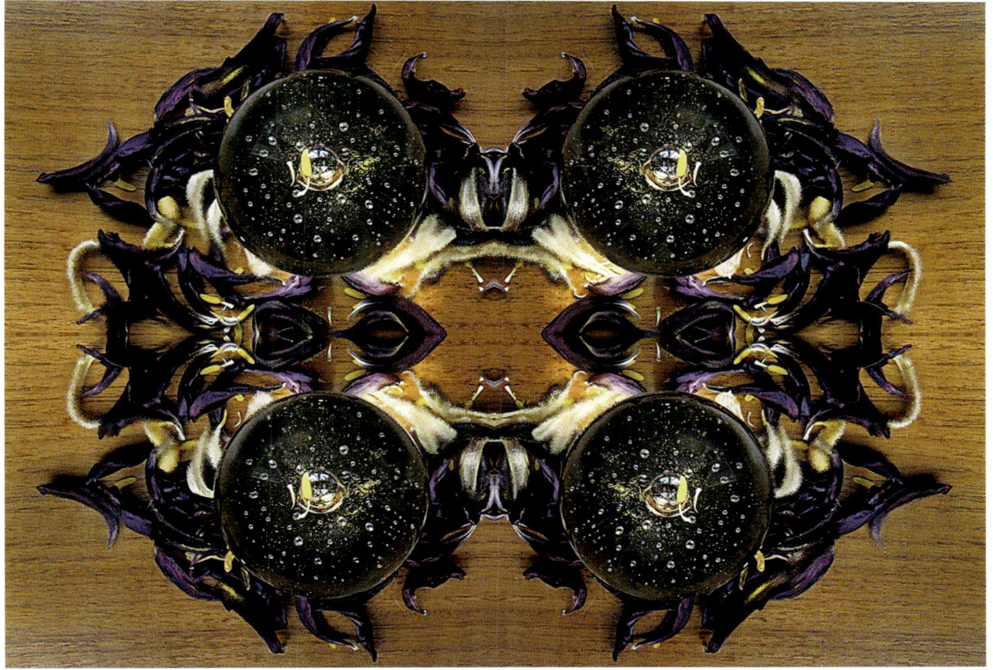

Figure 5.83 Paperweight pattern

Before digital imaging became widespread, I made many kaleidoscopic images by multiple printing on Cibachrome color paper. It was very difficult to join the four sections so that the joins remained invisible, but with digital imaging the process is much easier.

The image was first created in Photoshop, then the Photo brushes in Painter were used to sharpen key parts, to add saturation to others and to introduce some diffuse blur effects in some small areas to vary the textural finish.

You may notice that the picture is not exactly symmetrical. One of the nice things that you can do easily in digital is make changes that break the symmetry but are not immediately obvious.

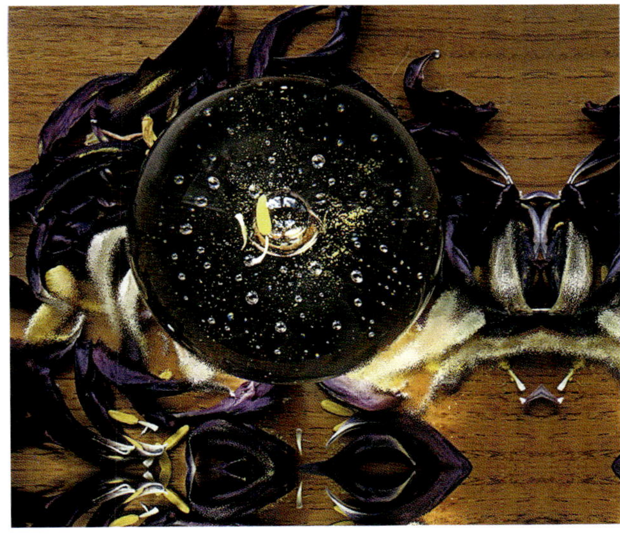

Figure 5.84 Detail

Sponges

In traditional painting, sponges are often used to dab on wet paint and add a textured finish, so they are not obvious candidates for cloning pictures. Most of these brushes can be used either in Cloning Method, which gives a patchy, but fairly realistic, picture or using Clone Color, where the image is reduced to dabs of color with little or no detail. The two Grainy Wet Sponge examples below illustrate the differences between the two methods.

As its name implies, the Smeary Wet Sponge smears the picture quite strongly.

Another way in which these brushes can be used very successfully is to apply them directly to the photograph; this is shown in the Wet Sponge example below.

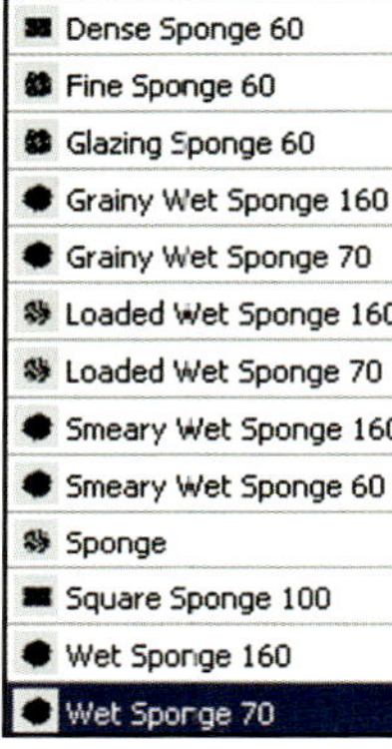

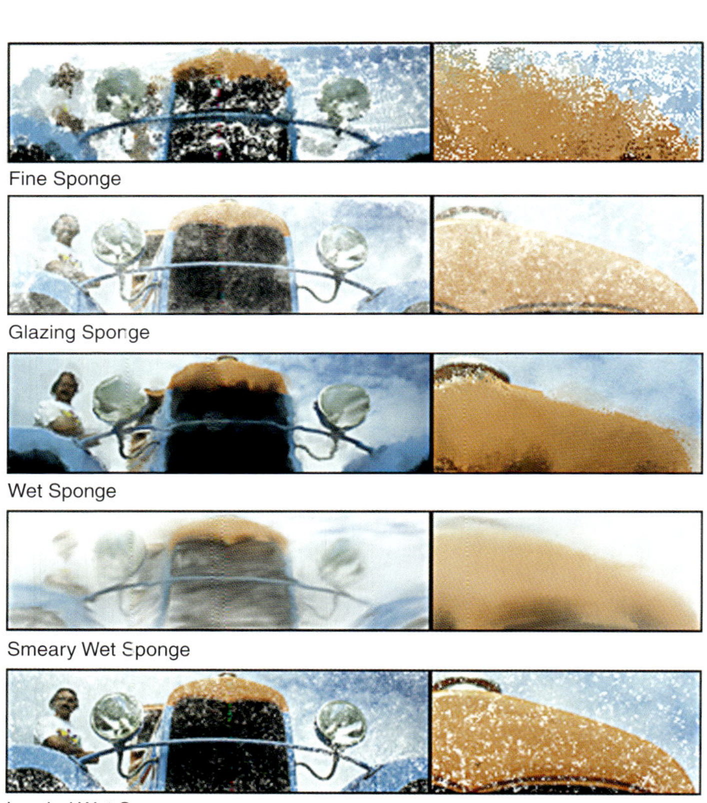

Fine Sponge

Glazing Sponge

Wet Sponge

Smeary Wet Sponge

Loaded Wet Sponge

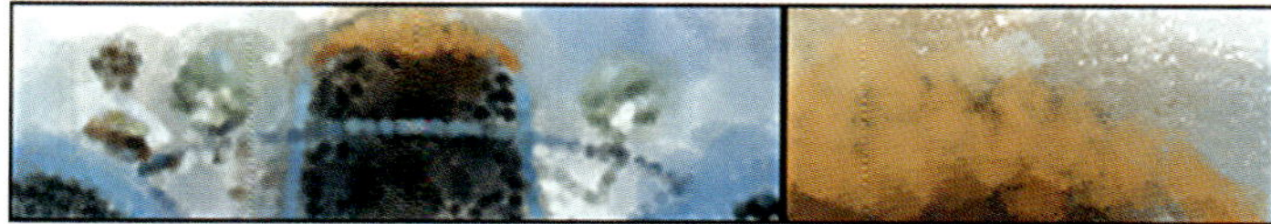

Grainy Wet Sponge – Clone Color

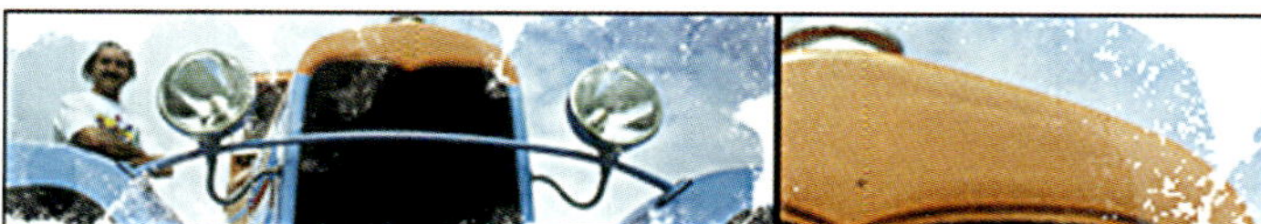

Grainy Wet Sponge – Cloning Method

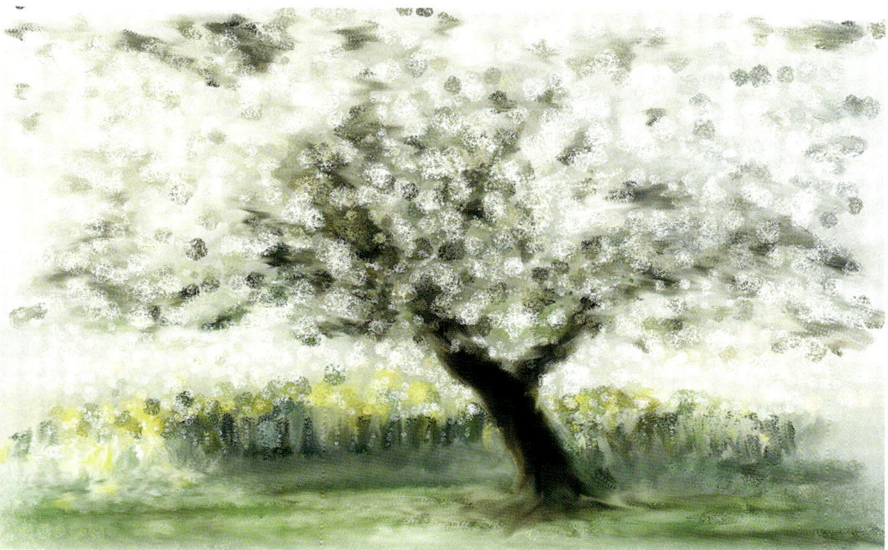

Figure 5.85 Springtime blossom

The stages of painting 'Springtime blossom' are shown below.

Stage 1 was a quick wash with the Smeary Wet Sponge using the Clone Color option. Stage 2 used the same brush, Clone Color was clicked off and the Method changed to Cloning to bring in more detail. The brush was then changed to Fine Sponge using the Clone Color option to add to the texture.

Stage 3 used the Smeary Wet Sponge, dabbing all over the picture to soften some of the detail. In Stage 4 (Figure 5.85), the Fine Sponge was used again and more dabs of color created.

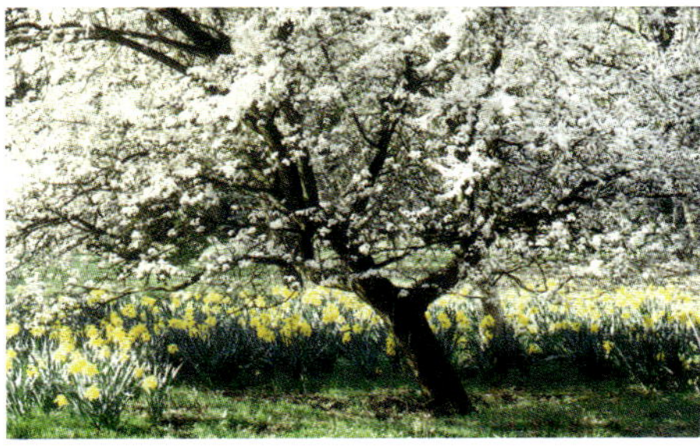

Figure 5.86 Original photograph

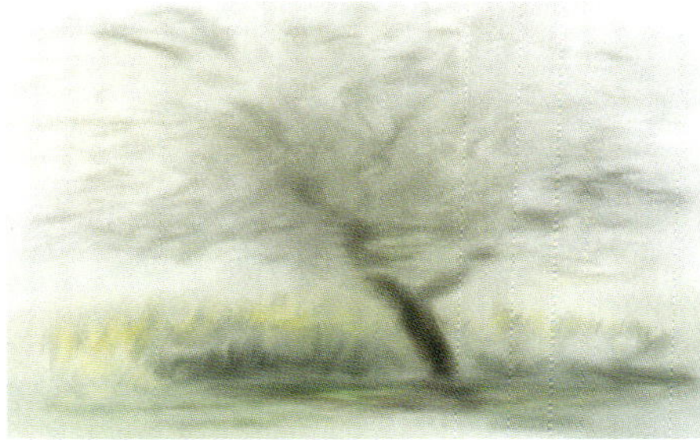

Figure 5.87 Stage 1

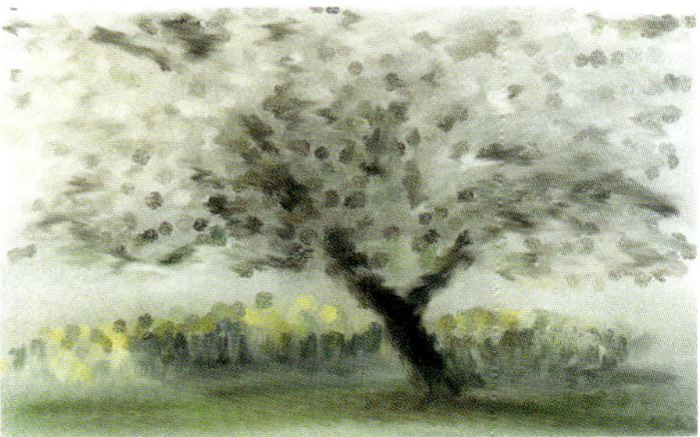

Figure 5.88 Stage 2

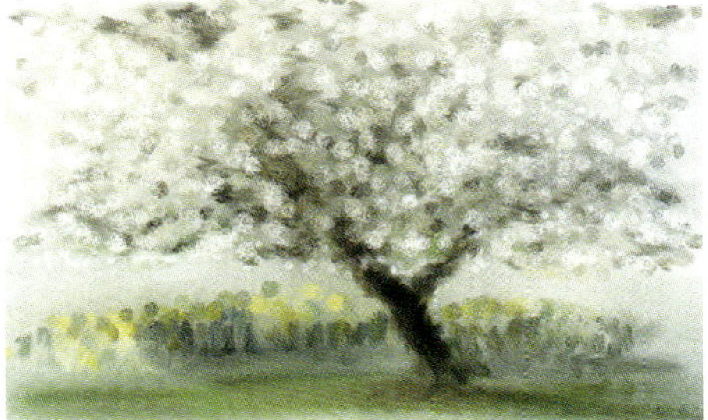

Figure 5.89 Stage 3

Sumi-e

Sumi-e is an unusual, distinctive brush that uses the rake stroke in most of its variants.

The Digital Sumi-e has the most pronounced rake style, but apart from the Flat Wet Sumi-e, all the others display this feature in varying degrees depending upon the brush type. All the examples have been used with the Clone Color option. The Fine Sumi-e is one of the few variants that can resolve fine detail.

The Flat Wet Sumi-e makes a very vivid colorful clone and, because it uses the Buildup Method, the colors intensify very quickly and will build up to black with over-painting.

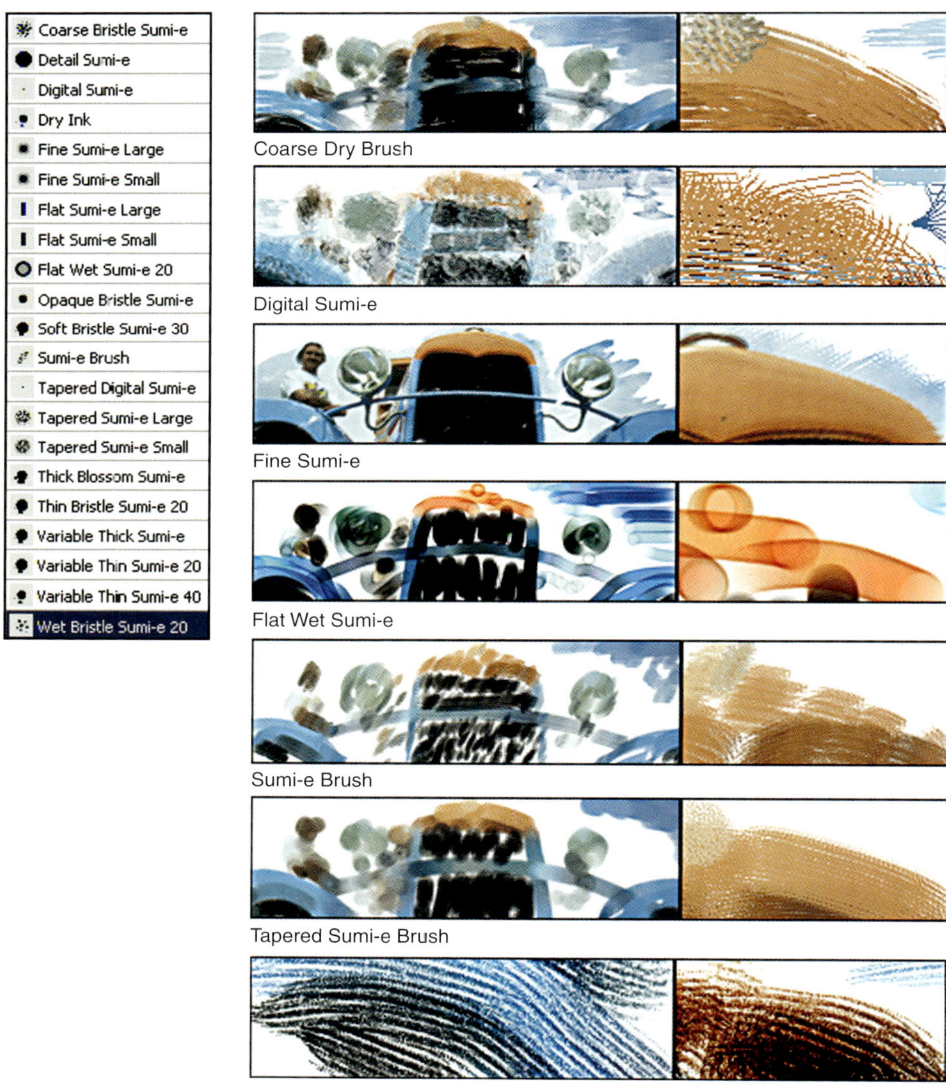

Coarse Dry Brush

Digital Sumi-e

Fine Sumi-e

Flat Wet Sumi-e

Sumi-e Brush

Tapered Sumi-e Brush

Wet Bristle Sumi-e

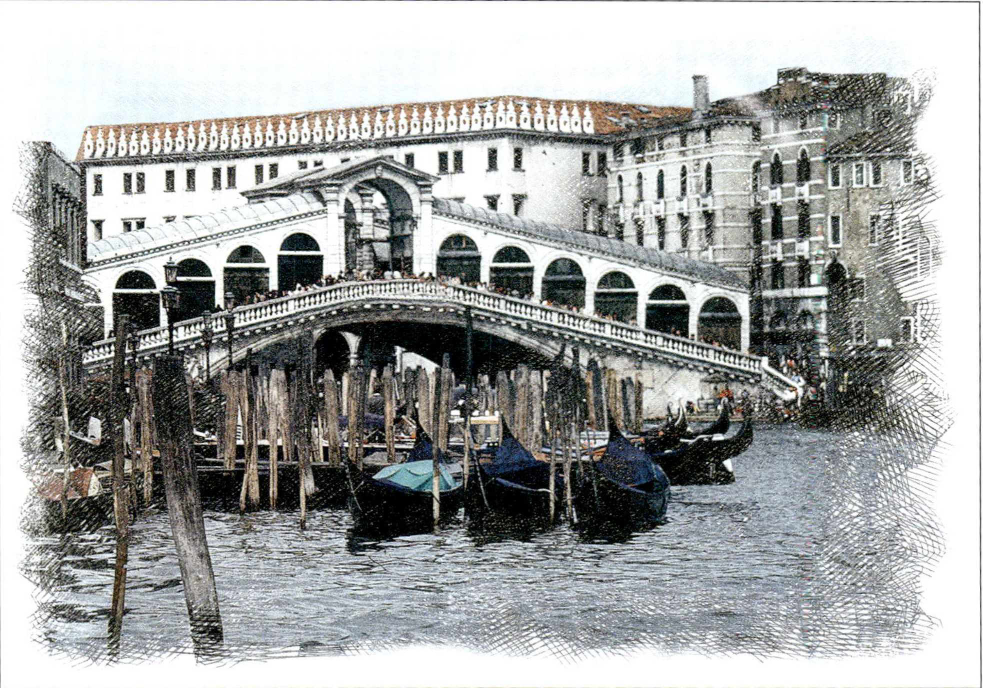

Figure 5.90 The Rialto Bridge, Venice

This picture of the well-known Rialto Bridge in Venice was made using the Digital Sumi-e brush.

This brush variant gives a distinctive rake type appearance and the enlarged detail shown in Figure 5.91 shows the brush strokes clearly.

The clone was made using a fairly large brush size with medium opacity, and cloning repeatedly until the image built up sufficient density.

It is on the outer parts of the picture where the brush marks are most evident. In the center, the picture has become much clearer by the overlapping of the brush strokes.

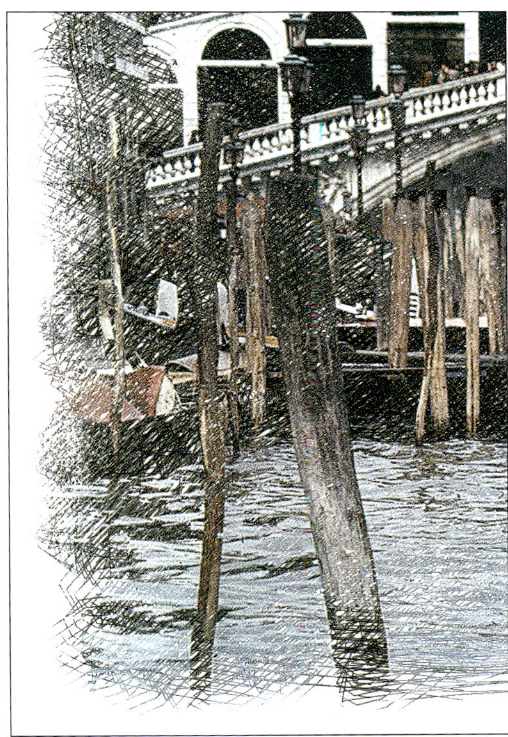

Figure 5.91 Detail of Sumi-e brush strokes

Tinting

This set of brushes is designed for tinting photographs. They all work in a similar way and their names indicate the differences: Oily, Grainy, Bristle, etc. In the illustrations below, the differences are not very apparent and I have rather arbitrarily chosen to repaint this car in some vivid colors.

The original monochrome photograph was kept on the Canvas, a new empty layer was created on top and the brush strokes painted onto that layer. It is essential to change the layer composite method to Color to avoid obscuring the original image beneath.

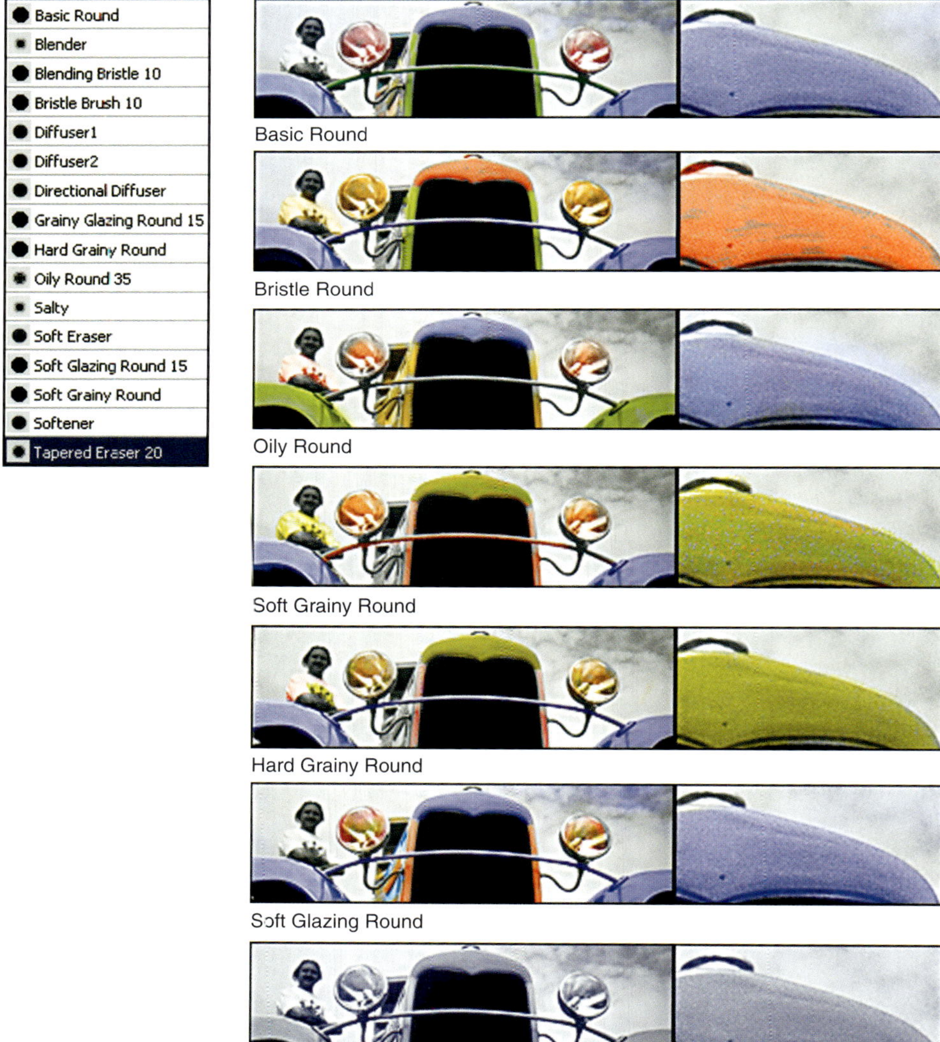

Basic Round

Bristle Round

Oily Round

Soft Grainy Round

Hard Grainy Round

Soft Glazing Round

Soft Glazing Round – Colorize

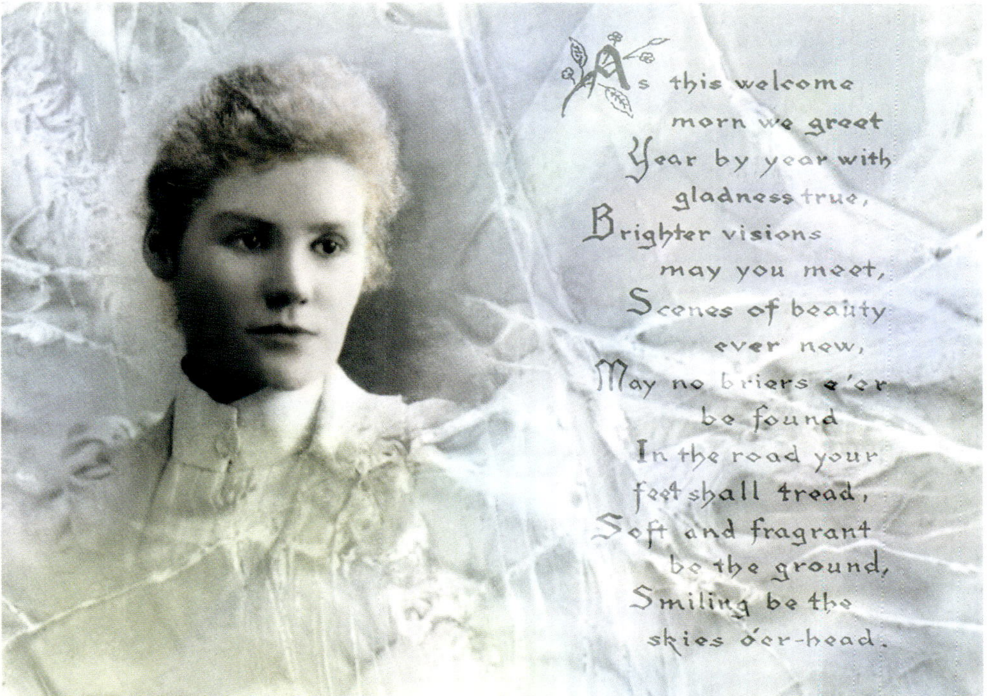

Figure 5.92 Ellen

A Soft Glazing Round brush from the Tinting brush category was used to tint this old family picture.

The brush opacity was only 1% or 2%, but the color was still too strong; however, as each section of tinting was put on a separate layer, this allowed the opacity of the relevant layers to be reduced where necessary. The Mixer palette was very useful in selecting the colors.

For a more detailed, step-by-step guide to hand tinting, refer to Chapter 12.

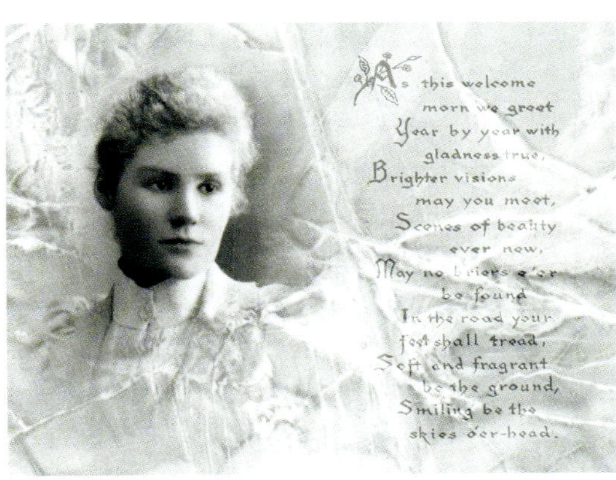

Figure 5.93 Original photograph

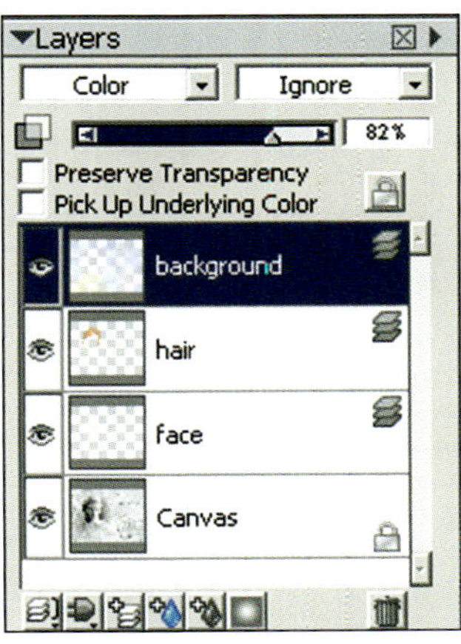

Figure 5.94 The Layers palette

Watercolor

As can be seen from the list of brushes on the left, the Watercolor category contains a huge range of variants, which cover many types of painting.

The Runny brushes use the traditional wet on wet style and run down the page leaving a highly diffuse picture.

The Dry Camel and Fine Camel give quite a clear clone with the brush stroke visible. The Dry Bristle brush is a good quick brush for a beginner to try. All the examples below use the Clone Color option.

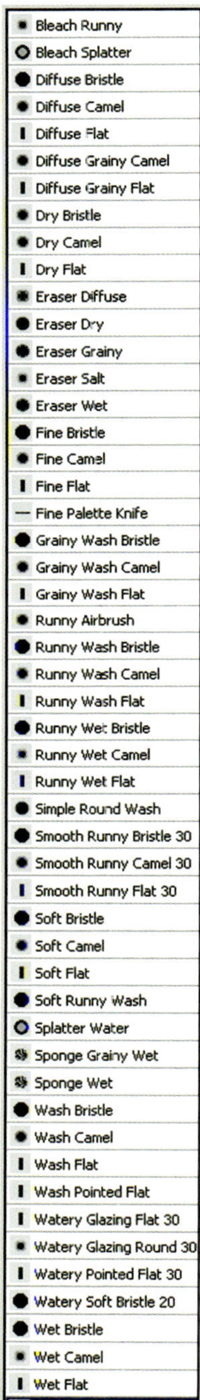

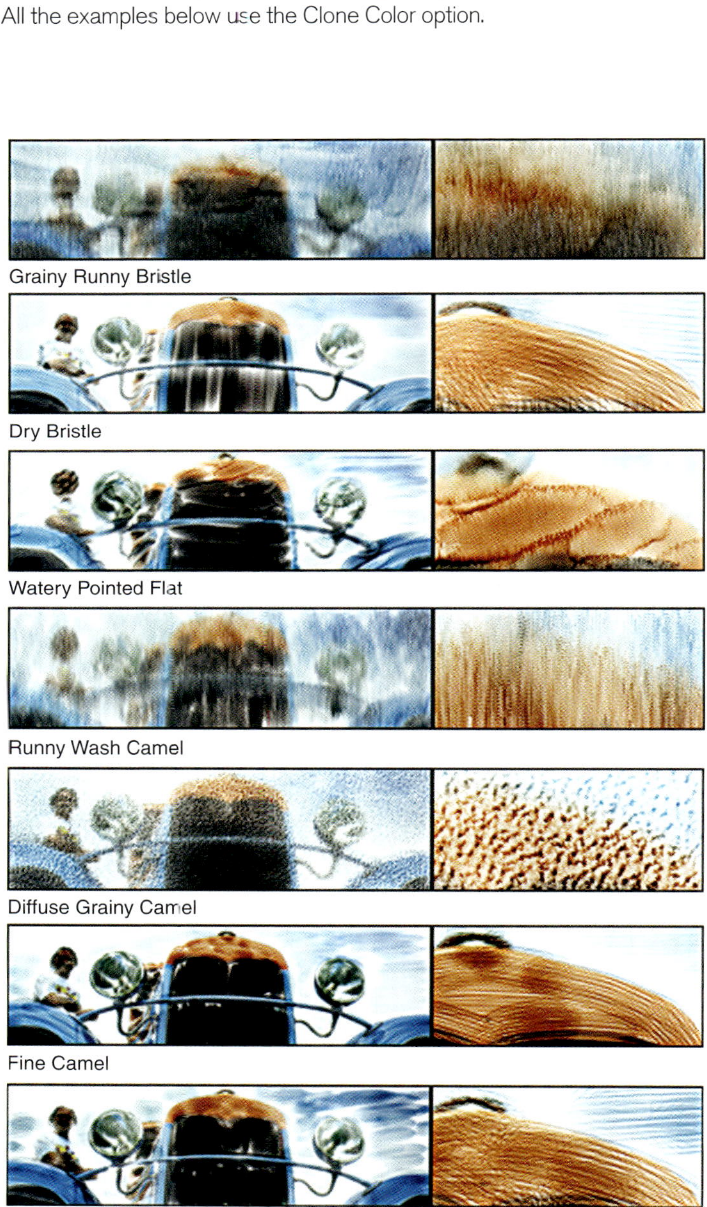

Grainy Runny Bristle

Dry Bristle

Watery Pointed Flat

Runny Wash Camel

Diffuse Grainy Camel

Fine Camel

Dry Camel

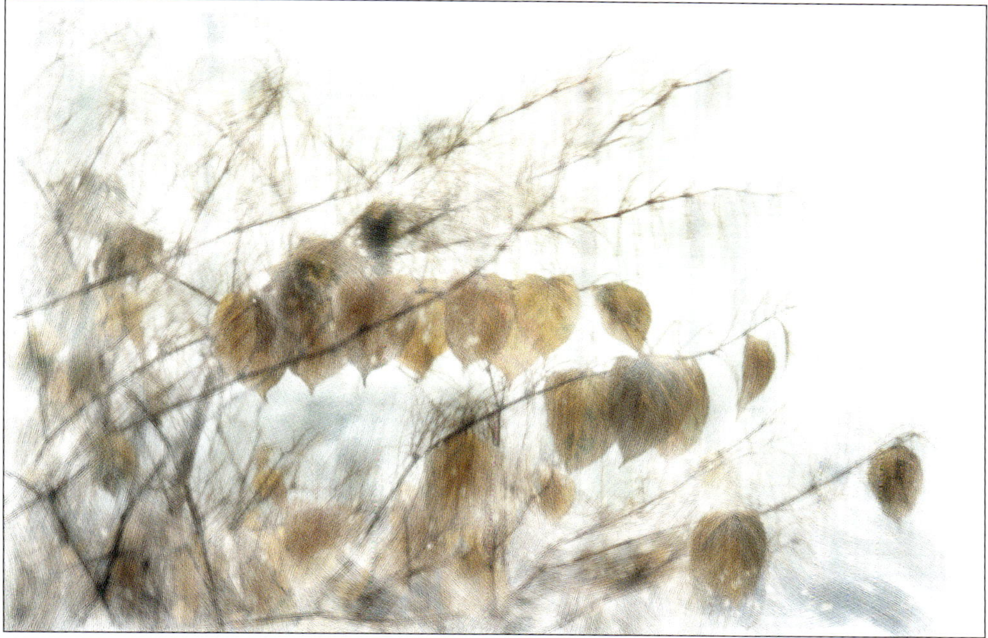

Figure 5.95 Leaves in the mist

'Leaves in the mist' was made with the Dry Bristle Watercolor brush, which is a good brush for pictures where the brush texture will enhance the image.

The paper used is Basic Paper from the Painter default set.

As you can see from the detail shown in Figure 5.97, the brush strokes are clearly visible and add to the overall texture.

When the clone was completed, the original image was copied and pasted on the top of the clone copy.

The Blur filter was applied to the layer and the composite method changed the layer to Screen at 30% opacity. This gave a luminous quality to the finished picture.

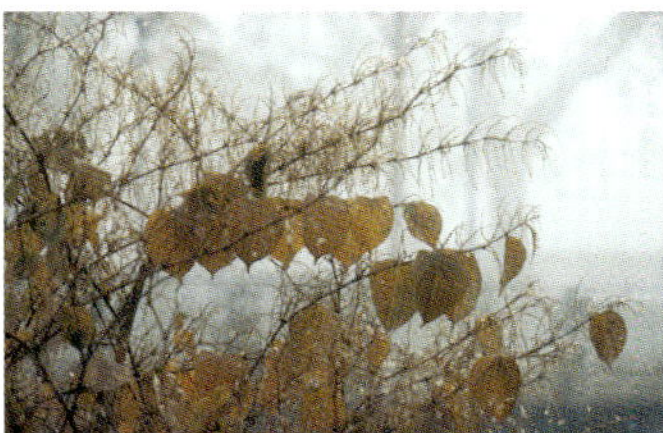

Figure 5.96 Original photograph

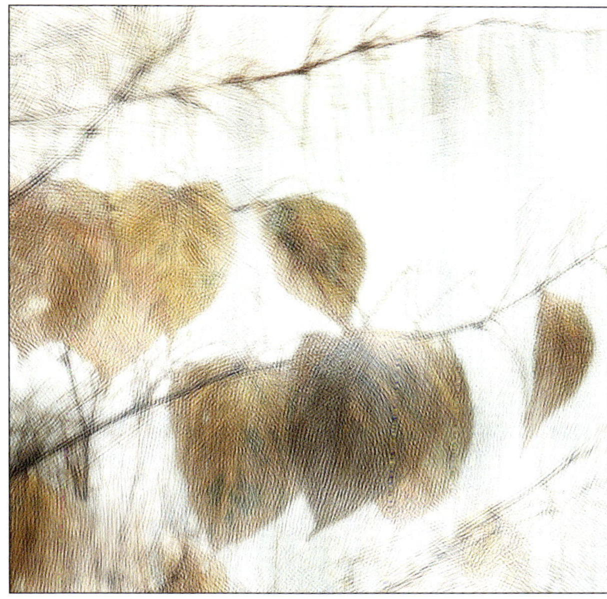

Figure 5.97 Detail showing Dry Bristle brush strokes

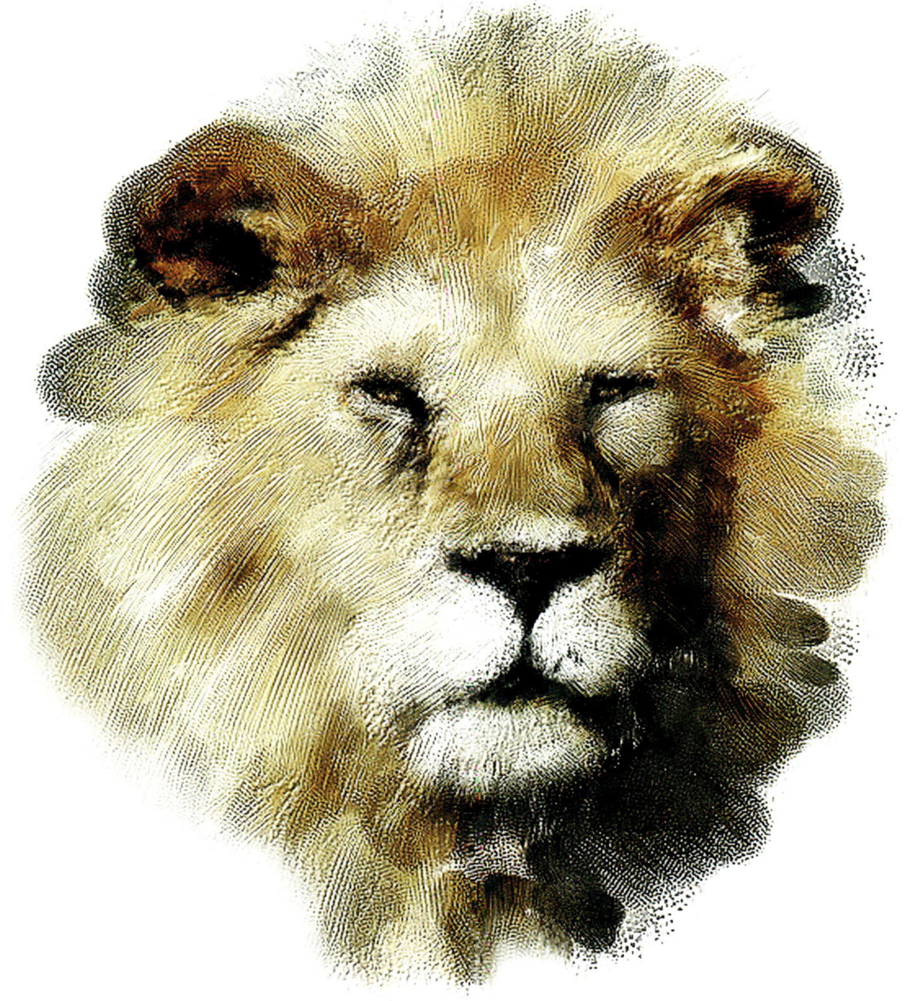

Figure 6.1 Lion

Chapter 6
Customizing brushes

The last chapter looked at the wide range of ready-made brushes available in Painter IX, but even with all these varieties it is still often necessary to customize them to get exactly the brush strokes required. The Brush Creator contains all the controls for customizing brushes and this chapter explains this in detail, together with many of the key controls that you will need to understand.

It is worth remembering that often the only differences between one brush and another are just a few settings in the Brush Creator. The brushes are, after all, just presets made by the creators of Painter for our convenience. In theory, you could use just one standard brush and, by changing the relevant options in the Brush Creator, have everything from a pencil to a watercolor brush. In practice, it is more convenient to use the standard brushes and change a few of the options to fine-tune the brush.

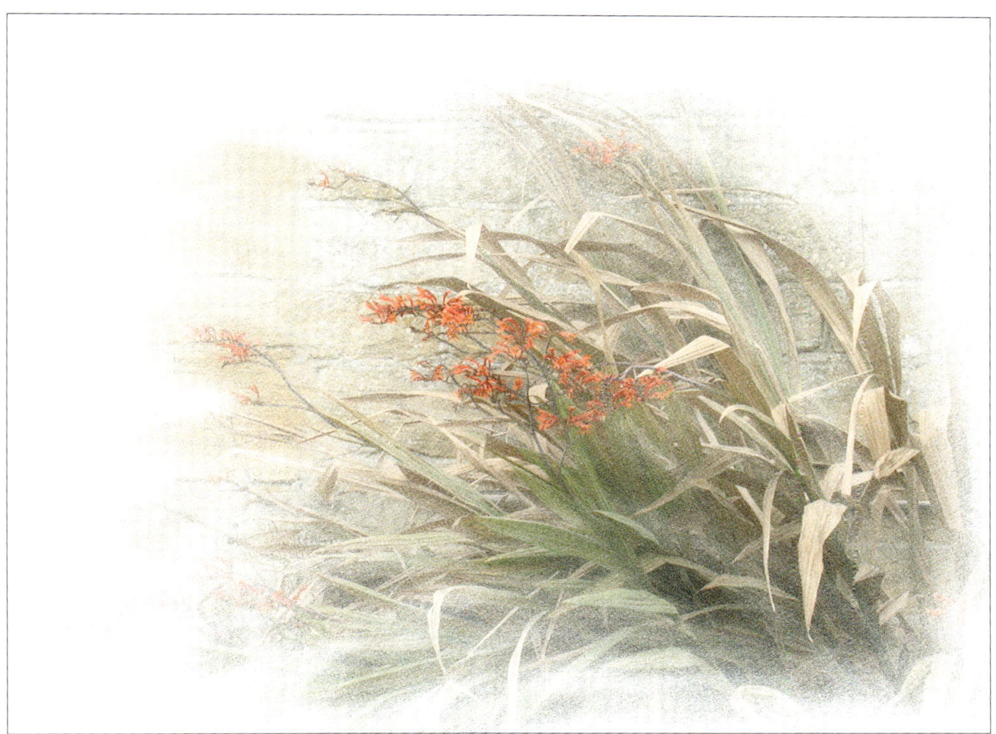

Figure 6.2 Crocosmia

The Brush Creator

The Brush Creator is the powerhouse for customizing brushes, as it brings together all the various palettes and commands into one easily accessible place.

Bring the palette on screen by *Window>Show Brush Creator* or by the shortcut *Ctrl/Cmd+B*. When you click back into the image, the Brush Creator drops back behind the document you are working on, which is a nice touch and saves time.

The Stroke Designer

Figure 6.3 shows the Brush Creator with the Stroke Designer tab active. This is where the many sub-palettes are stored.

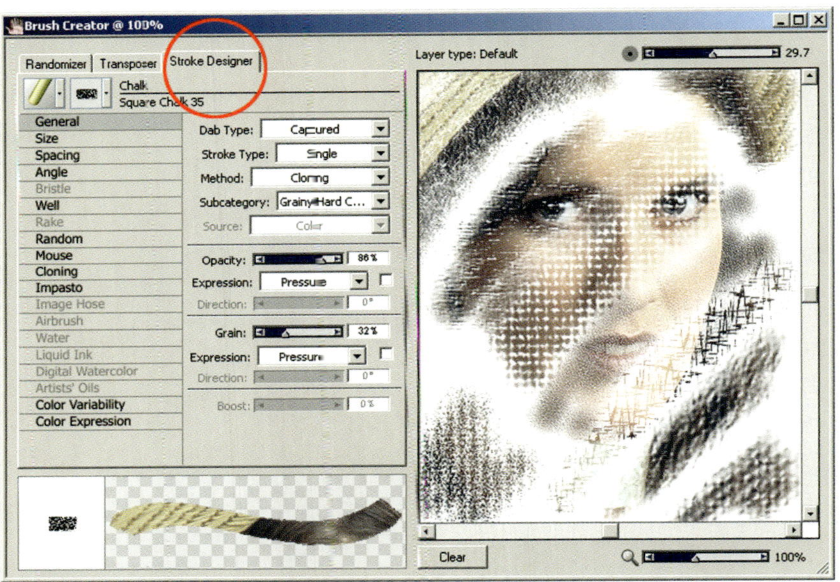

Figure 6.3 The Stroke Designer

In the Brush Creator, click the palette names on the left and the controls for that particular palette will appear to the right. Some of the palettes refer to specific types of brush and are grayed out if that brush is not in use.

At the bottom left is the Preview Grid; this shows a visual representation of the selected brush in both profile view (end on) and as a brush stroke.

The area on the right is the Scratch Pad and is where you can try out various brushes and options before making a final decision. This Scratch Pad reflects the paper texture in use and if you have a clone document active the brush will work in cloning mode. Remember that the clone is taken from the top left corner of the original, so nothing much will show if you have a blank area there!

The slider beneath the Scratch Pad will change the magnification; click the Clear button to delete the pad display. The slider above the Scratch Pad changes the brush size.

The Randomizer

Clicking on the Randomizer tab brings up another palette and here Painter suggests a set of variations on the current brush. As you can see in Figure 6.4, the brush strokes on the Scratch Pad show how the brush strokes would change in appearance. Click in the preview area on the left to try each variation. The slider beneath the display controls the amount of variation; move it to the right to get a bigger change. Click on the cogwheels to generate a different set of variations. In the Scratch Pad I have painted a brush stroke from each stage to illustrate the different variations.

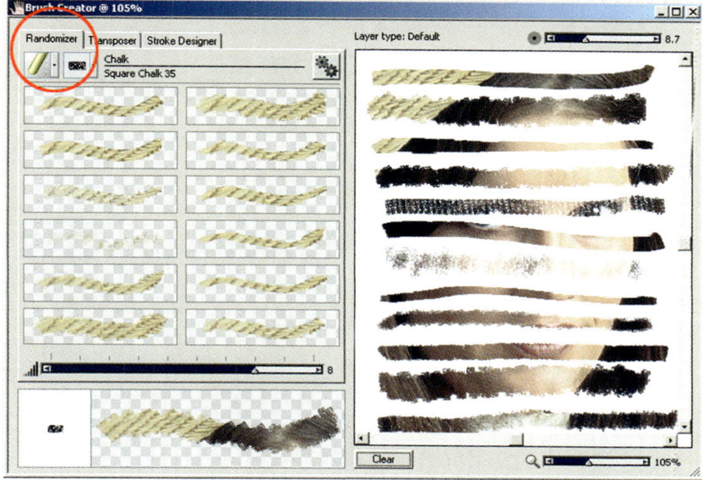

Figure 6.4 The Randomizer

The Transposer

Click on the Transposer tab to reveal another tool for creating alternative brush variants. In this case, Painter starts with your current brush, which is shown at the top of the display. and changes it to a

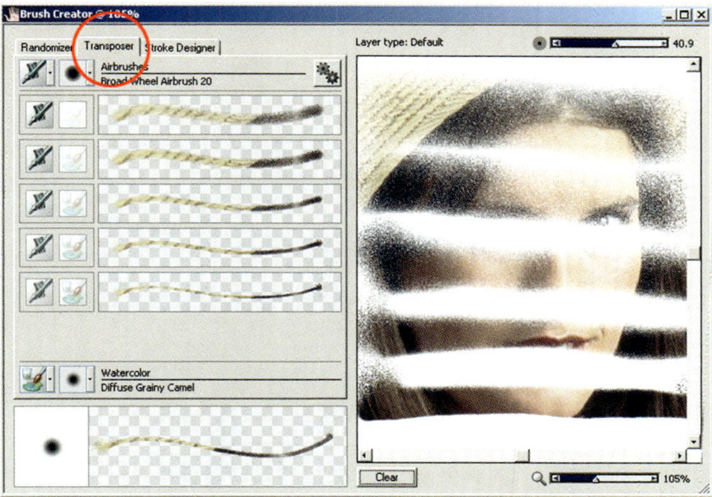

Figure 6.5 The Transposer

completely different brush in a series of steps. In Figure 6.5, the display shows how an Airbrush is changed to a Digital Watercolor brush, the Scratch Pad showing how the distinctive light spray of the Airbrush changed to become much denser. Try changing the starting and ending brushes to get a different result.

The Stroke Designer palettes

The next section looks at the main palettes within the Brush Creator; not all the controls are covered, just the ones that are most useful for cloning photographs.

Stroke Designer palettes – General

The General palette is the most regularly used of all the brush palettes.

It is worth knowing that all the individual palettes of the Brush Creator can be brought on screen separately in Painter IX; go to *Window>Brush Controls* and they will be listed separately there. Because the General palette is used so much, I have this on screen permanently; other palettes like the watercolor palette are on screen just when a watercolor brush is being used

Figure 6.6 The General palette

Dab types

The Dab is the mark that the brush makes when a single mark is made using the brush completely vertical.

Making alterations in this section will make a fundamental change to the brush, but don't worry if you mess it up as you can easily revert the brush back to the default setting by clicking the brush icon on the left of the Properties bar when the brush is active.

The chief dab types are as follows.

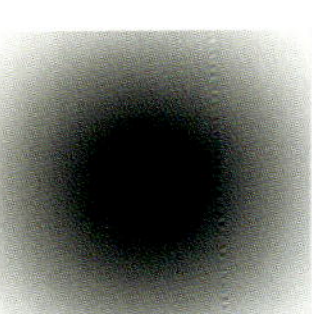

Circular dab types have a very smooth finish, and despite their name the brushes are often long and narrow. Soft clones use circular dab types, so this is a good option if you want a smooth, clear picture.

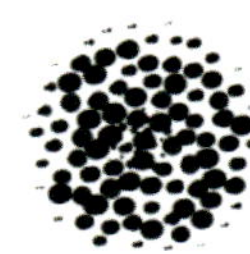

Static Bristle brushes are made up of individual bristles and therefore the brush lines are usually visible. This is the dab type to use if you want to emphasize the brush strokes.

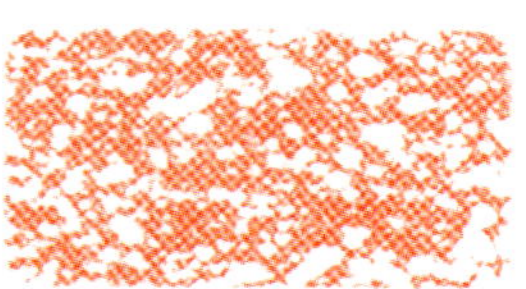

Captured means that the shape has been made from a design or image rather than using individual bristles. When you make your own dab type this is called Captured. The dab illustrated comes from a Chalk variant.

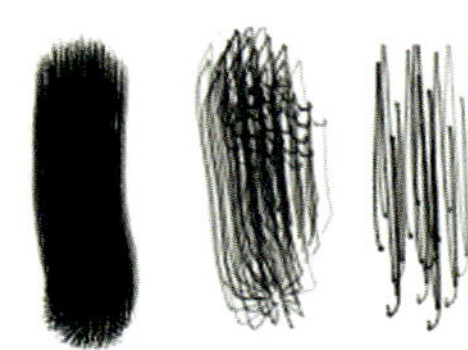

Camel Hair and Flat dab types use what are called Rendered dabs, which means that the brush is made up of individual bristles all computed separately. The brushes are often slow to operate, especially when smooth strokes are chosen. The Feature Slider in the Size palette controls the spread of the bristles. The illustration shows the Camel Hair brush with the Feature slider set at 2.1, 5.4 and 10.4.

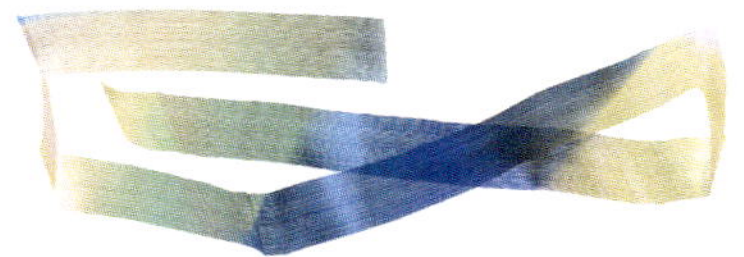

The Palette Knife has an elongated shape and can be used to move imagery around directly on a picture. When using this dab for cloning, the imagery will appear with the very distinctive knife-like shape.

The Rendered dab is rather like the Palette Knife in shape and is a difficult brush to clone with, as the image is distorted.

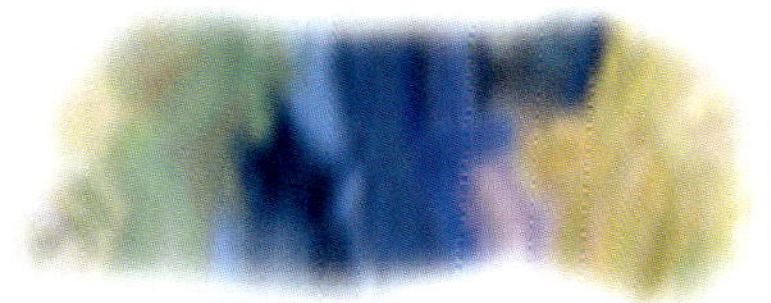

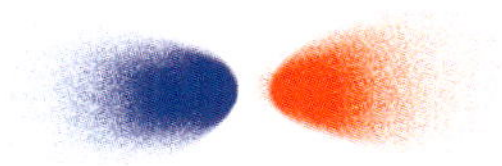

The Airbrush and the Pixel Airbrush both spray in the direction that the stylus is pointed, just like a real airbrush in fact. These two dab types are very similar, with a slightly different texture. The Pixel Airbrush is shown in red in the example.

The Line Airbrush sprays imagery and also severely distorts it. The Furry Clone uses this dab type.

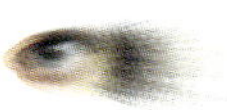

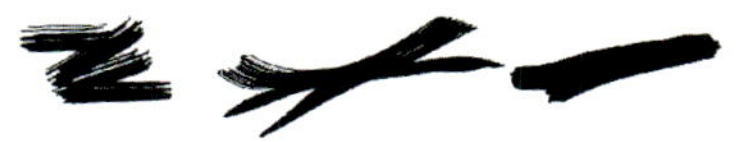

The Liquid Ink series of brush dabs are very smooth and dense, similar to pools of liquid ink on an even surface.

The Watercolor range of brush dabs varies depending upon the type of brush, but all paint in the wet method and will distort the cloned image to varying degrees.

Method

The Method controls how the paint is laid on the paper. Many of the choices are easy to imagine as they are descriptive. Cover will cover anything previously painted but will not become darker than the chosen color. Buildup will get darker as more brushstrokes are added, eventually going to black. Cloning is available on some, but not all, of the brushes; those which do use the Cloning Method will produce clear and accurate clones.

Buildup
Cover
Eraser
Drip
Mask (Cover)
✔ Cloning
Wet
Digital Wet
Plug-in

Subcategory

This section refines the chosen Method and in the case of Cloning offers four choices. The two that are used regularly for Cloning are Soft Cover Cloning, which has a smooth even finish with soft edges, and Grainy Hard Cover Cloning, which has a rough finish that shows paper grain. The Soft Clone is on the left and the Grainy Hard Cloning on the right. Drip Cloning does not usually work as it only used for certain brushes in earlier versions of Painter.

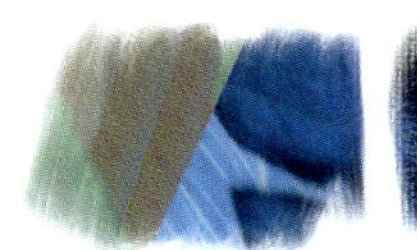

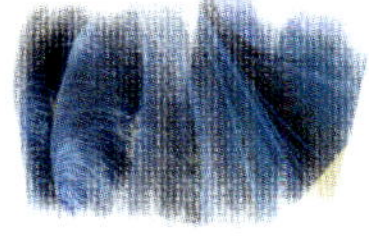

Grain

This slider controls the amount of grain that is revealed when brush strokes are applied to the paper.

The amount that is needed depends upon the combination of brush and paper being used. Generally, the control needs to be set at a very low level, sometimes as low as 1 or 2. It seems strange to be reducing the slider control to increase the amount of grain, but the slider really controls how much paint goes into the grain, so the higher the setting the less grain will be visible.

Stroke Designer palettes – Size

The size of the brush is usually set either on the Properties bar or in the Brush Creator, so the main reason for going to this section is to alter the shape of the brush tip. The top two rows are available for most brushes, while the bottom two rows are for the new Artists' Oils category.

The shape in the center of the second row is the watercolor brush tip; the raised edges will give the wet edge that characterizes watercolor painting.

Figure 6.7 The Size palette

Stroke Designer palettes – Well

The sliders in this section control whether or not the brush smears the existing artwork, or in the case of a clone, whether the clone is clear or completely blurred. The two sliders that control the level of diffusion are Resaturation and Bleed. Figure 6.9 shows, from top to bottom, brush strokes with the Resaturation slider at 12%, 50% and 100%.

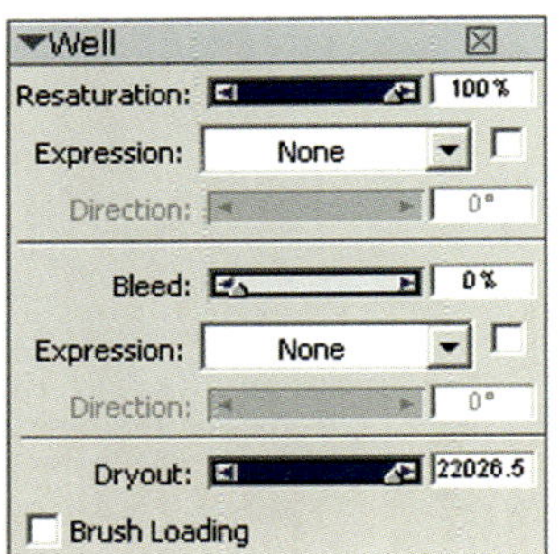

Figure 6.8 The Well palette

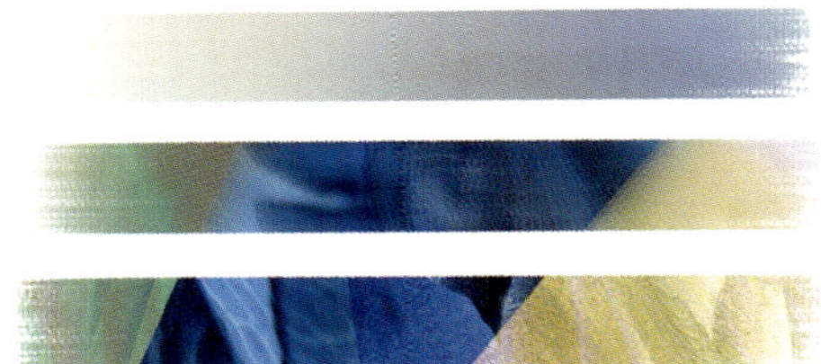

Figure 6.9 Resaturation and Bleed controls

Stroke Designer palettes – Spacing

Brush strokes usually appear to be continuous, but are really a series of individual brush dabs spaced very closely so they overlap. This palette adjusts the spacing between the dabs; Figure 6.10 shows the Wet Acrylic brush with spacing at 8%, 100% and 200%.

Figure 6.10 Brush spacing

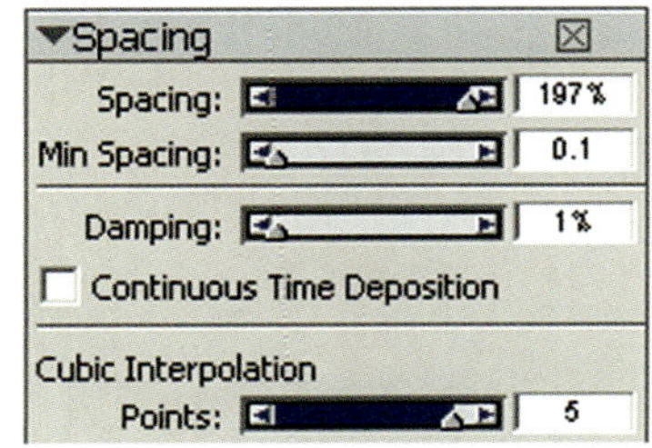

Figure 6.11 The Spacing palette

Stroke Designer palettes – Random

Computer brush strokes can often be too precise and accurate, unlike if we paint traditionally, when our hands flex and the stroke varies. The Random section gives us some controls which will reduce the regularity of the brush strokes. Figure 6.13 shows how the sliders affect the picture, from the left.

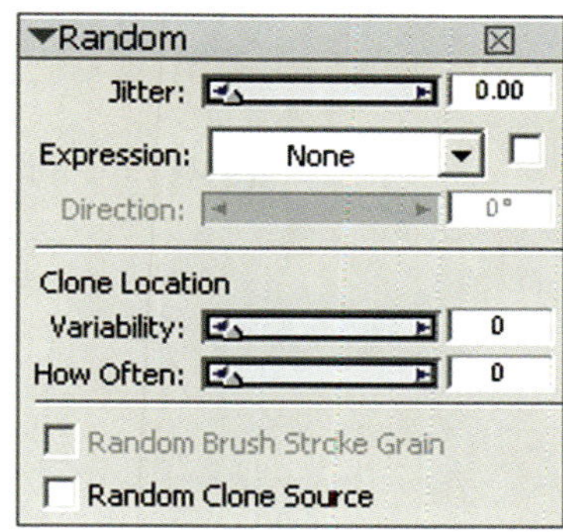

Figure 6.12 The Random palette

1 Using Square Chalk, the first is a normal stroke.
2 The Jitter slider is at 2.67, which places brush dabs at random places; the picture is still in register with the original clone source.
3 Clone Variability is set at 34. This control offsets the place from which the clone is taken. Moving the How Often slider changes the source more often.
4 Random Clone Source has been ticked, which takes each brush dab from a different part of the original clone but in a totally random manner. The result is a collage of elements from all over the picture.

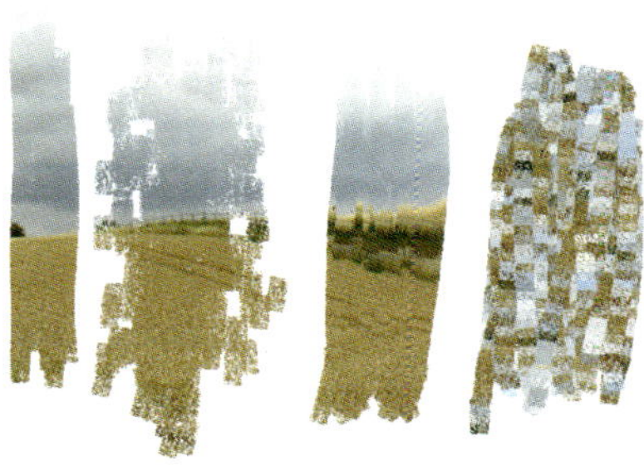

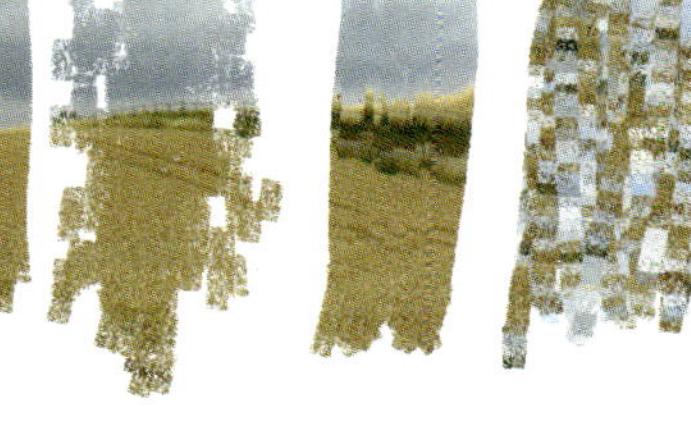

Figure 6.13

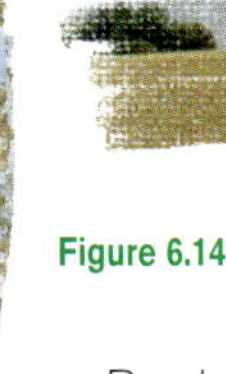

Figure 6.14

Random Brush Stroke Grain reduces the strength of the paper grain. Figure 6.14 illustrates this effect; the option has been ticked in right-hand example.

Stroke Designer palettes – Impasto

Impasto is a very thick viscous paint and in this palette the Impasto effect can be added or removed from brush strokes.

To add Impasto to your brush, open the Impasto palette and change the Draw To box to Color and Depth and the Depth Method to Original Luminance. The amount of the depth is controlled by the Depth slider and this will give the brush stroke a three-dimensional appearance.

Figure 6.15 shows the Grainy Cover Pencil with Impasto applied in the strokes on top and the default setting beneath. This effect will work with most brushes except Watercolor and Liquid Ink.

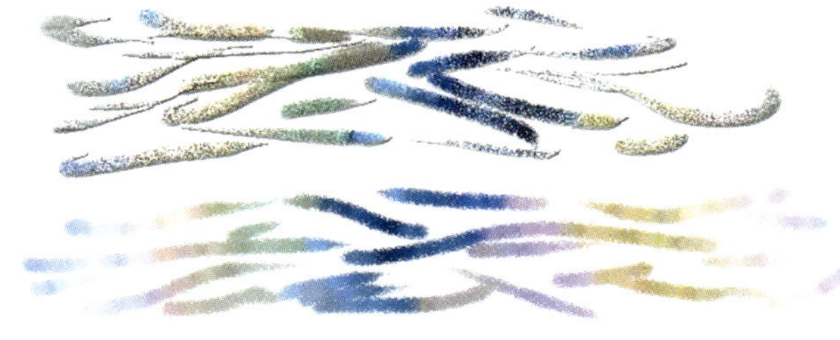

Figure 6.15

Saving brushes

Customizing a brush for a particular use can take some time, so it is sensible to save it for future use; Painter allows us to save brushes and also to make our own brush category.

The process is very easy; when you have customized the brush and are ready to save it, open the Brush Selector palette menu and click on Save Variant. Figure 6.16 shows the dialog box.

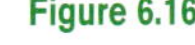

Figure 6.16

Give it a name different from the original and click OK. The new variant will be saved in the same brush category as the original.

If you want to delete the variant, use the same brush and choose Delete Variant. Painter will ask you to confirm that you really want to delete the brush; if so, click OK.

Making a new brush category

It is a good idea to make a new brush category for your own saved brushes; it helps to organize them and keeps them all in one place.

To make a new brush category and add brushes to it, follow the next set of instructions.

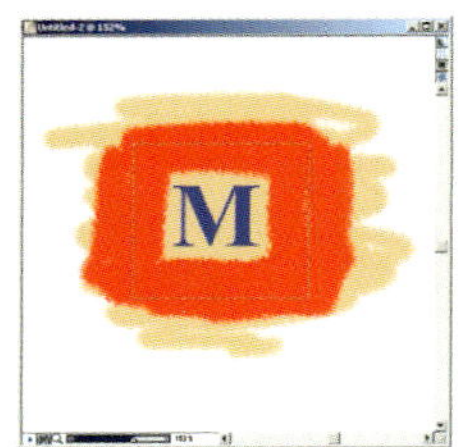

Figure 6.17

Step 1 The first step is to create an icon which will be used for the brush category. This can be an image or text, whatever you will recognize. For this example it will be an image with a single letter. Open an image or make a new document and, using the Type tool, type a single letter in capitals as in Figure 6.17, then Drop all the layers.

Step 2 Make a small square selection of the area with the Rectangular marquee (hold down the Shift key to keep it square).

Step 3 Open the Brush Selector palette menu and click on Capture Brush Category. A dialog box will appear and here you can type in a name for the category; click OK and the new category will appear in the brush category list.

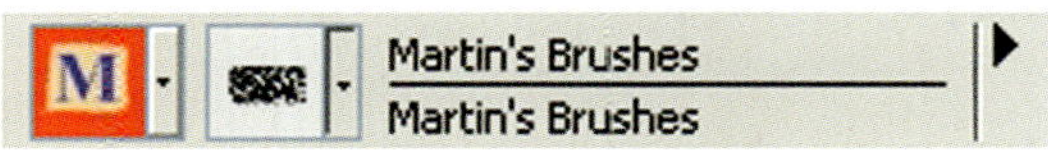

Figure 6.18

Step 4 To add a brush variant to your new category, open an existing brush in any category, make the changes to the brush variant and save the brush under a different name.

Step 5 To move it to your own brush category, go to the palette menu again and select Copy Variant. In the dialog box that appears, select your brush category from the drop-down list and click OK. Finally, go back to the original category and delete the entry there.

Another advantage with saving all your customized brushes in a new category is that you can save a copy in case you have to re-install the program. You will find that categories are not saved in the Program files section as you might expect, but in the Application Data or Application Support folder. This is also the only place where you can delete a brush category.

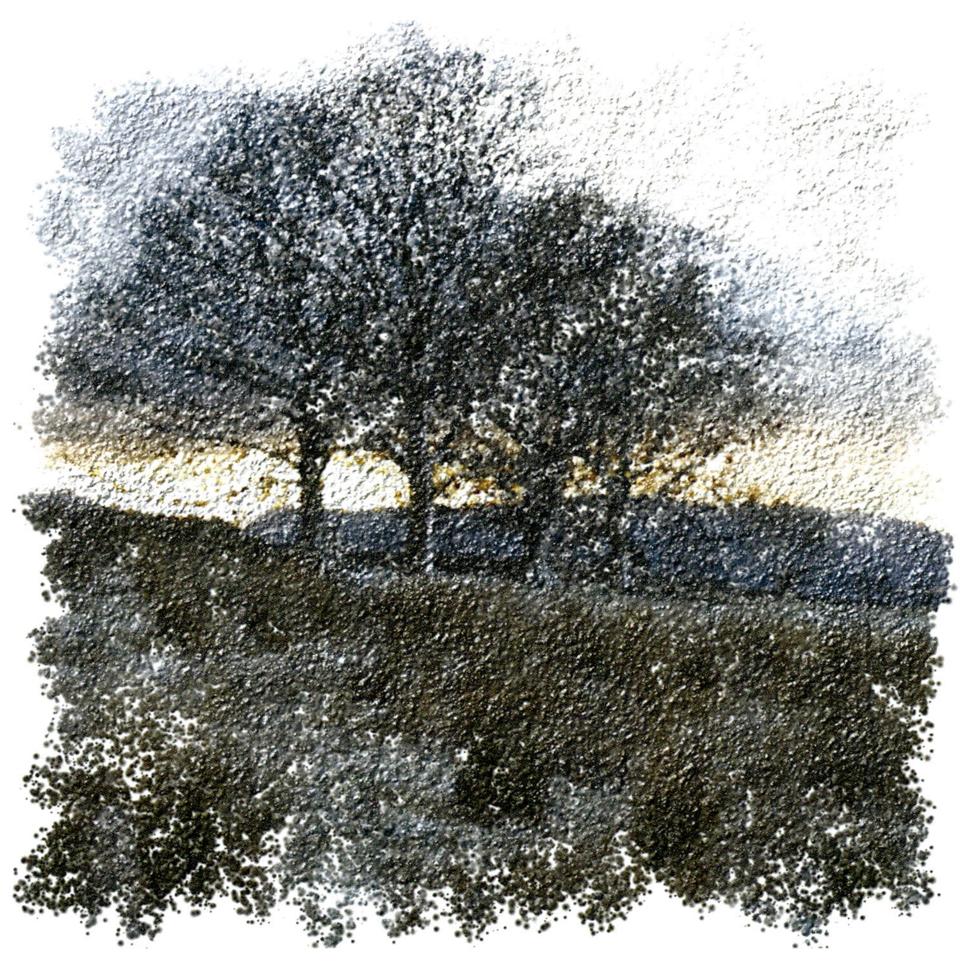

Figure 6.19 Trees in snow

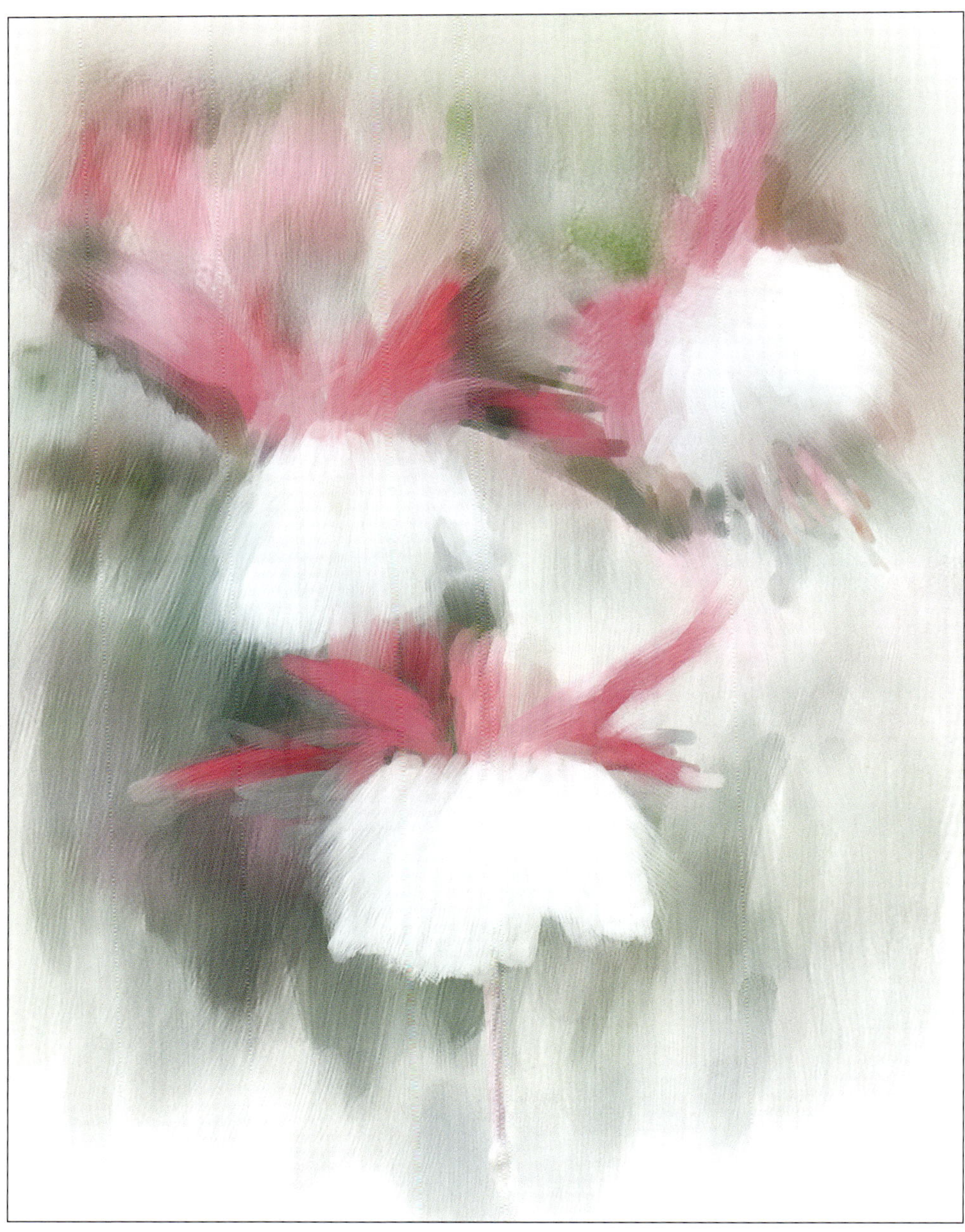

Figure 7.1 Fuchsias

Chapter 7
Cloning from multiple images

Using multiple originals from which to clone means that textures and imagery can be drawn from two or more photographs and parts of each photograph cloned into the final picture. As you will see from the examples in this chapter, it is easy to jump from one original picture to another, which means that the image can be modified as the picture is created, giving a lot of flexibility. Despite this flexibility, it is still very important to plan ahead, both from the technical requirements of image size and resolution and from the creative aspect.

The picture of fuchsias on the previous page was made from four different photographs, combined in Painter to make the final image.

The picture in Figure 7.2 was constructed from two original photographs, a portrait of a girl and a picture of a vase of flowers.

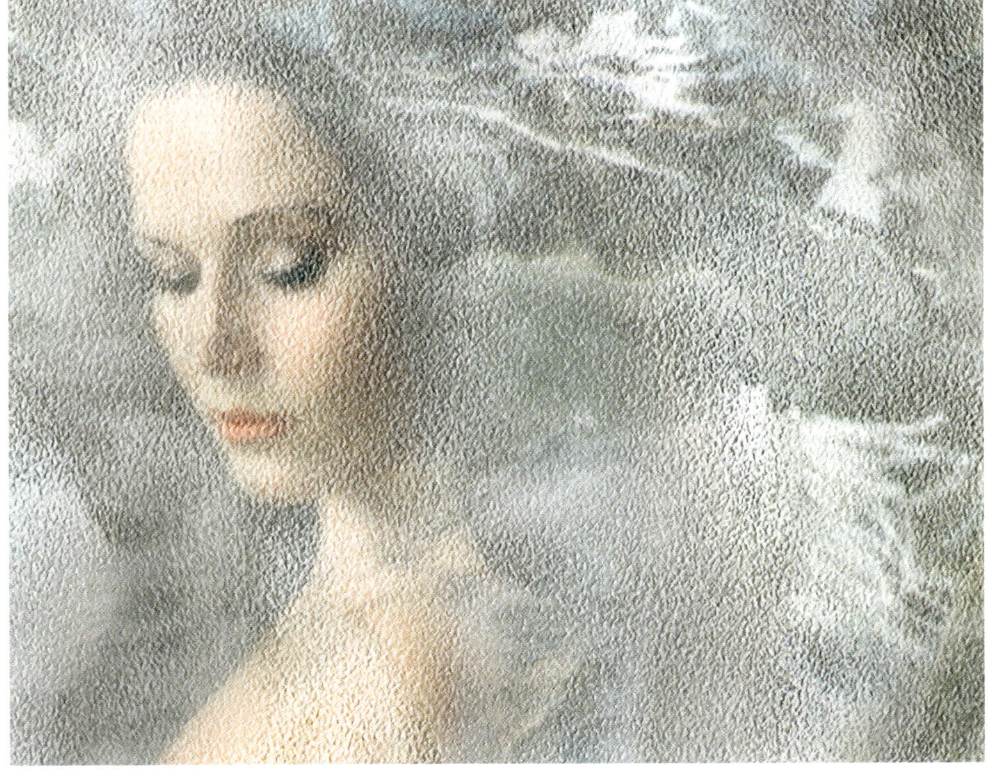

Figure 7.2 Water sprite

Cloning from two images

Phoenix

Step 1 *File>Open>CD>Step-by-step files>'07 Statue 3'.*

The original picture of the statue was scanned from a 35 mm slide and was originally in 24 × 36 mm format. The picture that it is going to be combined with is nearer 46 × 36 mm, so if you cloned from the original scan the statue would appear in the top left corner when it needs to be in the center. In order to clone it into a roughly square background, the canvas size had to be enlarged and the result can be seen in Figure 7.4, which is the image on the CD. The background has been filled with black to show the shape, but as you are not going to clone from that area the color is immaterial.

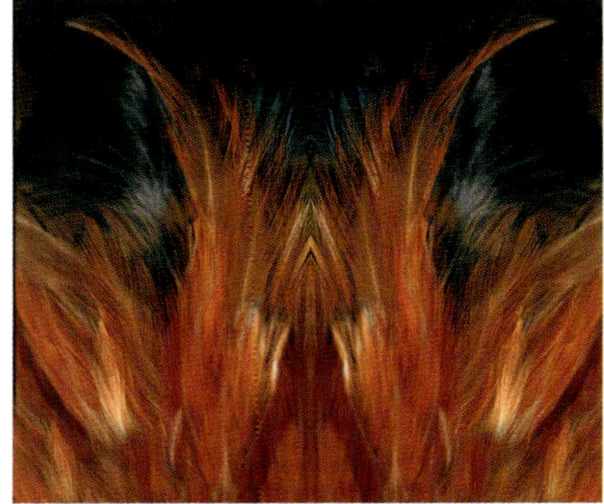

Figure 7.3 Feathers

Step 2 *File>Open>CD>Step-by-step files>'07 Feathers'.*

The picture that will be combined with the statue had already received some creative work in Photoshop. The original was a slide of cockerel feathers that had been copied and flipped to form an abstract design. The colorful feathers inspired the idea of flames from which the figure could emerge.

Step 3 Make the statue the active document by clicking in the image.

Step 4 *File>Clone*, which will make an identical copy of the original statue image; do not clear the clone copy.

Step 5 *File>Clone Source>Feathers.*

This last step changes the source of the clone, so the clone information will be taken from the feather image and painted into the portrait. There is no limit to the number of pictures from which you can clone and the clone source command allows you to toggle between them. Other pictures can be brought in at a later stage.

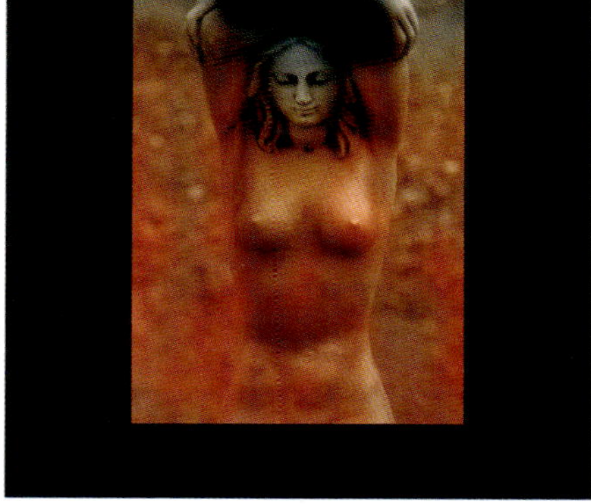

Figure 7.4 Statue 3

Step 6 *Select Acrylic>Opaque Acrylic 30* from the Brush Selector.

Step 7 In the General palette, change the Dab Type to Static Bristle, Method to Cloning and Subcategory to Soft Cover Cloning. Make the opacity 5% and the brush size 127.0.

Step 8 Click the Tracing Paper icon; this will overlay the feather picture.

Step 9 Paint lightly over the feathers, just enough to give some idea of where they are, then you can turn off the Tracing Paper to get a clearer view. This stage is shown in Figure 7.5.

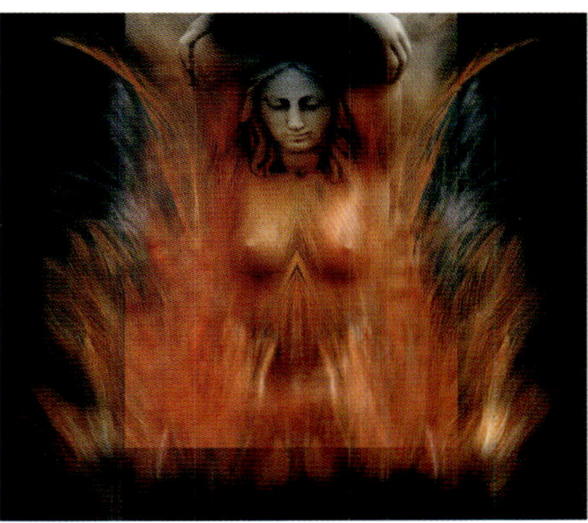

Figure 7.5 Step 9

Step 10 Gradually build up the density of the feathers and allow the 'flames' to reach up to and around the face. Don't worry if you overdo this, as it can be adjusted in the next step.

The edges of the smaller picture are visible and these need to be hidden, so increase the brush opacity to 15% and paint over these in the direction the feathers run. Paint over the hands at the top of the picture, as these are not needed.

Step 11 Decrease the brush size to 14.4 and increase the opacity to 62%. Use this brush to flick out brighter marks that will increase the contrast and texture.

Step 12 Change the clone source back to the statue (*File>Clone Source>'07 Statue 3'*) and paint any areas of the statue that have been covered unintentionally. Go back and forth between the two sources until the effect looks good.

In the final picture shown in Figure 7.6, some additional surface texture was added and this procedure will be covered in Chapter 10.

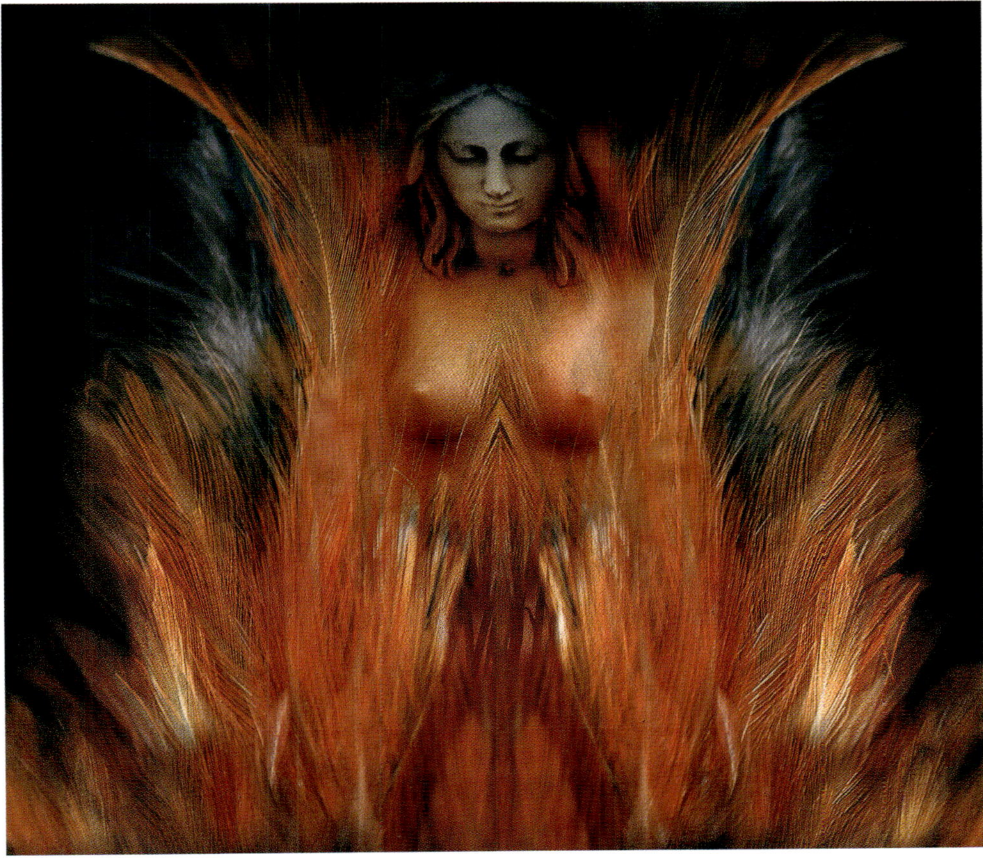

Figure 7.6 Phoenix

Cloning from three images

Try to visualize what you want to achieve before you start making a clone montage. These three elements were carefully selected to work together; the common element was trees of course, but using three very different scales will add a sense of mystery to the final picture.

The holes in the old leaf are particularly interesting and the way this hole punches through the more realistic landscapes will also emphasize the sense of unreality.

Tree and leaf montage

Step 1 *File>Open>CD>Step-by-step files '07 Leaf'.*

Step 2 *File>Open>CD>Step-by-step files '07 Tree'.*

Step 3 *File>Open>CD>Step-by-step files '07 Sky'.*

Step 4 *File>Clone* with the Leaf as the active document. This will make a clone copy of the Leaf picture without clearing the picture.

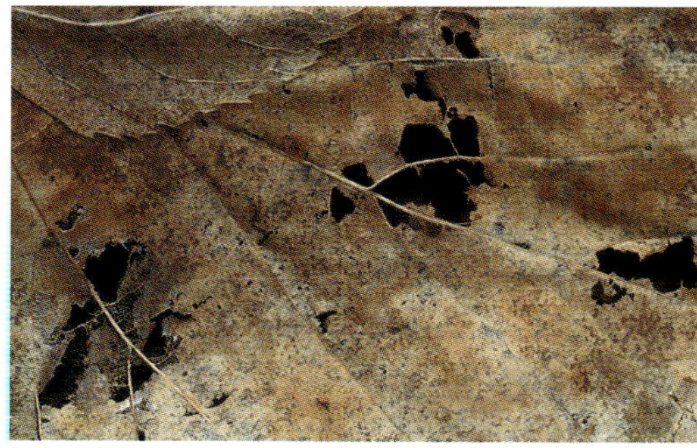

Figure 7.7 Leaf

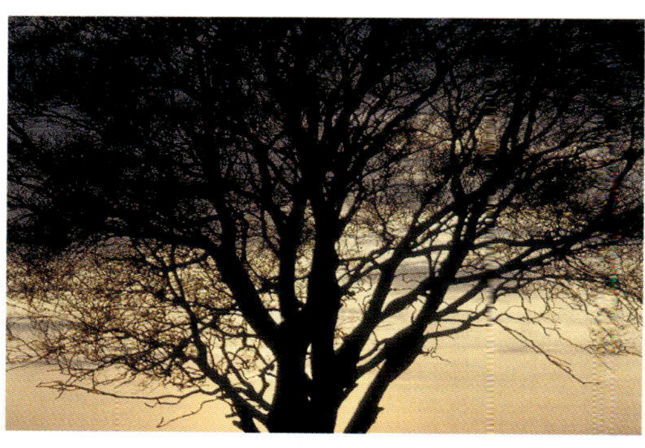

Figure 7.8 Tree

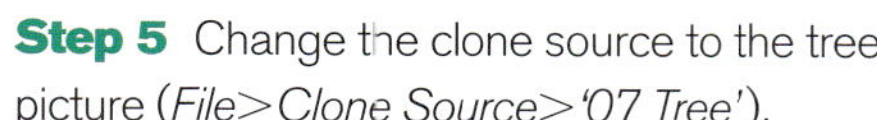

Step 5 Change the clone source to the tree picture (*File>Clone Source>'07 Tree'*).

Step 6 Choose the Graffiti brush from the Airbrush brush category. In the Colors palette, click the Clone icon and make the brush size 190.0 and the opacity 61%.

Step 7 Paint over the Leaf picture; the Graffiti brush will spray dots that will give the picture an attractive texture. Emphasize the lines of the tree trunk and branches as seen in Figure 7.10.

Step 8 Change the clone source to the sky picture (*File>Clone Source>'07 Sky'*).

Step 9 Change the brush to *Airbrush>Fine Tip Soft Air 50*, brush size 150.0 and opacity 4%.

In the General palette, change the Method to Cloning and the Subcategory to Grainy Soft Cloning. Paint in the sky and tree, giving it a dreamlike quality by cloning in some areas but not in others.

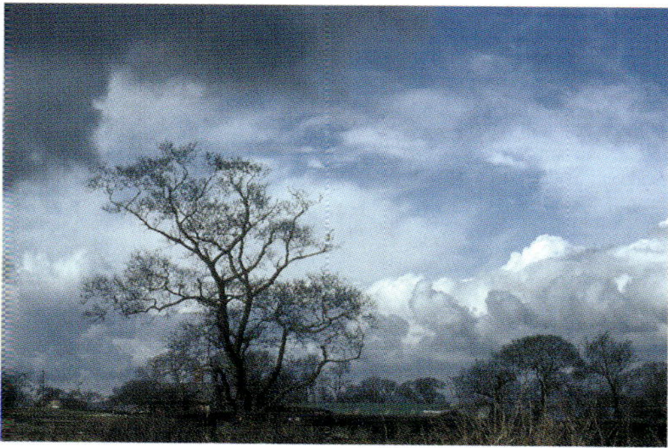

Figure 7.9 Sky

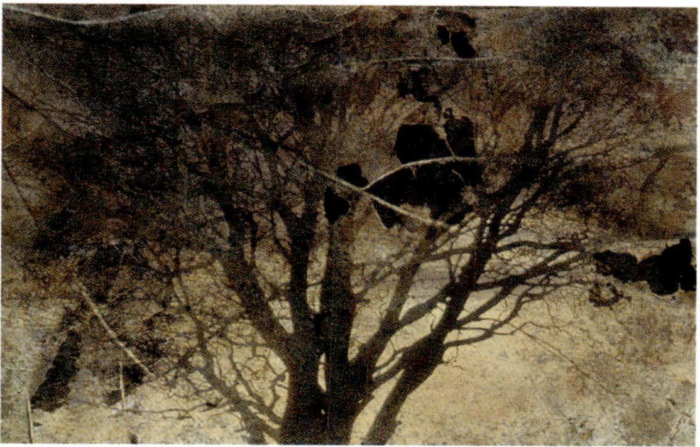

Figure 7.10 Step 7

Step 10 In the previous step it is difficult to get exactly the right amount of blue; it can also be too smooth, so change back to the Leaf as your clone source and return to the Graffiti brush used earlier. Brush over with this to get the right balance between the three images.

Continue to swap between the three original pictures by using the clone source option until the picture is to your satisfaction.

Step 11 Finally, you will need to crop the picture as the originals are not exactly the same size; you can see this by the line down the right side of the picture.

Select the Crop tool in the Toolbox, click in the top left corner and, dragging down to the bottom right, include all of the picture you want to keep. Adjust the edges by dragging them to the desired position and click in the picture to crop. The picture in Figure 7.11 has cropped the top and right quite substantially, which has strengthened the picture.

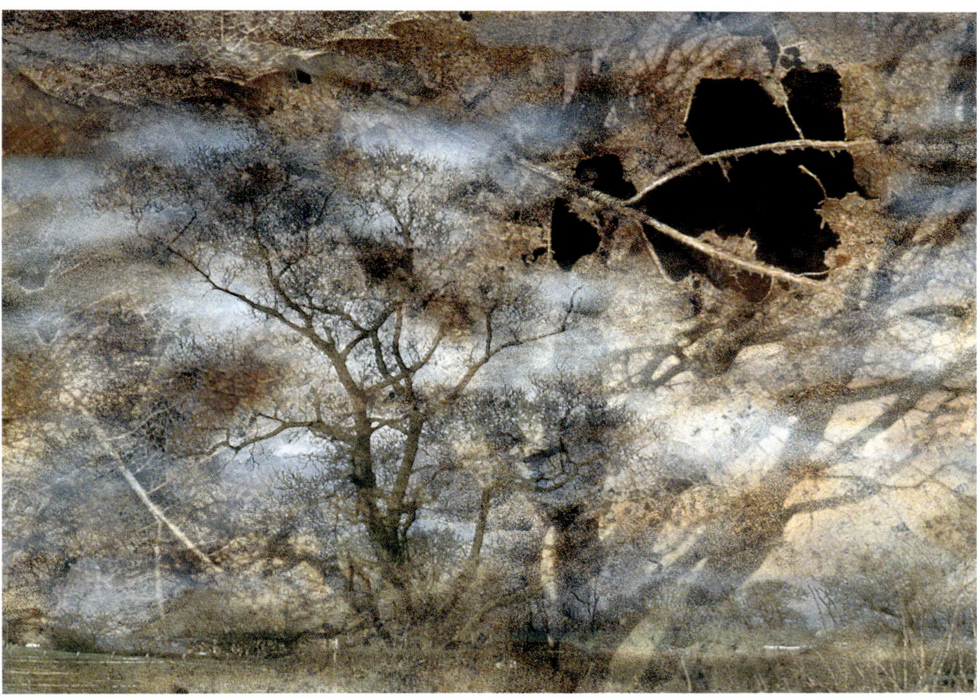

Figure 7.11 Tree and leaf

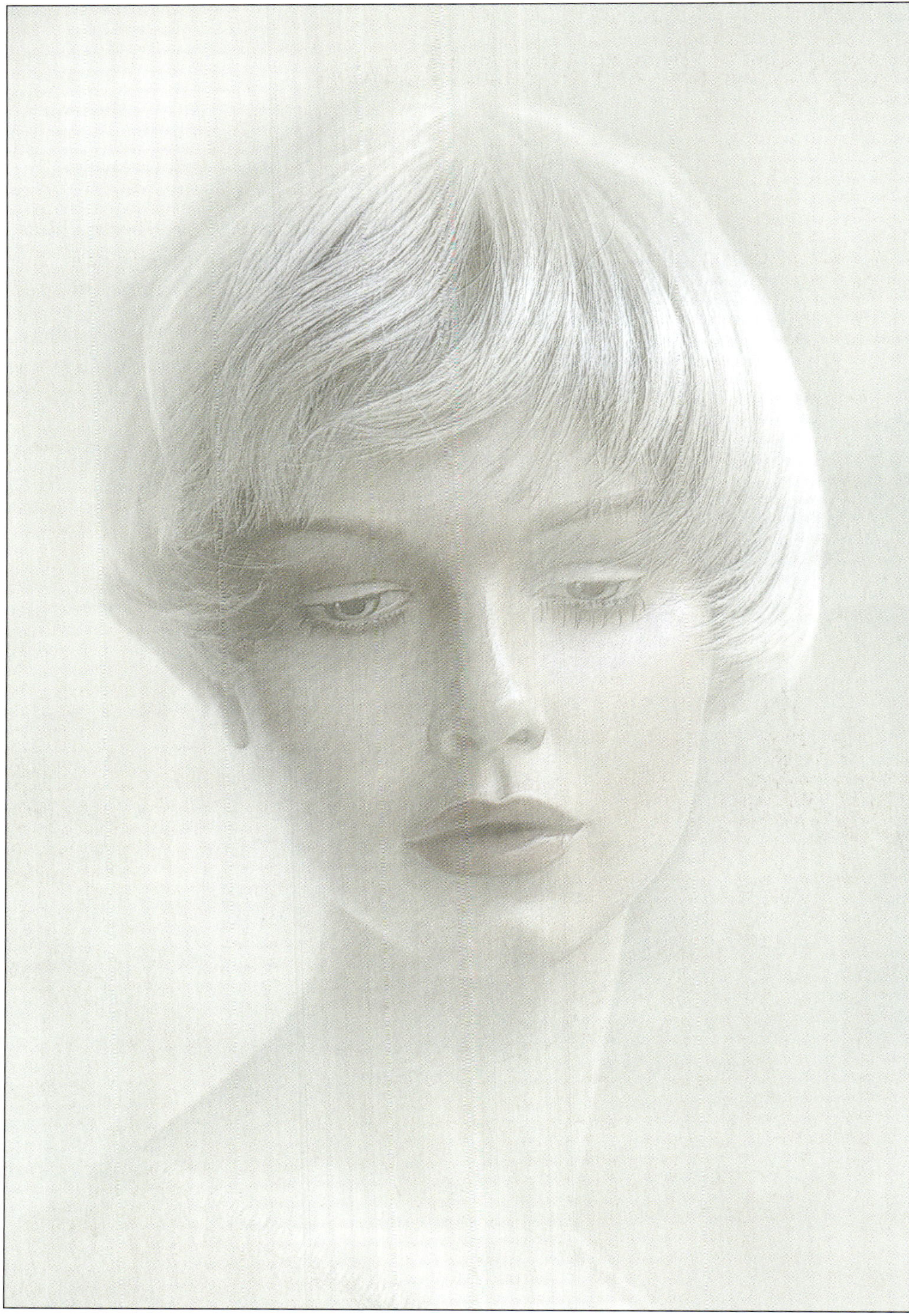

Figure 8.1 Dream ng

Chapter 8
Layers and montage

Layers are an important part of Painter and they give considerable additional flexibility, both in cloning and in bringing together elements from different photographs. If you are already familiar with using layers in Photoshop, you will find that Painter's Layers palette looks very similar; however, there are some differences, which you will need to be aware of.

This chapter is in three distinct sections.

Part 1 takes the form of a reference section that introduces all the main functions, which will enable you to follow and understand the step-by-step examples in the later sections.

Part 2 explains how to use layers as part of the cloning process. This will enable you to make several different versions and merge them together to make the final picture.

Part 3 is a step-by-step example of a montage consisting of several different images.

The portraits shown in Figures 8.1 and 8.2 were created with several layers of imagery and combined in the Layers palette using various layer composite methods; these are described later in this chapter.

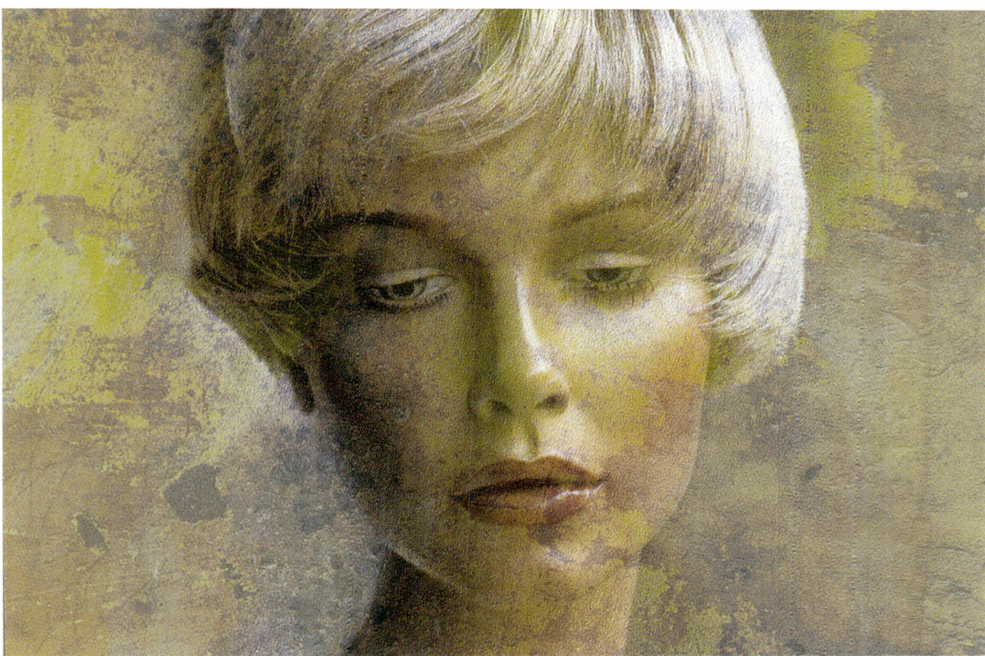

Figure 8.2 Dreamer

The Layers palette

The Layers palette will be in use throughout this chapter, so if the palette is not already visible on screen, go to *Window>Show Layers*.

Open the file on the CD called '08 Multi layered file', which is shown in Figure 8.3. This file has several layers already present, which you can use to follow the examples.

Layers can be thought of as clear sheets of acetate placed on top of the Canvas. The layer stack is being viewed from the top, so that when the top layer is full of imagery none of the layers beneath are visible.

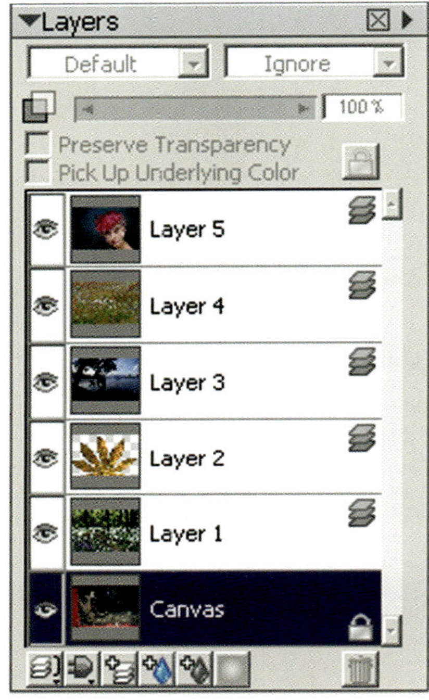

Figure 8.3 Layers palette

The active layer

Click on any layer and it becomes the active layer, which means that it can be edited, moved or painted on. Normally, only one layer can be active at any one time and the active layer is colored dark blue.

Layer visibility

Click the eye icon to the left of the top layer; this will turn the visibility of the layer off and reveal the layer below. Continue to turn off the eye icon of each of the layers until you reach the Canvas layer at the bottom of the stack. When a layer has its visibility turned off, it does not contribute to the picture and if the picture is printed the layer would be ignored.

The canvas

The Canvas is always at the bottom of the stack and is similar, though not identical, to the background in other graphics programs. This layer cannot be moved or have layer masks applied and is restricted in some other ways.

Making new layers

New layers can be made either by going to *Layers>New Layer* and selecting the type of layer required or by clicking one of the icons in the Layers palette, as shown in Figure 8.4.

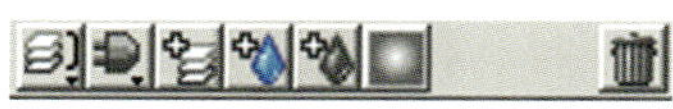

Figure 8.4

There are several types of layers, all of which have their own special characteristics. To make a new standard layer, click the third icon from the left. Standard layers can be painted on with most types of brush and are the ones that are mainly used for cloning.

The second icon will make a Dynamic Plug-in layer, which is a special effects layer that will make adjustments to the layer beneath. They are a bit like adjustment layers in Photoshop, as the settings can be changed at a later date; this type of layer is described in Chapter 13.

The fourth icon from the left, which has the blue droplet design, makes a new Watercolor layer; these are described in Chapter 9 and can only be used with Watercolor brushes.

The fifth icon from the left makes a new Liquid Ink layer, which may only be used for Liquid Ink brushes. A step-by-step example of Liquid Ink brushes appears in Chapter 11.

Deleting layers

Layers that are active can be deleted by clicking on the Trashcan on the far right of the new layer icons. This will immediately delete the currently active layer; there is no warning given, so be careful!

Merging and flattening layers

Generally, I recommend that you keep the layers intact rather than flattening the picture; however, if you do need to, click the icon on the far left and select Drop. This will merge the active layer with the Canvas. If you need to flatten all the layers, either go to the palette menu and select Drop All, or to the layers menu and select Drop All.

Grouping layers

It is sometimes convenient to store layers in groups; this is rather like keeping them in folders. Layers can be grouped and ungrouped by clicking the first icon at the bottom of the Layers palette and selecting Group or Ungroup; these commands are also available from the Layers menu and the palette menu. To collect several layers into a new group, select them before clicking on the group icon (hold down the *Ctrl/Cmd key* and click the layers needed to select them). The Collapse command will merge all the layers within a group. In Figure 8.5, Group 1 contains four layers and they are offset in the layer stack to show that they are contained in a group. Group 2 is collapsed and hides the layers within it to save space.

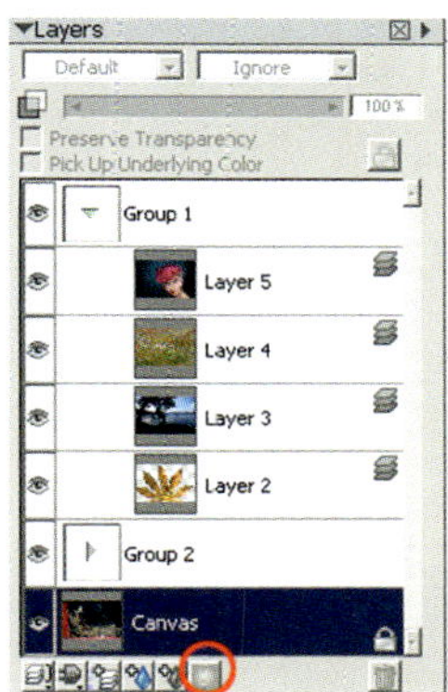

Figure 8.5

Layer masks

Layer masks work very much like their cousins in Photoshop. By painting into the mask with black, the contents of the layer are hidden. If you have not used masks before you may want to try the short step-by-step example below.

Step 1 *File>Open>CD>Step-by-step files>'08 Multi Layered File'.*

Step 2 Click the top layer to make it the active layer.

Step 3 Make a layer mask by clicking on the layer mask icon highlighted in Figure 8.5.

Step 4 Click on the layer mask itself to make it active; the mask thumbnail will have a black line around it. You must do this or you will be painting on the image itself rather than the mask.

Step 5 Select the *Pencils>Grainy Cover Pencil 3* with a size of about 65.0 and opacity 100%. In the Colors palette, make the painting color black.

Step 6 Paint with the brush in the picture area; you will see the face disappearing and the layer below being revealed. The Layers palette can be seen in Figure 8.6, while the resulting picture is shown in Figure 8.7.

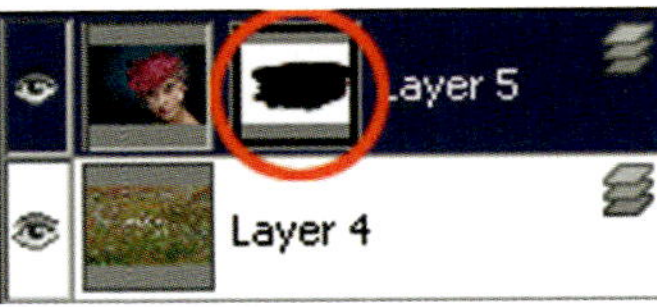

Figure 8.6 Layers palette showing the layer mask

Step 7 Reduce the brush opacity to 25% and paint again. Note that these strokes have only partially hidden the top layer; black hides the picture but shades of gray only partially hide the layers below.

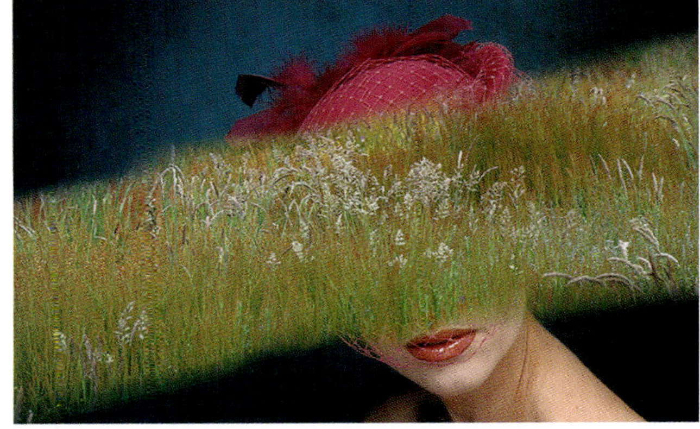

Figure 8.7 The effect of a layer mask on the top layer

Step 8 Change the painting color to white and paint over the masked area; this will reveal the original picture again.

To delete a layer mask, click on the layer mask to activate it then click on the Trashcan, which will delete the mask and leave the original layer intact.

Locking a layer

To lock a layer, click on the layer then depress the padlock symbol just above the layer stack. Locking is useful to prevent accidental erasure or painting on the wrong layer. Click the padlock icon again to unlock.

Duplicating layers

To duplicate a layer, go to *Layers>Duplicate Layer* or if you are using a computer which runs Windows you can right-click the layer and select duplicate from the pop-up menu.

The procedure to make a duplicate copy of the Canvas Layer is different and is shown below.

Step 1 Make the Canvas active.

Step 2 Select All (*Ctrl + A*).

Step 3 Make the Layer Adjuster tool active.

Step 4 Hold down the *Alt/Opt key* and click in the picture area. This will make a copy of the Canvas on a new layer at the top of the layer stack, leaving the Canvas layer intact. If you forget to hold down the *Alt/Opt key*, the picture on the Canvas layer will be erased and moved to the top of the stack as a layer. (Use the Undo command to correct this if needed.)

Layer opacity

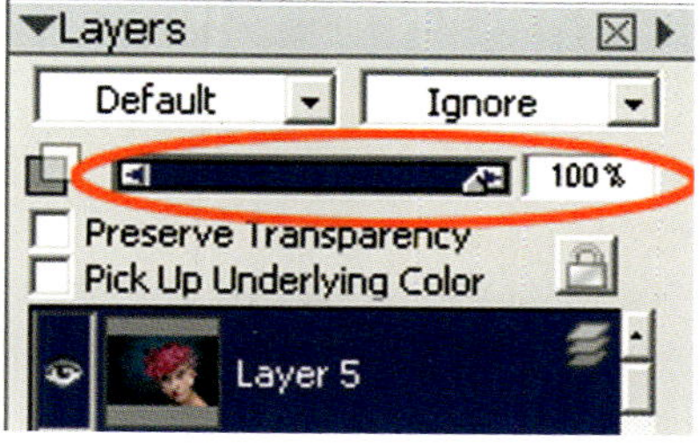

Figure 8.8

The slider near the top of the Layers palette controls the layer opacity; move the slider to the left to gradually reveal the layer beneath. With multi-layer images it is very useful to be able to fine-tune the opacity of each layer with this slider.

Figure 8.8 shows the slider at 100% opacity.

Layer Composite Depth

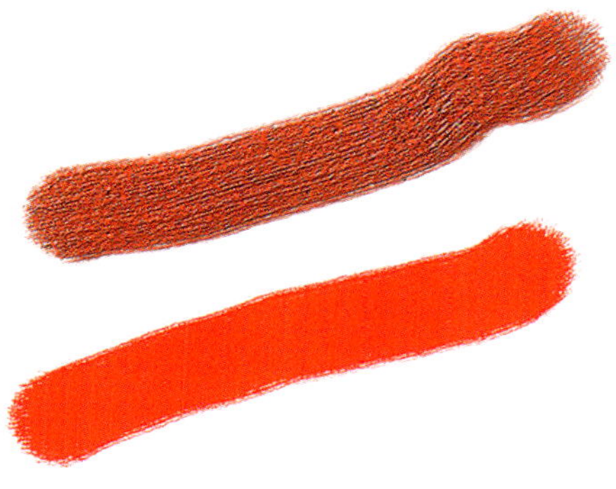
Figure 8.9

The box to the right of the layer blend mode is the Layer Composite Depth control. The default here is Ignore. This set of options is active when using brushes which have Impasto strokes that show depth and a three-dimensional appearance. We will be using Impasto brushes in Chapter 11, but if you would like to try the effect now, use the *Impasto>Thick Wet Round 20* brush with a brush size of about 40.0. Select a bright red color and paint into the picture; you will see how shadows have been added to the paint strokes, which give them a three-dimensional appearance. The Layer Composite Depth option will have changed automatically to Add when you used this brush; change it to Ignore and see the brush strokes flatten. Figure 8.9 shows the Impasto effect on the top brush stroke and the effect removed on the lower stroke.

Preserve Transparency

This option is used to protect areas of a layer that has no imagery and is often used to paint over objects on that layer without affecting an empty background.

To see how this works, make a new empty layer (*Layers>New Layer*) and select the *Pencils>Grainy Cover Pencil 3* with a size of about 35% and opacity 100%. Paint into the picture with any color but leave plenty of blank areas. Tick the Preserve Transparency box and change the paint color. Paint all across the layer and you will see that the paint has only recorded in the areas that already have some imagery, while the areas that were transparent have been preserved untouched, hence the name. Now turn off the Preserve Transparency option and paint again. This time the paint is laid down wherever the brush is used.

Renaming a layer

If you create several layers in a document it is often helpful to rename them to aid in identification. To rename an existing layer, open the palette menu and click on Layer Attributes and type the name there.

Painter/Photoshop compatibility

When moving image files from Photoshop to Painter and vice versa, most of the elements stay intact, including the layers, layer masks and selections. However, there are some special elements that do not work in the same way, so it is important to be aware of these differences.

Photoshop CS to Painter IX

Adjustment layers are not translated, so you will need to merge them in Photoshop prior to moving the file to Painter, otherwise the adjustment will be discarded. Type layers will become normal bitmap layers and will not be able to be directly edited again.

Layer blend modes that have the same names in both programs will translate well, but newer ones such as Hard Mix, Linear Light, etc. will change to the Default mode and look quite different.

Painter IX to Photoshop CS

The Canvas will translate as a background and Normal layers will stay the same. The specialist layers that include Watercolor layers, Liquid Ink layers, Dynamic Plug-in layers and Type layers will change to Normal layers.

All these special layers will be rasterized during the process of saving to PSD format. Rasterized means that they become normal bitmap layers and the special effects cannot be directly edited again. If you wish to keep any of these special layers to be edited at a later date, you must save in Painter's own file saving format, called RIFF.

In Painter go to *File>Save As* and select RIFF, and you will then be able to edit this layer in the future. If you are working in any of these special types of layers, you may wish to save two versions, one in RIFF format in case you need to change something later and another in PSD format to transfer immediately into Photoshop.

Layer composite methods will translate pretty closely into Layer Blend Modes in Photoshop. The modes that are exclusive to Painter will go to Normal mode, which will usually look totally different. If the mode fails to translate correctly, it may be necessary to flatten the picture within Painter before saving it.

Layer composite method

The layer composite method controls how a layer will interact with the layer beneath and offers many creative opportunities when using multi-layer files. The layer composite method box is at the top of the Layers palette and is highlighted in Figure 8.10, where it is shown in the default mode.

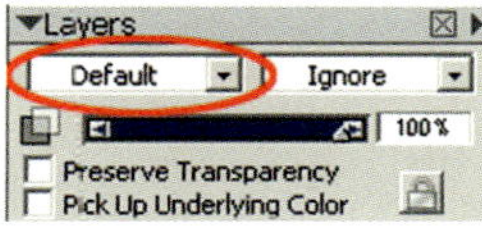

Figure 8.10

The first set of examples illustrates how the layer composite methods will combine layers with different images on each layer. This is extremely useful when making montages, as it allows you to mix image layers in ways that are not possible using any other method. Often this can spark off new directions in which to develop your image.

The following screenshots shown in Figure 8.11 will provide a brief insight into how each composite method works. The effect of the composite method will differ considerably depending upon the content of the two layers that are combined. The opacity setting will also change the appearance. Try this with the multi-layered file we used earlier in this chapter.

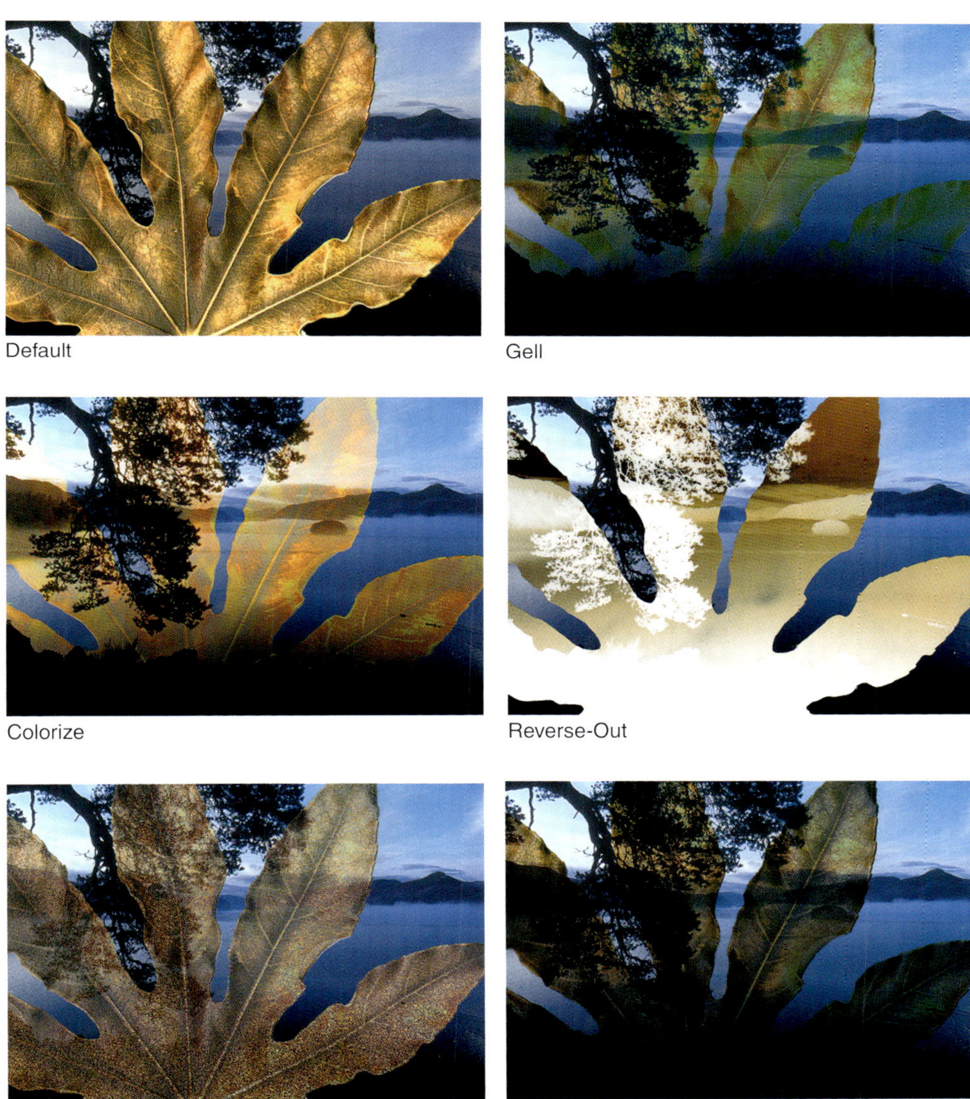

Figure 8.11

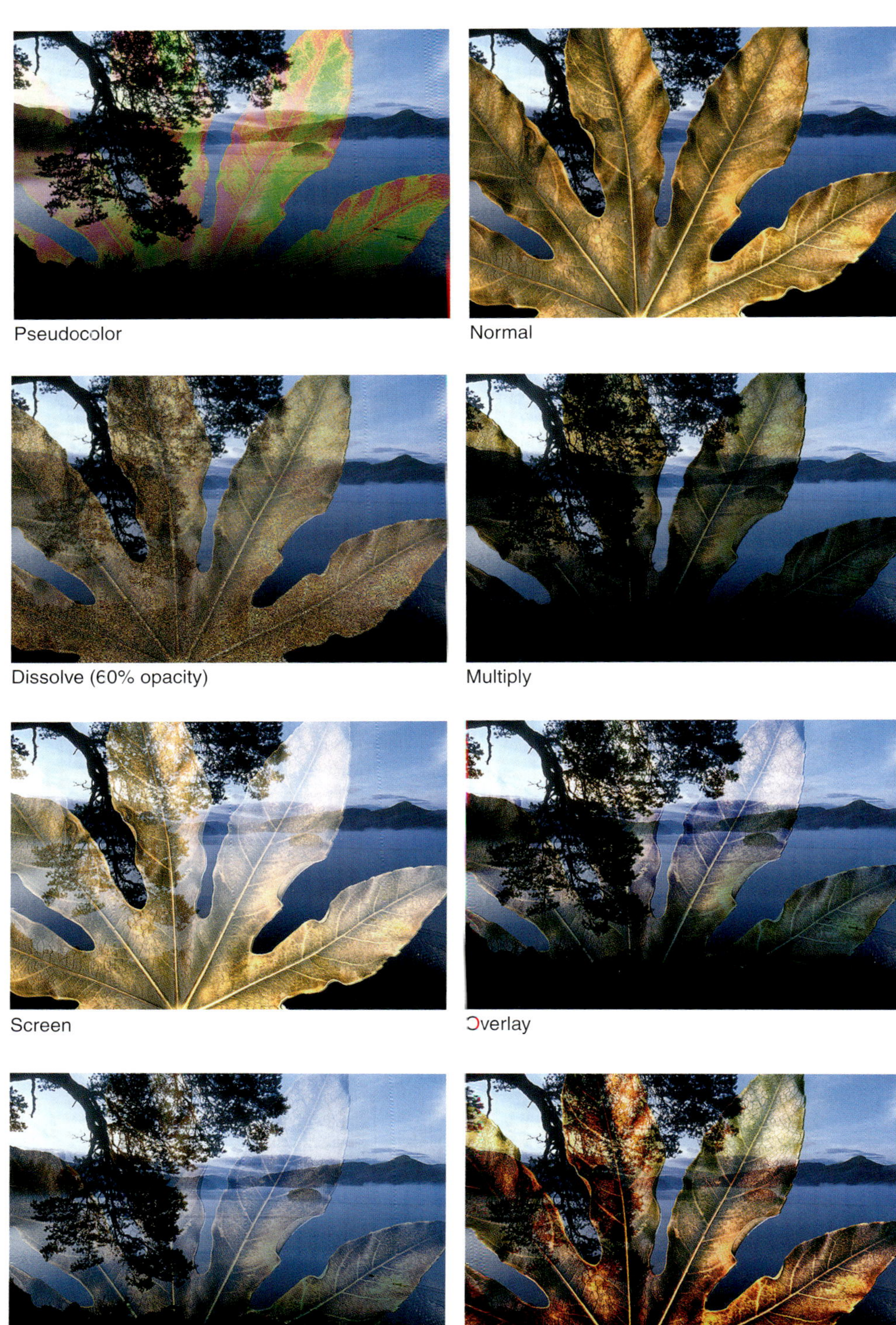

Figure 8.11 (*Continued*)

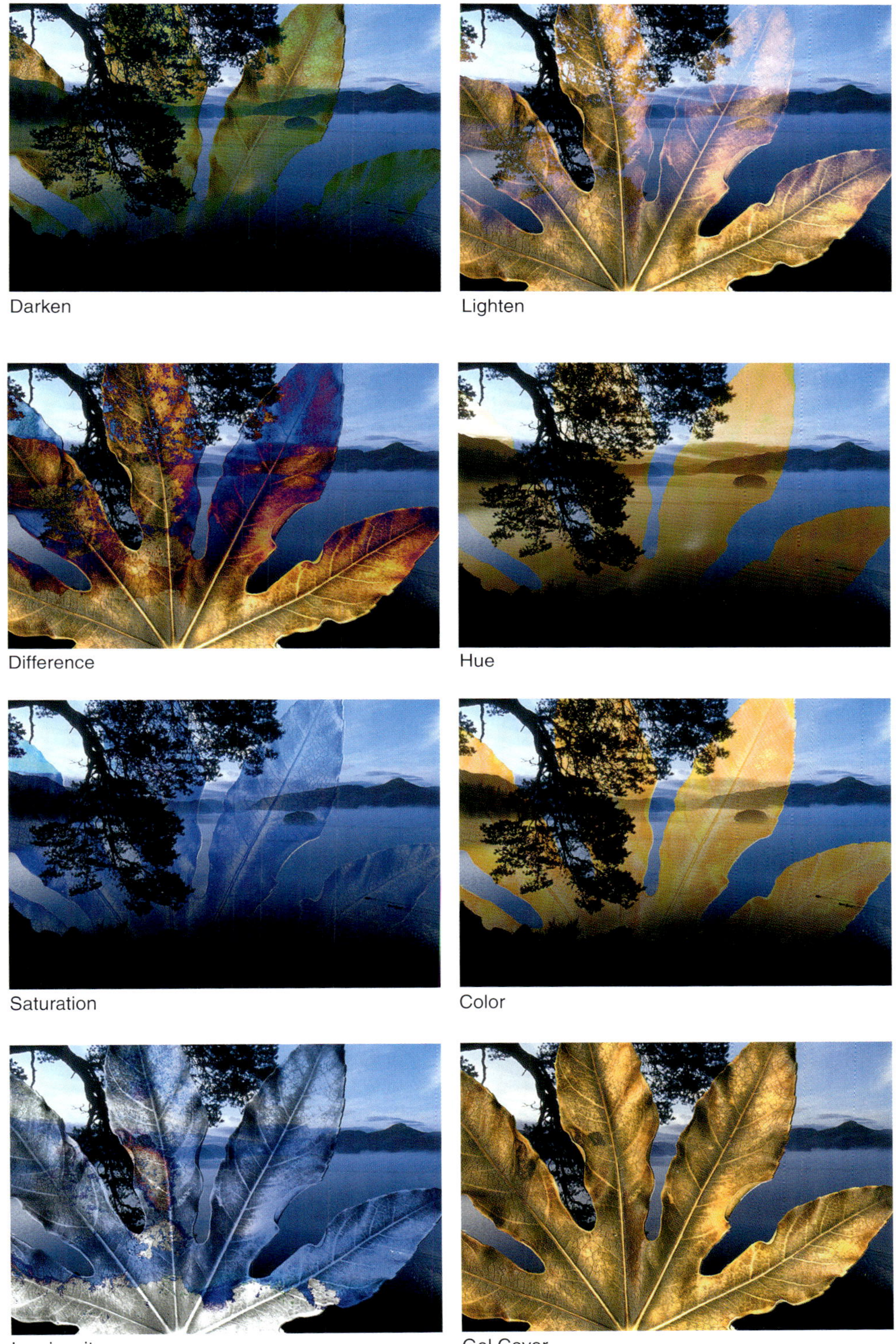
Darken
Lighten
Difference
Hue
Saturation
Color
Luminosity
Gel Cover

Figure 8.11 (*Continued*)

Altering tone and color with layers

The second set of examples use the layer composite method in a different way. This method uses a duplicate copy of the same layer (or a copy of the Canvas) and the composite method to adjust the layer beneath. Depending on which composite method is used, the picture can be made lighter or darker or the color changed. The following examples in Figure 8.12 give some idea of possible uses. Remember that the opacity slider will reduce the effect and should be used to fine-tune the result. A step-by-step example follows.

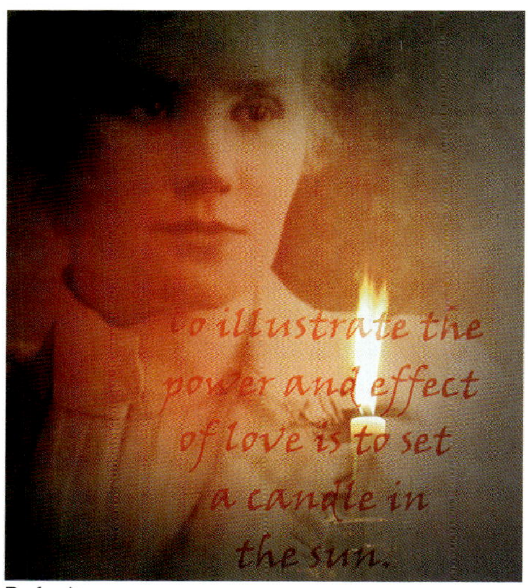

Default

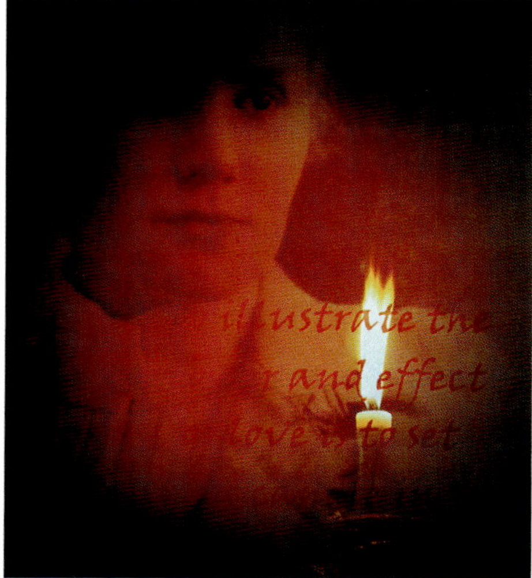

Multiply

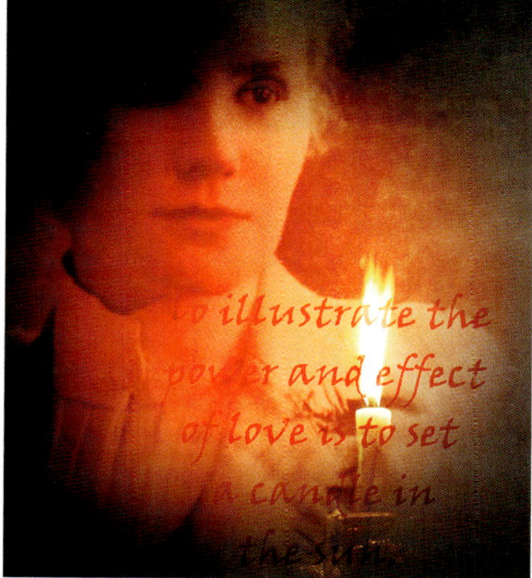

Overlay

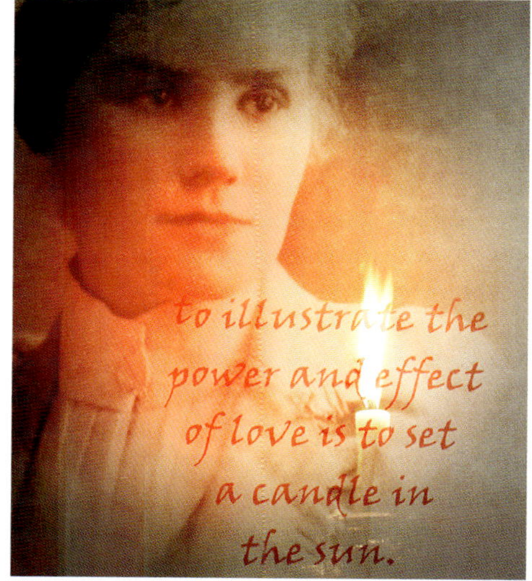

Screen

Figure 8.12

Candle in the sun (Figure 8.13)

Step 1 *File>Open>CD>Step-by-step files>'08 Candle in the Sun'.*

Step 2 *Select>All.*

Step 3 Make the Layer Adjuster tool active.

Step 4 Hold down the *Alt/Opt key* and click in the picture area; this will make a duplicate copy of the Canvas.

Step 5 Change the layer composite method to the one required.

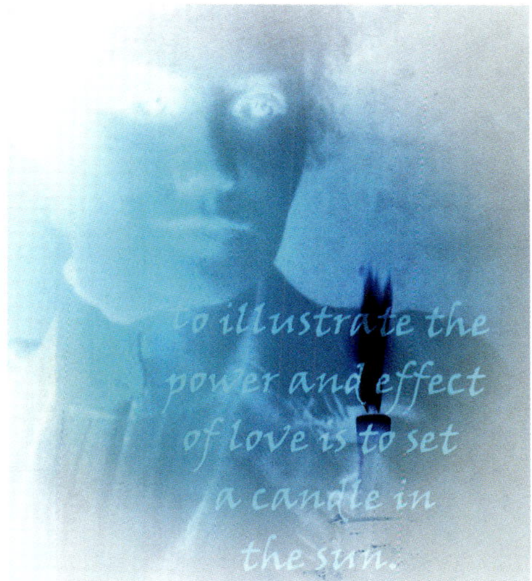

Reverse-Out

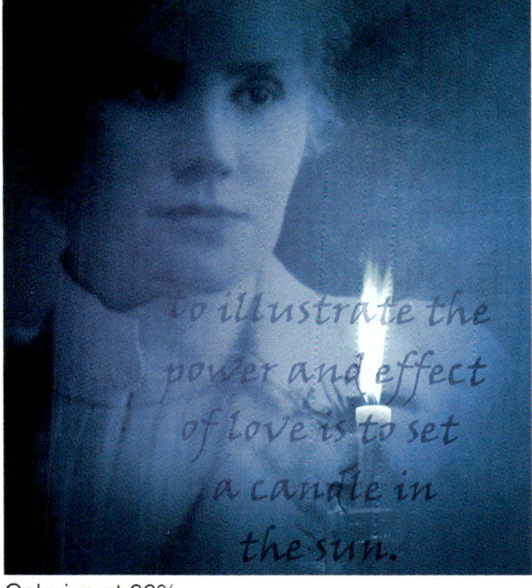

Colorize at 66%

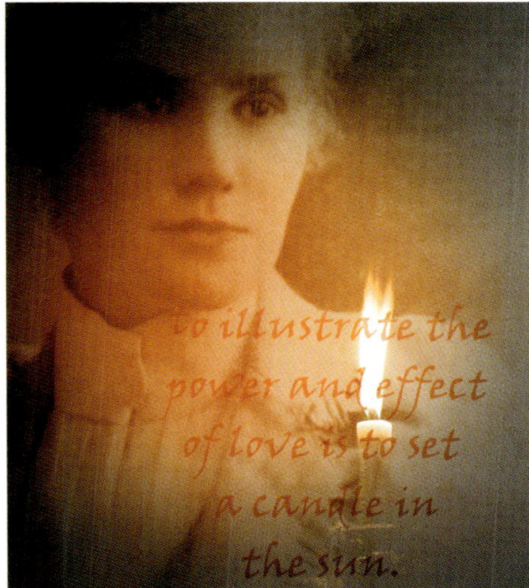

Hue at 73%

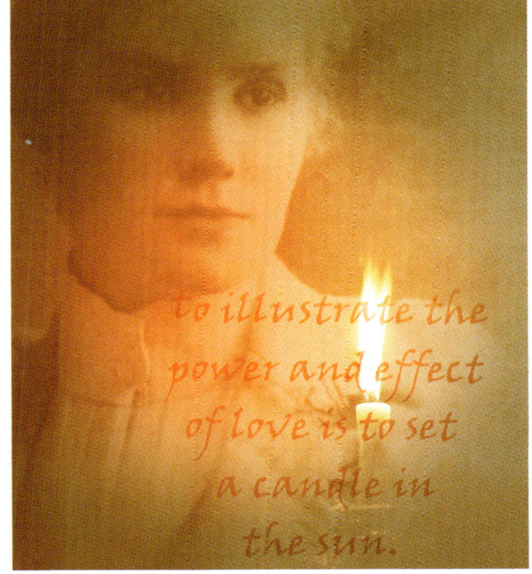

Screen at 73%

Figure 8.13

Using layers with cloning

Making a multi-layered picture

This step-by-step example will show you how to use the Layers palette while making clones. Several clone versions will be combined to make the final picture.

Step 1 *File>Open>CD>Step-by-step files>'08 Donna'.*

Step 2 *File>Clone.*

Step 3 *Select>All*, but do not clear the image.

Step 4 Activate the Layer Adjuster tool (top right in the Toolbox) and click in the main image with the cursor. This will lift the image off the canvas layer onto a new layer, leaving the Canvas plain white. The Canvas will provide a white backdrop for the new layers about to be created.

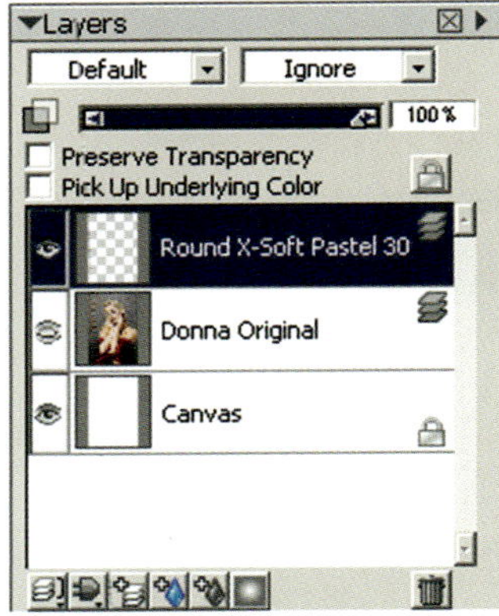

Figure 8.14

Step 5 *Layers>Layer Attributes* and change the name to Donna Original.

Step 6 Click the eye icon for this layer in the Layers palette to hide the picture. You should now have nothing showing in the picture area.

Step 7 Make a new empty layer by clicking on the new layer icon at the base of the Layers palette (third from the left). Open the Layers palette and click on Layer Attributes to rename this layer Round Soft Pastel 10.

Step 8 Click the top layer to activate; it is now ready to clone into. The Layers palette should now look like Figure 8.14.

Remember to save copies of your work at regular intervals; this is always good practice.

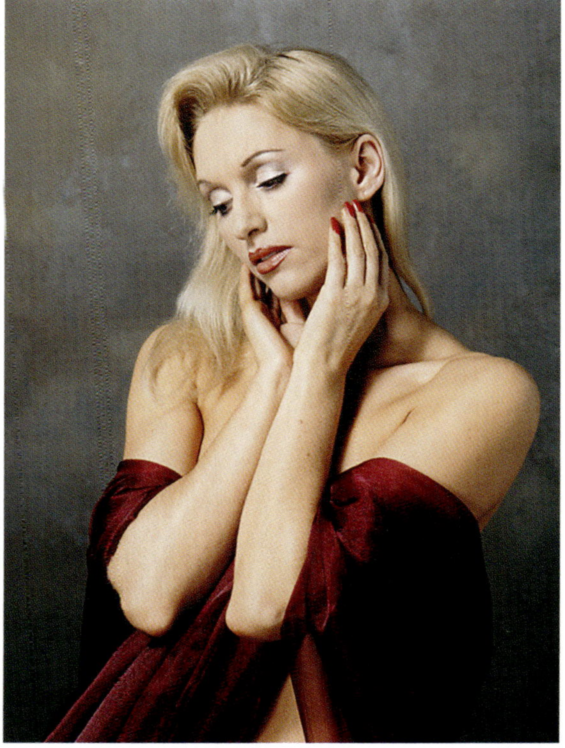

Figure 8.15 Original photograph

The first clone

Step 9 Select Thick Handmade Paper from the Papers palette; this is a fairly strong texture which will work well with the pastel brush.

Step 10 From the Brush Selector choose *Pastels>Round X-Soft Pastel 30*, brush size 60.0. This pastel brush has a captured dab, which means that it has been created from a shape or design.

Step 11 In the General palette, make the following settings: Dab Type Captured, Method Cloning, Subcategory Grainy Hard Cover Cloning, opacity 60%, grain 10%.

If the General palette is not on screen, go to *Window>Brush Controls>Show General*. The other palettes that open at the same time can be closed as they will nct be used here. This palette is also contained in the Brush Creator if you are using an earlier version of Painter.

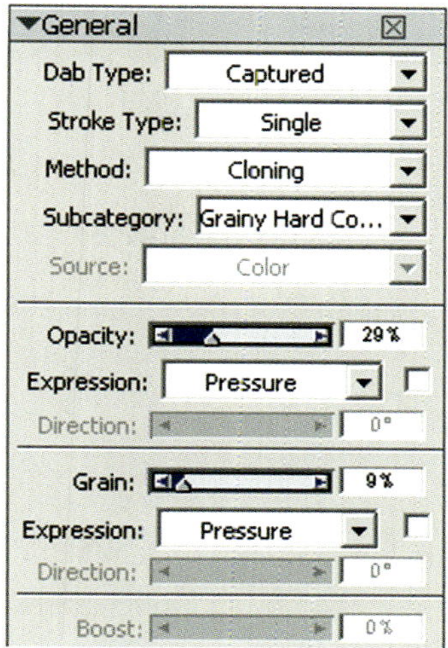

Figure 8.16

Step 12 Click back in the document and make a light clone of the head and shoulders. Paint over the face again to make it a little more distinct. Your picture should look something like the one in Figure 8.17.

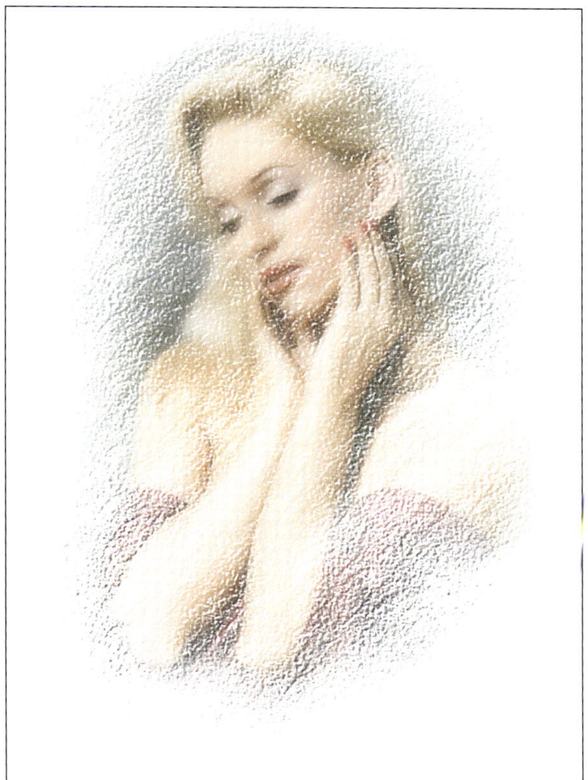

Figure 8.17

The second clone

Step 13 Click the eye icon of the newly cloned layer to hide it; the screen will be blank again.

Step 14 Make a new layer above the cloned layer. Rename it Square Chalk 35 in the Layer Attributes box.

Step 15 In the Papers palette, select French Watercolor Paper.

Step 16 Choose *Chalk>Square Chalk 35*, brush size 45.0.

Step 17 Make the following settings in the General palette: Dab Type Captured, Method Cloning, Subcategory Grainy Hard Cover Cloning, opacity 7%, grain 12%.

Step 18 Paint in the new layer and make a clone of just the head and shoulders as before. Figure 8.18 shows how this clone should look. Save the picture at this point.

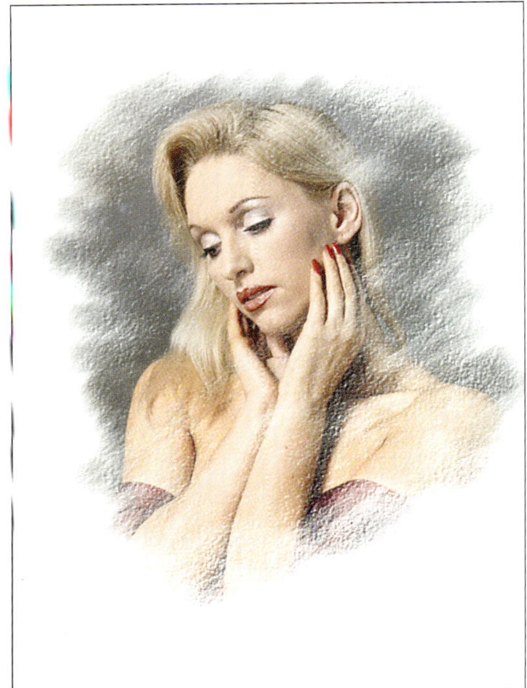

Figure 8.18

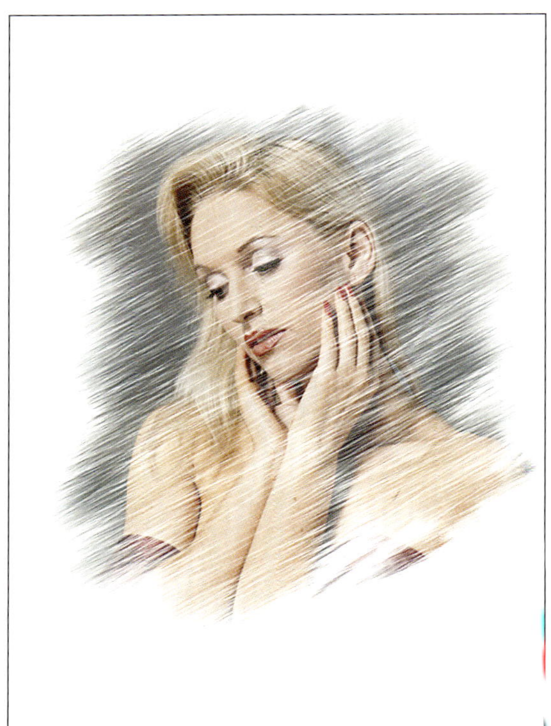

Figure 8.19

The third clone

The third clone uses a very different paper that you will have to load specially. If you have not already loaded a paper texture library, the full instructions are in Chapter 3.

Step 19 Click the eye icon of the newly cloned layer to hide it.

Step 20 Make a new empty layer on top of the cloned layer and name it Variable Width Chalk.

Step 21 Click the Papers palette menu arrow and select Open library from the drop-down menu. When the Open box appears, go to where your paper libraries are kept and choose Wild.

Step 22 With the new library loaded, select the paper called Streaks.

Step 23 Select the *Chalk>Variable Width Chalk*. Dab Type Circular, Method Cloning, Subcategory Grainy Hard Cover Cloning, opacity 24%, brush size 50.0. Make another clone as in Figure 8.19.

The fourth clone

For the final clone the brush changes to an airbrush that will give an even texture.

Step 24 Click the eye icon of the newly cloned layer to hide it.

Step 25 Make a new empty layer on top of the cloned layer and rename the layer Broad Wheel Airbrush 50. This airbrush does not use a special paper.

Step 26 Choose the Broad Wheel Airbrush 50 with the following settings: Dab Type Airbrush, opacity 44%, brush size 150.0. Click the Clone Color button in the Colors palette to change this to a cloning brush.

Step 27 Spray the airbrush lightly all over the picture concentrating in the center and allowing the spray to go each side. Figure 8.20 shows this version of the picture.

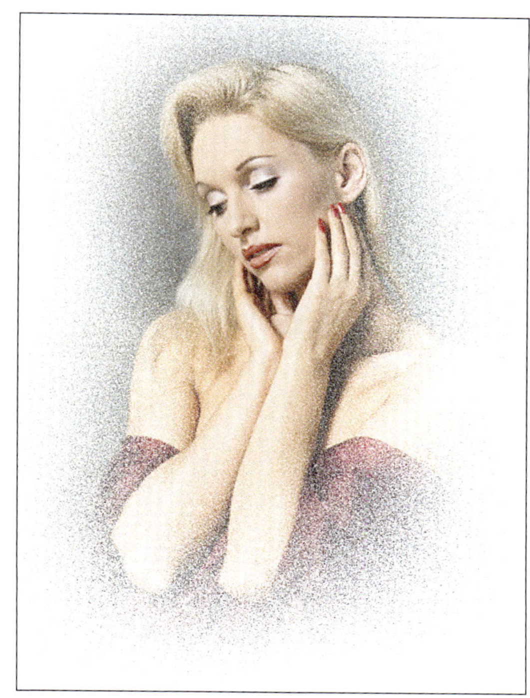

Figure 8.20

The final stage

The next stage is to look carefully at each clone layer and decide which of the layers are the most successful. Once you have done this you can adjust and combine them in several ways:

- Move the layers up or down the layer stack.
- Alter the opacity of the layers.
- Change the layer composite method.
- Use layer masks to hide parts.

This stage is very much about trying out the combinations that look the best; experiment and you will produce many different results. You may well decide that some layers are not required and delete them. If you are still not satisfied with the picture, then you could start another clone layer with a different brush or paper.

The Layers palette arrangement for my final version is shown in Figure 8.21 and the finished picture in Figure 8.22.

The layer settings, from the top, are:

1 Colorize composite method, 73% opacity.
2 Default composite method, 61% opacity.

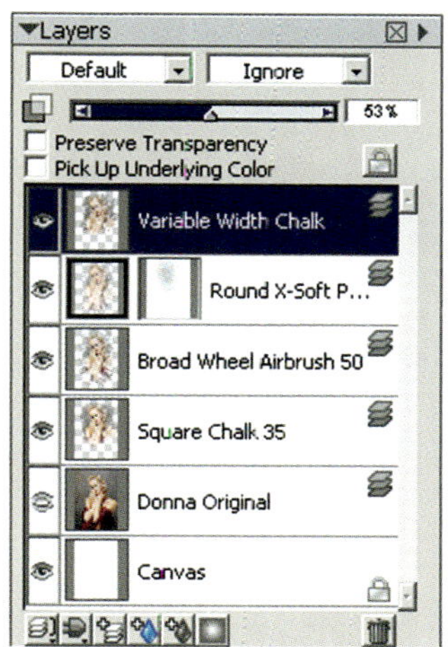

Figure 8.21

3 Default composite method, 77% opacity.
4 Hard Light composite method, 66% opacity.

The final layer is the original copy of the photograph and in this case it has not been used. It is, however, very useful on occasions to move the layer to the top of the layer stack and use a layer mask to hide or reveal parts of the original.

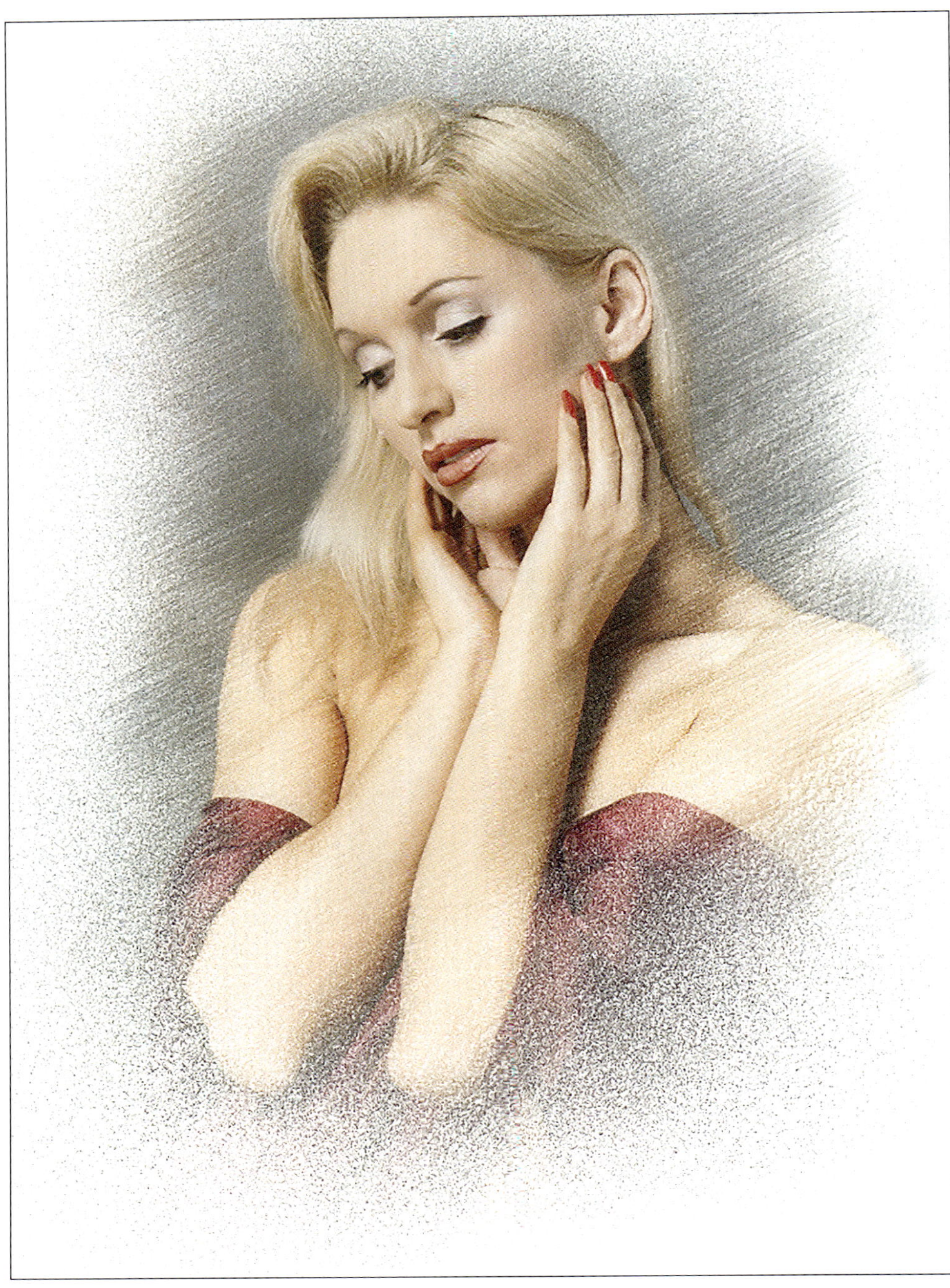

Figure 8.22 Donna

Creating a montage

One of the most interesting and exciting uses of layers is to make a montage. Montage is when several different images are combined in a way that makes the final result more than the sum of its parts. Montages can be used to get across a message, or to make an image that is interesting and satisfying in its own right using layers of texture and imagery.

Certainly, one of the most important things to do before starting work on a montage is to think really hard about the picture that you are intending to create. The more you can plan in advance the better, but that is not to say that you should not experiment as you go along; indeed, one of the great joys in making montages is that they can go off in directions not originally envisaged. Obviously, if you are working to a commercial brief you may not have this opportunity, but in personal work you are free to go where your imagination takes you.

Step-by-step montage

In the step-by-step montage you are about to embark on, there is no specific end planned, rather a choice of some interesting textures and imagery that should work well together. As you work through the steps you will use many of the techniques that have been described earlier in the chapter, plus some others. When you have completed the exercise you should have enough experience to make your own montage using photographs that will blend well together.

Remember to save your montage at regular intervals to avoid loss. I recommend that you use the Iterative Save (which is new in Painter IX) from the File menu, as this will save a new version each time and give them different reference numbers. When the picture is finished they provide a useful overview of how the montage has developed.

The first layer

Step 1 *File>Open>CD>Step-by-step files>'08 Montage 1'.*

Step 2 *File>Quick Clone.*

Step 3 Select the Square Chalk 35 brush and in the General palette change the Method to Cloning and the Subcategory to Grainy Hard Cover Cloning. Use brush size 40.0, opacity 13% and grain 10%. Clone the picture following Figures 8.23 and 8.24.

Step 4 Select the paper; use French Watercolor Paper from the Default set of paper textures.

Step 5 Paint the top half of the figure in fairly roughly, then reduce the opacity to 9% and complete the lower half including the blue towel. Go over any areas that need more emphasis.

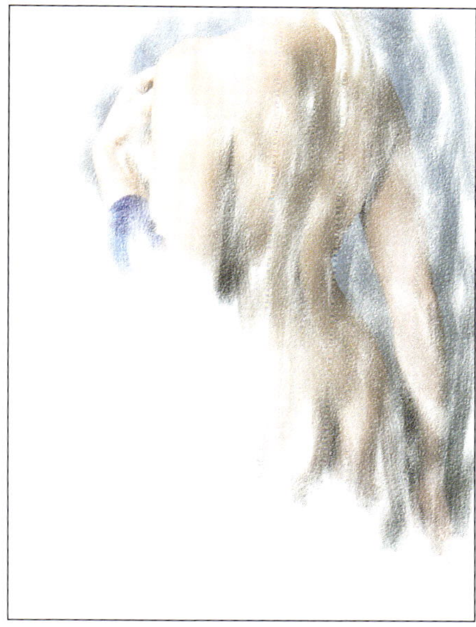

Figure 8.23

Adding the rock texture

Figure 8.25 is a photograph of a section of rock that has an unusual honeycomb texture and will make an interesting overlay for the figure.

Step 6 *File>Open>CD>Step-by-step files> '08 Honeycomb Rock'.*

Step 7 Make a new layer and rename it Rock Texture. Always use a new layer for each element so that you can adjust it separately.

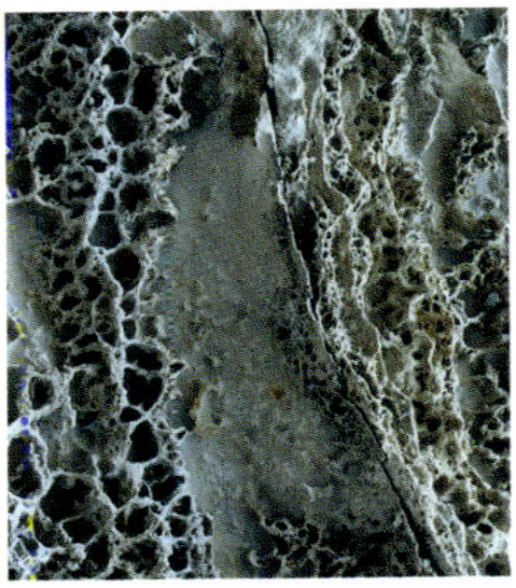

Figure 8.25

Step 8 Select the Broad Wheel Airbrush, brush size 76.8, opacity 44%, spread 40, flow 672. In the Colors palette, click the Clone Color icon.

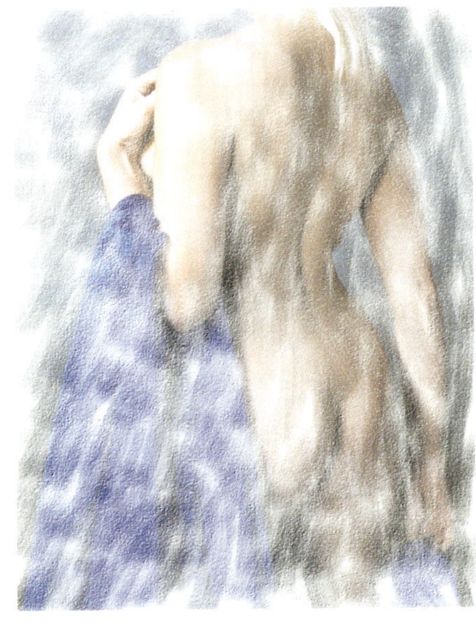

Figure 8.24

Step 9 *File>Clone Source>'08 Honeycomb Rock'.*

Step 10 Spray over the picture with the airbrush, paint from top to bottom and follow the flow of the rock pattern. You need not worry if it looks too strong, as the next step will enable you to adjust it.

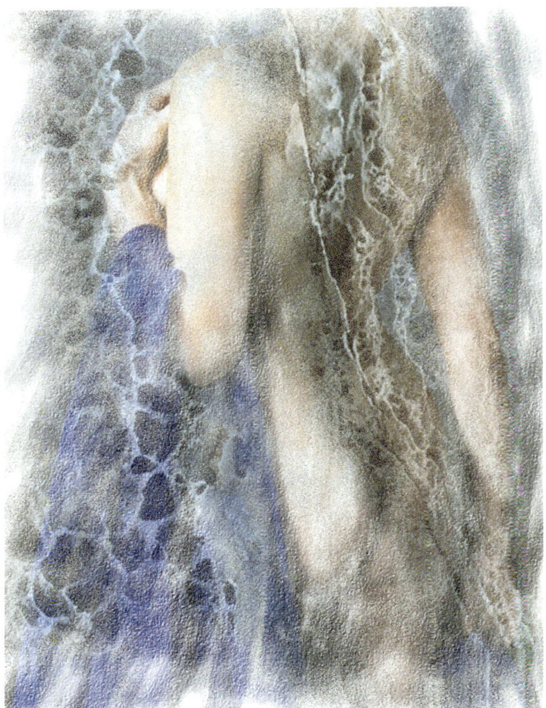

Figure 8.26

Using a layer mask to reduce the effect

Step 11 Click the layer mask icon in the Layers palette to add a layer mask to this layer, then click the mask thumbnail to activate it. Don't forget to click the mask, otherwise you will be painting onto the picture rather than the mask; this is an easy mistake to make!

Step 12 Using the same brush and settings, paint into the mask and hide parts of the rock overlay. Because you are using the same brush you retain the texture of your original brush strokes, or in this case airbrush texture. If you paint out too much, simply click the picture thumbnail to return to cloning as before. When you have finished this step your picture should look something like Figure 8.26. It will not look identical, as each version is always different and this is just to give you a guideline.

If you find that the texture that remains over the figure looks unattractive, change to the Med um Felt Tip Pens with black as the painting color and paint in the mask to remove some of the sootiness.

Changing the layer composite method

Now that you have completed this separate layer it is worth experimenting with changing the composite method to see the difference it can make. Check through the information and examples earlier in this chapter if you haven't used the composite methods before.

It is always very difficult to predict how each composite mode will affect the balance of a picture; experience helps and the names give some guidance, but until you try it you can never be sure.

Step 13 Take a good look at the picture, click the composite method box and try all of the options and decide which one looks best. Some will have very little effect while others are totally unsuitable. Try the following two in particular which should work well with this picture.

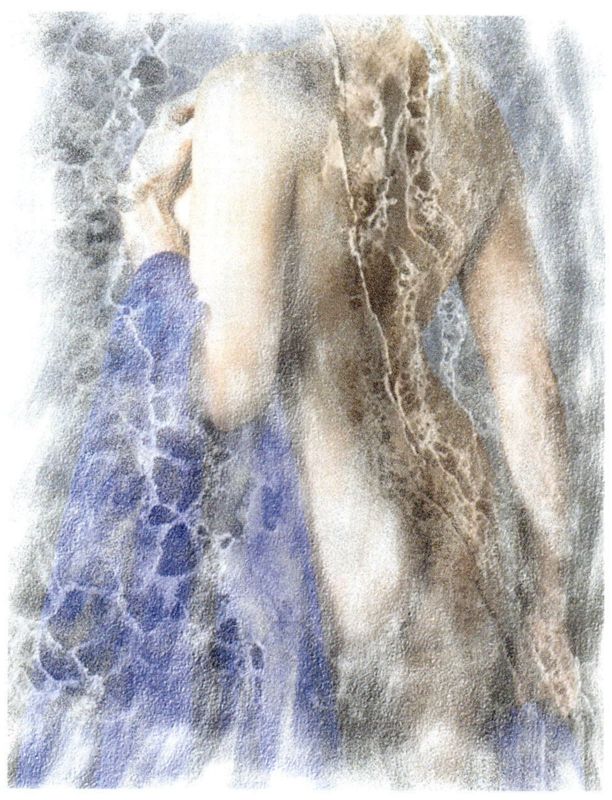

Figure 8.27

- Hard Light will give the picture a brighter appearance as it increases the contrast and removes some of the gray.
- Luminosity retains the contrast level and enhances the color slightly.

It is your choice, whichever looks best on your version. Remember that this is not final as it can be changed at any time. Before going any further you can close down all the other images, as they are finished with for the present. If you do need them again later, they can be re-opened and the clone source re-established by going to *File>Clone Source*.

Changing the color

The next stage is to alter the color tone; there are several ways of doing this, but one of the easiest and most effective is to create a colored layer.

Step 14 Make a new layer on the top of the layer stack.

Step 15 *Effects>Fill.* With the Fill palette open, go to the Colors palette and choose a light orange color; the color will change in the Fill palette as you click the colors. You can choose your own color, but if you prefer to use the one in the example, go to the Colors palette and to the right of the color wheel is a small readout which shows either RGB or HSV values. This display changes when it is clicked, so make it so that it shows HSV, which stands for Hue, Saturation and Value. Move the cursor in the outer color ring until the Hue reads 43%. Put the Saturation at 100% by keeping it on the top or bottom edge of the inner triangle. The value, or brightness, increases as the slider is raised, so take this to 70%. Figure 8.28 shows the color values in the Colors palette. Click OK in the Fill palette when you have chosen the color.

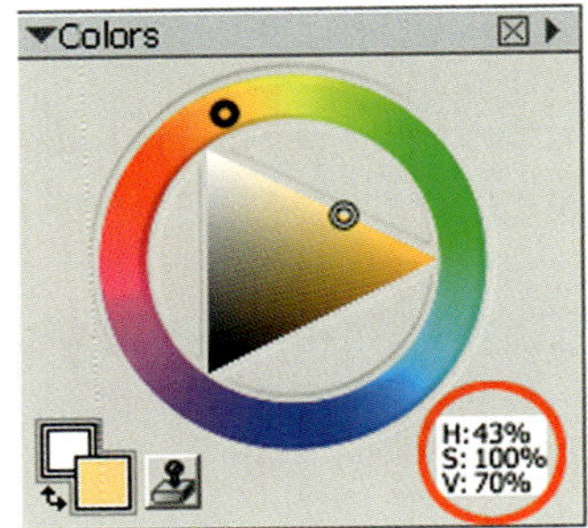

Figure 8.28

Step 16 The new color layer will block out everything else, so the layer composite method must be changed to Colorize, which will allow just the color values to change the layers below. The color will be too strong, so reduce the layer opacity to about 34%, which will allow some of the existing color to come through. A lighter depth of color could have been chosen in the Colors palette, but it is usually better to make it stronger and then reduce it via the layer opacity.

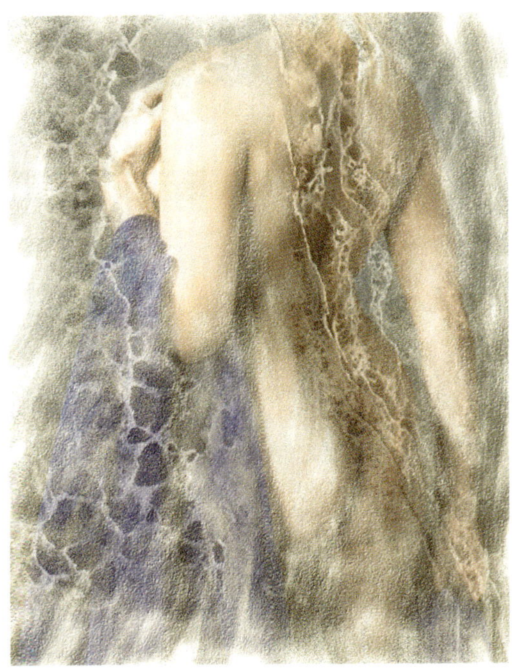

Figure 8.29

Overlaying a texture from another picture

The next stage is to take a handwriting sample and overlay it on the montage. This involves using the Apply Surface Textures command, which is explained in more detail in Chapter 10.

Step 17 Make a new layer at the top of the layer stack. *Edit>Fill*, and choose 50% gray in the Colors palette. You can select 50% gray by placing the cursor on the left edge of the inner triangle and moving it until the Value shows 50%. This will hide all the other layers with a gray color.

Step 18 *File>Open>CD>Step-by-step files>'08 Elizabethan Handwriting'* (Figure 8.30).

Step 19 Click back onto the montage document and go to *File>Clone Source>'08 Elizabethan Handwriting'.*

Step 20 *Effects>Surface Control>Apply Surface Texture.* In the dialog box that appears, change the Using box to Original Luminance and leave the other sliders on the default setting. Figure 8.31 shows the dialog box.

Click OK and the handwriting will appear as embossed on the gray layer. Change the layer composite method to Overlay and the gray will disappear and the embossed letters will be superimposed on top of the montage. There are two other composite methods that work with a gray layer: Soft Light gives a softer effect and Hard Light emphasizes the texture. Figure 8.32 shows the layer before the layer composite method is changed.

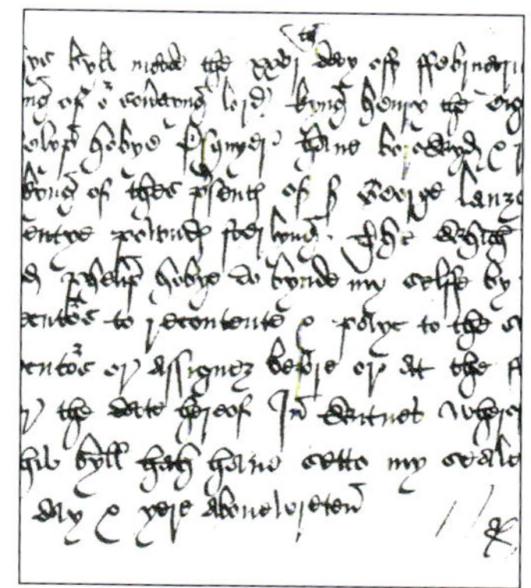

Figure 8.30

Step 21 Add a layer mask to this layer and using the Medium Felt Tip pen again, paint into the mask with a size 84.0 brush and 85% opacity. Make sure the painting color is black and that you are painting on the mask and not the gray layer. Remove the embossed letters from most of the figure, leaving it over the towel and background. If you remove too much, change the painting color to white and paint over again. Figure 8.33 shows the picture at this stage.

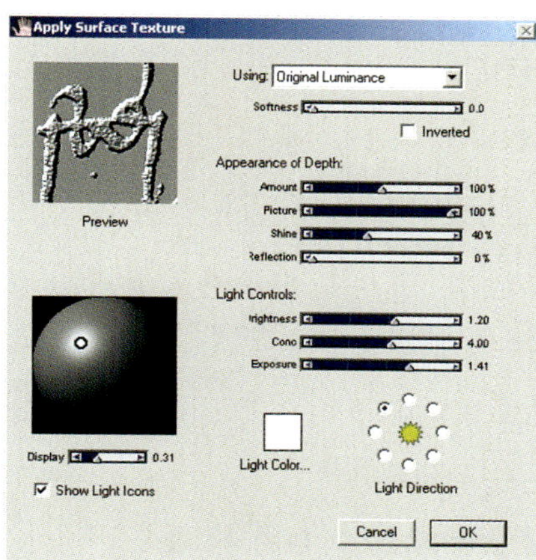

Figure 8.31

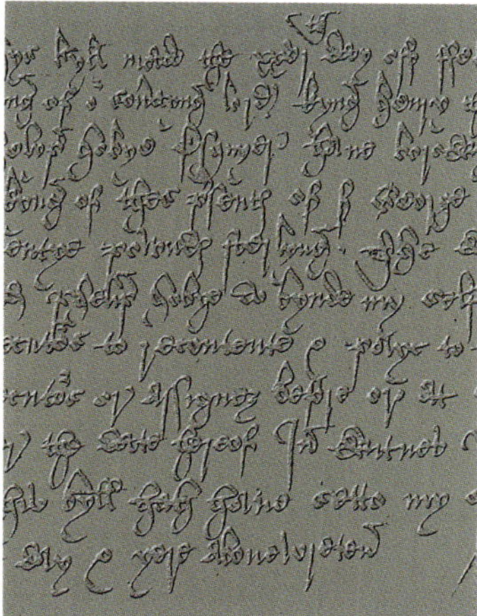

Figure 8.32

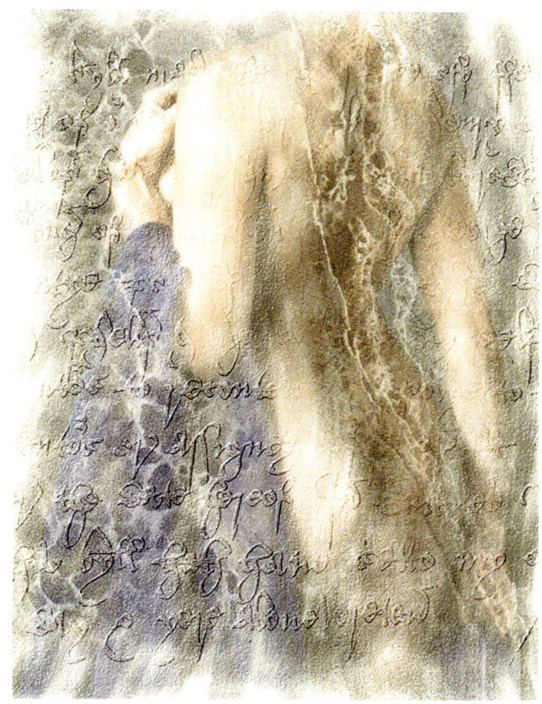

Figure 8.33

Adding extra imagery

Having reviewed the picture at this stage, the bottom of the picture is not as strong as the top and will require some additional material.

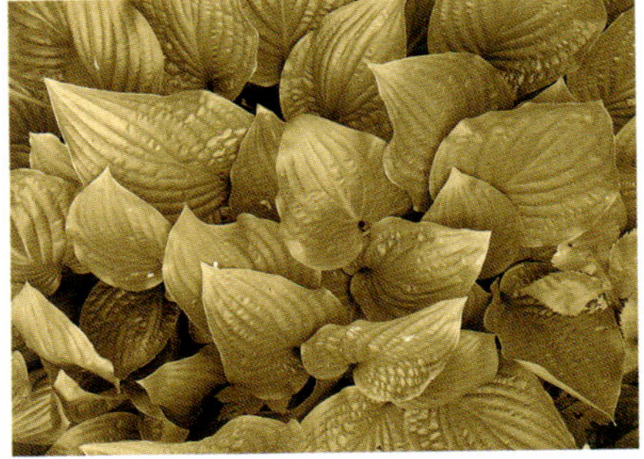

Figure 8.34

Step 22 *File>Open>CD>Step-by-step files>'08 Hosta Leaves'* (Figure 8.34).

Step 23 *Select>All*, then *Edit>Copy* and, returning to the montage document, paste it into the picture via *Edit>Paste*. This is the standard way of moving one photograph into another. Move this to above Layer 1 and change the layer composite method to Lighten. The incoming picture will have been placed in the center of the screen, so use the Layer Adjuster tool to move the picture down to the bottom.

Step 24 Make a layer mask and paint into the mask with the same Felt Tip brush as in the previous step. Use 100% opacity to paint out the leaves in the top left corner and to hide the hard edge, then reduce the opacity to 60% and paint to partially hide the other leaves. Check Figure 8.35 for the picture at this stage; you will see that the leaves are only just visible but help support the lower areas.

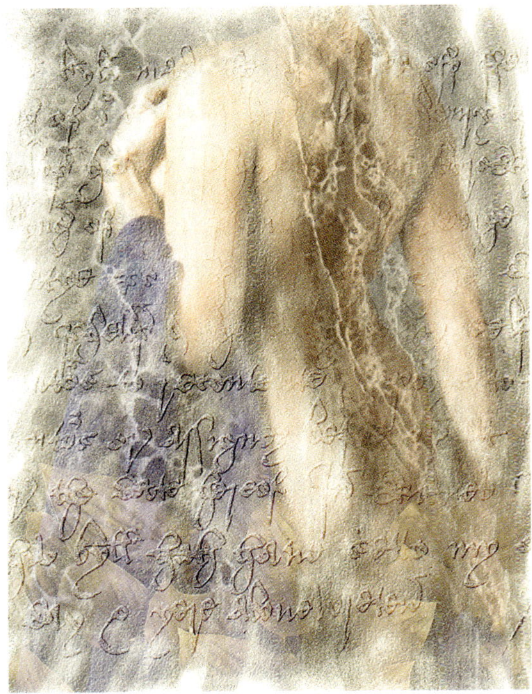

Figure 8.35

Finishing off the picture

This is the stage to step back and assess the picture and decide what needs doing before it is declared finished. Check if the colors are correct. Is the picture too light or too dark?

Step 25 You may well need to lighten some areas and darken others; an easy way to do this is to make another one of those very useful gray layers.

Make a new layer, fill with 50% gray as before and change the layer composite method to Overlay. Use the Felt Tip brush, opacity around 65% to start with. The way this works is that in Overlay method the gray disappears, but if you paint with a lighter gray it will lighten the picture and the opposite will happen with dark gray or black. Do that now to balance any areas that are too light or dark; adjust the layer opacity to adjust the effect.

Adjusting the saturation and contrast

Step 26 To reduce the color saturation make a new layer at the top of the layer stack and fill it with black. Change the layer composite method to Colorize; this will turn the picture to monochrome. Reduce the layer opacity to partially allow the color back. Use a layer mask if you want to restrict this muted color to certain areas of the picture.

Step 27 To increase the color and contrast, make a new layer at the top of the layer stack and fill it with black. Change the layer composite method to Overlay and adjust the layer opacity as required. The Layers palette at the end looked like Figure 8.36.

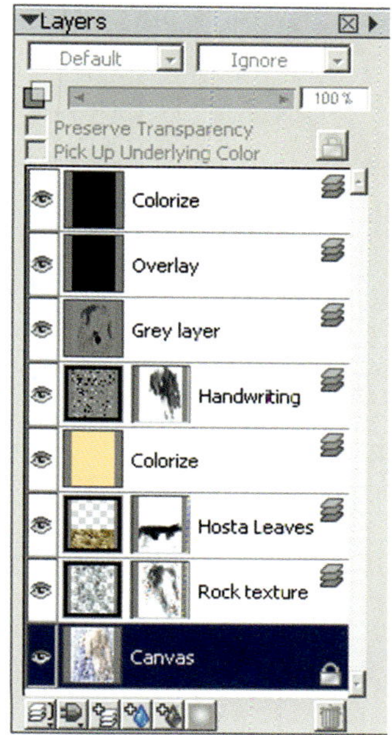

Figure 8.36

Creative cropping

When the picture is complete it is time to consider whether your picture needs cropping. It is very easy when working on a picture to accept the format and shape in which it was originally conceived. However, a picture can look good in several different ways of presentation, so it is worth spending a few minutes trying out several different crops. Try out some radical ones too; they can often be very interesting.

Some of the crops that I tried with this picture are shown in Figures 8.38–8.40, together with some from earlier stages of the montage (Figures 8.41 and 8.42).

This has been a long and complex set of instructions to follow, but I hope that it has given an insight into how a montage might be created. I have introduced several ways to blend images, through cloning, merging layers and the use of layer blending modes. The whole process is very much one of developing ideas as you go along and not being afraid to experiment. Not everything will work, but invariably something worthwhile will come out of the creative process.

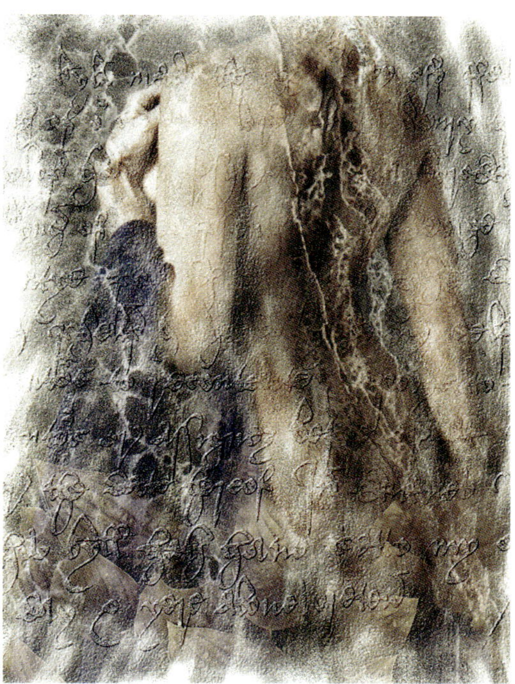

Figure 8.37

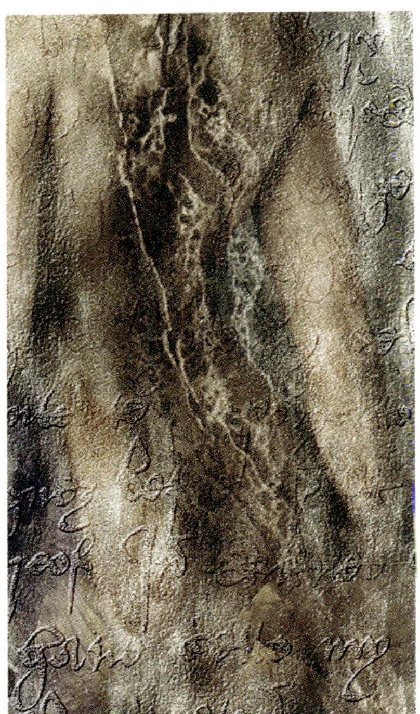

Figure 8.38

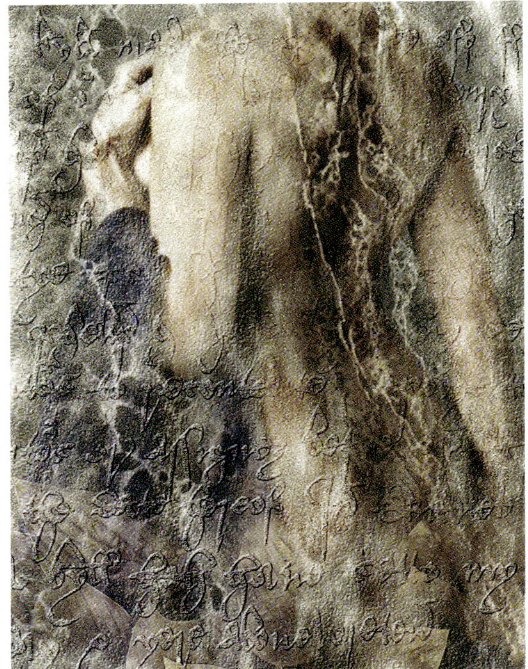

Figure 8.39

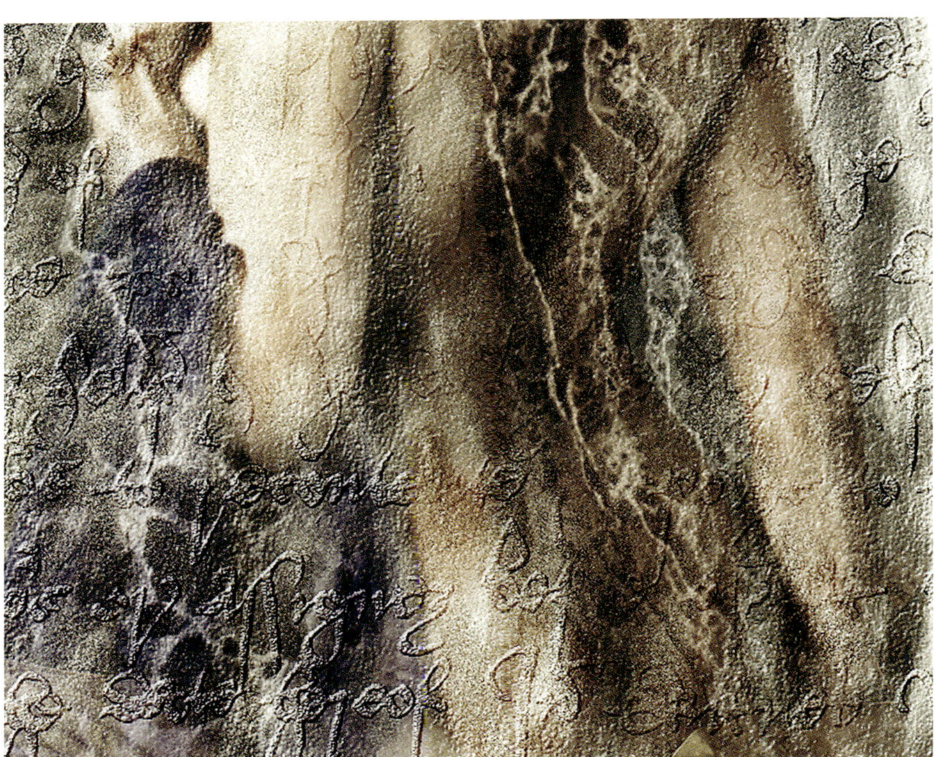

Figure 8.40

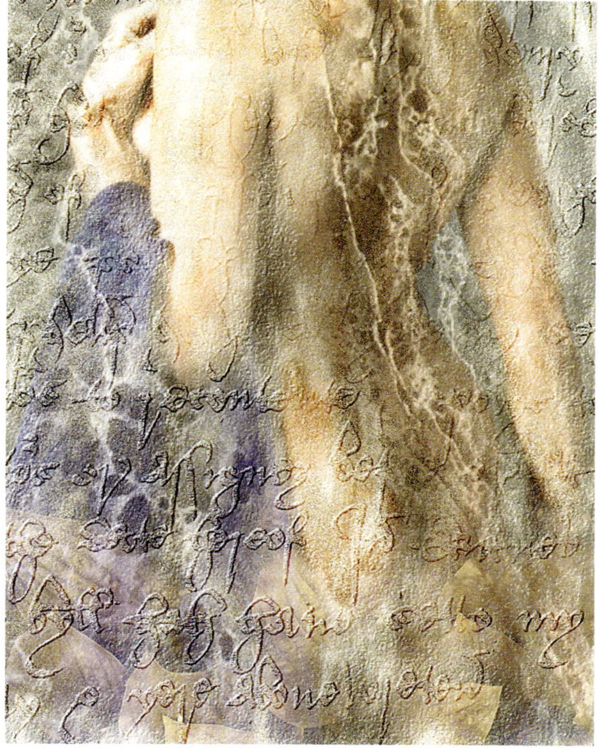

Figure 8.41

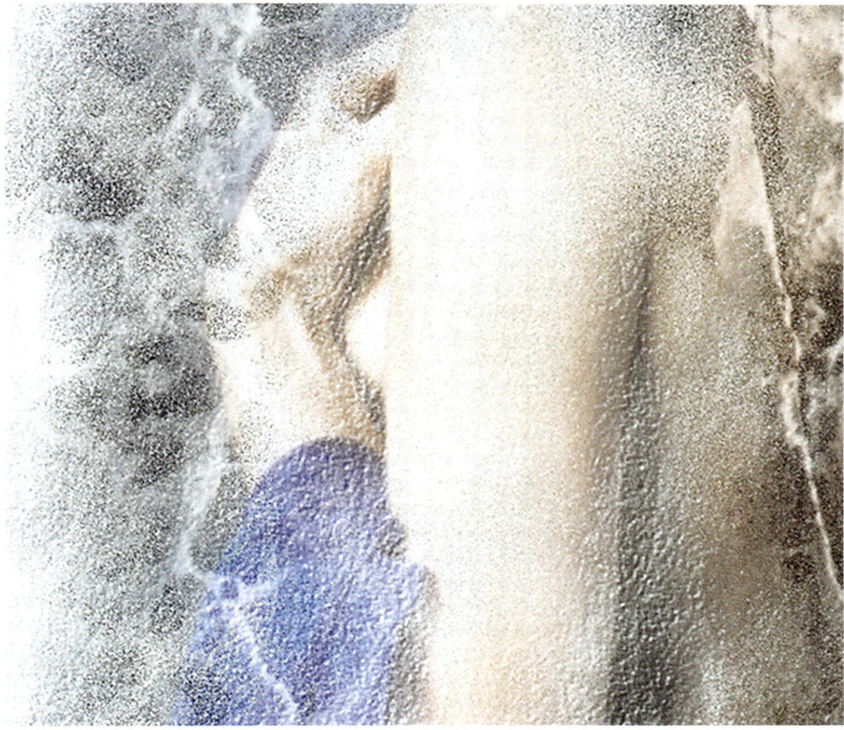

Figure 8.42

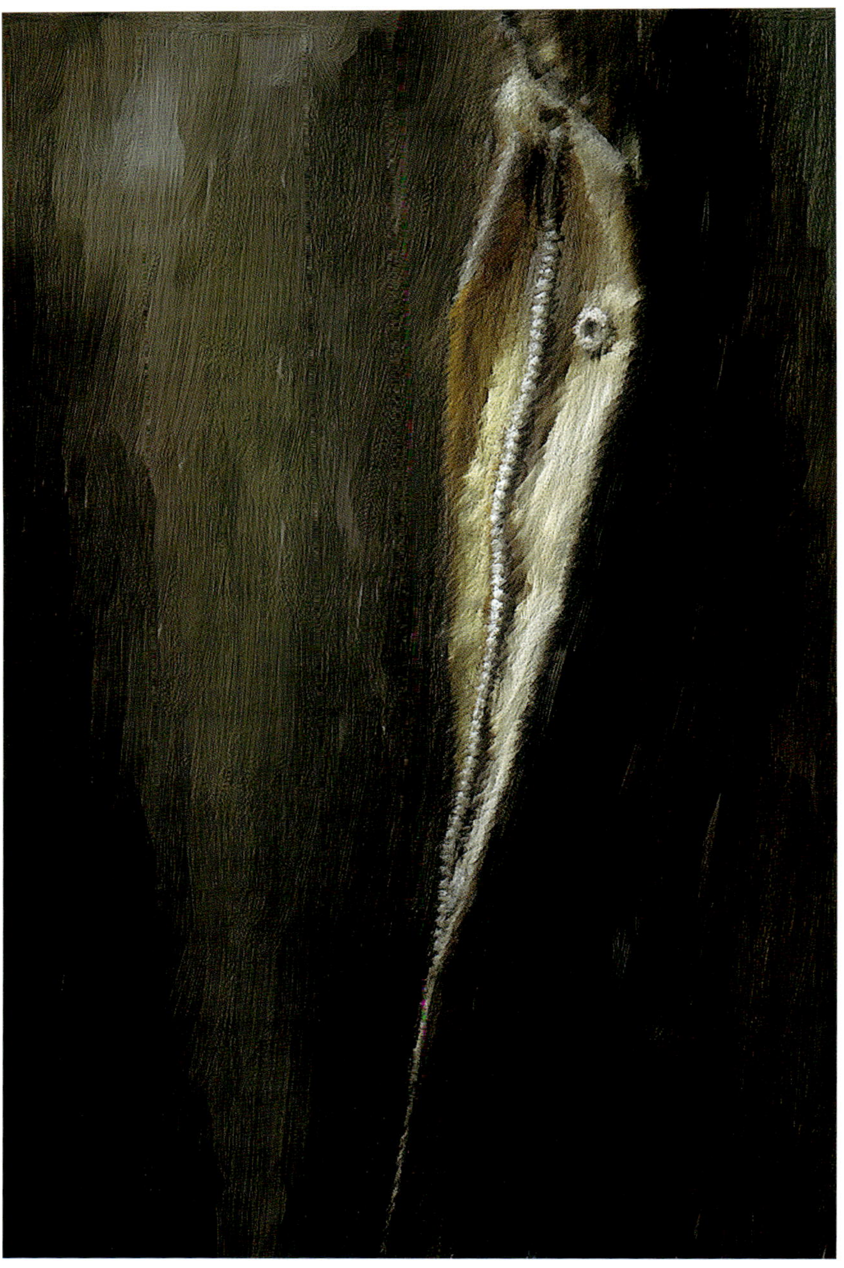

Figure 9.1 Zip

Chapter 9
Watercolor, oil and pastel

The step-by-step examples in this chapter will show you how to make clones using watercolor, oil and pastel brushes. These clones differ from those in earlier chapters in several ways; the method of building the image is to gradually bring in detail, and the result is a lot more like a traditional painting.

The picture on the facing page was made with the Thick Wet Oils brush and you can see very clearly the three-dimensional character of the brush stokes.

In Figure 9.2, the outer edges of the frame have been cloned with the Thick Wet Oils brush with the center area being left clear. The frame was made in Photoshop, which is better suited to this kind of presentational technique, while the painterly section was created within Painter.

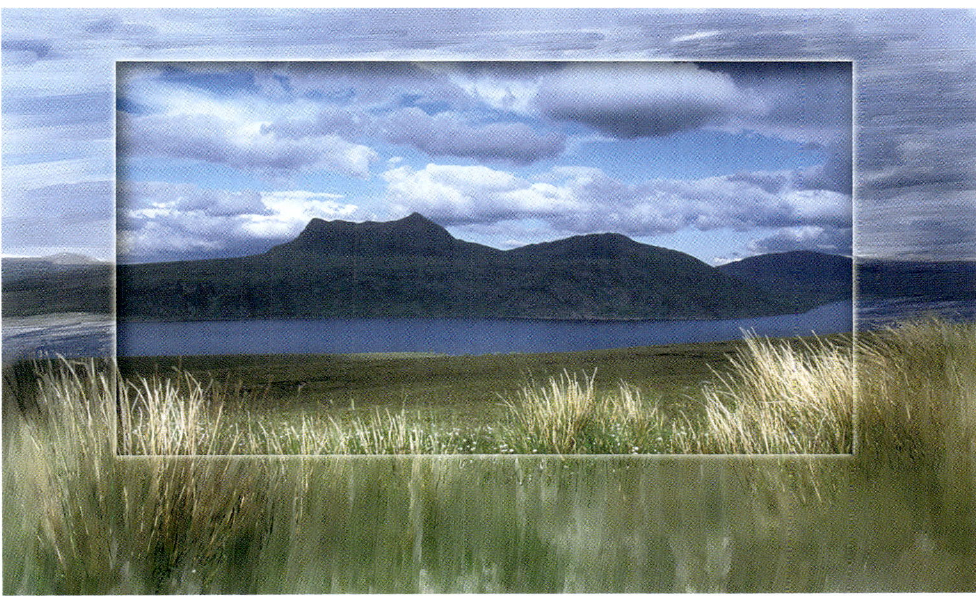

Figure 9.2 Mountain view

Watercolor or Digital Watercolor?

Painter has two categories of Watercolor brushes, one simply called Watercolor and the other Digital Watercolor, so what is the difference and which should you use?

The main difference is that Watercolor brushes have to be used on a separate layer and those layers can only be used for watercolor brushes. The digital version can be used on a standard layer and can be used like any normal brush. Digital Watercolor tends to be much quicker to use but the end result can look very similar depending on the choice of brush.

If you are painting from scratch, the Watercolor brushes have more controls to customize the brush and is probably the one to choose. If you are cloning from a photograph, Digital Watercolor is often more convenient. In earlier versions of Painter the two were very different; however, in Painter IX they are now operating in a more similar way.

Watercolor explained

Before you start work on the next step-by-step clone, it will be helpful to explore some of the very special features of the Watercolor brush category. This category has a lot of unique features and the following exercise will take you through some of the settings in the Water palette and explain how the brushes can be adjusted to suit the style of painting you need.

There are 52 brushes in the Watercolor category and each one has a particular arrangement of settings in the Water palette; with so many brushes available it is worth trying out several to find the one you need before you start to customize the brush.

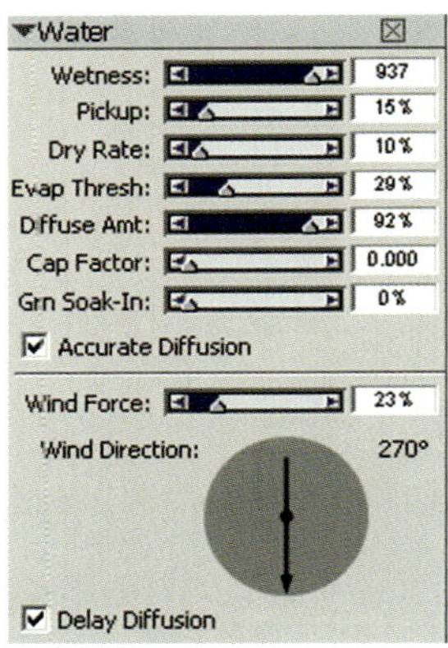

Figure 9.3

Step 1 Bring the Water palette on the screen; *Window>Brush Controls>Show Water* will bring all the brush control palettes to the screen. Drag the Water palette out of the stack and close down the remainder; it is useful to have this palette on screen when using the Watercolor brushes. This palette is also available in the Brush Creator.

Step 2 *File>Open>CD>Step-by-step files>'09 Old Building'.*

Step 3 *File>Quick Clone.*

Step 4 Select the Smooth Runny Flat 30 brush from the Watercolor brush category. Figure 9.3 shows the default Water palette for this brush. If your palette has different settings, then go to the Brush Selector palette menu and click on Restore Default Variant. You may find it useful to return to the default between each of the examples.

Step 5 Click the Clone Color option in the Colors palette, switch the Tracing Paper off and you are ready to try out the examples.

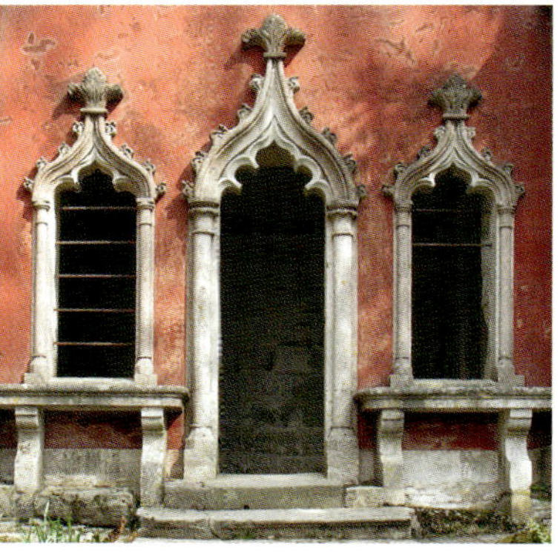

Figure 9.4 Old building

Watercolor layers

All the brushes in this category use a dedicated layer to paint on and this is automatically created when you select and use a Watercolor brush. These layers have some special characteristics – for example, because watercolor will blend when wet, you can return to these layers at a later date and, having wet the layer again, can paint over the image and paint 'wet on wet', a traditional watercolor technique. This is only possible if you save the picture in RIFF file format: if you save it in any other format this option is lost.

One other thing to be aware of is that the diffusion process to get the watercolor effect is very complex and brush strokes can take longer than usual. Check the Layers palette when you have used this brush for several strokes and you will see a blue water-droplet symbol (highlighted in Figure 9.5); when this is moving the brush effect is still being computed, so you will need to wait until it has finished.

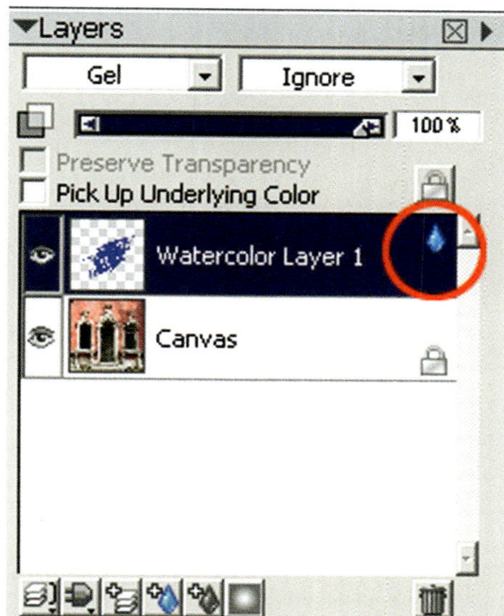

Figure 9.5

Water: Wetness

Make some brush strokes on the default Wetness setting, which is 937 for this brush, and see how the paint runs down the page. This blending of color washes is one of the special characteristics of traditional watercolor painting and is caused by the liquid nature of watercolor paint. To get this blending effect the paper is tilted downwards, and if you look at the bottom of the Water palette you will see under Wind Direction the arrow is pointing downwards; this is telling you that the paint will run down the page.

To understand how the Wetness slider affects the blending, make two more groups of brush strokes, one with the slider set at 500 and the other at 0. Figure 9.6 shows how the blending becomes less as the amount of Wetness is reduced.

Figure 9.6

Water: Dry Rate

The Dry Rate controls how quickly the paint dries and has a similar effect to the wetness slider at the extreme settings, but rather different at 50%. Make brush strokes at 8%, 50% and 100% to see the difference; Figure 9.7 shows these settings. Brush strokes at low settings will work more slowly.

The other difference that is not apparent in this example is that when the paint is applied on top of the previous brush stroke, the colors will blend if the paint is still wet. This is more noticeable when painting rather than cloning.

Figure 9.7

Figure 9.8

Water: Diffuse Amt

The Diffuse Amt slider controls the amount of diffusion; the top section of Figure 9.8 shows the brush at the default setting of 92%, which produces significant diffusion, while the others at 50% and 0% show very much less.

Figure 9.9 shows a detail where the brush strokes were applied at Diffuse Amt 92% and opacity 18%. More brush strokes were painted on top with the Diffuse Amt set to 33%. See how this has brought in more detail in a rather gentle manner.

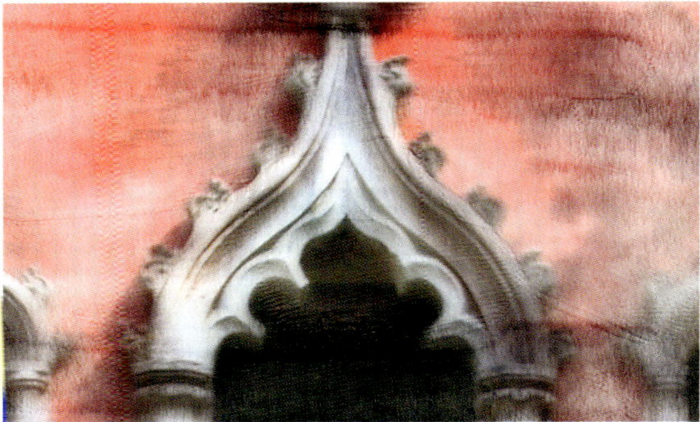

Figure 9.9

Water: Wind Force

This was mentioned earlier and is a fascinating feature that replicates the ability in traditional watercolor painting to angle the paper downwards so that a wet wash will run and mix with other washes. In Painter both the angle and direction of the movement can be altered.

Figure 9.10 shows three different examples of using this control. The top is with Wind Force at 0% so the diffusion had not significantly moved. The center shows the Wind Force at 50% so the diffusion has moved downwards. The final example is with Wind Force at 100% and the direction of the wind is now to the right, a real gale force in fact! This is really useful as you can control the final result very effectively.

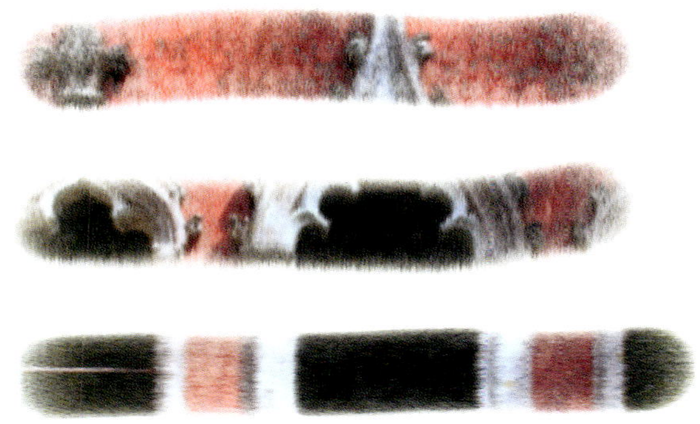

Figure 9.10

Water: other controls

There are several other sliders in the Water palette, not all of which affect this particular brush but will affect others.

Delay Diffusion, which is turned on in the default setting, allows the brush stroke to finish before the diffusion process starts. Try the two options to see the difference.

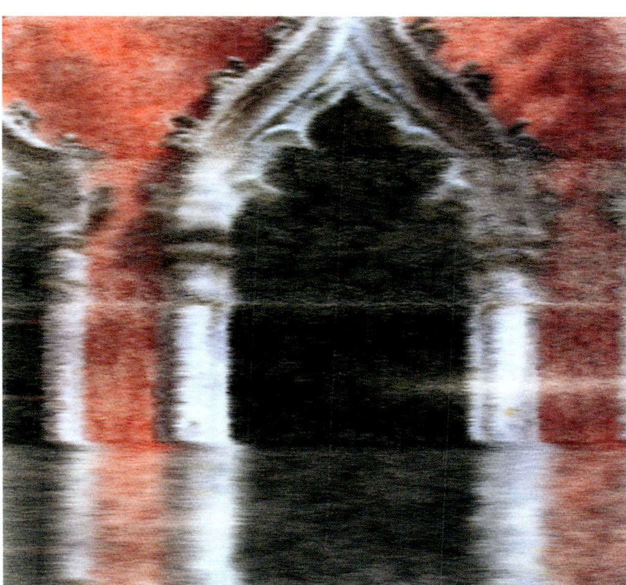

Figure 9.11

Accurate Diffusion results in the clone copy having more clarity. Untick this option to get a rougher impression that can be very useful for backgrounds. Figure 9.11 shows the result of this option; from the top the first and third bands have Accurate ticked, while the second and fourth do not.

Digital Watercolor

This first Watercolor clone step-by-step uses the Dry Brush technique, which is one of the easier Watercolor brushes to use. The painting method is to start with a Watercolor wash and then to use the Dry brush to gradually bring in more detail.

Step 1 *File>Open>CD>Step-by-step files>'C9 Lower Brockhampton Court'.*

Step 2 *File>Quick Clone.*

Step 3 Select the Digital Watercolor brush category and the Coarse Water variant. Use brush size 85.0 and opacity 1%. Click the Clone Color option in the Colors palette.

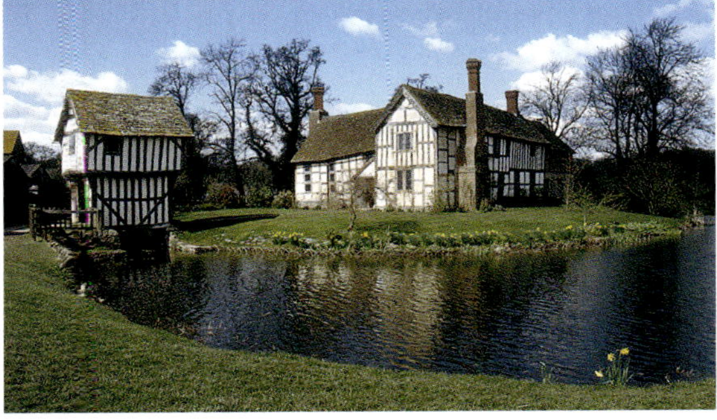

Figure 9.12 Original photograph

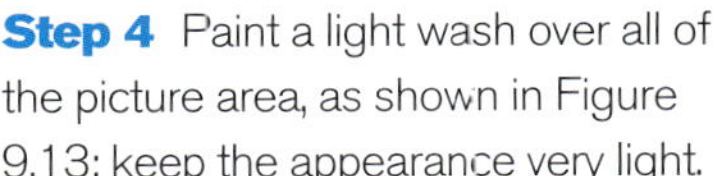

Step 4 Paint a light wash over all of the picture area, as shown in Figure 9.13; keep the appearance very light.

Step 5 Change the brush to *Digital Watercolor>Dry Brush*. Size 30.0, opacity 2%, grain 5%. Click the Clone Color option in the Colors palette. Select the French Watercolor Paper. Turn the Tracing Paper on and paint over all the main shapes. When you turn the Tracing Paper off you will see that the shapes are very rough; go over them to make them more defined. Figure 9.14 shows the picture at this early stage.

Figure 9.13

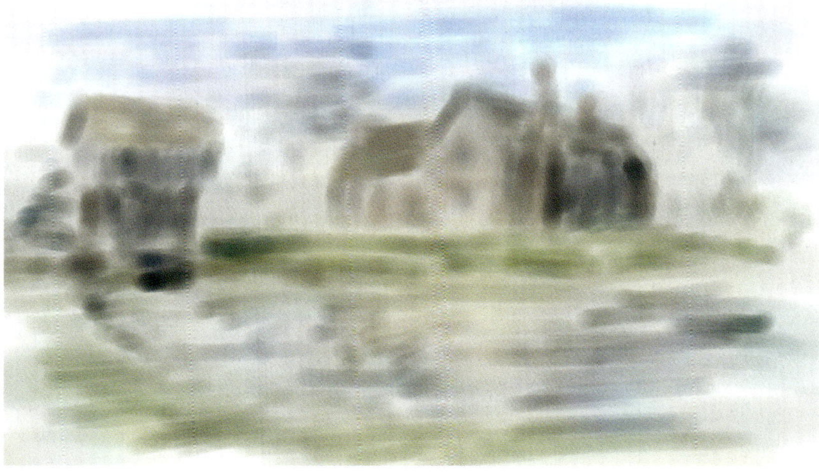

Figure 9.14

Step 6 Make the brush size 10.0, opacity 5% and go over the buildings again; keep switching the Tracing Paper on and off to check the detail. Figure 9.15 shows the house starting to show more detail.

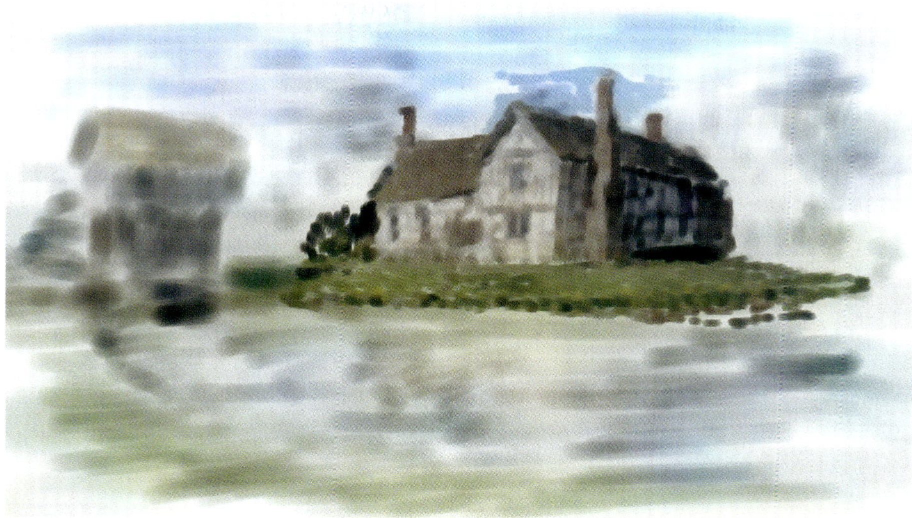

Figure 9.15

Step 7 Using the same brush, change the size to 23.0 and the opacity to 1% and paint over the remaining areas again to bring the picture together. Paint over the edges of the darker brush strokes you did earlier to integrate them with the lighter areas. Figure 9.16 shows the picture at this stage. You will need to vary the brush size and opacity to make the various parts of the picture blend well.

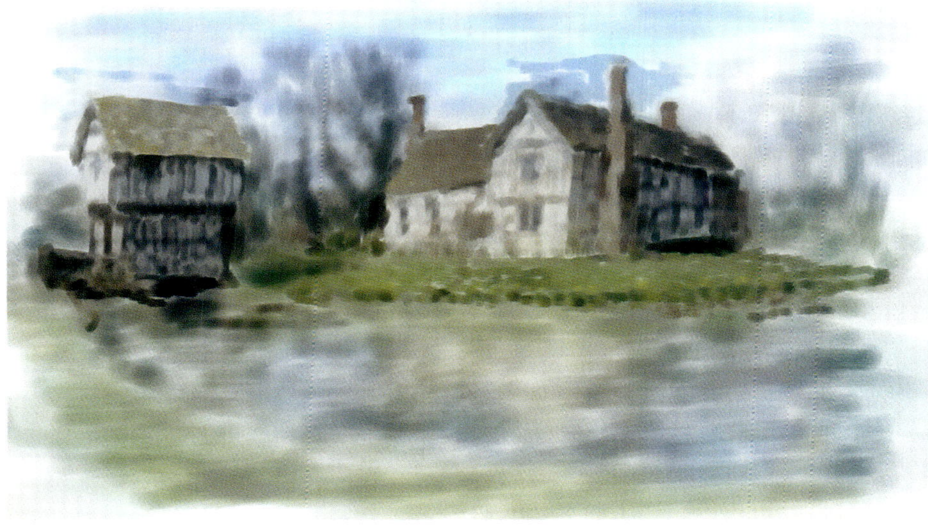

Figure 9.16

Step 8 Reduce the brush size to 4.3 and increase the opacity to 55%; this will put a lot more detail in the buildings. Follow the lines of the building to emphasize the dark wooden beams and the white areas between (magnify the picture to see more clearly). If this looks too harsh, go over it afterwards with a larger brush and lower opacity. Paint over the sky and foreground with brush size 23.3 and opacity 9%.

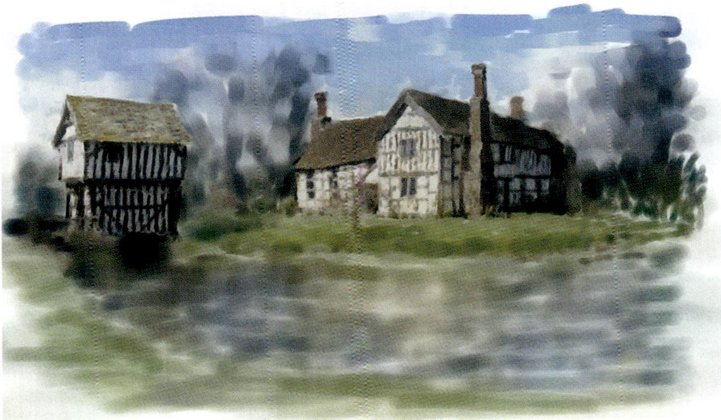

Figure 9.17

Step 9 Paint over the trees with brush size 8.2 and opacity 55% to emphasize the trunks and branches. Use brush size 12.0 and opacity 4% to paint over areas where different textures join and look wrong.

Step 10 In the General palette, change the Method to Eraser and the Subcategory to Soft Paint Remover, brush size 32.0 and opacity 10% and go around the edges to remove any dirty marks or brush strokes you would prefer were not there.

Increase the opacity between 60% and 100% and use this brush to add some sparkle to your picture, especially in the white areas of the buildings and in their reflection in the water.

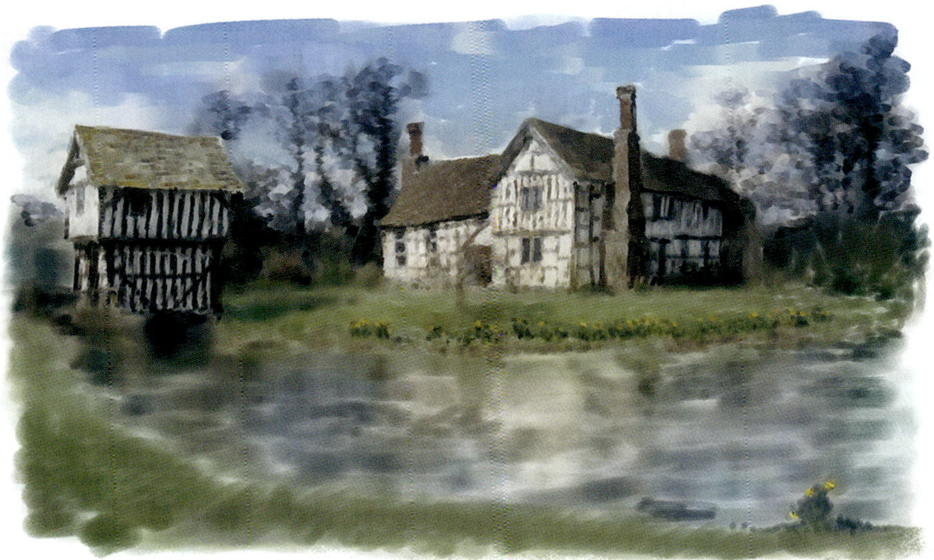

Figure 9.18 Lower Brockhampton Court

Soft Runny watercolor

Step 1 *File>Open>CD>Step-by-step files>'09 Slaters Bridge'.*

Step 2 *File>Quick Clone.* Turn off the Tracing Paper as it is difficult to see the detail in this very light clone.

Step 3 Select the *Watercolor>Soft Runny Wash brush*, size 100.0, opacity 2%. Click the Clone Color option in the Colors palette.

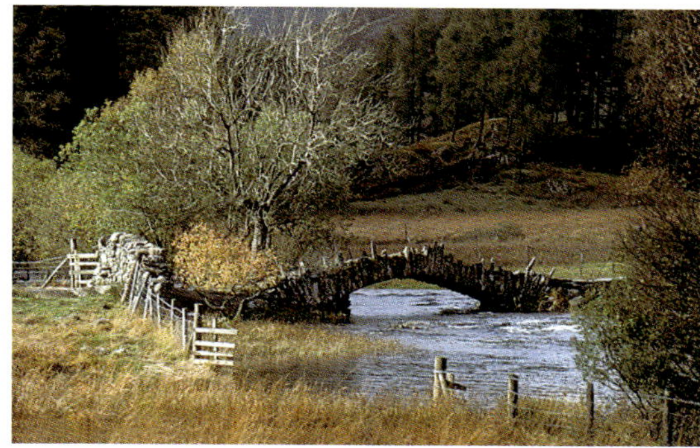

Figure 9.19 Original photograph

Step 4 Starting from the bottom, gently paint into the picture, allowing the picture to slowly reveal itself. This brush uses a lot of diffusion and is therefore very slow to use. Keep an eye on the watercolor symbol in the Layers palette and wait for it to stop moving before continuing to paint.

Step 5 Decrease the brush size to 50.0 and increase the opacity to 3% and paint over the key parts, which are the bridge, the foreground posts, the water and the trees. This will give the picture more shape while still maintaining the delicate overall appearance.

Step 6 If the picture looks too dark when finished, lower the opacity of the watercolor layer. Figure 9.20 shows the final version. The end result is very soft and delicate, and could be used as a base for a more detailed picture.

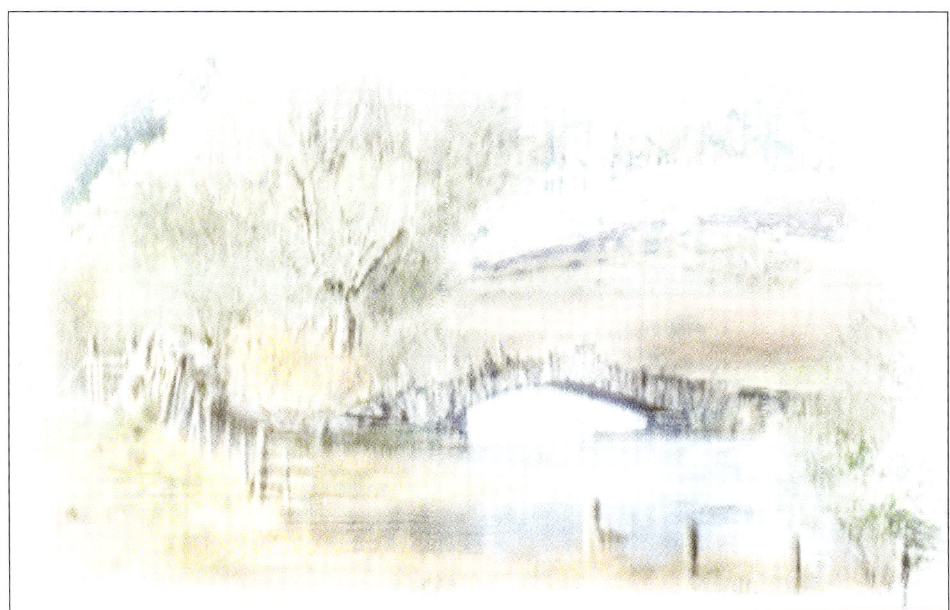

Figure 9.20 Slater's Bridge

Dry Bristle watercolor

Step 1 *File>Open>CD>Step-by-step files>'09 Slaters Bridge'.*

Step 2 *File>Quick Clone.*

Step 3 Select the *Watercolor>Dry Bristle brush* size 30.0, opacity 2%. Click the Clone Color option in the Colors palette.

Step 4 Brush over the main elements of the picture with the Tracing Paper on, then turn the Tracing Paper off and continue to paint in the picture. You will find this brush much quicker to use than the Soft Runny brush, as the paint does not diffuse as much.

Step 5 Increase the opacity gradually, paint with 3% then 4%, which should be sufficient to give you good density. Figure 9.21 shows the final picture.

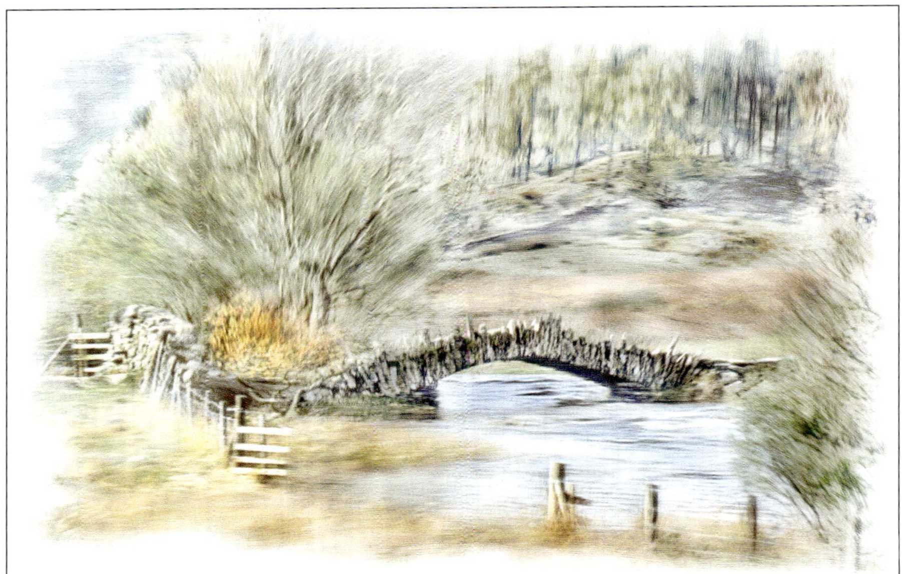

Figure 9.21

Figure 9.22 is an enlargement of the finished clone, where you will see the brush strokes in more detail.

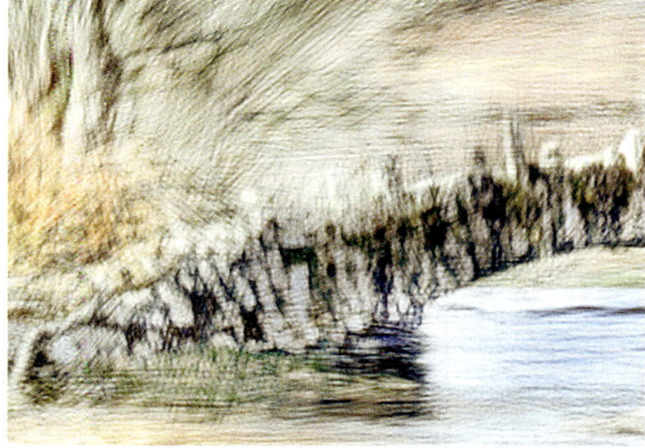

Figure 9.22

Oils

Many of the brushes in the Oils category have textured brush strokes and in this next step-by-step you will see how this can transform a photograph into an image which appears to have depth. The impression of depth is called Impasto, which is described in more detail in Chapter 6.

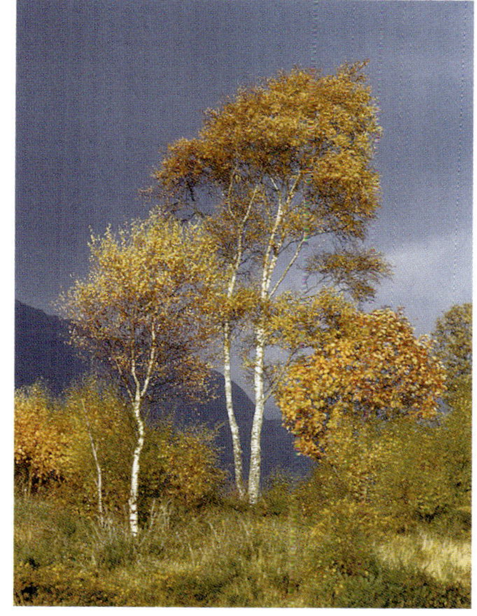

Figure 9.23 Original photograph

Autumn trees

Step 1 *File>Open>CD>Step-by-step files> '09 Autumn Color'.*

Step 2 *File>Quick Clone.*

Step 3 Select the Thick Wet Oils 30 brush, size 35.0, opacity 100%. Click the Clone Color option in the Colors palette. On the Properties bar, change the Resat box to read 100%; this change means that the brush will keep on painting with the full amount of paint rather than running out.

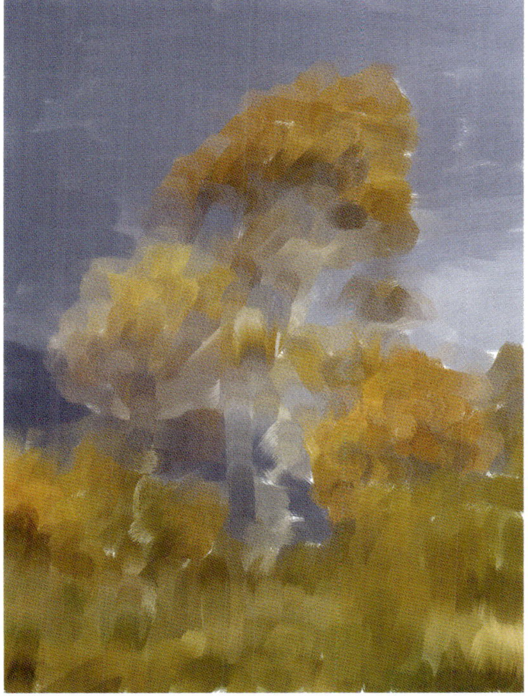

Figure 9.24

Step 4 Paint the entire picture with a layer of paint; this stage is shown in Figure 9.24. Paint the sky first, which will darken it considerably, then paint the rest of the picture using short brush strokes to give a textured effect. More detail can be seen in the enlargement shown in Figure 9.25.

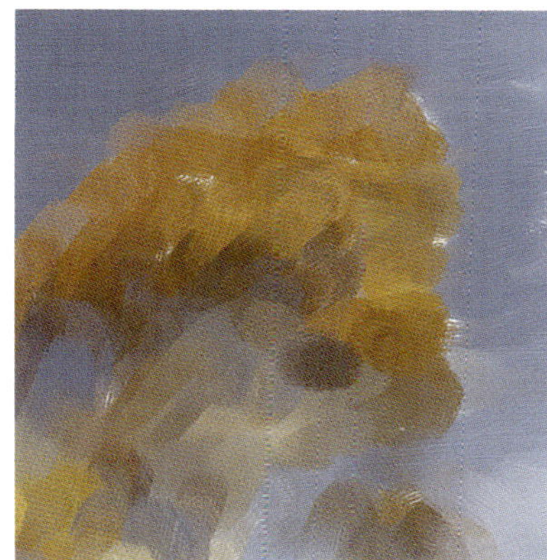

Figure 9.25

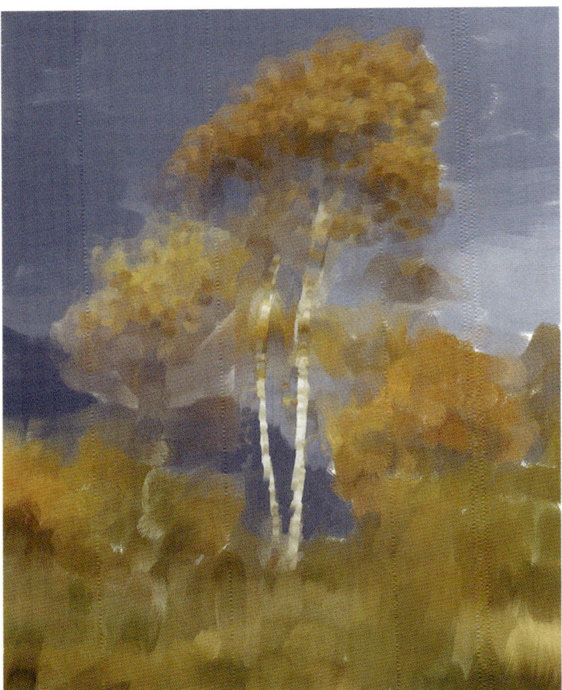

Figure 9.26

Step 5 Reduce the brush size to 15.0 and using very short brush strokes paint over the autumn leaves, pushing the brush strokes outwards from the center of the foliage. Enlarge the picture on the screen to work in greater detail and check the detail shown in Figures 9.26 and 9.27.

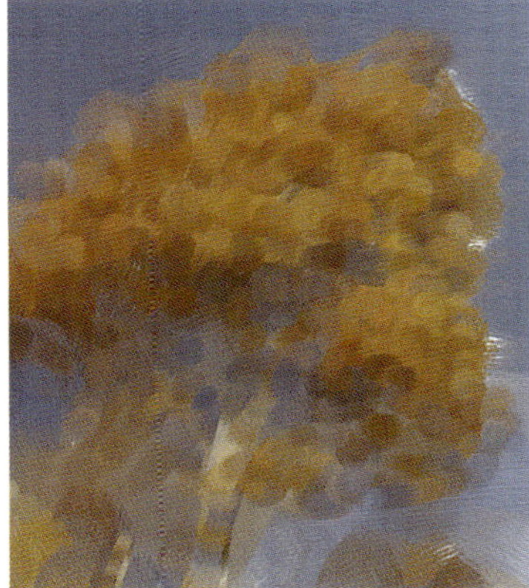

Figure 9.27

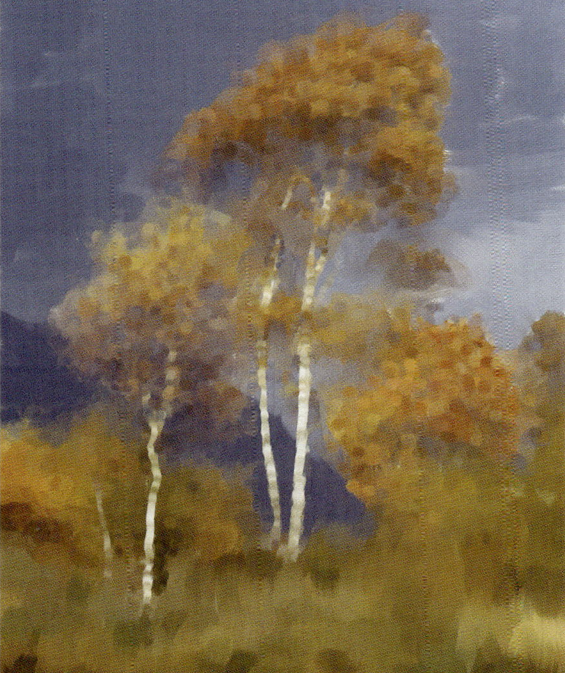

Figure 9.28

Step 6 Reduce the brush down more to between 8.0 and 10.0 and run the brush down the tree trunks to bring them out clearly. Paint the side of each tree trunk to emphasize the light and dark areas. Continue to paint over the leaves at varying brush sizes to give an interesting texture, as in Figures 9.28 and 9.29.

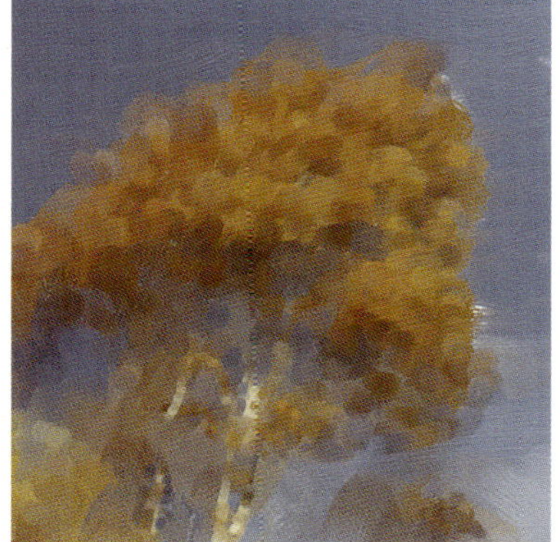

Figure 9.29

Step 7 Press *Ctrl/Cmd + B* or go to *Window>Show Brush Creator* and click on the Spacing tab. Change the Spacing slider from the default 8% to read 63%. This will space out the brush dabs and reduce the smoothness of the brush, which is useful to create a more individual texture on the leaves. Paint over the edges of the trees and look for groups of leaves to highlight. This brush will break up the edge and give more highlights. Figures 9.30 and 9.31 show this stage completed.

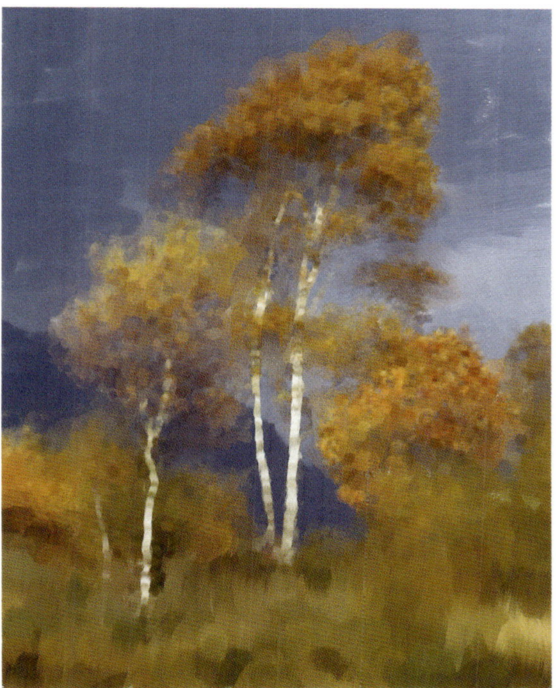

Figure 9.30

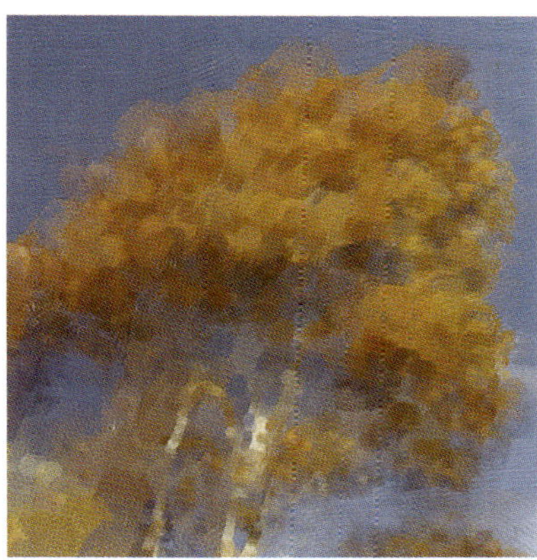

Figure 9.31

Changing the contrast of the original

The picture needs more contrast to make it spring off the page, but we cannot clone from the original photograph until it has been brightened, so the next stage is to alter the contrast of the original by making two extra layers.

Step 8 If the Layers palette is not on screen, bring it up via *Layers>Show Layers*.

Activate the original image by clicking in the picture and then select the Layer Adjuster tool from the Toolbox. *Select>All*, then holding down the *Alt/Opt key*, click in the picture to make a copy of the Canvas, putting it on a new layer.

Repeat this step to make a second copy of the Canvas.

Step 9 Click on the top layer and rename it Lighten (via the Layers palette menu).

Go to *Effects>Tonal Control>Brightness/Contrast* and move the sliders to the approximate positions shown in Figure 9.32.

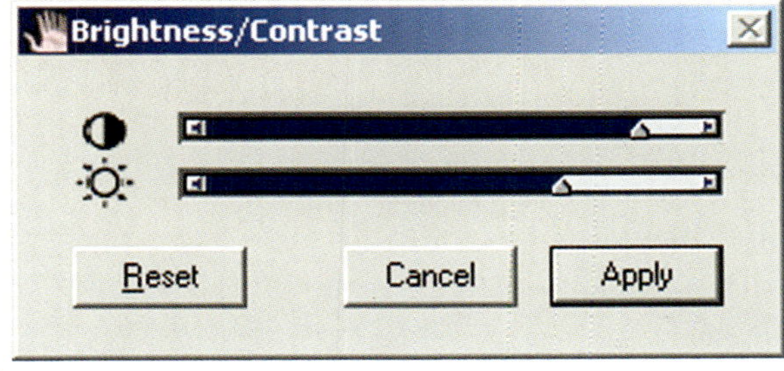

Figure 9.32

Step 10 Click the eye icon on the top layer to hide it, then click on the middle layer and rename it Darken.

Go to *Effects>Tonal Control>Brightness/Contrast* and move the sliders to the positions shown in Figure 9.33.

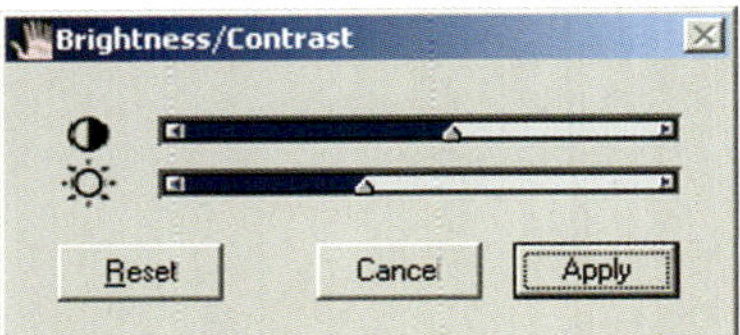

Figure 9.33

This has given us two extra versions of the original picture from which to clone. The two extra layers are shown in Figures 9.34 and 9.35, and the Layers palette in Figure 9.36.

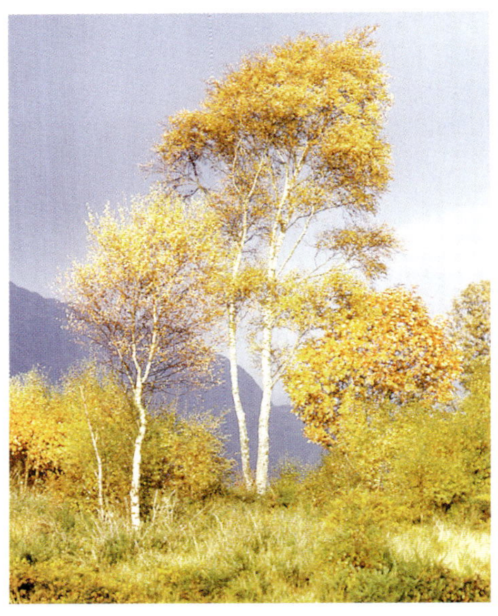

Figure 9.34

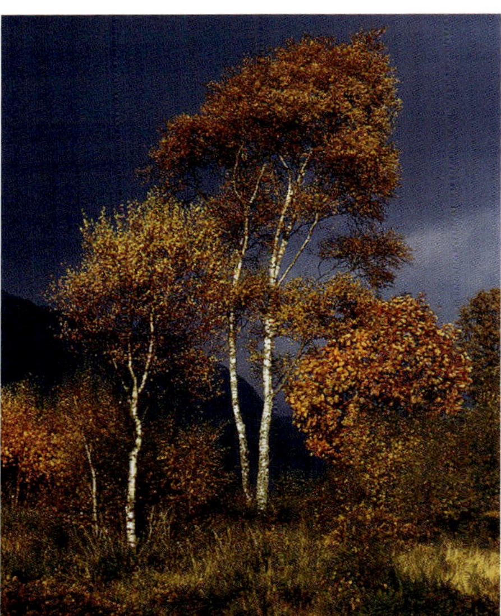

Figure 9.35

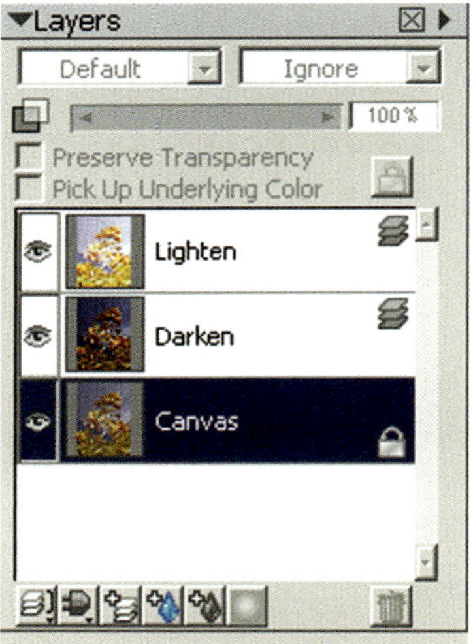

Figure 9.36

Step 11 Click on the Darken layer in the original image to make it active and turn off the visibility of the Lighten layer. Return to the clone copy and using brush size 12.0 and 33% opacity, brush some darker areas into the picture where you would expect to see shadows.

Step 12 Click on the Lighten layer in the original image to make it active and turn off the visibility of the Darken layer. Return to the clone copy and using brush size 14.0 and 33% opacity, brush highlights into the tops of the trees and in the groups of leaves. Increase the opacity to 65% and dab in more highlights. Increase the opacity to 100% and add just a few more highlights very carefully – don't overdo it!

The final cloned image after a small crop is shown in Figure 9.37. Some extra texture was added to complete the picture; the procedure for this is covered in the next chapter.

In the same way that these extra layers were created to increase contrast, the original image can be altered at any time – for instance, to clone out something distracting, to blur the picture or to change the color before continuing to clone.

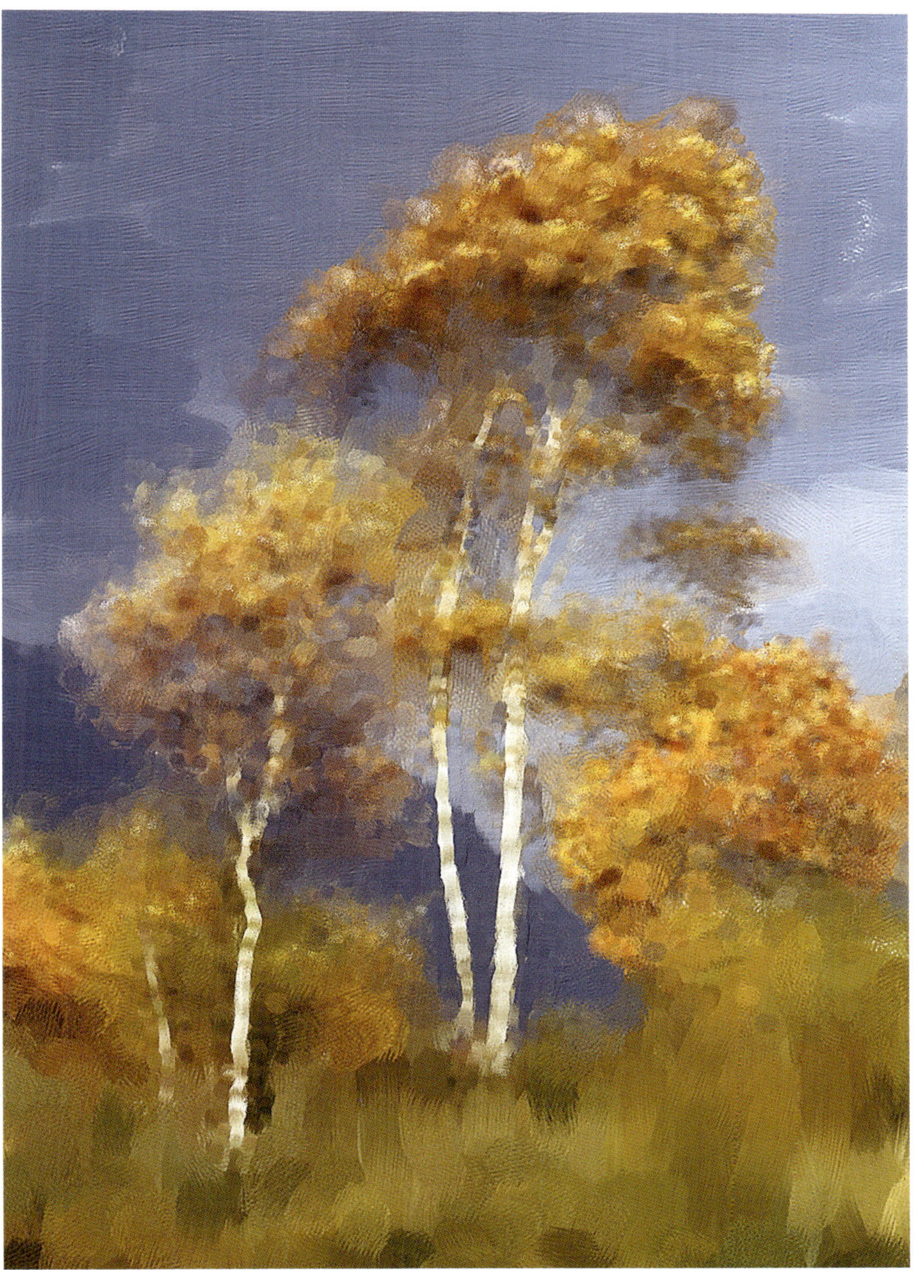

Figure 9.37 Autumn colors

Pastel

Pastel pictures have a very distinctive texture, as the Pastel interacts strongly with a textured paper. The choice of Pastel brush is critical as they vary considerably; hard pastels emphasize the paper texture while the soft ones blend into the paper but still have the texture present, particularly on the edges of the brush strokes.

The picture you are about to make uses a different method to the previous clones and you will soon see the potential of this technique. This method is not exclusive to Pastels and can be used with many other brushes. When you have completed this step-by-step, try making the picture again using the Opaque Bristle Spray from the Oils brush category; it gives a lovely soft silky finish.

Step 1 *File>Open>CD>Step-by-step files>'09 Dog'.*

Step 2 *File>Clone*; do not clear the clone copy.

Step 3 Select the Artist Pastel Chalk and click the Clone Color option in the Colors palette. Brush size 108.0, opacity 29%, grain 23%.

Step 4 The first step is to paint out the background and this large brush will do this quite quickly. Paint until the detail in the background is obscured; do not worry if the brush paints over the edge of the dog, as this will be brought back later.

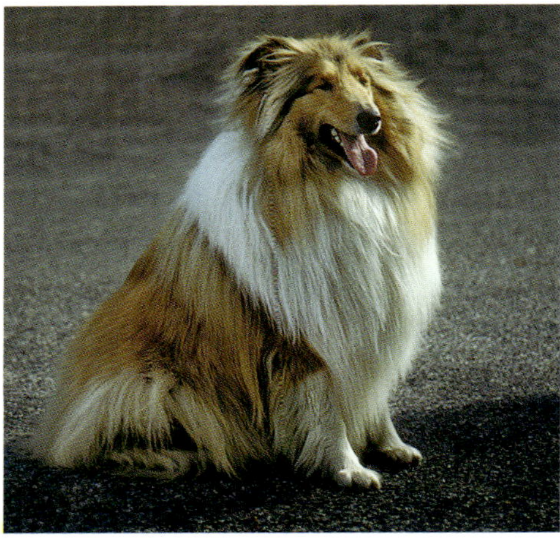

Figure 9.38 Original photograph

Step 5 Change the brush size to 8.2, the opacity to 50%, leave the grain on 23% and start to paint the hair on the front of the dog. The brush will clone in pastel strokes from the original clone source and you will be painting over the top of the clone picture. Most of the original picture will be covered as you paint. See Figure 9.39 for a detail of the brush strokes.

Throughout this exercise it is important to follow the lines of the hair, but within that general direction the strokes can vary in angle, which is in keeping with the way the hairs look on the original. Keep the brush strokes quite short and where the color changes bring the top color down over the lower one; again, this is in keeping with the way the hair falls. Flick out the brush strokes into the background at the edge of the dog.

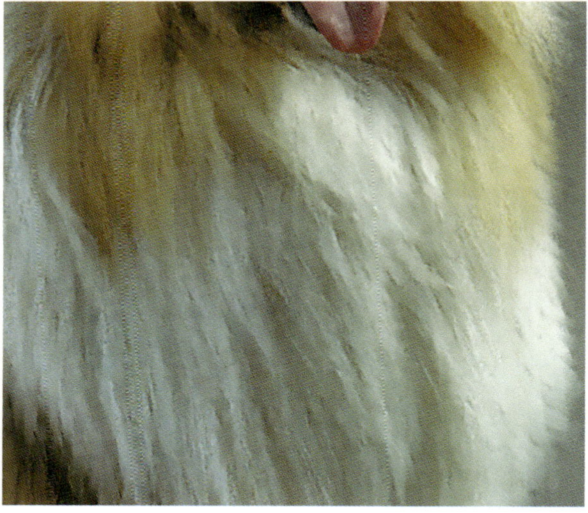

Figure 9.39 Detail

Step 6 Continue painting over the entire dog's coat except for the face; try increasing the brush size slightly to 10.0 or 12.0 for the lower parts of the dog. Use the Tracing Paper if necessary to clarify where the edges are.

Step 7 Decrease the brush size to about 7.0 to work on the head, using the same technique as before, but take extra care to identify which way the hair grows and ensure that your brush strokes emphasize these directions. Reduce the brush size to 4.8 and delicately go over the nose and eyes.

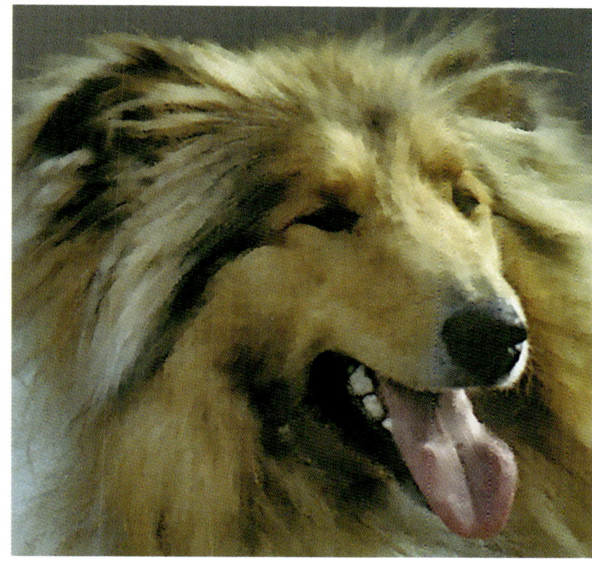

Figure 9.40 Detail

Step 8 Increase the opacity to 65% and paint over the edges to clarify the loose hairs. Increase the brush size again to 100% and go over the entire picture, picking out important areas to emphasize. This opacity setting will roughen up the texture where it has become too soft and introduce more contrast. Figure 9.40 shows the head in more detail.

If you need to clean up the edges, go over them with brush size 12.0 and opacity 17%; this should remove any dark or light marks. Return to the previous brush to go over the hairs again if necessary.

Figure 9.41 shows the final picture made with the Pastel brush.

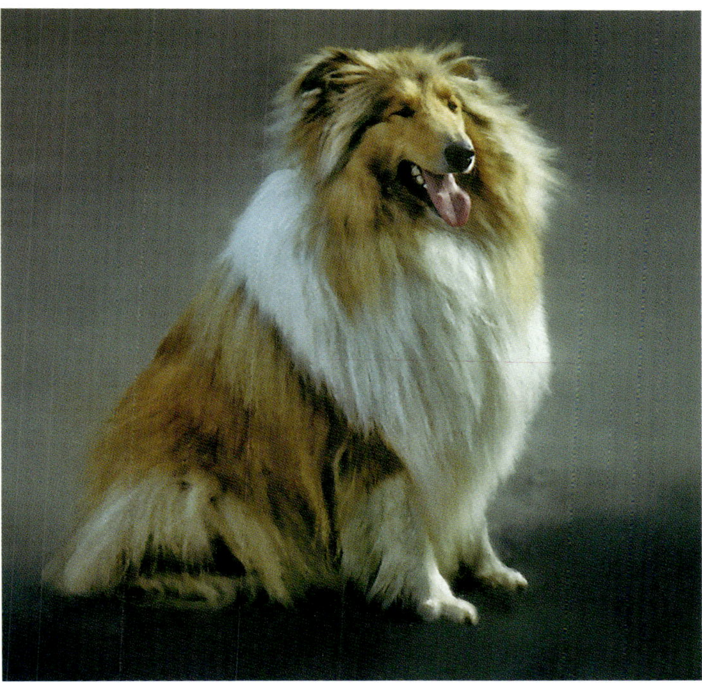

Figure 9.41 Dog

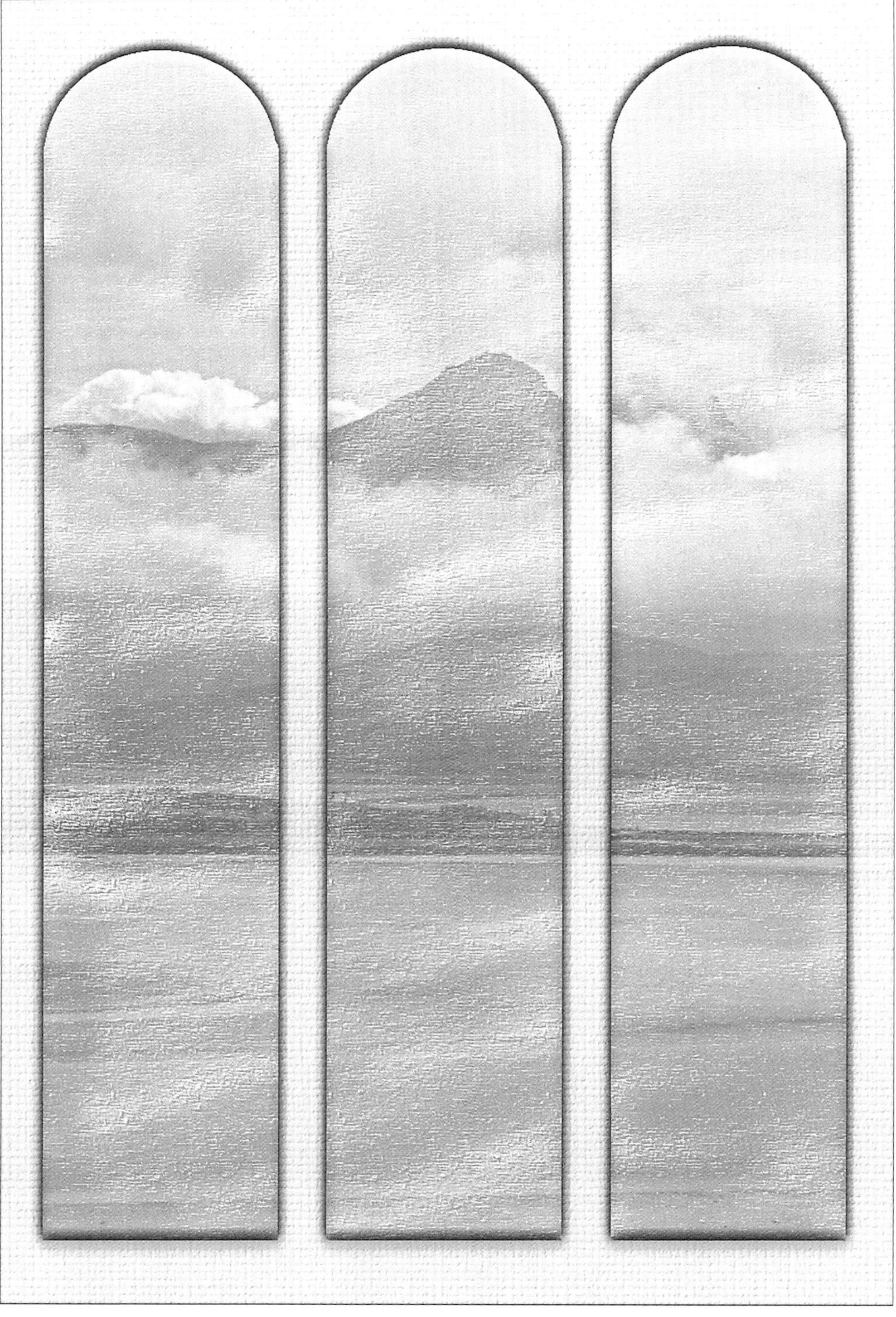

Figure 10.1 Mountain triptych

Chapter 10
Applying surface texture

Chapter 3 explained how textures could be applied when using a clone brush. This chapter takes this a stage further and you will discover how to apply these textures to your picture after it has been finished. The textures that you can apply are not confined to paper patterns, and the examples show how to apply textures based on both the clone picture and the original source image.

The picture on the opposite page illustrates how different textures can be applied to the same image. A rough paper texture was applied to the insets while the surround has received a canvas texture. This has helped to separate the elements and has made a more interesting design.

In Figure 10.2, the picture of the mannequin has had two applications of surface texture, one based on the image luminance, the other based on a paper pattern.

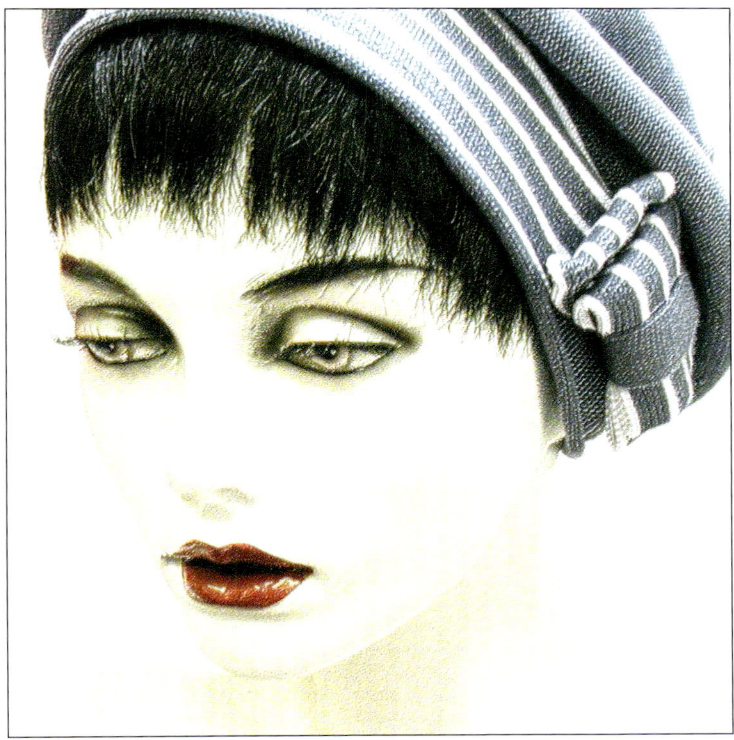

Figure 10.2 Mannequin

Apply Surface Texture – dialog box

Surface texture is usually applied at the last stage of creating a picture. There are several ways of applying texture and the dialog box, which is shown in Figure 10.3, is where all the adjustments are made. Before you start the step-by-step examples in this chapter, read through the explanations of the various controls, which are given below.

Open a picture first, one of your own or use '10 Vase of Grasses' from the CD.

To open the dialog box go to *Effects>Surface Control>Apply Surface Texture.*

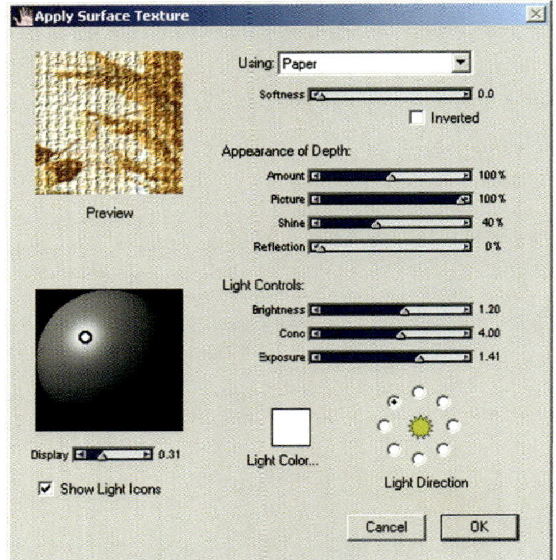

Figure 10.3 Apply Surface Textures dialog box

Using

The four ways of using the Apply Surface Texture command are found in the Using drop-down menu in the dialog box. They allow the texture to be based on several different sources.

- Paper uses the current paper texture.
- Image Luminance bases the texture on the cloned image.
- Original Luminance takes the texture from the original source image.
- 3D Brush Strokes calculates the difference between the original and the clone copy.

Softness and Inverted

The Softness slider controls how sharp the texture will appear; in most cases the slider is best left on zero to keep the detail.

The Inverted option changes the appearance of the texture from positive to negative. Figure 10.4 shows the normal texture and Figure 10.5 the texture after being inverted.

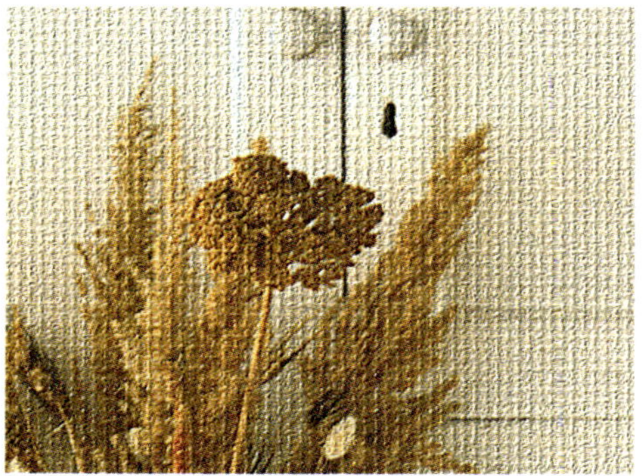

Figure 10.4 Normal texture

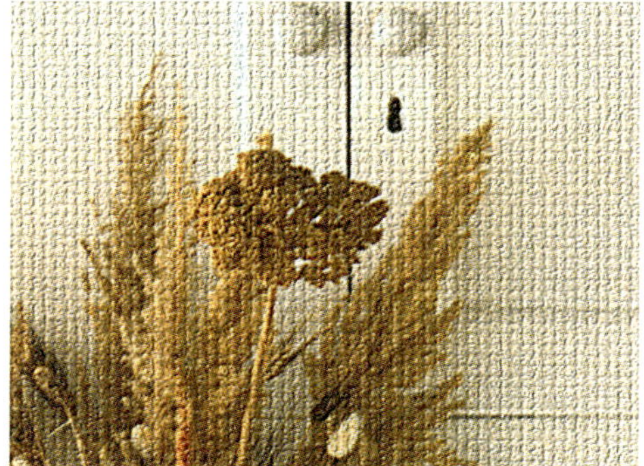

Figure 10.5 Inverted texture

Appearance of Depth

The Amount slider does just what is says – it controls the strength of the applied texture. Larger file sizes will need a higher setting and vice versa. In most cases the default amount is too strong; I suggest you try 50% and use the *Edit>Fade* command to fine-tune if necessary. Figures 10.6–10.8 show three settings of the Amount slider.

- Picture controls the balance of the picture in relation to the texture. At the minimum setting, the picture is virtually hidden by the texture. You can usually leave this on the default 100%.
- The Shine slider increases or decreases the amount of the highlights. Use this if the picture looks a bit dull after the texture has been applied.
- The Reflection slider moves the picture towards gray at the center point; at the far end only the texture is visible. You can usually leave this on the default setting of zero.

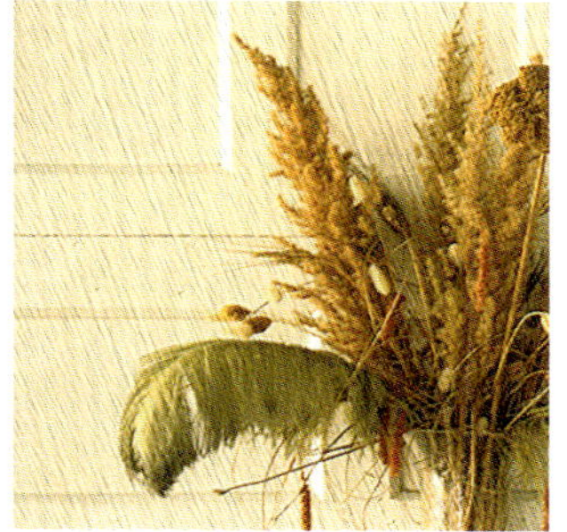

Figure 10.6 Amount at 40%

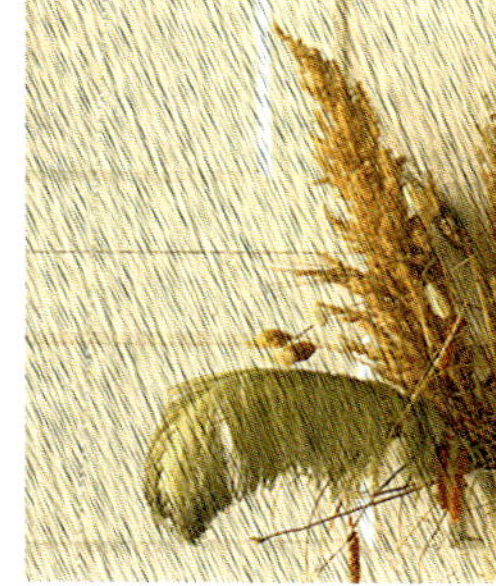

Figure 10.7 Amount at 100%

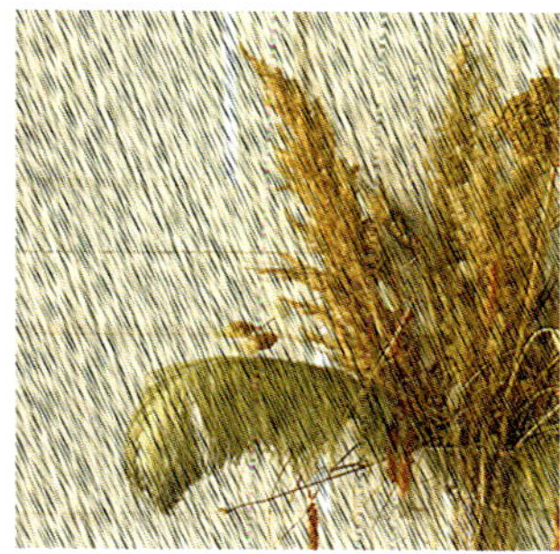

Figure 10.8 Amount at 200%

Light Controls

Surface texture is represented by light and shadow based on the image luminosity, and the Light controls will change the direction, intensity, color, exposure and balance of the lighting. Figure 10.9 shows the light direction coming from the top left, while in Figure 10.10 it is coming from the bottom right, which gives the frame a very different appearance.

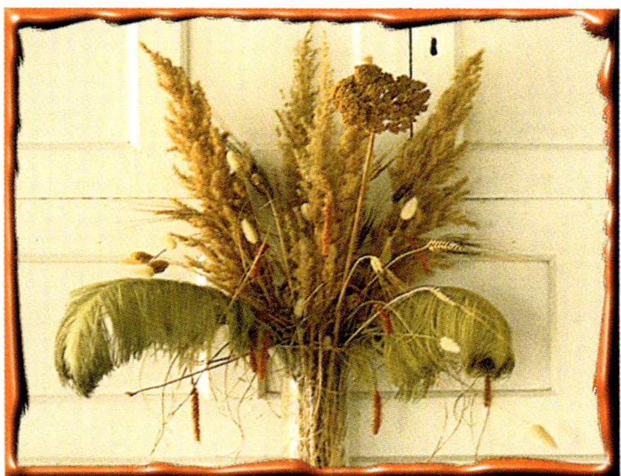

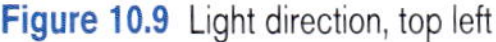

Figure 10.9 Light direction, top left

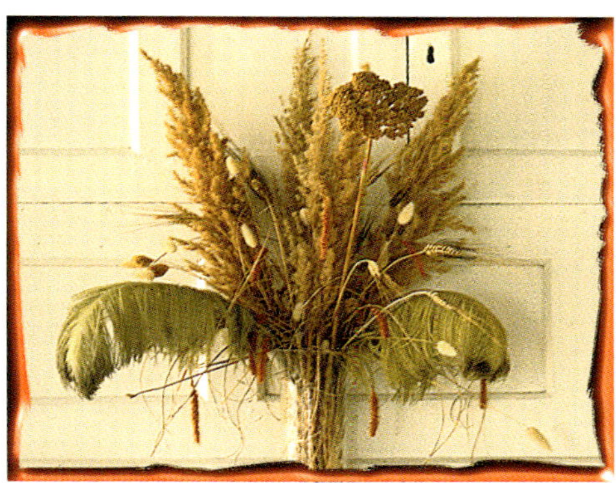

Figure 10.10 Light direction, bottom right

Using – Paper

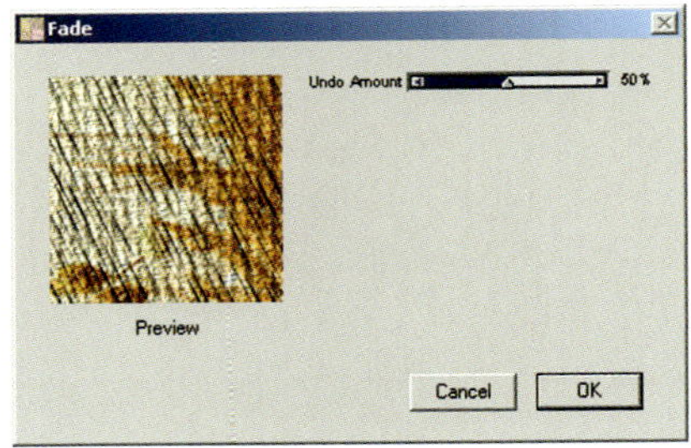

Figure 10.11

The first option in the Using box uses Paper as the source of the texture. Paper textures can be used from any of the many paper libraries, so the choice of texture is huge.

Step 1 *File>Open>CD>Step-by-step files>'10 Vase of Grasses'.*

Step 2 Select Artists Canvas from the Papers palette.

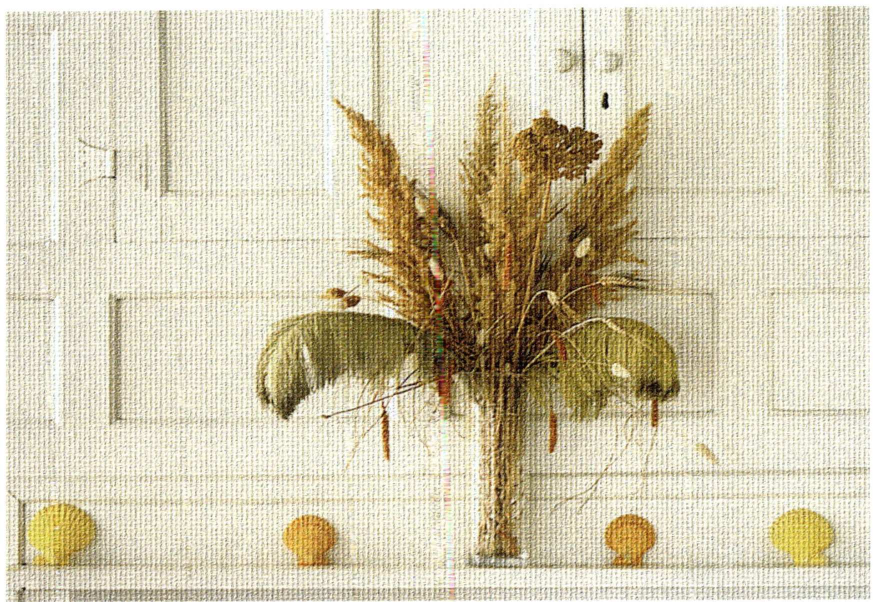

Figure 10.12 Vase with paper texture applied

Step 3 *Effects>Apply Surface Texture.*

Step 4 Select Paper in the Using box and 68% in the Amount slider. In the Preview square you will see the effect on the picture; click in the square to compare the before and after views. Before you click OK, try some of the other settings and see their effect in the preview window.

While the dialog box is on screen you can use the Papers palette to change the texture and see the updated result immediately. Figure 10.12 shows the result at the 68% setting.

It is often difficult to assess the amount needed as the preview window is small, so it is usually better to make the amount fairly strong and then to go to *Edit>Fade* to reduce the strength. This option to fade an action is really useful to remember, as it applies not only to this effect but to many actions throughout Painter, including individual brush strokes. Figure 10.11 shows the Fade dialog box.

Using – Image Luminance

The Image Luminance option bases the texture on the luminance or brightness of the image itself. In effect, this means that you are putting an embossing effect directly upon the picture. The effect is used to add depth and texture to a picture.

Step 1 *File>Open>CD>Step-by-step files>'10 Rose'.*

Step 2 *File>Quick Clone.*

Step 3 Select the *Cloners>Soft Cloner*, brush size 262.0, opacity 7% and make a soft clone as seen in Figure 10.14.

Step 4 *Effects>Surface Control>Apply Surface Texture.* Select Image Luminance from the Using drop-down menu and move the Amount slider to 30%. Leave the other settings on default. The picture will now have an embossed texture on top, as can be seen in Figure 10.15.

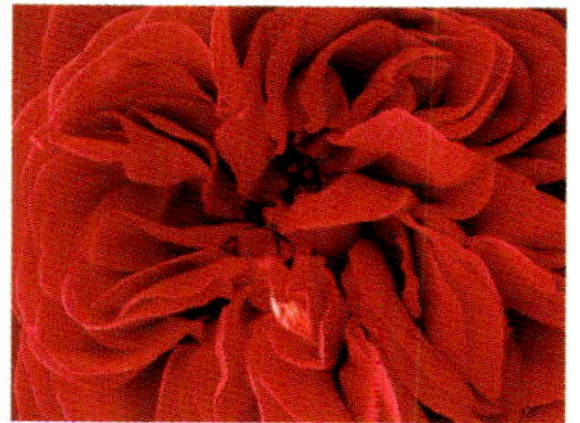

Figure 10.13

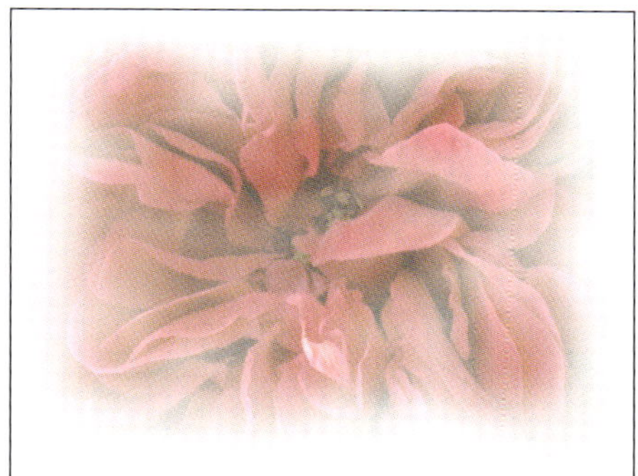

Figure 10.14

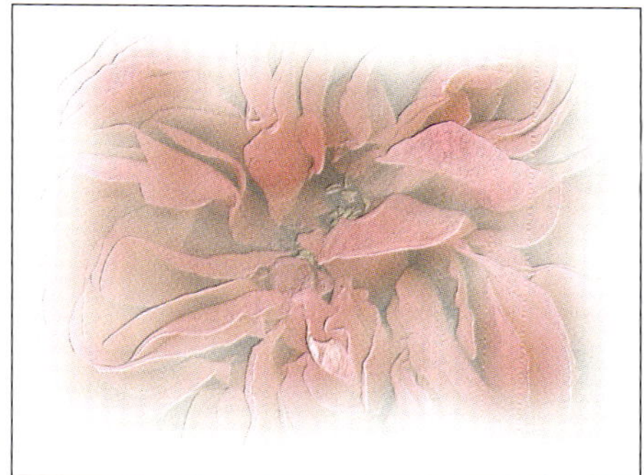

Figure 10.15

Figures 10.16 and 10.17 show another example of this setting; the texture in the old photograph album cover has been enhanced with the Image Luminance texture.

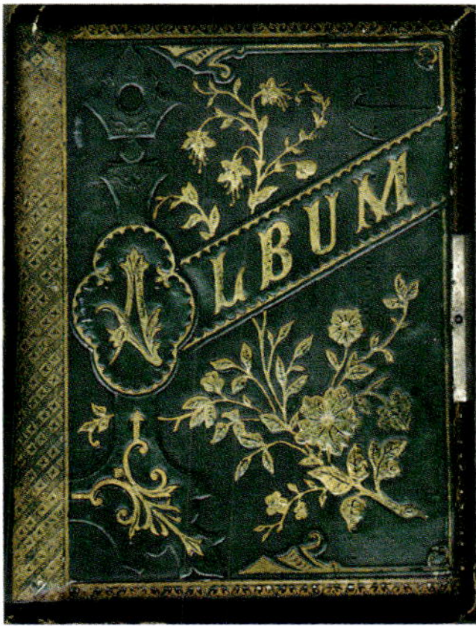

Figure 10.16

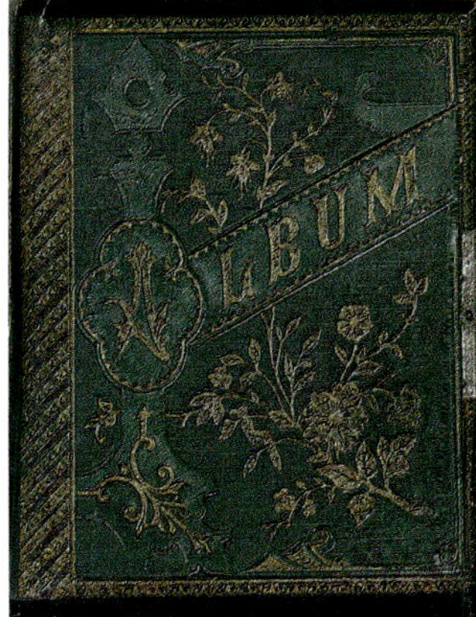

Figure 10.17

Using – Original Luminance

This option uses the original picture as the source of the texture and applies it to the clone copy. You must have the clone source active on the desktop and linked to the clone before the texture can be applied. The original and clone need not be the same picture, as the texture can be taken from any open image by changing the clone source in the Edit menu.

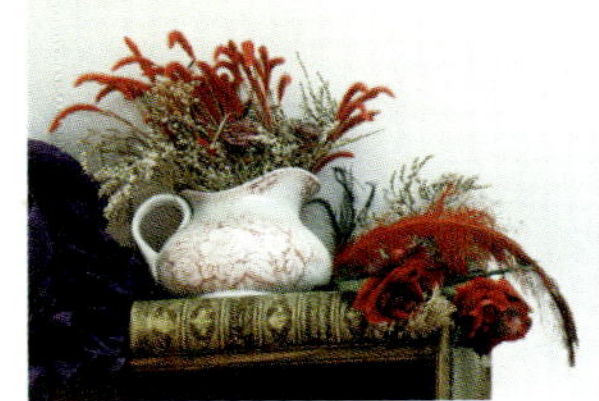

Figure 10.18

Step 1 *File>Open>CD>Step-by-step files>'10 Edwardian Corner'.*

Step 2 *File>Quick Clone.*

Step 3 Select *Cloners>Soft Cloner*, brush size 308.0, opacity 7% and make a soft clone as seen in Figure 10.19. Leave the edges clear so that you can see the effect clearly.

Step 4 *Effects>Surface Control>Apply Surface Texture*; select the Original Luminance option from the Using menu. Set the Amount at 20% and leave the other settings unchanged.

Figure 10.20 shows the result; look especially at the book and shelf support and you will see that an embossed texture has been created which is not present in the clone.

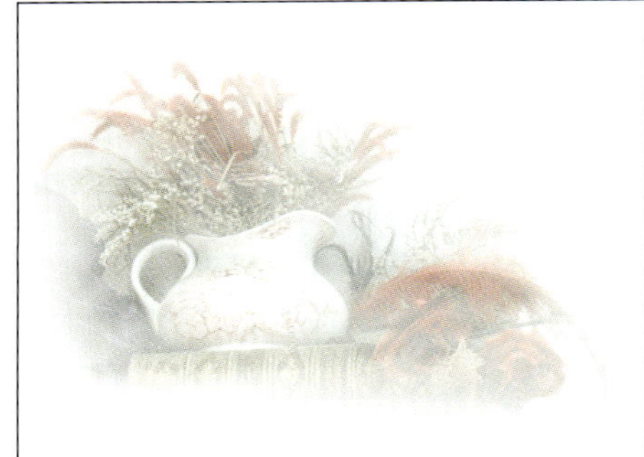

Figure 10.19

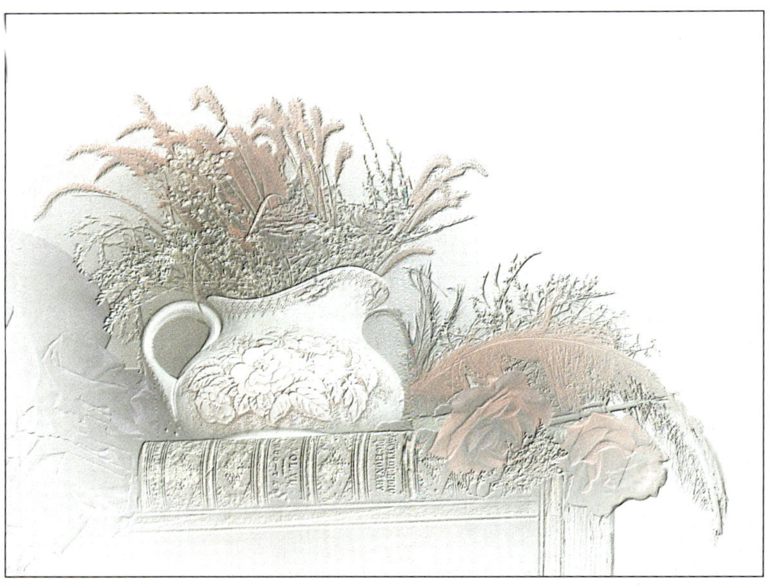

Figure 10.20 Clone with Original Luminance applied

Using – 3D Brush Strokes

This final option compares the original picture with the clone and puts the texture on the difference between the two. This is a little difficult to imagine but it does give a very 3D effect to the brush strokes, particularly when a rough brush and textured paper have been used. The illustrations below show the differences between the various options and by looking closely at the textures you will be see how each one can be used in a picture.

Figure 10.21 shows the original image before cloning. Figure 10.22 is the cloned image using the Bristle Brush Cloner.

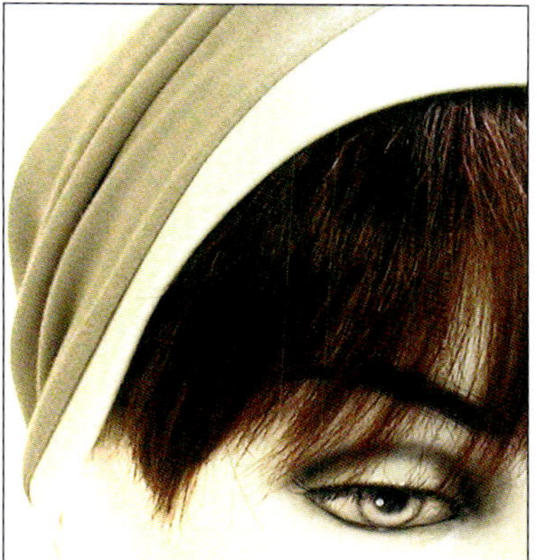

Figure 10.21

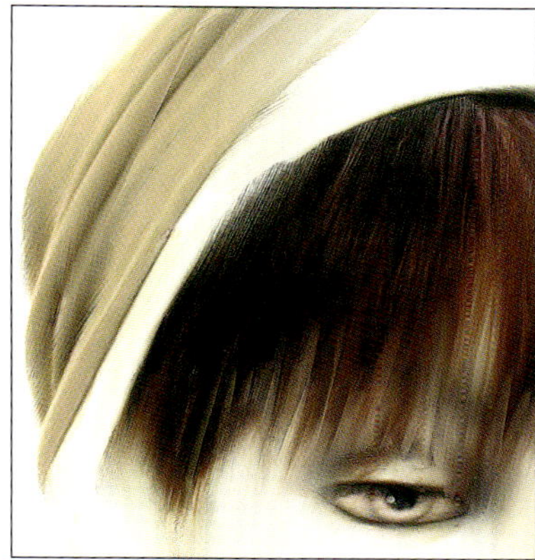

Figure 10.22

Figure 10.23 has had the Original Luminance option applied; note how the harder lines of the original image have been superimposed over the softer clone. Compare this with Figure 10.24, which has used the Image Luminance option; the image is softer as the texture has reinforced the cloned detail.

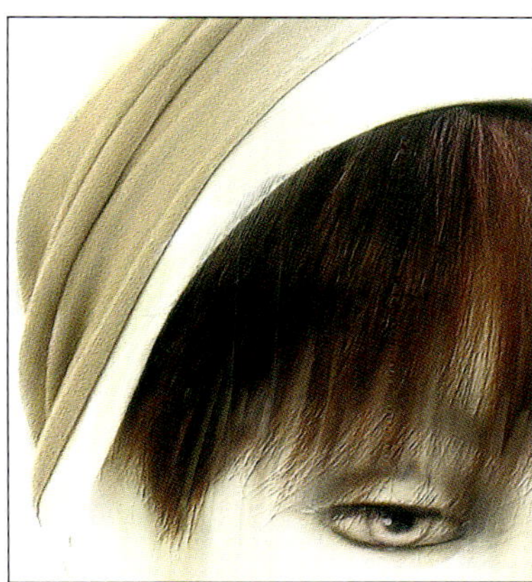

Figure 10.23

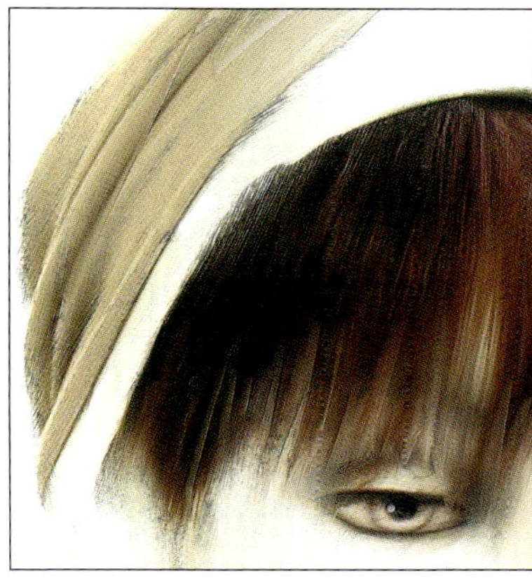

Figure 10.24

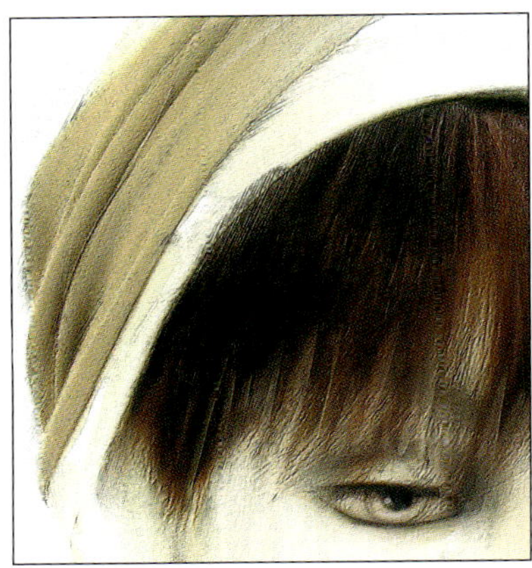
Figure 10.25

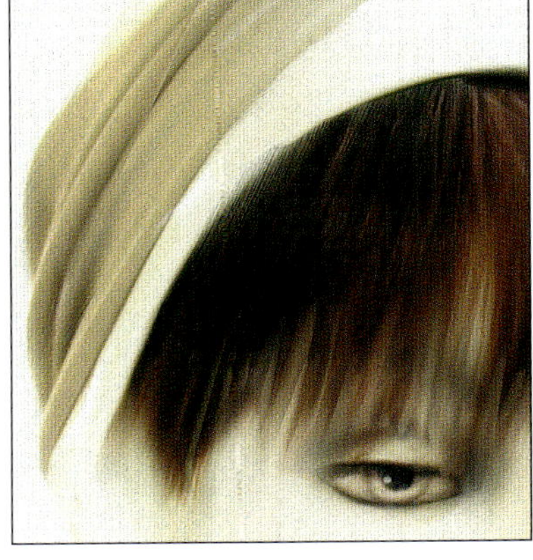
Figure 10.26

Figure 10.25 uses the 3D Brush Strokes option and the texture is somewhere between the Original and the Image Luminance examples above. Figure 10.26 uses the Paper option on the clone copy; the paper used is Artists Canvas.

At the printed size shown here, it may be difficult to see the subtle differences between these pictures; I have therefore added the examples to the CD so that you can open the images up in Painter to see the detail better. They are under the name AST in the Step-by-step files folder.

Applying texture to a soft clone

When a paper texture is applied to a clone image that has white areas around the edge, the texture can be intrusive, as Figure 10.27 shows. To stop the texture showing in the white vignette areas, take the following steps before applying the texture.

Step 1 *File>Open>CD>Step-by-step files>'10 Groynes Clone'.*

Step 2 Use the Magic Wand and click in the outer white area to select the edges.

Step 3 *Select>Feather 50 pixels* then *Select>Invert* to select the inner area.

Step 4 Apply the surface texture; this will now only affect the area enclosed by the selection. You may need to vary the amount feathered to ensure the edges are not visible. Figure 10.28 shows the picture with these steps carried out.

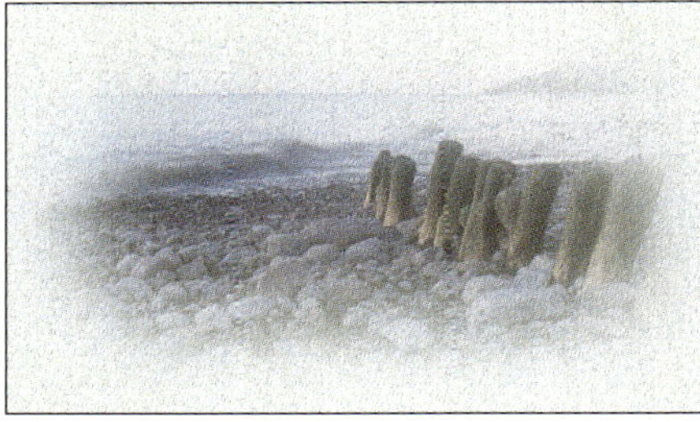
Figure 10.27

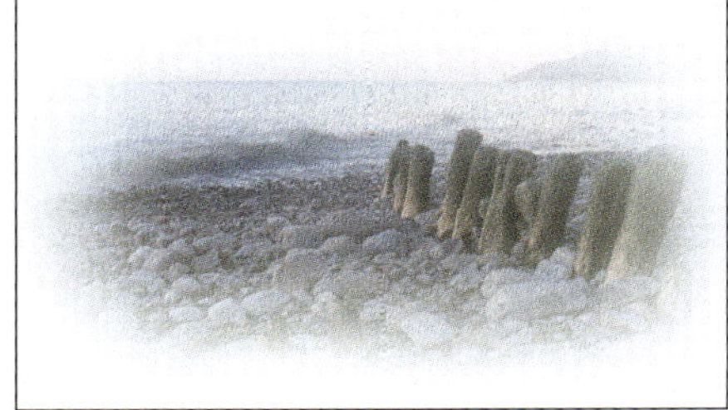
Figure 10.28

Applying texture to a layer

This technique applies the textures created in Apply Surface Textures onto a separate layer rather than putting them directly on the image. The advantage in doing this is that the image remains unchanged and the texture is adjustable at any time as it is not part of the picture.

There are several ways of achieving this. A duplicate copy of the canvas can be made, and the texture applied to this. Reducing the layer opacity will lessen the effect. Any type of texture can be applied and adjusted in this way.

The next step-by-step process will involve making a new layer and applying the texture to it.

Step 1 *File>Open>CD>Step-by-step files>'10 Window Model'.*

Step 2 *File>Clone.* Do not clear the image.

Step 3 Click the new layer icon to make a new layer.

Step 4 In the Colors palette, select 50% gray (click into the inner color triangle and slide the cursor halfway down the left side until the readout reads S 0% V 50%).

Step 5 *Effects>Fill* and choose Current Color.

Step 6 Change the layer composite method to Hard Light and the gray layer will disappear.

Step 7 *Effects>Surface Control>Apply Surface Texture.* Select 3D Brush strokes in the Using menu and make the Amount 100%. Click OK.

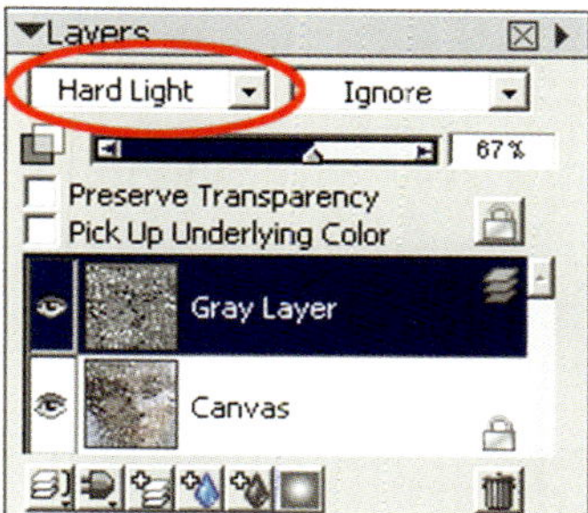

Figure 10.29

Now that the texture is on a separate layer it can be adjusted. Reduce the layer opacity to lessen the effect. Change the layer composite method to Overlay and Soft Light and see how the texture looks different each time; for more extreme changes try Multiply and Screen. Figure 10.30 shows the original and Figure 10.31 the applied texture in Hard Light composite method. Figure 10.29 shows the Layers palette with the gray layer in Hard Light composite method at 67% opacity.

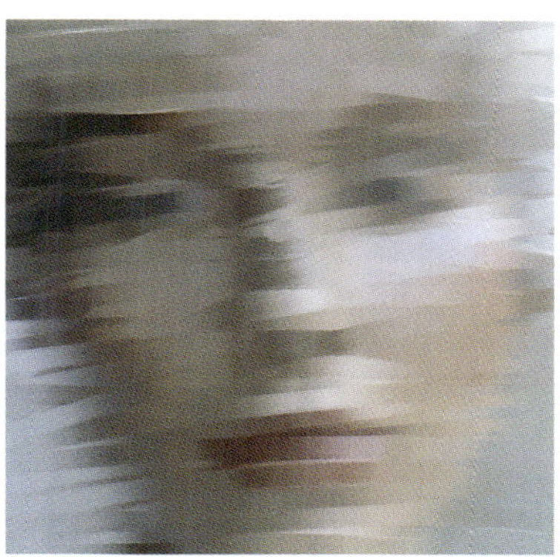

Figure 10.30

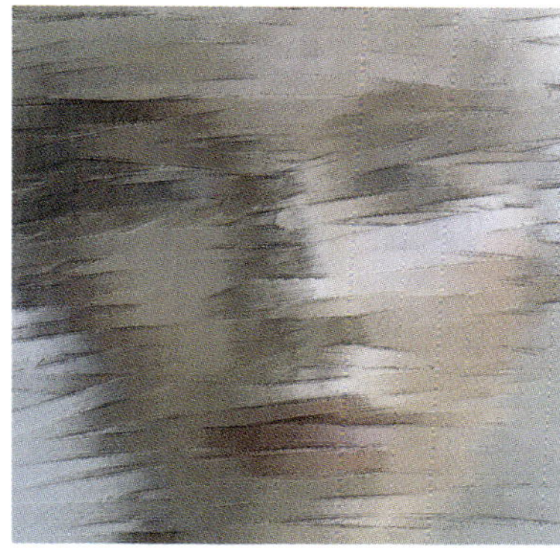

Figure 10.31

This technique can use the Paper, Original Luminance and 3D Brush Strokes textures, but cannot use Image Luminance as it is being applied to a layer empty of imagery.

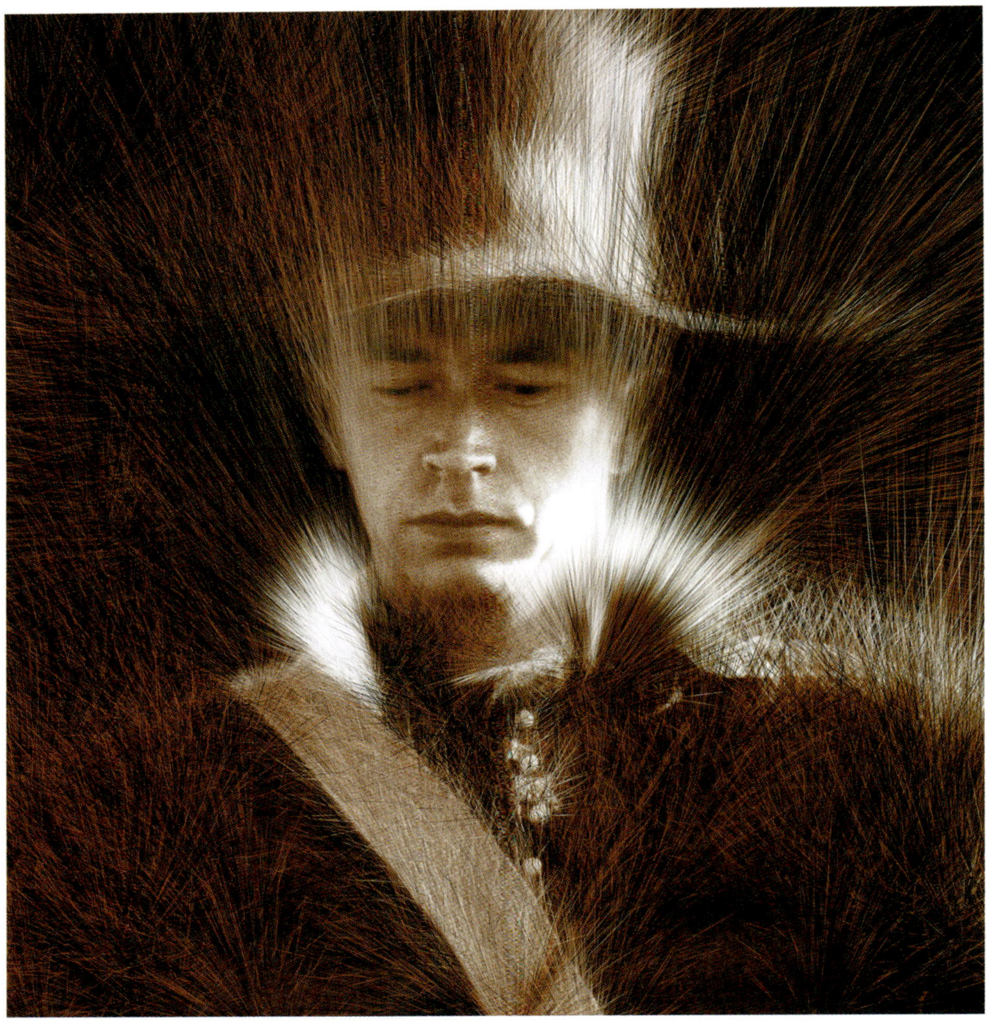

Figure 11.1 Gunner

Chapter 11
Mosaics and other clones

This chapter includes several clones that have not been explained in earlier chapters.

The step-by-step guide to making a mosaic clone will enable you to experiment with this unique picture-making method. This is not the uniform pattern imposed by mosaic filters in other programs; each tile is individually laid and adjustable and this results in a fascinating and satisfying image based on your own photograph.

Monochrome images are perennially popular and some ways of approaching these are explained in more detail, including using a Liquid Ink brush.

The final clone in this chapter uses the Furry brush and as its name indicates it creates some interesting fur-like textures. The picture on the opposite page was made with the Furry clone – have fun!

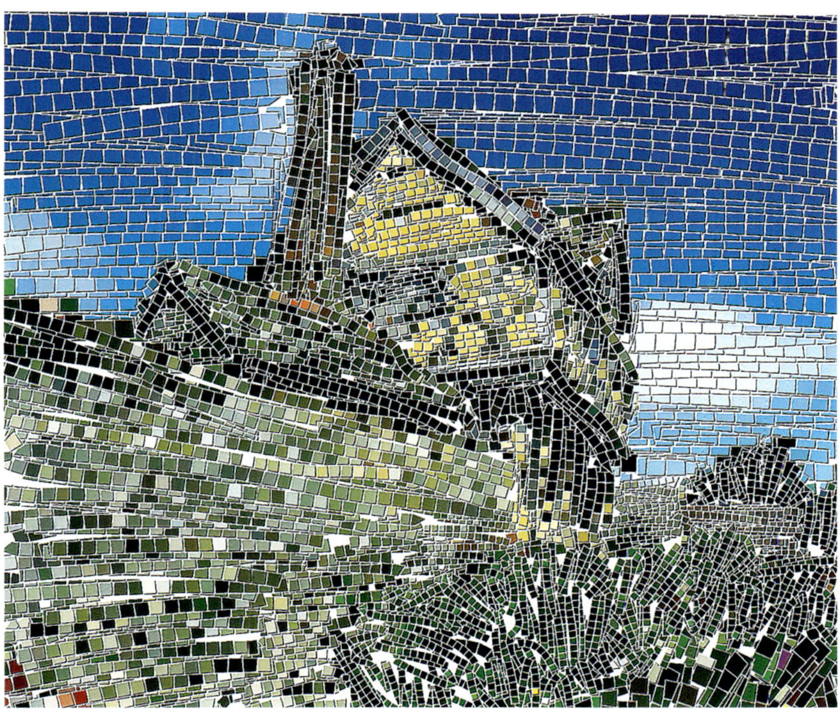

Figure 11.2 Manor house mosaic

Making mosaics

Mosaic clones work in a completely different way compared to all other clones. Most of the toolbox and palettes are not available when using mosaics, so all the controls you need are available from within the Mosaic dialog box. Choosing the right picture to make into a mosaic is important, as not all photographs are suitable; pictures with good strong shapes and lines usually work best.

Step 1 *File>Open>CD>Step-by-step files>'11 Quarry Truck'.*

Step 2 *File>Quick Clone.*

Step 3 The brush chosen is unimportant but you must click the Clone Color option in the Colors palette for the colors to be taken from the original image.

Step 4 *Canvas>Make Mosaic* will bring up the Mosaic dialog box. Click the icon on the left to start laying the tiles.

Figure 11.4 shows the Mosaic dialog box as it first opens. The left-hand icon (which is highlighted) in the dialog box is the one for applying mosaic tiles. The other icons are for removing, changing and selecting tiles after they have been laid.

The Width and Length sliders change the size and shape of the tiles.

The Pressure slider determines the variation of the tile size when using a pressure-sensitive stylus. A zero setting means the tiles vary from small to large; there is no variation at the maximum setting.

The Grout slider alters the space between each tile as it is laid. Clicking in the white box will change the color of the grout and effectively changes the background color. Figures 11.5 and 11.6 show the difference between the white and black grouts.

Before starting to make this picture it is worth trying out some brush strokes to see how the tiles are laid on the picture.

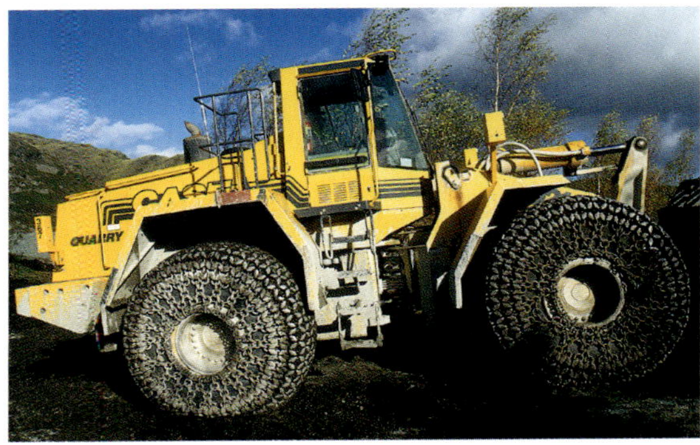

Figure 11.3 Original photograph

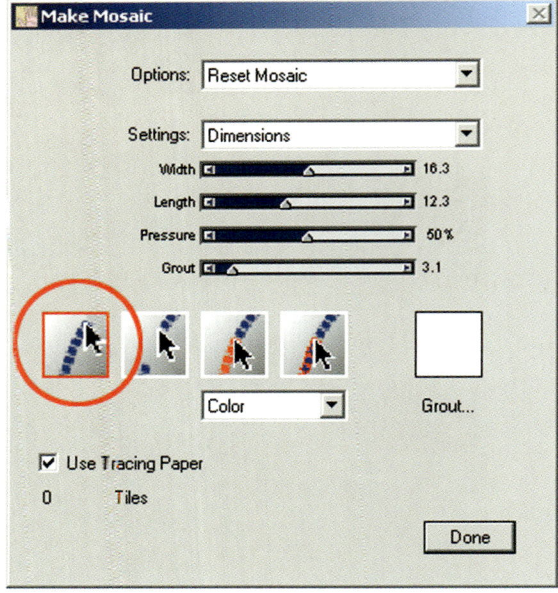

Figure 11.4 The Mosaic dialog box

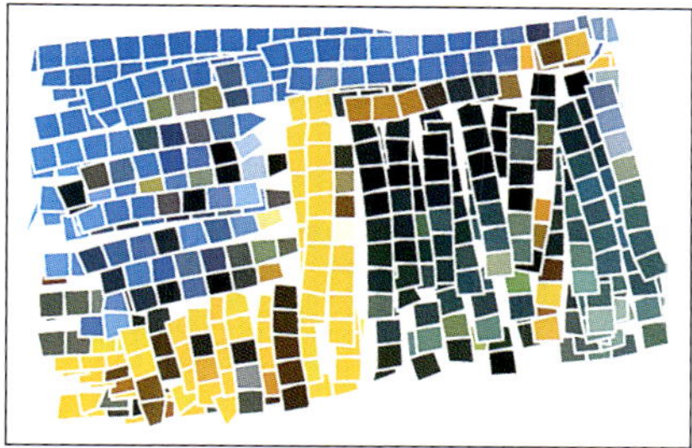

Figure 11.5 White grout

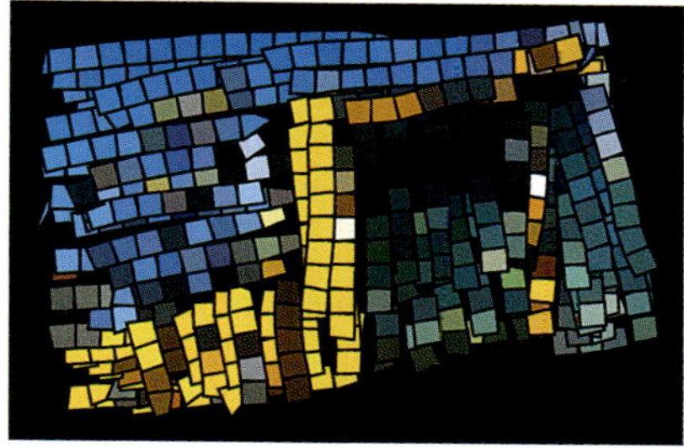

Figure 11.6 Black grout

You will quickly notice that it is impossible to lay one on top of another, just as in a real mosaic.

The Tracing Paper is turned on and off by ticking the option in the dialog box.

Tiles that you have already laid can be removed. Click the second icon and brush over the tiles; they can then be laid again.

To change the color of the tiles after they have been laid, untick the clone option in the Colors palette and select a color. Click the third icon (as in Figure 11.7) and paint over the tiles; they will change their color to the color selected in the Colors palette.

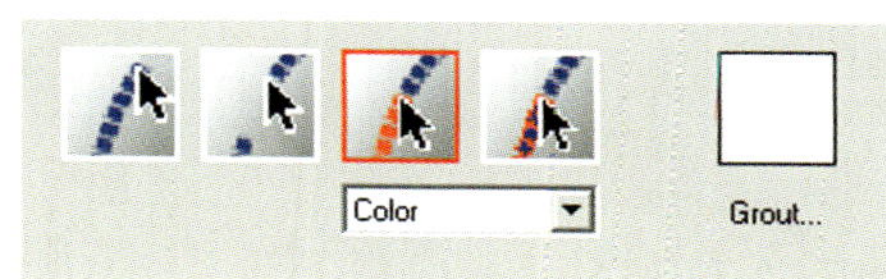

Figure 11.7

Remember to tick the clone option again before you start to clone more tiles.

Click in the box below the icons where it says Color and select one of the other options and the tiles will be darkened, lightened or tinted as you paint over them.

When you have tried out the options and are ready to start cloning the picture, close down the clone copy unsaved and make another Quick Clone. Usually you can clear a cloned image by *Select>All* and *Edit>Cut,* but in the case of mosaics this does not work. The image will be cleared but the memory of where tiles were laid is retained and makes it impossible to lay tiles in the same place.

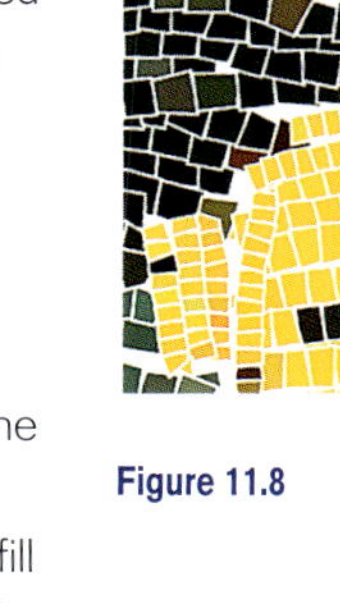

Figure 11.8

Step 5 Using the new clone copy and with the Tracing Paper turned on, paint over the picture using a tile size of about 25.0. How you lay the tiles depends on the picture, but generally it is better to follow the main lines of the picture and then to fill in the other areas afterwards. Figure 11.8 shows how the tiles can be laid in this way.

Step 6 As with all pictures you will want to save your work as you go along and when using mosaics this must be done using Painter's RIFF format. In any other

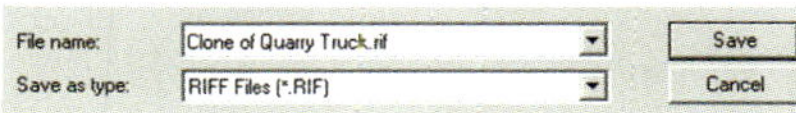

Figure 11.9

file type you will lose the ability to alter it later. *File>Save As* and select RIFF as the file type. When saved in RIFF format, the file can be opened again at any time and tiles added or altered, but make sure that you also re-open the original picture and set the clone source correctly. With the cloned picture open, go to *Canvas>Make Mosaic* and continue cloning.

Step 7 When you have finished making the mosaic picture there is one final operation, which is to add a texture to the mosaic, giving it greater depth. Select Render Tiles into Mask from the Options drop-down menu at the top of the dialog box and click on Done. This will not appear to have any effect, but it has made a mask that will be used in the next step. Figures 11.10 and 11.11 show the difference this mask makes.

Step 8 Go to *Effects>Surface Control>Apply Surface Texture* and in the Using menu select Mosaic Mask. This will add a three-dimensional impression to the tiles.

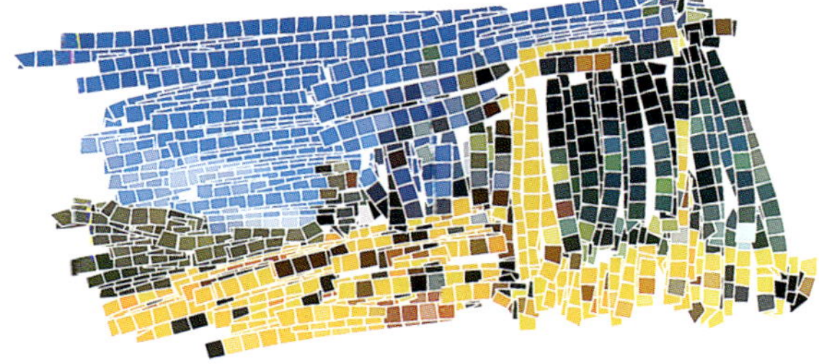

Figure 11.10 Without mosaic mask

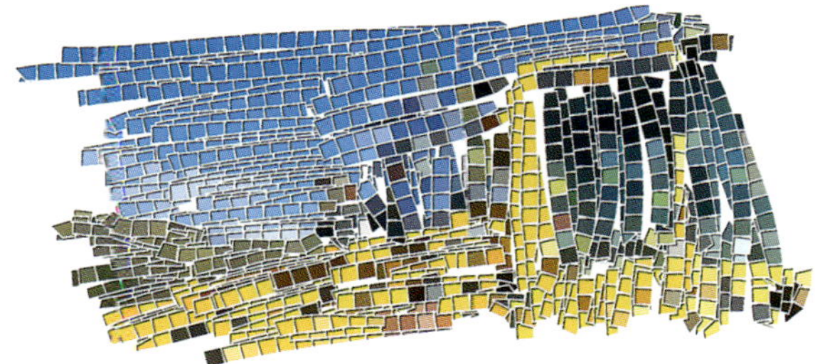

Figure 11.11 With mosaic mask applied

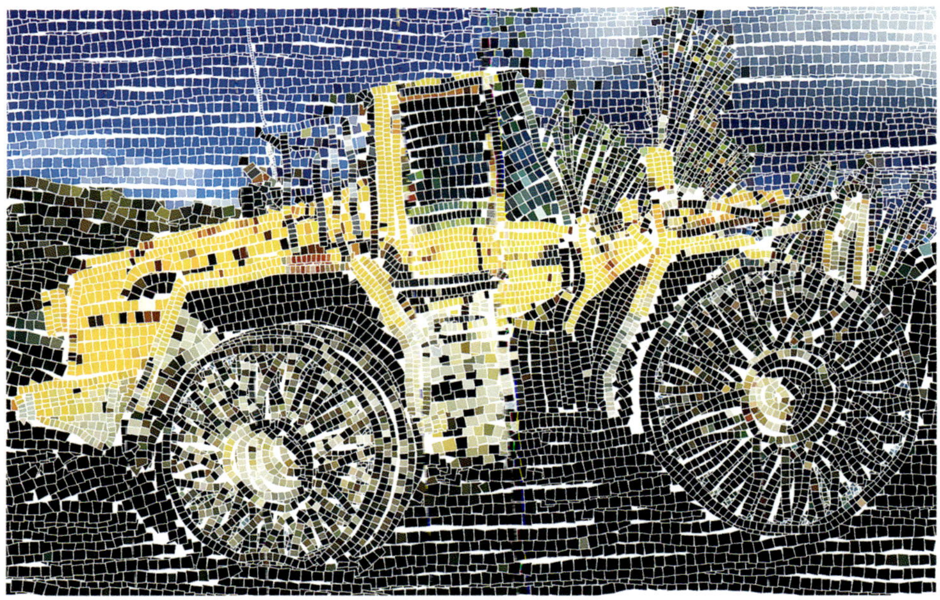

Figure 11.12 Quarry truck

Save the picture again as a RIFF if you want to adjust it later or as any other type of file when it will become a normal bitmap file type that can be opened in other imaging programs.

As a matter of interest, in the Mosaic dialog box Painter tells us how many tiles have been used in the picture, and in the quarry truck example I have used 10 530.

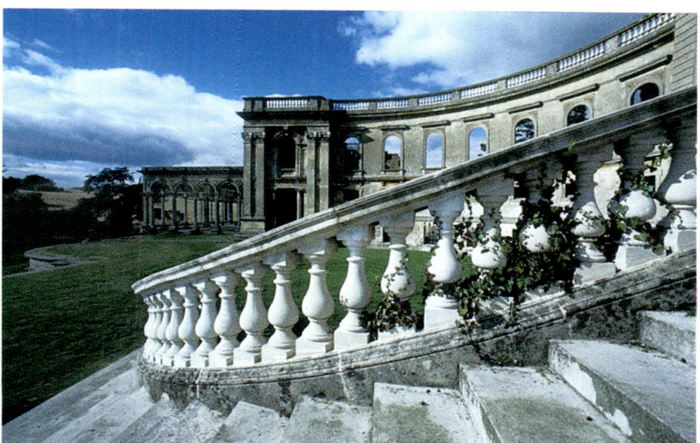

Figure 11.13 Original photograph

In this mosaic made from a picture of Witley Court (Figure 11.14), the picture had good lines to follow and although in this case the colors were quite muted, the mosaic was very successful.

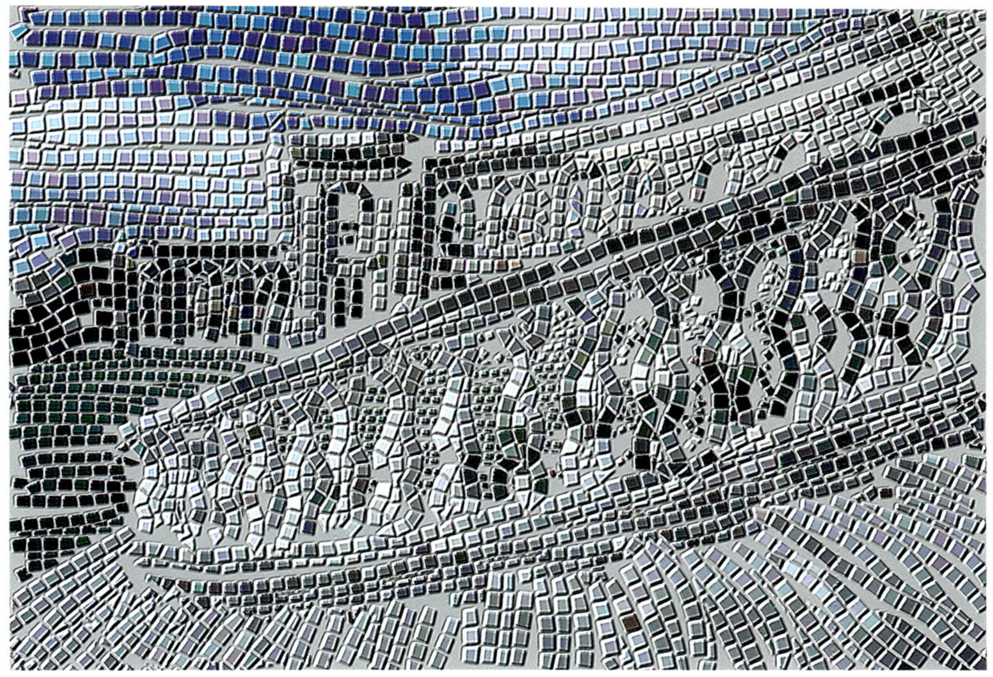

Figure 11.14 Witley Court

Monochrome clone

Clones using monochrome photographs can work very well. They need no special techniques apart from removing the color if your original picture is in color. This picture was originally photographed on Kodak Infra-Red film and that has given it a very grainy and contrasty appearance.

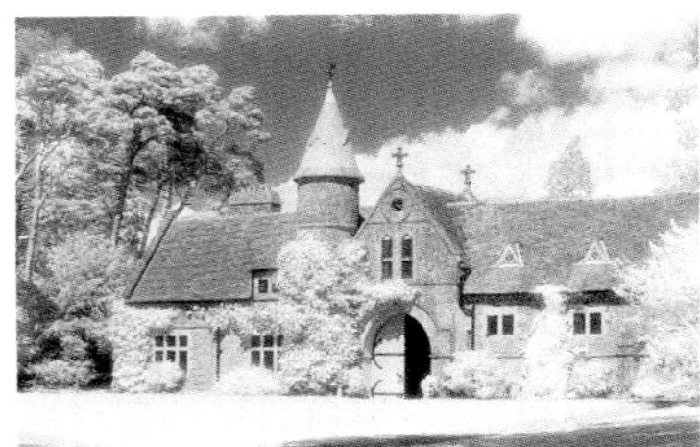

Figure 11.15

Step 1 *File>Open>CD>Step-by-step files> '11 Old Coach House'.*

If your own picture needs to be changed to monochrome, make a new empty layer above the canvas and fill it with black. Change the layer composite method to Colorize and click on Drop All in the palette menu.

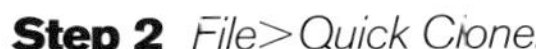

Step 2 *File>Quick Clone.*

Step 3 Select the Sketching Pencil 5 from the Pencils category, brush size 175.0 with opacity at 4%. In the General palette, change the Method to Cloning and Subcategory to Grainy Hard Cover Cloning.

Step 4 Select the Italian Watercolor Paper.

Step 5 Sketch lightly over the picture, leaving the edges white as in Figure 11.16.

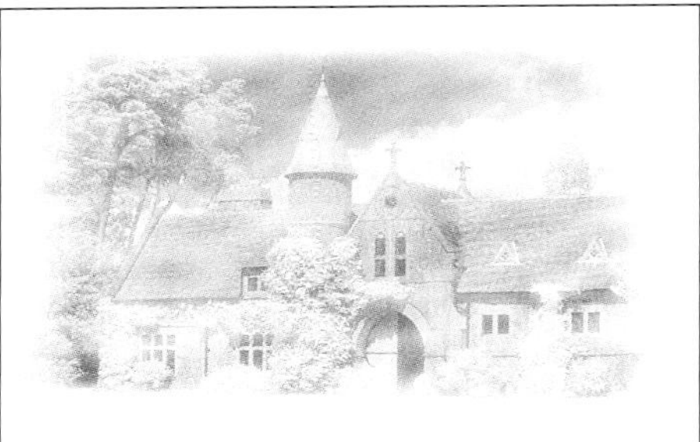

Figure 11.16

Step 6 Reduce the brush size to around 66.6, increase the opacity to 10% and paint over the picture, bringing out more detail where necessary.

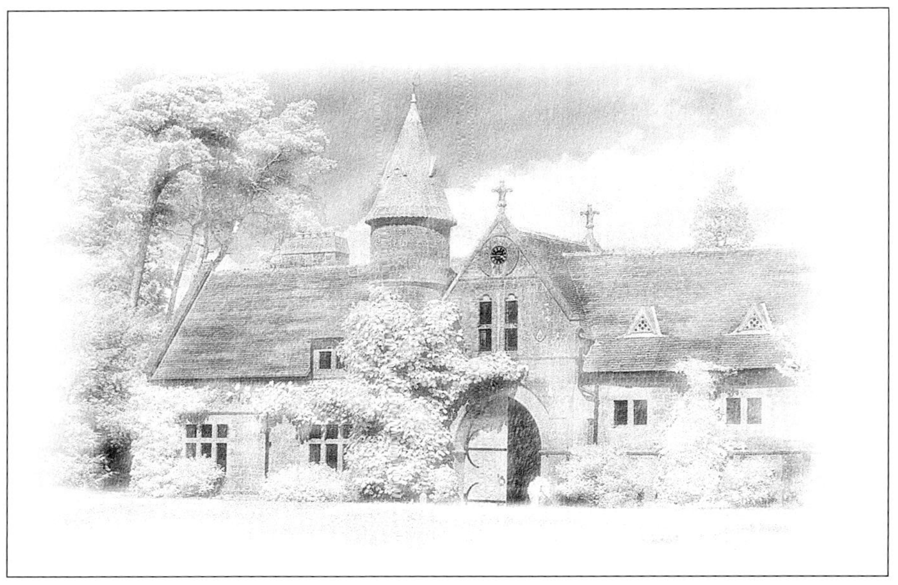

Figure 11.17 Old coach house

Liquid Ink

This next example uses a monochrome original and the unusual properties of a Liquid Ink brush to create a very hard rough finish. Like Watercolor clones, Liquid Ink uses a special layer which can be adjusted at any time. Because of this you will need to save the file in RIFF format until the picture is completed.

Step 1 *File>Open>CD>Step-by-step files> '11 Knight Statue'.*

Step 2 *File>Quick Clone.*

Step 3 Select the Coarse Bristle Resist brush from the Liquid Ink brush category, make the brush size 99.6, the opacity 12% and Smoothness 10%. This resist brush will put unseen marks on the layer that will stop ink from taking on the paper. This is like putting wax on a piece of paper then painting over with water-based paint; the wax will stop the paint from being absorbed.

Step 4 Make four brush strokes down the center of the picture with the resist brush. You will not see anything but the effect will become apparent in the next step.

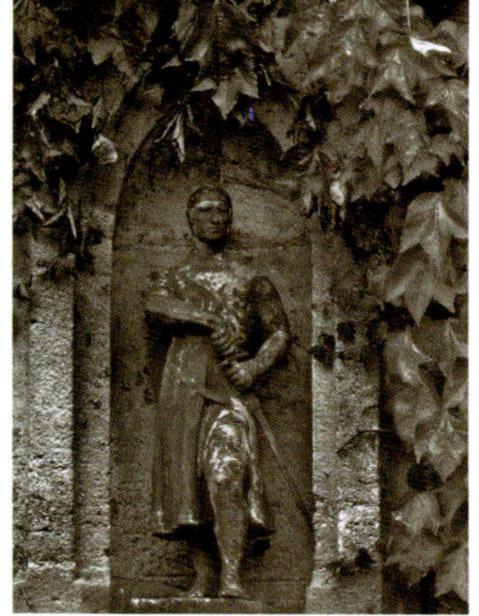

Figure 11.18

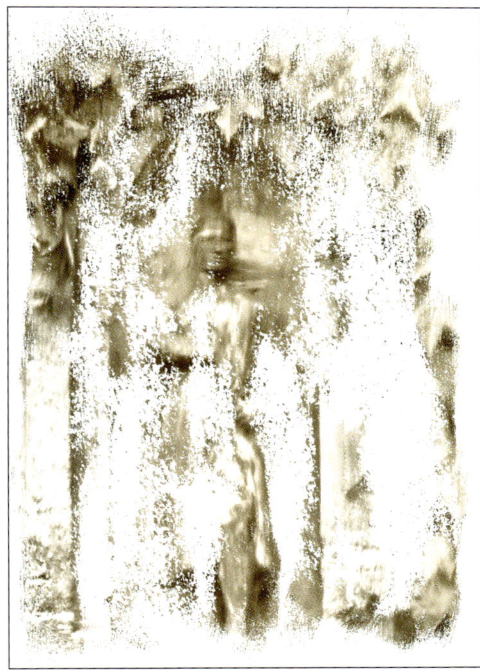

Figure 11.19

Step 5 Select the Coarse Bristle brush from the Liquid Ink category. On the Properties bar, make the brush size 44.4, opacity 30% and Smoothness 22%.

The change to the Smoothness slider will make this brush very rough. Click the Clone Color option in the Colors palette.

Step 6 Paint in short strokes from the top of the picture; give the brush time to finish each stroke, as this is a very complicated brush and works slowly. Don't allow the brush to linger in one place as the density will be too strong. As you can see in Figure 11.19, the picture is very broken up, partly due to the resist paint applied earlier. Change the layer composite method to Hard Light, which will increase the hardness of the texture.

Step 7 Make a new Liquid Ink layer by clicking on the new Liquid Ink icon in the Layers palette; the icon is the fifth from the left. Change this layer to Hard Light composite mode as previously.

Step 8 Use the same brush and paint again to show more of the picture. Figure 11.20 shows this layer seen with Layer 2 and the white Canvas (Layer 1 is turned off in order to show the layer separately).

Step 9 Make another Liquid Ink layer in Hard Light composite mode and paint more texture; fill in areas that are blank. Figure 11.21 shows this layer with just the white Canvas below; you will be working with all the layers visible and will therefore see the whole picture as it develops rather than one layer at a time as illustrated here.

The reason for making separate layers is that it allows more flexibility when the picture is being finished. The opacity and composite method of each layer may be changed.

The Layers palette is shown in Figure 11.22 and the final picture in Figure 11.23.

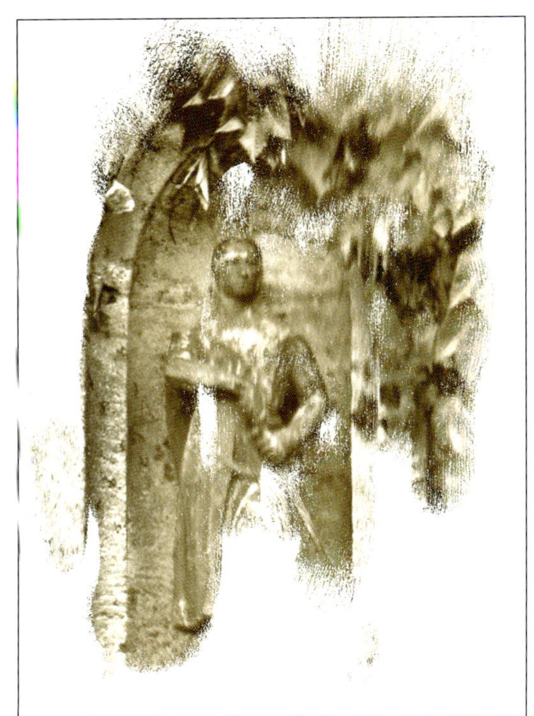

Figure 11.20

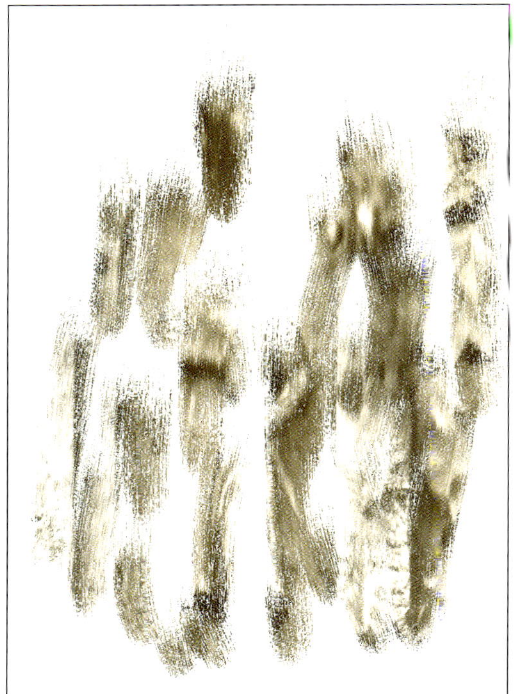

Figure 11.21

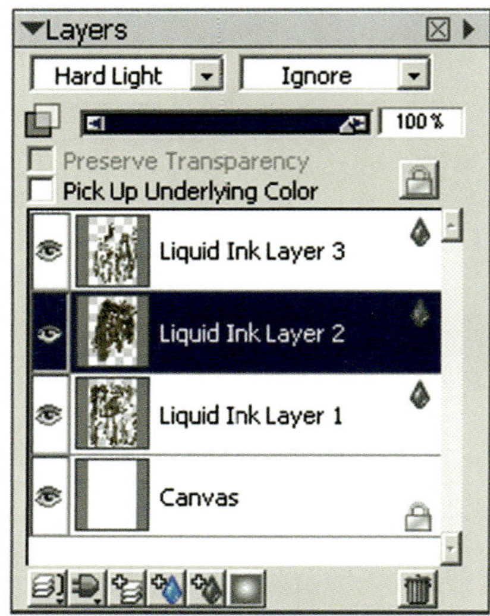

Figure 11.22

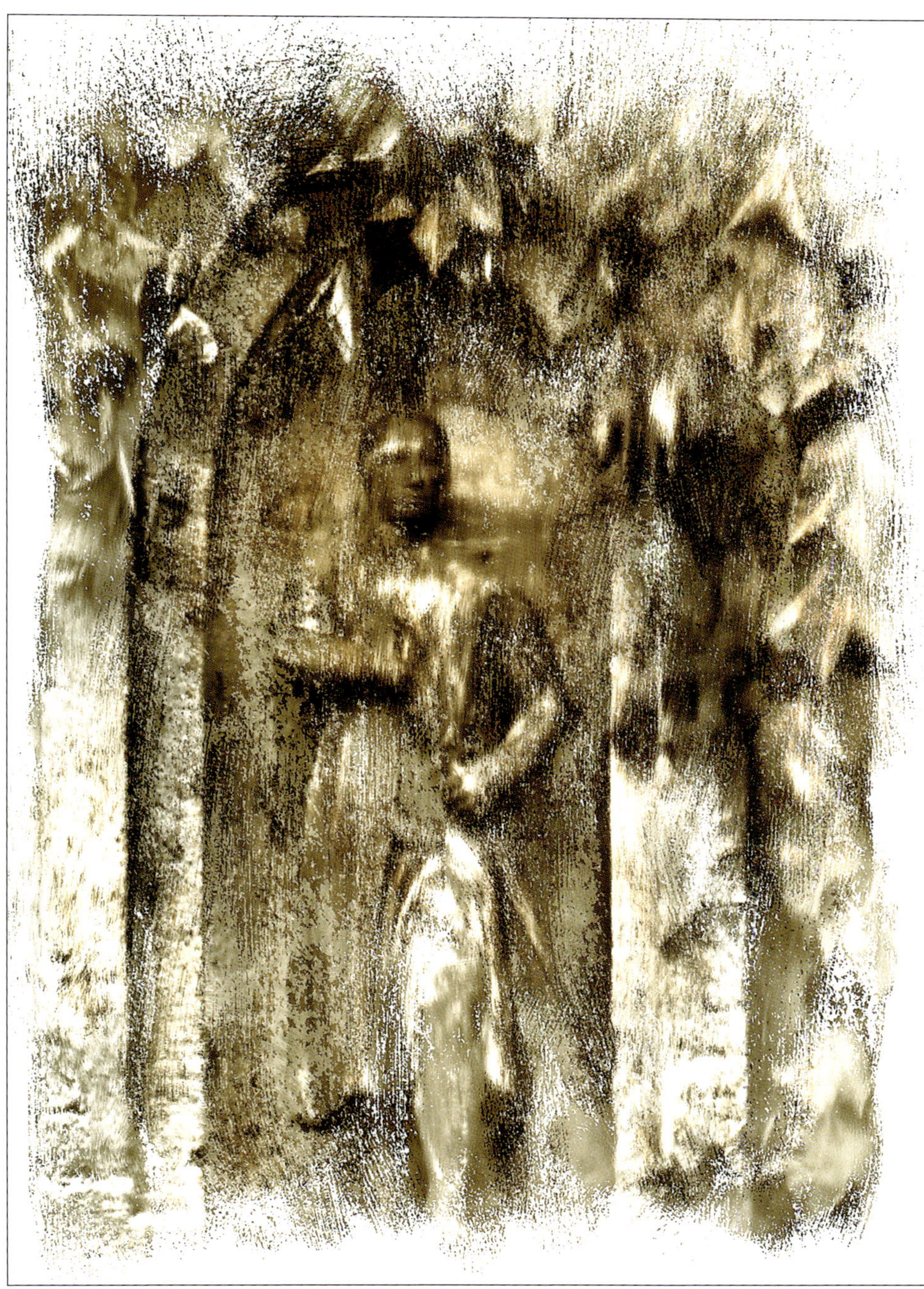

Figure 11.23 Knight statue

Furry clone

Furry clones are great fun to make, with streaks of fur shooting off in all directions; they also make some very interesting textures that can be suitable for backgrounds. The Furry brush uses the Line Airbrush dab type (see Chapter 6 on customizing brushes for more examples of dab types).

Autumn leaves

Step 1 *File>Open>CD>Step-by-step files>'11 Autumn Leaves'.*

Step 2 *File>Quick Clone.*

Step 3 Select the Furry Brush in the F/X brush category, brush size 48.2, opacity 100% and click the Clone Color option in the Colors palette.

Step 4 Hold your pressure-sensitive stylus at a shallow angle and allow the fur to spray outwards; paint all the background in this way. This fills the background with a loose coverage prior to painting the leaves in more detail. Figure 11.25 shows this step completed.

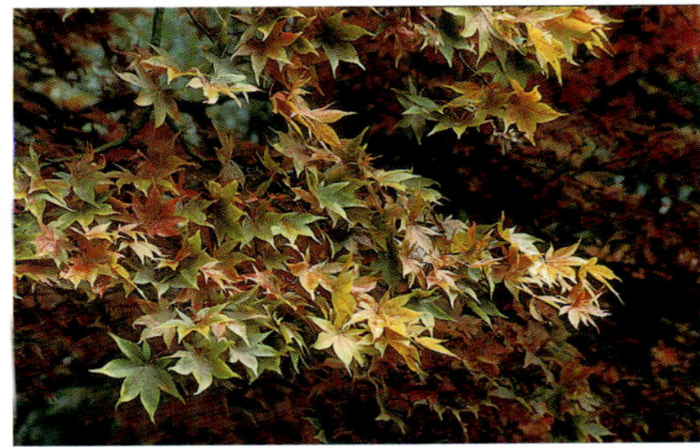

Figure 11.24 Original photograph

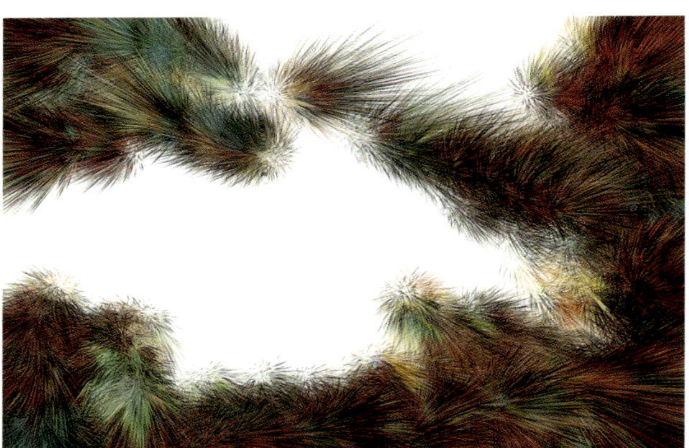

Figure 11.25

Step 5 Reduce the brush size to 15.5 and paint in the remainder of the picture, keeping the stylus at a shallow angle and pointed in the same direction as the leaves.

Step 6 Reduce the brush to 11.3 and go over the main leaves again using the Tracing Paper as a guide. The smaller brush will bring in more detail. Figure 11.26 shows this stage.

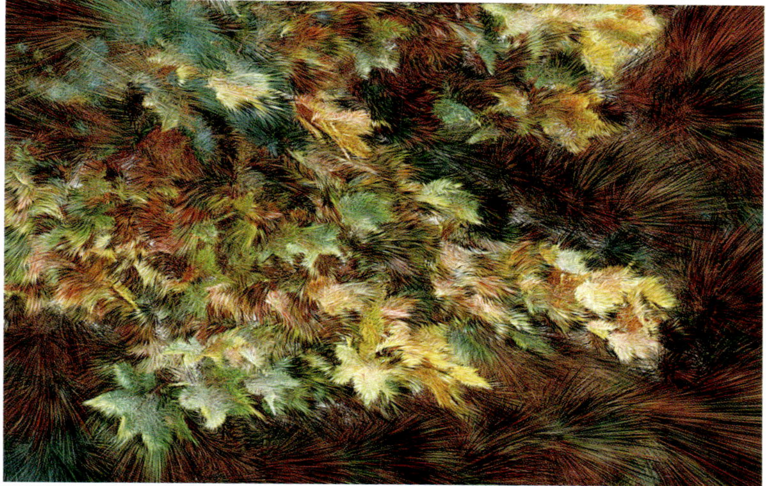

Figure 11.26

Step 7 The next step is to paste a copy of the original picture on top of the clone copy. Click back in the original picture to activate it and copy the picture by going to *Select>All, Edit>Copy*. Click back in the clone copy to activate that image and, holding down the Shift key, go to *Edit>Paste*. (Holding down the Shift key will keep the pasted picture in register with the one below.)

Step 8 Change the layer composite method of the pasted layer to Lighten and adjust the opacity if necessary. This will combine the clarity of the original with the softness of the clone copy. Figure 11.27 shows the completed picture.

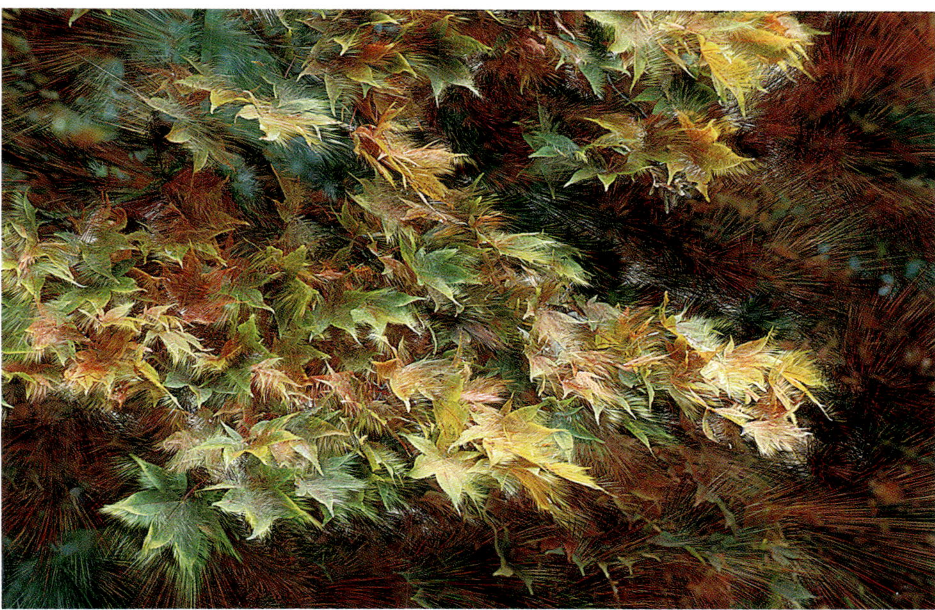

Figure 11.27 Autumn leaves

Furry clone as texture

This Furry clone uses the furry effect as a base texture and the original is brought back on top as an embossed texture using the Apply Surface Textures effect, which is described in more detail in Chapter 10.

Athena

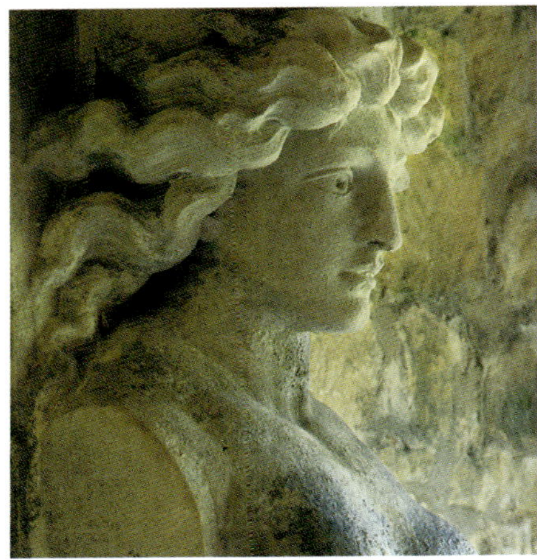

Figure 11.28 Original photograph

Step 1 *File>Open>CD>Step-by-step files>'11 Athena'.*

Step 2 *File>Quick Clone.*

Step 3 Select the Furry Brush from the F/X brush category. Set the brush size to 149.2 and opacity 100%.

Step 4 Paint over the whole picture, holding the stylus upright this time. The object is to make a background for the whole picture. The semi-abstract view at this stage is shown in Figure 11.29.

Step 5 Reduce the brush size to 29.7 and paint over the face and hair to bring in more detail from the original, but leave the background untouched. Reduce the brush further to 14.0 and paint over the face and hair, following the shapes at all times. Figure 11.31 shows this step.

To bring back some of the original texture the next step will be to make a copy layer and apply an embossed effect.

Step 6 Click on the Layer Adjuster tool. Go to *Select>All* and, holding down the Alt/Opt key, click in the picture area to make a copy of the Canvas.

Step 7 *Effects>Surface Control>Apply Surface Texture.* Change the Using option to Original Luminance and the Amount to 50% – click OK.

Step 8 Change the layer composite method of the copy layer to Lighten and reduce the opacity to about 80%.

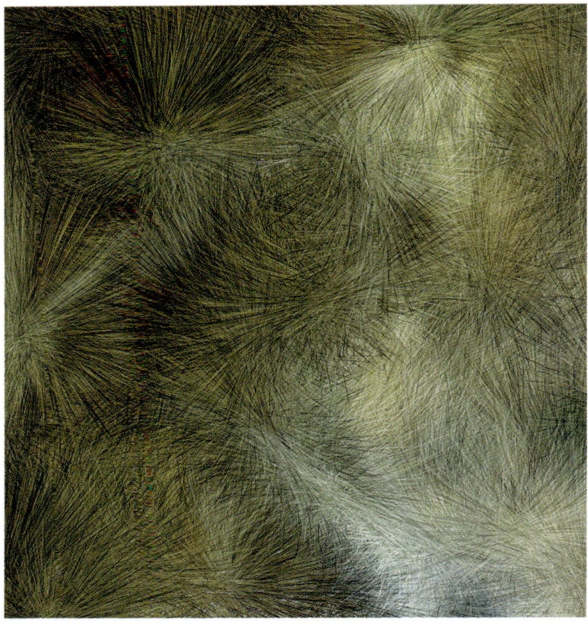

Figure 11.29

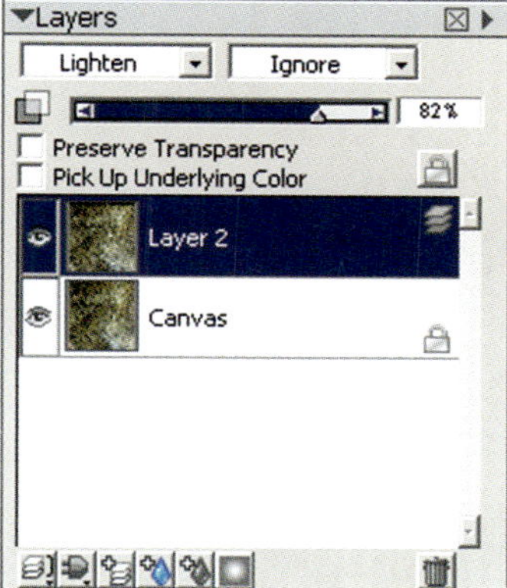

Figure 11.30

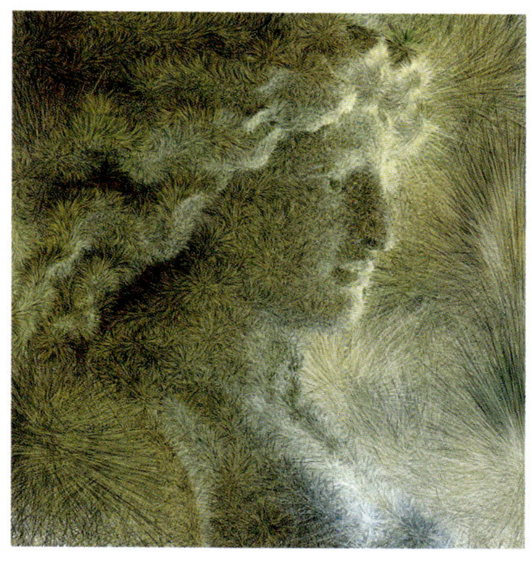

Figure 11.31

The Layers palette is shown in Figure 11.30 and the final picture in Figure 11.32.

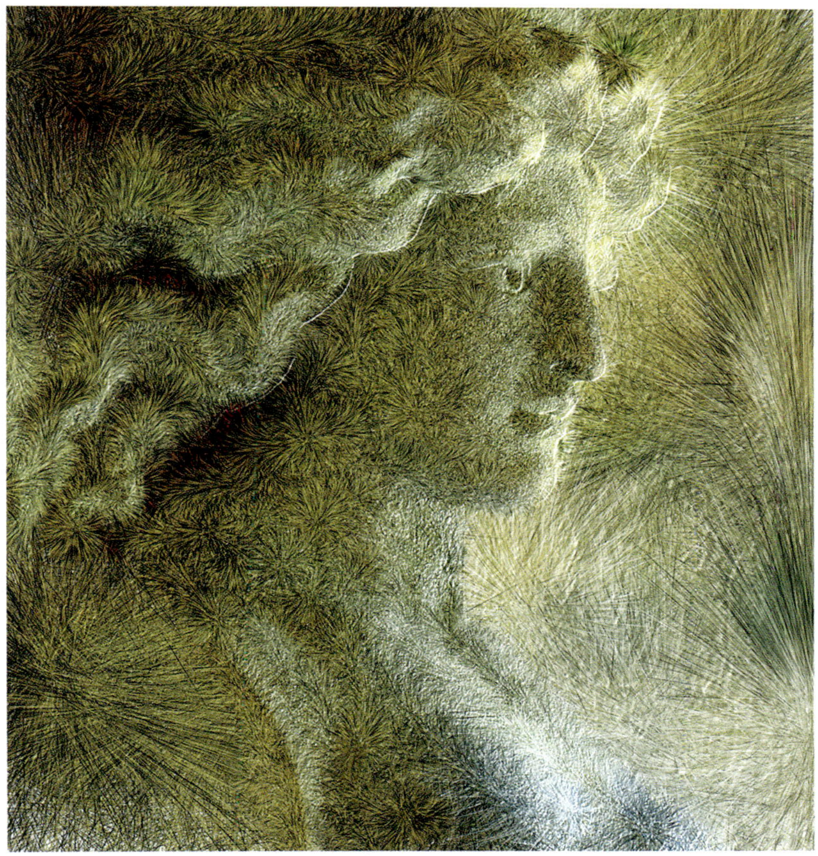

Figure 11.32 Athena

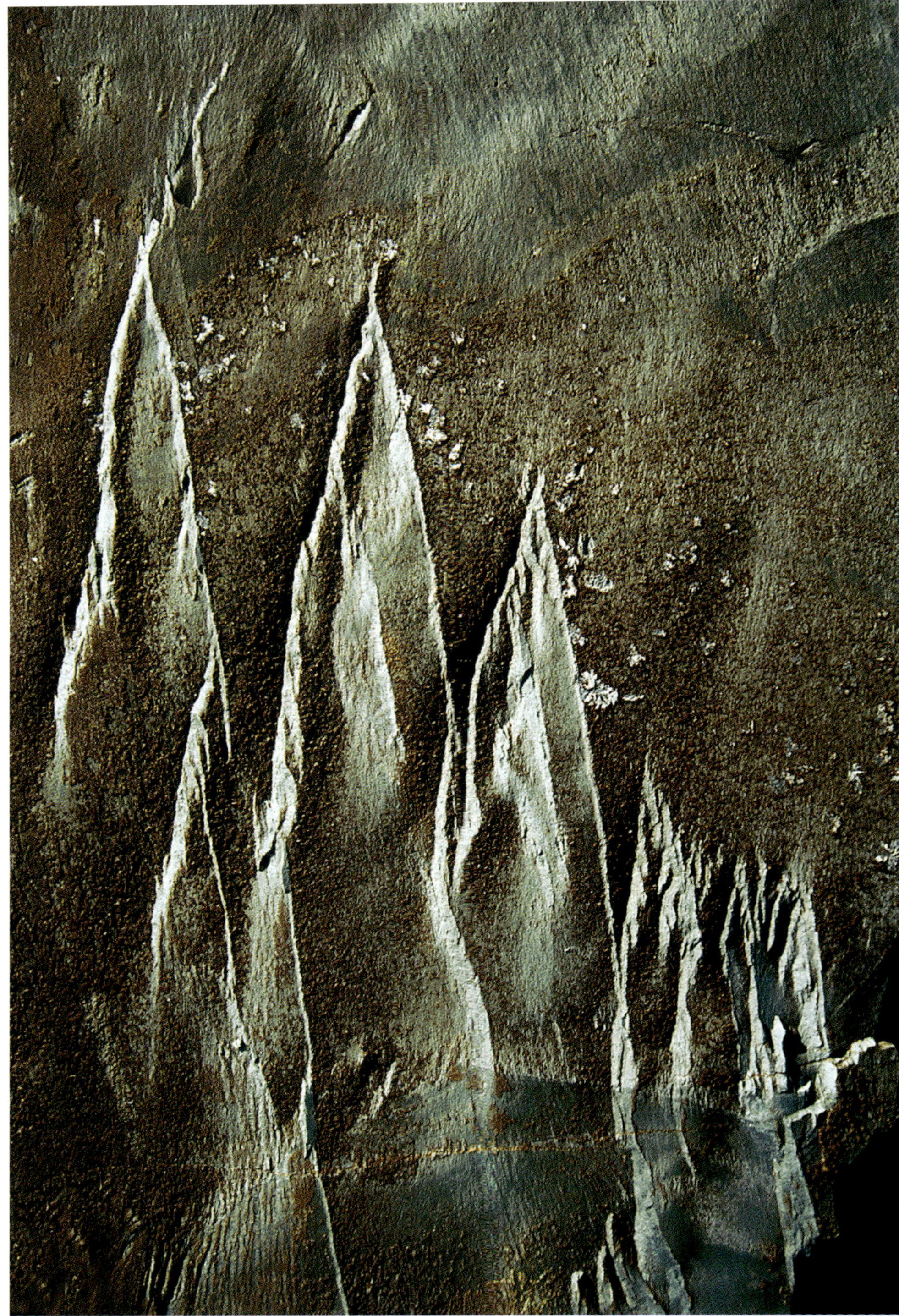

Figure 12.1 Rockface

Chapter 12
Hand coloring and toning

The chapter starts with a reference section on choosing colors using the various palettes and commands. Also included is a description of the Mixer palette that was first introduced in Painter 8 and improved in Painter IX, and which will be used in the hand coloring step-by-step examples.

Hand-colored pictures have a charm which is quite unique and in this chapter you will discover the best way to use this fascinating technique.

Allied to hand coloring is the ability to remove the color and tone photographs; this technique takes a picture a step away from reality, which often makes it that bit more special.

The scene in Figure 12.2 has been hand colored using the techniques explained in this chapter.

The picture on the left-hand page shows a detail of a piece of rock and the *Effects>Posterize* using Color Set command was used to tone the original photograph. The Color Set chosen was Muted Tones and the layer composite method was Shadow Map at 40% opacity.

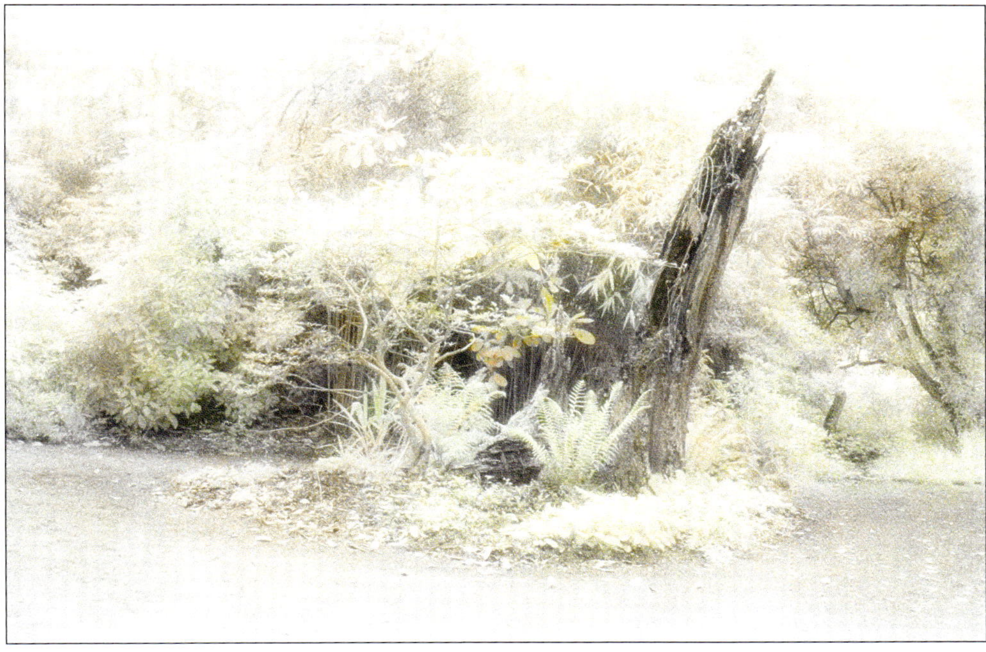

Figure 12.2 The lost garden

Choosing colors

Painter IX has a variety of ways to select and use colors whether for toning, painting or coloring, and is the ideal program in which to paint or hand tint photographs. Apart from the vast range of brushes, the ability to keep the palettes live while working is something that many other programs, including Photoshop, cannot do.

There are three principal palettes to use: Colors, which have been used many times before in this book; Color Sets; and the excellent Mixer palette

Colors palette

The Colors palette is shown in Figure 12.3; if this palette is not visible on the screen, go to *Window>Color Palettes>Show Colors.*

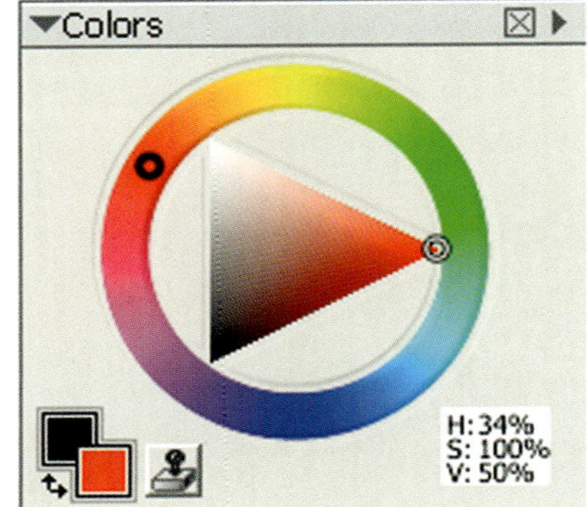

Figure 12.3 The Colors palette

This is the chief color picker for general use in Painter. Colors are chosen by first selecting the Hue and then the Value and Saturation. In case you are not familiar with the terminology, I will briefly explain what these terms mean.

Hue is the principal color and is chosen by clicking in the circular color ring. Value is the brightness of the color and is selected by moving the cursor up or down in the inner color triangle. Maximum value is white and minimum black. Saturation is the purity of the color. It is at its most intense on the far right of the inner triangle and as the cursor is moved to the left the color is diluted by being mixed with black or white.

The two squares bottom left show the Main and Additional colors. The Main color is the one that is used for painting and is the one in front. The square behind is the Additional color and is used for some special brushes that use two colors. It is not the same as the background color in some other graphics programs.

The small white readout in the bottom right corner shows the numerical values of the Hue, Saturation and Value of the color chosen. Click in this readout to change it from HSV to RGB. These readouts are useful if you need to know exactly how to replicate the color at a later date.

The rubber stamp icon is, of course, the Clone Color option, which we have used many times throughout this book, and makes the brush pick the color from the clone source instead of the Colors palette. When the Clone Color is selected the colors in the palette are muted.

Small Color palette

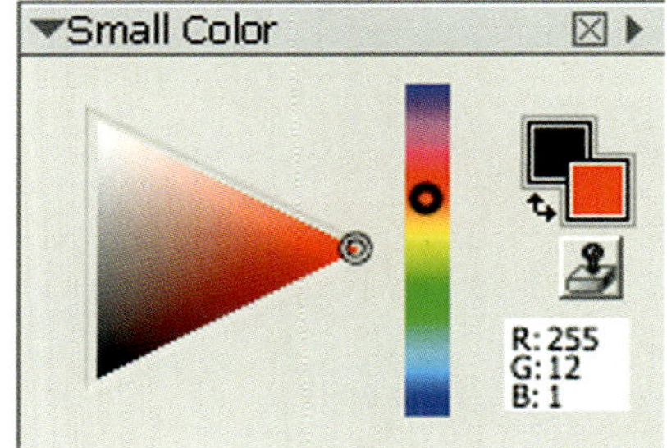

Figure 12.4

There is a smaller version of the Colors palette available; click in the palette menu and select Small Colors and the palette will change to that shown in Figure 12.4. It works in the same way as the standard Colors palette.

Color Info

The Color Info palette, which is shown in Figures 12.5 and 12.6, is very useful for making colors when you have the specific color values. Move the sliders or type directly in the boxes the color values you need. Click the palette menu to change the display between HSV and RGB. This palette will also list the values of any color when you click the eyedropper in a picture. This palette is available from *Window>Color Palettes>Show Info.*

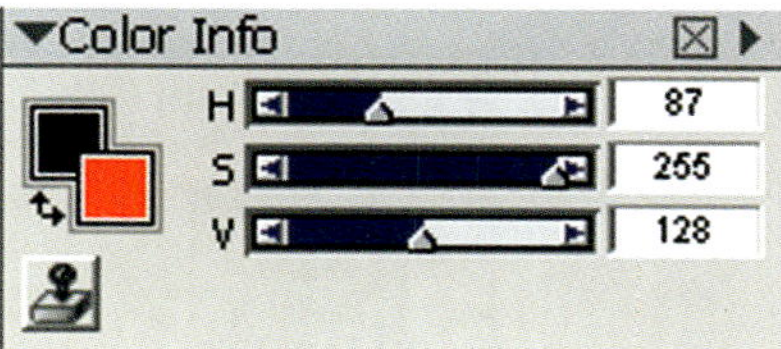

Figure 12.5

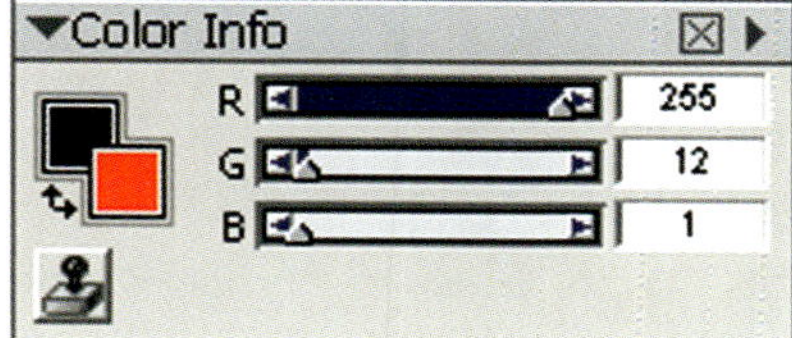

Figure 12.6

Color Sets

Color Sets is another way of picking colors and, like the other palettes, is displayed via *Window>Color Palettes>Show Color Sets.* Figure 12.7 shows the Color Sets palette with the palette menu extended.

It can be an advantage to choose a color from the Color Sets palette, as specific color shades may be more readily identifiable from the individual squares rather than from a continuous color range. To select a color, click on the square and the brush will paint with that color.

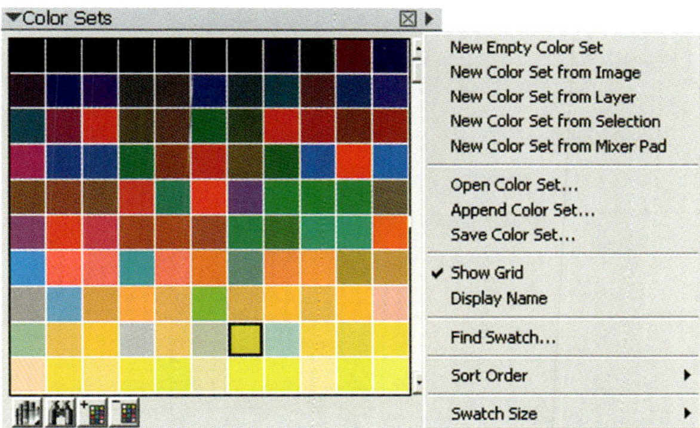

Figure 12.7 The Color Sets palette with extended menu

The palette menu shown in Figure 12.7 contains options for customizing the display. The first block of options is for creating new Color Sets from a variety of sources.

New Empty Color Set is for when you want to individually pick a range of colors and store them for future use. This could be useful if you are designing a layout or color scheme and want to keep all the colors used together. Click the New Empty Color option in the menu to make an empty set. Use the eyedropper to add colors, click on a color in the active image and then click the Color Set icon with the '+' symbol. Click the Color Set icon with the '–' symbol to remove a color.

New Color Set from Image creates a Color Set from the image currently active on the desktop. You could use this to restrict the number of colors in a new image to those of an existing one. The new Color Sets from Layers or Selections work in the same way but take the colors from the active layer or the active selection.

New Color Set from Mixer Pad takes the colors from the Mixer, which will be covered later in this chapter.

The default Color Set is only one of many sets available and Open Color Set will replace the current set with a different one. The extra Color Sets are loaded with the Painter program and when the open box appears it will normally take you straight to the relevant folder from where you can choose the new Color Set. If this does not happen you will need to navigate to where the Corel Painter program files are and go to the Color Sets folder.

There is a large selection to choose from, about 50 in all, and Figure 12.8 shows a few. From the top they are Black Walnut Ink, Vivid Spring, Gray Range, Flesh Tones and Rich Oils.

Append Color Set will add the new Color Set and not delete the existing one.

Save Color Set will save sets that you have created.

The other options are all self-explanatory; I will just mention the Swatch Size option, which controls the size of the swatches on screen. I find it very useful to view them at a larger size as the colors can be seen more easily.

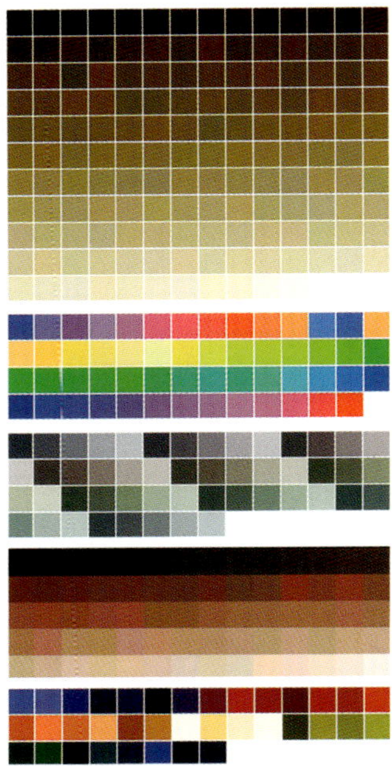

Figure 12.8 Some additional Color Sets

The Mixer

The Mixer was first introduced in Painter 8 and was a huge advance in recreating traditional techniques as it works like an artist's palette, where paints can be mixed together to form blended colors. Figure 12.9 shows the palette with the fly-out menu.

Click on the second brush icon and select a color from the selection at the top of the palette. Paint some brush strokes into the palette then select another color and paint some more; the slider will change the size of the brush that adds the color. The paint will mix together as it is layered on top of the previous brush strokes. When you have added several colors, click the palette knife icon and mix the colors together.

Figure 12.9 The Mixer palette with extended menu

When you are ready to paint, first click the eyedropper icon then click in the Mixer to select the color you need and paint into your picture.

The magnifying glass icon will enlarge the Mixer display to make blended colors more easily visible; double-click the icon to return to full view.

The hand icon will move the display when the mixer display is magnified.

The two other icons are used for the new Artists' Oils; see Chapter 5 for a description of the Artists' Oils brush category.

The palette menu has controls to save and import Mixer palettes and also the option to create a Color Set from the Mixer palette. Click on the Trashcan to clear and reset the palette.

Toning techniques

There are several ways to tone photographs in Painter and in this section you can try out some of these starting from a color original.

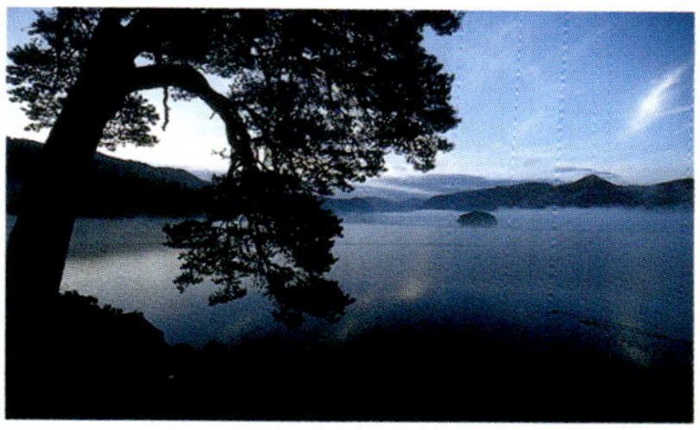

Figure 12.10 Original photograph

Lakeside view

This very blue early morning view will look more interesting as a toned picture and here is a very simple way of changing the tones.

Step 1 *File>Open>CD>Step-by-step files> '12 Lakeside View'.*

Step 2 *Effects>Tonal Control>Adjust Colors*; the dialog box is shown in Figure 12.11. Make the settings Hue −50%, Saturation −59%, Value 53% and leave the Using box on Uniform Color.

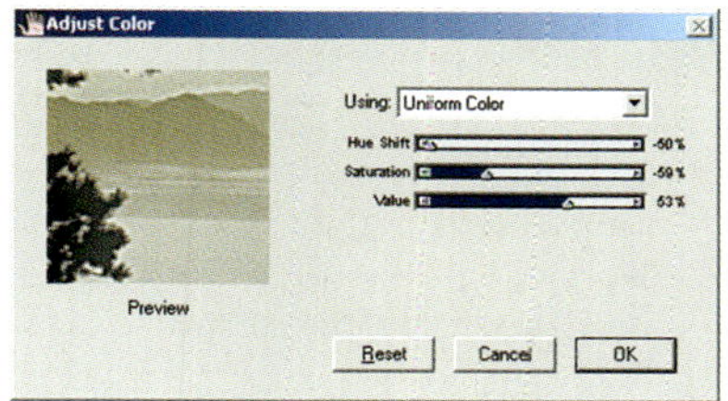

Figure 12.11 Adjust Colors dialog box

Figure 12.12 shows the final image; the strong blue has been transformed into a much more delicate picture.

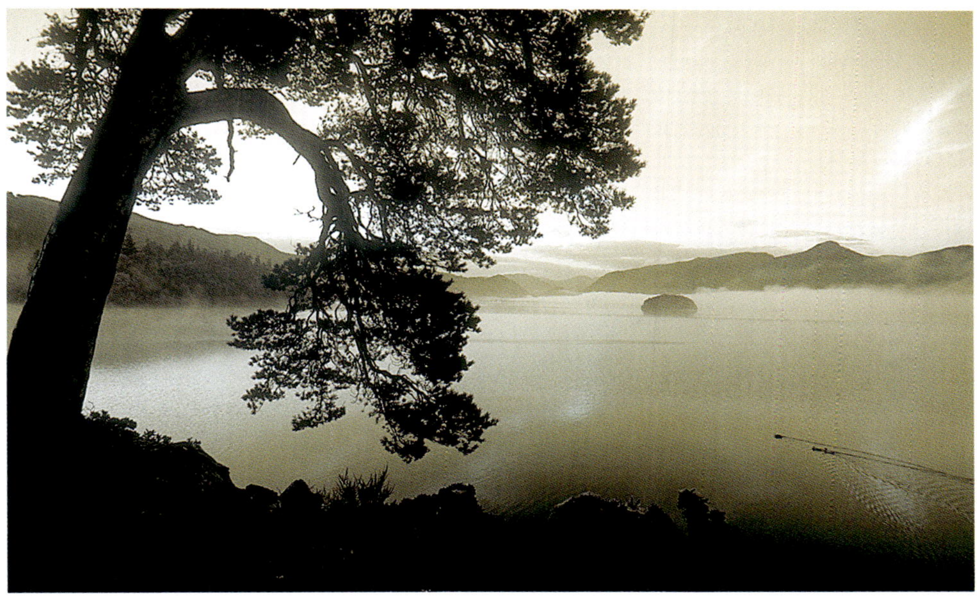

Figure 12.12 Lakeside view

The robe

Step 1 *File>Open>CD>Step-by-step files>'12 The Robe'.*

Step 2 To remove the color from a photograph, go to *Effects>Tonal Control>Adjust Color* and move the Saturation slider fully to the left (−139).

Step 3 Add a paper texture to the picture, *Effects>Surface Control>Apply Surface Textures*, select Paper in the Using box and 50% as the Amount. In the Papers palette, choose French Watercolor Paper. Figure 12.14 shows this stage.

Step 4 Choose a color in the Colors palette, a light orange or similar. Go to *Effects>Surface Control>Color Overlay.* Select Paper in the Using box, 100% opacity and Dye Concentration.

Step 5 The picture looks rather dull as you can see in Figure 12.15, so the next step is to brighten it and it is best to do this on a duplicate layer. Make the Layer Adjuster tool active, *Select>All* then, holding down the Alt/Opt key, click in the picture area. This will make a copy of the canvas.

Step 6 With the duplicate layer active, go to *Effects>Tonal Control>Brightness/Contrast* and move both sliders to the right.

Step 7 Certain parts of the picture, the arm in particular, will be over-bright, so click on the mask icon to make a layer mask. Click in the mask to activate it then, using the Digital Airbrush, size 242.2, opacity 2%, paint over the brightest areas with black and the mask will then reveal the original, darker layer beneath.

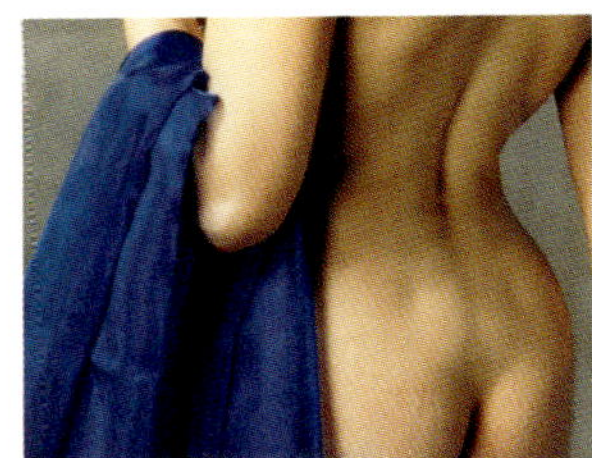

Figure 12.13

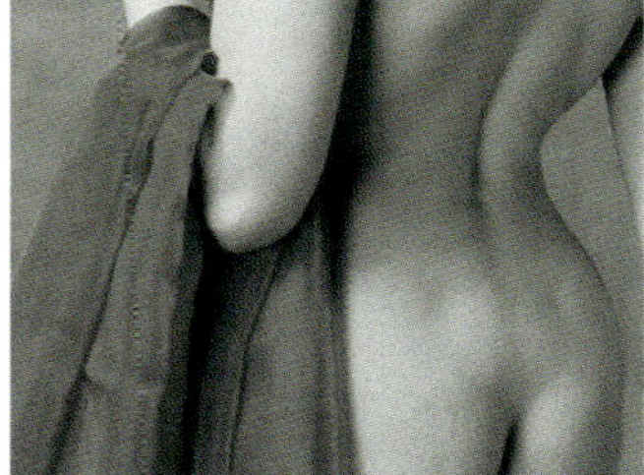

Figure 12.14

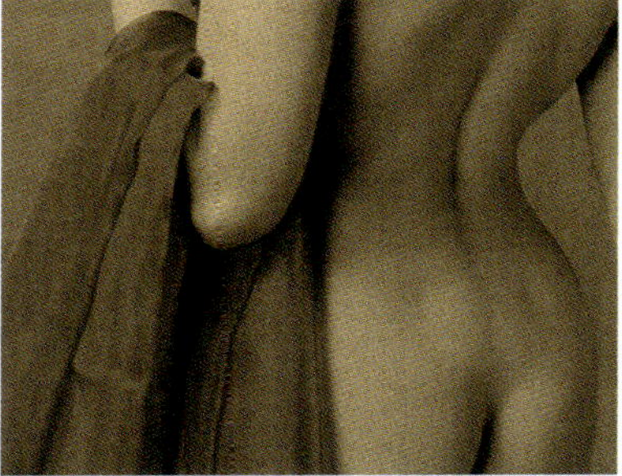

Figure 12.15

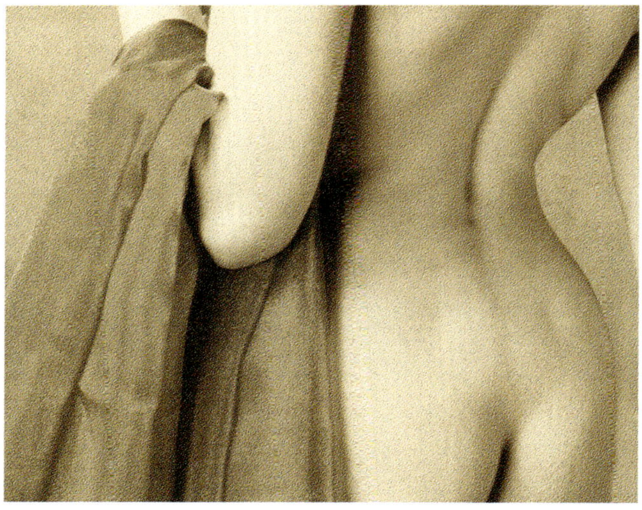

Figure 12.16 The robe

Hand tinting

Hand tinting photographs is as old as photography itself and in recent years has experienced a revival as artists and photographers seek to make pictures that have that very special magic that hand tinting can give. This step-by-step example will explain the techniques needed to get the right degree of color in the final picture.

The starting point is the picture of Hodge Tarn as seen in Figure 12.17. The original color slide has been desaturated and lightly toned in preparation for the hand coloring. It often helps to add a tone prior to hand tinting so that areas left unpainted will have a residue of color.

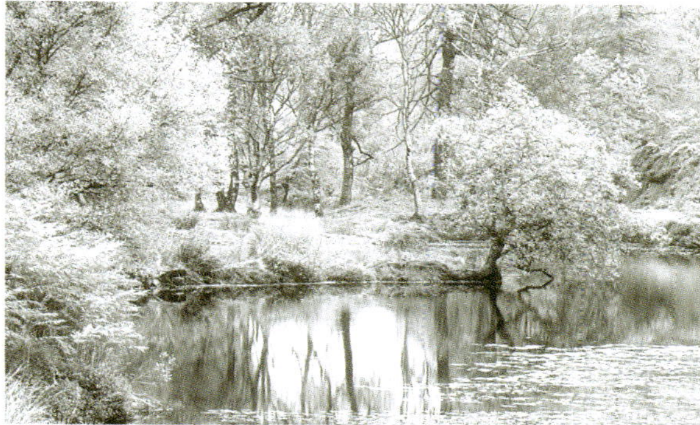

Figure 12.17 Original photograph after desaturation

Hodge Tarn

Step 1 *File>Open>CD> Step-by-step files>'12 Hodge Tarn'.*

Step 2 Open the Mixer palette, which is ideal for hand tinting. If it is not on screen, go to *Window>Color Palettes>Show Mixer.* You will also need the Colors and the Layers palettes open.

Step 3 Click the brush tool icon at the bottom of the Mixer palette and add a selection of colors to the mixing pad from the color swatches at the top of the palette. Figure 12.18 will give you a guide as to the range of colors needed. As you can see, the colors are mainly reds, greens and yellows for the trees and some blue for the sky.

Step 4 Click the palette knife tool and mix the colors together as in Figure 12.19. More colors can be added later on if you need to.

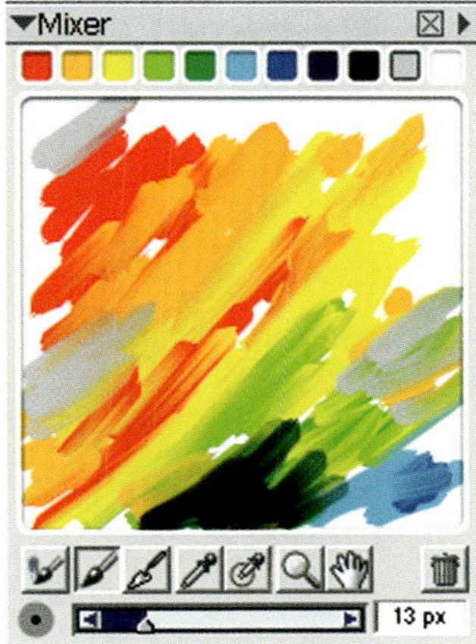

Figure 12.18

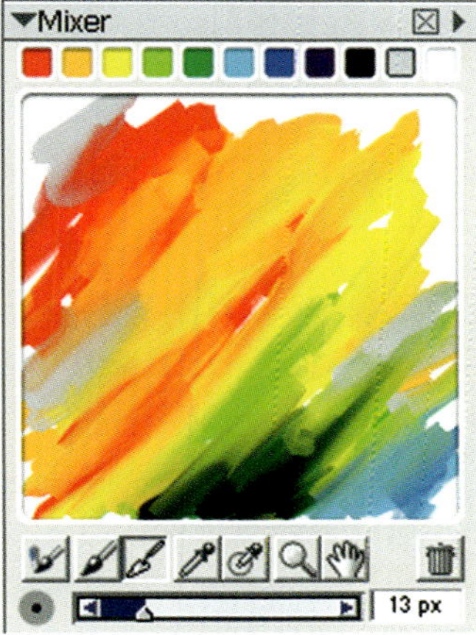

Figure 12.19

Step 5 Make a new empty layer by clicking the new layer icon. The color for each main element will be painted on a different layer; this retains maximum flexibility in the finishing stages as the layer opacities can be adjusted as necessary.

Step 6 Change the layer composite method to Color; this is an important step to take for all the layers, as it makes the paint translucent so that it does not cover up the picture beneath. Rename the new layer 'Grasses' via the *Layer>Layer Attributes* dialog box.

Step 7 Select the *Tinting>Bristle Brush 10,* brush size 4.6 and opacity 20%.

Step 8 Click on the eyedropper icon in the Mixer palette and then with the Tinting brush active, click into the mixer color to select the painting color. Paint into the grasses using short dabs rather than large brush strokes and change the color continually to get a wide variety of hues. Figure 12.20 shows how this should look.

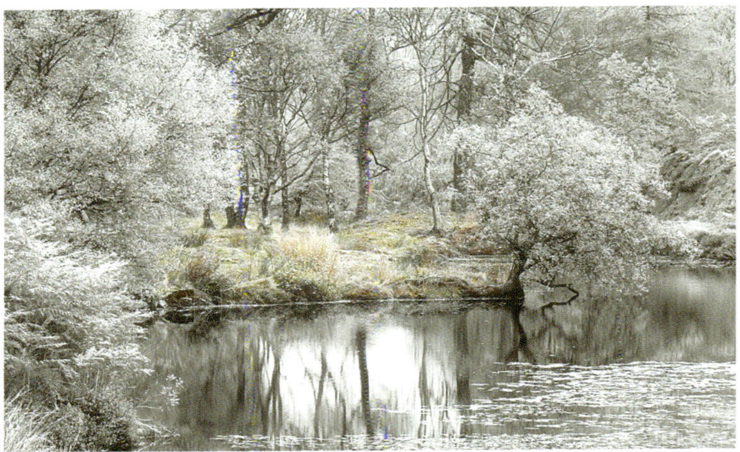

Figure 12.20

Step 9 When you have completed the grasses, make another new layer and name it 'tree on left'. Remember to change the layer composite method to Color.

Step 10 Change the brush to *Sponge>Sponge*, size 56.0, opacity 33%. This brush gives an attractive dappled texture that is ideal for trees and foliage. Dab the brush over the tree starting with bright yellow, then gradually changing to brown and red. If the colors in the mixer are not sufficient you can change the tones by moving the cursor in the inner triangle of the Colors palette either to the black corner to darken or towards white to lighten. Figure 12.21 shows the tree after tinting.

Step 11 Make another new layer in Color composite method and title it 'ferns'. Paint them using brown and bronze tones. Each of the main elements needs to have a slightly different color range in order for them to stand out from the other trees and bushes.

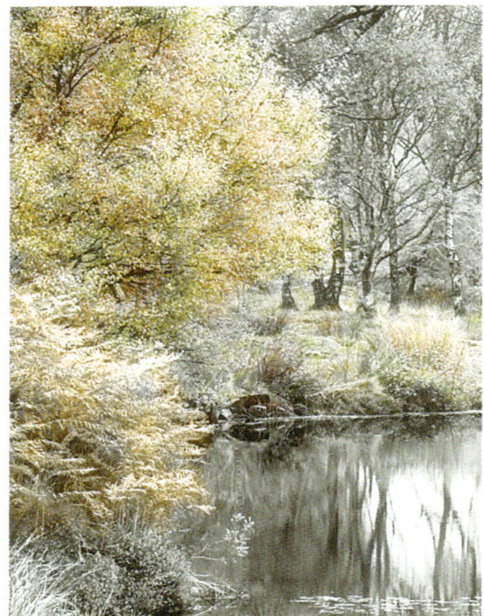

Figure 12.21

Step 12 Make another new layer in Color composite method and title it 'tree on right'. Use the Sponge brush again starting with yellow then moving into the green tones. Remember that trees are normally lighter at the top and darker underneath and that the leaves on some branches will not have changed color as much as others. Figure 12.22 shows the picture so far.

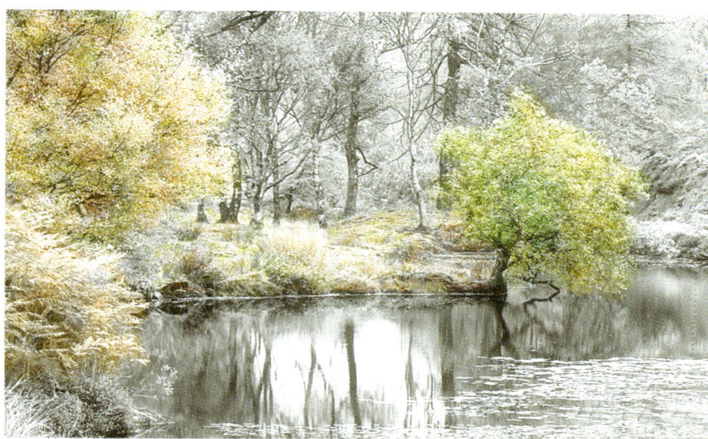

Figure 12.22

I have emphasized how important it is to change the layer composite method to Color while making a hand-tinted picture, so to illustrate the difference between the normal and color methods, Figures 12.23 and 12.24 show both types. In the picture on the left the mode is Default, while on the right it has been changed to Color.

At first sight the tree foliage may look pretty good in the Default mode, but when you look more carefully a lot of the branches have been obscured.

Step 13 Make another new layer in Color composite method and title it 'sky and reflection'. Use the Tinting brush again and lightly paint in bits of sky between the trees in the center then, using a deeper blue color, brush in the reflections in the water using downwards brush strokes.

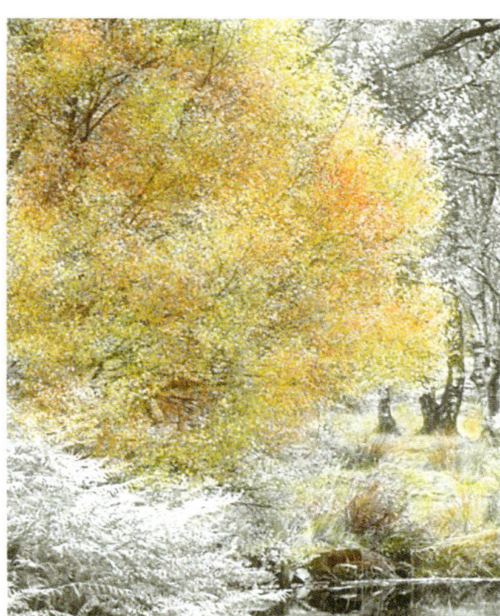

Figure 12.23 Default layer composite method

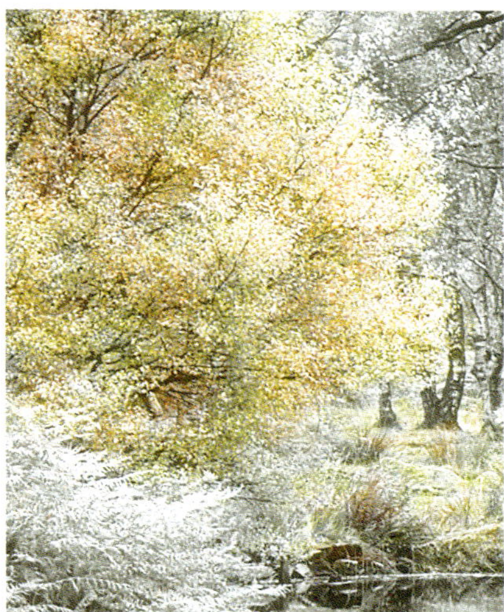

Figure 12.24 Color layer composite method

Step 14 Make another new layer for the background trees and paint them with the Sponge brush. Use a larger brush here, size 175.0 and opacity 5%, to cover the whole area lightly. Keep changing the colors, the brush size and opacity to get more variation.

Step 15 Make another layer for the reflections and the colors in the water and change the brush to *Airbrush>Soft Airbrush*, size 30.0, opacity 2%. This will give smooth gentle reflections. Repeat the colors that are in the bank and trees.

Figure 12.25 shows the Layers palette with separate layers for each element; the final picture is shown in Figure 12.26.

This completes the first part of the hand tinting exercise and, as you will have seen, the result is really very attractive. I have always found it very enjoyable to make these pictures and hope you do also.

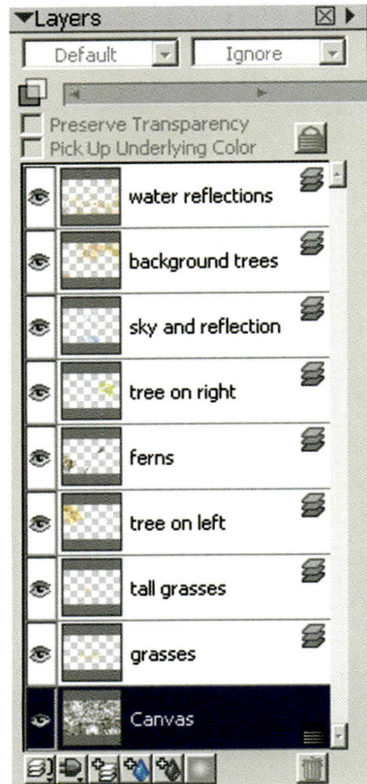

Figure 12.25 Final Layers palette

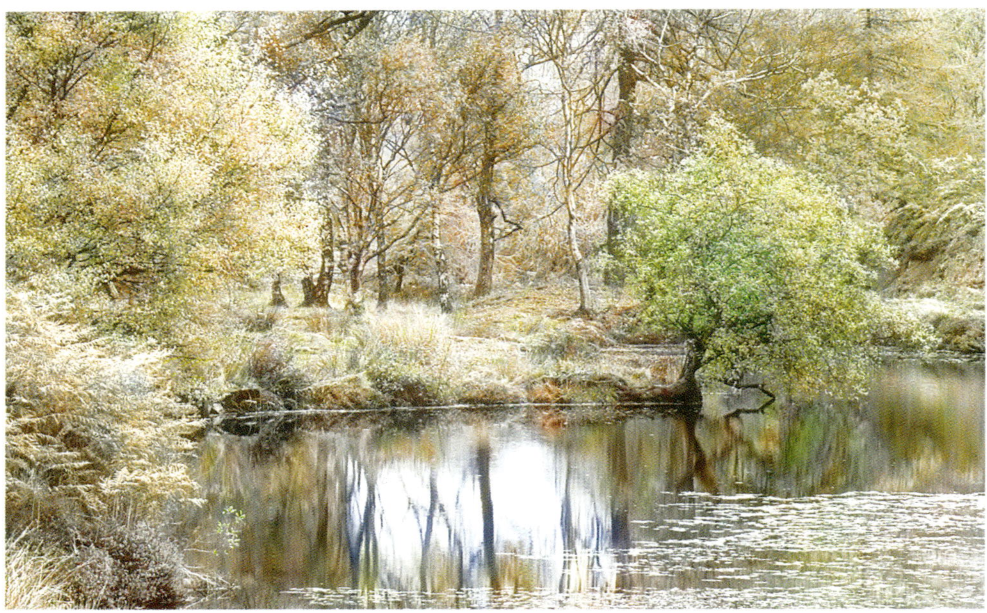

Figure 12.26 Hodge Tarn in autumn

Hand tinting – changing season

The next stage follows on from the previous exercise and illustrates how, with hand tinting, you can change the season at will. The first snowfall has arrived at our autumn scene and the brown and gold tones will soon be covered with a layer of snow. Many of the autumn leaves are still on the trees, so you can use your final version to build on or use the new starting version provided on the CD.

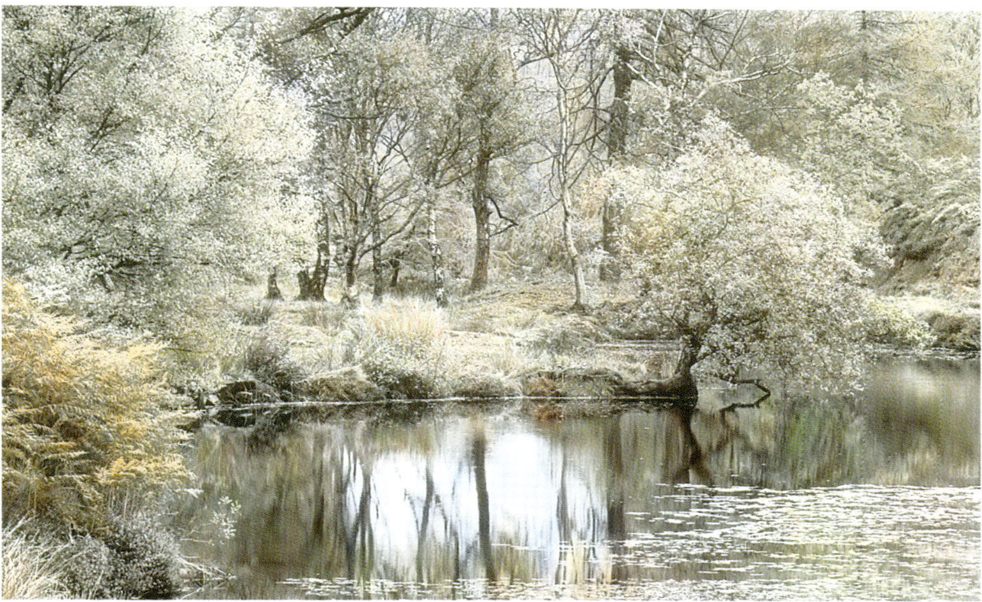

Figure 12.27 New starting photograph

First snow at Hodge Tarn

Step 1 *File>Open>CD>Step-by-step files>'12 First Snow at Hodge Tarn'.*

When you compare this starting version with the previously completed picture in Figure 12.26 you will see some differences, and if you are using your own version you will need to take the following steps.

Reduce the opacities of all the layers in your picture; the opacities will change to between 26% and 64%, and the intention is to lower the strength of color prior to adding the snow. The layer with the tree on the right that was still green in color will look completely wrong, so delete this layer. Make a new layer in its place and, with the Sponge brush, paint over a light covering of autumn colors to blend with the rest of the picture. This should now look like the starting picture in Figure 12.27.

Step 2 Open the Mixer palette and click the waste bin to remove any existing colors. Add blue and white into the Mixer in various shades and mix them together. Figure 12.28 shows the Mixer palette.

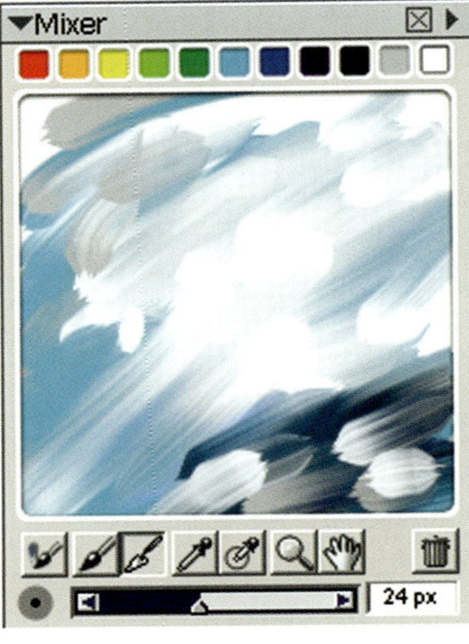

Figure 12.28 The Mixer palette

Step 3 Rather than using the Mixer palette again from which to paint, I would like you to make a new Color Set. If the palette is not on screen, show it from *Window>Color Palettes>Show Color Sets.* Click the Mixer palette menu and select New Color Set from Mixer Pad. This will make a Color Set which should resemble that in Figure 12.29 and can be used to select colors to paint the rest of the picture.

The blue shades will be needed to introduce cooler areas into the picture where the light is being reflected from the blue sky. As the brush will be used at a low opacity, the colors will also be much weaker than they appear in the Color Set.

Step 4 Make a new layer on top of the layer stack; if you are using your own multi-layered file it is advisable to make a duplicate document and drop all the layers to keep the file size down. This time the layers will be in the Default layer composite method rather than using Color, as the snow should look as though it is lying on top of the trees and grasses.

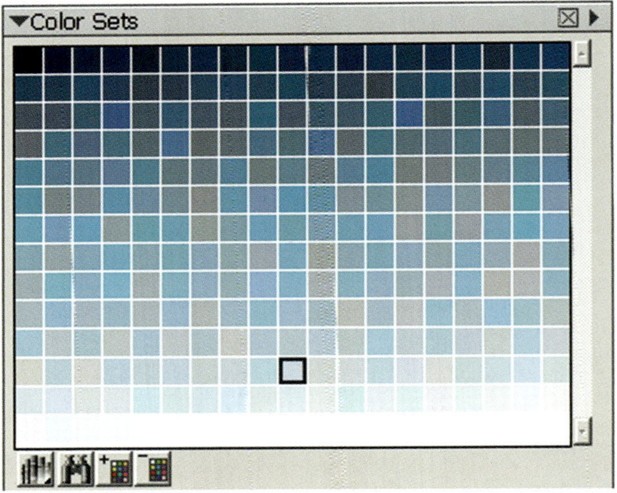

Figure 12.29 The Color Set created from the Mixer palette in Figure 12.28

Step 5 Select the *Sponge>Glazing Sponge 60*, brush size 60.0 and opacity 20%. Dab lightly over the picture with some blue shades to generally cool the atmosphere down. Change the color regularly by clicking in the Color Sets palette.

Step 6 Make another new layer and work on the tree on the left; use brush size 161.0 and opacity 44%. This brush will give a very textured finish, so keep making multiple brush dabs over the tree until the foliage texture looks good. Figure 12.30 shows the tree. At all stages, vary both the colors and the size and opacity of the brush to give more variety to the texture.

Step 7 Make a new layer again for the ferns and, using the same Sponge brush, dab these with a light blue color. Change the brush to Opaque Acrylic 10, size 5.4, opacity 65%. Use this small brush to make brush dabs with white following the lines of the ferns; we are effectively painting snow on the top of the fronds. Push the opacity up towards 100% on some of the most prominent fronds.

Figure 12.30 Tree on the left

Step 8 Make a new layer and paint the tree on the right with the Glazing Sponge, size 7.5, opacity 85%. Additional texture can be added with the Opaque Acrylic brush. Figure 12.32 shows the effect.

Step 9 Paint the background trees with the large Sponge brush, size 161.0, opacity 44%, lightly covering the area with white. Finish off the rest of the picture using the same brushes and finally use the separate layer opacities to balance the picture if required.

Figure 12.33 shows the final scene on a winter's day.

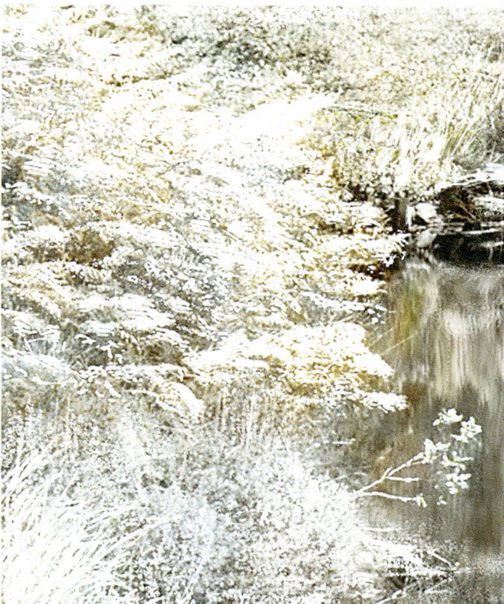

Figure 12.31 Ferns

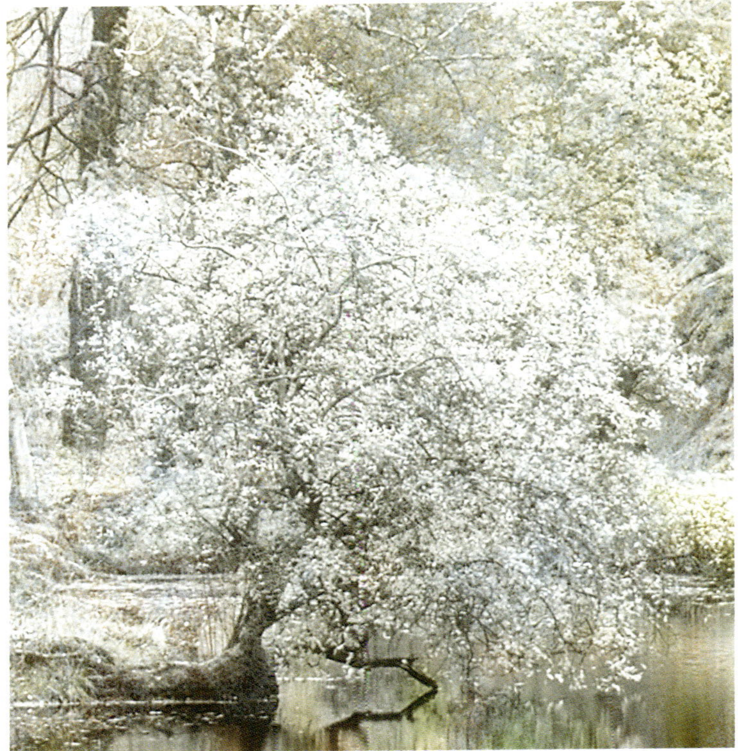

Figure 12.32 Detail of the snow-covered tree

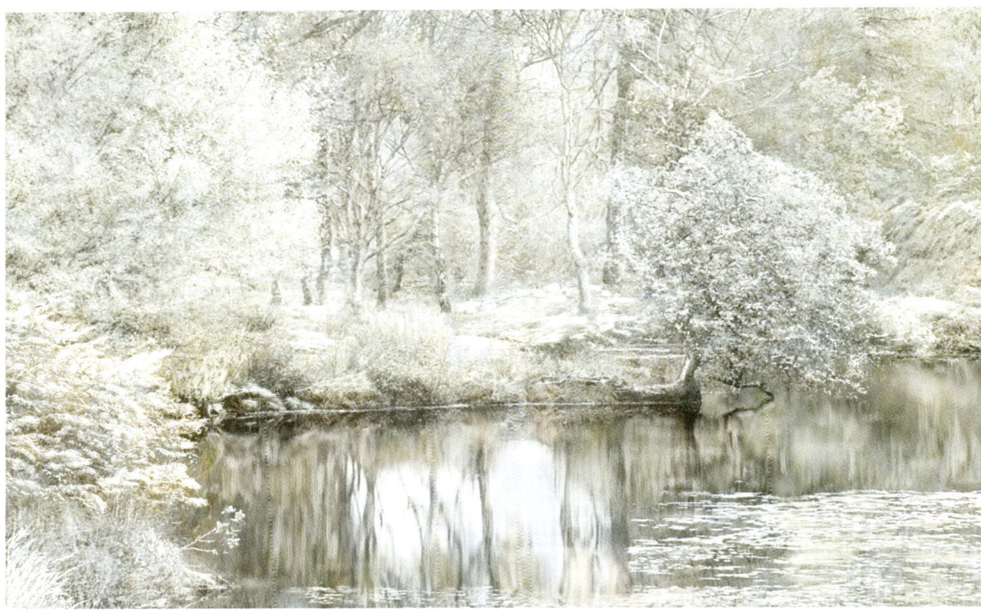

Figure 12.33 First snow at Hodge Tarn

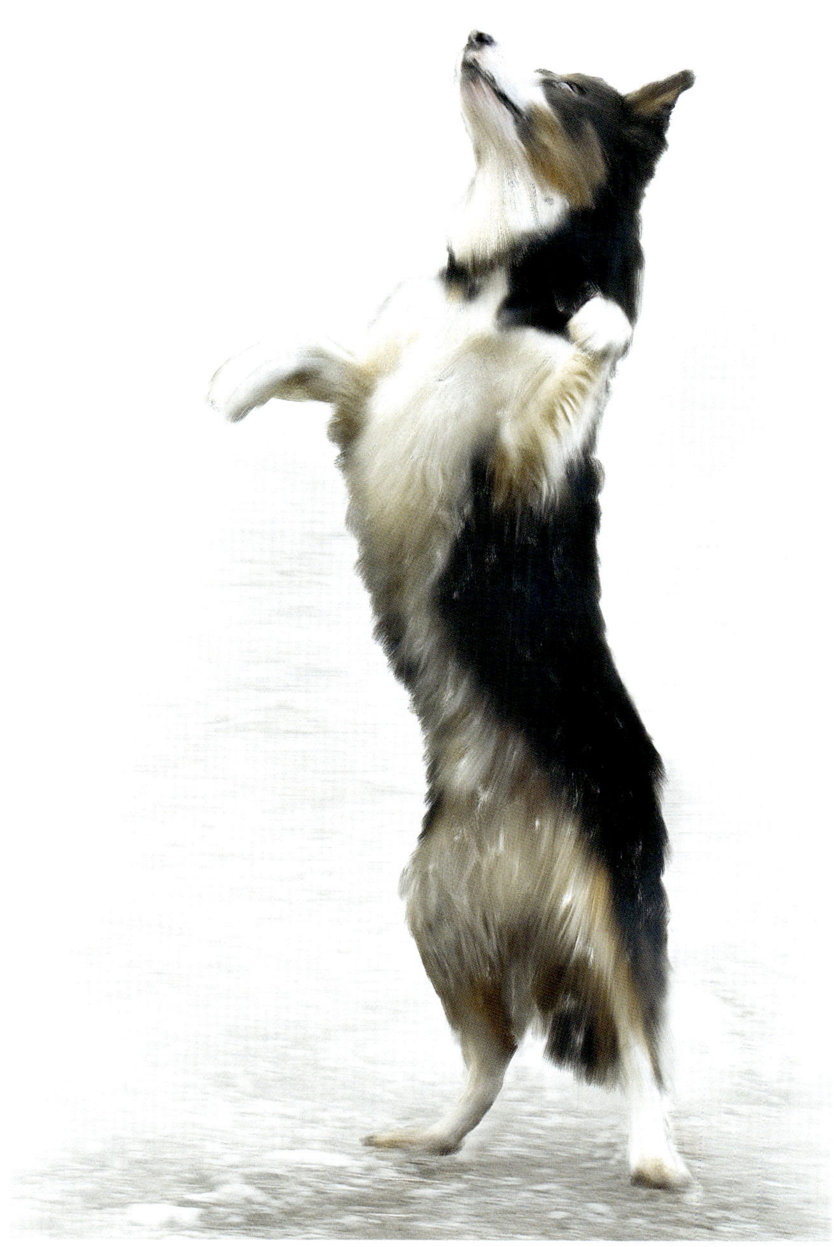

Figure 12.34 Dancer

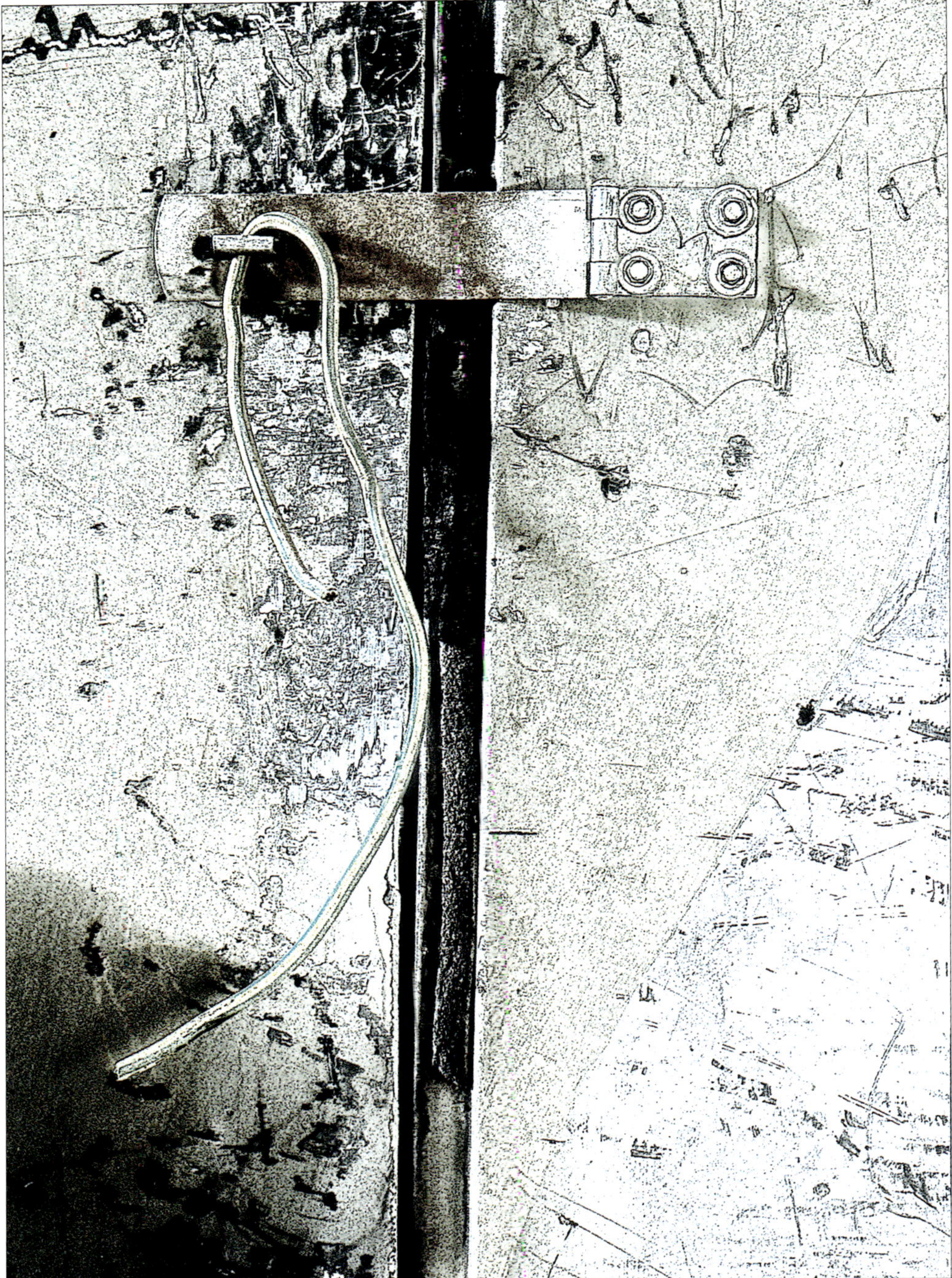

Figure 13.1 Makeshift fastener

Chapter 13
Special effects

The heart of Painter is in the vast range of brushes and art materials, which have been explored in earlier chapters, but the program also has a range of special effects and this chapter explores a selection of them.

Special effects in Painter come in many forms; some are in the Surface Control menu, while others come from the wonderfully named Esoterica section. Yet more are available from the Layers palette in the form of Dynamic Plug-in layers.

What is common to them all is the ability to make photographs look very different indeed.

The picture on the preceding page (Figure 13.1) used the Sketch effect, which is in the *Effects>Surface* Control menu.

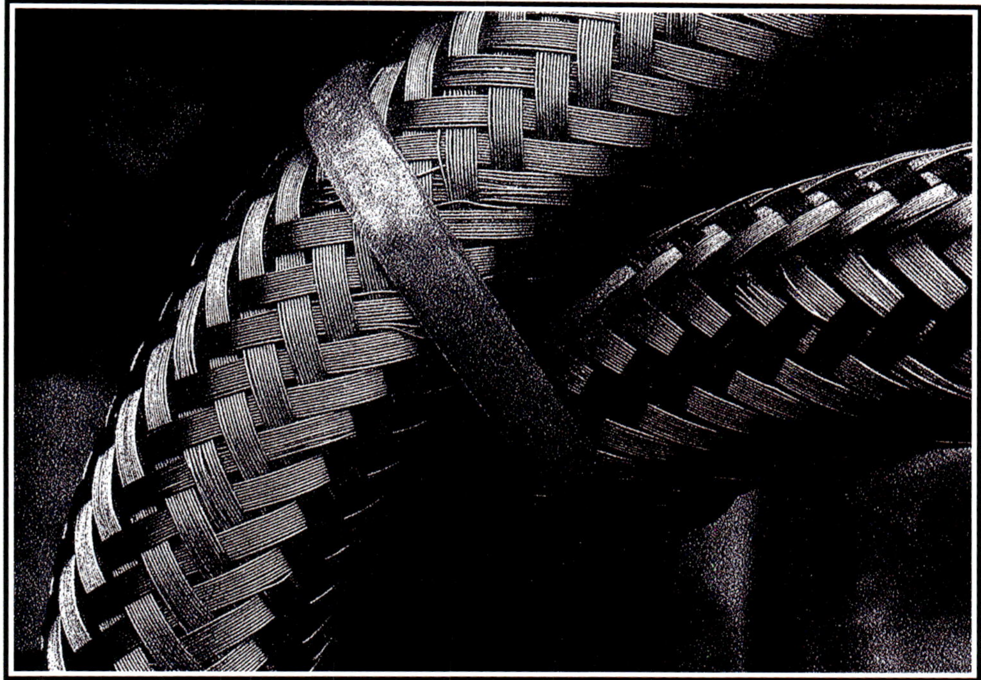

Figure 13.2 Cable

Glass Distortion

Glass Distortion will create distortions on the original photograph based on a huge variety of sources. The effect can be applied directly on a photograph; however, it is better to use a clone copy as it gives you the option of bringing back imagery from the original and blending with the distorted image.

Step 1 *File>Open>CD>Step-by-step files> '13 Autumn Leaves'.*

Step 2 *File>Clone.*

Step 3 *Effects>Focus>Glass Distortion.*

In the Glass Distortion dialog box, shown in Figure 13.4, the first option box is Using and the choice of where the texture comes from is identical to the Apply Surface Textures dialog box covered in Chapter 10.

The choices are Paper, 3D Brush Strokes, Image Luminance and Original Luminance. As the Paper option is based on the huge range of papers supplied with Painter, the choice is very wide indeed.

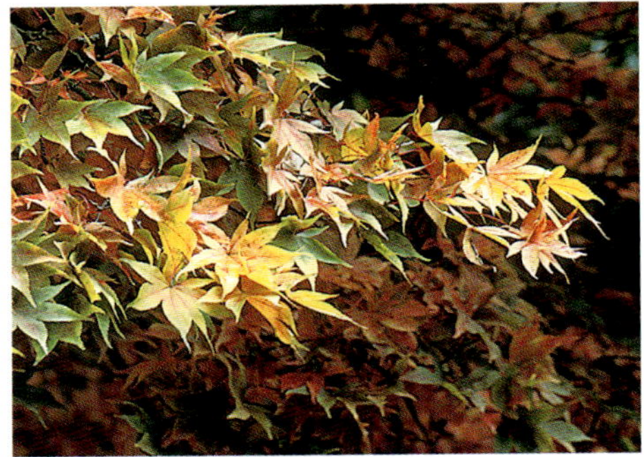

Figure 13.3 Original photograph

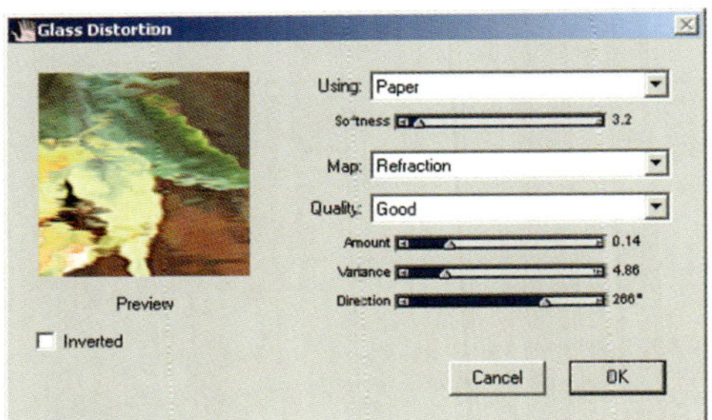

Figure 13.4

Map options are Refraction, Vector and Angle Displacement. The last two work in conjunction with Image Luminance in the Using box, which will result in powerful distortions of the image; you may have to increase the Amount to see the difference.

- Softness smoothes the distortions.
- Amount increases the overall effect.
- Variation distorts the pattern into less recognizable patterns.
- Direction works in conjunction with the Angle and Vector Displacement options.

Step 4 Select a paper of your choice; the one used here is Wavy Threads from the Textile Textures paper library. If you have forgotten how to load extra paper libraries, check back in Chapter 3. Return to the Glass Distortion box and set the Using box as Paper, Softness 3.5, Map Refraction, Amount – 0.54, Variation 3.0. The quality box stays on Good in all the examples and the Direction 266. Figure 13.5 shows the result of these settings.

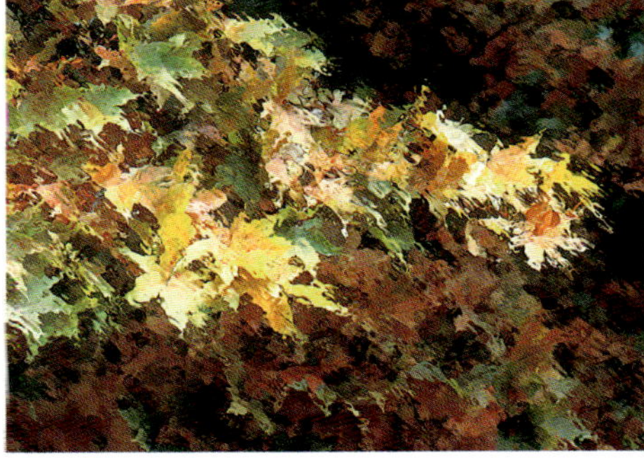

Figure 13.5

Step 5 To take this a stage further, go to *Effects>Apply Surface Texture* and select 3D Brush Strokes as the source. This compares the difference between the original and the now distorted clone image and bases the texture on that difference. The result is shown in Figure 13.6. In Figure 13.7, the paper used was Basket Weave from the Textile Textures paper library. Softness 3.5, Map Refraction, Amount 0.07, Variation 14.0.

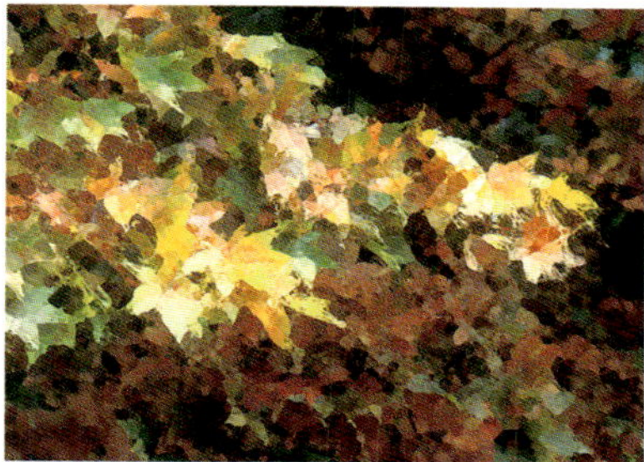

Figure 13.6

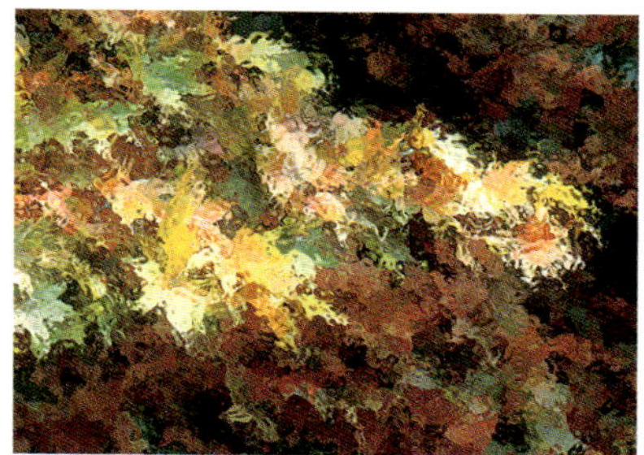

Figure 13.7

Figure 13.8 used Angle Weave paper from the Wild Textures paper library. Softness 3.5, Map Refraction, Amount 0.43, Variation 13.0. Figure 13.9 uses the Image Luminance option and has a low setting in the Softness box, which retains quite a lot of detail. The settings were Using Image Luminance, Softness 3.5, Map Refraction, Amount 0.43, Variation 13.0.

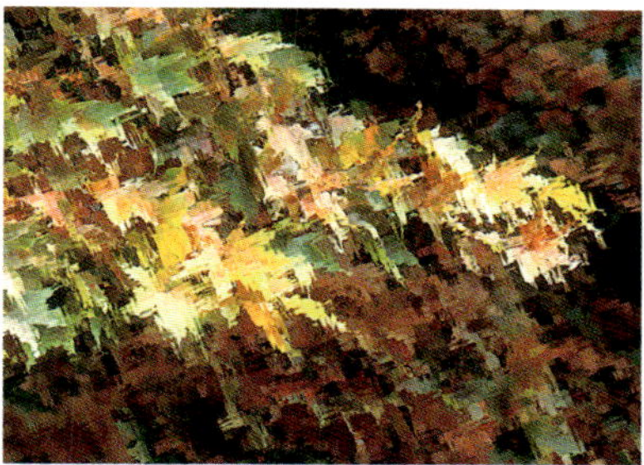

Figure 13.8

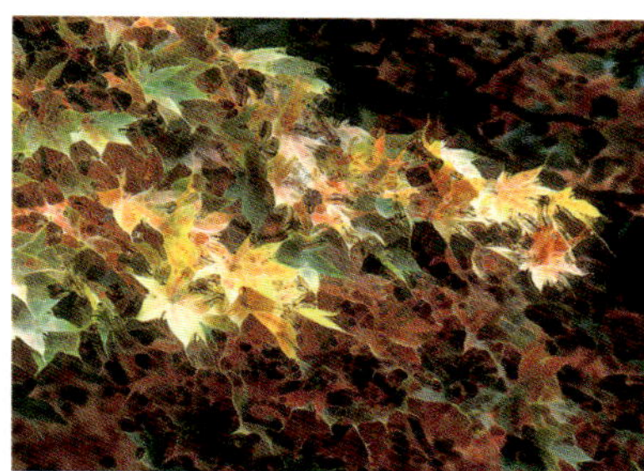

Figure 13.9

Figure 13.10 uses the Image Luminance again but has a higher softness setting and this produces a softer image with the leaves glowing from the refraction. Settings were Using Image Luminance, Softness 26.0, Map Refraction, Amount 0.59, Variation 13.0. Figure 13.11 uses Image Luminance, Softness 26.0, Map Refraction, Amount 1.72, Variation 2.0.

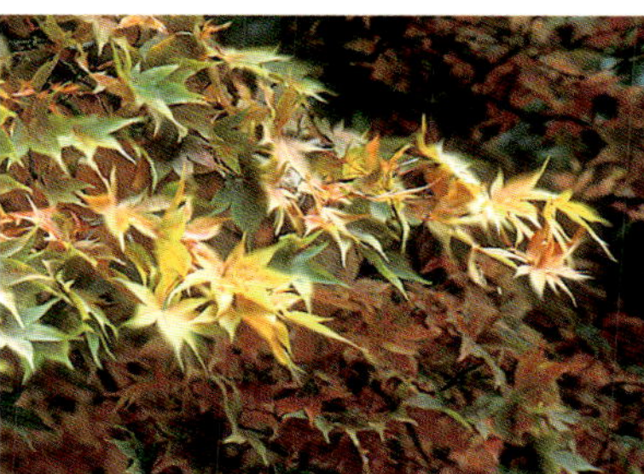

Figure 13.10

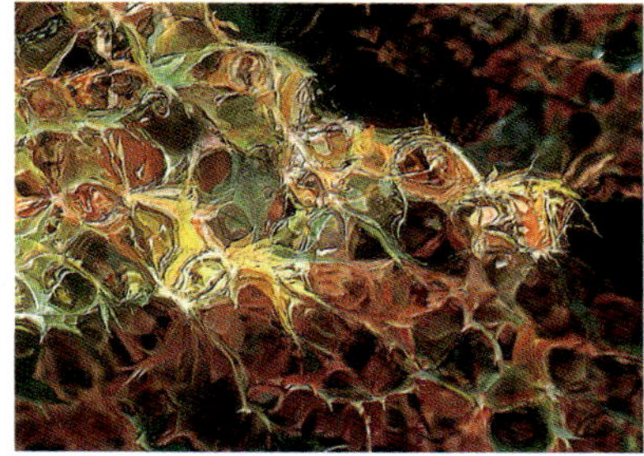

Figure 13.11

Sketch

The Sketch effect reduces a color photograph to a line drawing. It can be used on its own or in many cases the effect can be mixed back into the original photograph to give a delicate colored effect.

Steam traction engine

Step 1 *File>Open>CD>Step-by-step files>'13 Steam Engine'.*

Step 2 *File>Clone.*

Step 3 Make a copy of the Canvas on which to apply the Sketch effect (*Select>All*, then hold down the *Alt/Opt* key and click in the image with the Layer Adjuster tool).

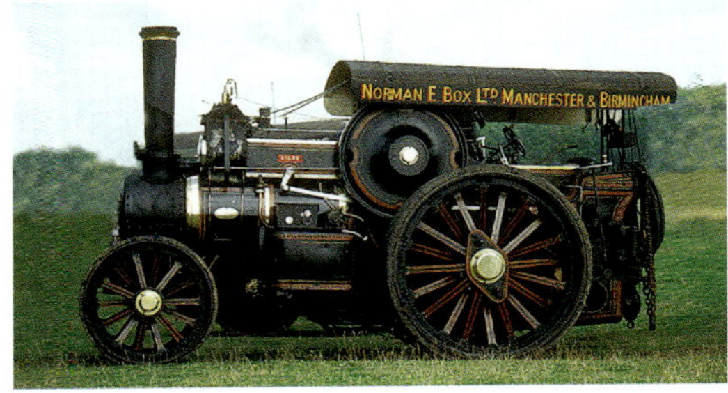

Figure 13.12 Original photograph

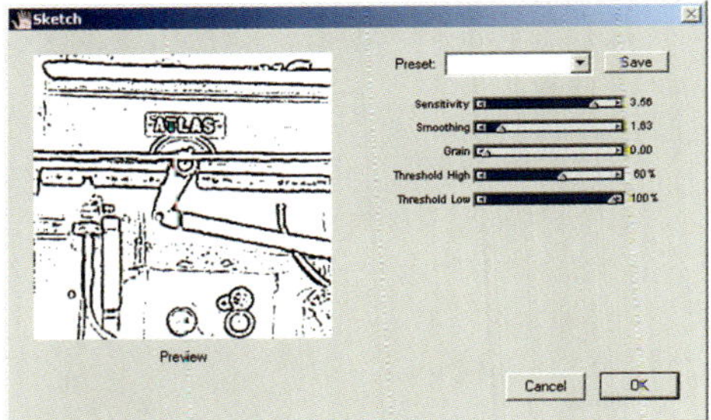

Figure 13.13 The Sketch dialog box

Step 4 *Effects>Surface Control>Sketch.* Enter the following settings: Sensitivity 3.56, Smoothing 1.63, Grain 0.00, Threshold High 60%, Threshold Low 100%.

Figure 13.14 shows the Sketch effect applied on the steam engine layer. The amount of noise in the background depends largely on the Threshold sliders; how you balance those two and the Smoothness slider will define the amount of detail in the sketch.

The Sketch effect as applied on this picture does not amount to much, but it provides a starting point to make a more satisfying picture.

Step 5 Change the layer composite method of the Sketch layer to Overlay; this will change the picture considerably, lightening and putting edge lines over the original.

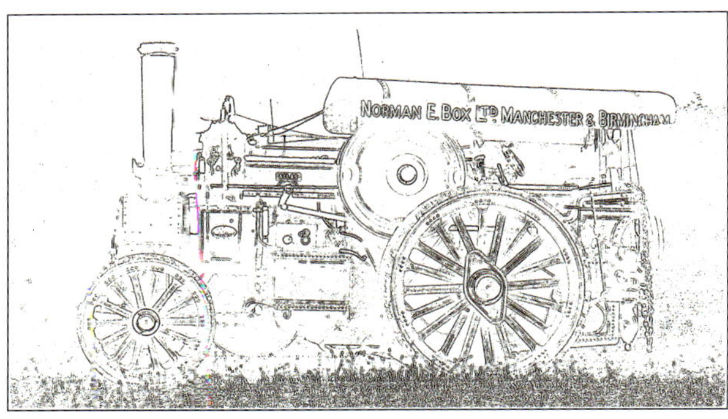

Figure 13.14

Step 6 Make a duplicate copy of the sketch layer via the Layers palette menu. Figure 13.15 shows how this extra layer, which is also in Overlay method, strengthens the effect. Reduce the layer to about 85% to bring back a little more color.

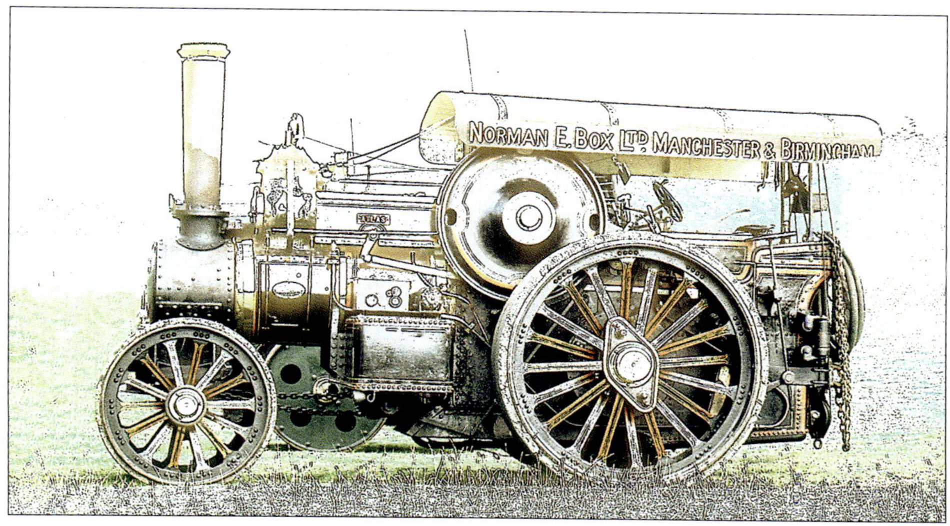

Figure 13.15

Step 7 Another change in the Layers palette will create an alternative version. Duplicate the Sketch layer again, move it to the top of the layer stack and change the layer composite method to Pseudocolor. Adjust the layer opacity to around 75% to reduce the intensity of the blue. Figure 13.16 shows this version.

One point to note regarding the last step: if you are saving the picture in Photoshop file format, the Pseudocolor layer composite method will not be recognized and the picture will completely change color. The way around this is to drop the layers prior to saving in PSD format.

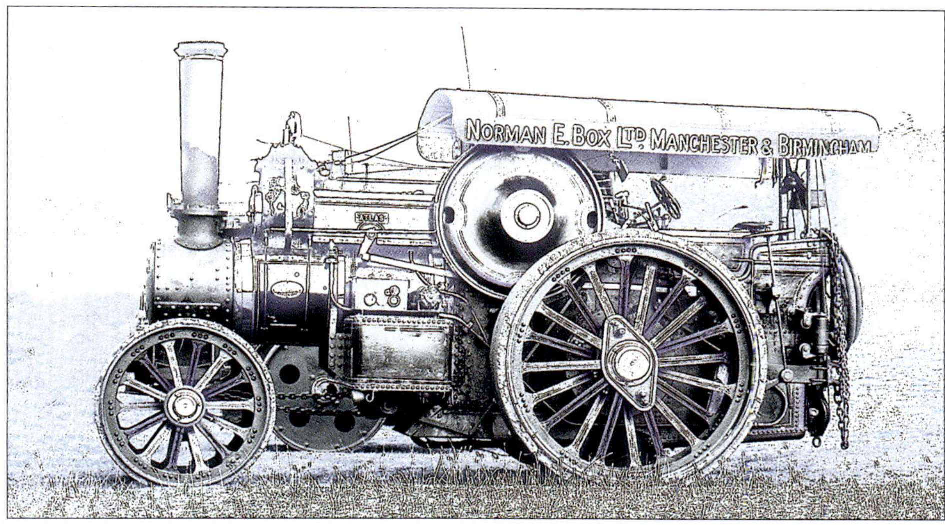

Figure 13.16

Woodcut

Woodcut, as its name suggests, creates a very excellent woodcut effect from an original photograph. It initially creates a black and white result but can be colored quite easily. The steam traction engine picture used for the Sketch effect is also the starting point for this exercise.

Traction engine

Step 1 *File>Open>CD>Step-by-step files> '13 Steam Engine'.*

Step 2 *File>Clone.*

Step 3 *Effects>Surface Control>Woodcut.*

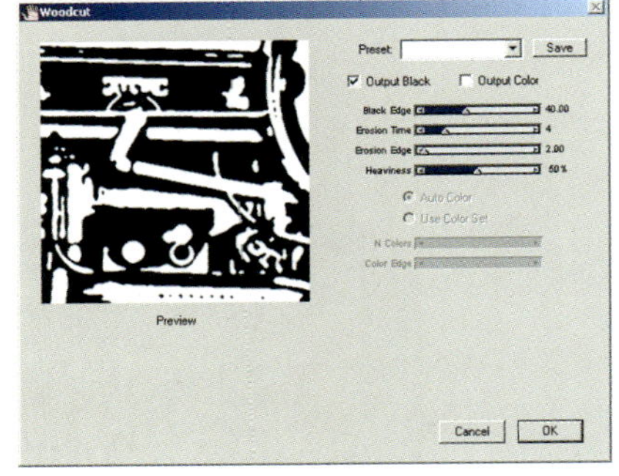

Figure 13.17

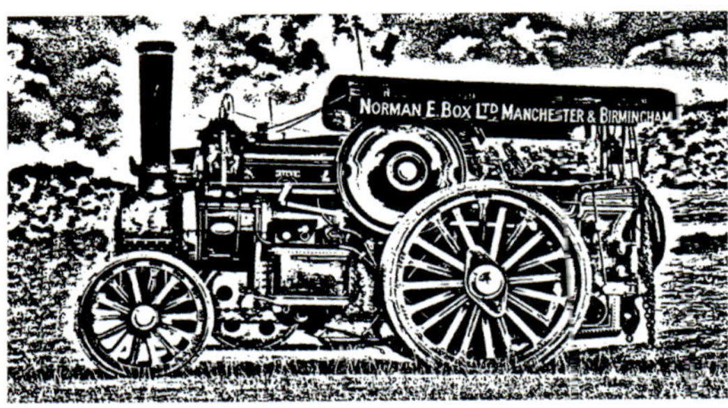

Figure 13.18

The settings for this are as shown in Figure 13.17: Black Edge 40.00, Erosion Time 4, Erosion Edge 2.00, Heaviness 60%.

Output Black should be ticked but not the Output Color. This will produce the black and white picture shown in Figure 13.18.

Step 4 The woodcut effect will now be combined with the original picture to create a colored version in the same way as we did with the Sketch effect. Change the layer composite method of the Woodcut layer to Overlay. Figure 13.19 is the result.

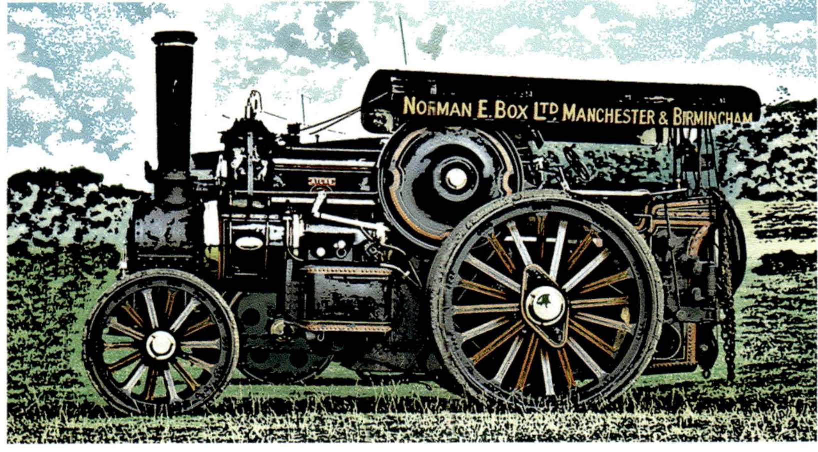

Figure 13.19

Step 5 Colored versions are also available from within the Woodcut dialog box. Make a new clone copy to start afresh.

Step 6 *Effects>Surface Control>Woodcut.* The settings for this are the same as last time: Black Edge 40.00, Erosion Time 4, Erosion Edge 2.00, Heaviness 60%, but tick the Output Color as well as the Output Black. Ticking this option reveals a further block of controls in the palette.

With Auto Color ticked, the woodcut will be colored using the selection of colors shown under the preview window. The number of colors to be used can be altered by using the N Colors slider; usually it is more effective to use a limited range of colors, but try moving the slider to see the difference. Figure 13.20 shows the effect using 26 colors.

Instead of using the default set of auto colors, you can also choose another color set to base the colors on. Tick the Use Color Set option. Open the Color Set palette and load the Black Walnut Ink set. This will give a dark sepia tone to the picture. Figure 13.21 shows the effect with this color set applied.

Figure 13.22 shows the same picture using the Rich Oils color set. The settings for this version are Black Edge 62.88, Erosion Time 0, Erosion Edge 26.70 and Heaviness 0.

The final example shown in Figure 13.23 has used the grayscale color set on one layer, the Flesh Tones on the layer above and the layer composite method of the top layer changed to Luminosity. This has produced a monochrome version that is very different to the one shown in Figure 13.18.

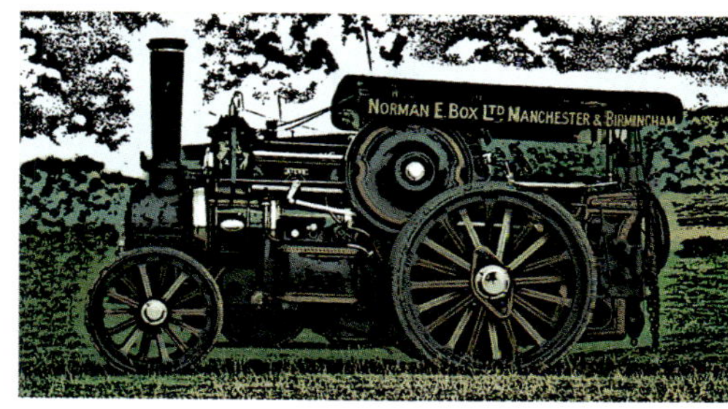

Figure 13.20

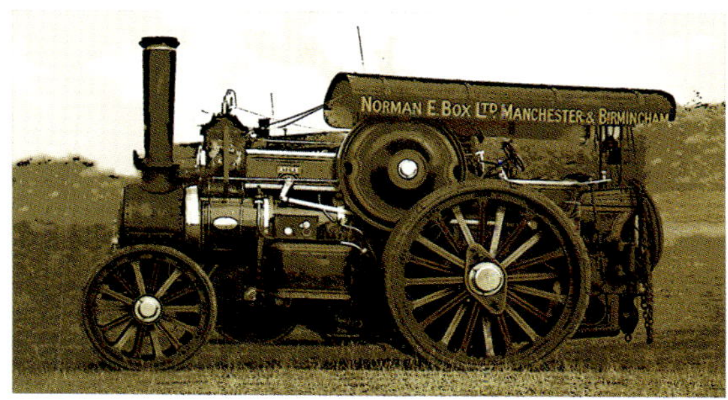

Figure 13.21

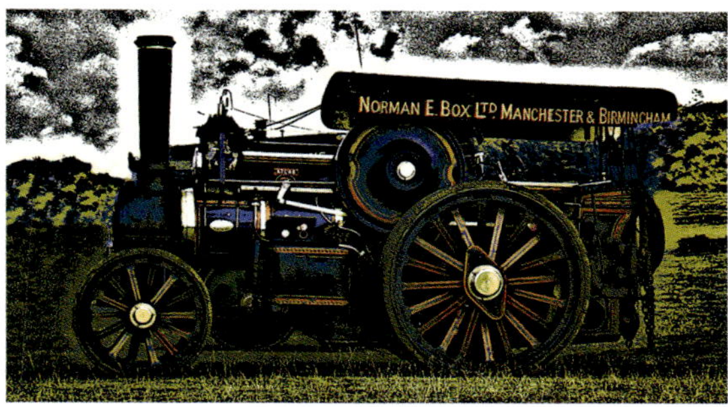

Figure 13.22

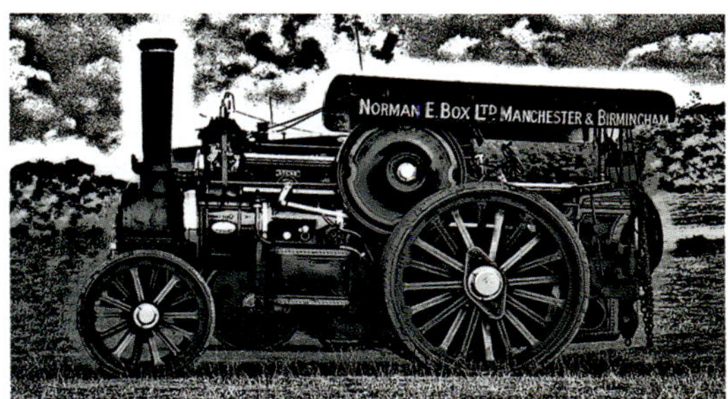

Figure 13.23

Distress

Distress is in the *Effects>Surface Control* menu and can make powerful graphic statements from your photographs. Most of the detail will be etched away and replaced with heavy grain. A clear strong picture is needed to get the best out of this effect.

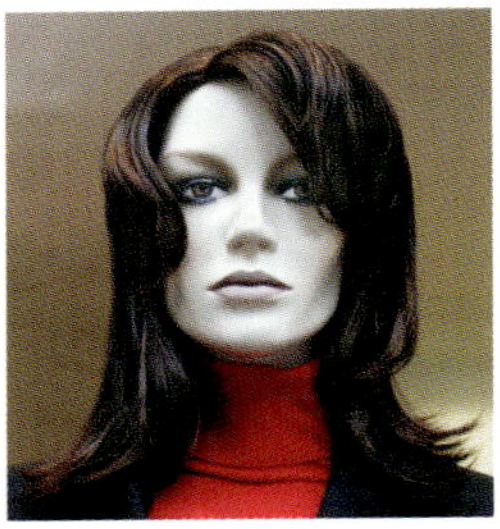

Step 1 *File>Open>CD>Step-by-step files>'13 Distressed'.*

Step 2 *Effects>Surface Control>Distress.*
Use the following settings: Edge Size 63.47, Edge Amount 57%, Smoothing 1.96, Variance 128%, Threshold 50%.

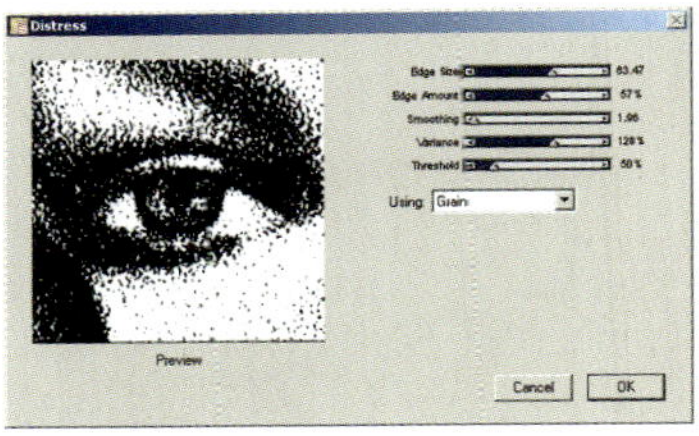

Figure 13.24

Figure 13.25

Step 3 Select Grain in the Using drop-down menu and Basic Paper as the paper texture.

Step 4 Click OK, then go to *Edit>Fade* and move the slider to 50%; this will fade the effect and allow some of the original color to show through.

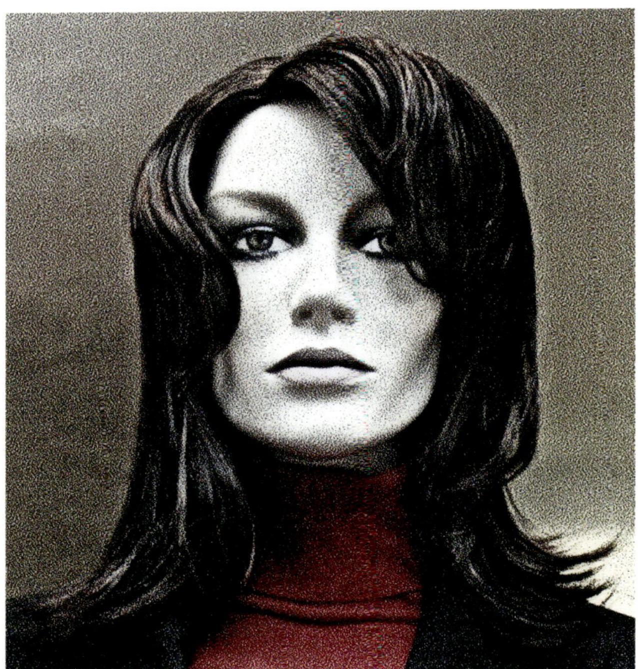

Figure 13.26 Distressed

The sliders interact with each other to get a balance of detail and overall exposure. Some of the sliders require very small movements to make a dramatic difference.

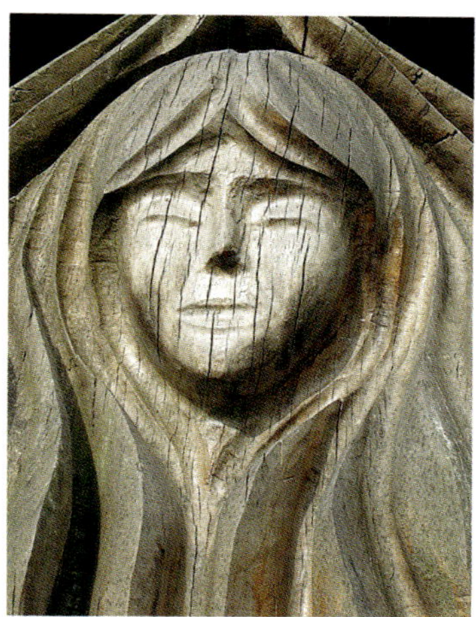

Figure 13.27 Original photograph

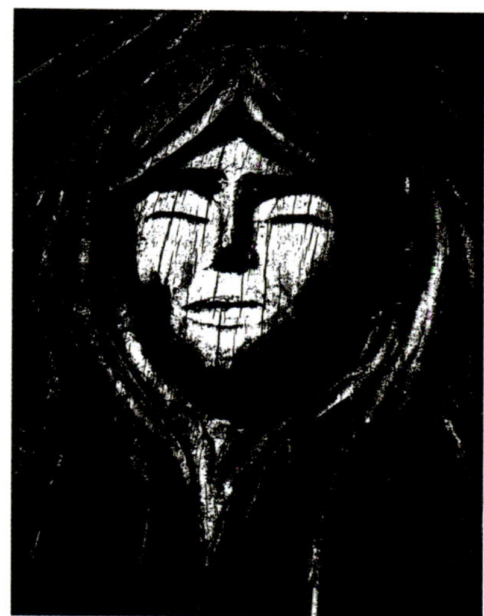

Figure 13.28

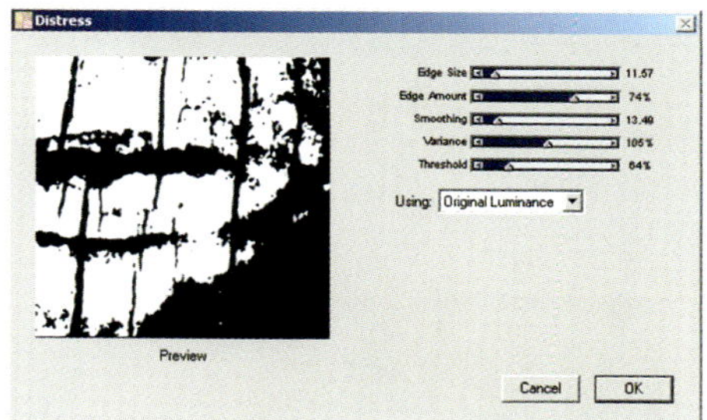

Figure 13.29

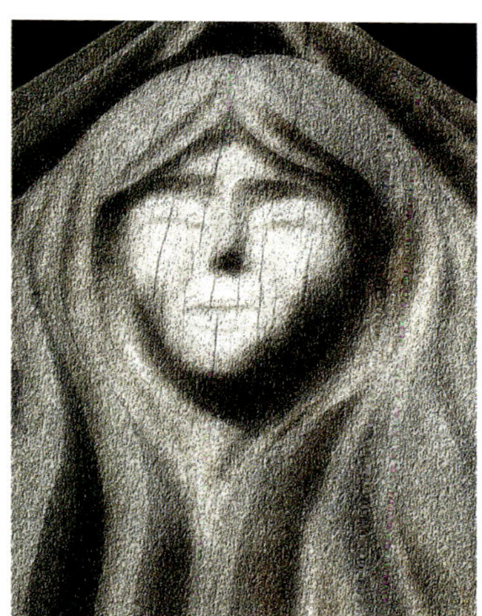

Figure 13.30

As in many other effects dialog boxes, Distress can be based on either the current paper texture or the Luminance of the picture.

The sliders interact with each other and control the size and amount of the edges, the smoothness of the image and the amount of grain added.

Threshold alters the amount of black and has a very powerful effect on the result. Remember that for fine adjustments of all sliders, click the small arrows at each end.

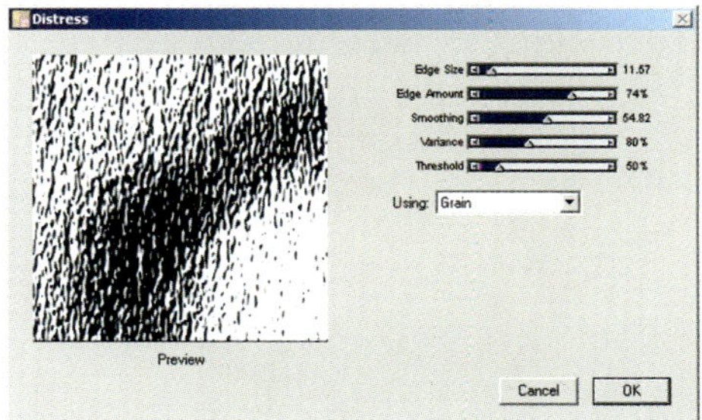

Figure 13.31

This photograph is on the CD if you wish to try this out; it is called '13 Wooden statue'.

Figure 13.28 used the Image Luminance as the source; the settings are shown in Figure 13.29.

Figure 13.30 used the Paper source with the settings shown in Figure 13.31.

After Distress had been applied, the picture has had the effect reduced by 50% in the *Edit>Fade* command. This both reduces the Distress effect and brings back some of the original detail and color.

Apply Screen

Apply Screen is another technique which creates a strong graphic appearance. The luminance values are split into three tones which can be set in the dialog box and will add new colors to the picture.

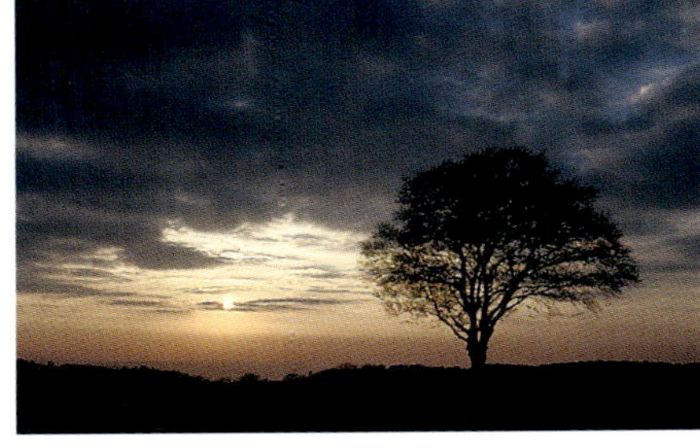

Figure 13.32 Original photograph

Step 1 *File>Open>CD>Step-by-step files>'13 Sunset'.*

Step 2 *Effects>Surface Control>Apply Screen.*

Step 3 Enter the following settings in the dialog box. Using: Image Luminance. Threshold 1: 92%. Threshold 2: 52%.

Click the left colored square and a color picker will appear (Figure 13.34); select three colors to tone the picture. If you want to use the same color but in different densities, choose a dark color for the first square then move the vertical slider on the right to select the next two colors.

The Threshold 2 slider controls how much of the first color will be shown in the image while the Threshold 1 slider controls the amount of the second and third colors.

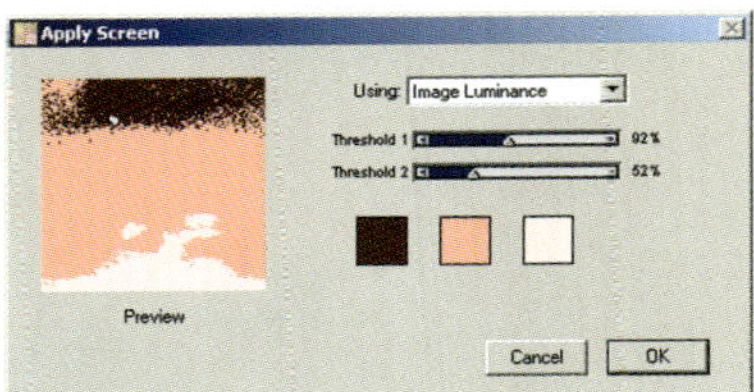

Figure 13.33

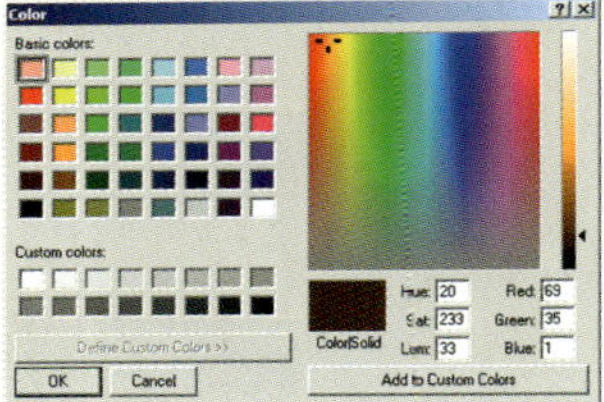

Figure 13.34

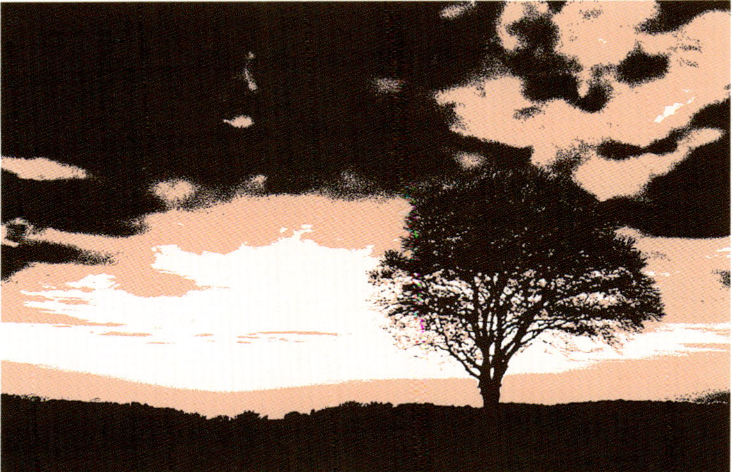

Figure 13.35

Apply Screen can be applied in many different ways and will benefit from some experimentation to find the most useful settings for any particular picture. The examples on this page show a dramatic interpretation of the building and also a monochrome version.

Step 1 *File>Open>CD>Step-by-step files>'13 Coughton Court'.*

Step 2 *Effects>Surface Control>Apply Screen.*

Step 3 Enter the settings in the dialog box as shown below.

In the first example, the paper has been changed to Charcoal. The second example uses the Image Luminance option and the colors chosen were black, gray and white.

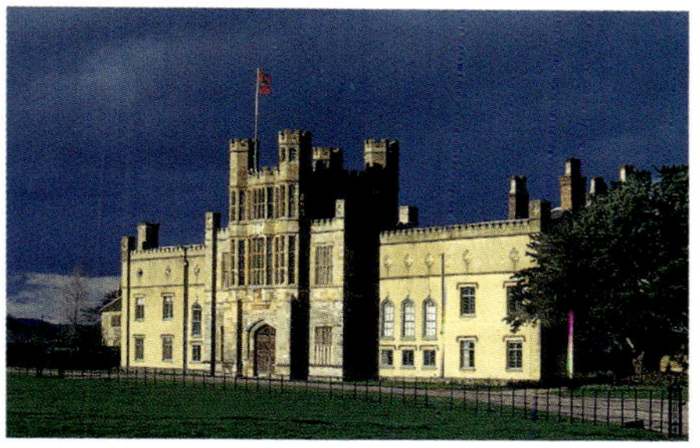

Figure 13.36 Original photograph

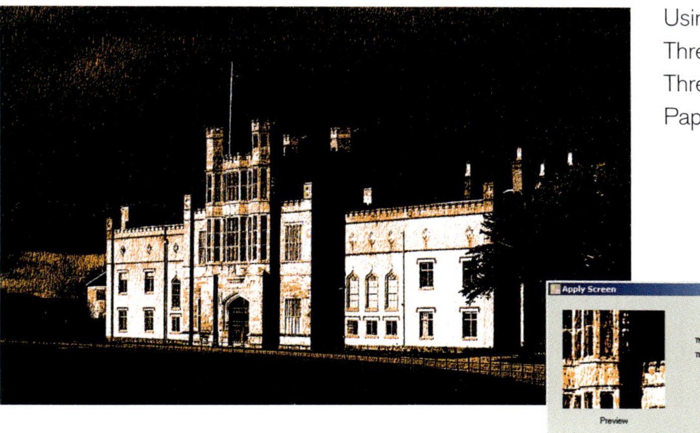

Figure 13.37

Figure 13.38

Using: Paper.
Threshold 1: 116%.
Threshold 2: 94%.
Paper: Charcoal

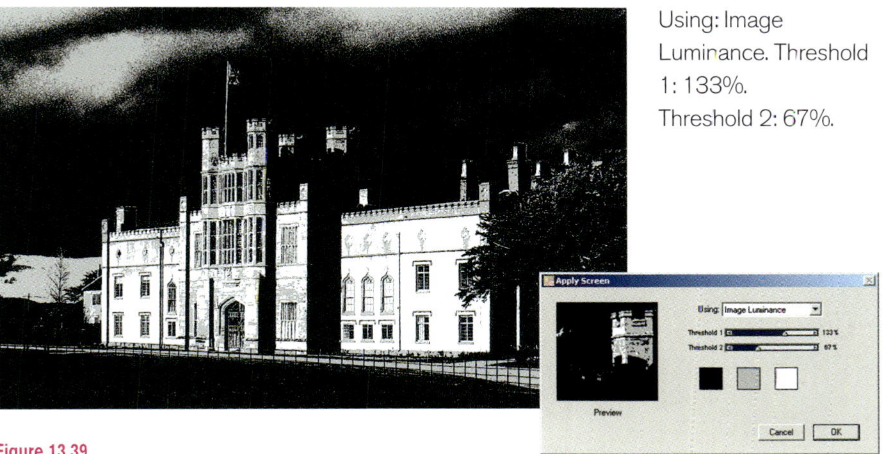

Figure 13.39

Figure 13.40

Using: Image Luminance. Threshold 1: 133%.
Threshold 2: 67%.

Burn

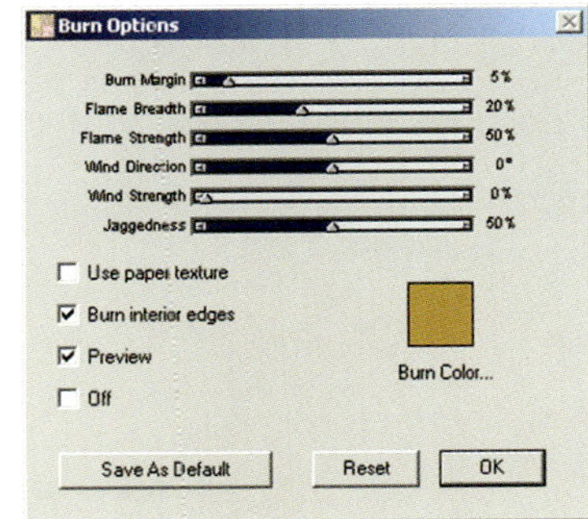

Figure 13.41

Burn is a Dynamic Plug-in layer, which means that the layer can be re-activated at a later date and the settings changed.

Step 1 *File>Open>CD>Step-by-step files>'13 Text Montage'.*

Step 2 The burn effect will be based on a selection, so *Select>All* to burn the edges of the whole picture.

Step 3 Bring the Layers palette on screen and click the second icon from the left, with the shape of a plug. In the drop-down menu select Burn.

Step 4 When the dialog box appears (it can take a while), leave the settings unchanged and click OK.

Step 5 A new Dynamic Plug-in layer will have been created; hide the Canvas layer to see the burnt edges. The sliders can be changed to give a different color and edge effect. Figures 13.42 and 13.43 show some different settings.

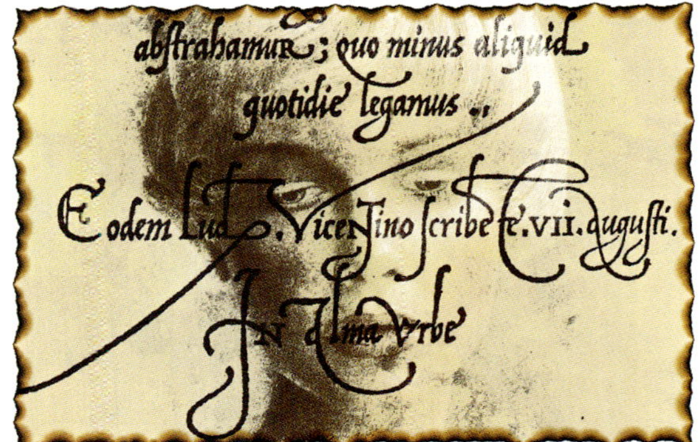

Figure 13.42

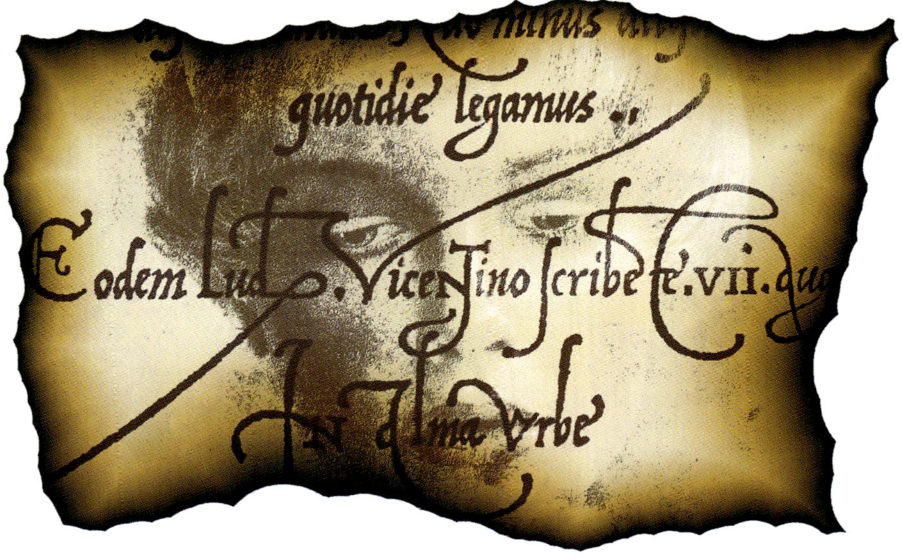

Figure 13.43

Bevel World

Bevel World is another Dynamic Plug-in and can be used to make bevels of all types, whether simply to add a border to a picture or to make a creative montage.

Step 1 *File>Open>CD>Step-by-step files>'13 Donna 4'.*

Step 2 The bevel effect will be based on a selection, so *Select>All* to add a bevel to the whole picture.

Step 3 Bring the Layers palette on screen and click the second icon from the left, with the shape of a plug. In the drop-down menu select Bevel World.

Step 4 When the dialog box appears (it can take a while), change the settings to those shown in Figure 13.44, or choose your own. The changes to the settings are slow, so you will need to wait to see the result which is visible on the picture.

In Figure 13.45, the original has been brought back on top to enhance the contrast.

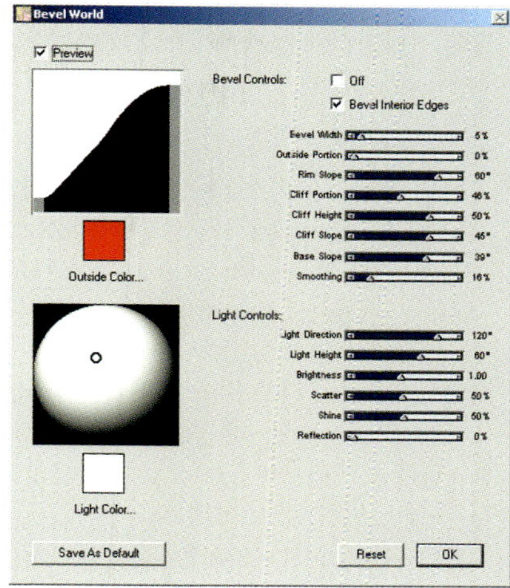

Figure 13.44

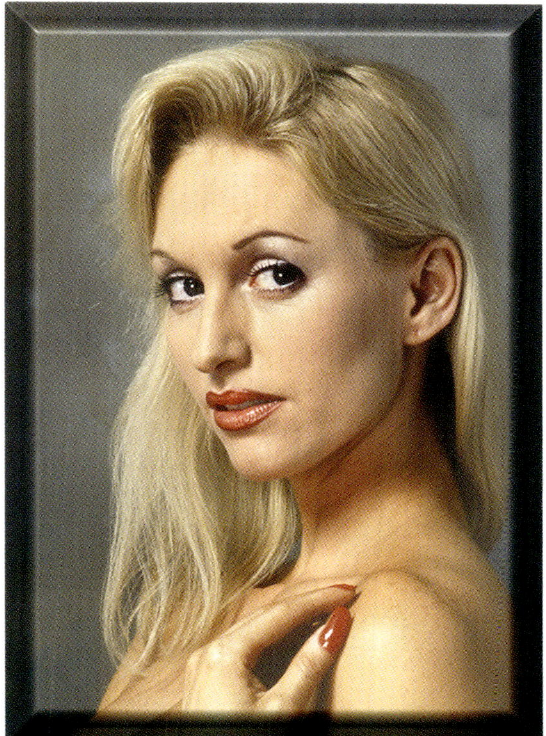

Figure 13.45

Liquid Lens

Liquid Lens is definitely one of the fun effects in Painter; it does what it says, it turns your precious photograph into liquid and then distorts the picture by using the various controls.

Step 1 *File>Open>CD>Step-by-step files>'13 Two Statues'.*

Step 2 Bring the Layers palette on screen and click the second icon from the left, with the shape of a plug. In the drop-down menu select Liquid Lens.

The icons in the dialog box distort in particular ways when painted in the picture.

The first icon simulates the effect of a droplet falling into water; select the icon then click and drag in the picture to increase the distortion.

The icons to the right twist the image to the right or left.

The two icons immediately below these will make the picture bulge or contract.

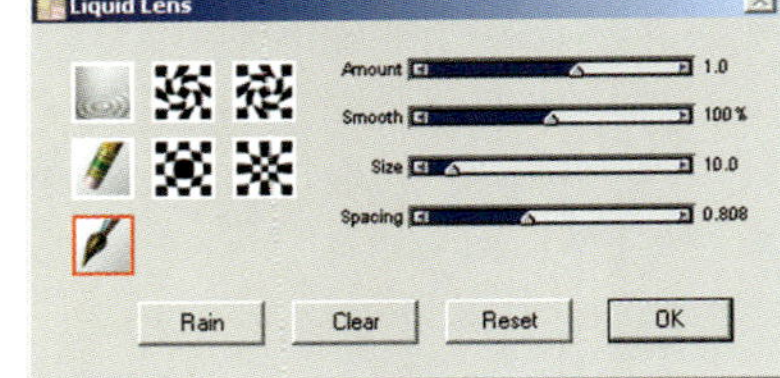

Figure 13.46

The eraser icon removes any distortion, returning the picture back to its original state.

The brush icon will distort as the brush is dragged over the picture.

The sliders modify the options and will alter the amount of the distortion, the smoothness, the brush size and how the dabs are spaced.

The four buttons will clear the picture of distortion; reset the sliders to their default setting and OK accepts the picture. The less obvious button is called Rain, which is explained on the next page.

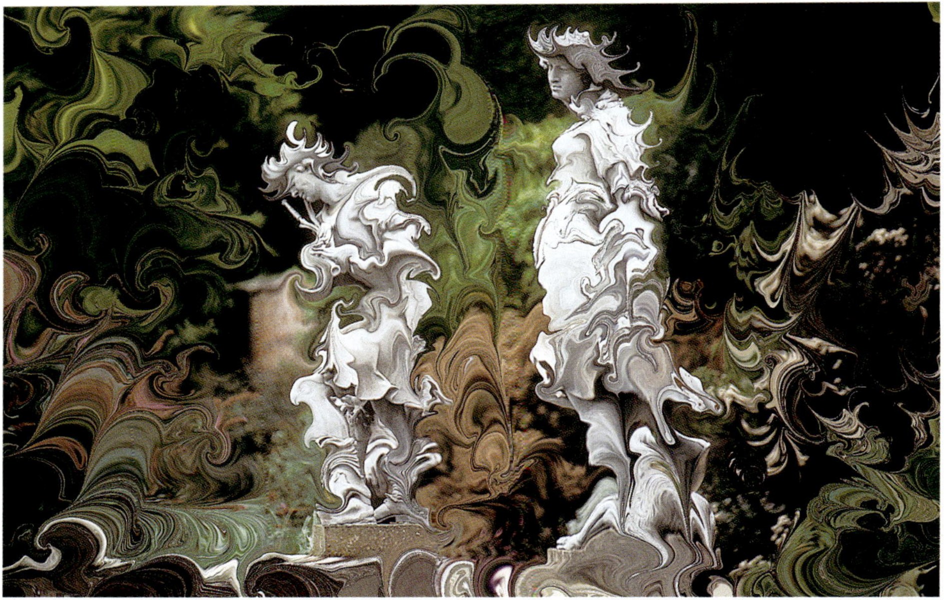

Figure 13.47 Using the Liquid Lens

The pictures running down the right side of the page have been made by pressing the Rain button in the dialog box.

Click the button now and see what happens: droplets of water start falling on the picture, which is gradually dissolved by the rain. The rain will continue until you click in the picture area; if you leave it raining for a long time the whole picture will eventually disappear.

The raindrops can be controlled by the sliders.

Move the Amount slider to the left and the droplets will drop straight down; move it to the right and the rain will run down from the top.

The size slider sets the size of the droplets and therefore the area which is affected.

Move the smoothness slider to the left and the droplets will form hard circles on the picture, while at the other end of the slider they will slide smoothly downwards.

Have fun!

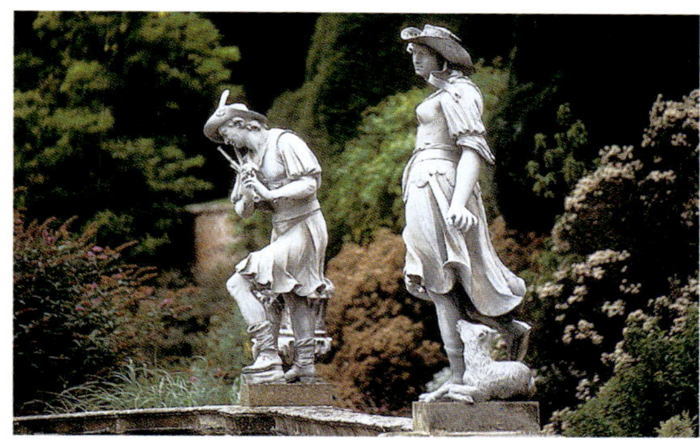

Figure 13.48

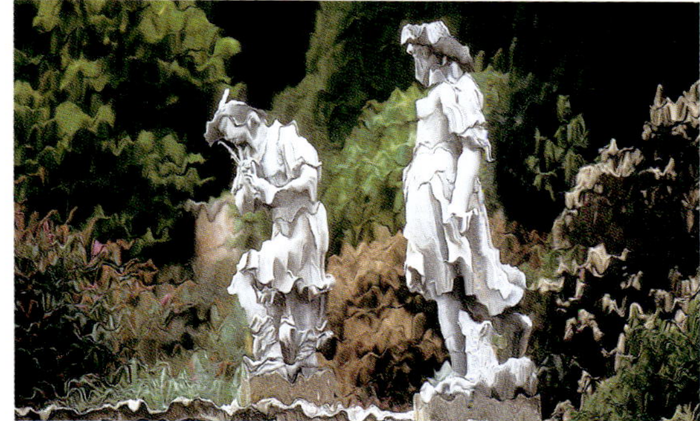

Figure 13.49

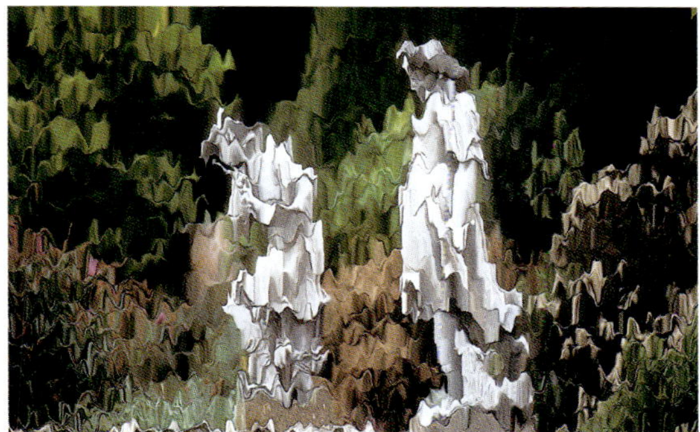

Figure 13.50

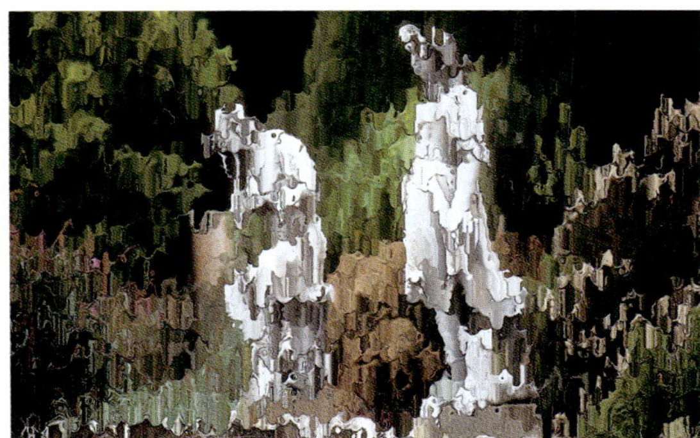

Figure 13.51

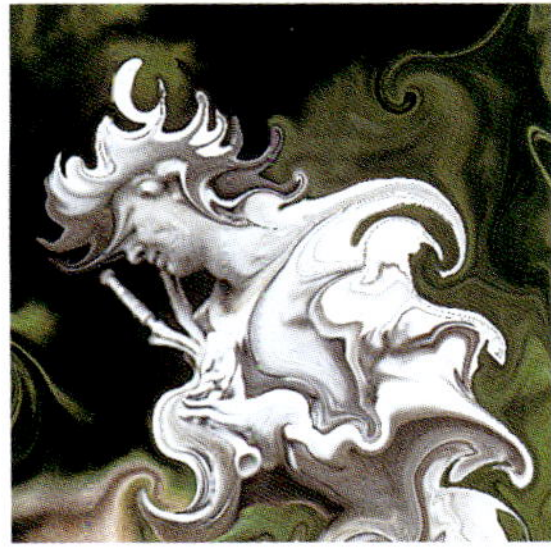

Figure 13.52

Kaleidoscope

Kaleidoscopic images are great fun and with Painter are incredibly easy to make. Try this out with the photograph on the CD or try one of your own; the steps are below.

Step 1 *File>Open>CD>Step-by-step files>'13 Rusty Metal'.*

Step 2 Bring the Layers palette on screen and click the second icon from the left, with the shape of a plug. In the drop-down menu select Kaleidoscope.

Step 3 In the dialog box change the size to 300 pixels; the default size is 100, which is too small for this picture.

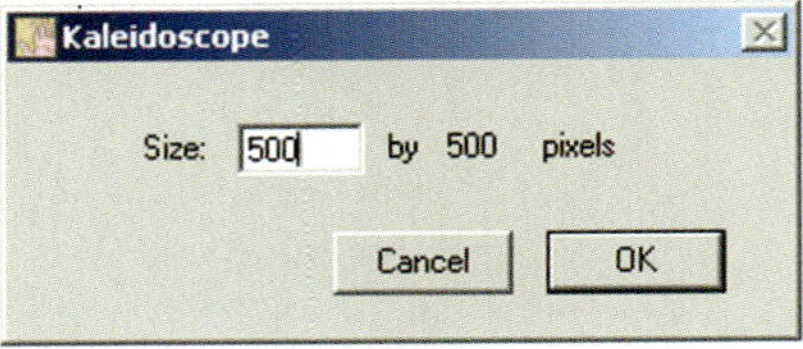

Figure 13.53

Step 4 Click on the kaleidoscope and move it around the picture; the pattern changes constantly as it is moved.

The effect works best on photographs with strong colors and good contrast, although subtle patterns can also work very well.

Every time the kaleidoscope icon is clicked, a new layer is made; this means that you can apply a kaleidoscope over the top of another kaleidoscope, thereby making even more complex designs.

The patterns shown in Figure 13.54 have been created using photographs of rust, a building and a bark pattern.

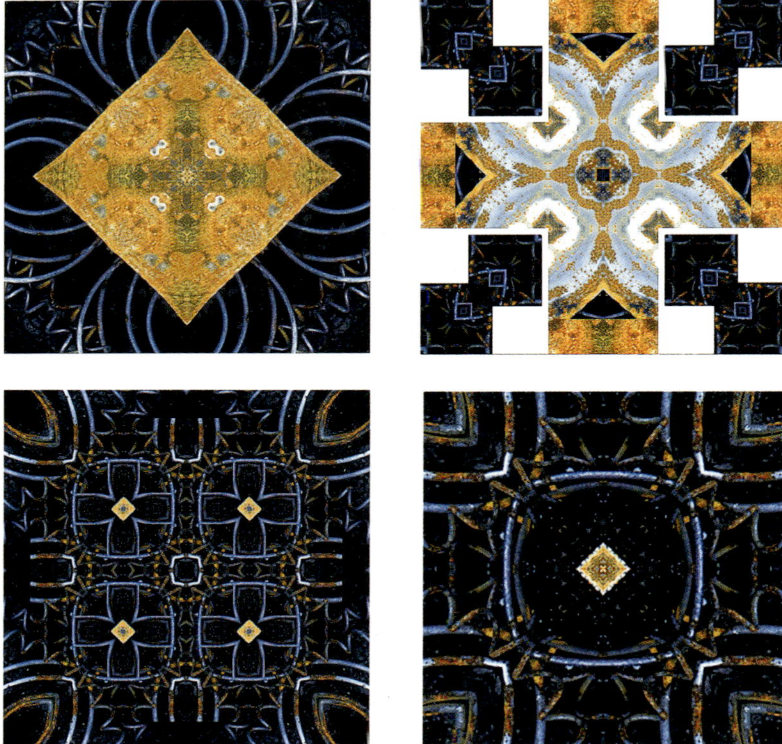

Figure 13.54

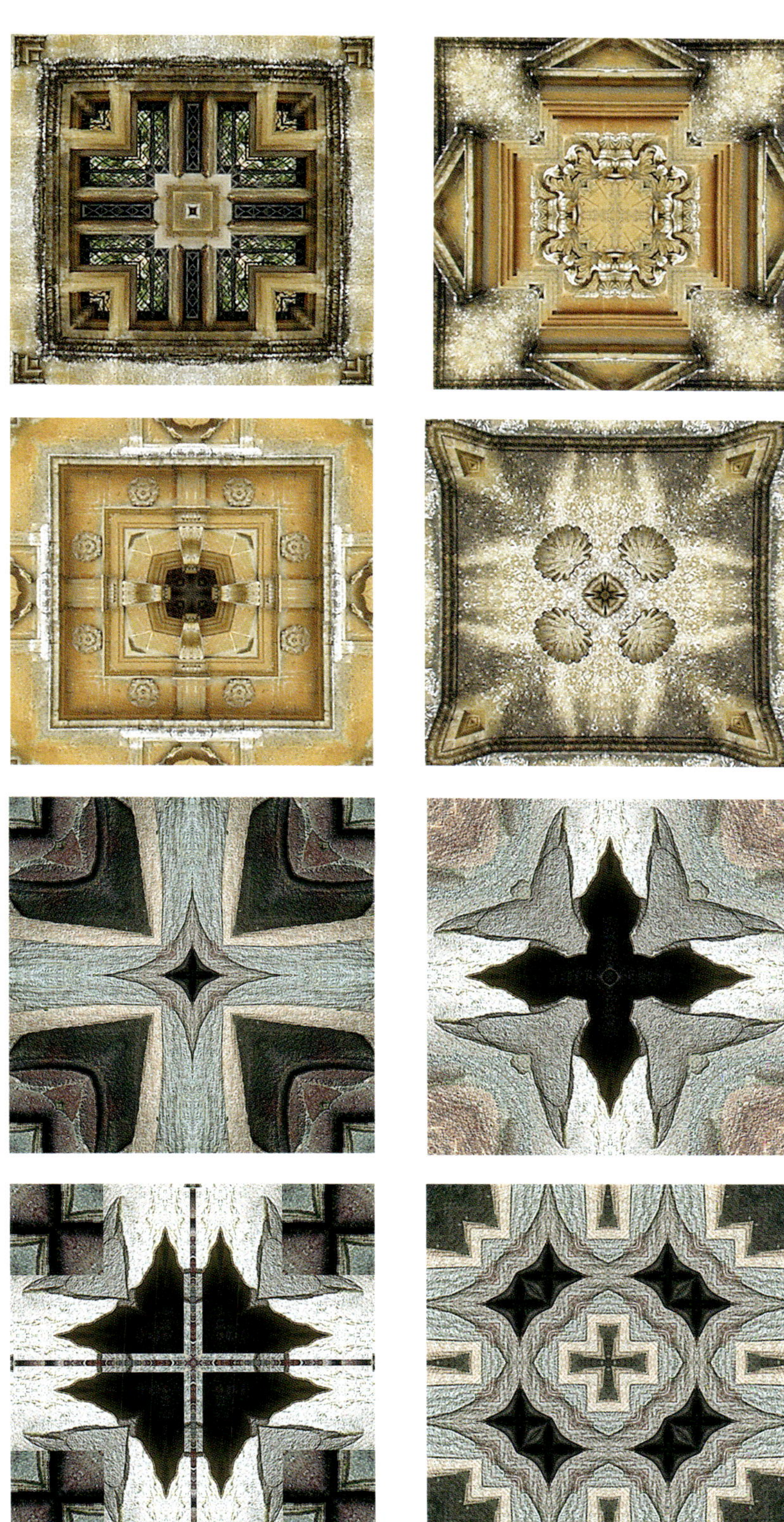

Figure 13.54 *(Continued)*

Marbling

Marbling is a traditional technique that involves mixing colored dyes and using combs to pull through the dyes, which creates the distinctive marbling pattern. Painter recreates this effect with the Apply Marbling command.

Step 1 *File>Open>CD>Step-by-step files>'13 Topsy'.*

Step 2 *Select>All, Edit>Copy.* This is ready for the next step.

Step 3 *Effects>Esoterica>Blobs.* This step will add blobs to the picture, which will aid the distribution of colors within the marbling pattern. Figure 13.57 shows the dialog box. Alter the settings to: Number of blobs 60, Minimum size 50.0, Maximum size 100.0.

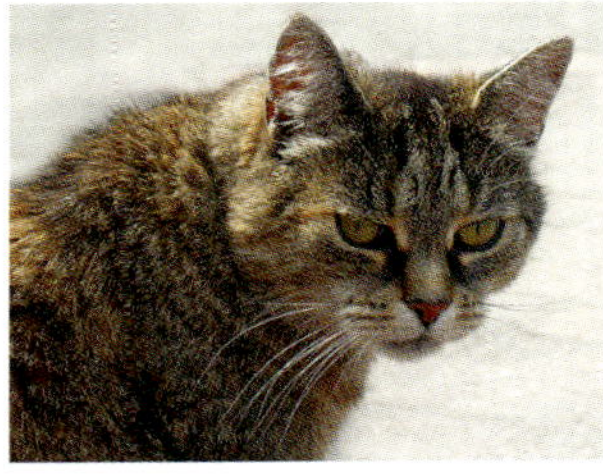

Figure 13.55 Original photograph

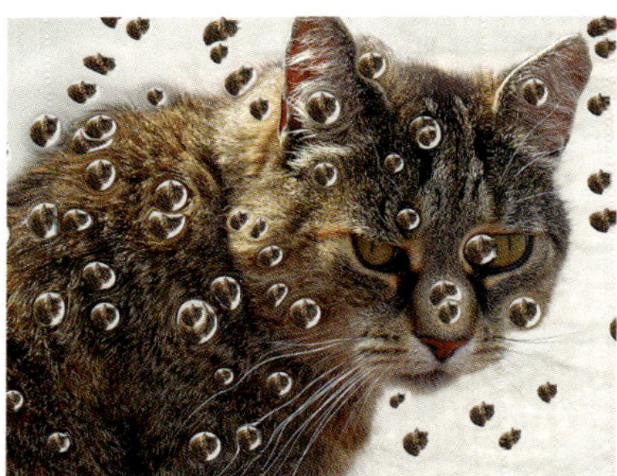

Figure 13.56

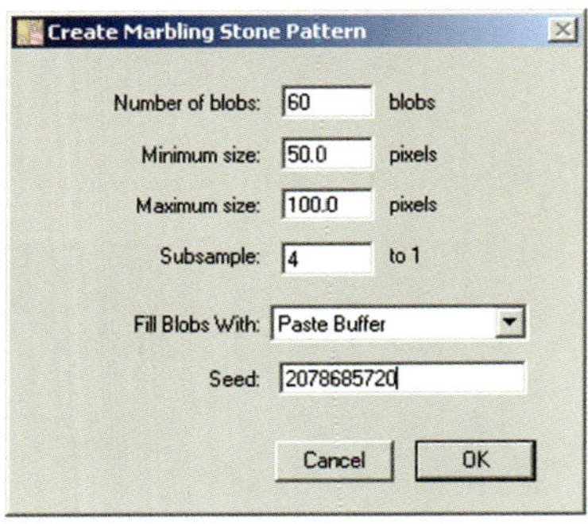

Figure 13.57 Creating blobs

Change the Fill Blobs With option to Paste Buffer, which will use the selection that was made in step 2. Click OK and the poor cat will be covered with blobs as in Figure 13.56.

Step 4 *Effects>Esoterica>Apply Marbling.* Apply the following settings (Figure 13.58): Spacing 0.17, Offset 0.00, Waviness 0.50, Wavelength 0.25, Phase 0.00, Pull 0.50, Quality 4.00.

Make the Direction Left-to-Right and click OK.

Repeat the step with the same settings just changing the direction to Right-to-Left.

Figure 13.59 shows the marbling pattern after being cropped. As you can see, the original picture has completely disappeared and been replaced by a marbled design.

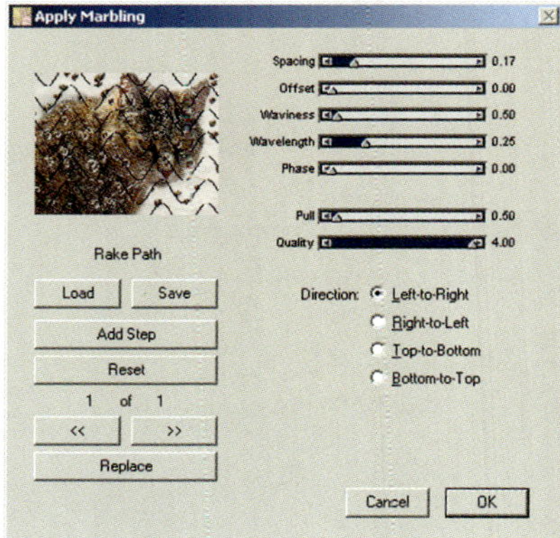

Figure 13.58

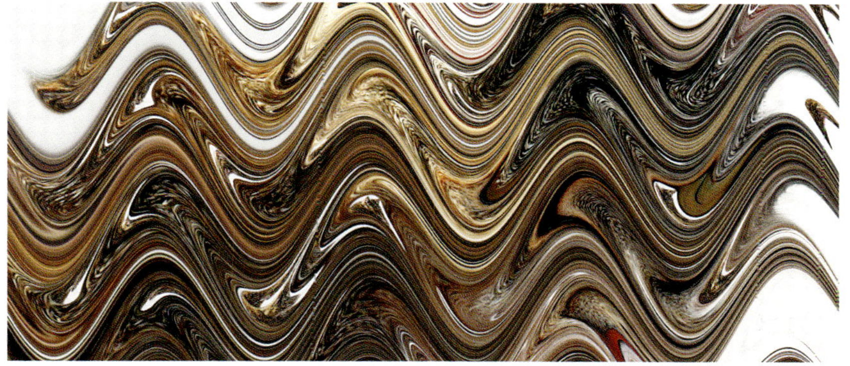

Figure 13.59

In addition to making patterns by experimenting with the controls in the dialog box, there are also some preset marbling patterns within the Painter program.

In the dialog box, click on Load and choose from the menu that appears. Some of the preset marbling patterns are shown below.

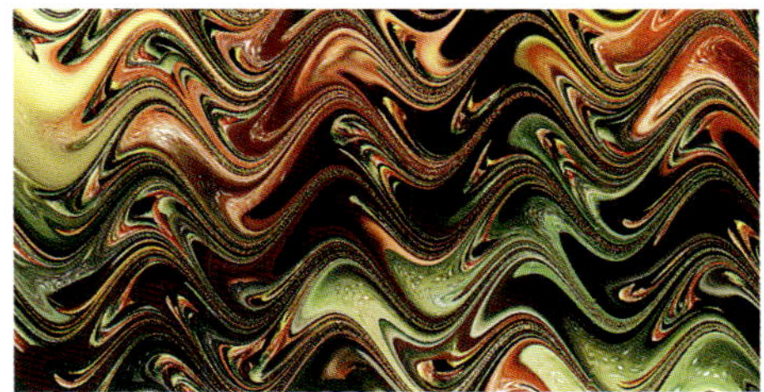

Figure 13.60

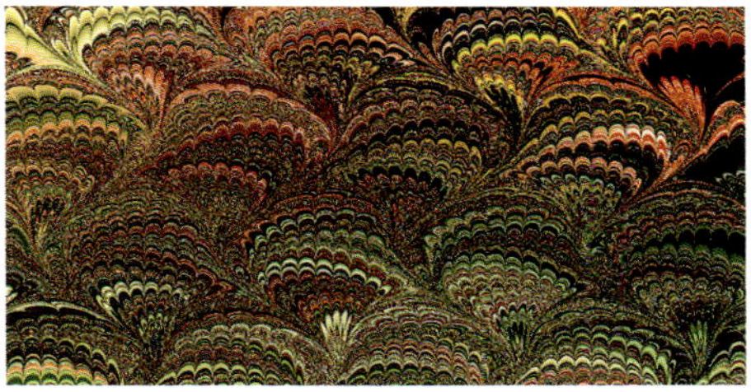

Figure 13.61

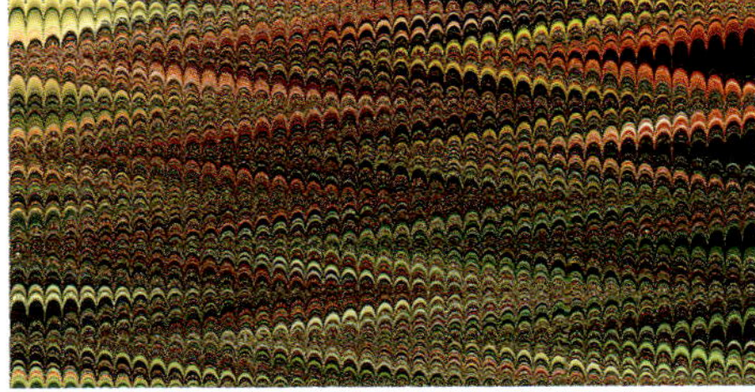

Figure 13.62

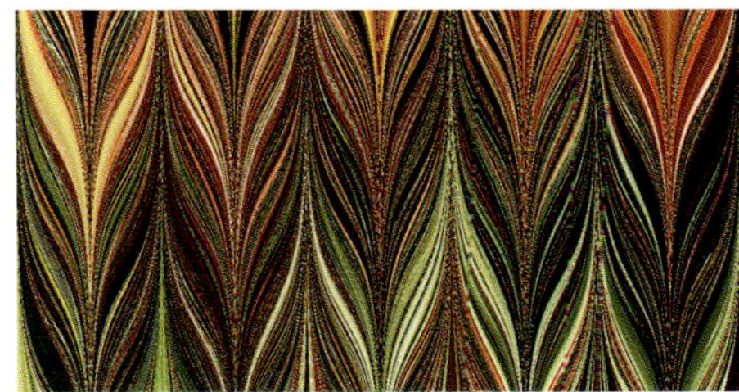

Figure 13.63

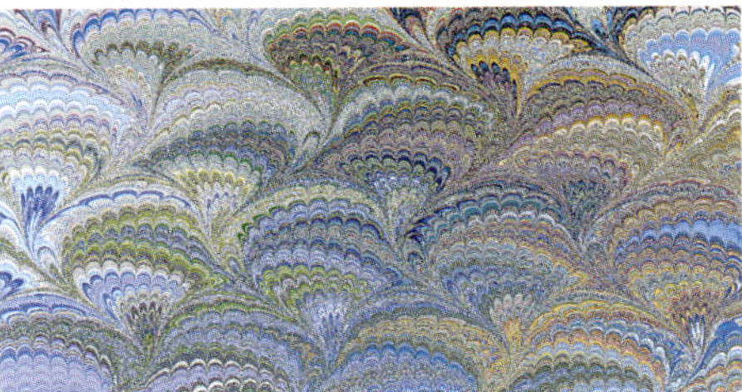

Figure 13.64

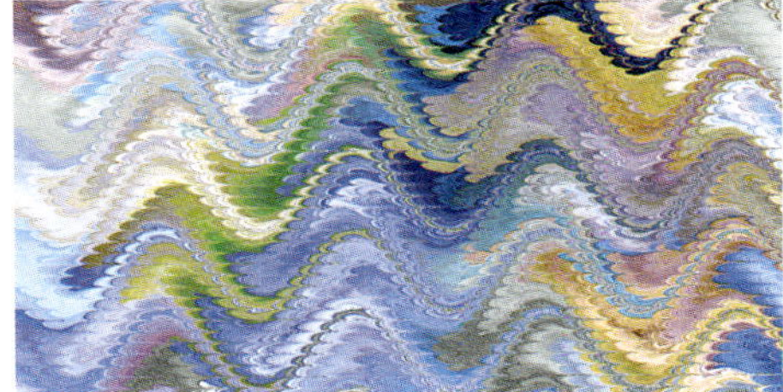

Figure 13.65

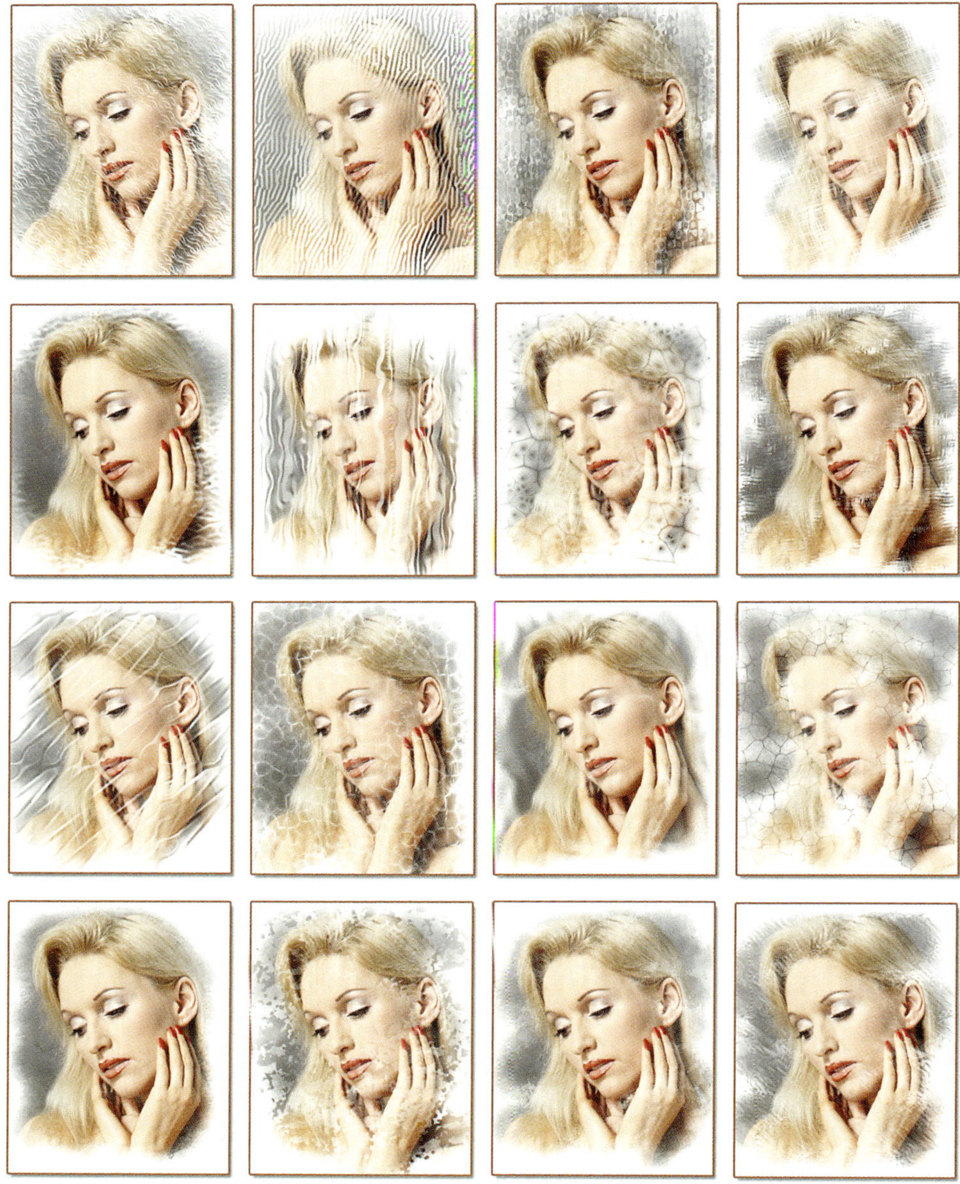

Figure 14.1 Portrait of Donna cloned with papers from 16 different paper libraries

Chapter 14
Paper libraries

Papers are used extensively throughout Painter, but there is no available reference where all of the papers can be easily viewed. This chapter illustrates all the papers available in the Painter IX program, including the additional libraries available on the Painter CD.

Details of how to load the extra papers from the CD are given in Chapter 3.

When you look at all the different papers available (and some of them are quite strange), try to imagine how they will look imposed on your own picture. It is important not to overwhelm the picture you are making with the pattern, as the paper should support and enhance the image. Sometimes, of course, the paper texture can be used in a way that is an integral part of the image, as in Figure 14.2, which used the River Map paper from the Weird library.

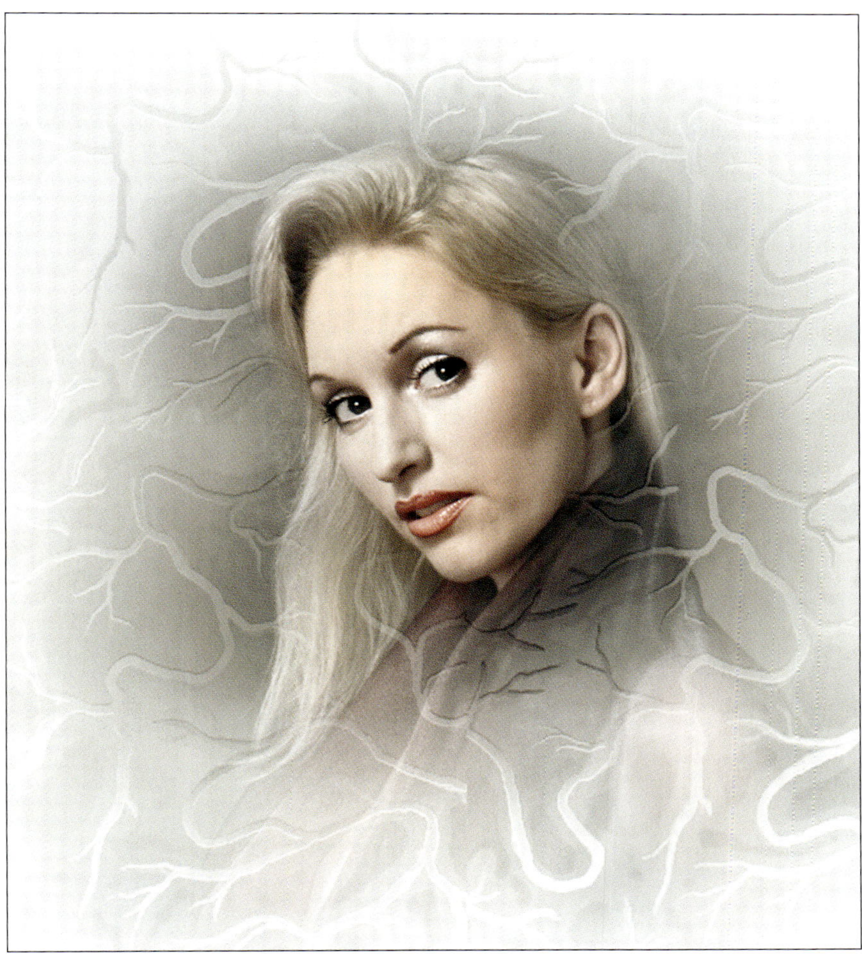

Figure 14.2 Cocooned

Painter IX default papers

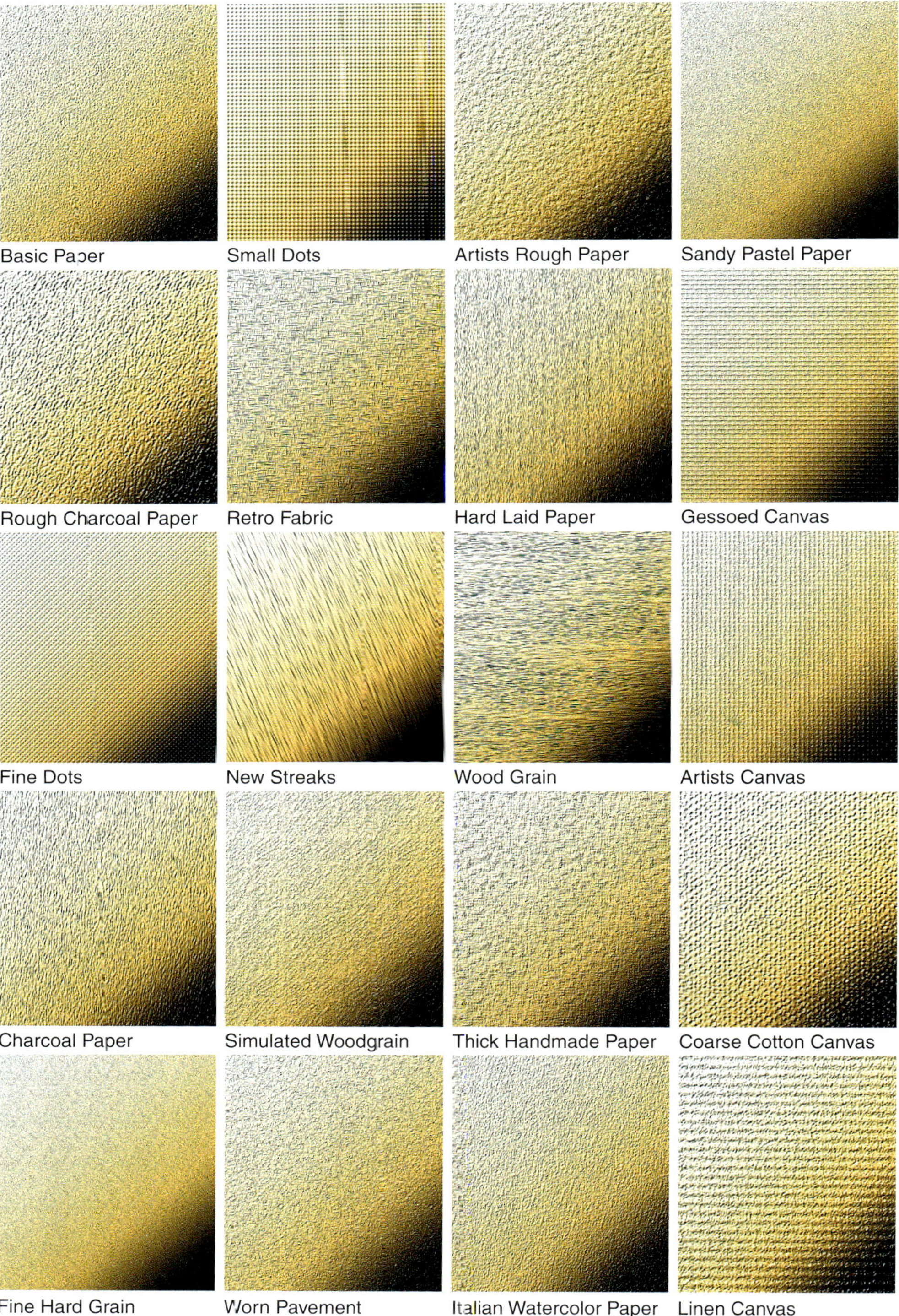

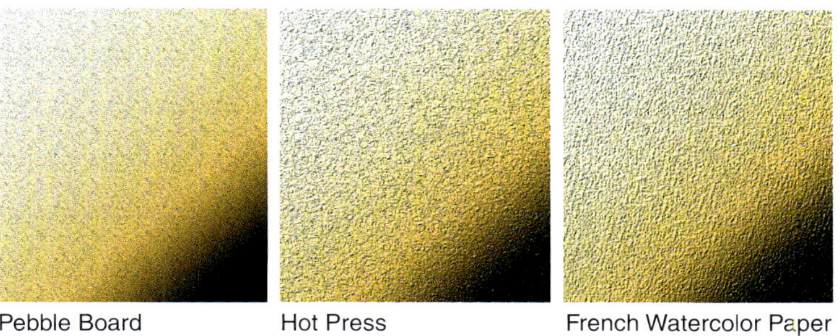

Pebble Board | Hot Press | French Watercolor Paper

Assorted textures 1

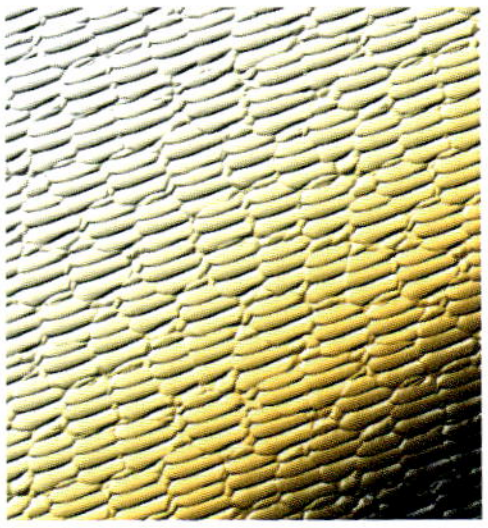

Sea Life 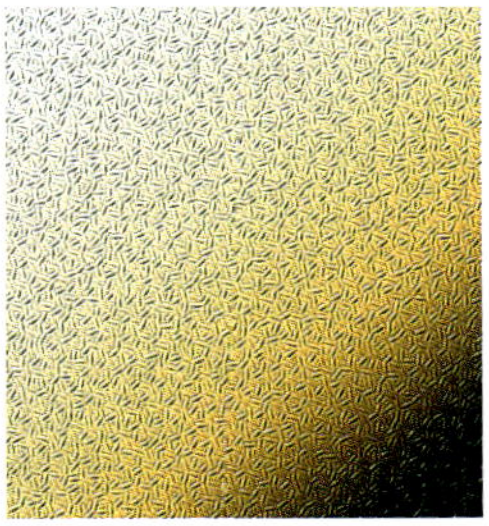 | Chain Link | Wriggle Lines 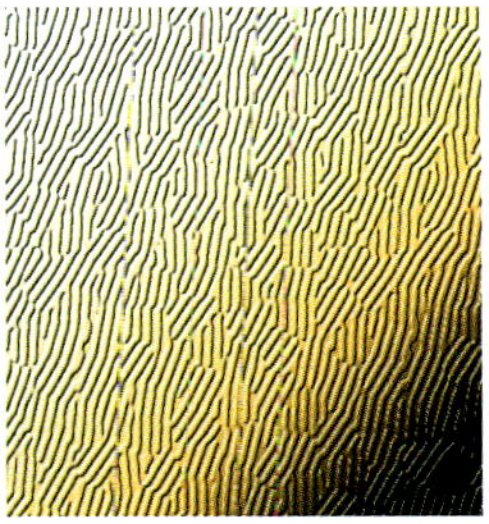 | Wheat Stalks

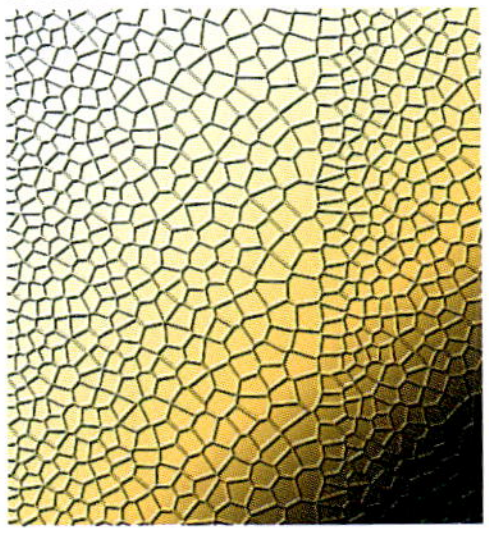

Basic Lizard | Basketball Hide 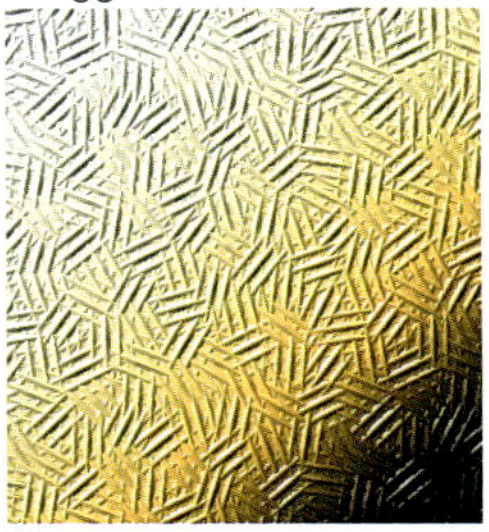 | Nightmare 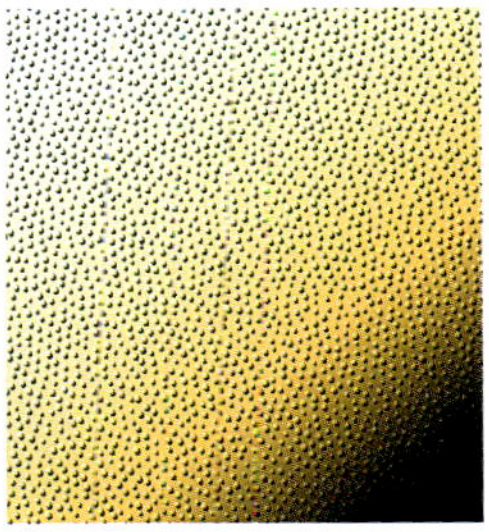 | Starry Sky

Alien Bamboo 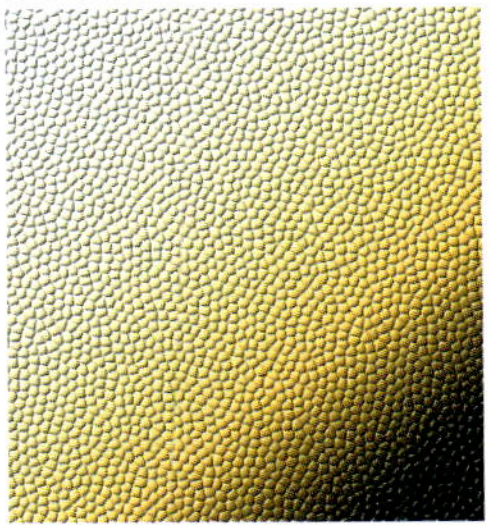 | Mosaic | Ribbed Pastel 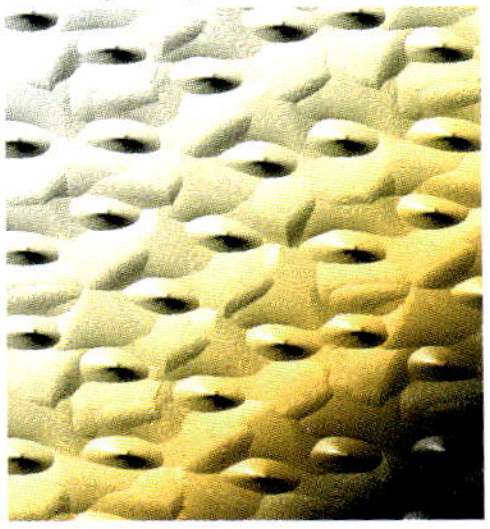 | Pearly Worms

Assorted textures 2

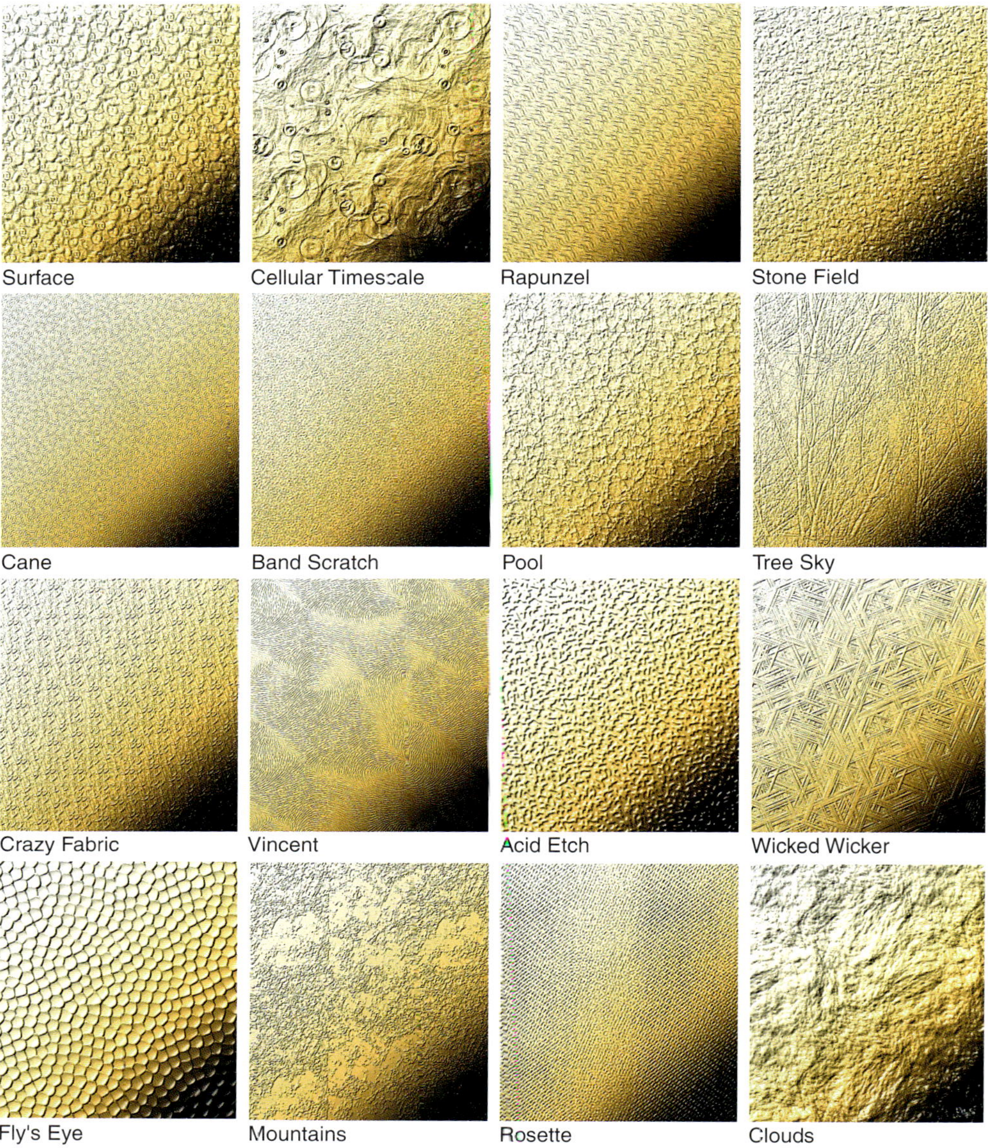

Surface
Cellular Timescale
Rapunzel
Stone Field
Cane
Band Scratch
Pool
Tree Sky
Crazy Fabric
Vincent
Acid Etch
Wicked Wicker
Fly's Eye
Mountains
Rosette
Clouds

Awesome textures

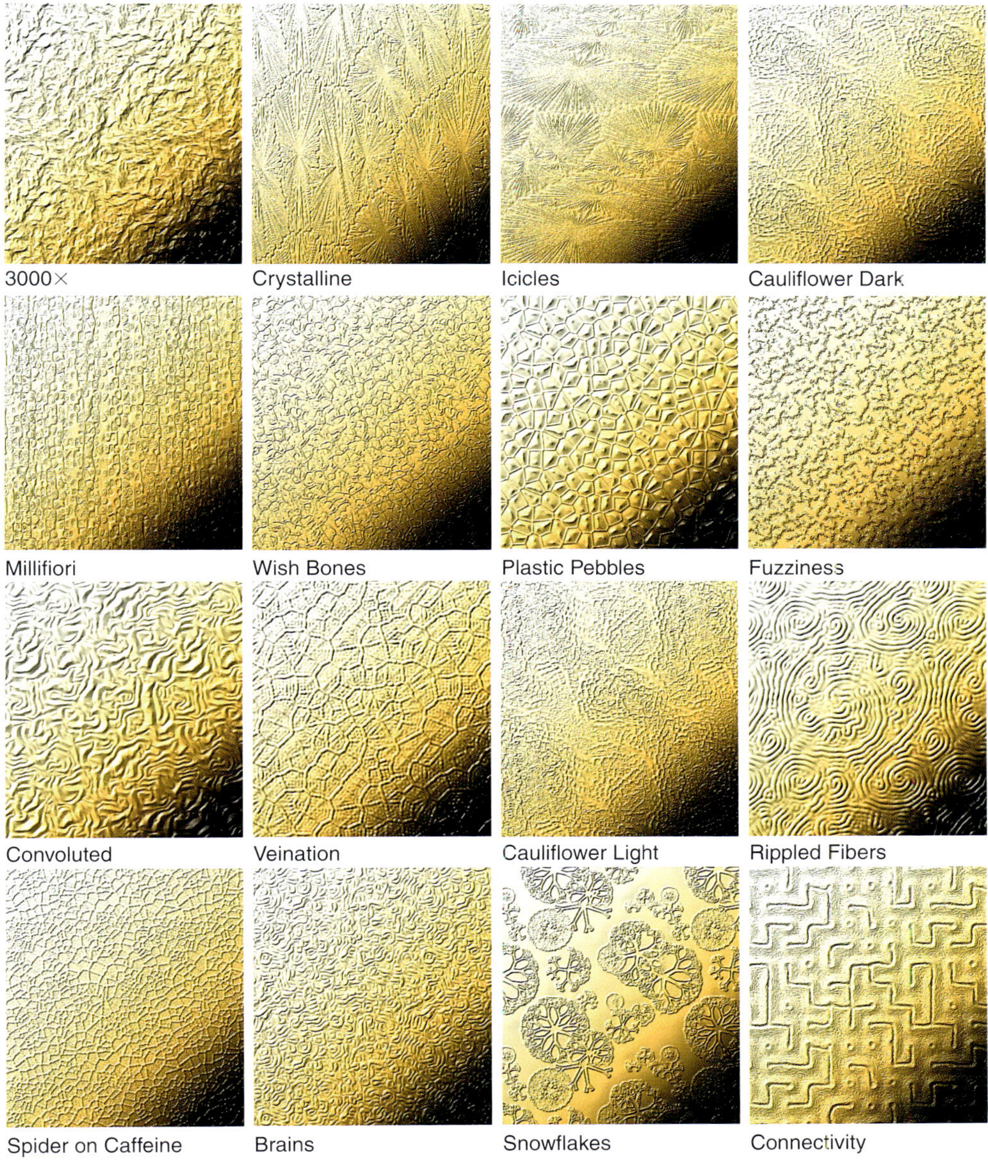

3000×, Crystalline, Icicles, Cauliflower Dark

Millifiori, Wish Bones, Plastic Pebbles, Fuzziness

Convoluted, Veination, Cauliflower Light, Rippled Fibers

Spider on Caffeine, Brains, Snowflakes, Connectivity

Biological textures

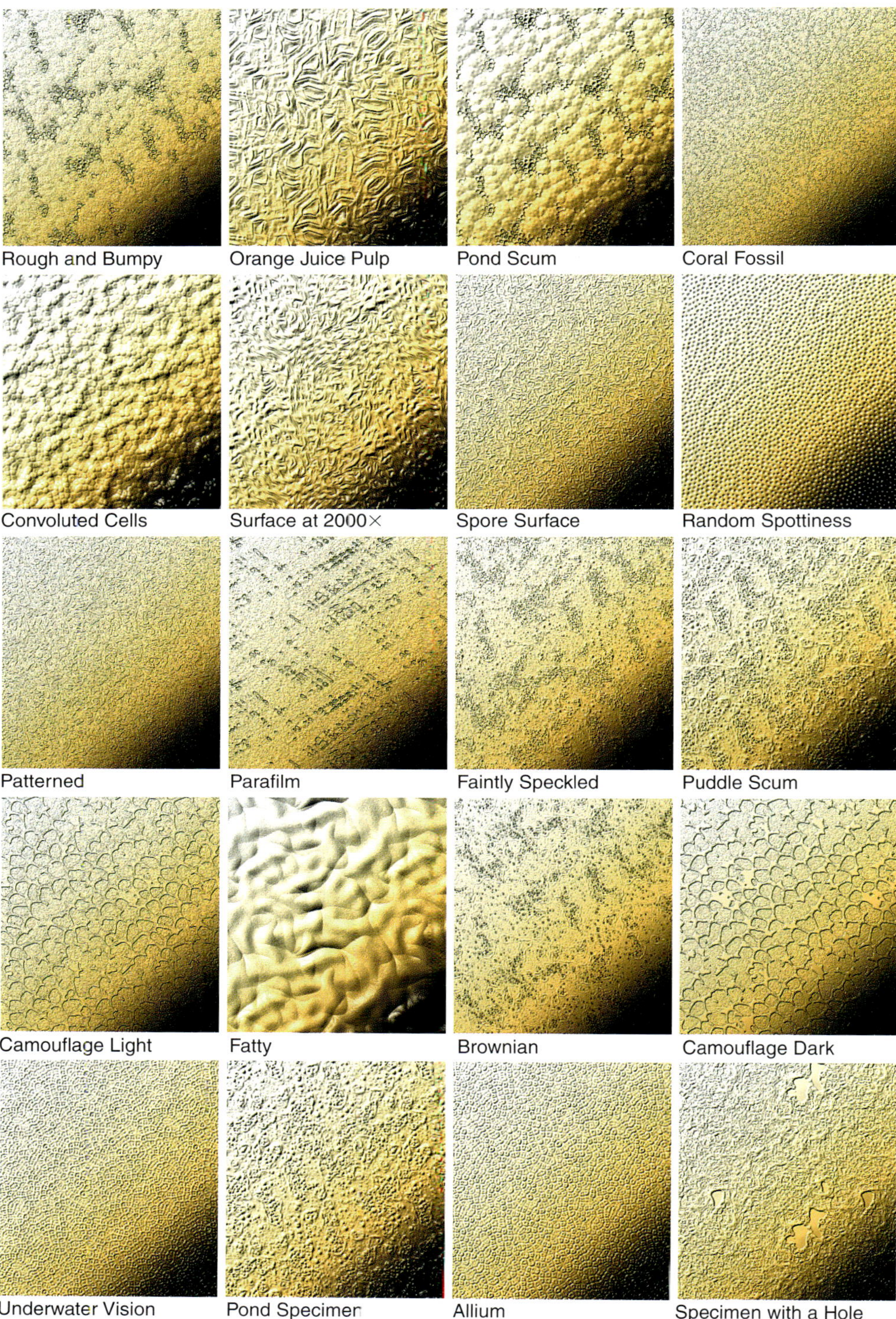

Rough and Bumpy | Orange Juice Pulp | Pond Scum | Coral Fossil

Convoluted Cells | Surface at 2000× | Spore Surface | Random Spottiness

Patterned | Parafilm | Faintly Speckled | Puddle Scum

Camouflage Light | Fatty | Brownian | Camouflage Dark

Underwater Vision | Pond Specimen | Allium | Specimen with a Hole

Branched textures

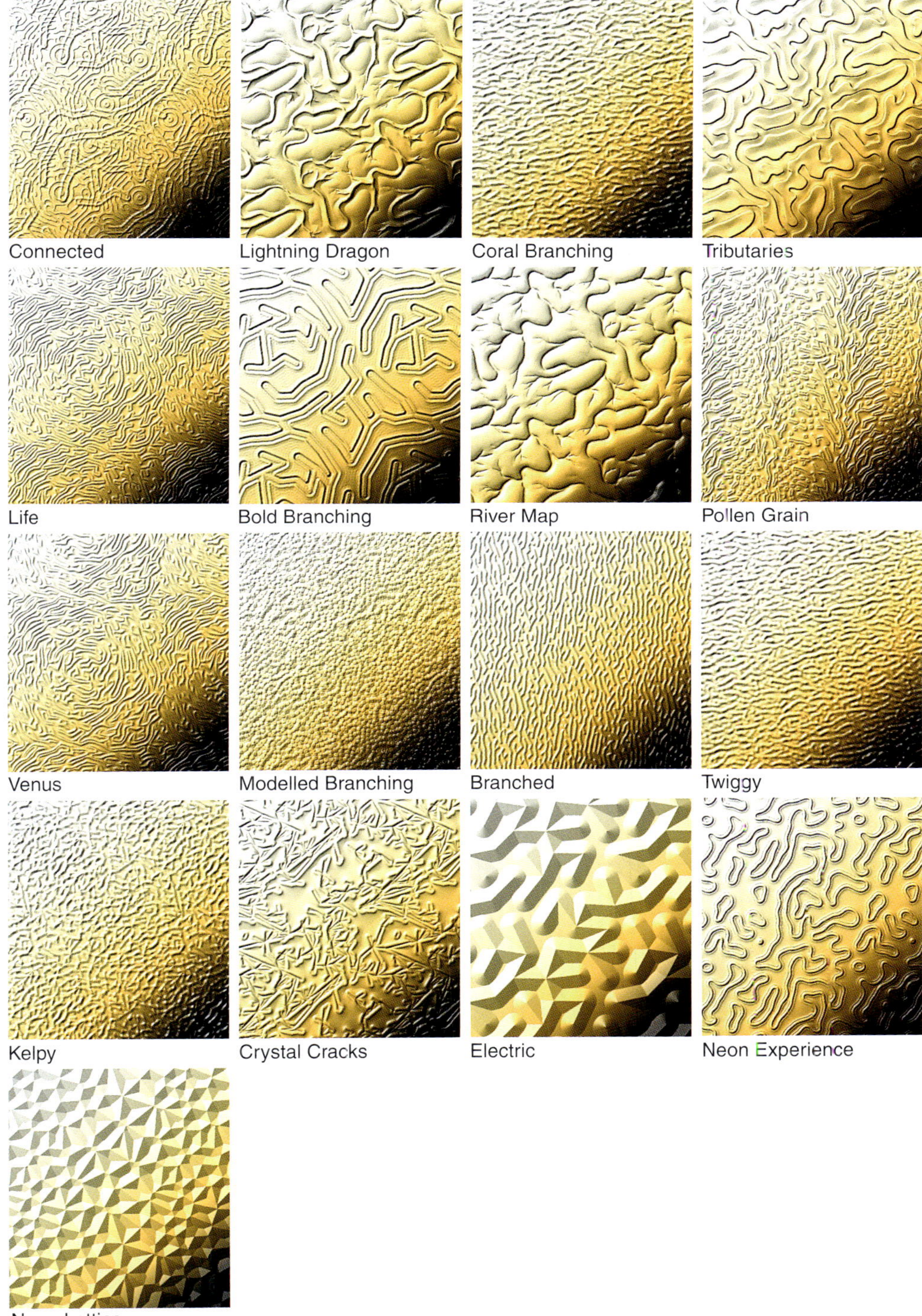

Connected
Lightning Dragon
Coral Branching
Tributaries
Life
Bold Branching
River Map
Pollen Grain
Venus
Modelled Branching
Branched
Twiggy
Kelpy
Crystal Cracks
Electric
Neon Experience
Neon Lattice

Contrasty textures

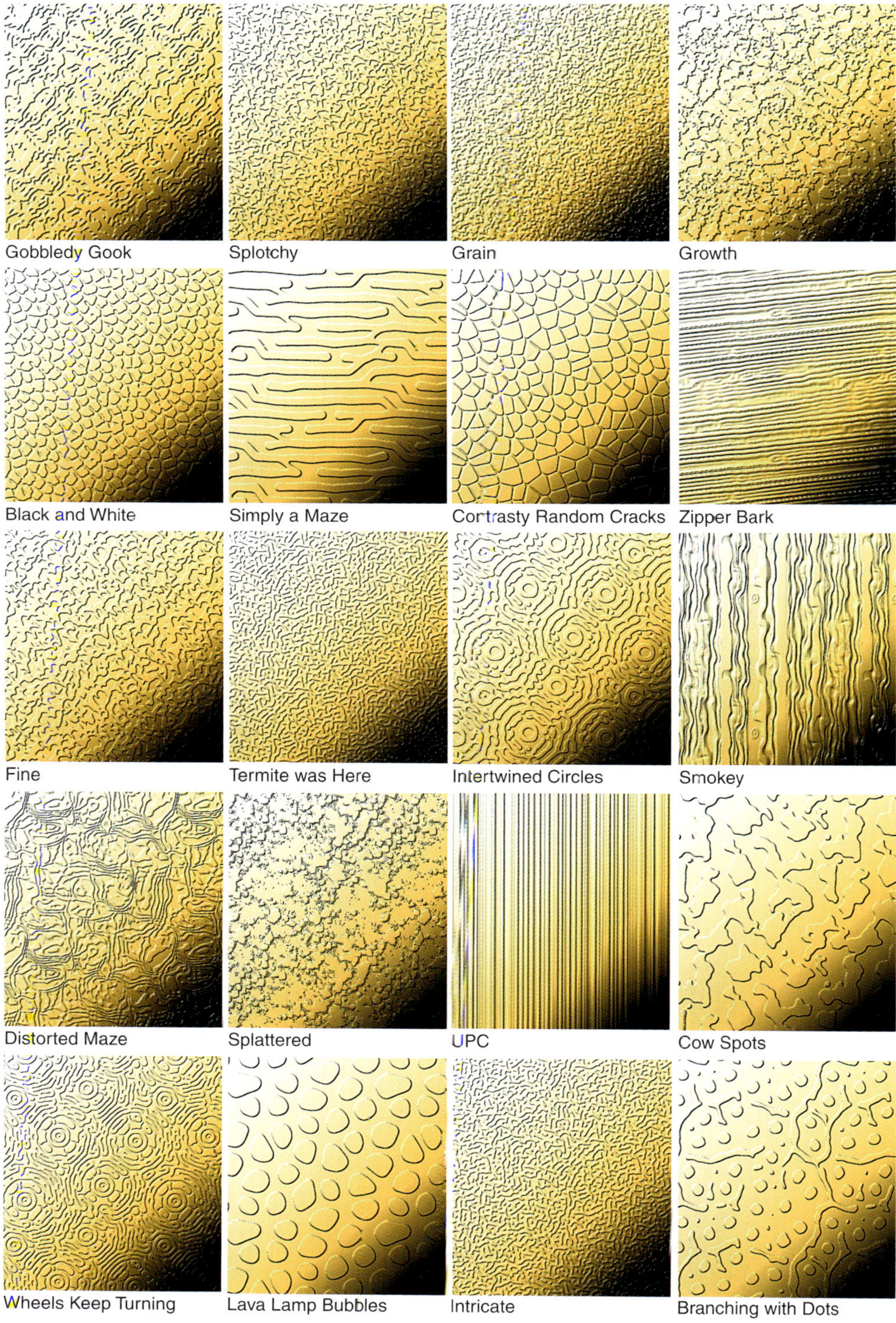

Gobbledy Gook | Splotchy | Grain | Growth

Black and White | Simply a Maze | Contrasty Random Cracks | Zipper Bark

Fine | Termite was Here | Intertwined Circles | Smokey

Distorted Maze | Splattered | UPC | Cow Spots

Wheels Keep Turning | Lava Lamp Bubbles | Intricate | Branching with Dots

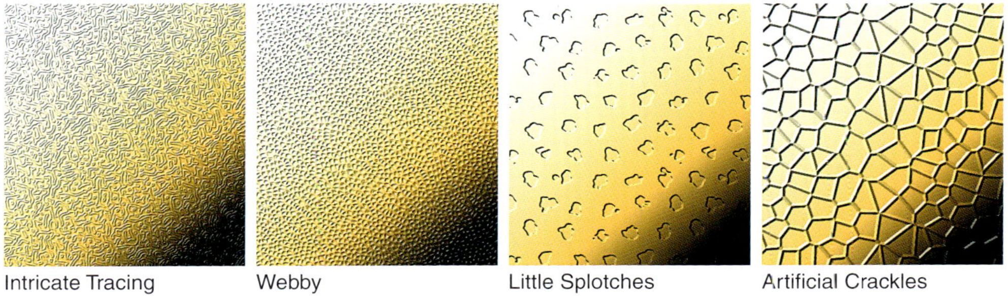

Intricate Tracing | Webby | Little Splotches | Artificial Crackles

Crack textures

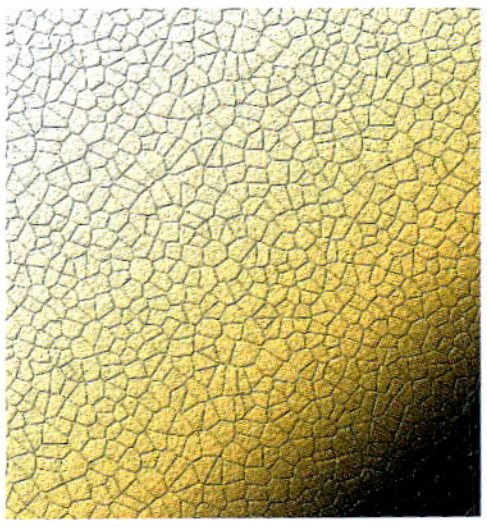

Crackle

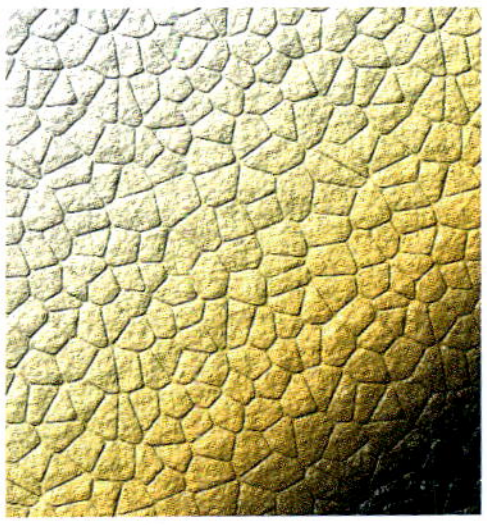

Subtle Cracks

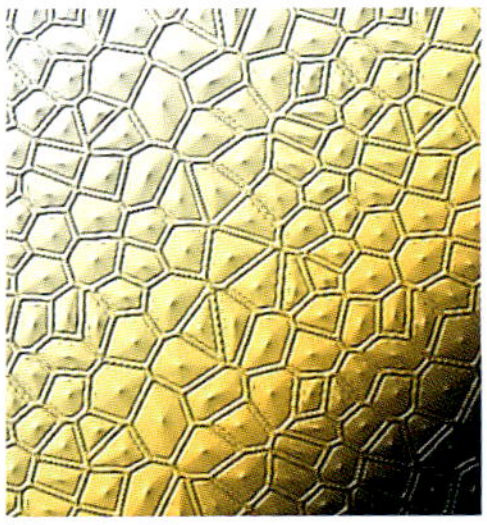

Plastic Plasma

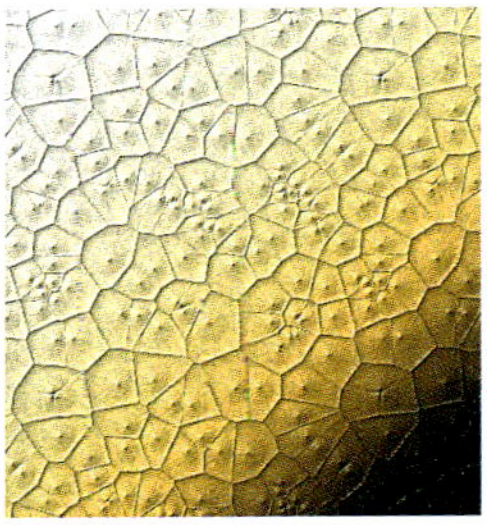

Grainy Iguana Skin

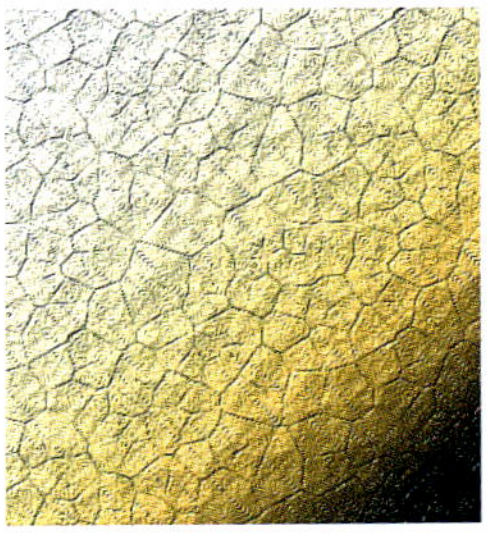

Onion Cracks

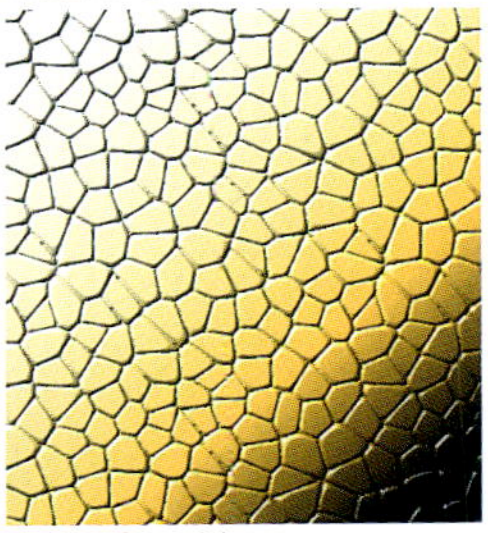

Light Crackle

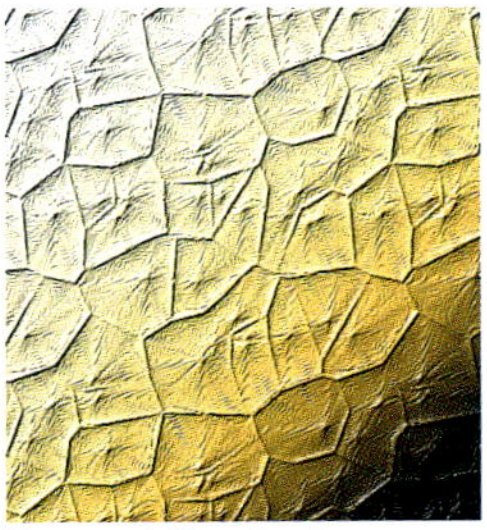

Dry and Cracked

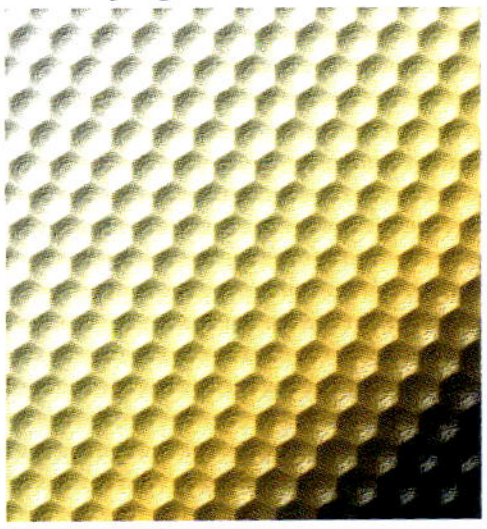

Honey Comb

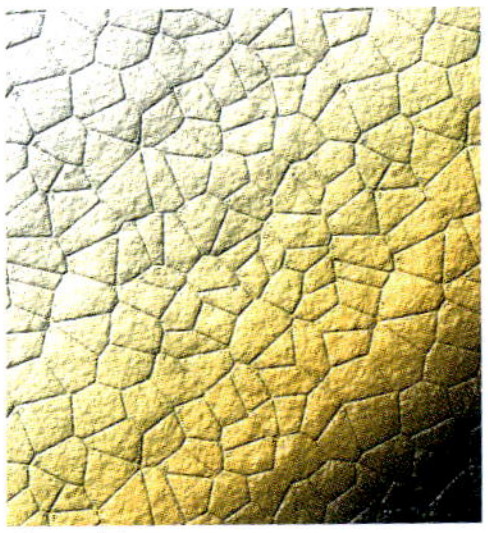

Cracking

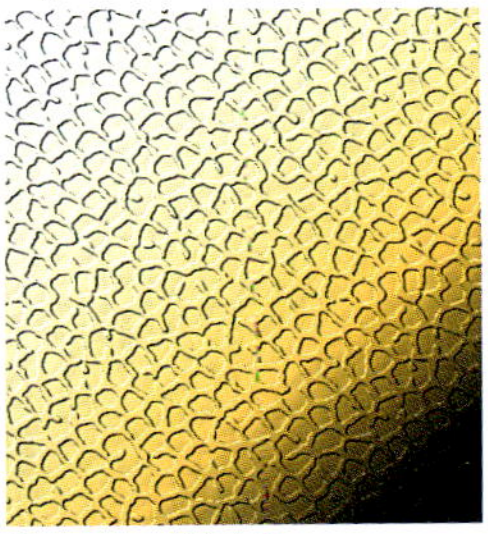

Gray and White

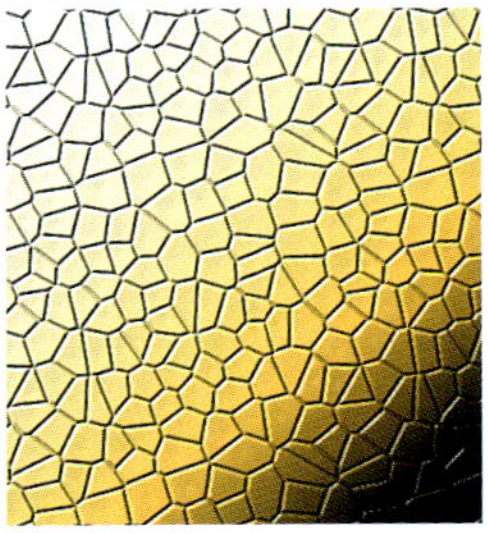

Fade to Crack

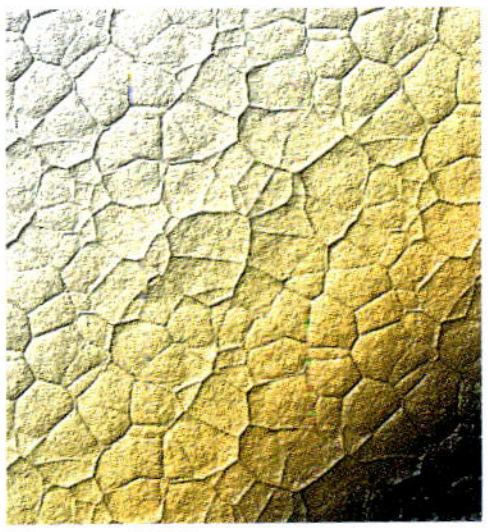

Natural Phenomenon

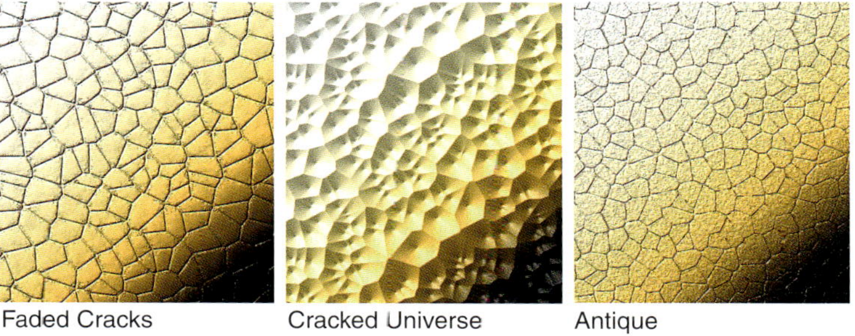

Faded Cracks | Cracked Universe | Antique

Crazy textures

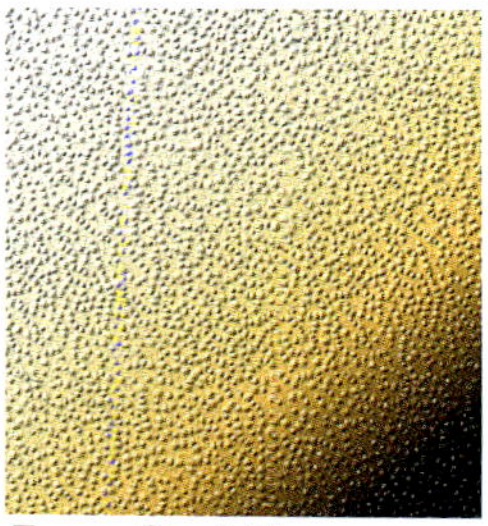

Fuzzy Confetti 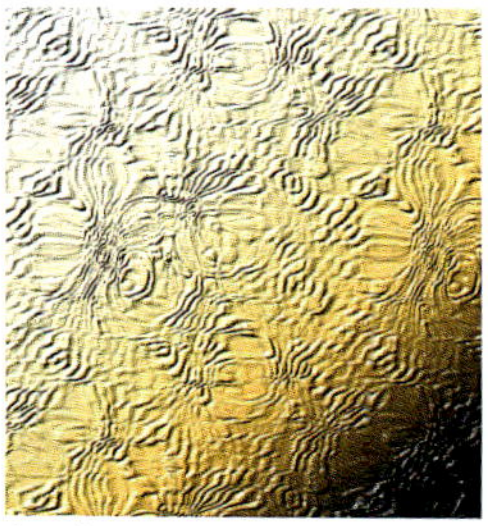 | Lost 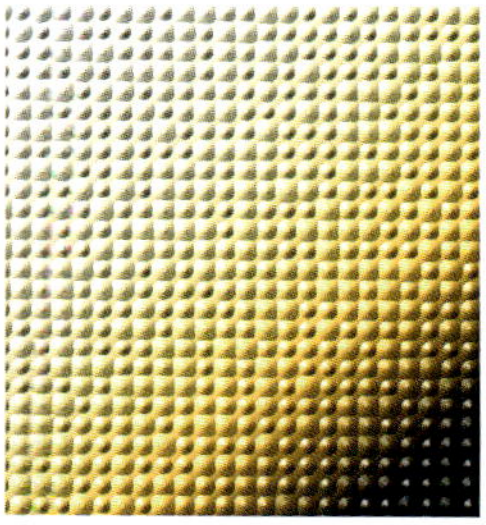 | Op 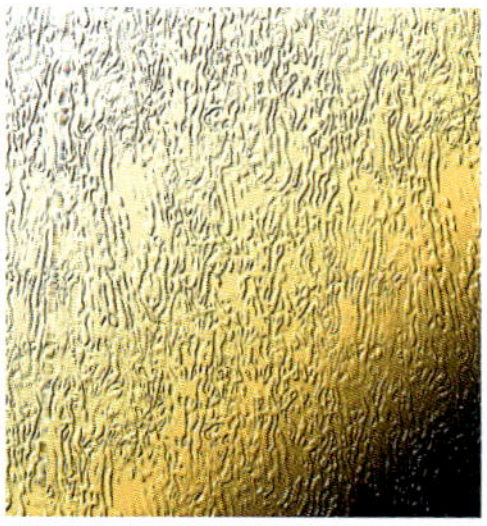 | Refracted

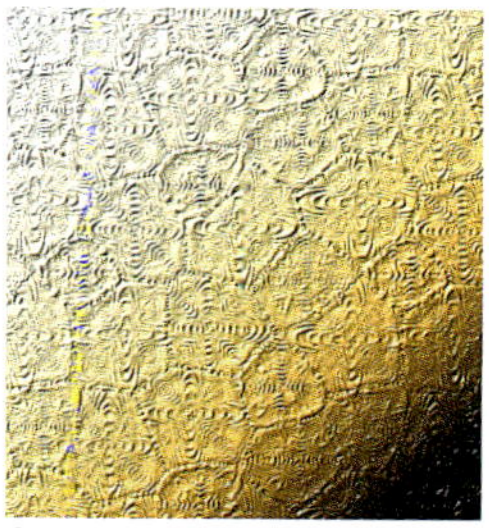

Crazy Quilt 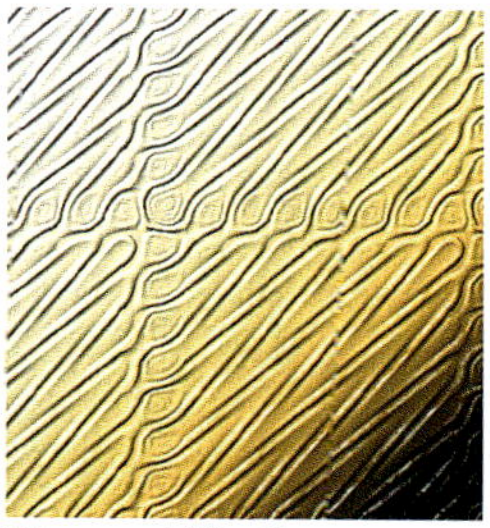 | Diagonal Zig Zags 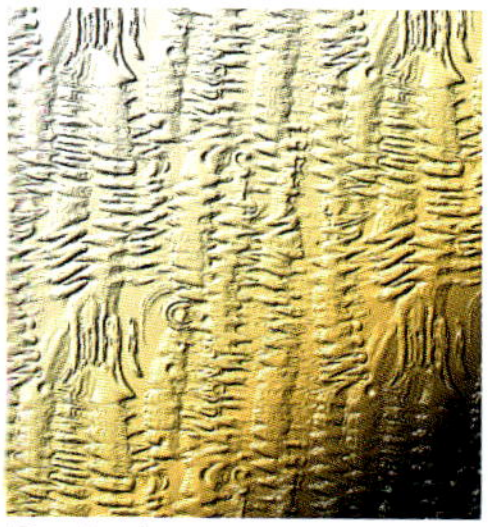 | Squiggly 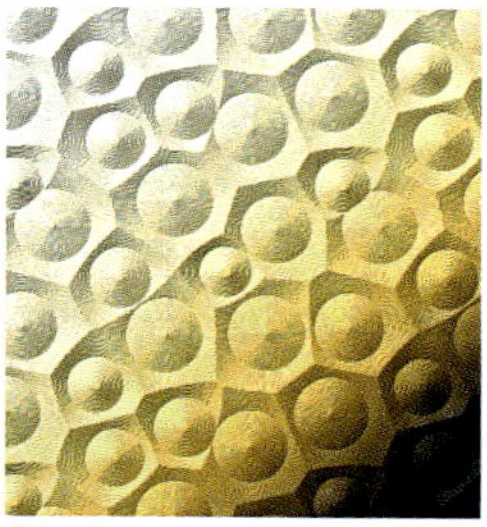 | Pin Ball

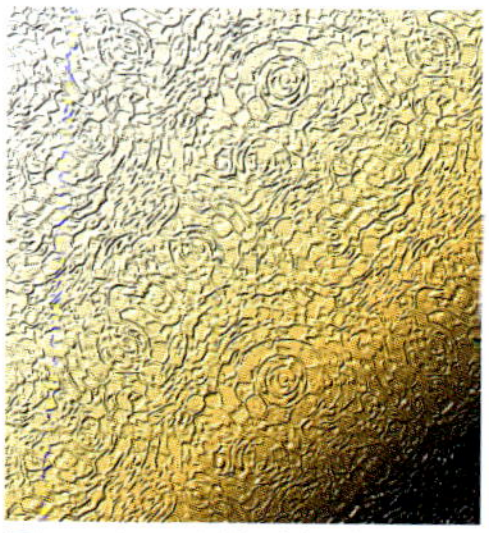

Tuned and Swirled 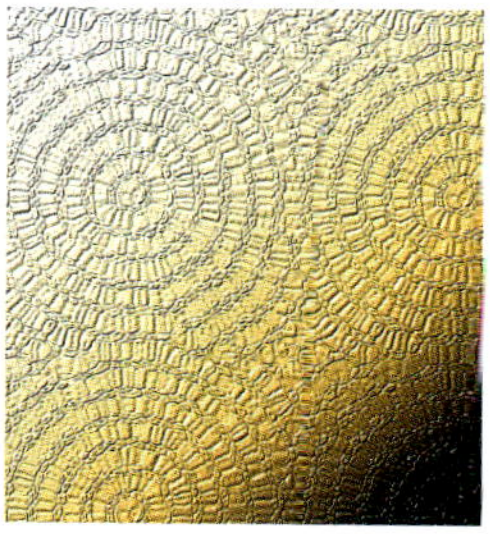 | Concentric 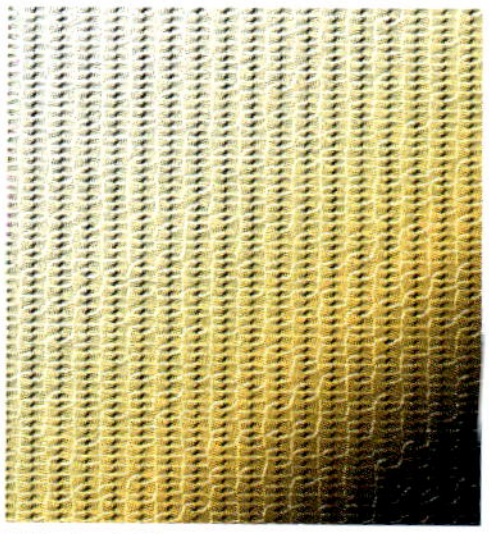 | Weird One 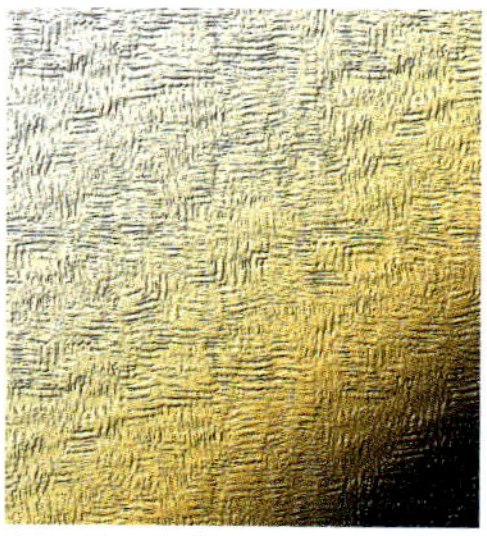 | Hatched Glass Grain

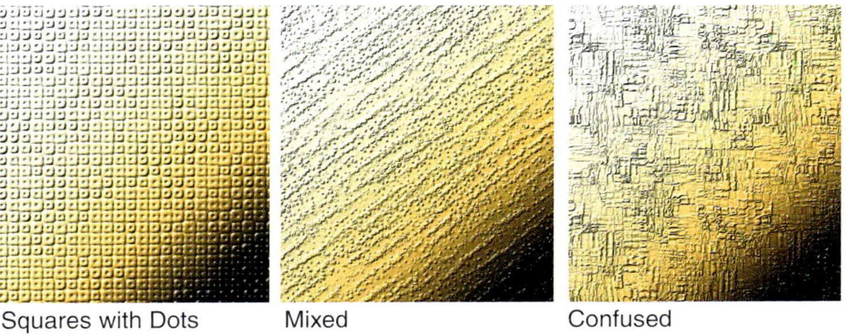

Squares with Dots | Mixed | Confused

Drawing Paper textures

Raw Pulp

Big Bumps

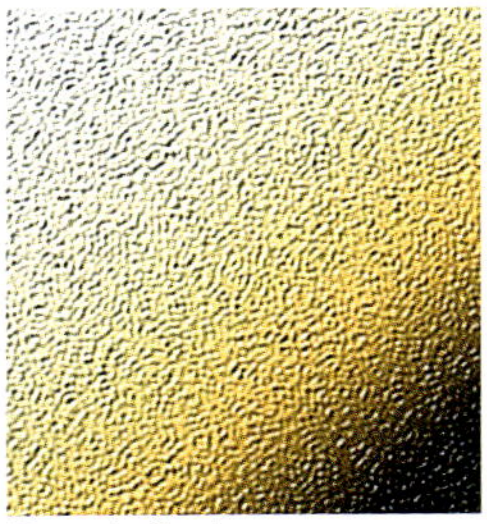

Rough Grain

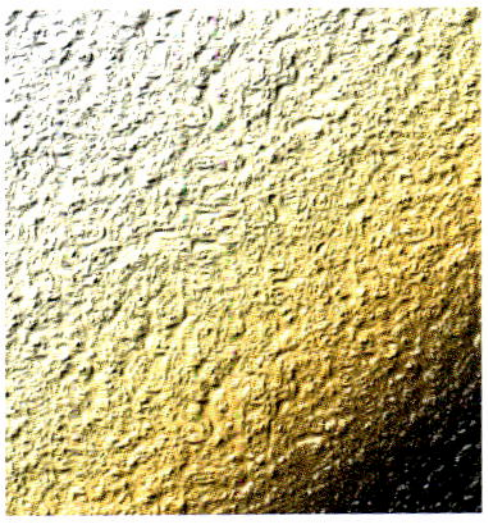

Medium

Water Color

Fine Paper

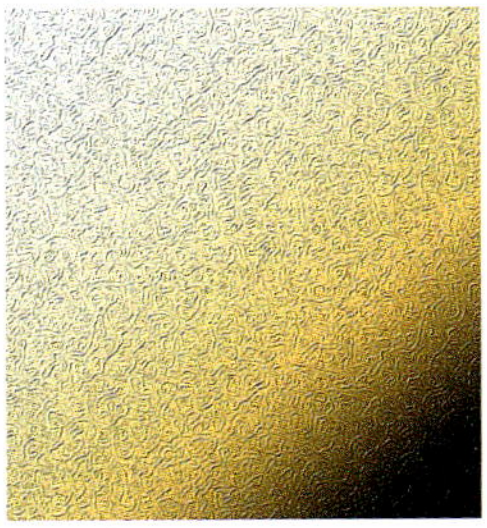

Nebulous

Plain Grain

Ultra Fine Grain

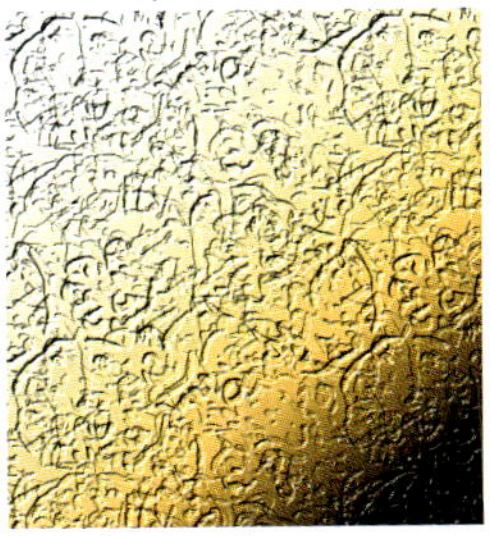

Termite Motif

Pulpy Handmade

Fine Strings

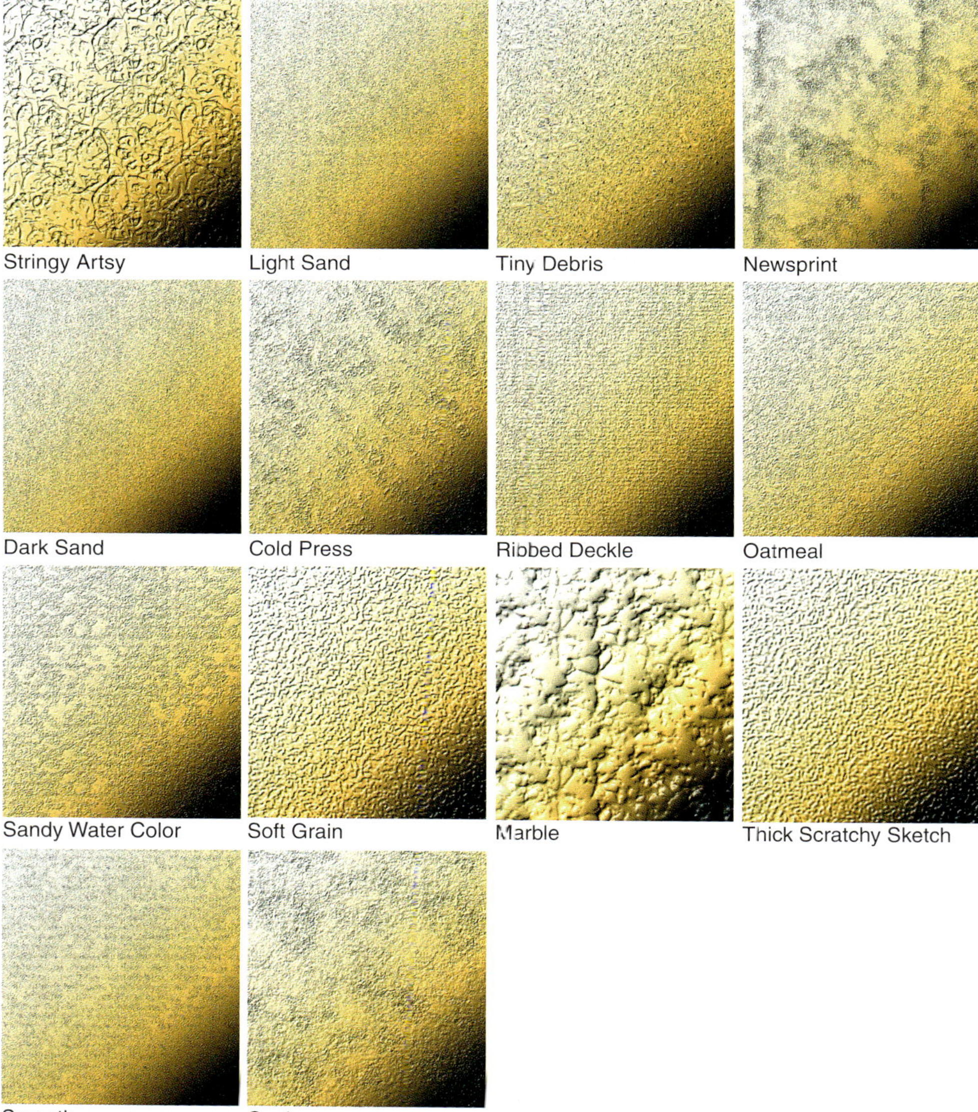
Stringy Artsy
Light Sand
Tiny Debris
Newsprint
Dark Sand
Cold Press
Ribbed Deckle
Oatmeal
Sandy Water Color
Soft Grain
Marble
Thick Scratchy Sketch
Smooth
Cool

Molecular textures

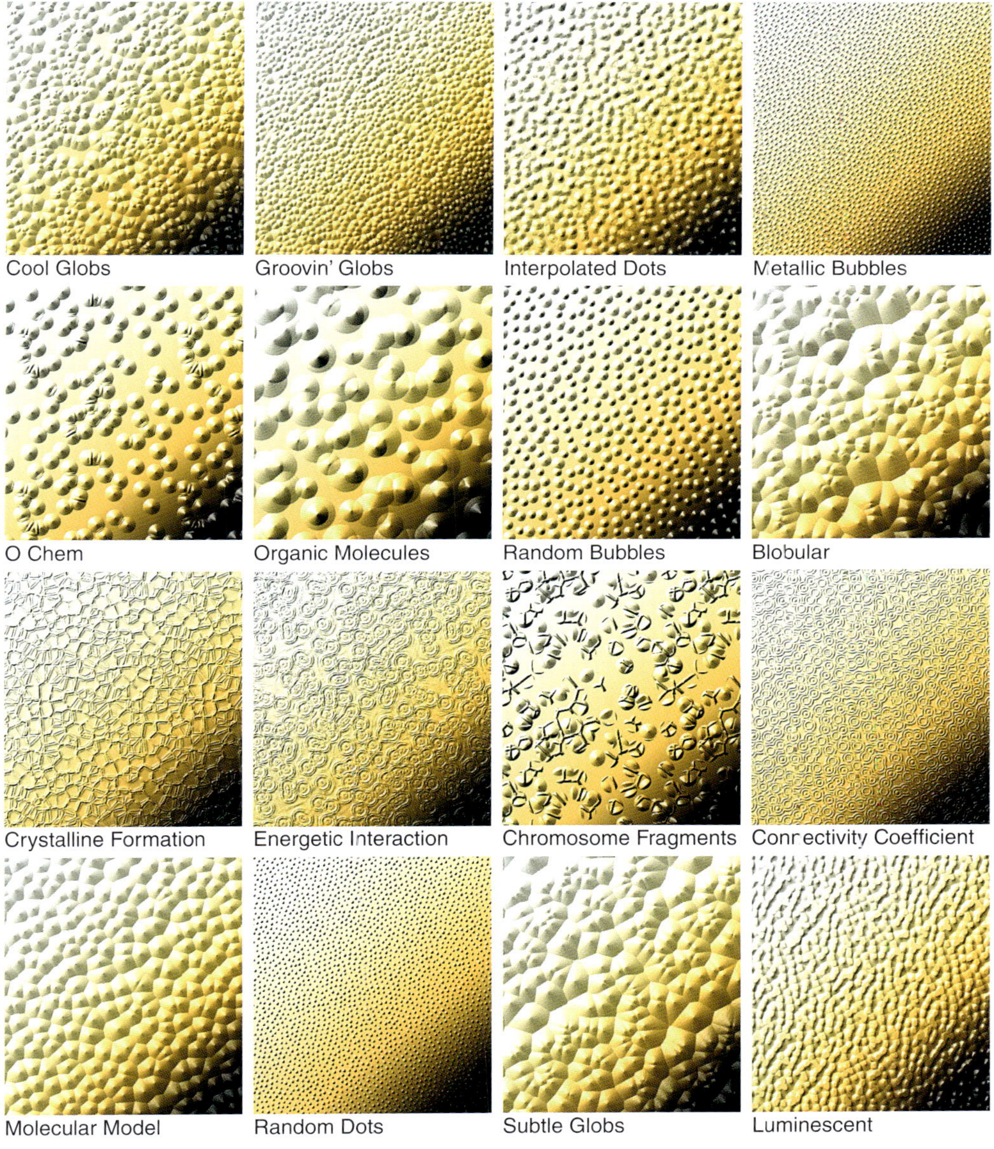

Cool Globs | Groovin' Globs | Interpolated Dots | Metallic Bubbles

O Chem | Organic Molecules | Random Bubbles | Blobular

Crystalline Formation | Energetic Interaction | Chromosome Fragments | Connectivity Coefficient

Molecular Model | Random Dots | Subtle Globs | Luminescent

Organismal textures

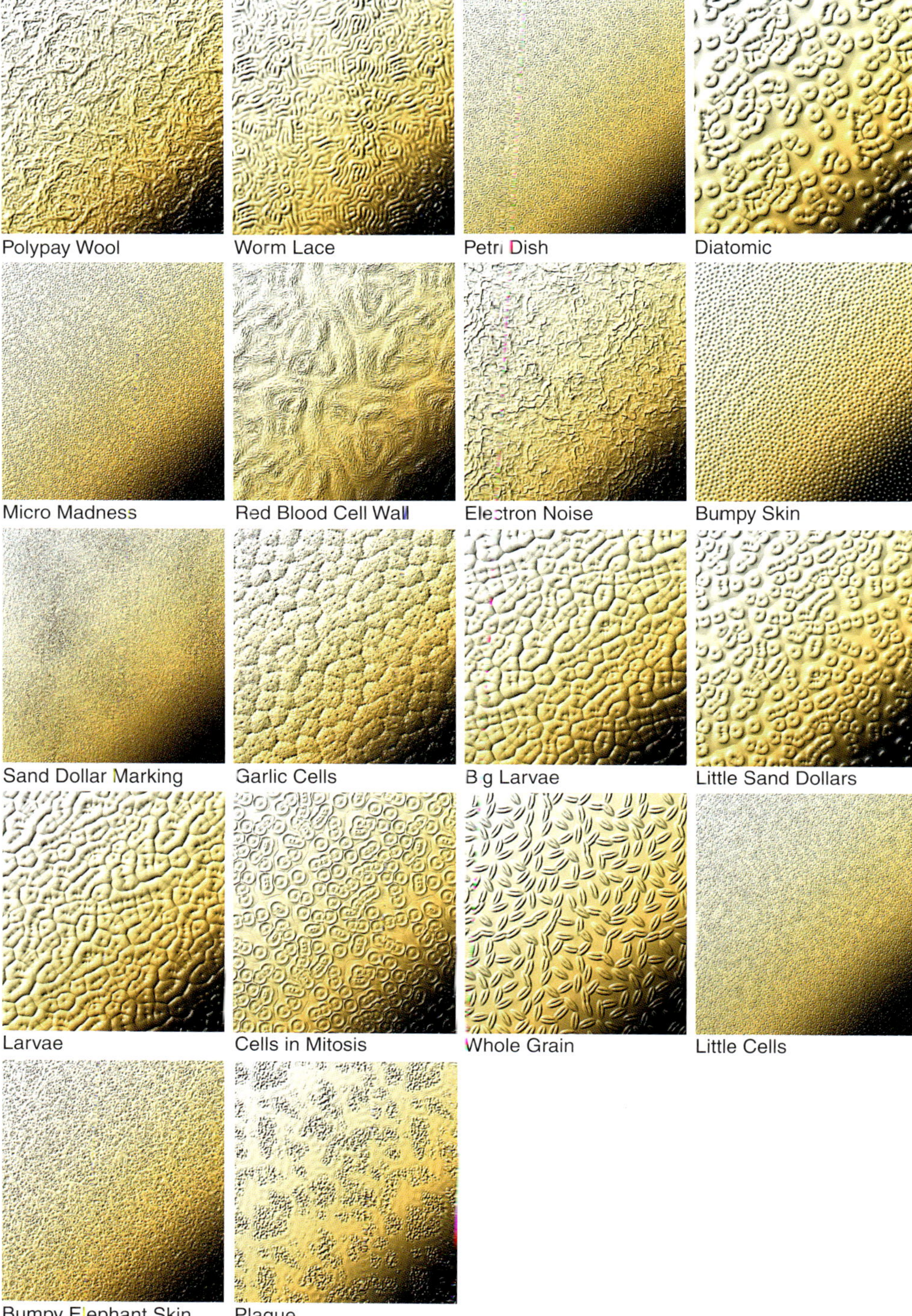

Polypay Wool
Worm Lace
Petri Dish
Diatomic
Micro Madness
Red Blood Cell Wall
Electron Noise
Bumpy Skin
Sand Dollar Marking
Garlic Cells
Big Larvae
Little Sand Dollars
Larvae
Cells in Mitosis
Whole Grain
Little Cells
Bumpy Elephant Skin
Plaque

Painter 5.5 textures

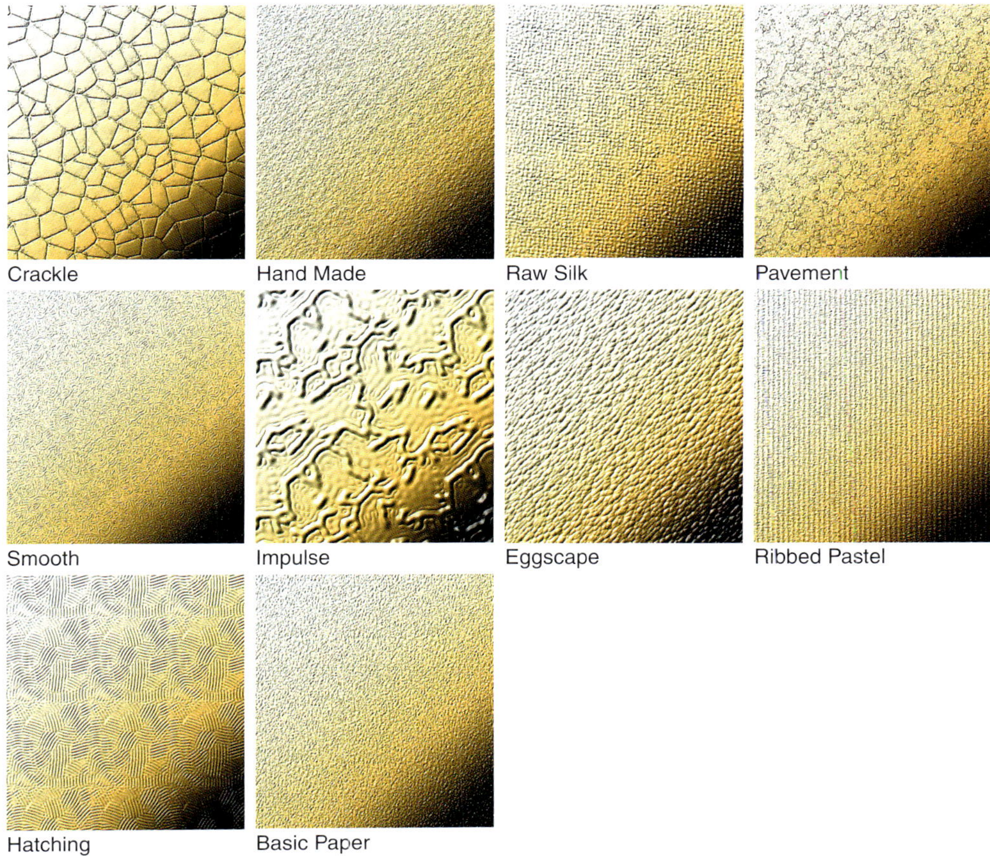

Crackle | Hand Made | Raw Silk | Pavement
Smooth | Impulse | Eggscape | Ribbed Pastel
Hatching | Basic Paper

Painter 6 textures (where different to Painter 5.5 textures)

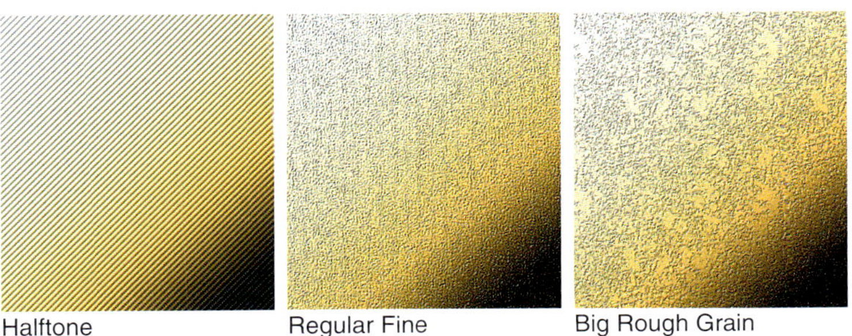

Halftone | Regular Fine | Big Rough Grain

Painter 7 textures

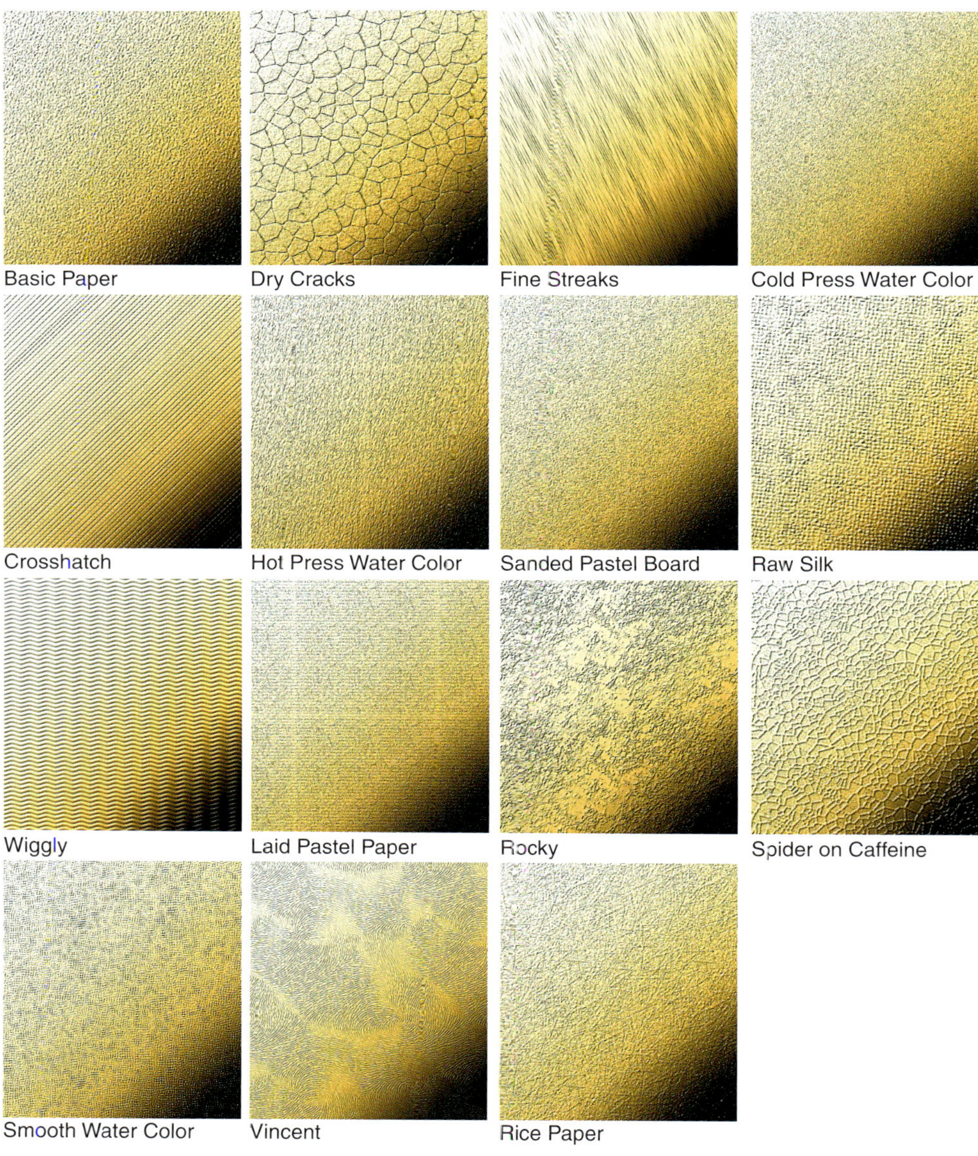
Basic Paper
Dry Cracks
Fine Streaks
Cold Press Water Color
Crosshatch
Hot Press Water Color
Sanded Pastel Board
Raw Silk
Wiggly
Laid Pastel Paper
Rocky
Spider on Caffeine
Smooth Water Color
Vincent
Rice Paper

Paper textures

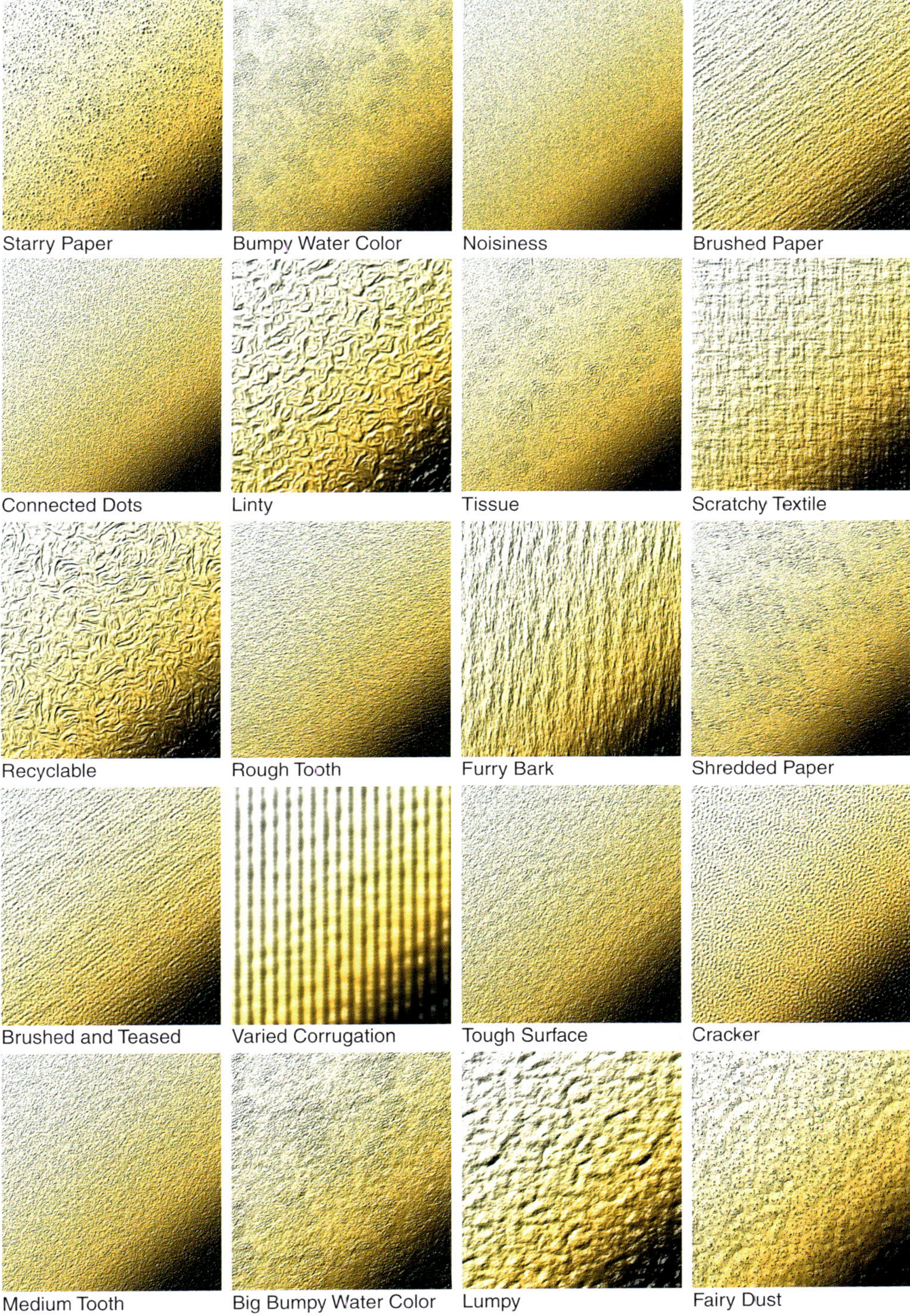

Paper textures 2

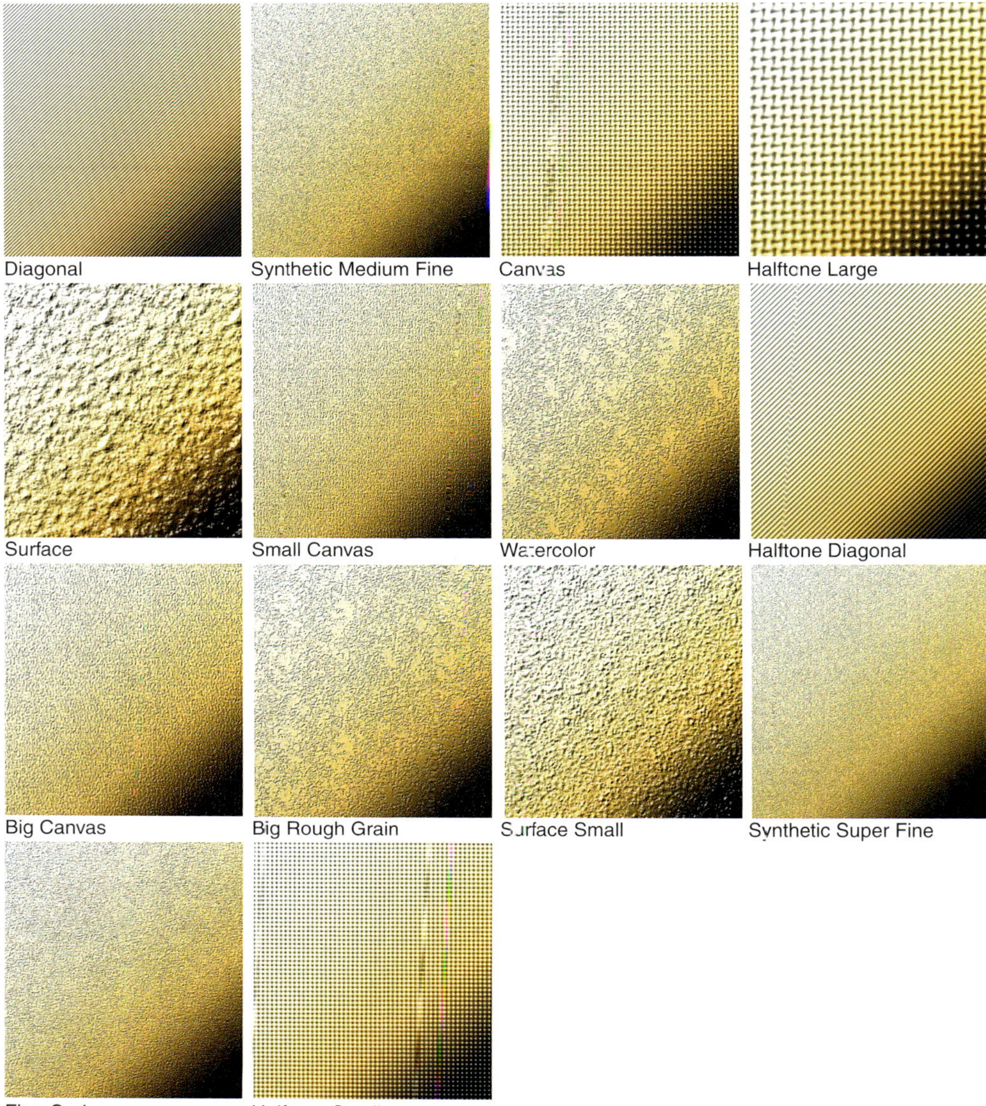

Diagonal

Synthetic Medium Fine

Canvas

Halftone Large

Surface

Small Canvas

Watercolor

Halftone Diagonal

Big Canvas

Big Rough Grain

Surface Small

Synthetic Super Fine

Fine Grain

Halftone Small

Relief textures

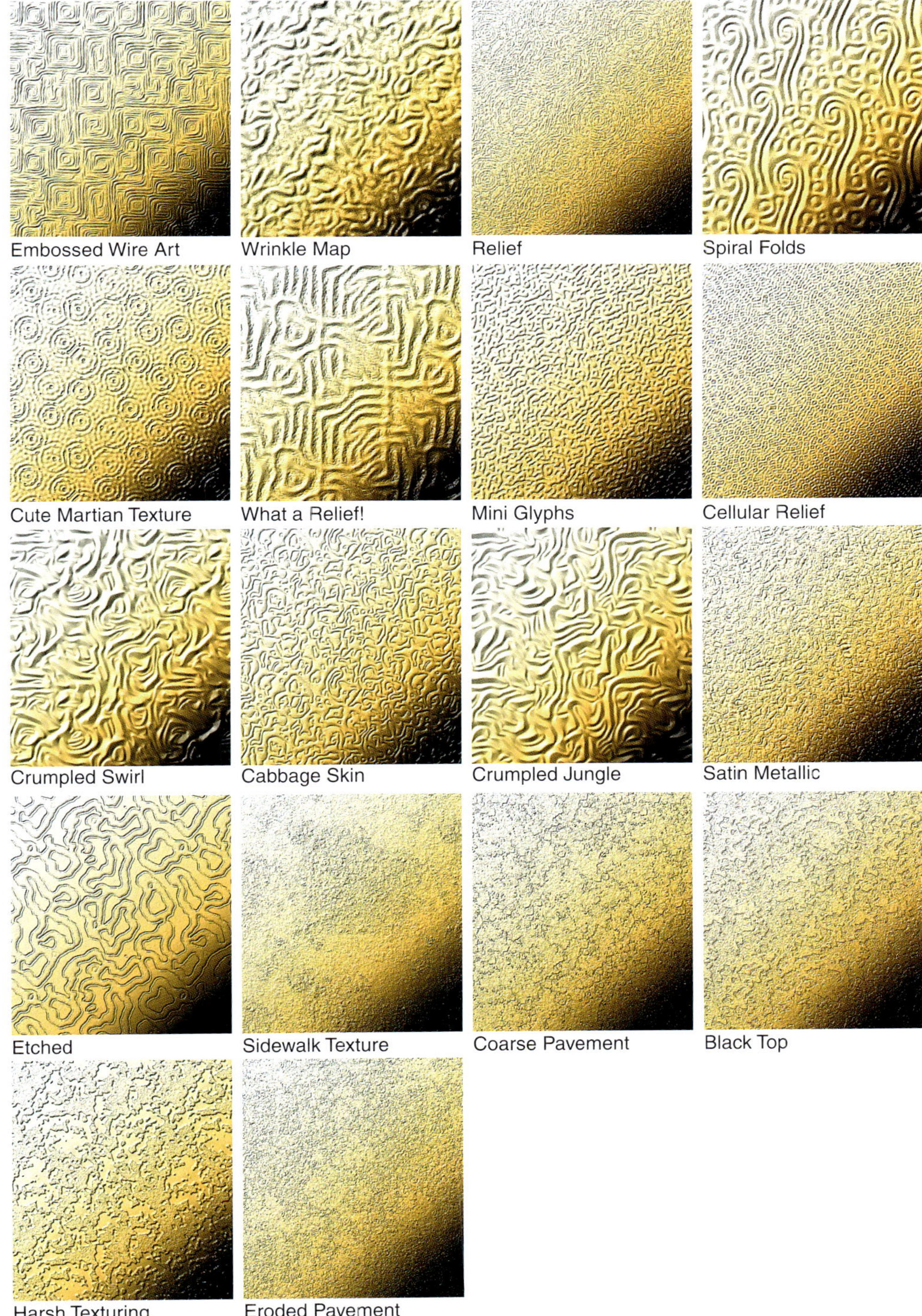

Embossed Wire Art
Wrinkle Map
Relief
Spiral Folds
Cute Martian Texture
What a Relief!
Mini Glyphs
Cellular Relief
Crumpled Swirl
Cabbage Skin
Crumpled Jungle
Satin Metallic
Etched
Sidewalk Texture
Coarse Pavement
Black Top
Harsh Texturing
Eroded Pavement

Subtle textures

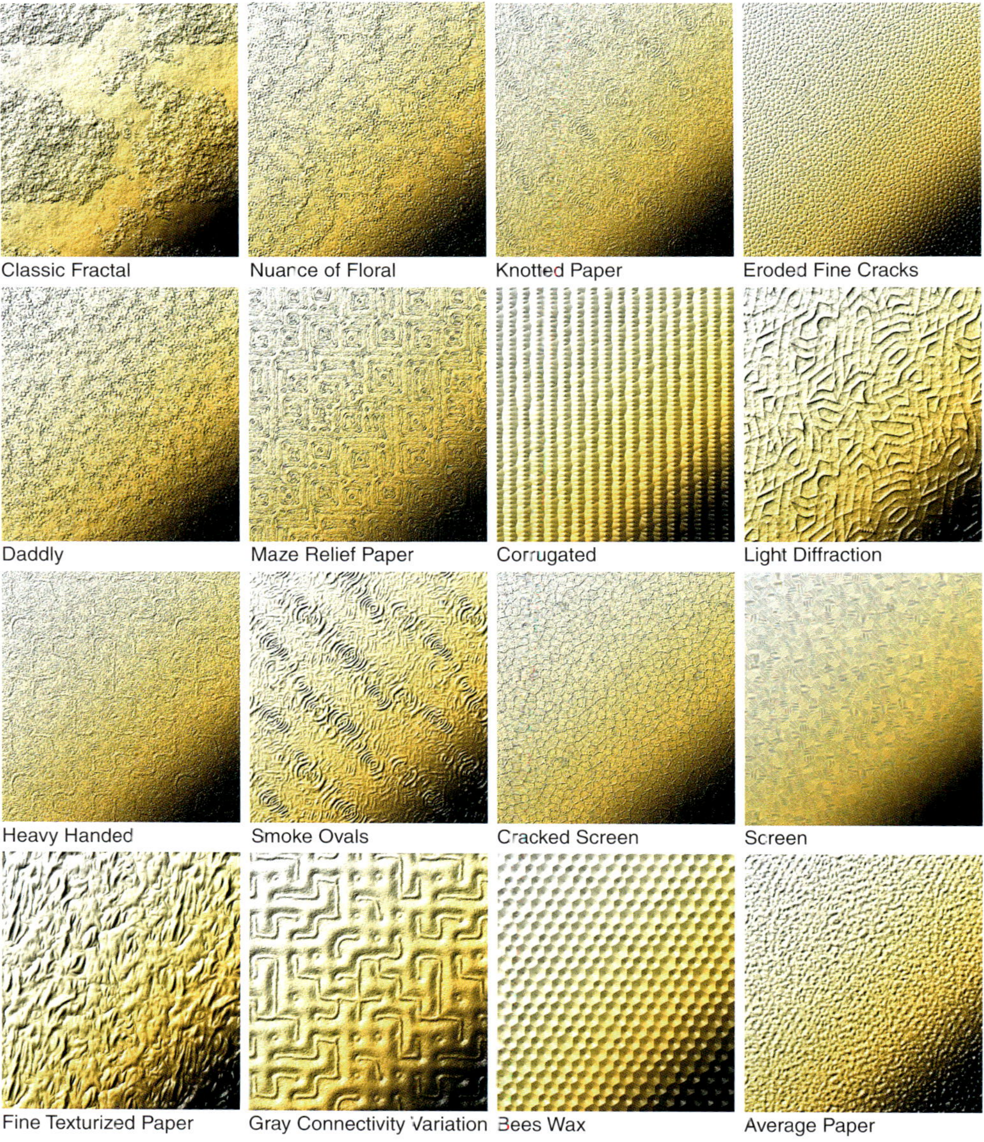

Classic Fractal
Nuance of Floral
Knotted Paper
Eroded Fine Cracks
Daddly
Maze Relief Paper
Corrugated
Light Diffraction
Heavy Handed
Smoke Ovals
Cracked Screen
Screen
Fine Texturized Paper
Gray Connectivity Variation
Bees Wax
Average Paper

Textile textures

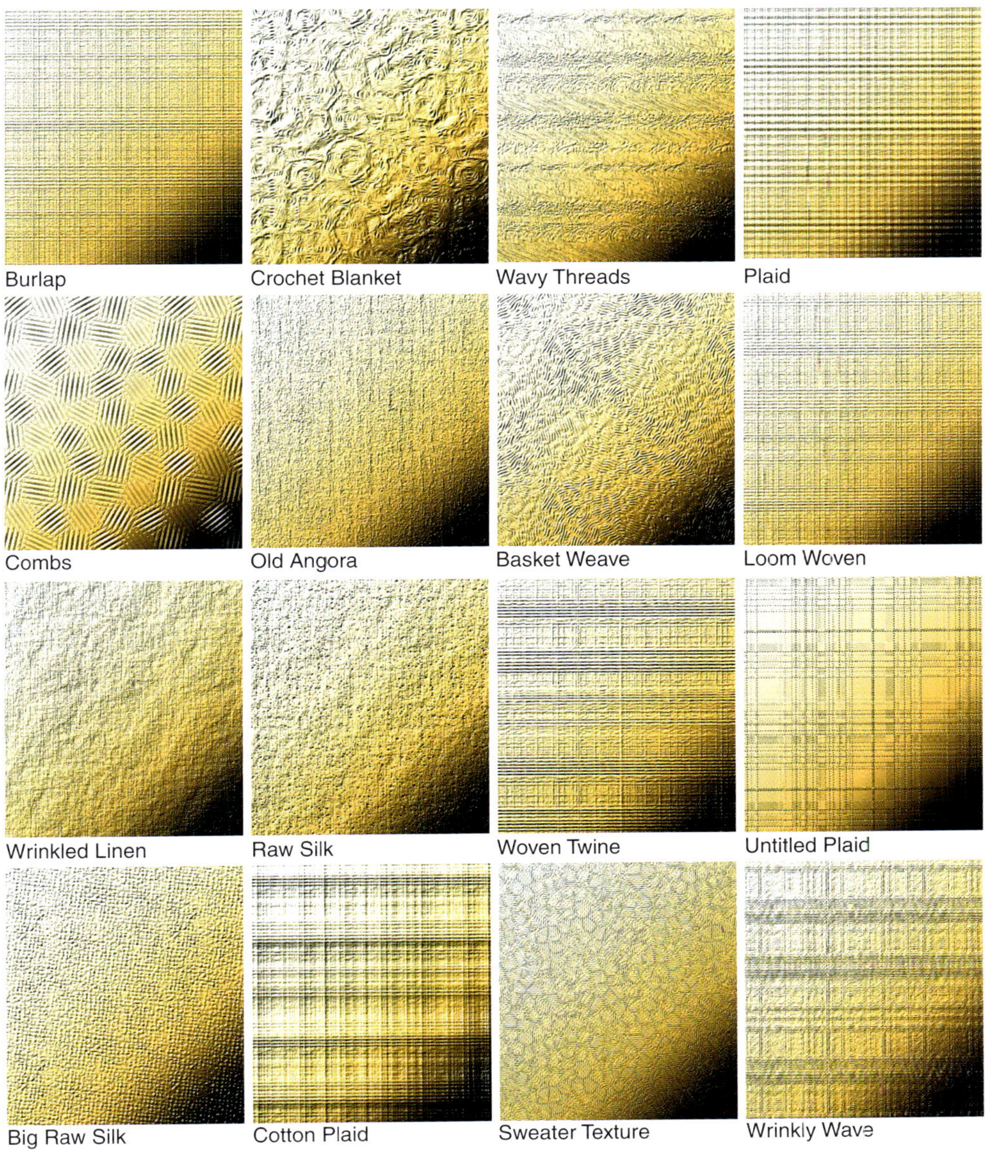

Burlap | Crochet Blanket | Wavy Threads | Plaid
Combs | Old Angora | Basket Weave | Loom Woven
Wrinkled Linen | Raw Silk | Woven Twine | Untitled Plaid
Big Raw Silk | Cotton Plaid | Sweater Texture | Wrinkly Wave

Weird textures

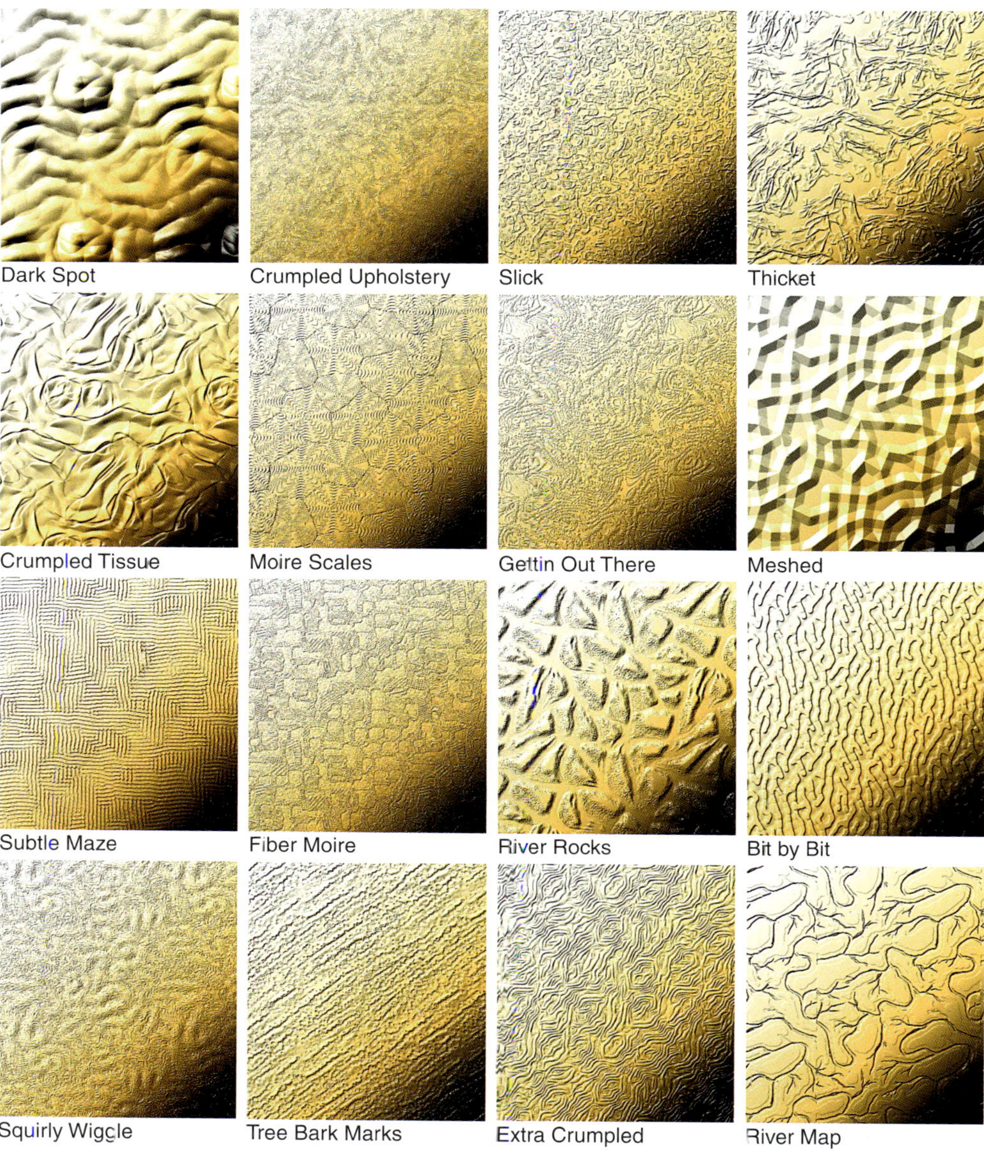

Dark Spot | Crumpled Upholstery | Slick | Thicket

Crumpled Tissue | Moire Scales | Gettin Out There | Meshed

Subtle Maze | Fiber Moire | River Rocks | Bit by Bit

Squirly Wiggle | Tree Bark Marks | Extra Crumpled | River Map

Wild textures

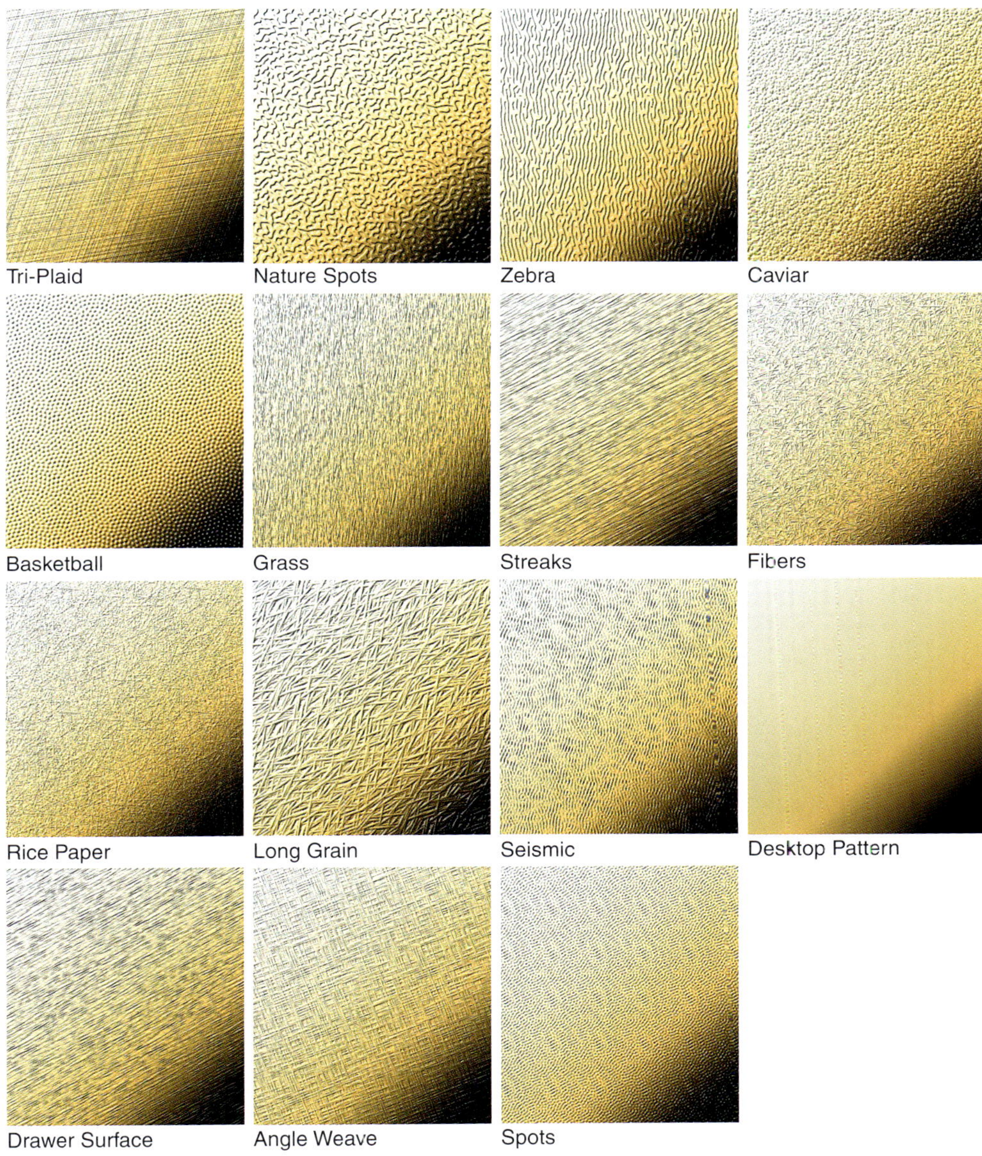

Tri-Plaid | Nature Spots | Zebra | Caviar

Basketball | Grass | Streaks | Fibers

Rice Paper | Long Grain | Seismic | Desktop Pattern

Drawer Surface | Angle Weave | Spots

Wild textures 2

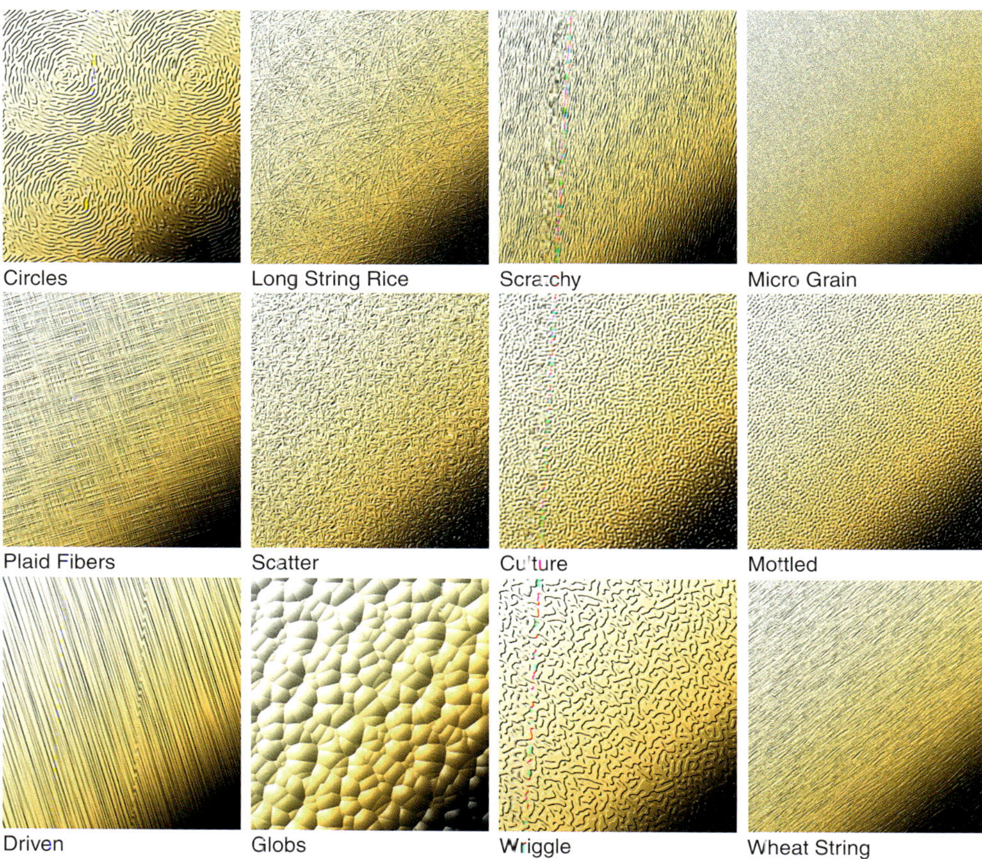

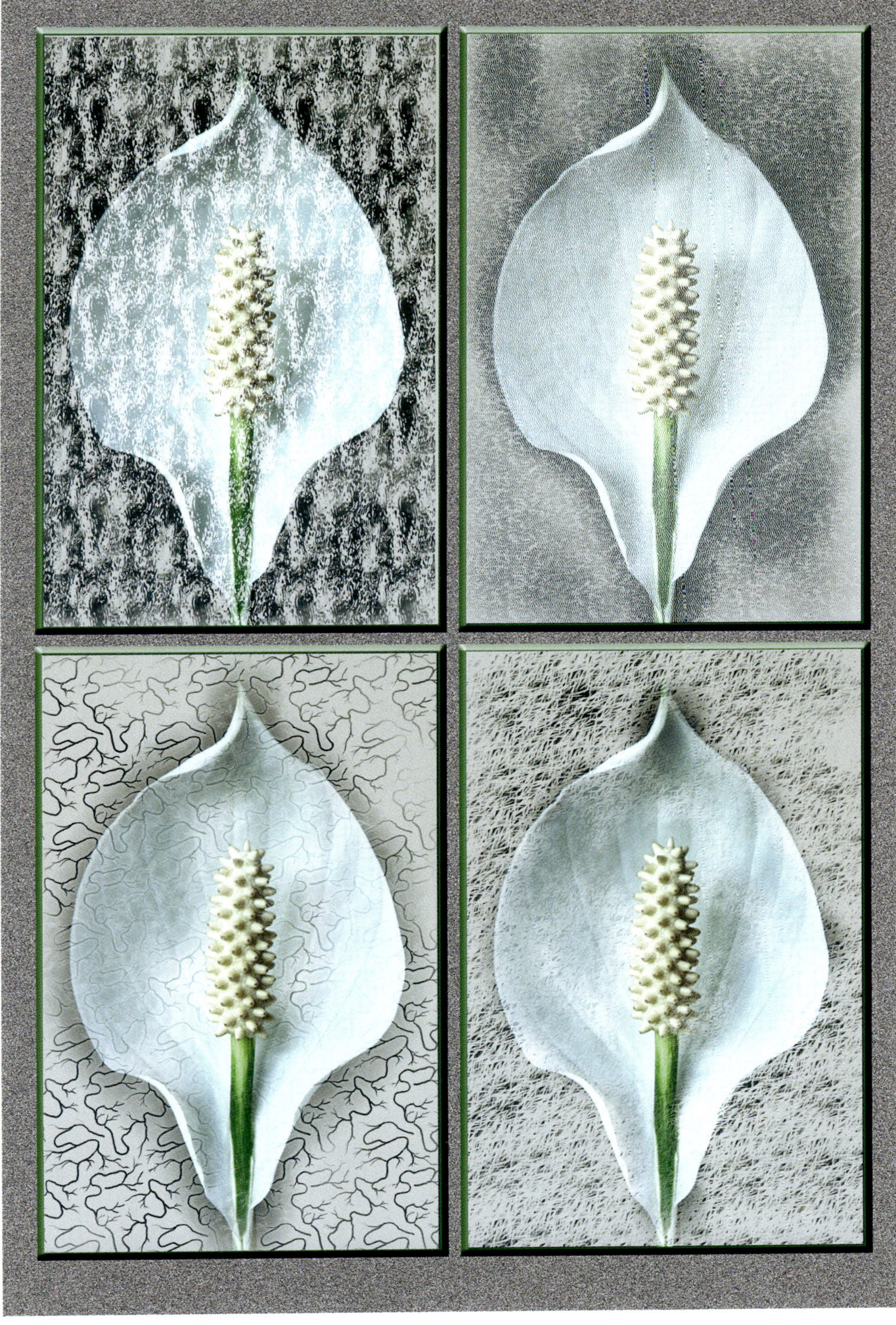

Figure 14.3 Flower design using four different paper textures

Index

Italic page numbers refer to illustrations